BORDERWATERS

BRIAN RUSSELL ROBERTS

BORDERWATERS

....

Amid the Archipelagic States of America

DUKE UNIVERSITY PRESS *Durham & London* 2021

© 2021 Duke University Press All rights reserved
Designed by Matthew Tauch
Typeset in Garamond Premier Pro by
Westchester Publishing Services

Library of Congress Cataloging-in-Publication Data
Names: Roberts, Brian Russell, author.
Title: Borderwaters : amid the Archipelagic states of America / Brian Russell Roberts.
Description: Durham : Duke University Press, 2021. | Includes bibliographical references and index.
Identifiers: LCCN 2020031375 (print) | LCCN 2020031376 (ebook)
ISBN 9781478010739 (hardcover)
ISBN 9781478011859 (paperback)
ISBN 9781478013204 (ebook)
Subjects: LCSH: United States—Insular possessions—History. | United States—Territories and possessions—History. | Caribbean Area—History. | Islands of the Pacific—History. | Philippines—History. | United States—Colonial question.
Classification: LCC F970 .R634 2021 (print) | LCC F970 (ebook) | DDC 973—dc23LC
recordavailableathttps:// lccn.loc.gov/2020031375
LC ebook recordavailableathttps:// lccn.loc.gov/2020031376

Cover art: Brian Russell Roberts, *From the Center of Spiral Jetty—Salt Crystals, Brine Shrimp, Red Algae*, 2019. Linocut. Courtesy of the artist.

For Johnny Frisbie and the slate carvers at Topaz.

For Norma and William and Sierra,

who read and talked about Frisbie and visited Topaz with me.

For an archive like the waves of the sea.

CONTENTS

ACKNOWLEDGMENTS · ix

Introduction · 1
Archipelagic Thinking and the Borderwaters: A US-Eccentric Vision

Chapter One · 45
Interlapping Continents and Archipelagoes of American Studies

Chapter Two · 82
Archipelagic Diaspora and Geographic Form

Chapter Three · 111
Borderwaters and Geometries of Being Amid

Chapter Four · 159
Fractal Temporality on Vulnerable Foreshores

Chapter Five · 202
Spiraling Futures of the Archipelagic States of America

Conclusion · 248
Distant Reading the Archipelagic Gyre: Digital Humanities Archipelagoes

NOTES · 275 / BIBLIOGRAPHY · 323 / INDEX · 359

ACKNOWLEDGMENTS

I am fortunate to have benefited from the insight and goodwill of many friends, colleagues, communities, groups, students, and institutions while I wrote *Borderwaters*. Most immediately influential have been the phenomenal scholars with whom I worked while editing, with Michelle Ann Stephens, the collection *Archipelagic American Studies* (Duke University Press, 2017). I found many of *Borderwaters*' major contours in the process of reading, commenting on, pushing, and being pushed by the essays contributed to that volume by Lanny Thompson, Elaine Stratford, Craig Santos Perez, Etsuko Taketani, Susan Gillman, Yolanda Martínez-San Miguel, Joseph Keith, Nicole A. Waligora-Davis, John Carlos Rowe, Cherene Sherrard-Johnson, Brandy Nālani McDougall, Hsinya Huang, Ramón E. Soto-Crespo, Alice Te Punga Somerville, Matthew Pratt Guterl, J. Michael Dash, Birte Blascheck, Teresia K. Teaiwa, Ifeoma Kiddoe Nwankwo, Allan Punzalan Isaac, and Paul Giles. Of course, as Michelle and I collaborated in conceptualizing and writing the introduction for *Archipelagic American Studies*, and as we have brainstormed and presented together over the years, her keen thought, insights, and friendship have been indispensable to my own thinking.

I have also benefited from the thought of friends and colleagues involved in other overlapping collaborative projects. I am grateful to have worked collaboratively with Mary Eyring, Hester Blum, Iping Liang, Chris Lynn, and Fidalis Buehler to edit the 2019 special forum "Archipelagoes/Oceans/American Visuality," published in the *Journal of Transnational American Studies*. During the editing process, I was inspired by the work of our many featured scholars and artists: Ryan Charlton, L. Katherine Smith, Emalani Case, Cherene Sherrard-Johnson, Kathleen DeGuzman, Zachary Tavlin, Matthew Hitchman, Tashima Thomas, Christo Javacheff, Jeanne-Claude Denat de Guillebon, Tiara R. Na'puti, Robert Smithson, Glenda León, Juana Valdes, Steve Mentz, Mary Mattingly, Humberto Díaz, Hi'ilei Julia Hobart, Yuki Kihara, Kalisolaite 'Uhila, Caroline Sinavaiana Gabbard, Brandy Nālani McDougall, Chris

Charteris, Maile Andrade, Ibrahim Miranda, Michelle Ann Stephens, James Cooper, and Jamilah Sabur. The *Journal of Transnational American Studies* forum grew in part from collaborations between the Archipelagoes/Oceans/Americas research group at Brigham Young University (BYU) and the Archipelagoes Seminar at Rutgers. In addition to the friends and colleagues already mentioned, thanks to several colleagues who participated in these groups or their symposia: Cody Arnall, Jessica Swanston Baker, Tiana Birrell, Charlie Cohan, Trent Hickman, 'Anapesi Ka'ili, Scott Miller, Sarah DeMott, Aaron Eastley, Daniel Elam, Susan Stanford Friedman, George Handley, Enmanuel Martínez, Kyle McAuley, Anjali Nerlekar, Lisa Swanstrom, and Mike Taylor.

I have also benefited from conversations, encouragement, and feedback from numerous readers and fellow travelers along the way.

Lisa Lowe and Jamin Rowan read and commented on a draft of *Borderwaters* for a book manuscript workshop sponsored by the BYU Humanities Center. Their enthusiasm for the manuscript sustained me as I finished the project, and their keen suggestions have enhanced my thinking on topics and chapters throughout.

Michelle Ann Stephens, Yolanda Martínez-San Miguel, Marlene Hansen Esplin, Keith Foulcher, and John Butcher each offered insightful comments on writing that eventually found its way into the introduction. John was generous in sharing a map of the Philippines that visualizes the lines specified by the 1898 Treaty of Paris with a few subsequent emendations. The introduction was also strengthened as a result of conversations with Madeline Y. Hsu on the topic of the Asiatic Barred Zone Act and by questions from students and faculty at the University of Rhode Island for whom I presented the Rumowicz Maritime Annual Endowed Lecture in 2019. During her 2015 visit to BYU, I also benefited from conversations with Mari Yoshihara on the significance of *American Quarterly*'s move to Hawai'i. Tiffany Tsao kindly exchanged emails on her Oddfits series and this series' place in the introduction. Canoeing and talking with Roland Roberts and Norma Roberts among shifting islands near Breeze Point on Yellowstone Lake enhanced some of the introduction's discussions of archipelagoes and temporality. A small portion of the material in the introduction is drawn from my essay "What Is an Archipelago? On Bandung Praxis, Lingua Franca, and Archipelagic Interlapping," in *Contemporary Archipelagic Thinking: Towards New Comparative Methodologies and Disciplinary Formations* (2020), and I thank Rowman and Littlefield for permission to republish this adapted material.

I am indebted to Shelley Fisher Fishkin not only for her enthusiasm for the project in general but also for discussing with me, during her 2016 visit to BYU, chapter 1's reading of *Adventures of Huckleberry Finn*. Chapter 1 is also indebted to Teresia K. Teaiwa for pointing me toward Florence "Johnny" Frisbie's important work. I was honored to have the chance to sit down with Johnny at her home in 2014, to talk about her books and thoughts on many topics, including the idea of America. During that trip to Honolulu, as I prepared for and reflected back on my conversation with Johnny, Craig Santos Perez, Alice Te Punga Somerville, and Paul Lyons were each extraordinarily generous, talking with me over meals and inviting me, in Paul's case, to attend a session of his graduate course on Pacific and African American intersections. Gratitude also goes to the Rutgers Archipelagoes Seminar and the Grupo Interdisciplinar LyA at Universidad de Castilla–La Mancha: thank you for the opportunities you afforded me to try out some of my ideas on Huck, Jim, and the island as I was planning and drafting this chapter. Cathy Roberts's insights into *Miss Ulysses from Puka-Puka* were helpful as I considered how to proceed, and Phil Snyder's insights, enthusiasm, and friendship were also important as I drafted chapter 1.

Early drafts of chapter 2 were enhanced by conversations with Billy Hall, George B. Handley, Ifeoma Kiddoe Nwankwo, Elizabeth M. DeLoughrey, and Bill Maxwell. Thanks also to the students of Michelle Ann Stephens's 2013 graduate seminar Archipelagic American Studies for feedback on the article version as it appeared in *American Literature* earlier the same year. The chapter appears in *Borderwaters* in much-revised form by courtesy of Duke University Press. Further thanks go to Sonya Posmentier for her insightful use of, and commentary on, the article version of this chapter in her 2017 book *Cultivation and Catastrophe: The Lyric Ecology of Modern Black Literature*. Her comments helped me further refine and clarify this chapter's conceptual and practical implications. Thanks also go to Seth Bramson, company historian of the Florida East Coast Railway, for discussions of the Oversea Railway—hoping that you, as well, have a Miami nice day.

I had the chance to try out the arguments, histories, and conceptual frames of chapter 3 in several forums and with various colleagues. Thanks to Ben Fagan and Juliane Braun not only for enlightening conversations over several years but also for inviting me to participate in the Transoceanic Studies Symposium held at the German Historical Society in Washington, DC, in 2018. Through this symposium, a portion of chapter 3 benefited from feedback and discussions with Michelle Burnham, Hester Blum, Maria Windell, Martha Elena Rojas, and Christopher Connery. Thanks also to Yuan Shu and Kenneth Dean for inviting me to participate in the America's Asia, Asia's America Conference at the National University of Singapore held later that same year. In Singapore, my thinking on chapter 3 benefited from discussions with Paul Giles, John Carlos Rowe, Tina Chen, Wai Chee Dimock, Prasenjit Duara, Janet Hoskins, Lily Rose Tope, Bayu Kristianto, and graduate students from the American Studies Program at Universitas Indonesia. Several friends and colleagues have also done me the favor of reading and commenting on the chapter in part or in whole: Emron Esplin, John Alba Cutler, John Carlos Rowe, Keith Foulcher, Adrian Vickers, Yolanda Martínez-San Miguel, and Tiara R. Na'puti. Jens Temmen and Nicole Waller gave insightful feedback on a small portion of this chapter as I prepared it for their "American Territorialities" special forum for the *Journal of Transnational American Studies*. The chapter had part of its earliest genesis in 2013 when I visited Indonesia and spoke with John McGlynn not only about Richard Wright's 1955 travels in Indonesia for the Bandung Conference but also about Pramoedya Ananta Toer's relation to archipelagic thought and Indonesia's work to champion Wawasan Nusantara within the United Nations Convention on the Law of the Sea (UNCLOS). Thanks to Cristina Meisner, research associate at the Harry Ransom Center, for locating the pamphlet that Miguel Covarrubias illustrated for the Information Office of the Republic of Indonesia in New York City, and thanks to Covarrubias's niece, María Elena Rico Covarrubias, for the graciousness with which she handled permissions for the chapter. Thanks also to Roger Knight for digging into the family collection of his father's papers to share a copy of the US Navy's publication *Roster of Officers, Enlisted Men, Civilians and Dependents*, which to my surprise adapted some of its illustrations from Covarrubias's work.

As I began thinking about and working on chapter 4, I benefited from conversations with Cathy Schlund-Vials and Chris Vials, initially after my 2016 talk for the Asian and Asian American Institute Seminar Series at the University of Connecticut and later at the 2018 Modern Language Association Convention. I am grateful for the insight and goodwill of many others as the chapter unfolded. Scott Miller, Heidi Moe Graviet, and Jack Stoneman consulted with me on the kanji characters associated with the Topaz slate carvers' inkstones and on broader questions regarding the stones' puns and relation to Japanese aesthetic conventions.

Delphine Hirasuna shared insight on Homei Iseyama's work, and a big thank you is due to Iseyama's granddaughter, Carolyn Holden, for sharing insights as well as looking through the family's collection of Iseyama's stone carvings in California. Jamie Henricks, archivist at the Japanese American National Museum in Los Angeles, helped locate Toranosuke Mifune's inkstone, and Evan Kodani of the museum's media arts center photographed it. As a research assistant, Heather Randall shared insights on stones, shells, and water as discussed in the *Topaz Times*, *Trek*, and Julie Otsuka's novel *When the Emperor Was Divine*. Cherene Sherrard-Johnson offered important reading suggestions as I was considering how to think about—and with—trilobites. Matt Wickman, Jonathan Pugh, Greg Robinson, Mari Yoshihara, and Dennitza Gabrakova did me the favor of reading the chapter at different stages of its development. And thanks to Wai Chee Dimock for her enthusiasm in sending out an early draft of chapter 4 to the listserv STEAM: Integrating Arts and Sciences and for talking with me about the chapter when we presented together during the BYU Humanities Center's 2018 symposium, On Being Vulnerable: "Crisis" and Transformation. Niles Eldredge, whose work has intrigued me since my AP biology course in high school, read the chapter, offered feedback, and fielded several questions on geology and evolutionary biology. I am further indebted to students in the back-to-back senior seminars on Topaz that I taught for BYU's American Studies Program and English Department. These students (Sarah Adams, Melodie Jackson, Ann Johnston, Hannah Lee, Jillian Manley, Marcus Vanderholm, Elizabeth Young, Abby Beazer, Moe Graviet, Jamie Mortensen, Eliza Schow, Summer Weaver, Matt Webb, and Tate Wright) provided me with an academic year's worth of smart discussion on Topaz's history as well as its literary and broader aesthetic cultures. Thanks to Emily Roberts for several conversations on *Korematsu v. United States*, and thanks to Ross Storey for sharing his talents, traveling to the Topaz Museum with me to photograph Toyo Suyemoto's brooch and Shigematsu Ishizaki's inkstone. Sincere thanks to Gregory Ishizaki, grandson of Shigematsu Ishizaki, for his generosity in sharing family history and other contexts. A big thanks to Jane Beckwith, director of the Topaz Museum, for making the inkstone and brooch available for photographing and for reading and commenting on this chapter, in which some geologically oriented writings of her grandfather Frank Beckwith Sr. feature prominently.

Chapter 5 benefited from many interlocutors. Andrea Westermann shared a prepublication version of her chapter "A Technofossil of the

Anthropocene: Sliding Up and Down Temporal Scales with Plastic," which was an inspiration in terms of my own chapter's structure. Joseph Kraft and Hikmet Sidney Loe shared photographs of *Spiral Jetty*, and Kathryn Knudsen and Alex Knudsen offered generative comments as I thought about the jetty and temporality. My sister Whitney Ehle and her family have shared a fascination with Utah's rocks and geology. Ryan Camacho and Jason Pollack read and offered feedback, from the perspective of physicists, on the chapter's discussions of Boltzmann brains, and my brothers, David and Michael Roberts, let me engage them in conversations on various streams of math and science. After hearing my description of Boltzmann brains, Emron Esplin bought me a copy of Jorge Luis Borges's *Collected Fictions* and bid me read. As I began thinking about ocean plastic, Alice Te Punga Somerville and Ramón E. Soto-Crespo's essays in *Archipelagic American Studies* were an inspiration, as were the presentations of Fiona Allon, Ruth Barcan, Liz Hansen, Karma Chahine, Anja Schwarz, Kylie Crane, and Nicole Waller for the 2016 Waste Matters Symposium at the University of Potsdam. I'm grateful for the invitation to participate in and present at this symposium. Thanks to the geologist Brenda Bowen for her presentation on plastic at the University of Utah's Re-valuing the Ocean symposium and for reading and commenting on chapter 5's discussion of plastic. My sister Emily Roberts offered useful legal perspective as I considered the 1906 Antiquities Act and the creation of national monuments. As for the chapter's final section: thanks to Paul Cox for answering email questions on the creation of the National Park of American Samoa, to Tina Chen for introducing me to Timothy James M. Dimacali's work, and to Dimacali and John Raymond Bumanglag for permitting me to use an excerpt from the front cover of the comic-book version of "Sky Gypsies."

The book's conclusion couldn't have unfolded as it did without, foremost, the energy and work of Brian Croxall (working together with Lorin Groesbeck and Jeremy Browne) in terms of data collection and visualization. Thanks also to Lalitree Darnielle of Duke University Press for creating the final graphs as they appear in the book. Lisa Swanstrom, Billy Hall, and Miriam Posner offered useful perspectives as the work was taking shape, and drafts of the conclusion benefited from reading and comments from Croxall, Alex Gil, and Sarah DeMott.

A semester in 2015 as a Fulbright senior scholar, teaching American studies courses at Universitas Sebelas Maret in Solo, Indonesia, heightened my attunement to the general project of rethinking the study of US and broader American cultures from archipelagic perspectives. Thanks especially to several friends and colleagues with whom I worked closely: Susilo Rini, Taufiq Al Makmun, Sri Kusumo Habsari, Agus D. Priyanto, Karunia Purna, Yusuf Kurniawan, Rarastesa Zita, Fitria Primasita, Rini Riana, and Halimi Mustofa. Thanks also to my students, Sri Mulyati, Tri Pujianto, Irene Yolanda Sembiring, Guruh Putra Tama, Hutomo Mukti Widanarso, and Cahyo Adi Nugroho.

Research funding for the project stemmed from a fellowship with the BYU Humanities Center, a professorship with the BYU Humanities College, and a grant from the David M. Kennedy Center for International Studies. I am indebted to Drew Hemsley for providing working translations from Édouard Glissant's French, to Daryl Lee for further perspectives on translations from French, and to Scott Miller and Jack Stoneman for consultations and translations from Japanese. Translations from Spanish and Indonesian are my own. My research assistant, Emily Jones Nichols, collaborated in checking citations. As always, Courtney Berger and Sandra Korn at Duke University Press have been a dream to work with throughout the process. Thanks to the manuscript's anonymous readers for their enthusiasm and suggestions as it moved toward production. Norma Roberts did me the favor of reading and commenting on the full manuscript, and—to understate things—has done me the favor of being a brilliant interlocutor on many topics during the two decades we have been married. The examples of a handful of mentors, past and present, have profoundly influenced my approach to this project and to thinking more generally: Eric Lott, Deborah McDowell, Marlon Ross, and Matt Wickman.

Family and friends, many of whom are mentioned in these acknowledgments and the book's dedication, have my greatest gratitude.

INTRODUCTION

Archipelagic Thinking and the Borderwaters: *A US-Eccentric Vision*

An Ocean Nation and Its Noncanonical Borders

In 2013 two scholars at the Massachusetts Institute of Technology published a "Territorial Map of the World" that drew attention to the boundaries that currently exist between and among all of the planet's sovereign nation-states. As one would expect, in representing the United States, the map registers the US-Mexico border to the south and the US-Canada border to the north. These two borders, of course, are *the* borders of the United States, canonized within traditional and popular thought. And as is intoned by the well-known patriotic hymn, between these two canonical borders the United States extends "from sea to shining sea"—it extends as a vast continental nation of fruited plains and purple mountains and fields of grain, with a manifest destiny whose only east-west limits have been the seemingly nonnational and apolitical blank spaces of the Atlantic and Pacific Oceans. And yet the "Territorial Map of the World," created by Rafi Segal and Yonatan Cohen, offers a substantial jolt to the traditional continental US narrative precisely because it does not represent shorelines as naturally imposed boundaries but instead moves toward an apprehension of the United States as a nation whose boundaries extend into heretofore uncanonized waters. As the creators explain, "This political map of the world depicts the extent of territories, both on land and at sea . . . , which are under the control of all independent nations. The map incorporates Exclusive Economic Zones (EEZs), which are sea zones whose resources belong to their coastal ... nations. International law defines these zones as lying within a 200 nautical mile ... geometrical offsetting" from a nation's coasts.[1] As one might imagine, however, many coastal countries are not able to claim the full two hundred nautical miles of ocean without having their claims bump into those of their neighboring nation-states, and consequently, as Segal and Cohen note, we see international assumptions and treaties that demarcate sometimes ambiguous maritime boundaries. Furthermore, as their map bears out, we see a proliferation of borders—a proliferation that takes us far beyond the United States' canonized borders with Mexico and Canada. In the Caribbean, aside from bordering Mexico, the United States borders Cuba, the Bahamas, the Dominican Republic, the United Kingdom, the Netherlands, and Venezuela (see fig. I.1). (The United States also has borders with Haiti and Jamaica, though the "Territorial Map of the World" does not register the contested US claim to Navassa Island that makes this so.) Meanwhile, in the Pacific the United States unexpectedly borders Japan, the Federated States of Micronesia, the Marshall Islands, the Independent State of Samoa, Tokelau, the Cook Islands, Niue, Tonga, New Zealand, and Kiribati (see figs. I.2 and I.3). Still another portion of the map reminds us that in the north the United States borders not only Canada but also Russia (see fig. I.4).

While popular discussions in US media often use the phrase *the border* as an unambiguous stand-in for the US-Mexico border, and while more attentive conversations may remind us that the boundary between the US and Canada is *also* a border, and while certain leaders in government may occasionally refer to the entire Caribbean as the United States' "third border," few US citizens or US watchers throughout the world will recognize the version of the United States of America—with its unforecasted surfeit of borders revealing it to be contiguous with some twenty-one countries—that becomes visible when we examine US maritime claims as they appear on Segal and Cohen's map.[2] And yet it is not as if this version of the United States were a secret, as if this terraqueous view of the country were accessible only via an archive one might become privy to through a Freedom of Information Act request. Indeed, as of the present writing, the US National Oceanic and Atmospheric Administration (NOAA) makes all of this clear on its website, on a page titled "Maritime Zones and Boundaries." On the topic of the two-hundred-mile EEZ, NOAA draws from the 1982 United Nations Convention on the Law of the Sea (UNCLOS):

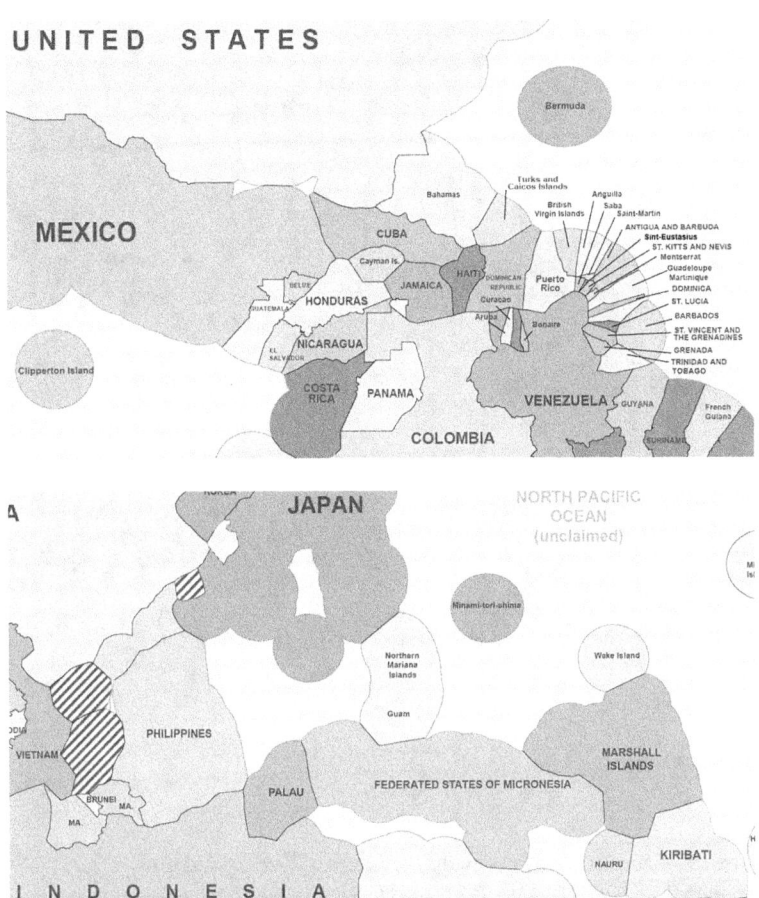

FIGURE 1.1 — US borders in the Caribbean. In this excerpt from Rafi Segal and Yonatan Cohen's "Territorial Map of the World," we see the US continent's land and maritime borders with Mexico but also the continent's maritime borders with Cuba and the Bahamas; also, via Puerto Rico and the adjacent US Virgin Islands, we see that the United States borders the Dominican Republic, the United Kingdom (via the British Virgin Islands and via Anguilla at a single point), the Netherlands (via Saba), and Venezuela. The map does not, however, register the US claim to the uninhabited Navassa Island, situated between Haiti and Jamaica, which affords the US a maritime border with both of those countries as well. This and other excerpts are from Rafi Segal and Yonatan Cohen, "Territorial Map of the World," *openDemocracy: Free Thinking for the World*, October 7, 2013, https://www.opendemocracy.net/en/territorial-map-of-world/. Courtesy of Rafi Segal and Yonatan Cohen.

FIGURE 1.2 — Some US borders in the Pacific, from "Territorial Map of the World." Via the Northern Mariana Islands and Guam, the United States borders the Federated States of Micronesia and Japan; via Wake Island, it borders the Marshall Islands.

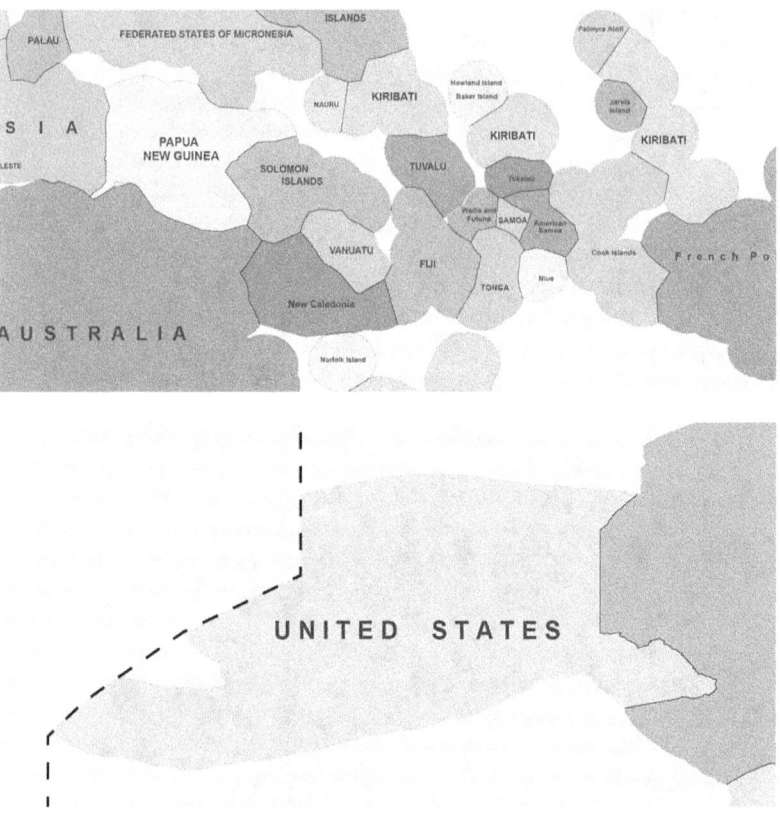

FIGURE 1.3 — Further US borders in the Pacific, from "Territorial Map of the World." Via American Samoa, the United States borders the Independent State of Samoa, Tokelau, the Cook Islands, Niue, and Tonga (thus, it borders New Zealand as well; although Tokelau, the Cook Islands, and Niue are regarded as sovereign countries, their residents are citizens of New Zealand). The United States also borders Kiribati, via the US territories of Palmyra Atoll, Jarvis Island, Howland Island, and Baker Island.

FIGURE 1.4 — Alaska's borders with Russia and Canada, from "Territorial Map of the World." Segal and Cohen's map is divided in such a way that it does not foreground Alaska's proximity to Russia, but the dotted line in this detail of the map indicates where Russia abuts the US EEZ. Meanwhile, to the east we see some of the United States' land and maritime border with Canada.

> Within its EEZ, a coastal State has: (a) sovereign rights for the purpose of exploring, exploiting, conserving and managing natural resources, whether living or nonliving, of the seabed and subsoil and the superadjacent waters and with regard to other activities for the economic exploitation and exploration of the zone, such as the production of energy from the water, currents and winds; (b) jurisdiction as provided for in international law with regard to the establishment and use of artificial islands, installations, and structures, marine scientific research, and the protection and preservation of the marine environment, and (c) other rights and duties provided for under international law.[3]

The discussion explains that the United States has subscribed to the maritime doctrine of the EEZ since 1983, and NOAA provides readers with a map of the US EEZ that is titled "The United States is an Ocean Nation" (see fig. 1.5).[4] Though it does not represent the countries with which the United States shares its maritime boundaries, this map on the NOAA website outlines approximately the same EEZ as is found on Segal and Cohen's 2013 map, and it offers the following caption: "The U.S. exclusive economic zone (EEZ) extends 200 nautical miles offshore, encompassing diverse ecosystems and vast natural resources, such as fisheries and energy and other mineral resources. The U.S. EEZ is the largest in the world, spanning over 13,000 miles of coastline and containing 3.4 million square miles of ocean—larger than the combined land area of all fifty states."[5]

Consider the contrast between that caption's uncharacteristic sense of US oceanic nationalism and the deeply conventional continental nationalism that persists into the present within the current US passport, the very document that regulates US citizens' ability to move beyond the United States' few land borders and its preponderant number of water borders. The passport's continental nationalism surfaces pronouncedly in many of the historical quotations that appear as epigraphs on the visa pages. Whereas NOAA directs readers to a map that trumpets the United States' oceanic EEZ as "the largest in the world," the US passport advances Horace Greeley's famous nineteenth-century endorsement of continental manifest destiny: "Go west, young man, and grow up with the country." Whereas NOAA points readers to a map that outlines an oceanic territory that is "larger than the combined land area of all fifty states," the passport has President Lyndon B. Johnson reminding US Americans of the specific landed forms of the United States' fundamentally continental geography: "For this is what America is all about. It is the uncrossed desert and the unclimbed ridge."[6] And whereas NOAA turns our image of the United States

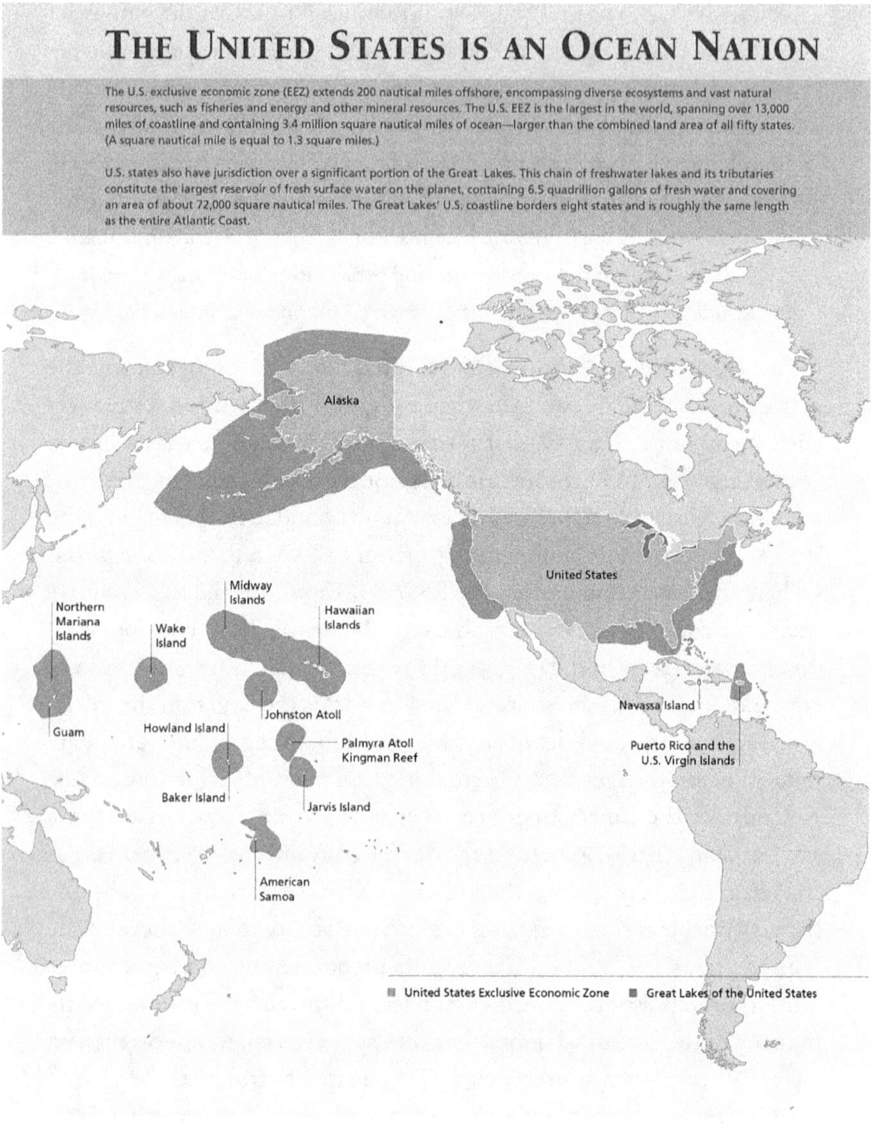

FIGURE 1.5 — Map portraying the United States as an ocean nation. "The United States is an Ocean Nation," NOAA Office of General Counsel, accessed August 24, 2020, https://www.gc.noaa.gov/documents/2011/012711_gcil_maritime_eez_map.pdf.

inside out by calling it "an ocean nation," the passport showcases two quotations on the transcontinental railroad. Jessamyn West, a US novelist, describes this railroad as "a big iron needle stitching the country together," while on another visa page we read the aspiration inscribed on the Golden Spike at Promontory Summit in Utah: "May God continue the unity of our country as the railroad unites the two great oceans of the world." But lest we forget that what is geographically central is not the uniting of two oceans but rather the continental landmass that extends from sea to shining sea, the passport advances Theodore Roosevelt's words: "This is a new nation based on a mighty continent, of boundless possibilities."[7]

Of course, even as Roosevelt imagined the United States as firmly based on the continent, he believed the country had claim on a new form of seagoing manifest destiny that was not hemmed in by the continent's shorelines.[8] During the final decade of the nineteenth century, with the Spanish-American War, a US imperial archipelago became the very object of what Roosevelt famously described as the United States' manly dedication to maintaining a "strenuous life."[9] "We cannot avoid," he intoned in the introduction to his 1900 volume *The Strenuous Life*, "the responsibilities that confront us in Hawaii, Cuba, Porto Rico, and the Philippines."[10] Yet even as manifest destiny overflowed the continent and mixed with the oceans—indeed, even as Roosevelt called for "the isthmian canal . . . which will enable us to have our say in deciding the destiny of the oceans of the East and the West"—he reaffirmed, in 1917, the continent's primacy: if there was a destiny to be had in the saltwater, the United States nevertheless remained stalwartly "based on a mighty continent."[11] Still strenuous after all these years, these are the continental presumptions now enshrined on the visa pages of the US passport.

One need not look far for the material ramifications of the United States' long-running and dual movement of seeking destiny in the oceans even while denying—on the stage of popular and judicial politics—full national identity to the noncontinental accruals of the country's seagoing manifest destiny. Looking back to the late nineteenth and early twentieth centuries, one may recall the US Supreme Court's Insular Cases, which determined "that the US Constitution does not apply fully to territories acquired through conquest after the Spanish-American War and the signing of the Treaty of Paris in 1898," with the "practical effect" even today of "refusing application of constitutional protections . . . to people recognized as US citizens."[12] The Insular Cases' ramifications are showcased in CHamoru (Chamorro) poet and activist Craig Santos Perez's 2017 poem

"Guam, Where America's Voting Rights End," in which Perez reminds us that even if the United States has a president like Barack Obama, invested in "civil rights" and hailing "from the Pacific," the island of Guam (a US territory to which the Insular Cases apply) "remains a forgotten name," a place where US citizens live without US constitutional protections. Perez's poem flatly recalls that "Obama only visited Guam once," a lackluster visit in 2011 during which "his plane landed at night on the air force base, / refueled, then departed."[13]

Of course, President Obama, at the time of his 2011 stopover, was grappling with difficulties that stemmed in part from the very Pacific connections that Perez mentions in his poem. It was no doubt anti-Black racism that undergirded birtherism's bad-faith contention, during and around the Obama presidency, that Obama was not born in the United States and hence was ineligible for the office to which he had been elected. Yet this racism existed in a state of interanimation with the subtler and less recognized tradition of viewing *only* the continental United States as properly *the* United States, while viewing archipelagic spaces as irretrievably foreign. Consider the Twitter feed of birtherism's most visible and influential proponent, who peppered his birtherist conspiracy theories with references to Hawai'i and Indonesia, the former being Obama's birthplace and the latter being one of his homes as a child.[14] (Had President Obama been white, been born on the US continent, and attended grade school for a time in continental Europe, would anyone have cast suspicion on his birth in the United States? The case of Franklin Delano Roosevelt stands as a stark counterpoint.) In light of this anti-insularity, it was unsurprising, a few years later, that when President Donald Trump's religiously discriminatory attempt to ban people from several predominantly Muslim countries was blocked by Judge Derrick Watson of the federal district court in Hawai'i in April 2017, the head of the US Department of Justice, attorney general Jeff Sessions, spoke in a way that mixed the Trump administration's overt efforts at religious discrimination with continental exceptionalism's enmity toward island spaces. "I really am amazed," reeled the head of the US Department of Justice, "that a judge sitting on an island in the Pacific can issue an order that stops the president of the United States."[15]

As a Caribbean-oriented follow-up to Sessions's remarkable dismissal of the US state of Hawai'i for its geographic situation as an archipelago in the Pacific, we saw the Trump administration's reaction to Hurricane Maria as it devastated the US territory of Puerto Rico in September of the same year. While reactivating stereotypes of Latinas/os as lazy ("They want everything to be done for them," tweeted the commander in chief), President Trump made landlocked and continentalist excuses for his administration's torpid response to the hurricane: "This is an island, surrounded by water. Big water. Ocean water." At another point: "It's very tough, because it's an island. ... In Texas, we can ship the trucks right out there. ... But the difference is, this is an island sitting in the middle of an ocean. And it's a big ocean; it's a very big ocean."[16] About a year later, after a death toll of nearly three thousand lives in Puerto Rico came into focus, Fabiola Santiago of the *Miami Herald* pointed out the anomaly of Trump's self-congratulatory stance regarding what he continued to describe as his "fantastic" response to Hurricane Maria. Santiago wrote, "Let the astonishing statistic for a small island of 3.7 million people sink in, and ask: Would anyone be congratulating themselves on the rescue and recovery job done if this had happened in Florida or anywhere else in the continental United States?" Santiago continued, gesturing to the fact that the United States has the most powerful navy in the world, "Nor is it impossible for a country like the United States with extremely well-funded military operations to get quick aid to an island just because it's surrounded by water, as Trump said in his childish explanation of why it took so long to appropriately respond to the disaster."[17]

As salutary as the US institution of liberal democracy can often feel, minorities in the United States—whether racial, ethnic, religious, political, LGBTQ, or others—have long needed to contend with what Alexis de Tocqueville once called "the tyranny of the majority," a tyranny that permits the majority, many times by design but often without thinking, to pass laws, make policies, and advance cultural norms that place minority populations at still greater disadvantage.[18] Indeed, this tyranny functions, as Lisa Lowe has pointed out, to buoy up liberal democracy's capital-driven commitment to "the social productions of 'difference,' of restrictive particularity and illegitimacy marked by race, nation, geographical origins, and gender."[19] As I discuss further in chapter 2 of this study, within the United States the demographically based tyranny of the majority has operated in tandem with a geographically based analogue—the tyranny of the continent, which has fetishized continental vastness and coded islands as inferior, espousing the exceptional status of the US continental state even while functioning to legitimize imperialism among islands and oceans beyond the continent's shores. Thomas Paine's 1776 pronouncements in *Common Sense* offer something of an origin story for the mode of continental tyranny that has extended from the country's beginnings into the present day. "Small islands," Paine argued, are proper "for kingdoms to take under their care; but there is something very absurd, in supposing a continent to be perpetually governed by an island."[20] Here we see that the blueprint for US sovereignty from insular England was sketched in big structures across the vast continent, while the political-geographic logic for a future US empire of "small islands" was already in place at the US founding, giving rise to a project that has, to borrow from Walter D. Mignolo and Catherine E. Walsh, "engendered coloniality and disguised it by the promises and premises of modernity."[21] This logic and project set up the preconditions for President Obama's 2011 stopover in Guam and the Trump administration's dismissal of Hawai'i and dilatory response to devastation in Puerto Rico.

We see a tension between the country's canonical and mythic continental borders and its noncanonical and material oceanic borders. As much as the tyranny of the continent has remained active in US political rhetoric as we enter the third decade of the twenty-first century, and even as it has had profound material consequences for the emergence and continued existence of a US empire of small islands, the United States' fetishization of its continental vastness lost its geographically material warrant in 1983, when the country became, as relayed by NOAA, "an ocean nation," embracing the doctrine of the EEZ and thereby claiming an ocean area larger than the land area of all fifty states. In other words, while present-day US demographers take pains to accurately forecast a date in the future when the United States will no longer be a majority-white country (and while prominent modes of demagoguery in the United States seek to mobilize white voting and vigilante constituencies by playing on white fears of the new tyrannies that a future nonwhite majority may usher in), scholarly and popular perception of US geography has largely fallen asleep with regard to a crucial shift that has long since taken place: owing to the EEZ's interactions with the islands and archipelagoes that are claimed as US territories, the United States lost its hallowed geographic status as a majority-continent nation nearly four decades ago.[22] It became a majority-ocean nation.

In the introduction to our edited collection *Archipelagic American Studies* (2017), Michelle Ann Stephens and I traced some ways in which the US transformation from majority-continent to majority-ocean was underway long before the arrival of UNCLOS in 1982. We have pointed to several watershed moments as preconditions for this transformation: the

Guano Islands Act of 1856, the Spanish-American War of 1898, the illegal annexation of Hawai'i in the same year, the purchase of American Samoa in 1899, and US control of the Trust Territory of the Pacific Islands after World War II and into the 1980s and 1990s. We argued that "as the energies of Manifest Destiny shifted from wayfaring across the continent to seafaring in the Caribbean and the Pacific, the United States constructed an imperial archipelago that deformed—stretched, twisted, and finally fractured—[the country's] entity status to the point of a topological shift," wherein a shift in the topology or form of national geography constituted a shift in national ontology.[23] With this ontological shift, the United States has moved from Paine's vision of US American sovereignty stemming from its fundamental continental form, to Roosevelt's affirmation that the imperial United States of the early twentieth century continued to be *based* on a continent, to NOAA's astounding assertion that (as stated by the map title) "The United States is an Ocean Nation." The iconic stars that spangle a field of blue: these have represented US states to generations of schoolchildren. But might NOAA's articulation of the country admit a new symbology, wherein the canonized US states and the territorial US states may be seen to flow into one another, to mingle and grate against each other in the blue waters, amid the storms and stresses of an ocean nation that has, contra Paine, no nature-inscribed logic for sovereignty, coherence, or existence? The flag's star-spangled blue ocean, then, becomes a site amenable to the existential seeking described in 1946 by the US American writer Carlos Bulosan, who was a US national because he was born in the US territory of the Philippines but who was nonetheless ineligible for US citizenship. Bulosan at one point envisioned stars floating in the blue ocean—in desperation and hope at what he found while reading literature in the continental United States, he imagined "boring through the earth's core, leveling all seas and oceans, swimming in the constellations."[24] What constellations might we swim among, in an ocean spangled with a gyre of canonical and noncanonical US states? What are the borders and waters that imperfectly divide and incompletely unify these states of grating coalitions and dissensions, histories and futures?

Whether or not we adopt NOAA's phrase "ocean nation," the purpose of the present study is not to play into the notions of geographic majority and minority that have undergirded the tyranny of the continent during the course of centuries. *Borderwaters* does not seek to usher in continental tyranny's mirror image, a tyranny of the ocean, by simply presenting readers with a version of national geography in which the United States is the largest oceanic nation in the world, with claims to oceanic territory that exceed its claims to continental territory, and with claims, furthermore, to only a minority share of the very continent to which it has staked its popular geographic self-perception as a nation. As close as that view might hew to the materiality of the lands and waters that the United States claims as its territory, modes of predictable and unpredictable demagoguery would lurk within this tack's continued fetishization of geographic size. Hence, *Borderwaters*, even as it works to undercut continental exceptionalism, does not pit the ocean or the island against the continent. And it is certainly not an endorsement of any past or present US land or water claims, many of which have been and continue to be legitimately contested by Indigenous groups, and all of which (however permanent the present-day borders of the United States may seem) will certainly shift and even disappear in the future, depending on how distant a future we set our sights on. Rather, *Borderwaters* is concerned with what the volume *Archipelagic American Studies* describes as "'the archipelagic Americas,' or the temporally shifting and spatially splayed set of islands, island chains, and island-ocean-continent relations which have exceeded US Americanism and have been affiliated with and indeed constitutive of competing notions of the Americas since at least 1492."[25] Within that collection's model, the archipelagic Americas span over five centuries and are not circumscribed by US imperialism, US territorial claims, or US existence. Consequently, essays in that volume interrogate the archipelagic Americas in space-times ranging from seventeenth-century Mexico to twenty-first-century New Zealand and Canada and from the Great Pacific Garbage Patch to the francophone Caribbean. Distinct from *Archipelagic American Studies* in scope and purpose, *Borderwaters* speaks to a more focused set of coordinates in space and time, redescribing the United States and its planetary embeddedness in a way that finds touchstones in twentieth-century cultural-ecological events: epoch-defining scholarly narratives regarding the United States, nuclear weapons that rescript warfare and wreak environmental devastation, hurricanes in the Pacific and Caribbean, literary writings that are geoformally attentive, US deployments of non-Euclidean geometries amid the oceans, the World War II–era carving of stone containing fossils of half-a-billion-year-old sea creatures, a world's fair that turned the Pacific into a pageant. These and other events set up the preconditions for the United States' late twentieth-century territorial shift to a terraqueous national ontology and the early twenty-first-century possibilities of its emergence as self-conscious regarding this shift. In so doing, *Borderwaters* disrupts the continent's exceptionalist and even tyrannical claims by giving place to the interrelated land-water complexes of the archipelago and the borderwaters.

What Is an Archipelago?

Because I do not want to pit the preponderant materialities of US ocean and island spaces against the enduring if geographically unmoored metaphor of the United States as a fundamentally continental nation, I gravitate in this study toward the term *archipelago*, along with its adjectival form, *archipelagic*. (Pronouncing the latter term can be a bit tricky for many English speakers, but it is central enough to this study that it warrants mention that, based on the guidance of reputable dictionaries, speakers of US and British English should pronounce *archipelagic* so that the initial *arch-* rhymes with *snark* and the final *-lagic* rhymes with *magic*.[26]) The term *archipelago* has the benefit of operating very clearly at the intersection of the material and the metaphorical. It also admits, like the allied term *terraqueous*, both water and land (including, as we shall see, continents) to its suite of ontological and epistemological concerns. In its entry for the term *archipelago*, the *Oxford English Dictionary* (*OED*), in both the second edition of 1989 and the current online edition, notes that the word derives from the Italian *arcipelago*, with *arci-* signifying "chief, principal" and *-pelago* signifying "deep, abyss, gulf, pool." The entry clarifies that the term, while drawing on Greek roots, does not derive from "ancient or mediæval Greek" but developed first in early modern "western languages" such as Italian, Spanish, Portuguese, and French. From there, it was imported into Modern Greek. The *OED*'s first definition for *archipelago* appears as follows: "The Ægean Sea, between Greece and Asia Minor," with the first such usage listed as occurring in 1268 in a treaty "between the Venetians and the emperor Michael Palaeologus." The term's second definition points toward the planetary deployment of the first definition as a metaphor: "Hence (as [the Aegean] is studded with many isles): Any sea, or sheet of water, in which there are numerous islands; and [in a transferred sense] a group of islands." The dictionary's examples for this latter usage date from 1529 to about 1860, with the term *archipelago*, this erstwhile synonym for the Aegean, applied to island groups situated in what we now think of as Indonesia, the Arctic Ocean, the Pacific, and the North Atlantic.[27] Interestingly, the definitions and examples provided by the *OED*'s second and online editions remain unchanged from those included in the dictionary's first edition (1933) and, looking further back, unchanged from those included in the *OED*'s late nineteenth-century forerunner, *A New English Dictionary on Historical Principles* (*NED*). Indeed, as of the present writing, the online *OED* repeats verbatim the *NED*'s original definition and usage examples for *archipelago* as first offered in the 1880s.[28]

Within discussions of archipelagoes (whether in the humanities, social sciences, jurisprudence, or diplomacy), these 130-year-old definitions and etymologies, or their derivations, are widely cited. Indeed, we might consider the *NED/OED* as having provided a baseline narrative within archipelagic thought, namely, that the term *archipelago* arose as a name for the island-studded and material Aegean Sea and was subsequently applied metaphorically to other island-studded seas and to island groups throughout the world. This narrative is at once compact (contained in a single sentence) and astonishingly sweeping, unfolding over the course of centuries (from the thirteenth century to the twenty-first century) and comprehending, though only obliquely acknowledging, the planet-spanning conflicts (material and epistemic) that have been concomitant with continua of Indigenous knowledges; varied approaches and responses to colonization, empire, and liberalism; myriad processes of creolization and *mestizaje*; postcolonial and decolonial thought and practice; developments in human perception of terraqueous materialities and objects, including oceans, islands, and continents; efforts in linguistic and cultural translation; and schemes of active and passive miscommunication, genocide, enslavement, liberation, trans-Indigenous solidarities, and cultural reconstitutions and grapplings with neoliberalism. These vectors, together with uncounted other events that contribute to a skyward-growing pile of what the proverbial Benjaminian angle of history might see as debris, constitute the backdrop that informed, and was reciprocally informed by, the processes by which a term for the Aegean Sea came to be applied metaphorically to groups of islands that span the planet.[29]

I have underscored a contrast between, on the one hand, the pat and unchanging definition of *archipelago* as conveyed by the *OED* and, on the other hand, the messy and mercurial historical, epistemological, and ontological struggles and processes that exist not as a dynamic backdrop for a static term but as the historical dynamo for what I also take to be the dynamic, shimmering term *archipelago*. In other words, as intriguing and useful as the *OED*'s historically informed and etymologically based definitions are, the dictionary definition is far from adequate for this study's approach to a long twentieth century's US American subset of the archipelagic Americas. I am unaware that any scholar has undertaken, to any substantial degree, a project that has sought to document the multilanguage historical processes that undergird the archipelagic narrative implied in the *NED/OED*. Such a project would require a facility not only with English, Italian, Spanish, Portuguese, French, Dutch, and other colonial languages but also with the host of Indigenous languages spoken by the many groups whose members in various ways resisted, succumbed to, and stood apart from invasion and colonization by speakers of the colonizing languages. How might Taíno epistemologies regarding island interconnection have interacted with Spanish projections of Caribbean islands as a New World archipelago analogous to the Aegean? How have Polynesian methods of island grouping interacted with traditions of French archipelagic thought? What Indigenous notions of island linkages and separations have been lost or have persisted in the face of the Spanish and subsequent US American application of the archipelago concept to island groups such as the Philippines and the Marianas? How did the Dutch term *archipel* interface with fourteenth-century Javanese and later twentieth-century Indonesian notions of Nusantara?

Various facets of the answers to such questions must be acknowledged as, to borrow a phrase from George B. Handley, having "inevitably and irrevocably fallen into historical oblivion."[30] But for many of these questions, the oblivion is revocable, with its revocation contingent on scholars' linguistic facility. Still, the very question of linguistic facility presents a conundrum: imagine a Venn diagram illustrating the overlap between scholars with a research agenda in archipelagic thought and scholars who have facility with at least ten of the languages germane to planetary archipelagic research. I suspect that such a diagram would showcase a very limited degree of overlap. (I, for one, would not be present in the overlap.) And yet, to my mind, a sprawling comparative project—multilingual, long-durational, transregional, and involving multiple participants—would be one of the most urgent of all projects that could be undertaken in the realm of archipelagic thinking. Unsurprisingly, the Martinican philosopher Édouard Glissant has suggested that "translation is ... among the elements most important within ... archipelagic thought."[31] Far beyond the *NED/OED*'s concise historical definitions and sparsely documented usage examples, such a project would move toward asking and answering, in deeply material and culturally aware ways, a question that must lie at the very foundation of research into archipelagic thinking: What is an archipelago?

Derek Walcott once contemplated an analogous question: "What is the nature of the island?" He concluded he was not ready to answer it: "Except by hints. Contradictions. Terrors. The opposite method to the explorer's."[32] Neither does *Borderwaters* undertake anything close to the project that would be required to begin to answer such a question regarding the nature or natures of an archipelago. What this project *does*, however, is side with the messy and the mercurial—delving into, at various points, thought regarding issues of island-ocean-shoreline-continent relations as it has developed and at times cross-pollinated in English, French, Spanish, Indonesian, Japanese, and other languages, including, if it may be called a language, mathematics. Thus, readers will find that a definition of what an archipelago *is* grows by accretion throughout this study's five chapters, as *Borderwaters* traces various things that an archipelago *does* or is capable of doing, materially and epistemologically. But it is nonetheless worth stating at the outset certain assumptions that I am making about the nature—or multiple natures—of an archipelago, beyond the layperson's definition of an archipelago as a group of islands.

To start with, I have an exceedingly difficult time accepting the idea that an archipelago exists independent of some form of subjectivity. If an archipelago is a group of islands, then the grouping of material islands must take place by means of some subjective and relational heuristic. We see this in the postcolonial nationalism that became Indonesia's archipelagic heuristic, while Enlightenment racial classification became Melanesia's (the latter name referring to "the region of islands inhabited by darkskinned peoples").[33] Elsewhere, we see commonality of magnitude among islands, as in the Lesser Antilles, or linguistic relation, as in Polynesia or the francophone Caribbean. In this way my understanding of an archipelago is allied with what we see in the Hawaiian language, which has two terms, *pae 'āina* and *pae moku*, that may be translated into English as *archipelago*. Brandy Nālani McDougall has explained that these two terms "conceive of multiple lands as interconnected" and so "imply active human and state intervention in the creation of an archipelago."[34] And together with human and state interventions, I also admit alien, weird, or otherwise nonhuman subjectivities such as those exhibited by island-hopping birds, large monitor lizards swimming among islands, or the coral polyps that form the islets that constitute the archipelagic formation of an atoll—for this latter case, it might be said that the living islands themselves exhibit alien forms of thought capable of thinking archipelagically.[35] Analogous to the islands that make up an archipelago, the logs that make up a raft don't tie themselves together—someone or something is lashing the cords. Yet an archipelago is not made up of islands alone—it is a terraqueous complex that is also crucially constituted by the waters in which the islands exist. The OED's etymological history informs us that centuries ago the term originally referred to the Aegean, or the *chief sea*, and only incidentally to the sea's many islands. During their decades-long fight for recognition as an "archipelagic State," diplomats from Indonesia resurrected the term's lost terraqueous definition and melded the NED/OED definition with some Indonesians' Indigenous traditions of referring to their archipelago as *tanah air*, a term usually translated into English as "homeland," in which *tanah* refers to land and *air* refers to water (more on this in chapter 3). Since the finalization of UNCLOS, which liberally incorporates Indonesian notions of archipelagic space into its definition of an "archipelagic State," the populations of every nation-state on the planet have been impacted by Indonesia's success in grafting the term *archipelago* onto an Indigenous etymology that situates water as a nonnegotiable component of archipelagic space.[36] Nodding toward the archipelago as a water-land complex, Juan Carlos Quintero Herencia has stated that an archipelago exists as the "consequence of activities and experiences that interweave themselves into interpretations" that then flow onto and into "islands and their waters, lands and their seas."[37]

Further, moving beyond descriptions of archipelagoes as groups of islands or island-water complexes, I take continents and temporality as crucial and in some ways interlinked components of an archipelagic frame. I am persuaded by Glissant's observations on continents *archipelagizing*, or reconfiguring themselves such that they attain a set of archipelagic relations within and among themselves but also with islands and oceans. Here Glissant is, to draw on Michael Wiedorn, taking the "exceptionality of the Caribbean as a template for the future of the world."[38] While I do not embrace Glissant's vision of the Caribbean as *the* exceptional template for relations across the planet, I nonetheless see acuity in Glissant's vision, for instance, when he looked at Europe and claimed, "Europe is turning into an archipelago. That is to say that beyond national barriers, we see many islands taking shape in relation to one another. . . . I feel it acutely in European life, which is becoming a sort of archipelago with [regional cultural] islands maintaining relations among themselves."[39] Elsewhere, he has observed that this process is occurring throughout the world, including in the Americas: "What I am seeing today is that continents are 'archipelagizing,' at least from an outsider's point of view. The Americas are archipelagizing—they are made up of regions *par-dessus les frontières nationales*."[40] I have permitted the closing phrase of this quotation to remain in Glissant's French because translating it outright would not do justice to what I see as its relation to the archipelagic United States. Most simply, the phrase might be translated as "beyond national borders," which for Glissant, in this context, likely points toward a proliferation of subnational entities or cultural islands whose cultures overflow national boundaries and thereby ask us to see beyond the borders of the nation-state.[41] And yet Glissant's statement on the archipelagization of the continental Americas might also be taken, in the context of the United States of America, as adumbrating the nation-state's constitution to a large extent by island-ocean regions that exist, to try out another translation, "beyond national frontiers," a phrase evocative of US American national frontiers that are classically continental. The terraqueous regions beyond the nation's continental frontiers may be cultural islands in the Glissantian sense. But they are also archipelagic spaces constituted by material oceans and material islands whose existence is in turn to a large extent constitutive of the United States of America and whose suite of archipelagic relationalities has transformed the continental United States into a swath of continental land that is and has been archipelagizing. Conventionally, archipelagic thinkers (whether in international law or cultural criticism) have started at the shoreline and asked how far seaward we might find archipelagic waters and archipelagic relationalities; in tandem, and also with the shoreline as a starting place, I ask how far inland we might find these archipelagic waters and relationalities. If the continent is archipelagizing, can archipelagic waters and relationalities be traced up a river, moving upstream like salmon swimming toward an ancestral spawning creek? Can they be engraved on a golden spike that unites two oceans, evocative of Walt Whitman's vision of "the earth to be spann'd, connected by network, / .... The oceans to be cross'd, the distant brought near"?[42]

Can they flood continents and turn hills into islands or even transform mountain ranges into island chains? To the topic of continents as archipelagoes, François Noudelmann has appended the question of temporality: "The continent itself can become an archipelago if we think of it differently, as . . . continually changing."[43] This is an image of archipelagic islands as not simply existing within a shimmering ocean but also, themselves, shimmering with change through their dynamic interrelations with the ocean, each other, and archipelagic continents. But this image of islands' shimmering temporalities does not agree with UNCLOS's definition of an island, which is also time dependent but at the same moment seems to bracket temporality by insisting on a definition based on a snapshot taken at one specific point within the tide's cycle. "An island is a naturally formed area of land, surrounded by water, which is above water at high tide," states UNCLOS in Part VIII, "Regime of Islands."[44] *Borderwaters* sides with the shimmering, with the temporal messiness of which UNCLOS is very much aware but that it wishes to forestall by recourse to a snapshot view that defines islands as only those entities that exist at high tide. Amid the messiness, an archipelago might consist of a set of islands that exist for only five minutes—all that is needed for a series of waves during a rising tide to break a sandbar into multiple pieces and then wash them away. Or, to compress things further, an archipelago might last a few milliseconds—constituted by the set of pebbles momentarily exposed near a shoreline as one ripple pulls back and another fillips forward. Moving into much vaster timescales, we might consider the work of Columbia University geologist Marshall Kay, who in the 1940s "made the connection between modern-day 'island arcs' (such as Japan, the Aleutians, the Philippines, the outer archipelago of Indonesia) and the fully consolidated linear mountain belts that we see on the continents."[45] Relating to this observation on the geographic form or topology held in common by mountain ranges and archipelagoes, Kay published a 1951 map visualizing the "paleogeography" of North America as he retrojected that it would have appeared just after the Cambrian period about half a billion years ago (see fig. 1.6). On the map, the swath of land that would later become the continental United States is submerged hundreds of miles inland in many places, so that present-day mountain ranges become archipelagoes that flank North America to the east and west, while all of the remaining lands of the (future) continental United States appear not as fruited plains but as "coastal plain[s]" that span from archipelago to shining archipelago.

The archipelago of millisecond duration and the aeonic archipelagoes of North American paleogeography could not seem further from each other in terms of temporal duration, and yet geoformally the archipelago of the millisecond could stand in for the archipelago of the geologic age (a set of rocks off the coast). And indeed both of these archipelagoes—seemingly so far removed from a scale relevant to humans—could stand in geoformally for any number of archipelagoes that currently exist on a human temporal scale, whether these are archipelagoes that tragically

FIGURE I.6 — "Paleogeography of Early Medial Ordovician of North America," drawn by Erwin Raisz. From Marshall Kay, *North American Geosynclines*, Geological Society of America memoir 48 (1951; repr., New York: Geological Society of America, 1963), xii.

may be on their way out (certain islands in the Pacific disappeared by extractive capitalism's global warming) or archipelagoes that are on their way in (California or the Carolinas literally archipelagized by that same global warming). The archipelago, then, as it shimmers through time and water, becomes a geographic form that permits human temporalities to link up—perhaps even to archipelagize—with nonhuman temporalities that have traditionally been bracketed rather than grappled with in the humanities and social sciences. In this version of the archipelago, humans may find access to that which is so temporally microscopic that it lies beyond the ken of even the most abusive of traditional close readings, as well as access to geologic and cosmological temporalities far beyond the multidecade spans of Franco Moretti's distant-reading projects, so vast as to evoke nihilistic reconceptualizations of humans as meaningless specks of dust floating across the stage lights of aeonic dramas.[46] In this way, the archipelago emerges as an answer to Wai Chee Dimock's question, as posed in a conversation on temporality with Mark McGurl, "Isn't it possible that the macro and the micro might be connected . . . [by] a layer of mediation we have yet to theorize, going back and forth between the micro and the macro, maintaining a nonrigid but also nontrivial distinction between the two?"[47]

Material, metaphorical, translational, terraqueous, archipelagizing, geoformal, and temporally scalar: these are some of the attributes of an archipelago that I assume at the outset. And if a shorthand definition of *archipelagic thinking* might be thinking that takes the archipelago as a thought template or even intellectual collaborator, then this same list of attributes would also be salient within archipelagic thought.[48] Further elaborations on archipelagic thinking will grow by accretion, and in dialogue with archipelagic thinkers hailing from various archipelagoes, throughout the chapters of this study. But with these initial attributes in mind, we may approach an important US Geological Survey publication that was issued seven times during the long twentieth century that *Borderwaters* addresses.

With a title that shifted over the decades, this publication originally appeared in 1885 as *Boundaries of the United States and of the Several States and Territories* and had its final publication in 1976 as *Boundaries of the United States and the Several States*.[49] The table of contents for the 1885 edition lists, beyond the eastern slice of the continent claimed by war and treaty from Great Britain and Indigenous nations, the following "additions to the territory of the United States": the Louisiana Purchase, Florida, Texas, the first Mexican cession, the Gadsden Purchase, and Alaska.[50] Between this first edition in 1885 and the final edition in 1976, we see many changes, with a proliferating variety of geographies added and taken away, as well as a dizzying variety of modes of governmentality vis-à-vis these geographies. The table of contents for the 1900 edition adds Hawai'i, Puerto Rico, Guam, and the Philippines.[51] The 1904 edition adds American Samoa.[52] In 1923 the table of contents adds several new entries: Wake Island, the Panama Canal Zone, the US Virgin Islands, the Guano Islands (involving many nineteenth-century island claims in the Caribbean and Pacific), and claims related to Guantanamo, Wrangell Island, Tonga Islands, Yap Island, extraterritorial holdings such as diplomatic missions, and "territorial waters" that extend about three nautical miles off the coast.[53] The 1930 version adds discussions of the Isle of Pines off Cuba, the Great and Little Corn Islands off Nicaragua, Bennett Island

and others north of Siberia, islands in the North Pole region, and "air space over a state or nation."[54] In the 1966 version, the Philippines have disappeared from the list, while other geographies are added: Midway and Johnston Islands and Canton and Enderbury Islands (among the Guano Islands), as well as a new section that describes "interests of the United States beyond its borders," which includes Antarctica, military and naval bases, the Trust Territory of the Pacific Islands, and the underwater or submerged lands of the continental shelf.[55] When this publication was first issued (in 1885), the United States professed no boundaries except the seashore and those negotiated (often violently) with other entities on the North American continent.[56] In contrast, the 1976 version of *Boundaries of the United States and the Several States* explains, "In this paper, the phrase 'territory of the United States' includes areas under the sovereignty or jurisdiction of the United States. These areas extend over a large part of the earth; from Barrow, Alaska, on the north to American Samoa on the south, and from the Palau Islands in the western Pacific to the Virgin Islands in the Atlantic."[57] These four geodetic markers, so to speak, range from an Arctic town in a continental (albeit noncontiguous) US state to the islands of an unincorporated US territory in the Pacific where the flag flies without offering full constitutional rights, and from another such territory in the Caribbean to an archipelago that abuts Indonesia and is paradoxically referred to as US territory even while it is, as part of the Trust Territory of the Pacific Islands, described in the same publication as one of the "interests of the United States beyond its borders." Amid these four ultima Thules of US American territory, as the entire run of this publication makes clear, we see an incredible variety of modes of US governmentality: states, commonwealths, districts, territories (incorporated and unincorporated, organized and unorganized), leases (perpetual, hundred-year, terminable only by mutual agreement), military bases and coaling stations, extraterritorial demarcations associated with diplomacy, US jurisdiction without US sovereignty, territory that lies paradoxically beyond borders, commercial claims to underwater lands, "territorial sea" that is legally beyond US boundaries, speculations on airspace, and entities of blurred or joint sovereignty owing to competing national claims. This list could go on, and it certainly has as we have moved past 1976, with the emergence of UNCLOS in 1982 and the EEZ, as well as the termination of the Trust Territory of the Pacific Islands, which has been partially replaced with a new governmental mode of "free association" between the United States and the Federated States of Micronesia, the Republic of the Marshall Islands, and the Republic of Palau.

The scenes that come into view via this survey of *Boundaries of the United States and the Several States* should draw attention to commentary by Alyosha Goldstein in the introduction to *Formations of United States Colonialism*, wherein he reminds us that "the United States of America has never been a uniform or unequivocal geopolitical entity.... Rather, the United States encompasses a historically variable and uneven constellation of state and local governments, indigenous nations, unincorporated territories, free associated commonwealths, protectorates, federally administered public lands, military bases, export processing zones, *colonias*, and anomalies such as the District of Columbia."[58] Also turning his sights on this multifarious version of the United States, Paul Lai has played on the phrase *contiguous United States* to coin the term *discontiguous states of America*, framing the United States as a geopolitical entity whose "discontiguous" qualities permit only a "discontinuous logic of unity, one in which leaps of logic are necessary to create a semblance of wholeness."[59] Drawing on Lai's terminology to assess not only "the discontiguous American Empire" but also the ways in which studies of US American cultures have themselves become discontiguous in assessing imperial and other US discontiguities, Craig Santos Perez has looked toward archipelagic American studies, asserting that an "archipelagic turn offers a promising analytic to navigate the transnational, transatlantic, transpacific, transindigenous, and transhemispheric turns in the now discontiguous archipelago of American studies."[60] Bringing the US Geological Survey's "several states" and Lai's "discontiguous states" into the ambit of what Perez has referred to as an "archipelagic turn," the present study, as its subtitle suggests, limns a set of analytic categories that may aid us in assessing cultural formations that have arisen amid the *archipelagic states of America*, a phrase I use to refer to the archipelagic portions and aspects of the United States of America. This is a postcontinental redescription of the United States that asks vast and unintegrated ocean and island territories to speak from their points of disjunction and quandary, placing pressure as well on archipelagic spaces that have generally been seen as continental. Here the archipelagic as a framework does not promise to integrate these points or to make them anything other than discontiguous, and yet it does offer, as Perez suggests, a navigational heuristic, one that permits studied and dexterous movement among, to borrow from Cuban theorist Antonio Benítez-Rojo, their discontinuous conjunctions.[61] These are the conjunctions and discontiguities of the US borderwaters, realms where weird sovereignties and nonsovereignties range from those showcased in the Insular Cases to those infusing the seaborne plastic shards lodged in the digestive tracts of Laysan albatrosses.

Borderwaters: A Stone Skipped across the Sea

To this point in the introduction, the question of borders has been an initiating conceit and subsequently woven throughout discussions of the United States as an oceanic and archipelagic nation. The boundaries of the EEZ have given rise to the image and fact of a United States that claims more ocean space than it does land space, a United States that unexpectedly borders twenty-one other countries, a Glissantian United States that archipelagizes beyond the continental frontier and beyond its maritime borders with paradoxical claims to territory outside of its own borders. This is a United States whose shifting boundaries are recounted rhythmically by the US Geological Survey across several editions of *Boundaries of the United States and the Several States*. Certainly, in this light, and in light of the near-universal recognition and sense of utility the term *borderlands* has attained within analyses of US and broader American cultures since the 1990s, one might feel justified in suggesting that the archipelagic states of America constitute a borderland or a set of borderlands. For me, this question came to a head at the 2012 American Studies Association Convention, held in San Juan, Puerto Rico, where Stephens and I organized a session titled "Archipelagic American Studies" and where I attended a topically allied session titled "Islands of Resistance: Taiwanese American Studies in the Twenty-first Century." After island-oriented presentations by Philip Deloria, Rob Wilson, Birgit Däwes, and Hsinya Huang, the session commentator, Iping Liang of National Taiwan Normal University, gave excellent commentary in which she, in passing, described islands as "borderlands," joining other critics whose work has gravitated toward this same land-oriented critical framework to describe archipelagic and oceanic spaces.[62] During the audience comment period, I pointed out the terrestrial bias inherent in the term *borderlands* and wondered, advancing a term I had just begun using that year, what a *borderwaters* framework would look like in the context of the session's titular "Islands of Resistance."[63] Liang's reply at the moment was a rather cagey caution against essentializing geographic forms in ways that mark a distinction between terrestrial and watery surfaces. But since 2012 I have continued to wonder whether terrestrial metaphors such as border*lands* and cross*roads* do not already stack the epistemological deck against—if not fully essentialize— our grapplings with archipelagic spaces and vast swaths of the planet that are, in Patricia Yaeger's words, "not geo- but aquacentric."[64]

In making our way toward the aquacentric notion of the borderwaters, it is useful to note that, at least according to my reckoning, iterations of the border*lands* paradigm have run along three distinct but sometimes converging or intersecting terrestrial tracks. Within the arena of North American history, borderlands studies has existed for a century, with beginnings in the landmark 1921 study by Herbert E. Bolton, *The Spanish Borderlands: A Chronicle of Old Florida and the Southwest*, followed by Bolton's expansion of "borderland researches" as applicable to the history "of the entire Western Hemisphere," including such topics as the "relations of New England and the Maritime Provinces of Canada."[65] Within the field of American history at the end of the twentieth century, the term had come to describe "the contested boundaries between colonial domains," a model in which "inter-imperial struggle" proceeded developmentally and teleologically toward "international coexistence" and thus turned "borderlands into *bordered* lands."[66] Here, in narrating "tales of economic exchange, cultural mixing, and political contestation at the edges of empires, nations, and world systems," the "borderlands are places" where "master American narratives" tend to "come unraveled," even as, according to some historians, early twenty-first-century "Americanists [have] run the risk of loving borderlands to death" by turning everything into a borderland.[67] In enacting this love, American historians have, since the late 1980s, taken inspiration from a Chicana/o track of borderlands studies that has also existed quite separately as a field of its own, with basic assumptions that can stand in stark contrast to those of American historians. Whereas historians in the Bolton stream have seen a model in which the borderland arrives first and the border follows (i.e., wild borderlands are domesticated into *bordered* lands), Gloria Anzaldúa's influential book *Borderlands/La Frontera* (1987) advanced an inverted model in which the border, "a dividing line," arrives on the scene first, followed by an epiphenomenal "borderland," "a vague and undetermined place created by the emotional residue of an unnatural boundary."[68] As Mary Pat Brady has noted, Anzaldúa's formulations were intentionally universalizing and have—analogous to American history's borderlands framework—been taken up widely in studies far beyond the US-Mexico border and its epiphenomenal borderlands, even as within Chicana/o studies (as John Alba Cutler observes), borders themselves have come unmoored from the territorial dividing line and have begun "emerging from multiple sites of racial, economic, and gendered contestation."[69] Concomitant with these moving borders, "the borderlands" of Chicana/o studies are "extending to places in the interior of the United States."[70]

A third track, like that of the American historians, also takes inspiration from Chicana/o borderlands studies. This body of work surrounds Walter D. Mignolo's decolonial border thinking/gnosis/epistemology, which "is a critical reflection on knowledge production from both the interior borders of the modern/colonial world system (imperial conflicts, hegemonic languages, directionality of translations, etc.) and its exterior borders (imperial conflicts with cultures being colonized, as well as the subsequent stages of independence or decolonization)."[71] Although it has the term *border* as its focal point, it does not often use the term *borderland* aside from its regular citations of Anzaldúa. Even so, it continues to see the border in landed terms, as depending on "massive appropriation of land accompanied by the constitution of international law that justified the massive appropriation of land."[72] And to date its thinking has been continentally driven to a large extent, as evidenced, for instance, in the preponderance of continent-based languages in Mignolo and Madina V. Tlostanova's list of languages that the "decolonial epistemic shift" might call upon: "Mandarin, Japanese, Russian, Hindi, Urdu, Aymara, Nahuatl, Wolof, Arabic, etc."[73] Aside from its nod to Japanese, this list either completely disregards languages with centers of gravity among what Du Bois called "the islands of the sea," or it compresses them into the term *etc.*[74] Still, even in its continentally minded and landed present, border thinking with its aspirations toward decoloniality, or its commitment to struggling "from and within modernity/coloniality's borders ... to build a radically distinct world," is invested in what has been an archipelagic keyword, *relationality*, which Mignolo and Catherine E. Walsh take to mean the "ways that different local histories and embodied conceptions and practices ... can enter into conversations and build understandings that ... cross geopolitical locations and colonial differences."[75] Hence, it is unsurprising that, even as Mignolo has based his border gnosis primarily on the continental foundations of "the Chicano/a experience" and "African *gnosis*," he at one point permits himself the tangent of considering the Barbadian poet and theorist Edward Kamau Brathwaite's "search for a rhythm that would match his living experience in the Caribbean"—a rhythm, as Mignolo mentions, that Brathwaite found "when skipping a pebble on the ocean."[76] The tangential quality in Mignolo's work of this stone skipping on the ocean is perhaps where border thinking/epistemology/gnosis hits its limits—limits that border thinkers of this track have been aware of, given that this mode of border thinking is self-consciously not universal, self-admittedly unable to "account for all experiences and geo-historical violence and memories."[77]

Rather than being tangential to my own project, Brathwaite's image of a stone skipping on the ocean is a crucial component of what I am here describing as the borderwaters. This image found its way into the first stanza of Brathwaite's poem "Caribbean Theme: A Calypso" (1956), which imagines a stone skip as the genesis for the Caribbean archipelago:

> The stone had skidded, arc'd, and bloomed into islands
> Cuba and San Domingo
> Jamaica and Puerto Rico
> Grenada, Guadeloupe and St. Kitts
> Nevis, Barbados and Bonaire.
> Speed of the curving stone hissed into coral reefs
> White splash flashed into spray
> Wave teeth fanged into clay
> Bathsheba, Montego Bay.[78]

Here we see not a pebble skipping through the waves a few dozen feet offshore but a stone skimming across the entire Caribbean Sea, from the waters off North America to the waters off South America, and wherever it strikes, an island grows up out of the sea to mark the site where stone and water have met. Intriguingly, if we take the catalog of islands as our guide to the procession of stone strikes, the stone is not proceeding in a smooth arc but is zigzagging: it first hits Cuba and then skips east to San Domingo (Hispaniola) before zigging back west to hit Jamaica; it then sails over San Domingo to hit Puerto Rico, the easternmost of the Greater Antilles, before plummeting toward Grenada among the southernmost islands of the Lesser Antilles; it then zags back north, to the northernmost of the Lesser Antilles, hitting Guadeloupe before proceeding to St. Kitts and Nevis; finally, it skips back to the southern Lesser Antilles, hitting Barbados, and then, in a final long zag, it flies all the way west to Bonaire. In thinking through the unpredictable zigging and zagging of the stone, and in contemplating the mythic image conveyed in these lines of poetry,

I find useful a term Brathwaite employs in the opening pages of his 1974 book *Contradictory Omens: Cultural Diversity and Integration in the Caribbean*. This book describes the Caribbean as a place of "inter-lapping," a relational state that in Brathwaite's specific commentary plots a Caribbean relationality to North America and Africa that is distinct from conventional *over*lapping.[79] Brathwaite does not elaborate on his definition of *interlapping*, but the term, when brought to bear on the erratic stone skip in "Caribbean Theme," seems to point toward an unpredictable cutting back and forth, as well as a type of mutual overlap or, better, of mutual palimpsest between earth and ocean, where earth (the stone) arrives from above and skips across the sea below, instigating an eruption of land, now arriving from below the sea, pushing through the sea to emerge as a set of islands that on a map seem to write over the ocean. But on the shore, the ocean again laps up onto the islands, while various components within the archipelagic ocean-island complex of the borderwaters reciprocally and cyclically inscribe and reinscribe themselves on each other. Brathwaite's skipping stone—an image of interlapping islands and waters—is evocative of Gilles Deleuze's commentary on certain islands as offering a "reminder that the sea is on top of the earth," while other islands remind us that "the earth is . . . under the sea, gathering its strength to punch through to the surface," with earth and sea "in constant strife."[80] Or, treating the same interlapping dynamic but without Deleuze's antagonistic imagery, Elizabeth Bishop offers a less assured version: "Land lies in water . . . / Or does the land lean down to lift the sea from under . . . ?"[81] Within the borderwaters, both sea and land are interlapping; to borrow from Brathwaite's description of Caribbean English, they are "submerged/emerging."[82] Meanwhile, borderwaters connections among the islands are also interlapping, excessive beyond a graceful arc and instead cutting back and forth in desultory, unforecasted motions among south and north, east and west.

This interlapping of land and water, of east and west, of north and south, has certain resonances with images conveyed by Anzaldúa and Glissant. *Borderlands/La Frontera* opens with Anzaldúa standing on the seashore, "at the edge where earth touches ocean / where the two overlap," imagining that "the sea cannot be fenced, / *el mar* does not stop at borders."[83] In turn, Anzaldúa's image of the ocean as something that does not love a fence seems to flow effortlessly into Glissant's allied image of the "unfenced archipelago of the world totality."[84] The unfenced archipelago and the unfenceable ocean constitute one vector, a decolonial vector, that we might find in the borderwaters—if not in the quiddity of the islands and waters themselves, then in certain cultural interactions with these forms and materialities, consistent with Philip Schwyzer's view of the "archipelagic perspective" as having its essence "in a willingness to challenge traditional boundaries."[85] And yet to envision islands and seas as somehow inherently conducing toward an annihilation of boundaries would be at odds with the human-archipelago interactions of the long twentieth century, during which oceanic borders have not been swallowed amid decolonial or transnational waves and spume but have proliferated in ways that indeed feel alien compared to traditional land borders, with stark implications for human individuals as well as larger human and nonhuman populations. This point was driven home to me during a conversation with the i-Kiribati American visual artist Fidalis Buehler, who told of growing up in American Samoa and going to help relatives who had been stranded at sea, nearly starving even though ships were passing them on a regular basis—it turned out these were non-US ships fishing in the United States' EEZ, with crews who feared that offering aid would draw attention to their unauthorized activities within an economic zone that was supposed to be exclusive to the United States.[86] Elsewhere, we might look at the mid-twentieth-century disagreement between New Zealand and the Philippines. This disagreement hinged on whether, when the US-Spanish Treaty of Paris drew a box around the Philippines in 1898, that box should be taken to mark the maritime borders of what would become the postcolonial Philippines or whether it should simply be taken to signify that the islands inside the box were considered Philippine territory (see fig. 1.7).[87]

We see another weird human-archipelago interaction in the US Immigration Act of 1917, also called the Asiatic Barred Zone Act, which drew a line in the ocean with the intention of excluding "natives of islands not possessed by the United States adjacent to the continent of Asia" (see fig. 1.8).[88] As one US senator explained of the boundary, "What we desired to avoid was the naming of all the little islands in the archipelago running along the Asiatic coast . . . , [hence choosing] merely to draw certain geographical lines and to say that none within those lines should come."[89] Also pertaining to maritime boundaries and immigration, it has been suggested that the United States' "wet feet, dry feet" policy, which from 1995 to 2017 permitted asylum only for Cuban immigrants who set foot on US soil, functioned to undercut the United States' own maritime claims regarding the sovereignty of its twelve-mile territorial sea (see fig. 1.9).[90] Today, furthermore, one can hardly look at the tension-ridden territorial

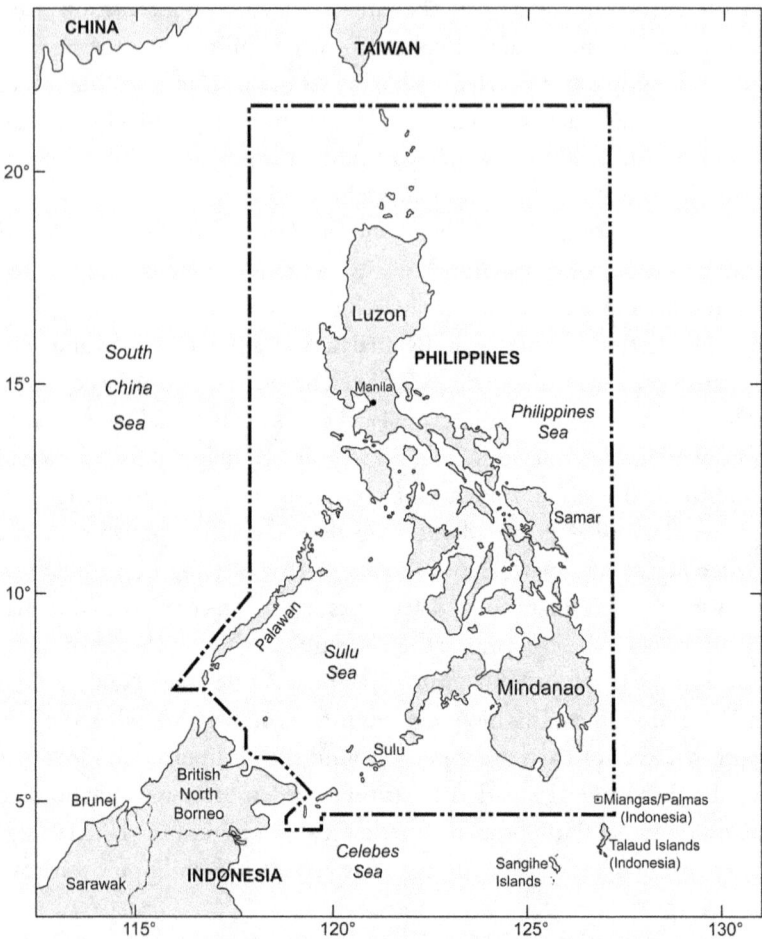

FIGURE 1.7 — The line around the Philippines as set in the 1898 Treaty of Paris and slightly revised in the run-up to the Philippines' assertion of the line as a border. The 1898 treaty stated, "Spain cedes to the United States the archipelago known as the Philippine Islands, and comprehending the islands lying within the ... line" (quoted in United States Bureau of the Census, *Census of the Philippine Islands Taken Under the Direction of the Philippine Commission in the Year 1903*, vol. 1 [Washington, DC: Government Printing Office, 1905], 49). The treaty was careful not to specify the line as indicating a border within the water, but the Philippines reimagined the line as the border in innovating the new international category of the "archipelagic State," with borders in the water. From John G. Butcher and R. E. Elson, *Sovereignty and the Sea: How Indonesia Became an Archipelagic State* (Singapore: National University of Singapore Press, 2017), 53. Courtesy of National University of Singapore Press.

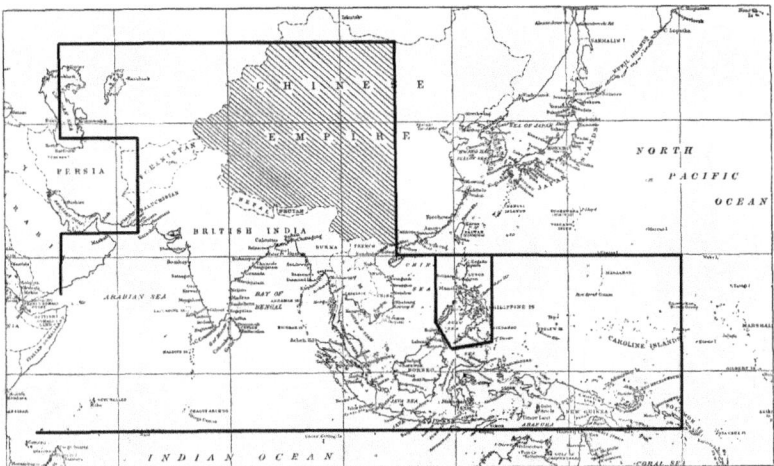

FIGURE 1.8 — Asiatic barred zone. This map was originally published with the following caption: "MAP SHOWING ASIATIC ZONE PRESCRIBED IN SECTION THREE OF IMMIGRATION ACT, THE NATIVES OF WHICH ARE EXCLUDED FROM THE UNITED STATES, WITH CERTAIN EXCEPTIONS. (Section indicated by diagonal lines covered by treaty and laws relating to Chinese. The Philippine Islands are United States possessions and therefore not included in the barred zone.)" Drawn by the US government across vast swaths of land and ocean, the Asiatic Barred Zone Act's line was not a border that marked territorial holdings, but it functioned as a border to the extent that it became the boundary that determined who could enter the United States and who was barred. Line is enhanced for ease of viewing. From US Department of Labor, Bureau of Immigration, *Immigration Laws (Act of February 5, 1917): Rules of May 1, 1917* (Washington, DC: Government Printing Office, 1917), map inserted between pages 32 and 33.

claims made in the South China Sea and suggest that there is something inherent in the ocean that does not love a border (see fig. 1.10).[91] And, peering into the future, two US national security experts have written a novel titled *Ghost Fleet: A Novel of the Next World War* (2015), which looks to the coming decades and imagines World War III having its initial stirrings at the bottom of the Mariana Trench, inside the United States' Marianas Trench Marine National Monument, as state-sponsored Chinese scientists search for natural gas deposits in ocean space that is inside the US EEZ and therefore considered international waters for scientific purposes but US territory for purposes of fishing and mineral extraction.[92]

Unlike the inverted border/borderlands models in the fields of American history and Chicana/o studies, the watery borders and borderwaters interlap—that is, one is not neatly epiphenomenal to the other, but

INTRODUCTION · 31

FIGURE I.9 — Would-be immigrants from Cuba attempting to enter the United States by crossing the Florida Straits on an old Chevy truck attached to oil barrels, July 17, 2003. According to the "wet feet, dry feet" policy, such travelers would be eligible for asylum if they reached US soil, but if the Coast Guard found them while they were in US territorial waters or the US EEZ, they would be returned to Cuba. This particular group was intercepted within forty miles of the US coast and sent back to Cuba. Later Luis Grass, who in 2003 had repurposed the truck as a vehicle for water travel, crossed into the United States by land with his family in 2005. See "Truck-Sailing Cubans Finally Reach U.S.," NBC News, March 22, 2005, http://www.nbcnews.com/id/7267457/ns/us_news/t/truck-sailing-cubans-finally-reach-us/#.XXfuHihKiUk. Photograph by US Coast Guard fireman Greg Ewald. From Defense Visual Information Distribution Service, https://www.dvidshub.net/image/1077912/cuban-migrants. The appearance of US Department of Defense (DoD) visual information does not imply or constitute DoD endorsement.

rather they cut back and forth, zigging and zagging, mutually writing and rewriting, like islands on a map seeming to sit on top of the water while the water laps back up onto the islands. In this way, compared to their land-based counterparts, watery borders and borderwaters are weird, with their weirdness showcased in the suite of confounding borders already mentioned. The treaty-negotiated boundary around the Philippines might not be a border but rather evoke thousands of island-circumscribing borders that are nature-fixed and nature-fluxed by the shorelines of thousands of Philippine islands. The United States might claim a sea-based border

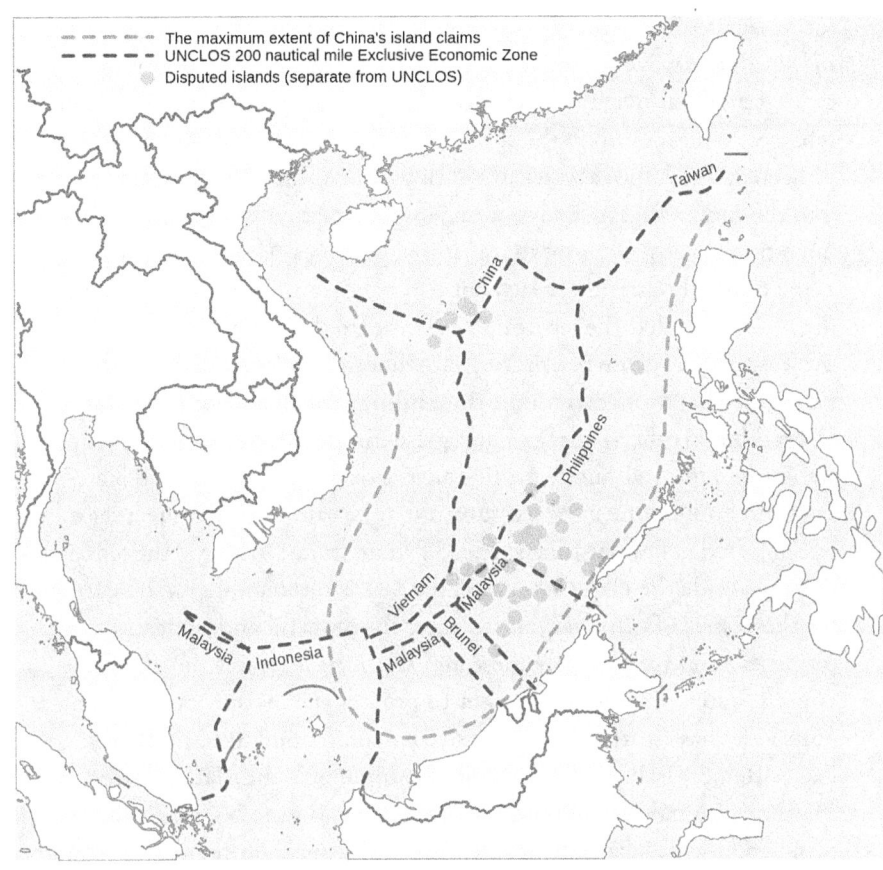

FIGURE 1.10 — The tangle of borders in the South China Sea. The lines with country labels represent the EEZ-based territorial claims of China, Vietnam, Malaysia, Indonesia, Brunei, and the Philippines. The curved line that swoops from around China's EEZ line throughout the South China Sea shows what is known as China's "nine-dash line," representing a Chinese claim to sea territory that emerged in the wake of World War II. China's nine-dash line conflicts with the claims of every nation with an EEZ in the South China Sea. Magnifying territorial tensions in the region, the United States, in an effort to reaffirm its stance that the nine-dash line is illegitimate and that other nations' EEZs are not off-limits to military ships, maintains an active military presence in the South China Sea. Map by Goran tek-en, 2014, https://commons.wikimedia.org/wiki/File:South_China_Sea_vector.svg.

for its territorial sea that is based on its own moving shorelines, asserting sovereignty over a twelve-mile band of ocean, but for over two decades it might also deny its own oceanic sovereignty by requiring Cuban refugees to set foot upon the shoreline from which the watery border is projected. The United States might draw a line through the Pacific and into the Indian Ocean, and that line might function as a border for immigration purposes but not for territorial purposes. Meanwhile, the EEZ, as the swath of waters that reach out two hundred miles from a shoreline, functions much like the territorial sea border to the degree that it involves the seaward projection of a shifting shoreline, but at the same time it functions like the 1898 box around the Philippines, like a border in some respects but in others simply a line representing the idea that animals, vegetables, and minerals inside the line are the territory of the United States. Now a school of one hundred tuna might be said to constitute a set of one hundred swimming tuna-shaped US borders just so long as the school remains inside the EEZ. Otherwise, the EEZ is international waters, free for the vessels of other nations to enter for peaceful and nonextractive purposes. And yet strangely these are *international* waters in which the United States (because of its right to protect the marine environment of its EEZ) has created several massive *national* monuments, such as the Pacific Remote Islands Marine National Monument, the Marianas Trench Marine National Monument, the Rose Atoll Marine National Monument, and the Papahānaumokuākea Marine National Monument (see fig. 1.11). Compounding the alien quality of these watery borders: because the United States claims the right to operate military ships in the EEZs of other countries (believing that "military activities are" not "inherently non-peaceful"), it must therefore also tolerate other countries when they have indirect military interests inside US marine national monuments.[93]

In some places the aquatic border becomes a function of moving shorelines. Elsewhere, it melds with the skin of living tuna or the entrails of Laysan albatrosses, and foreign trespasses against these borders might involve a hook in the mouth of a fish or a shard of plastic, carried by a current from thousands of miles away, lodged in the digestive tract of an albatross. In this way, we might say, the borderwaters complex becomes an instantiation of what Bruno Latour has referred to as "nature-culture," a "seamless fabric" that interweaves that which is "*real, like nature*" with that which is "*narrated, like discourse*."[94] Hence, unlike Chicana/o borderlands scholarship as crystallized by Anzaldúa, the project of *Borderwaters* is not to map humans' presumably *natural* "emotional residue" in response to

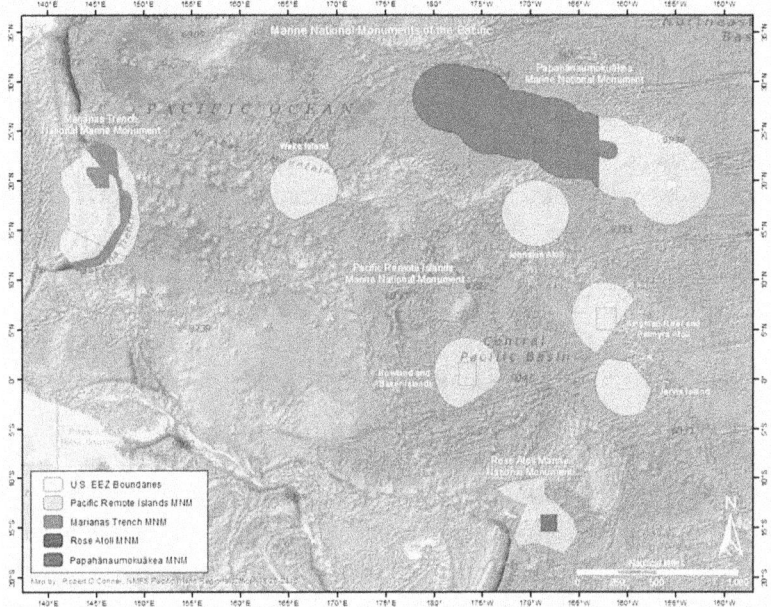

FIGURE I.11 — Some of the United States' island-based EEZ boundaries in the Pacific, together with the boundaries of US marine national monuments, which are sometimes coterminous with the EEZ and sometimes smaller. The Marianas Trench Marine National Monument is the westernmost monument on the map. From "Marine National Monuments in the Pacific," NOAA Fisheries, accessed August 24, 2020, https://www.fpir.noaa.gov/MNM/mnm_index.html.

the imposition of an "unnatural boundary."[95] Rather, like a stone skipping across a sea and evoking an archipelago, *Borderwaters* seeks to cut back and forth, to hit upon sites of US American interlapping between earth and ocean, surface and depth, nature and culture—to trace a set of archipelagic prehistories of the United States' emergence as a majority-ocean nation, a status that as yet seems more natural (residing in the nonhuman terraqueous materiality that the US government claims) than cultural (residing in a living set of cultural mythologies regarding the state's claims to those materialities). But in *Borderwaters* the United States' terraqueous prehistories assertively punch, as if charging up from the seafloor, into its archipelagic present. And at other times, less in the mode of Deleuze's description and more in the mode of Bishop's, the present shorelines lean down into the water to lift the prehistories up from under. In the context of a borderwaters framework, a reference to the "interior" of the United

INTRODUCTION · 35

States might be less likely to speak to places like Iowa or Missouri and more likely to speak to the waters that exist between the ocean surface and the ocean floor. And yet even as *Borderwaters* is a project addressing the archipelagic states of America, it participates in a planetary project of decontinentalization, one that operates simultaneously at the level of how we know what we know about the surfaces and depths of the planet, and at the level of how we permit the ontologies of the planet's terraqueous features to participate in structuring how we act.

Something That Can't Be Found by Covering More Ground

Recently, Leslie Elizabeth Eckel asked an important and clarifying question regarding the project of archipelagic American studies, wondering whether scholars who have written in this vein "rely on the type of nation-centered model that they intend to unsettle."[96] This question is urgent in the wake of nearly three decades of what has usually been called *transnational American studies*. As is clear to any of us who have participated in it, this latter mode of American studies has seen much hand-wringing, as scholars have wondered if the field's new transnationalism has only been an academic superstructure built on global neoliberalism's economic base, or as scholars have inevitably come up short as they have approached what still seems to be the definitionally impossible task of writing in the field of American studies without engaging the United States in some way.[97] Above all, transnational Americanists have wondered—and Eckel's question regarding archipelagic American studies' apparent US-centered analyses is a variation on this theme—"Are we being transnational yet?"[98] I see *Borderwaters* and much of archipelagic American studies as emerging from the wake, rather than the midst, of transnational American studies, at a place where such questions have hit a point of exhaustion. Some transnational Americanists may indeed see *Borderwaters* as US-centric. This is unavoidable, and in substantial ways accurate, because the book is fundamentally concerned with the United States of a long twentieth century and with the natural-cultural prehistories of the country's emergence as an ocean nation. It is, furthermore, interested in taking seriously—though definitely not endorsing—the implications of the United States' present and historical claims to archipelagic territory. This is a project that exists in dark waters—waters where President Trump could not go because continental exceptionalism's anti-insularity did not permit him to see the

US imperial archipelago as US American, and waters where some postcolonial and decolonial scholars have been less likely to go because they also, like Trump but with antithetical rationales, would prefer *not* to see the US imperial archipelago as US American.⁹⁹ No doubt, in tracing these prehistories, the study must zigzag from the Mississippi River to the Cook Islands, from Florida to Haiti, from Indonesia to the US Trust Territory of the Pacific Islands, from Utah's Sevier Desert to the Cambrian ocean that half a billion years ago submerged what would become the Sevier Desert, and from the US Virgin Islands to Guam and the Great Pacific Garbage Patch. Along the way it must draw on English, Indonesian, French, Spanish, and Japanese. One could say, then, that transnationalism weaves itself throughout *Borderwaters*. But the purpose of *Borderwaters* is certainly not to *be* transnational. It is to turn the narrative of the United States of America inside out, and in this way it moves away from *striving against a US-centric view* and toward *striving for a US-eccentric vision* of the United States as an archipelagic and oceanic nation-state with interlapping natural-cultural lives that are also archipelagic and oceanic.

As a US-eccentric study, *Borderwaters* finds kin in the interlinked novels *The Oddfits* (2016) and *The More Known World* (2017), part of the Oddfits series by Tiffany Tsao, a US-born novelist who spent her formative years in Singapore and Indonesia and now lives in Australia.¹⁰⁰ In the Oddfits series, the island of Singapore becomes present-day readers' point of entry to a nether-dimensional version of the planet Earth that was originally settled by a group of Pacific Islanders who centuries ago, during an oceanic expedition, accidentally slipped into this other dimension (which is called "the More Known World") and found themselves on an island in a lake.¹⁰¹ Within the novels, the present-day project of cataloging the More Known World is headed by a woman hailing from the Maluku Islands, the present-day Indonesian islands that were the fabled Spice Islands that Christopher Columbus was looking for when he encountered the Caribbean.¹⁰² Amid this massive cataloging effort, there is a phrase that circulates vaguely among a few characters—it is aspirational and subversive to the project of cataloging: "Something that can't be found by covering more ground."¹⁰³ In its drive against cataloging, the phrase resonates with Walcott's musing on "the arrogance of an Old World botanist" giving a name to "an unknown plant" and Walcott's belief that his own "ignorance is more correct than [the botanist's] knowledge."¹⁰⁴ Resembling the anticataloging impulse that circulates in Tsao's novels, the chapters in *Borderwaters* are not a catalog or set of representative case studies—not a set of explorations conducted to create a grid-facilitated map of the US borderwaters according to intersecting latitudinal and longitudinal lines. *Borderwaters* finds kin in Tsao's aspirational phrase for still other reasons. If continental and multicontinental approaches to US and broader planetary cultures are seeking something by covering more ground (not a single continent but two, three, four, five, etc.), then *Borderwaters* seeks something that can't be found by covering more ground. When it walks the quasi-ground of the shoreline, it walks fractally, walking the same beach in multitudinous ways (like a human, like a mouse, like an ant, like a mollusk)—ways that become nether-dimensional according to how continentally minded humans typically apprehend space and place. Further, it seeks wet, aquacentric modes of knowing and being that are not beholden to the geocentric notion that the *ground* is the necessary epistemological or ontological foundation. Submergence in water and the churnings of shorelines become foundational. The chapters might be considered a series of waves in which archipelagic thought and archipelagic materiality are tumbling, knocking against each other, even as they churn up and churn with US-centric and US-eccentric self-perceptions and cultural forms.

Chapter 1 directs readers toward archipelagic churnings in the interdisciplinary field of American studies, which during the mid-twentieth century afforded academic and broader popular thought with widely influential and iconic images of the continental United States as a virgin land, a garden inhabited by a machine-building American Adam, a manifest destiny spanned and fulfilled by a sublime transcontinental road. In juxtaposition with this backdrop, the chapter, titled "Interlapping Continents and Archipelagoes of American Studies," begins by discussing two archipelagic moments of the early twenty-first century: a heightened interest in archipelagic spaces and archipelagoes per se among Americanist scholars and the relocation of *American Quarterly* (the flagship journal of the American Studies Association) to the University of Hawai'i. The chapter speaks to both an emergent set of archipelagic Americanists and a traditional set of continentally trained Americanists, seeking to trace a heretofore unexamined archipelagic backdrop of twentieth-century Americanist continentalism, while reciprocally advancing projections on where the continent might fit within a self-consciously archipelagic American studies of the twenty-first century. In tracing these conceptual questions, I place pressure on specific scenes from Mark Twain's *Adventures of Huckleberry Finn* (1884) and from the lesser known Cook Islands writer

Florence "Johnny" Frisbie's memoir, *Miss Ulysses from Puka-Puka: The Autobiography of a South Sea Trader's Daughter* (1948). My readings of specific scenes from these two books showcase heuristics for understanding, retrospectively, the place of the archipelago within twentieth-century Americanist continentalism and, prospectively, potential positionalities of the continent within twenty-first-century approaches to the archipelagic states of America. These retrospective and prospective continental-archipelagic relationalities find theorization via the notion of *interlapping*, and the chapter concludes with a discussion, based on my 2014 conversations with Frisbie, of US America's simultaneously variegated and ontologically flat geographic expanse.

Building on this first chapter's work on archipelagic thought in space and time (continent and archipelago, retrospect and prospect), the ensuing four chapters bring further focus to archipelagic thinking vis-à-vis spatial and temporal categories. Although space and time cannot be peeled apart or otherwise disentangled from one another, chapters 2 and 3 of this study are more oriented toward archipelagic thinking's upshots for spatial engagement, while chapters 4 and 5 are more oriented toward archipelagic thinking and its implications for temporal engagement. Even so, across the chapters, the spatial and temporal categories are copresent and mutually contingent, with shifts in focus being matters of degree and proportion rather than bracketing either space or time. These general shifts in spatial and temporal focus permit *Borderwaters* to underscore archipelagic thinking's material implications, ranging from viewing human-Earth relations by means of the category of form, to accessing multiple modes of practical thinking regarding borders in relation to oceanic and terraqueous space, to understanding citizenship and vulnerability in relation to deep geologic pasts measured by floods and periods of drying, to striving toward new modes of life and being by contemplating the archipelagic states of America in relation to near-term and inconceivably long-term futures.

Leaning toward the spatial dimension, chapter 2, titled "Archipelagic Diaspora and Geographic Form," marks a distinction between standard culturally materialist and newer formally materialist approaches to geography within the study of US American culture. The distinction is crucial because, as the previous chapter illustrates, culturally materialist approaches to geography are not lacking in formalist components—rather, they are less cognizant of their geographically formal investments and, consequently, tend to acquiesce to a traditional continentalist status quo even when that status quo runs contrary to their cultural and political commitments. The chapter juxtaposes this tendency with a geoformally attentive approach to Zora Neale Hurston's *Their Eyes Were Watching God* (1937), a novel that engages in a project of theorizing the geographic form and spatial materiality of the vast archipelago that W. E. B. Du Bois, in his description of the planetary color line, referred to as "the islands of the sea."[105] The insular spaces on which the novel relies include Key West, Palm Beach, the Caribbean, Hellas, Indonesia, and others. Each of these spaces exerts parallax influence on *Their Eyes*' evocation of the horizon space that Janie, the novel's protagonist, uses to animate her travels in the context of the 1928 hurricane-induced breach of the dam containing Florida's massive Lake Okeechobee. The hurricane sets Janie amid a flood in which continents and islands are, quite literally, moving. This attentiveness to Hurston's varied reliances on insular and archipelagic spatial forms helps make accessible Hurston's investments in critiquing and ironizing the fundamental geographic claims of US sovereignty. Ultimately, the chapter argues that the form of the archipelago offers a window into a new geographic formalism—complementing studies that rely on cultural geography—that lends pivotal modes of legibility to cultural texts as well as to reading practices.

Chapter 3, titled "Borderwaters and Geometries of Being Amid," furthers the book's spatial tack, offering an elaboration on the general discussion and definition of the term *borderwaters* that appears in this study's introduction. Generally speaking, the border/borderlands complex has evinced a spatial imagination in which the border is an unnatural and Euclidean line attended by an epiphenomenal borderland characterized by an organic set of contestations that direct their energies against the state's superimposed Euclidean geometry/geography. In contradistinction to this model, chapter 3 links a salient aspect of the borderwaters to governments and broader human cultures' engagement in and with modes of *non*-Euclidean spatial perception, in which the spatial imagination of boundaries has been a partial function of the aqueous and terraqueous materialities to which governmentality has tended to affix marine borders. As human imaginations have innovated aqueous and terraqueous notions of the border by burrowing into and engaging with arenas of nature that are better described in terms of non-Euclidean geometries (such as fractal and Indigenous geometries), watery borders and their attendant borderwaters have become places where humans interact with other humans on terms set by nonhuman and non-Euclidean spatial models. In making these arguments, I turn toward the archipelagic and oceanic work of the Greater Mexican visual artist Miguel Covarrubias, whose midcentury visual and written formulations—of Indonesia, of the United States' Trust Territory of the Pacific Islands, and of Indigenous Caribbean populations—help contextualize and theorize state, Indigenous, and nonhuman cultures as they have converged and diverged across non-Euclidean modes of imagining boundaries, nonboundaries, and spatial area on a terraqueous planet. The chapter is interested in Covarrubias's work per se but is equally interested in the geometric vistas with which his work intersects. Geometric questions may feel abstruse to some in the humanities, but as the chapter emphasizes, questions of geometry have stark implications for how we think of the meaning of boundaries, the existence of US territory, potential solidarities between transarchipelagic populations, and the terrifying ramifications of nuclear testing in the United States' interlapping southwestern borderlands and southwestern borderwaters.

Chapter 4 builds on the spatially fractal qualities of the borderwaters to move the form of the archipelago—and the project of archipelagic thinking—into fractal temporalities that link human and geologic timescales, with the question of time functioning to push the borderwaters frame into what would normally be considered a landlocked portion of the North American continent. Titled "Fractal Temporality on Vulnerable Foreshores," this chapter orients itself around the notion of the *foreshore*, a term that typically describes the portion of the shore between the tide's high- and low-water marks. But here *foreshore* is generalized to describe space that exists between *any* two high- and low-water marks, evoking the apprehension of a temporally fractal procession of foreshores, ranging from those produced by the blip-like ripple of a millisecond all the way to those created by inundations and desiccations associated with shifts in climate and plate tectonics that are measured in hundreds of millions or even billions of years. With this understanding of the fractal temporality of the foreshore, the chapter examines the illuminating archipelagic theorizing that took place at the Topaz internment camp (officially the Central Utah Relocation Center), which the United States built during World War II in Utah's Sevier Desert as an unconstitutional prison for people of Japanese descent, whether they were US citizens or noncitizens. As the prisoners well understood, they were living on the bed of an ancient and very large lake that had dried up about ten thousand years previously, at the end of the most recent ice age. Looking back much further in time, they also understood that they were living on the floor of the Cambrian ocean of some half-billion years ago. Engaging in beachcombing tens of thousands and even hundreds of millions of years after the fact, the prisoners at Topaz collected mollusk shells from the lake and fossils from the ocean, creating art—ranging from shell brooches to stonework to poetry—that incorporated these lithic items as a mode of theorizing human situatedness within geologic periods that are fractal in their inundations and desiccations. The prisoners' archipelagic theorizings—particularly as they pertain to human meaning in geologic time—showcase the urgency of the borderwaters to thinking through human ethics and agency, as the prisoners' aesthetic works unspooled questions of human suffering at the hands of an unjust government in relation to the aeonic sociality of stones and shells on geotemporal foreshores.

A fifth and final chapter, titled "Spiraling Futures of the Archipelagic States of America," moves away from chapter 4's retrospective orientation toward deep times of the past and instead plots archipelagic thought in a prospective frame, in reference to the temporalities—deep and shallow—of multiple futures, ranging from the US Virgin Islands' perhaps unexpected relation to the heat death of the universe in the exotically distant future, to the Anthropocene's examination by posthuman Black oceanographers of perhaps a hundred thousand years hence, to spacefaring humans of perhaps a century from now who descend from seafaring earthlings. Against the legacies of Georg Wilhelm Friedrich Hegel's nineteenth-century view of past and future history as requiring the continent as its fundamental stage, this chapter seeks methods of decontinentalizing the future, reading archipelagic futures against the continental grain. In so doing, it leans on Robert Smithson's earth- and waterwork *Spiral Jetty* (1970) together with future-oriented archipelagic theorizing of the Caribbean and the Pacific, locating future archives of the borderwaters in cosmology's predicted fluctuations in entropy, albatross-curated collections of seaborne plastic, and asteroids near Mars. Along the way, the genre of the *short* story becomes a paradoxical form through which *long* futures are thought, ranging from US Virgin Islands writer Tiphanie Yanique's "The Bridge Stories" (2005), to British writer A. S. Byatt's "Sea Story" (2013), to Filipino writer Timothy James M. Dimacali's "Sky Gypsies" (2007). Within this archipelago of stories, metonymic of a future of mind-bogglingly numerous US American and post–US American stories, the archipelagic states of America fade in and out of existence, meeting their temporal borders across prospective and fractal times.

A conclusion, "Distant Reading the Archipelagic Gyre: Digital Humanities Archipelagoes," reflects on convergences between the digital humanities and archipelagic thought in terms of distant and close reading. Here, for instance, Moretti's use of the geographic form of the archipelago to theorize distant reading interfaces with Glissant's direct address to a "distant reader" as he contemplates commensurabilities and incommensurabilities between the fractal granularities of a single island and the unfenced totality of the world archipelago. With these convergences in mind, I closely read the data produced by the computer-facilitated distant reading of the entire runs of three Americanist journals: *American Quarterly*, *American Literature*, and *Journal of American History*. Focused on a set of archipelagic keywords (*island, archipelago, ocean, sea, continent, mainland,* and *transnational*), this melding of close and distant reading draws on the work of the preceding chapters, commenting on *Borderwaters'* place within Americanist scholarship and wider work in archipelagic thought. Rather than calling for an archipelagic turn in Americanist thought or suggesting there has been such a turn, the conclusion emphasizes the urgency that Americanists engage with an archipelagic gyre, or a set of island- and ocean-oriented philosophical currents that have neither descended from nor depended on the United States for their genesis and vitality.

CHAPTER ONE

Interlapping Continents and Archipelagoes of American Studies

Archipelagizing American Studies

One of the farthest-ramifying essays in American studies of the past half century appeared in 1981 in the flagship journal of the American Studies Association: Nina Baym's "Melodramas of Beset Manhood: How Theories of American Fiction Exclude Women Authors." The essay's extraordinary impact does not reside simply in the several hundred times it has been cited in journals and books in fields including American studies, American literary studies, and American history. Rather, Baym's essay has had extraordinary ramifications for understandings of US literature and broader culture because, on the heels of publishing this agenda-setting piece, her work in scholarship attained a distinctly public face, as she appeared on the editorial board and eventually became the general editor of *The Norton Anthology of American Literature*. Bringing the urgency and incisive arguments of "Melodramas of Beset Manhood" to bear on her capacity as editor of the anthology for some three decades (from its second edition in 1985 to its eighth edition in 2012), Baym's work on the *Norton* helped introduce millions of undergraduate students (often in general education and introductory literary surveys) to a new version of US literary and cultural history, presenting a "diverse and balanced" view, advancing a narrative of the US past in ways that have both reflected and restructured an ever-shifting present.[1]

Although many scholars of US culture are familiar with Baym's 1981 article, her arguments merit some rehearsal here, because recalling them in detail brings crucial perspective to some tectonic shifts in the study of US and broader American cultures that have taken place much more recently, during the 2000s and 2010s. These shifts are emblematized perhaps most vividly in the 2015 move of the journal *American Quarterly* (the original venue for Baym's essay) from its continental US home at the University of Southern California to the University of Hawai'i at Mānoa, located within the United States' only canonized archipelagic state. Indeed, Baym's 1981 essay speaks in unexpected ways to *American Quarterly* editor Mari Yoshihara's 2015 commentary on the journal's relocation to Hawai'i. As Yoshihara observes, "To those on the continental United States and other parts of the globe, Hawai'i may not appear to be the most natural center for American studies. Yet we believe that precisely because of our geographic location, history, and lived experience on the islands . . . we bring perspectives and voices of critical importance to the field."[2]

Corresponding to Yoshihara's geographically oriented commentary on islands and continents, Baym's concern in "Melodramas of Beset Manhood" was the decidedly continental geographic processes that "led to the exclusion of women authors from the [US] canon."[3] Explaining that critics had been engaging in "the search for [US American] cultural essence," Baym was responding to such figures as Henry Nash Smith and R. W. B. Lewis, who in *Virgin Land: The American West as Symbol and Myth* (1950) and *The American Adam: Innocence, Tragedy, and Tradition in the Nineteenth Century* (1955) had seen the essence of US America in "the doctrine that the United States is a continental nation" and in the figure of Adam inhabiting and settling land that was a "new continent" and a "new garden."[4] Baym summarized the continental thesis of Smith, Lewis, and others as involving Euro-American man inhabiting "this new land, untrammeled by history and social accident."[5] Within this traditional Americanist mode of geographic thought, the west-stretching continent's other names were *virgin land, the frontier, the wilderness,* and *the garden.* And, as Baym explained, US literary and cultural critics had seized on national literary narratives that took "the essential quality of America . . . to reside in its unsettled wilderness," with the masculine hero taking flight into the feminized and putatively virgin wilderness to escape an equally feminized and "entrammel[ing] society."⁶ Relying on Richard Poirier's quotation in which the United States' foundational American narrative becomes a masculine retreat from a feminine society and an "expansion of national consciousness into the vast spaces of a continent," Baym argued that Americanist critics' privileging of the mythic continental wilderness had functioned to exclude women from the canonized narratives of US American literature and culture.⁷

Thus argued, "Melodramas of Beset Manhood" helped set the stage for two major epistemological interventions, only one of which attained field-wide recognition during the ensuing decades. First was a recovery of many women writers that the United States' continental American narrative had excluded. This indispensable turn occurred within numerous arenas, including with Baym's first appearance on the *Norton* editorial board; the second edition of the *Norton Anthology of American Literature* (1985) offered diversified content and a preface implying that the conceptual points Baym made in "Melodramas of Beset Manhood" were now being brought into practice: "A major responsibility of this Norton anthology is to redress the long neglect of woman writers in America."⁸ Since then, the *Norton* has continued to diversify, attentive (as stated in the preface to the eighth edition in 2012) to the "enlarged ... number and diversity of authors now recognized as contributors to the totality of American literature."⁹

But in spite of the *Norton*'s professed commitment to the totality of US literature, a second and more geographically foundational epistemological intervention suggested by Baym's 1981 essay remains largely unrealized today. Rather than questioning the mythologized image of the United States as a fundamentally continental nation, the *Norton* permits the continent to continue standing in for that which is fundamentally US American. Recall, as outlined in this book's introduction, that the United States, largely by virtue of its extensive and widely dispersed island possessions, claims more archipelagic and oceanic space than it does continental space and that it claims to possess more archipelagic and oceanic space than any other nation-state. And juxtapose this fact with a second fact: that the ninth edition of the *Norton Anthology of American Literature* (2016), whose over six thousand pages suggest a dedication to thoroughness, includes no writers from the state of Hawai'i, nor from the US Commonwealth territories of Puerto Rico and the Northern Mariana Islands, nor from the current US territories of American Samoa, Guam, and the US Virgin Islands, nor from the former US territory of the Philippines, nor from the former trust territories now freely associated with the United States: the Federated States of Micronesia, the Republic of the Marshall Islands, and the Republic of Palau.[10] Indeed, within this popular anthology that both mirrors and shapes general perceptions of what the United States is and has been, non-US islands (including Great Britain, Nevis, Cuba, Jamaica, Java, Antigua, and Hispaniola) appear as places *from* which to come to the United States, while the archipelagic states of America are absent as places *in* which to be from the United States.[11] No doubt Baym's editorial and other work, such as her *Women Writers of the American West, 1833–1927* (2011), have contributed to the absolutely crucial project of reenvisioning US American literary and cultural history so that women become visible within the continental narrative. But this diversified continental image has not delivered on the full epistemological promise of her 1981 essay to the degree that the continent remains entrenched (in the *Norton* and broader US American cultural narratives) as the most American of geographic forms.

And yet such continental exceptionalism feels increasingly belated. During the 1990s and 2000s, the field of American history saw a surge in discussions of oceans and seas, the culmination of various efforts toward an "American maritime history."[12] Meanwhile, Americanist literary historians and scholars have long discussed a "literature of the sea," more recently in conjunction with an "oceanic turn," a "blue humanities," and a "transoceanic" frame, drawing on currents beyond the realm of Americanist scholarship.[13] Such turns toward the oceans, together with heightened attentiveness to transnational and anti-imperial Americanist frameworks, have brought continent-based scholars of US culture and history into dialogue with the archipelagic spaces of US empire and, reciprocally, have prompted recognition that thinkers of the archipelagic states of America have already been engaged in thinking through and theorizing versions of the United States from positionalities alien to continental history and expressive culture's gravity.[14] One such positionality is vividly illustrated in Gary Y. Okihiro's 2008 book *Island World: A History of Hawai'i and the United States*, which upends the "customary narrative of the United States acting upon Hawai'i" by telling a story of "the Islands' press against the continent, causing it to move and endowing it . . . with historical meaning."[15] Okihiro's narrative joins the narratives of myriad Caribbean and Pacific thinkers, telling US and broader American and Pacific histories in ways that recognize the "initiative, weight, and intellect" of "islands."[16] Indeed, island-based and island-oriented thinkers (of the archipelagic states of America, the broader archipelagic Americas, and archipelagoes across the planet) have been crucial, as both participants and foundational thinkers, to a postcontinental structure of feeling that has arrived at a point of supersaturation within the Americanist water. This structure of feeling and sense of supersaturation become apparent when, in tandem with Yoshihara's editorial commentary on the significance of island positionality within American studies, we consider the surge in uses of the term *archipelago* in *American Quarterly* from the journal's founding in 1949 to the 2010s—moving from only seven articles during the journal's first half century to nearly fifty articles during the 2010s alone.[17]

Indeed, during the 2010s, commentary in *American Quarterly* became self-consciously archipelagic, looking toward a postcontinental model that underscores the potential to undertake, albeit in a highly belated way, the epistemological decontinentalization that Baym's *American Quarterly* essay presaged four decades ago. This new attention to the archipelago as an Americanist geography and framework appears throughout the decade but most prominently in *American Quarterly*'s special issues of 2014 and 2015, which were pivot points—respectively, the final special issue produced at the University of Southern California and the first special issue produced at the University of Hawai'i. Introducing the "Las Américas Quarterly" special issue in 2014, editors Macarena Gómez-Barris and Licia Fiol-Matta explain that the issue's final section, titled "Archipelagic Thought," contains four essays that refuse to permit "islands [to] do the work of clarifying inter-America relationships" while still remaining "occluded from knowledge-production in the Americas."[18] In assuming this stance, Alexandra T. Vazquez's essay in "Las Américas Quarterly" frames itself as contributing to work "in the surround of Archipelagic American studies," which Michelle Ann Stephens and I have described as an Americanist approach "dedicated to tracing the interrelations of America (as a contingent and elastic space constellated by oceanic waterways, two continents, and uncounted islands both within the hemisphere and beyond via the sinews of empire) and the broader planetary archipelago," a "tracing of the interactive and constitutive relationships between (to borrow a phrase from W. E. B. Du Bois) 'America and the islands of the sea.'"[19] A year after Gómez-Barris and Fiol-Matta's special issue, Craig Santos Perez, in the award-winning 2015 "Pacific Currents" special issue, points toward the archipelago's rise in American studies, while issue editors Paul Lyons and Ty P. Kāwika Tengan gesture toward the geographic form of the archipelago as a model for investigating US American and Pacific "undercurrents that extend to the conceptual."[20] They conclude by asking about potentially intersecting undercurrents of relationality among islands: "How will Islanders and Islands—inclusive of Turtle Island (North America) and its peoples—move at the points of their convergence?"[21] According to Yoshihara, "Pacific Currents" points toward "the kinds of critical intervention the Hawaiʻi-based editorial team seeks to bring to *American Quarterly*."[22]

A key component of these archipelagic Americanist visions has been an effort to think postcontinentally, not in the sense of exiling the continent from an Americanist geographic imaginary but in ways that mitigate continental gravitas such that islands, archipelagoes, shorelines, and oceanic spaces come into view not as the United States' geographic aberrations or anomalies but as jointly and powerfully constitutive of its foundational geographies. Allied but not congruent with oceanic scholars' work in disrupting "gazes fixed on land," this is an emergent Americanist postcontinentalism that seeks points of convergence among island-ocean archipelagic spaces and those spaces that have traditionally seemed continental.[23] In fact, building on Lyons and Tengan's reminder (via certain Native American groups' Turtle Island creation narratives) of the North American continent's occasional perception as an island, I would argue that Americanists in search of convergences between archipelagic and continental spaces should look toward some of the field's most seemingly continental moments. These moments run from Frederick Jackson Turner's landmark speech at the 1893 Columbian Exposition to Wai Chee Dimock's 2006 *Through Other Continents: American Literature across Deep Time*, and they are indispensable to the project of considering how Americanist continentalism relates to the heightened attentiveness to archipelagic thinking as it has surfaced in the twenty-first-century study of US and broader American cultures. By means of this undertaking, archipelagic American studies might emerge as a critical framework that plots unexpected convergences among islands and continental spaces as well as unforecasted continuities (uncanny and sometimes disturbing) running from the myth-symbol school to the present era's transnationalism.

These convergences and continuities come into high relief when conceptualized via what Matthew Pratt Guterl and Susan Gillman have recently drawn attention to as *the American Mediterranean*, or a Caribbean-centered region that Guterl describes as a "network of rivers, seas, and waterways that [has] served as the lifeblood of the New World."[24] As Gillman explains, this archipelagic region in the Caribbean is literally *mediterranean* (or set amid landmasses) in relation to North and South America and has also been an American analogue of *the* Mediterranean for various thinkers, including Cuban novelist Alejo Carpentier, Jamaican nationalist W. Adolphe Roberts, Prussian naturalist Alexander von Humboldt, and many others.[25] But here I want to stretch and complement Guterl's and Gillman's American Mediterranean frame, moving it beyond the Caribbean, offering an *archipelagic thought*, a mode of thinking that according to Édouard Glissant "distracts and sets adrift," undoing regional and continental thinking.[26] This is a thought that reminds Americanists of the ways a distinctly archipelagic Mediterranean has inhabited the study of US and American cultures even at moments when that project has waxed most continental. It is a thought that interlinks the Mississippi River and US Guano Islands claims in the Pacific, myth-symbol Americanists and transnational Americanists, the continental United States and the archipelagic United States, and Mark Twain's hypercanonical *Adventures of Huckleberry Finn* (1884) and Florence "Johnny" Frisbie's lesser known book *Miss Ulysses from Puka-Puka: The Autobiography of a South Sea Trader's Daughter* (1948). Ultimately, it projects some ways in which precontinental perceptions of the space now known as America might become templates for postcontinental and archipelagic perceptions among twenty-first-century Americanists.

Mark Twain's Archipelagic American Fable

Adventures of Huckleberry Finn begins and ends with the continental narrative that Baym critiques in "Melodramas of Beset Manhood." In chapter 6, as the action is beginning, Huck does not "want to go back to the widow's any more and be so cramped up and sivilized," so he plans to "run away"—not to raft down the river but to "just tramp right across the country, . . . and hunt and fish to keep alive, and so get so far away that . . . the widow couldn't ever find me any more."[27] By the time Huck delivers the book's famous closing lines, he is finally ready to undertake the journey he describes at the novel's beginning: "I reckon I got to light out for the Territory ahead of the rest, because aunt Sally she's going to adopt me and sivilize me and I can't stand it. I been there before" (362). It would seem that such a novel, one that begins and ends with a continental frontier fantasy, was ripe for recuperation and admission to candidacy as the great American novel during the myth-symbol era of American studies, a time when Henry Nash Smith traced the United States' mythic development vis-à-vis "the pull of a vacant continent," when Leo Marx described the machine set amid the garden of a "new continent," and when Alan Trachtenberg narrated the Brooklyn Bridge as the triumph of "a civilization which had begun its career on a virgin continent."[28] Indeed, based on Huck's yearning for the continental territory, C. Merton Babcock in his 1965 *The American Frontier: A Social and Literary Record* situated *Huckleberry Finn* between James Fenimore Cooper's Leatherstocking Tales and "cattleman's frontier" fiction, ranking Twain's novel among "classic studies of frontier America," as "Huck Finn is forever lighting out for the territory in a mad flight from respectability and decency."[29]

But strangely, given *Huckleberry Finn*'s strong uptake during this era of Americanist continental fervor, the novel does not showcase a continental narrative. Rather, it is a watery hiatus from the continent, offering the famous story of Huck and Jim's raft journey down the Mississippi, moving them ever closer to where the river empties into the sea near New Orleans, a city that US journalist A. J. Liebling in 1961 described as existing, "like Havana and Port-au-Prince," "within the orbit of a Hellenistic world. . . . The Mediterranean, Caribbean and Gulf of Mexico form a homogeneous, though interrupted, sea."[30] Looking at the homogeneity amid interruption that Huck and Jim experience upriver from New Orleans, I would suggest that in some ways the raft journey attains, if possible, an even more precise relation to the Mediterranean Sea than the Caribbean or the Gulf of Mexico: the main currents of *Huckleberry Finn*'s terraqueous geography (the Mississippi River itself together with its long chain of islands and littoral stops) assume the archipelagic quality of Odysseus's Aegean, while the riverine setting becomes a precise match for the literal definition ("inland, far from the coast") of the classical Latin term *mediterrāneus*.[31] Analogous to the islands of Odysseus's Aegean, the islands of *Huckleberry Finn*'s American Mediterranean extend from Huck and Jim's initial hideout on Jackson's Island, to the island on which they discuss King Solomon after witnessing the steamboat wreck (92, 94), to the small island (or towhead) that foils their plans to board a steamboat and head north (99), to the island on which Jim hides while Huck falls into the Grangerford-Shepherdson feud (154), to the long series of towheads to which they tie the raft while resting during days on the river (156), to the island where Jim poses as a "*Sick Arab—but harmless when not out of his head*" (203, 259), to Spanish Island, where Huck hides the raft after realizing he can't pray a lie and where Jim helps the doctor treat Tom's gunshot wound (343, 271, 352–54).

Within *Huckleberry Finn*'s episodic archipelago of riverine islands, chapter 15 stands out most prominently for my purpose of seeking a heuristic view of archipelagic space within traditional Americanist thought. Indeed, chapter 15 is centered specifically on the question of islands and their interpretation. In drawing attention to chapter 15, I am not suggesting that Twain left an archipelagic Easter egg for us to find over 130 years after the novel's publication. Rather, I want to frame *Huckleberry Finn*'s chapter 15 as attaining acute explanatory power—as providing a current critical allegory—for two groups of present-day Americanists: for archipelagic Americanists contemplating ways of relating to a larger field that has seemed to define itself vis-à-vis the continent and for Americanists whose training and research have been built around continental spaces and who, perhaps curious about a structure of feeling that has hit a point of supersaturation, may wonder about possible convergences between the borderwaters and the discipline's traditional continental terrain. This critical allegory shapes the present chapter's subsequent genealogy of intertwined continental and archipelagic modes of thought, currents that have run from the late nineteenth through the early twenty-first century.

Chapter 15's fable begins as Huck and Jim become separated on the river amid thick fog, Huck in a canoe and Jim on the raft. They try to find each other again by "whooping," and readers watch Huck flounder as he attempts to home in on the source of Jim's whoops, which he finds impossible to locate because it keeps "changing its place." The whoops at first seem to come from ahead and then from behind. Finally, while following a series of whoops, Huck runs into the riverbank, as if somehow Jim were no longer even floating on the river but had taken to the land. After sitting momentarily confused in the current and fog, Huck realizes why Jim's whoops have been so difficult to follow and why he has just crashed into the riverbank: "That cut bank was an island and Jim had gone down t'other side of it. It warn't no tow-head, that you could float by in ten minutes. It had the big timber of a regular island; it might be five or six mile long and more than a half a mile wide" (100). After this realization, Huck floats downriver, navigating the spaces between many small islands while passing the large island that separates him from Jim. Eventually, in the water past the foot of the large island, Huck finds Jim asleep on the raft and tricks him into believing the episode was all a dream. Thinking he has just had the most powerful dream of his life, Jim insists on interpreting it and assigns a variety of meanings to the currents and various islands featured in the episode (104). But, finally, Huck points to some debris—some "trash"—that accumulated on the raft as a result of the same strong current that separated them. Huck asks for an interpretation of this trash. Deeply hurt by what he now recognizes as Huck's mocking deception, Jim replies, "Dat . . . dah is *trash;* en trash is what people is dat puts dirt on de head er dey fren's en makes 'em ashamed" (105).

Critics have frequently recognized Huck's subsequent apology as central to the book's representation of his increasing sense of Jim's humanity, but I want to bring focus to another set of interpretive possibilities within the episode, particularly as these relate to the potentialities of a postcontinental American studies seeking convergences between continental and archipelagic spaces.[32] When Huck follows Jim's whoops and crashes into the island's shoreline, he immediately assumes he has bumped into the continent. This assumption is consistent with the continental telos of Huck's horizon of expectations, which from beginning to end is bent on lighting out for the continental territory. Taking Huck's confusion between continent and island as instructive, I would suggest that some Americanists have been critically analogous to Huck, crashing into islands and confusing them with the continent, such that many of American studies' most seemingly continental moments have exhibited a con*fusion* between island and continent in which the fusion of the two grows out of unacknowledged convergences. Recovering these convergences is crucial to pointing out how archipelagic Americanists might find something like an archipelagic tradition within a tradition that has conceived of itself as continental and, reciprocally, how continentally attuned Americanists might map a coherence between a seemingly continental tradition and the archipelagic borderwaters.

Within what many may assume to be the main currents of Americanist thought, Americanists have fused islands and the continent at some of the field's most foundational moments. Consider Frederick Jackson Turner's monumental 1893 speech, "The Significance of the Frontier in American History," which famously discusses an "advance across the continent" in which "American settlement westward" serves to "explain American development."[33] If no moment has done more for the continent's uptake within the foundational US myth of America, one must also recall the speech's closing lines, within which Turner (like Huck) looks at islands in a double movement of continental confusion and archipelagic recognition: "What the Mediterranean Sea was to the Greeks, breaking the bond of custom, offering new experiences, calling out new institutions and activities, that, and more, the ever retreating frontier has been to the United

States."[34] Here, as Turner frames it in no uncertain terms, the continental frontier is the American Mediterranean—the United States of America's Mediterranean.

Nor is Turner's American Mediterranean conceit a flight of fancy vis-à-vis the traditions of continental thought on which he was building. It is moored in historical and mythologized representations of the United States' continental frontier, as is evident in the frontier's description in the opening pages of James Fenimore Cooper's 1827 novel *The Prairie*:

> The earth was not unlike the ocean when its restless waters are heaving heavily.... There was the same waving and regular surface, the same absence of foreign objects, and the same boundless extent to the view.... Here and there a tall tree rose ... like some solitary vessel; and ... far in the distance appeared two or three rounded thickets ... like islands resting on the waters.... As swell appeared after swell and island succeeded island, there was the disheartening assurance that long and seemingly interminable tracts of territory must be passed.[35]

Building on such models of the continental frontier as a space of oceans and islands, Turner again took up an archipelagic American Mediterranean frame in his 1914 speech "The West and American Ideals," which explains that "as we turn from the task of the first rough conquest of the continent there lies before us a whole wealth of unexploited resources in the realm of the spirit."[36] After hearkening back to "the ships of Columbus" and deploying the metaphor of a "ship bound on a voyage of discovery," Turner's speech concludes by averring that the perduring spirit of US America's western frontier finds its "symbol" in the travels of Ulysses (as mediated by Alfred Lord Tennyson's famous poem): "Push off, and sitting well in order smite / The sounding furrows; for my purpose holds / To sail beyond the sunset, and the baths / Of all the Western stars until I die."[37] Here we see a genealogy in which the Western-continental cliché of riding off into the sunset has routes in a Mediterranean oceanic journey. In reading Turner, Americanists have for decades believed that they have been gazing at one of the continental frontier's great enshriners. And we have. But, like Huck bumping into an island and mistaking it for a continent, we have been seeing a continent to the exclusion of Turner's island- and sea-oriented myth: an American Mediterranean breaking up traditions like the Greek Mediterranean, a metaphor structured by mythic images of Odysseus's archipelagic travels among networked islands and seas.

Dedicated to elaborating Turner's seemingly continental thesis, Henry Nash Smith in his 1950 study *Virgin Land: The American West as Symbol and Myth* explains, "The doctrine that the United States is a continental nation . . . has had a formative influence on the American mind and deserves historical treatment in its own right." Hence, as Smith outlines, "The present study traces the impact of the West, the vacant continent beyond the frontier, on the consciousness of Americans and follows the principal consequences of this impact in literature and social thought down to Turner's formulation of it."[38] Yet in lighting out for the territory on his way to the main continental sections of his book (on "overland expansion" and the "idea of a continental empire"), Smith first bumps into the island, as it were, writing *Virgin Land*'s opening section on a vision of American "empire as command of the sea," bent on "'passage to India'" via the Pacific.[39] In this first section, he traces recurrent colonial and US American desires to reactivate Columbus's initial quest, citing a variety of seventeenth- through nineteenth-century thinkers. As quoted by Smith, these thinkers yearned "to find out the East India Sea," to attain the "spices rare / Of Philippine, Cœlebe [the Indonesian island of Sulawesi] and Marian[a] isles," to become like "Amsterdam . . . great . . . in power . . . all upon the East India trade."[40] They yearned (as showcased in Smith's quotation from Walt Whitman) to salute "the flowery peninsulas, and the spice islands," and revel in a godlike man "coloniz[ing] the Pacific, the archipelagoes," in a future that has "the oceans to be cross'd, the distant brought near, / The lands to be welded together."[41] Analogous to Huck Finn's narrative, Smith's book begins by announcing an intention to light out for the continental territory, but first it unexpectedly takes to the water and crashes into the islands. This is a fittingly watery course, given *Virgin Land*'s dedication to elaborating Turner's unexpectedly Mediterranean thesis.

Published nearly a decade and a half later, Leo Marx's famous *The Machine in the Garden: Technology and the Pastoral Ideal in America* (1964) takes up Smith's image of the continental garden and follows Smith and Huck by bumping into an island while putatively en route to the continent. After the book's introduction, Marx begins with a chapter titled "Shakespeare's American Fable," which reads *The Tempest* and comments that "so far as [Shakespeare] allows us to guess [the island] lies somewhere in the Mediterranean off the coast of Africa."[42] But Marx Americanizes this Mediterranean isle, framing it as a symbol of "the raw continent," explaining that "the island, like America, could be Eden *or* a hellish desert."[43]

Later in *The Machine in the Garden*, the island reappears, this time in Marx's treatment of *Huckleberry Finn*, which, as Marx observes, begins "with the hero's urge to withdraw from a repressive civilization," so that Huck "flees to Jackson's Island."[44] Then, repeating the island-continent legerdemain of his opening chapter, Marx looks at the island and treats it as a continent, using language saturated with frontier continentalism when he explains that Huck and Jim "are able to penetrate the innermost recesses of the island," making the island stand in once again as a microcosm of Marx's continental garden.[45] Subsequent to his discussion of Huck and Jim's penetration of this putative minicontinent, Marx's interpretation not only transforms the island into the continent but also converts the entire raft journey into a continental expedition. He explains, "The raft becomes a mobile extension of the island."[46] Here Marx's syllogistic logic is implicit even as it is absolutely crucial to his continental argument: if the raft is the stand-in for the island, and if the island is the stand-in for the continent, then the raft journey can conform to midcentury Americanists' continental-frontier thesis. And here Huck becomes a fable of Marx himself, as both figures crash into an island and (owing to their continental horizons of expectation) interpret the island as the continent. Finally, Marx's reading of the island as the continent, and of Huck and Jim's river journey as a continental expedition, overlays a powerfully continentalizing framework on a novel that has repeatedly been discussed as an American *Odyssey*, permitting Marx to sublimate the novel's archipelagic structure into a continental mythos and, like Turner, evoke the continent as US America's Mediterranean.[47]

One might have thought this midcentury continental horizon of expectations would have faded during the decades since 1964, especially in light of what Amy Kaplan once described as the newer Americanists' replacement of an older Americanist "notion of wholeness," moving instead toward innovative attention to "race, gender, class, ethnicity, and sexuality" as producing "a more complex, if de-centered," "concept of interconnectedness."[48] Kaplan's description of interconnectedness—implying simultaneous separation and fusion—in some ways resembles Cuban theorist Antonio Benítez-Rojo's description of "the character of an archipelago, that is, a discontinuous conjunction."[49] And yet, rather than recognizing the archipelago as an allied alternative geography, many newer Americanists may have taken the geographic status quo of the continent as the "common ground" that George Lipsitz once hypothesized to exist between the older Americanists of Marx's generation and the subsequent Americanists of his own.⁵⁰ Indeed, newer Americanists—multiculturalized and eventually transnationalized—have continued, for reasons attributable both to a deeply structuring Americanist tradition and to what I would frame as the inertia of a little-perceived Euro-American metageography, to stage the continent as American (and planetary) geography's center of gravity.⁵¹

Though I could point toward numerous examples, Wai Chee Dimock's widely influential book *Through Other Continents: American Literature across Deep Time* (2006) stands as a vivid case in point, offering important inspiration to the present study's work in deep temporality even as it also operates according to the continent/island dynamic I have been discussing. The book begins by noting newer Americanist work in transnationalism and explaining, "*Through Other Continents* reflects this sea change." In addressing the sea change, Dimock describes "'American' literature" not as "a discrete entity [but] . . . as a crisscrossing set of pathways, open-ended and ever multiplying, weaving in and out of other geographies, other languages and cultures."⁵² Dimock explains, "I would like to propose a new term— 'deep time'—to capture this phenomenon. What this highlights is a set of longitudinal frames, at once projective and recessional, with input going both ways, and *binding continents and millennia into many loops of relations*, a densely interactive fabric."⁵³ Hence, within Dimock's formulation, the deep time of millennia finds its spatial analogue and coconstituent in the deep space of a very specific geographic form: the continent. Within Dimock's transnationalized continentalism, the mono-continentalism of Turner, Smith, and Marx has become too limiting. One senses that the old continentalism has now seemed too small, too isolationist, too island-like, as if it were now time to read Marx's Shakespearean fable anew: the old Americanist mono-continentalism really was like being stuck on an island. The continent, as numerous transnational Americanists have described it, was "insular," an isolating island in a far sea.⁵⁴ From within this view, one now imagines *The Tempest*'s island-continent populated by old Americanist island dwellers (Smith, Marx, Trachtenberg, and other Calibans and Ariels) who had no commerce with the wide world. But now, in dialogue with *other continents* (as Dimock says, the "African, Asian, and European" continents), newer Americanists (Prosperos, Mirandas, and Ferdinands?) may shed the insularity of the field's old continentalism to truly apprehend America as a *continental* continent (not an *insular* continent) among its worldwide continental peers.⁵⁵ As Dimock frames it, these are deep continental epics linked by correspondingly deep millennial epochs.

But amid this linking of vast continents and vast millennia as spatiotemporal analogues, one notes that the term *deep time* arises in conjunction with Dimock's engagement of Fernand Braudel's notion of history of a *longue durée*. She quotes Braudel, explaining that this is "a history to be measured in centuries . . . : the history of the long, even of the very long time span, of the *longue durée*."[56] Of course, Braudel's famous test case for long-durational history was the Mediterranean world, as seen in his monumental two-volume study *The Mediterranean and the Mediterranean World in the Age of Philip II*, first published in 1949. In the opening of the study's English translation, Braudel speaks of "a history in slow motion." Geography, he explains, "helps us to rediscover the slow unfolding of structural realities, to see things in the perspective of the very long term. Geography . . . helps us to discover the almost imperceptible movement of history, if only we are prepared to follow its lessons and accept its categories and divisions."[57] But what are the geographic categories and divisions that Braudel accepts for his test case in history of the longue durée? They are the Mediterranean's "mountainous peninsulas," which he calls "miniature continents," interrupted by "vast, complicated, and fragmented stretches of sea, for the Mediterranean is not so much a single entity as a 'complex of seas.'"[58] For Braudel, the seas and coasts are "the heart of the Mediterranean," in which the "islands are more numerous and above all more important than is generally supposed," with major islands and island groups existing in tandem with the fact that "there is hardly a stretch of the Mediterranean shore which is not broken up into islands, islets and rocks."[59] "Whether large or small," Braudel explains, "these islands of all sizes and shapes make up a coherent human environment."[60]

Hence, in Dimock's reliance on deep time, we once again have a seemingly continental Americanist bumping into an island (or, better, bumping into a geotemporal framework that Braudel predicated on a set of archipelagic relationalities), followed by the transformation of that island into a continent (or in Dimock's case, a vision of continental planetarity). And like Turner's old continentalism, this newer Americanist continentalism is, counterintuitively, Mediterranean; *deep time*'s Mediterranean basis is reflected in the fact that Dimock's "crisscrossing set of pathways, open-ended and ever multiplying," resembles the relationality among islands and coastal seaports within Braudel's analysis. Indeed, *Through Other Continents* does go island-hopping at points, speaking of the "oceanic . . . process of 'drifting,'" ranging from the Sea Islands to Coney Island to Turtle Island, drawing on Derek Walcott's and Edward Kamau

Brathwaite's poetry and observing that "Americanists have much to learn from this Caribbean poetics."[61] Within Dimock's study, this recognition constitutes the beginning of an archipelagic thought. And yet *Through Other Continents* frames such thought according to a strong continental telos, as working "across continents" and undertaking the search for "intercontinental pathways."[62] Dimock's overarching recourse to the long tradition of Americanist continentalism is ultimately reflected in her fundamentally continentalist framing of deep time, dedicated to "binding continents and millennia into many loops of relations." As a continental revision of Braudel's archipelagic geography, Dimock's "deep time" Americanizes its Mediterranean template. Hence, her widely cited transnationalist framework emerges, strangely, as the American Mediterraneanization of a planet schematized along specifically continental lines, with archipelagoes surfacing even as they are folded into a continental model.[63]

No doubt the folding of, say, the Caribbean into the American continent is consistent with a standard practice of imagining islands as continental appendices: according to the modes of European metageographic thought that have been naturalized throughout the world, the island of Britain is appended to the continent of Europe, the island of Madagascar is appended to the continent of Africa, the islands of Indonesia are appended to the continent of Asia, and the Caribbean is appended to the continent of America. But this mode of continental imagination is not without practical consequences. If an island or archipelago does not manage to attain status as at least a continental appendix (a dubious status from the outset), it is often erased altogether from mental and physical maps that depend on continental models of planetary perception. As Martin W. Lewis and Kären E. Wigen observe in their important 1997 study *The Myth of Continents: A Critique of Metageography*, "Many islands and archipelagos . . . remain for the most part little-known anomalies."[64] Offering commentary that illustrates this anomalous situation, CHamoru poet Craig Santos Perez explains, "On some maps, Guam doesn't exist; I point to an empty space in the Pacific and say, 'I'm from here.' On some maps, Guam is a small, unnamed island; I say, 'I'm from this unnamed place.'"[65] The crux of Perez's predicament is a continentalized worldview that Lewis and Wigen explain has culminated in "the sevenfold continental system of American elementary school geography" and has functioned to afford planetary priority to "Europeans and their descendants overseas."[66] This is the worldview of which Filipino legal scholar Jay L. Batongbacal spoke while helping to form the University of the Philippines' Archipelagic Studies and Ocean Policy Program in 1998. He observed that archipelagic space presents "challenges that have largely been ignored under the weight of decades of biases brought about by training in disciplines developed and dominated by Western continental countries."[67] Batongbacal was perhaps too cagey to specify precisely which Western continental countries he was referencing, but given the United States' specific position vis-à-vis the Philippines and much of the world more generally, it is fair to suggest that a US-based American studies, running from the early twentieth to the early twenty-first century, has drawn on and helped reinforce the Western continentalism that Batongbacal critiques.

And yet, as indicated by the Americanist genealogy I have traced to this point, some of US continentalism's most influential narratives have unsuspectedly depended on figurations of the American continent as an archipelagic American Mediterranean. Hence, one might feel justified in asserting, in analogy to Bruno Latour's famous articulation of the modern, that *we (Americanists) have never been continental.*[68] But one of the fruits of *being continental* involves the ability to crash into an island and perceive it as a continent, or to make that which is archipelagic stand in service of the continent (e.g., as metaphor, as metonymy, as anomaly). Hence, the main currents of Americanist thought (from Turner to Smith to Dimock) have always been continental precisely and especially because, in the face of their archipelagic attributes and reliances, they have identified themselves (by means ranging from mythic formulations to transnationally oriented book titles) as continental.

The present chapter, then, as it points out Huck's (and Americanists') misrecognition of the island as the continent, works to intervene in the very Americanist fable it identifies. This geoformal redescription of Americanist genealogy seeks to advance (again, following Glissant) an *archipelagic thought*—that is, a mode of thought analogous to the thought that permits Huck to dismiss his continental assumptions and recognize that he has bumped into an island. This mode of thought moves away from a core-periphery world system and toward island- and water-oriented thinking that (as Glissant suggests) is "set in opposition to systemic thought" and does not confine itself to a "single imperious direction" but rather "bursts upon all horizons."[69] Indeed, a phrase I have been using throughout this chapter (*the main currents of Americanist thought*) intentionally and ironically echoes the title of Vernon Louis Parrington's three-volume study *Main Currents in American Thought: An Interpretation of American*

Literature from the Beginnings to 1920, a landmark early twentieth-century study that seemed to take the continent as its bedrock. And yet the allusion to Parrington, routed through Huck's and Glissant's archipelagic thought, seeks a recognition that Americanists who have inhabited what seem to be the main currents of continental thought have been *navigating a set of currents*. US American historical and cultural lives should not be conceived as a unidirectional transcontinental east-to-west overland trek followed by a second transcontinental move through other continents; rather, these lives have ridden a set of currents—complete with bends, swirls, eddies, vortices, rapids—studded with labyrinths of islands.

Here the archipelagic thought constitutes a recognition that for too long the continent has been regarded as the systemic building block of world history, as encoded classically, for instance, in Georg Wilhelm Friedrich Hegel's *Lectures on the Philosophy of World History* (1837), which reads world history through four continents: Europe, Asia, America (Hegel's "transatlantic continent"), and Africa. Of course, Hegel infamously called Africa "an unhistorical continent," but in his continental-historical schema, Africa at least met the continental precondition for consideration as historical.[70] Meanwhile, the geographic form of the island found a different fate within Hegel's schema: "World history takes account only of those nations which have formed themselves into states. But we must not imagine that this can occur on a desert island."[71] Against such continentalist world-historical dismissals of the island, the archipelagic thought becomes something analogous to W. E. B. Du Bois's post-Hegelian rewriting of geography's place in history: "The problem of the twentieth century is the problem of the color-line,—the relation of the darker to the lighter races of men in Asia and Africa, in America and the islands of the sea."[72] Here we see Africa become historical, while Europe as a continent disappears. But Du Bois's phrase "the islands of the sea" may constitute his famous statement's most radical world-historical revision, supplanting Hegel's ahistorical "desert island" with a world of islands and archipelagoes ranging from the Philippines to the Antilles and from Madagascar to Taiwan or Guam. As islands and archipelagoes attain status within history, the archipelagic thought constitutes an invitation to participate in a multidirectional and unpredictable Americanist nissology (or an Americanist island studies), engaging with the archipelagic states of America and the broader archipelagic Americas on their own terms and not as misperceived or microcosmic continents.[73]

Miss Ulysses on the Other Side of the Main Currents

Within the economy of *Huckleberry Finn*'s narrative, the main currents are those in which Huck floats while searching for the source of Jim's whoops. Meanwhile, readers have no firsthand access to another set of currents that carry Jim as he floats on the other side of the big island. Rather, readers hear about these currents—and the islands that stud their waters—only after Huck and Jim are reunited and only in the context of Huck's cruel joke, as Jim is apparently persuaded that the currents he floated on were part of a prophetic dream.[74] Based on what Huck reports of Jim's words, readers know Jim "got mix' up in de islands" and at some point "bust[ed] up agin a lot er dem islands en [had] a turrible time en mos' git drownded" (103). According to Jim's interpretation of the so-called dream, "the first tow-head [stands] for" an ally they will meet, while the current stands for someone who will try to draw them away from the ally. Meanwhile, Huck's whoops, which Jim hears in the putative dream, represent providential or magical "warnings" they will receive along the way, while "the lot of tow-heads [is] troubles we [is] going to get into." Finally, "the big clear river" that appears after the fog subsides represents "the free States" (104). Yet Jim's ascription of meaning to the archipelagic currents is always already framed as moot because readers know, with Huck, that Jim is interpreting a dream that has not occurred. And Jim's interpretation of the archipelagic currents also proves moot within the novel's larger trajectory: the novel's subsequent events do not correspond to Jim's prophecies. Indeed, the ending of *Huckleberry Finn* seems to reaffirm the sense (as conveyed in chapter 15) that Jim's attentive reading of archipelagic space has been an episode of buffoonery.[75]

Underscoring Twain's representation of Jim as an archipelagic figure—indeed as the novel's most engaged reader of archipelagic space—recalls Leslie Fiedler's troubling yet foundational 1948 article "Come Back to the Raft Ag'in, Huck Honey!," wherein Fiedler repeatedly frames Jim as analogous to a Native Hawaiian—that is, analogous to Richard Henry Dana's character Hope, who in *Two Years before the Mast* (1840) emerges as the dear Kanaka (or Kanaka Maoli, or Native Hawaiian) friend of the book's Euro-American narrator.[76] Though Fiedler's comparisons were drawn along flat-footed racial lines (i.e., both characters are nonwhite), a reminder of Twain's varied bibliography may suggest a more archipelagic poetics for Fiedler's apprehension of similarities between Jim and Dana's Kanaka character: as Twain was completing *Huckleberry Finn*, he was also at work on a novel of Hawai'i, leading him to "saturate ... [him]self with knowledge of that unimaginably beautiful land & that most strange & fascinating people."[77] Twain's Hawaiian novel was never published, existing today as a mere seventeen extant pages.[78] The preserved portion of the book's opening chapter showcases purple prose regarding "the true Isles of the Blest," juxtaposed with a seemingly prophetic foreboding of the literary aphasia that perhaps resulted in the novel's unpublished and nearly disappeared state: "You move through a very paradise; & you say nothing, because you cannot put into words, even to yourself, the deep charm & solace & beauty of it."[79] Indeed, the unpublished and incomplete Hawaiian novel bears a certain resemblance to Jim's archipelagic (yet always already moot) interpretive work. *Huckleberry Finn*'s rendering of Jim in this scene, in a way that idealizes him as Huck's victim and hence undercuts Jim's serious work in archipelagic interpretation, mirrors the Hawaiian novel's incomplete attempt—its ultimate false start—at treating the archipelagic space that Twain once romanticized as "the loveliest fleet of islands that lies anchored in any ocean."[80]

To think about how to navigate a complex set of archipelagic Americanist currents that are alluded to but incompletely articulated in Huck's cruel joke, I want to look away from Twain's Mississippi and indeed away from Hawai'i, turning toward another book, *Miss Ulysses from Puka-Puka: The Autobiography of a South Sea Trader's Daughter*, written by Florence "Johnny" Frisbie, daughter of Ngatokorua à Mataa of Pukapuka in the Cook Islands and Robert Dean Frisbie, a white US American of Cleveland, Ohio, who spent nearly all of his adult life living among and writing about the islands of the Pacific.[81] Published in New York by Macmillan in 1948, *Miss Ulysses* appeared during what Jonathan Arac has described as *Huckleberry Finn*'s post–World War II moment of hypercanonization, and Johnny Frisbie's book bears some notable comparisons to Twain's.[82] Both books are generic splicings of novel and memoir: while *Huckleberry Finn* is a novel written in the form of a memoir, *Miss Ulysses* is a memoir written in the form of a novel, leading Teresia K. Teaiwa to rank it among the earliest novels by a Pacific Islander.[83] These two memoir-novel splicings have adolescent narrators: Huck describes himself as "thirteen or fourteen or along there" (134), and Johnny's father noted that she "started writing her story in January, 1945, when she was 12 years old, and I typed the final copy in July and August, 1946."[84] Both books detail their narrators' episodic journeys on waters studded with intermittent islands, through what some might perceive as the edge of the United States: for Huck this is the river touching the nineteenth century's fabled frontier west of the Mississippi, and for Johnny this is a Pacific Ocean that had been a watery US American frontier for several decades. Even before the late nineteenth-century rise of what Lanny Thompson has termed the United States' "imperial archipelago," Johnny's home atoll of Pukapuka was claimed by the United States in 1859 under the US Guano Islands Act of 1856; within the action of her book, the waters and islands among which she navigates are emerging during World War II as a watery frontier of US sea power and Pacific dominance.[85] Johnny's epic Pacific journeys (beginning at her home atoll of Pukapuka, circulating among numerous Pacific atolls and islands, and finally arriving at Pago Pago in the US "territory" of American Samoa) bear a formal resemblance to Huck's travels (beginning at his hometown of St. Petersburg, Missouri, weaving among the Mississippi River's islands and shorelines, and finally seeking the US American "territory" stretching toward the Pacific). Indeed, these archipelagic correspondences are manifest in the books' converging American Mediterranean settings, reflected in *Huckleberry Finn*'s previously mentioned mid-twentieth-century popularity as a US American epic hearkening back to the *Odyssey* and Johnny's mid-twentieth-century self-framing via the *Odyssey*, as she notes that she is "an American girl" (91) and also declares herself to be, as stated by her book's title, *Miss Ulysses from Puka-Puka* (see fig. 1.1).

But whereas *Huckleberry Finn* presents its most intense work in archipelagic interpretation as always already moot, *Miss Ulysses*'s narrator articulates an archipelagic entanglement and engagement between human consciousness and practice and a nonhuman environment of sprawling waters and islands, surfaces and depths. Originally written by Johnny Frisbie in the languages of Rarotongan, Pukapukan, and English (and translated and edited by her father), *Miss Ulysses* presents readers with variegated epistemological baselines that position the book as a promising starting point for considering archipelagic Americanist modes of interpretation and the place of the continent within those modes.[86] In *Miss Ulysses*, Johnny's transregional archipelagic and navigational comparisons become key to accessing and thinking through the ways precontinental perceptions of the space now called America might become pivotal to postcontinental Americanist approaches. This is a move away from continentalist models of coherence and toward modes of perception in which, as was on display during my 2014 conversation with Johnny, a variegated US Americanness of waters and lands, territories and states, exists polyvalently within a critical commitment to what I discuss as a flat US American ontology.

FIGURE 1.1 — Photograph of Florence "Johnny" Frisbie from the inner flap of the book jacket for *Miss Ulysses from Puka-Puka* (1948). The caption states, "Although Johnny Frisbie's life story is distinctly unusual, she herself has grown to be a normal young lady whose greatest pleasure is in the moving pictures, or in riding horseback on the South Sea cattle ranches. She wants some day to go to a real show in the U.S.A., to visit the zoo and see a circus. These things are much more exciting to her than hurricanes on uninhabited islands, flights among the clouds, and long dreamy voyages in the tropic seas." Courtesy of Florence "Johnny" Frisbie.

Writing her book in Apia, Samoa, Johnny recalls younger days when she flew kites on the beach and listened to Rakuraku, an elder from one of Pukapuka's villages, who "would chant by the hour one of our *makos*, which are epic poems of the old wars and voyages of discovery" (14), and she projects that "some day I will fill a book with those stories I heard at night on the beach . . . , particularly about the heroes who sailed their canoes to distant lands where they had as exciting adventures as Ulysses" (25).[87] Johnny's Pukapukan-Odyssean equivalency reflects that at the same time as she was memorizing the navigation-oriented oral traditions of the archipelagic Pukapukan makos, she was also internalizing another set of orally delivered navigational and archipelagic adventures. As Johnny explained in February 2014, "My father shared [the *Odyssey*] on nights when we would lay on the beach awaiting the appearance of the first star. It became a ritual. The written version became my bible in my teens so I was able to compare it to my father's [oral] version!"[88] Within *Miss Ulysses from Puka-Puka*, this dual education in Greek and Pukapukan epics further surfaces in a passage I take as key to a current critical project of figuring an archipelagic frame in relation to the notion of a continental America:

> I like ships and the sea and the anticipation of arrival. . . . I guess it's in my blood, this wandering spirit. On my mother's side I am descended from navigators as bold as the vikings. I have read in schoolbooks about how Captain Cook discovered some of the South Sea Islands and Bougainville discovered

others. What nonsense! My people discovered all Polynesia centuries before Cook and Bougainville were born. When the white men were living in caves my ancestors were sailing their double canoes in the Great Migration from Asia to the Pacific islands; when Ulysses was returning from Troy, the Polynesians were having equally thrilling adventures in the Great South Sea; and when Columbus set out to *re*discover America, the great navigator Kupé had already sailed from Tahiti to explore the Cook Islands and then pressed on to discover New Zealand. Many a time in Puka-Puka Grandpa Mataa chanted for us an old *mako* which told of a voyage to Te Tawa o te Langi, a place of cold winds and beautiful flowers, surrounded by a dark sea on which white stones floated. Perhaps the stones were icebergs, and the land America! And why not? A voyage to America would be no farther than a voyage to Easter Island, which the Puka-Pukan voyagers called Te Pito o [te] Wenua—"The Navel of the Earth." (65)

Here, Johnny's commentary presages the instigating question of David A. Chang's 2016 book *The World and All the Things upon It: Native Hawaiian Geographies of Exploration*: "What if, instead of conceiving of global exploration as an activity just of European men such as Christopher Columbus or James Cook or Ferdinand Magellan, we thought of it as an activity of the people they 'discovered'?"[89] Against canonical narratives of European exploration and colonization that some understand to have culminated in a world system in which oceans are nonspaces whose sole function is to connect lands and thereby "subject . . . all societies to a single, continuous geography," Johnny posits archipelagic and navigational equivalencies— an analogous "wandering spirit," to use her phrase—among Polynesians, Vikings, and Odyssean Greeks.[90]

In the context of these transregional archipelagic equivalencies, *Miss Ulysses*'s representation of the space that has come to be known as America is of particular note. When Johnny frames Columbus as a *re*discoverer of America, she is positing a Pukapukan priority over canonical European narratives of American space, asserting Pukapukan knowledge of, interaction with, and historical codification of America avant la lettre. Her claims to priority are self-consciously analogous to those that have frequently been made regarding the Vikings, whom Johnny sees as navigational peers of the Polynesians. As Johnny would have understood, Vikings arrived in what is now called North America nearly five centuries before Columbus, as recorded in the Vinland sagas, Norse narratives that were conveyed orally before being transcribed during the thirteenth and fourteenth centuries.⁹¹ Similar to the Vikings' Vinland sagas, the Pukapukans' Te Tawa o te Langi makos had an extended oral life before they were written down by the ethnologists Ernest and Pearl Beaglehole, who gathered material in Pukapuka during the mid-1930s.⁹² In their 1938 study *Ethnology of Pukapuka*, the Beagleholes recorded Pukapukan accounts of two ancient voyages undertaken by navigators sailing east among many islands and finally reaching Te Tawa o te Langi, meaning "the side of the sky," or the place where "the sky meets land or sea at the horizon."⁹³ The first voyage was undertaken by the navigators Tu and Longo of Ngake village. After landing on a few islands as they traveled east, "their next landfall was Te Tawa-o-te-langi (Side-of-the-sky), where everything was beautiful, rocks, flowers, and trees particularly so. Here they sought to gather the beautiful things they saw about them and bring them back to Pukapuka to show the people. They filled up the canoe with all manner of things and put to sea, but before going far, the flowers had all wilted. They put back to land to gather more, but the flowers wilted again. A third time they gathered flowers, but again they turned to ugliness, so they sailed on without going back."⁹⁴

A second voyage to the same place is recounted, undertaken by the navigators Tonu and Taea from the village of Loto, also toward the east: "At the place called Te Tawa-o-te-langi (Side-of-the-sky) the navigators tried to pick the flower called *tokolangi*, which is the same plant as was unsuccessfully gathered by the expedition of Tu and Longo."⁹⁵

In interpreting the Te Tawa o te Langi makos as referring to America and thereby evoking archipelagic and navigational equivalencies between Polynesians and Vikings, Johnny was joining the Māori politician and anthropologist Te Rangihiroa, who a decade earlier, writing under the name Peter H. Buck, had published the 1938 study *Vikings of the Sunrise*, a history of Polynesian cultural dispersion containing an opening chapter that references one of the Vinland sagas, *Eirik the Red's Saga*, and its account of the Viking Leif Ericsson, who, as Te Rangihiroa describes it, "coasted south to some part of what is now New England and named it Vineland."⁹⁶ Subsequently marking Polynesians' still greater achievement, Te Rangihiroa states, "Long before Columbus made his great voyage, a stone-age people, in efficient crafts, had crossed the Pacific from continent to continent across its widest part and had colonized every habitable island within its vast interior."⁹⁷ In 1938 Te Rangihiroa pointed to botanical evidence of Polynesian travel to America: the South American sweet potato's pre-Columbian presence in Polynesia.⁹⁸ And now Johnny, a decade later, was interpreting the Pukapukans' Te Tawa o te Langi makos as offering a proleptic description of America, undertaking a course that is structurally analogous to a project frequently undertaken in relation to Vinland, namely, the effort to interpret pre-Columbian oral (and subsequently written) traditions in relation to post-Columbian notions of a continental America.[99] This tack of taking the modern notion of a continental America as the telos of pre-Columbian oral narratives is also similar to a gesture by the Tuscarora writer David Cusick, in his 1828 *Sketches of Ancient History of the Six Nations*. In this translation and transcription of Iroquois oral traditions, Cusick recounts the world's watery beginning and the way "a large turtle" rose from within "the great water," so that the "turtle increased every moment and became a considerable island of earth," eventually "increas[ing] to a great Island" and finally becoming "the Great Island" possessed by humans.[100] Notably, in the subtitle to his book Cusick interpreted the Great Island in continental American terms, specifying that *Sketches* contains a *Tale of the Foundation of the Great Island, (Now North America)*.

I am interested here in convergences among Vinland, Te Tawa o te Langi, and the Great Island, less for what they can tell us about pre-Columbian priority *in America* and more for what becomes apparent in these locales' ex post facto interpretation *as America*.[101] To interpret Vinland, Te Tawa o te Langi, and the Great Island as the American or North American continent (even if these interpretations may be considered accurate along proleptic lines) requires the uptake of a continental teleology—as if the modern and contingent notion of an American continent were the ultimate historical horizon of these oral and subsequently written traditions, as if the American continent were an ontological constant, as if thinking continentally could be an epistemological stand-in for the ways of knowing encoded in the Pukapukans' Te Tawa o te Langi, the Iroquois's Great Island, or the Vikings' Vinland. Recalling Glissant's narrative of a monological continental telos that "forg[es] ahead, ordaining cities, then states, then nation-states," might we more responsibly conceptualize these spaces as, to draw language from George B. Handley, "spaces of oblivion that . . . inevitably resist and fundamentally change the direction of and perhaps render unpredictable the historical outcomes" we may plot?[102] If we acknowledge that, as John R. Gillis has persuasively argued, the modern notion of a continent developed among Europeans only over the course of the sixteenth through eighteenth centuries, we may then ask what it would look like to undo the predictability of continentalist

American historiography.[103] To return to Lyons and Tengan's question about convergences among islands and islanders, "inclusive of Turtle Island (North America) and its peoples," I suggest that these sites cannot predictably converge with each other on any American continent that can be taken for granted.[104] Rather, they remain removed from each other, converging in the way their mutual physical, epistemological, and ontological disparities gesture toward a noncoherent precontinentalism whose critical apprehension offers a template for present-day postcontinental Americanist thought.

The project of taking precontinental epistemologies as a template for postcontinental thought hinges on understanding the American continent not as fact but as geographic perception. In a move that papered over multitudinous and disjunct Indigenous cosmogonies and epistemologies within what is now thought of as continental America and that also operated against earlier European perceptions of "the Indies" and of "a vast archipelago . . . which would surely lead to Asia," "America had to be intellectually 'invented' as a distinct parcel of land—one that could be viewed geographically . . . as equivalent to the other continents."[105] It was a process of imagining into existence "a single 'new world' landmass."[106] Françoise Lionnet has described this imagination of continental singularity—which takes the "continental landmass" to be a "closed system"—as operating according to a logic of *E pluribus unum*, funneling the multitudinous into a "sacred notion of the 'one.'"[107] Elsewhere, Nelson Maldonado-Torres has denaturalized and critiqued "monolithic nations" and "supposedly natural continents" as predicated on spurious "ontological unity," while Glissant has referred to "continents" as "intolerant landmasses focused on a single truth."[108] The effects of an ontologically and epistemologically totalizing American continental perception can be seen in moments ranging from Turner's 1893 thesis on the frontier as the United States' central engine of development, to Smith's notion of the continental "American West" as "a physical fact" on which the central US American myth is predicated, to the vision of Gilles Deleuze and Félix Guattari in their 1980 *A Thousand Plateaus: Capitalism and Schizophrenia*: "America is a special case. . . . There is the rhizomatic West, with its Indians without ancestry, its ever-receding limit, its shifting and displaced frontiers."[109] Deleuze and Guattari's vision of US America's continental frontier frames the American continent as so exceptional that, although they elsewhere aver that a rhizome has "no points" ("there are only lines"), the rhizomatic American continent becomes "the pivot point" for the entire planet, where moving west takes you to the East and moving east takes you toward the West.[110] Within these various figurations, America's continental coherence stands as a physical fact or uninterrogated assumption. And it is from within this mode of thought that one may say *Columbus discovered/invaded America*—as if he had some wet paint on the bottom of his boot (the paint of discovery/invasion) and when he first stepped onto land in the so-called New World, this paint not only colored the specific ground on which he stood (a footstep's worth of seastrand on an island) but spread automatically (via the continent's alleged status as a coherent and indeed dimensionless "point") throughout the entire hemisphere. Within this continentalist frame, Columbus somehow discovered/invaded it all, ranging from what we now think of as Patagonia in the south to Alaska in the north, from Plymouth Rock to the unceded territory of the Musqueam people now overlaid by British Columbia.[111] This dimensionless logic of American discovery/invasion showcases what Glissant critiques as "continental thinking," which has "the whole persist ... in your mind" "if you are in any part."[112] When the Pukapukans, the Vikings, and the Iroquois are perceived via this continental American thinking and mythology, it might be said that they all spoke *from* different places while all speaking *of* America.

But Edward Kamau Brathwaite's term *interlapping*, as discussed in this study's introduction and further elaborated here, is useful to thinking through the interrelation among these three precontinental landings on what postcontinental thought seeks to *unsee* as the American continent. To visualize the relationality among Te Tawa o te Langi, Vinland, and Turtle Island by recourse to an interlapping structural form, as seen, for instance, in the architectural tradition of reciprocal framing (see fig. 1.2), is to set aside present-day continental teleologies and the related political expediencies of claiming pre-Columbian priority in arriving at or occupying what is now thought of as an American continent. Here the negative space that may appear to be the center of the interlapping structure—the space that attracts eyes habituated to looking for a center—is not a continent. Rather, within the epistemological, ontological, and spatial architecture of the interlap, we view Te Tawa o te Langi, Vinland, and the Great Island as precontinental and noncentered, interlapping in ways that invite us, postcontinentally, to *imagine how not to imagine* the negative space as a center or a coherent continent.[113]

This mode of pre/post/noncontinental imagination is showcased later in *Miss Ulysses*, as Johnny recalls the navigators Tu and Tonu, who led

FIGURE 1.2 — An interlapping matchstick model showcasing a reciprocal frame structure at its simplest. Beyond suggesting the mutual palimpsest of islands and oceans as discussed in the introduction, the notion of interlapping is structurally instantiated by the noncentered quality of what has been described as "reciprocal frame architecture," or a mode of architectural framing "consisting of mutually supporting sloping beams." Innovated independently by many cultures and societies throughout the world, reciprocal framing does not rely on a central nexus or pillar but rather makes use of an interlapping structure so that the beams "do not meet in a central point." Larsen, *Reciprocal Frame Architecture*, 1, 3. Image by PeterEastern, 2009, https://commons.wikimedia.org/wiki/File:Three_stick_reciprocal_frame.JPG.

the two expeditions to Te Tawa o te Langi, or to "America" (according to Johnny's earlier interpretation of that site). But now, later in her book, Johnny mentions these navigators solely as "great navigators" who "explored the remotest islands in the Pacific" (104). In advancing a view of Tu and Tonu that highlights their major accomplishment as reaching islands, Johnny elides a continental telos from their set of accomplishments, which is not to say that she necessarily elides the space now conceived of as continental America from their list of destinations. As she explains, "To [Pukapukans] the earth is the planet holding Puka-Puka—also some other 'islands' like 'Lonitoni' and 'New Yawka'" (105). Although she was writing before the 1957 emergence of the allegedly pre-Columbian map

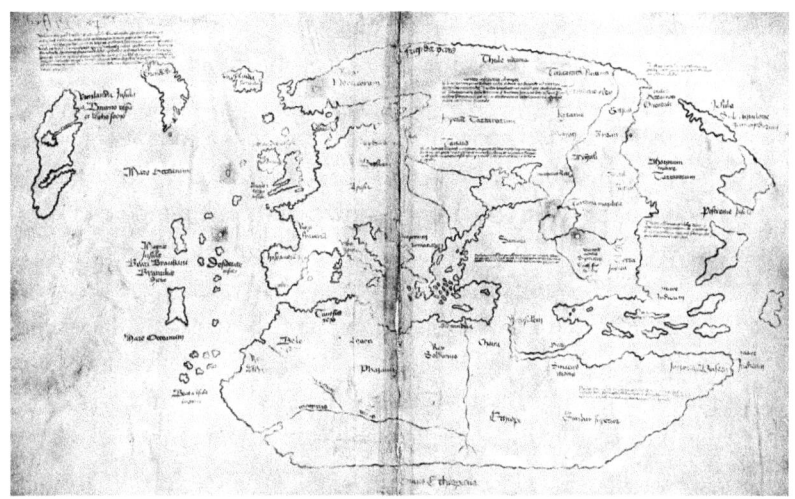

FIGURE 1.3 — The Vinland Map. Beinecke Rare Book and Manuscript Library, Yale University, via https://upload.wikimedia.org/wikipedia/commons/d/dd/Vinland _Map_HiRes.jpg. ઐ Some believe this map, held by Yale University's Beinecke Rare Book and Manuscript Library since 1965, to be "the earliest known [European] representation of any part of the New World" and to have originated "in Northern Europe during the 15th century." Others have concluded that the map is "a modern forgery" ("Vinland Map," Beinecke Rare Book and Manuscript Library, Yale University Library, accessed August 25, 2020, http://brbl-dl.library.yale.edu/vufind/Record/3520245). Regardless of its provenance, the mapmaker inhabited—either genuinely or in a feigned way for purposes of forgery—a precontinental stance regarding America and the world. In the center and to the right, the lands we now may perceive as continents (Europe, Asia, and Africa) are represented according to the precontinental model of the "world island," or *Orbis Terrarum* (on the world island see Okihiro, *Island World*, 207, 209; and M. Lewis and Wigen, *Myth of Continents*, 26). Meanwhile, Vinland is represented as an island in the map's top left corner. Translated into English from Latin, the caption above Vinland and Greenland recounts in part: "By God's will, after a long voyage from the island of Greenland to the south toward the most distant remaining parts of the western ocean sea, sailing southward amidst ice, the companions Bjarni and Leif Eiriksson discovered a new land, extremely fertile and even having vines, the which island they named Vinland" (Skelton, Marston, and Painter, *Vinland Map*, 140). This precontinental view of what we now may think of as America is not inhabited by a continental telos. In other words, Vinland is represented as an island and not as the known tip of a vast and yet-unexplored continent. This view contrasts starkly with the famous conclusion of F. Scott Fitzgerald's novel *The Great Gatsby* (1925), which has Nick Carraway anachronistically superimposing a continental telos on the thought of early European explorers upon first encountering Long Island: "For a transitory enchanted moment man must have held his breath in the presence of this continent, compelled into an æsthetic contemplation he neither understood nor desired, face to face for the last time in history with something commensurate to his capacity for wonder" (Fitzgerald, *Great Gatsby*, 189).

of Vinland (see fig. 1.3), Johnny's islanding of Te Tawa o te Langi (and of London and New York) constitutes a postcontinental imagination that interlaps with the precontinental imagination of the Vinland map's anonymous maker. These two noncontinental figurations also interlap with a pan-tribal trend that, beginning in the 1960s, saw "the term 'Turtle Island' spread through the fugitive Native American newsletters and other communications," so that "the term is now standard in a number of Native American periodicals and circles": "Whereas 'North America' is the home of colonizers, for whom the land is something to be tamed and mastered, 'Turtle Island' is a place where Indigenous cultures, with their emphasis on environmental balance and stewardship of the land, remain vital and respected."[114] Recovering and drawing on precontinental phenomenologies of spatial perception, Johnny, the Vinland mapmaker, and the Indigenous peoples of Turtle Island have envisioned interlapping modes of postcontinental geographic perception that promise to become key to archipelagic and other postcontinental modes of approaching the study of US American and planetary cultures.

Regarding these interlapping modes of decontinentalizing, *Miss Ulysses* offers what I take as a compelling and illustrative episode. Johnny's novelistic memoir revolves around her family's months-long sojourn on the otherwise uninhabited Anchorage Island, among the twenty-six islands and islets of Suvorov Atoll in the Northern Cook Islands. Titled "Cowboys in the Jungle," the chapter that narrates the family's arrival frames Anchorage as a version of the United States' continental American frontier: the children are cowboys exploring the island, and subsequent chapters have them "play[ing] Indian" (137), making an "Indian trail" (133) and "wigwams" (136), and generally emerging as, to redeploy Deleuze and Guattari's language, "Indians without ancestry" within a US American frontier that is "shifting and displaced" in ways that stretch far beyond the intentions of *A Thousand Plateaus*.[115] But this island version of the mythic American continent is washed away on February 21, 1942, as a hurricane crashes through the islands of Suvorov Atoll. For the Frisbie family on Anchorage Island, the situation is so dire that, as Johnny recounts, her father ties his children and himself to tree branches that he hopes will be strong enough to withstand the storm: "For twelve hours the sea had flooded the land, often ten feet deep on the highest part of Anchorage Island, where we were lashed to the limbs of one of the five tamanu trees. With all the jungle gone we were truly isolated in a treetop in mid-ocean, surrounded by violence and destruction" (154). Finally, the hurricane and ocean subside, leaving Johnny and her family sleeping "huddled together in the lee of a pile of coconut logs" (156). The next morning, as Johnny explains, they wake up to a different island, one that looks worse than an island that "the United States Army, Navy, Marine Corps, and Air Force had blasted . . . to smithereens" (156). Johnny states, "The Suvorov we had known was gone forever. . . . Of twenty-six islets strung along the reef only six were left. Even when the sea rebuilt the islets and the jungle grew again—which, of course, it would—Suvorov would be a different land. . . . A new spirit would be born with the growth of the new island, but the old one was gone forever" (158).

I take Johnny's account of Suvorov's Anchorage Island as this chapter's third iteration of a critical fable. Previously, I have pointed toward Marx's deployment of *The Tempest*'s Mediterranean island as a stand-in for the American continent, and I have subsequently suggested that the transnational turn that assesses America *through other continents* has in effect performed a rereading of Marx's island, such that Marx's generation is stuck on an isolated continent that is too insular, while transnational Americanists have managed to get off the island, so to speak—to read America through the intimacies of other continents, thereby transforming transnationalism's American continent from an *insular* continent into a fully *continental* continent among continental peers. In juxtaposition to this first fable involving Marx's insular continent and its transnational variations, I have offered a second fable, in which Americanists have been analogous to Huck Finn, crashing into islands while thinking they are crashing into continents, followed by an archipelagic thought, a recognition of the islands. On the heels of these two fables, I take Johnny's account of the hurricane as offering a further iteration of the archipelagic thought, emerging not from Huck's putatively main currents but from the archipelagic currents of the other side, useful to conceiving of a postcontinental American studies. Here the tempest and the ocean wash away the Frisbies' built-up continental mythology regarding the US American continental frontier (e.g., the cowboy explorations, the Indian trails, the wigwams), while the subsequent image of the family's tamanu tree sticking up out of the ocean heightens a sense of US America as existing in archipelagic states, not forming a solitary island but made up of many islands surrounded, bridged, washed away, built up, and constituted by water over and over again. To invert the literal meaning of *mediterranean* as "set amid land," the United States becomes *set amid water*—the United States of America becomes the archipelagic states of America. To be clear, I am

CONTINENTS AND ARCHIPELAGOES · 75

not suggesting that Americanists ought to begin viewing "the continent" as surrounded by water and consequently a metaphorical island—such a view has been standard enough in US national hymnody (e.g., "from sea to shining sea") and in foreign policy and national defense discussions.[116] Rather, an *archipelagic-states* view admits (borrowing from Ian Bogost) a type of "flat ontology" among proliferating US locales, permitting a view of various land- and water-oriented topographies (territory, commonwealth, national monument, exclusive economic zone, state, territorial waters, etc.) as US American. To retorque Bogost's commentary on flat ontology for an Americanist context: "Things can *be* many and various, specific and concrete, while their *being* remains identical[ly American]."[117] I would elaborate that their beings may be multiple and contested: a physical and human geography may be simultaneously US American and Taíno and Puerto Rican and generally American, for instance, so that modes of spatial being interlap with each other as they interlap with place. This variegated but flat ontological view registers the archipelagic states of America as constitutive of the United States, recognizing that numerous cultures, societies, communities, and land- and seascapes are noncontinental while at the same time existing as flatly and contingently US American.

Those skeptical of this type of flat but variegated US American ontology might argue that the US imperial archipelago—because its archipelagic sites are not the United States but have been contingently occupied by the United States—should not find integration into ontological accounts of US America. Such a stance admirably acknowledges the postcolonial and decolonial nationalisms that archipelagic writers, politicians, and activists have expressed, as is showcased, for instance, in Hōkūlani K. Aikau and Vernadette Vicuña Gonzalez's collaborative collection *Detours: A Decolonial Guide to Hawai'i* (2019). And yet on the question of contingency, of all points, the US imperial archipelago is not an exception among US territorial claims. Rather, acknowledging a flat ontology contributes to projects seeking to denaturalize territorial assumptions of continental coherence and the related assumption of the continent as inalienably US American, reminding us that nearly every point circumscribed by US borders has been occupied and contested.[118] Indeed, an *archipelagic-states* view departs from the mode of nondimensional continental thinking that equates stepping on a seastrand with stepping on an entire continental hemisphere; it disrupts the continental thought process by which landing on, stepping on, or living on the part is tantamount to landing on, stepping on, or living on the whole.

The Lands and Waters Have Been Shifting

Commenting on the shifting cultural lives of lands and waters, the Anishinaabe scholar and poet Margaret Noodin has observed that "in the 1500s, the terms 'America,' 'Pacific,' and 'Atlantic' became common, but they are only new stories layered over old stories. What the scientists call North America, the elders call *Mashkiki-minis*, Turtle Island. The land, like the truth, has always been, and will always be, shifting."[119] The perpetually shifting lands and waters of the archipelagic states of America were on display during my February 2014 conversation with Johnny Frisbie at her home in Honolulu.[120] The shifts had taken place over the course of decades, and they were taking place over the course of minutes as well.

As part of our larger conversation on her travels and relation to the United States, I asked, "As I understand from [reading] *Miss Ulysses*, you're an American citizen?" She answered, "I was born an American citizen, just the year before [... the] policy changed.... After 1932, ... a child born of an American parent outside of the United States had to live in the United States five years before his twenty-first birthday." She explained that she herself was not subject to the five-year residency requirement, but her younger sister, Elaine, had been.[121] Our conversation at the dining room table continued, and a few minutes later, while discussing American Samoa and Puerto Rico as US territories, I mentioned I had recently learned that the United States had laid claim to her home atoll of Pukapuka until the early 1980s. At that point, she stepped away from the table and disappeared down the hall. She returned with a photograph in hand and affirmed, "Yeah, [the United States] laid claim to all the northern group" of the Cook Islands. Showing me the photograph, she explained it was "the signing of the treaty" by Cook Islands "Prime Minister Tom Davis, with a US representative, reclaiming the [Northern] Cook Islands." We were looking at a photo of the June 11, 1980, signing of the Treaty between the United States of America and the Cook Islands on Friendship and Delimitation of the Maritime Boundary between the United States of America and the Cook Islands, which came into force on September 8, 1983 (see fig. 1.4). Through this treaty, the United States affirmed the Cook Islands' claims to the northern islands, relinquishing US claims to the atolls of Pukapuka, Nassau, Manihiki, Rakahanga, and Penrhyn, which it originally claimed via the Guano Islands Act and which it, before the treaty, regarded as existing within a common maritime boundary with American Samoa.[122]

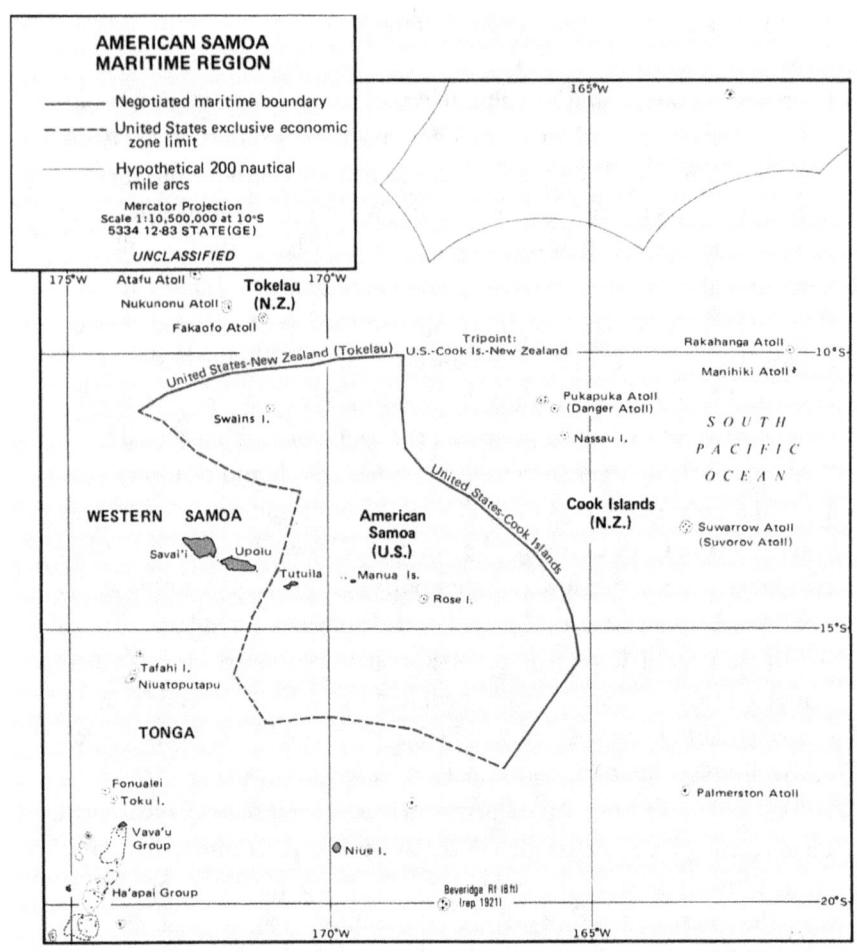

FIGURE 1.4 — The maritime boundary between the United States and the Cook Islands, as outlined in the June 11, 1980, Treaty between the United States of America and the Cook Islands on Friendship and Delimitation of the Maritime Boundary between the United States of America and the Cook Islands. For perspective, note the location of Johnny Frisbie's home atoll of Pukapuka and of Suwarrow Atoll (Suvorov, according to *Miss Ulysses*'s spelling) in relation to American Samoa. From Office of The Geographer, Bureau of Intelligence and Research, *Maritime Boundaries: United States–Cook Islands and United States–New Zealand (Tokelau)* (Limits in the Seas, No. 100; December 30, 1983), 20.

As our conversation on the United States and the idea of America continued, I paraphrased the passage from *Miss Ulysses* (quoted earlier) in which the posthurricane Anchorage Island looks worse than an island that "the United States Army, Navy, Marine Corps, and Air Force had blasted ... to smithereens."[123] I then asked, "What has the idea of America meant to you over the years?" I had assumed we might pick back up on a critique of US imperialism that she had offered earlier in the day before the recorder was on, but she replied, "I was sent here to go to school ... because that was what my father [before he died in November 1948] had wished for me." She explained that she made the trip according to a prior arrangement between her father and some of his admirers in Hawai'i: "I came to Hawai'i thinking I was coming to another island, like Pukapuka. It was a great disappointment at the airport. I cried and cried all the way to Lanikai. But when we got to Lanikai I saw lots of coconut trees and tamanu and I was happy." In a later account, published in 2016, she wrote of living in Lanikai "near a lagoon that reminded [her] of many of the atoll lagoons" of the Northern Cook Islands.[124] She had arrived in America, in the US Territory of Hawai'i, on April 25, 1950, two months before her eighteenth birthday, about two years after publishing *Miss Ulysses*, and about a year and a half after her father's death in Rarotonga in the Cook Islands.[125]

What strikes me about these moments in the conversation is the way Johnny was holding in suspension multiple and shifting modes of being US American and being in US America, with new stories layered over and interlapping with older stories. Within the conversation, she attained US citizenship through her US American father, while her sister, Elaine, born after the policy change, attained US citizenship by relocating and living in the United States for five years. Yet, ironically, Elaine was born on Pukapuka, an atoll that the United States regarded as part of its territory.[126] As we spoke, Johnny was well aware of US claims to Pukapuka—witness her immediate recourse to the photograph of the signing of the 1980 treaty. And even though she had grown up on an island over which (as is attested to in the text of the treaty) the United States had "maintained a claim to sovereignty," when I in a different context asked about the idea of America, Pukapuka did not apparently register as America.[127] Instead, she located America using the phrase "I was sent here," wherein "here" referred to Hawai'i, a locale that represented her arrival in the United States but, at the time of her 1950 landing in Honolulu, was a nonstate, a US territory, another set of islands that the United States regarded as existing within its

FIGURE 1.5 — *Bamboo Roof*, by the Japanese architect Shigeru Ban, exhibited at Rice University from November 9, 2002, to May 11, 2003. The installation showcases how the interlapping structure of reciprocal framing may expand into an extensive lattice as multiple interlapping structures link up and subsequently interlap with one another, pointing toward the repetitions and multiplicities of archipelagic thought and being. Courtesy of the Woodson Research Center Special Collections and Archives and Shigeru Ban Architects.

boundaries.[128] But still, Pukapuka and the Hawaiian island of Oʻahu were connected in her mind (she thought she "was coming to another island") and then simultaneously dissevered (perhaps by Honolulu's modernity?) and sutured (geoformally and botanically by Lanikai's lagoon and coconut and tamanu trees). Here, washed into the ocean by the tempest, the pat cowboys-and-Indians image of Anchorage Island gives way to an archipelagic image of US America in which interlapping definitions of inside and outside are contingent and shifting by the minute, in which being in one US American spatiotemporal configuration does not imply being in another, in which the monological continent and the canonical US states do not function as US America's benchmark states.[129]

In this version of the United States—that is, in the archipelagic states of America—a person may (be compelled to) selectively forget or remember their interiority or exteriority to US America, whether prompted by personal ethical commitments or by imposed governmental designs. Johnny discussed multiple ways of being in multiple and contradictory US Americas, with a sensibility convergent with Glissant's mode of archipelagic thinking: you may "find yourself in some part of [the] archipelago without being in the entire archipelago, without being troubled by this."[130] Johnny's archipelagic states of America have been multiple and interlapping: a US America "synonymous with the U.S. state," as Paul Lyons has critiqued, and yet an "'America' [that] is not so easy to find anymore," as Rob Wilson has described; a United States whose "present configuration is not an immutable fact," as projected by Tiara R. Na'puti and Michael Lujan Bevacqua, and a US America whose present configuration isn't fully *present* but is instead riddled with alter/native undercommons, as Stephanie Nohelani Teves has addressed.[131] To expand on Glissant's archipelagic thinking: more than being in a part of the archipelago without being in the entirety of the archipelago, archipelagic thinkers may find themselves in—and find ways to recognize, negotiate, embrace, contest, and exist plurally within—portions of multiple and interlapping archipelagoes at once (see fig. 1.5).

In this interlapping of old and new stories, in this *shifting of being* amid shifting lands and waters, we see realms of the borderwaters that look toward geographic form—the form of the island, the form of the shoal, the form of the archipelago—and imagine new relationalities among, for instance, the archipelagic Pacific, archipelagic Blackness, the archipelagic states of America, and the always already archipelagic form of Turtle Island.[132] These borderwaters are places of the geo-ontologically plural and amphibious: islands and oceans, riverine archipelagoes and archipelagic thoughts, the American Mediterranean and a US America set amid water, Pukapuka and Puerto Rico, main currents and cruel jokes, retrospect and prospect, archipelagic currents and hurricanes—and, not least among these, interlapping pre- and noncontinental imaginaries as keys to a postcontinental imagination of the archipelagic states of America.

CHAPTER TWO

Archipelagic Diaspora and Geographic Form

Repeating Islands

Zora Neale Hurston's 1942 autobiography *Dust Tracks on a Road* begins with a dream. Before the age of eight, Hurston receives a prophetic vision, which forecasts the book's narrative arc and sets young Zora apart: "It gave me a feeling of terrible aloneness. I stood in a world of vanished communion.... I stood on a soundless island in a tideless sea."[1] Hurston—who was a leading light of the Harlem Renaissance during the early twentieth century, was nearly forgotten during the mid-twentieth century, and was recovered and canonized as a major US author during the late twentieth century—had a history strewn with variations on the island space surfacing in *Dust Tracks*. In 1935 she gathered folk songs on a coastal island in Georgia. Her collaborator, Alan Lomax, later recalled, "We were ... in an isolated community on St. Simon's island.... We felt when we left St. Simon's island that we had ... heard and recorded some genuine Afro-American folk-music of the middle of the nineteenth century."[2] In 1940 Hurston traveled to the South Carolina sea island of Port Royal to study religious trances. She hoped her efforts would complement other anthropological research into trances on the island of Bali.[3] Five years later, she compared the fight for African American civil rights to the anticolonial nationalism erupting in Bali's larger archipelago—that is, the Malay

Archipelago or (as it was often known before Indonesia's emergence as a postcolonial state) the Dutch East Indies. She wrote of "a certain Javanese man who sticks up for Indonesian Independence" from the Netherlands, and she allied herself with "this contrary Javanese."[4] In her 1938 book *Tell My Horse*, Hurston told of traveling from Haiti to the nearby island of La Gonâve: "I found on this remote island a peace I have never known anywhere else on earth."[5] She found this place of peace immediately after completing her novel *Their Eyes Were Watching God* in 1937.[6]

I have presented this arc of islands so as to mimic one of archipelagic space's foundational structures—namely, a repeating insular form whose recursions are discursively ordered in reference to national, racial, imperial, tectonic, or other heuristics. Here the heuristic is authorial, specifically Hurston. The islands enumerated—spanning from the West Indies to the East Indies—constitute only a small subset of Hurston's larger archipelago, which extended temporally during her lifetime from the Soundless Island of *Dust Tracks* to Merritt Island, the Florida coastal island on which she lived in the 1950s, near the end of her life. As is intimated by the connection between La Gonâve and Hurston's peace upon completing *Their Eyes*, Hurston's islands also repeated throughout her expressive writings. This chapter foregrounds the methodological and critical utility of mapping the portion of Hurston's archipelago that emerges as a crucial component of what I think of as *Their Eyes*' geosemiotic project, or its efforts at engaging the planet's material features (land- and waterscapes) as they signify in relation to the planet's cultural features (human traditions, institutions, and formations).

In recent years, much exciting work on *Their Eyes* has been indebted to various cultural geographies that seek to disrupt the exceptionalist claims of the US nation-state. Prescient of this scholarship has been Hazel V. Carby's 1990 essay "The Politics of Fiction, Anthropology, and the Folk: Zora Neale Hurston," which positions *Their Eyes* as an effort "to rewrite the geographical boundaries of representation" by situating the Black folk of the US South "in relation to the Caribbean rather than the northern states."[7] In the wake of Carby's observations, scholars have drawn on *Their Eyes*' Caribbean routes to describe the novel as engaging a set of cultural geographies unbeholden to US borders. Such geographies have included diasporic modernisms, circum-Caribbean spaces, a South that is local and global, and continua of Vodou influence.[8] Yet even as these geographies have illuminated *Their Eyes*, the critical emphasis on cultural continuity across borders—and indeed across physical or geoformally constituted features such as islands, archipelagoes, continents, and oceans—leaves unaddressed the underpinnings of the novel's engagements with the planet's material geography. If heuristics such as the circum-Caribbean and Global South have evoked cultural continua that are mapped in ways untrammeled by the land- and waterscapes composing the planet's geoformal features, then what might the study of Hurston's novel—and US culture in a planetary context more generally—look like when the question of formal geography attains an interpretive weight that mirrors the heft typically afforded to cultural geography?

Particularly instructive in accessing some of *Their Eyes*' geoformal preoccupations is the work of Antonio Benítez-Rojo, whose phrase *repeating island* forecasts my opening gesture toward Hurston's archipelago. Benítez-Rojo takes the archipelago as a geographic entity whose splayed physical ontology is key to theorizing Caribbean society as a discontinuous conjunction.[9] He advances an image of the Caribbean's archipelagic logic (of discontinuous conjunction) disseminating itself globally, so that the Caribbean no longer exists solely as the subset of islands washed by the Caribbean Sea but rather as an expansive set of land and water spaces that chaotically repeat across the entire planet. In theorizing the Caribbean not as a localized subset but as a planetary continuum, Benítez-Rojo coins the term *meta-archipelago*: "as a meta-archipelago," the Caribbean "has the virtue of having neither a boundary nor a center. Thus the Caribbean flows outward past the limits of its own sea," with its extreme limit "found on the outskirts of Bombay, near the low and murmuring shores of Gambia, in a Cantonese tavern of circa 1850, at a Balinese temple, in an old Bristol pub, in a commercial warehouse in Bordeaux at the time of Colbert, in a windmill beside the Zuider Zee, at a cafe in a barrio of Manhattan, in the existential *saudade* of an old Portuguese lyric."[10] Here the Caribbean interlinks world cultures because its history is a crucible of world cultures. Adding to a late twentieth-century discourse that privileged the Caribbean as an exceptionally useful model for understanding the new globalized culture, Benítez-Rojo acknowledges Hellas and the Malay Archipelago as meta-archipelagoes of the past but positions the Caribbean as "the last of the great meta-archipelagoes."[11] The Caribbean alone takes the expanse of the planet as its compass.

While I admire Benítez-Rojo's attentiveness to the forms of the island and the archipelago, I want to resist the exceptionalism embedded in a view of the Caribbean as the last great meta-archipelago. This view is disrupted by the fact that the Greek, Malay, and other archipelagoes have generated cultures that continue to overflow their purported cartographic boundaries. But still more troubling to the Caribbean's archipelagic exceptionalism is the Caribbean's participation—together with all other sea islands—in a truly decentered and planetary archipelago. Often referred to as *the islands of the sea*, this meta-archipelago has been fetishized by colonists, missionaries, and anthropologists—and also at times by islanders, including decolonial and other liberation-oriented thinkers. During the early twentieth century, furthermore, the global archipelago was a critical component of some of US America's most avant-garde thinking on race relations. Consider, as alluded to in the previous chapter, W. E. B. Du Bois's post-Hegelian assertion that "the problem of the twentieth century is the problem of the color-line,—the relation of the darker to the lighter races of men in Asia and Africa, in America and the islands of the sea."[12] Here the islands of the sea emerge as a planetary meta-archipelago constituted by archipelagic subsets ranging from the Antilles to Hawai'i and from the Philippines to the Azores. Tracing this meta-archipelago's discontinuous conjunctions (among the islands and in relation to oceans and continents and shoals) becomes crucial to accessing the planet's unwieldy tangles of racialized power relations.

The archipelagic component of Du Bois's century-old pronouncement suggests that although recent trends in the transnational study of US literature and culture have positioned themselves in implicit contradistinction to the insular form, *insularity* must be recognized as a formal geography that is key to interpreting US and broader American literatures and cultures. During the past three decades, postexceptionalist versions of US and American cultural and literary studies have gained ascendancy under the rubrics of the transnational and the postnational, the hemispheric and the planetary.[13] Postexceptionalist scholars have drawn productive critical attention to the splayed island spaces of the de jure and de facto empires of the United States, but the postexceptionalist discourse also has positioned itself in methodological contradistinction to the insular form, with influential voices encouraging "internationalist" projects in opposition to an outdated "American Studies that is . . . insular and parochial."[14] Postexceptionalist voices have emerged contra "the insularity of an American studies that imagines the nation as . . . fixed . . . and self-enclosed."[15] They have sought a "complex hemispheric history" in opposition to "insular and nationalist" accounts.[16] They have, to recall a fable from the previous chapter, imagined the field's older scholars as stuck on a desert island while the newer, transnationalized Americanists have escaped the island's putatively claustrophobic topography. If galvanizing voices in the development of postexceptionalist US American cultural and literary studies have paired the island's defining geoformal quality with devalued categories such as the fixed, self-enclosed, nationalist, and parochial, then one must wonder to what extent the field is equipped to access the archipelagic topographies of the hemisphere and planet it takes as its extensions. As immensely enlightening as the postexceptionalist discourse has been, a Cuban or Hawaiian cultural geography will be inadequately mapped to the degree that island space's geoformal qualities meet with analytic lenses announcing themselves as somehow anti-insular.

On one level, then, this chapter's recourse to *Their Eyes* seeks to project the potential for critical insight forgone by analyses that comment on insular sites without developing a corresponding attentiveness to the project of reading insular form as a complex of water- and land-evoked connectivity. Whereas several scholars have read Hurston as implicated in US and anthropological imperialism, recourse to *Their Eyes'* engagements with island space permits a view of Hurston as theorizing and participating in what I describe as *archipelagic diaspora*.[17] In a way that contrasts, but may also interlock, with imperial, racial, and religious modes of theorizing the planet, archipelagic diaspora creates a sense of planetary connectivity not by identitarian heuristics or imperial superimposition but by connection, via unanticipated formal recognitions, across spatially perceived ontological difference. Indeed, tracing the dynamics of archipelagic diaspora becomes a means of layering the question of geographic form into this study's ongoing and accretive work in outlining some of the contours of archipelagic thinking.

Speaking to broader methodological questions, the chapter argues for a greater attentiveness, within the realm of geography as cultural-critical discourse, to what George B. Handley describes as "the phenomenological encounter with natural forms."[18] Focused on cultural flows rather than formal and material topographies, Americanist studies in postcolonialism, the Global South, the Atlantic world, the borderlands, the transpacific, and the planet generally have evidenced a cagey reluctance to fall into latter-day iterations of the suspect environmental determinism that, ranging from the Enlightenment through the late nineteenth and early twentieth centuries, embraced ideas ranging from "the *temperate zone*" as the necessary "theatre of world history" to the stance that "man is a product of the earth's surface."[19] Yet, increasingly, work by Katherine McKittrick, Tiffany Lethabo King, Paul Giles, Christopher Tilley, Robert T. Tally Jr., and scholars of oceanic studies has demonstrated the urgency of attending to the materiality of geography.[20] Adding to this materialist and variously formally engaged line of inquiry, I argue for a critical geoformalism that brings to geographically oriented critical discourse a heightened willingness to take literary studies' waning and waxing attentiveness to literary form (with its shifting and culturally determined conventions and horizons of expectations) as a template for reading cultural engagements with a material horizon that comprises formal features ranging from shoreline to timberline, from comparative elevation to comparative magnitude of land or water space. Cultivating a new attentiveness to geographic things—and indeed an attentiveness to the ways in which a sense of geographic form is produced through subjective engagements with the planet's physical features—lends pivotal modes of legibility to literary texts, cultural formations, material topographies, and our own critical (re)reading practices.[21] The geoformal underpinnings of Hurston's recovery in the 1970s, together with her many rereadings during the ensuing decades, offer an occasion to examine and meditate on some of these legibilities.

Parallax Zones, Insular Allotopia

The Hurston-based persona who narrates *Dust Tracks on a Road* discloses that Janie and Tea Cake's relationship was modeled on a "love affair" between Hurston and a man "born of West Indian parents" in New York City (207). This love, explains the narrator, was mutually destructive and prompted Hurston to accept a Guggenheim Fellowship for anthropological research in Jamaica and Haiti. Her Caribbean travel was an effort "to release him, and fight myself free" (210). Hurston's narrator recalls, "I wrote *Their Eyes Were Watching God* in Haiti. It was dammed up in me, and I wrote it under internal pressure in seven weeks" (175). She explains, "I tried to embalm all the tenderness of my passion for him in *Their Eyes Were Watching God*" (211).

The cultural contexts of Hurston's Haitian writing session and Caribbean-descended love interest are suggestive in relation to the nexus between *Their Eyes* and island space. Yet attending to insular form demands more immediate focus on the continuity that *Dust Tracks* alleges between its own narrator and the narrator of *Their Eyes*, especially in light of the former narrator's assertion that her foreknowledge caused a "vanished communion" and placed her "on a soundless island in a tideless sea."

Of course, the narrators of *Dust Tracks* and *Their Eyes* bear no easy conflation; they are separated by the temporal differences between the 1930s and the 1940s, the generic differences between novel and autobiography, and the perspectival differences between first and third person. Yet these vanished communions—when contextualized with *Dust Tracks*' assertion of narrative continuity—open Hurston's personae to being read as narrating from separate sites that might be thought of in reference to what Paul Giles describes as "parallax zones," or spaces that lack physical proximity but nonetheless achieve a set of interconnections to one another.[22] In theorizing a mode of planetary analysis independent of the "myth of presence" embedded in Mary Louise Pratt's "contact zone," Giles references the phenomenon of parallax (or the disjunctive visual effect produced by viewing one object from two different points of view) to remind us that events transpiring at antipodal geographic removes from one another will reveal themselves as interconnected to the degree that these regions (or parallax zones) are linked to a common and third point of reference.[23] In this view, events as spatially disparate as US independence and Pacific exploration become interlinked through a shared yet parallax relation to colonial Britain.[24] Drawing on Giles, I read Hurston's two narrators as assuming parallax views of the Soundless Island, with *Dust Tracks* taking the island as an immediate site of narrative positionality and *Their Eyes* situating the island as a far-flung object of geographic desire. Whereas Leigh Anne Duck has remarked that *Their Eyes*' apparent existence "outside the time of the nation" creates "the chronotope of [the novel as] relatively allotemporal," attending to *Their Eyes*' relation to the Soundless Island places pressure on the other variable within the chronotope's spatiotemporal equation.[25] The Soundless Island's distant exertions infuse *Their Eyes* with a sense of allotopia, a sense of other-place-ness reified in Janie's fixation on and imagination of the horizon.

Janie is inducted into this allotopic spatial economy after watching a "bee sink into" a pear-tree blossom.[26] Her ensuing ill-timed kiss with Johnny Taylor leads Janie's grandmother to decide that her sixteen-year-old granddaughter will marry the local farmer Logan Killicks. When Janie resists, Nanny slaps her and offers an initial lesson on race, gender, and allotopic geography:

> "Honey, de white man is de ruler of everything as fur as Ah been able tuh find out. Maybe it's some place way off in de ocean where de black man is in power, but we don't know nothin' but what we see. So de white man throw down de

load and tell de nigger man tuh pick it up. He pick it up because he have to, but he don't tote it. He hand it to his womenfolks. De nigger woman is de mule uh de world so fur as Ah can see. Ah been prayin' fuh it tuh be different wid you." (14)

Contextualizing Nanny's speech within Hurston's Caribbean routes, scholars have linked Nanny's hypothesized "place way off in de ocean" to postrevolutionary Haiti.[27] Certainly, even if Nanny is less aware of her words' import than are the novel's readers, Nanny's reference to a place in the ocean where "de black man is in power" recalls Haiti as the world's first Black republic, a revolutionary entity whose fame had long circulated on a common wind that ran through the islands and continents of the Americas and Europe and which had been a persistent if vexed beacon of Black liberation to people of African descent in the United States.[28] But Nanny's mapping of the known (white, male) world in relation to an unknown world also gestures toward a second space beyond the island where "de black man is in power." As an imperfectly fathomable and unseen site within a planetary grid constituted by intersecting gendered and racialized lines, the second space is a phantom island on which Black women are empowered. This is Hurston's "soundless island in a tideless sea" imagined from a vast distance, with soundlessness and tidelessness emerging as apt expressions of its isolation. Its soundlessness resides in its unpresentable distance from the known world's coast and its consequent incapacity to form a sound in relation to what presently appears to be the mainland. Its tidelessness sets it apart from the cyclic motions of the global ocean, thereby distancing the phantom island from material islands' well-documented sea-facilitated intercourse with other planetary spaces.[29] Nanny's hypothetical island is antipodal in both senses: as a site of unpresentable distance from the known world and as a site of emancipatory inversion in relation to that world.

Of course, for Nanny, this antipodal and hypothetical island is moot ("we don't know nothin' but what we see") and has no bearing on the imperative that Janie marry Logan in early twentieth-century Florida. But for Janie, the phantom island is the sublime object of "an imagination striving to figure even that which cannot be figured," or perhaps, to adapt phrasing from McKittrick, it is a Black geography "so inconceivable, . . . so radically outside our archives, that [it is] merely [a] psychic impression . . . of life and livingness."[30] Whatever the case, two decades and two husbands after Nanny's speech, Janie continues contemplating her grandmother's theories of space and practicality. By now, Janie has married Logan and left him for Jody Starks. Janie and Jody have lived in the Florida town of Eatonville, where Jody has spent years as mayor before dying. Now Janie realizes she has wasted her life following Nanny's dreams:

> She hated her grandmother.... [Janie] had been getting ready for her great journey to the horizons in search of *people*.... But she had been ... run off down a back road after *things*.... Some people could look at a mud-puddle and see an ocean with ships.... [But] Nanny had taken the biggest thing God ever made, the horizon—for no matter how far a person can go the horizon is still way beyond you—and pinched it in to such a little bit of a thing that she could tie it about her granddaughter's neck tight enough to choke her. (89)

The difference between Nanny's known-world practicality and Janie's allotopic yearning is the difference between a land journey ("down a back road") and a sea journey ("an ocean with ships") toward the horizon. Intriguingly, in placing the horizon on a continuum of *things* as "the biggest thing God ever made," *Their Eyes* transforms the horizon from a passive object into a vast and active *thing*, or an object asserting itself in relation to human subjects by issuing scripts that invite humans to take action, to move and travel.[31] Nanny's horizon, then, is one of objective circumscription, while Janie's is a sublime and vital thing—what Jane Bennett might call a nonhuman *actant* or *operator*—whose geoformal unattainability (perpetually "way beyond you") produces a beckoning sense of planetary infinitude.[32] It behaves like a hyperobject, a thing "massively distributed in time and space relative to humans," and yet attains the appearance of massive distribution as a line that shifts—and indeed exists—in relation to the subjective perception and striving movement that it invites.[33] Ultimately, it is a thing that looks similar to the imperial imagination that the young Hurston absorbed through reading *Gulliver's Travels*, *The Swiss Family Robinson*, and works by Robert Louis Stevenson (*Dust Tracks*, 38–39).

Archipelagic Diaspora—Suitors, Spice, Battleships

While Janie's gaze at first glance may seem to allude to the spatial imagination of such colonial texts as *The Swiss Family Robinson*, her gaze also begs for distinctions. These distinctions become apparent in a description of Janie and Tea Cake's courtship that is attentive to what scholars have discussed as the difference between empire (as a global projection of the state) and diaspora (as a global relationality involving a stateless polity).[34] As the courtship develops after Jody's death, empire wanes while diaspora waxes and converges with the form of the archipelago. For over six months, Janie is surrounded by "hosts of admirers," but "not one suitor . . . ever gain[s] the house porch" (92, 91). One day, however, she meets Tea Cake and feels a connection with this man who, unlike her typical "stiff" suitors (92), has no car and admits he hitches train rides—"money or no money" (97). During one conversation, Tea Cake says he's found work "four days dis week and got de pay in mah pocket." Janie teases, "We got a rich man round here, then. Buyin' passenger trains uh battleships this week?" He answers, "Which one do *you* want?" Janie cautiously replies, "Ah'll take de passenger train. If it blow up Ah'll still be on land." But Tea Cake can see she wants something different and responds, "Choose de battleship if dat's whut you really want. Ah know where one is right now. Seen one round Key West de other day. . . . Ah'd git dat ship out from under [the admiral] so slick till he'd be walkin' de water lak ole Peter befo' he knowed it" (101). Finally, Tea Cake is the suitor who makes it past the porch (101–6). The next day, Janie's thoughts return to him: "He could be a bee to a blossom—a pear tree blossom in the spring. He seemed to be crushing scent out of the world with his footsteps. Crushing aromatic herbs with every step he took. Spices hung about him" (106).

Trucking in suitors, spice, and battleships, this courtship is intriguing in its metonymic interlinking of what Benítez-Rojo references as the planet's three meta-archipelagoes—Hellas, the Malay Archipelago, and the Caribbean. In a Penelopean scene, Janie keeps her proliferating suitors at bay in fidelity to an Odysseus who at first seems nonexistent. Certainly, this is Tea Cake's initial appearance rather than an Odyssean return after twenty years away. Yet Janie's emplotment of Tea Cake within her life's narrative creates him as emblematic of the pear-tree event of two decades earlier. He could be a bee to a blossom, she thinks. Like Odysseus returning disguised as a beggar after years traveling throughout the Greek isles, Janie's bee-to-a-blossom is disguised as a traveler so poor he "can't do nothin' but help [Janie] spend whut she got" (111).[35] But Tea Cake brings traces of travels that exceed Hellas's archipelagic horizon. He carries a redolence of spices. Janie's figuration of Tea Cake via the trope of spice recalls Richard Wright's observation on the poetics of spice in colonial modernity's wake. "Spices were what Christopher Columbus had been looking for in 1492 when he had sailed forth," Wright observed; to "many European minds[,] the islands of the Atlantic and Pacific . . . still mean . . .

spices."³⁶ Tea Cake's scent gestures toward the Malay Archipelago's Spice Islands, the insular space in the East Indies for which the Caribbean, as the West Indies, has served as a far-flung analogue since 1492. Indeed, 1492's meta-archipelagic moment—its transhemispheric fusion of distant archipelagoes—is reproduced in the couple's banter on battleships. If Janie's suitors suggest Tea Cake as an Odyssean figure returning from adventures throughout the Greek archipelago, and if Tea Cake carries the Malay Archipelago's redolence, then his glib promise to commandeer a battleship off Key West brings the Caribbean into a meta-archipelagic relationality with these other island chains. Tea Cake's promise intimates that in him Janie has found her passport to what Du Bois and many others have called the islands of the sea, a planetary space promising to reveal the antipodal and hypothetical island that Nanny, years ago, gestured toward and dismissed. In choosing Tea Cake, Janie rejects the known-world train and seeks the ship's allotopic promise. She defends this decision: "Ah done lived Grandma's way, now Ah means tuh live mine" (114). Janie's way is an ocean with ships.

Yet significant slippage exists between Tea Cake's battleship and the ship Janie envisions as conducing toward the unpresentable island space that structures her allotopic desire.³⁷ Tea Cake's battleship has imperial routes in the Key West naval station, which during and after the Spanish-American War became important as a base for US vessels threatening intervention in the Caribbean.³⁸ Structurally, Tea Cake's promise to commandeer the battleship—to install himself in place of the admiral—is a promise to maintain the known form of empire while becoming empire's new content. Hence, the battleship is a false cognate of the ship Janie wants. Unexpectedly linked to the known-world railroading space of the passenger train, the battleship is of a piece with the known horizon: Tea Cake would have traveled to Key West by hitching a ride to the farthest point of the 128-mile Oversea Railway, a marvel of early twentieth-century engineering that connected continental Florida to an island lying closer to Havana than to Miami (see figs. 2.1 and 2.2).³⁹

Requiring a vehicle distinct from Tea Cake's imperial ship, Janie's allotopic desire is diasporic in geophenomenological ways, or in ways that rely on interrelations among humans and the planet's material and formal features. Her desire finds its form in the meta-archipelagic relationality broadly encoded in the couple's courtship, which figures Janie and Tea Cake's union in terms of an interlinking of Hellas, the Caribbean, and the Malay Archipelago. Access to the courtship's geophenomenology is

FIGURE 2.1 — Florida East Coast Railway passenger train traveling across Seven Mile Bridge on the Key West extension of the Oversea Railway in the early twentieth century. Black and white photoprint, 7 × 9 in. Florida Memory: State Library and Archives of Florida (RC 06890).

enhanced by recourse to Hurston's book *Tell My Horse*, which, like *Dust Tracks*, assumes a parallax relation to *Their Eyes* inasmuch as it offers another view of the island space that is crucial to the novel's geoformal investments. Conveying a narrative of Hurston as anthropologist, *Tell My Horse* documents the fieldwork Hurston performed during a yearlong stay in the Caribbean, a sojourn during which she supplemented her anthropological work with what she described as the seven-week writing spree resulting in *Their Eyes*.

Tell My Horse's geoformal preoccupations become most pronounced in the chapter "Isle de la Gonâve," which describes the island to which Hurston retreated immediately after completing *Their Eyes*. Here Hurston recounts the myth of the Vodou god Damballa, who sent his wife, Cilla, to relay to the people of Haiti "the formula for peace."[40] As Damballa's envoy, Cilla traveled on the back of a whale that carried her so smoothly she fell asleep and became an island in the waters off Port-au-Prince. Hurston explains, "Anyone in Port-au-Prince who looks out to sea can see [Cilla] lying there on her back with her hands folded across her middle sleeping

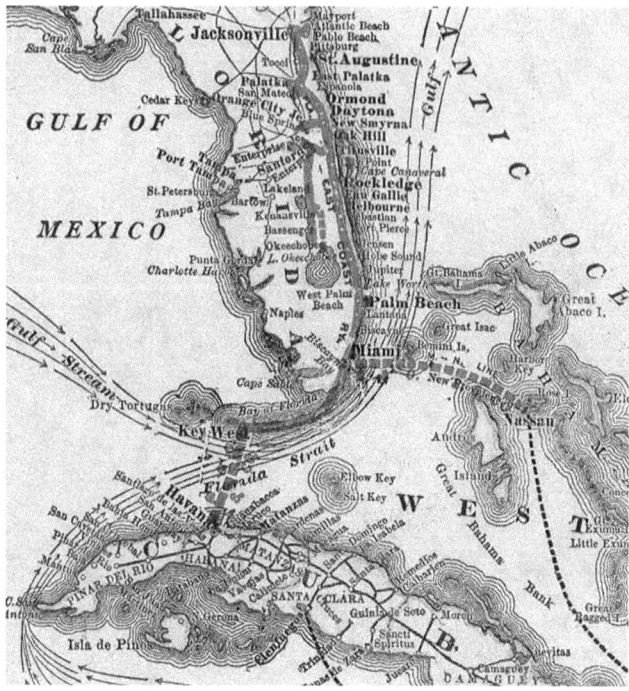

FIGURE 2.2 — The extent of the Oversea Railway, with its Key West terminus situated closer to Cuba than to Miami. Dotted lines between Key West and Havana, as well as between Miami and Nassau, indicate routes traveled by the Peninsular and Occidental Steamship Company. Note also Lake Okeechobee (sometimes called "Florida's inland sea") in the center of the peninsula, where Janie and Tea Cake work with the Bahamian laborers and where the levee breaks and drives them to West Palm Beach. Map excerpted from Florida East Coast Railway's *Map of the Peninsula of Florida and Adjacent Islands* (1912). From Geographicus: Rare Antique Maps, accessed August 25, 2020, https://www.geographicus.com/P/AntiqueMap/FloridaEastCoastRail-matthewsnorthrup-1912.

peacefully."[41] The chapter narrates Hurston's sea voyage to "the island of the sleeping woman," where she finds "a peace I have never known anywhere else." La Gonâve's "outlines which from Port-au-Prince look like a sleeping woman are prophetic."[42] Hurston's subjective encounter with La Gonâve, which is precipitated by an insular topography whose profile gains signifying content through Haitian myth and formal correspondence to Hurston's own body, offers a glimpse at a mode of subject-earth relations in which insular landscape and imaginative subject oscillate between subject and object positions, between bestower and receiver of profile lines and content. If the island's sleeping profile is prophetic of Hurston's peace after her December 1936 completion of *Their Eyes*, then *Tell My Horse*'s description of an intersubjective experience with La Gonâve is prophetic of how a young Gilles Deleuze, in the early 1950s, would describe the encounter between human creative consciousness and the insular form. Discussing desert islands, Deleuze observed, "Those people who come to the island . . . , were they . . . sufficiently creative, . . . would give the island only a dynamic image of itself, such that . . . the island would be only the dream of humans, and humans, the pure consciousness of the island." These would be "absolute creators, . . . a woman who would be a goddess, . . . a pure Artist, a consciousness of Earth and Ocean, an enormous hurricane."[43] Deleuze's and Hurston's converging visions of insular form are illuminating in regard to a novel whose completion presaged a singular moment of shared consciousness between artist and island, a moment when the artist envisioned the shape of her interior state as identical to the profile of the island itself and when earth and ocean coalesced in ways evoking, for Hurston, an unforecasted feeling of peace upon completing a novel whose climax revolves around the eye of an enormous hurricane.

Hurston's encounter with the insular form presents an instance of what I call *archipelagic diaspora*, a mode of planetary relationality that evokes cohesion not through racial or religious commonality but through phenomenological encounters, facilitated by unforecasted formal congruities, across radical difference. While it operates in a different register than diasporas that may look toward religious or racial commonality, it inevitably enters into complementary, defamiliarizing, and interanimating dynamics with these formations.[44] Indeed, reminiscent of Du Bois's 1926 intimations regarding aesthetic objects as potential agents in compelling "recognition" between object and human, and hence human and human, archipelagic diaspora relies on the ways geographic things (islands, archipelagoes, other formal features) play a role in compelling recognition, as is the case with La Gonâve's parallax mediations among Hurston, her readers, and residents of Port-au-Prince.[45]

The interconnective qualities of this mode of diaspora find an allegory in the cultural and etymological history of the archipelagic form. To briefly recap the OED's narrative, the Italian term *arcipelago* (with *arci-* signifying "principal or chief" and *-pelago* signifying "pool or abyss") arose during the thirteenth century. It emerged as a name for Hellas's chief sea, the island-studded Aegean, and by metonymy came to describe not the sea but the Aegean's intermittent island spaces. During Europe's so-called Age of Discovery, explorers traveling to other regions (regions existing at radical removes in terms of spatial proximity and cultural epistemology) experienced an uncanny formal recognition of the Aegean in the island-studded zones they now beheld. Consequently, the term *archipelago* ceased naming a specific sea and began structuring and describing a formal relation to material geographies spanning the planet, with the originary reference as a proper name for the Aegean largely forgotten. More than presenting the history of a metaphor that died during the era of colonial modernity, this etymology reveals the form of the archipelago as an instructive analogue in relation to the dying metaphor *diaspora*, which during the late twentieth and early twenty-first centuries has been unrelentingly distanced from its origins as a description of Jewish dispersion. Tasked to describe dispersions of groups ranging from Africans to Albanians, *diaspora* has, finally, emerged as a demographic form capable of referring to "any and every nameable population category that is to some extent dispersed in space."[46] To describe diaspora as archipelagic recalls *archipelago*'s analogous history of evoking formal recognitions across ontological difference, among any and all island-studded regions. As a description, then, the term *archipelagic diaspora* retools diaspora so as to deemphasize in-group identitarian heuristics and foreground diaspora's recent history of evoking proliferating formal analogies among the planet's seemingly unrelated diasporan populations, much as the tropes of *archipelago* and *Indies* have sustained long-durational, formally driven analogies among local and global spaces across the planet. Archipelagic diaspora's connections are less reliant on attachments to specific cultural homelands and what Alexander G. Weheliye refers to as "a transcendental racial bond" and more indebted to perceptions of formal correspondences among humans and material topographies that exist at spatial removes from one another.[47] Archipelagic diaspora resonates with—or trembles with—what Glissant in *La cohée du Lamentin* (2005) referred to as archipelagic thought's alliance with "the trembling of our world," a trembling which, as the Japanese cultural anthropologist Ryuta Imafuku summarizes, "seeks ... magnetic ties between the lands, the land and the people, and among the people."[48]

On one level, I am discussing the way in which archipelagic diaspora arises as La Gonâve's profile is viewed from parallax zones inhabited by Hurston and the Haitian informants who explained the whale and Cilla's transformation into an island. But looking toward a broader arena, consider the way in which the Mediterranean's Aegean—as the originary crucible of the planetary archipelago trope—has effaced itself as any type of a homeland or racial beacon while evoking multiple modes of recognition based on perceived formal correspondences among water-land complexes of islands and even continents. Such correspondences are showcased in the previous chapter, in Florence "Johnny" Frisbie's self-framing as Miss Ulysses from Puka-Puka and Frederick Jackson Turner's conceptualization of the US American frontier as the Greek Mediterranean, but also in Saint Lucian poet Derek Walcott's famed interface with *The Odyssey* in his epic *Omeros*.[49] In tandem with such transnational and interregional interlacings by recourse to parallax relations with the Aegean, many other modes of archipelagic diaspora have arisen, as seen in proposed interlaps among the Pacific Islands, the Caribbean, and Turtle Island. Elsewhere, this appears in, for instance, the decision of the editors of *A New Oceania: Rediscovering Our Sea of Islands* (the 1993 volume that first published Epeli Hau'ofa's watershed essay "Our Sea of Islands") to begin the collection with an epigraph from Walcott's poem "The Sea Is History." The epigraph represents and figures an archipelagic-diasporic consciousness evoked not only by a common postcolonial relation to archipelagic seas and shores but also, and more immediately, by a shared relation to "the salt chuckle of rocks," "sea pools," and "the reef's moiling shelf"—in which the Caribbean's and the Pacific's material rocks, pools, and reefs are antipodean to one another but nonetheless elicit Caribbean-Pacific identifications by means of geographically formal correspondences.[50] Certainly, such formal correspondences also play a role in the convergence between Janie's yearning for "an ocean with ships" and Johnny Frisbie's enthusiasm for the "wandering spirit" that impels her toward "ships and the sea and the anticipation of arrival."[51]

In meditating on the emergence of diasporic consciousness within the ancient Greek Mediterranean, Irad Malkin has described a Greek identity "without a homeland," made up of "communities with no contiguous territory and no single political center." In a process he describes as experiencing "Diaspora in the reverse," Greeks came into existence not from a common center but from "a variety of mother cities . . . and only then created their virtual center."[52] Allied in its lack of a homeland and inverted relation to traditional notions of centered diasporic dispersion, archipelagic diaspora has a dispersion narrative similar to the dispersion narrative that is poetically encoded in frequent descriptions of archipelagoes as made up of *scattered*, *splayed*, or *far-flung* islands. Archipelagic diaspora's humans, landscapes, and seascapes have not been scattered (broken away and dispersed from a prior state of physical contiguity) any more than islands in an archipelago have been scattered. Rather, *scattering* becomes a metaphor for perceptions of formal links among archipelagic diaspora's subjective and material topographies.[53]

In its formal linking of human subjects through the contours of an island, Hurston's "Isle de La Gonâve" chapter offers a parallax glance into *Their Eyes* as advancing a story-based theorization of archipelagic diaspora.[54] This theorization takes place in the novel's representation of Janie and Tea Cake's courtship, which geoformally joins two persons of radically different stations: the mayor's widow and a traveling badman. Their courtship is a commingling of suitors, spice, and battleships that constitutes—and finds constitution through—a meta-archipelagic ordering of far-flung island chains including Hellas, the Malay Archipelago, and the Caribbean. Janie and Tea Cake are distant islands interlinked, and their archipelagic relationship jolts the town of Eatonville (110), much as the interlinking of Mediterranean, Pacific, and Atlantic islands might confound a complacent cartographer. The courtship, however, is only a preliminary moment in the novel's theorization of archipelagic diaspora.

Submerged Ontologies of US Geography

Although Tea Cake's appearance prompts *Their Eyes*' movement toward archipelagic diaspora, he himself is oriented toward more traditional modes of identity-based diaspora. He assumes a race-based diaspora function when, rather than commandeering a battleship, he takes Janie to the Everglades, to a place on the muck near Lake Okeechobee. Here Janie and Tea Cake befriend the "Saws"—or "Bahaman workers"—who like themselves have traveled to the muck to find agricultural work. Janie and Tea Cake's quarters become a meeting place for African Americans and Saws, with many African Americans learning Bahamian "fire dances" and enjoying "it as much as the 'Saws'" (154). Framing the 'Glades as a contact zone has been key to critical readings that attend to *Their Eyes*' investments in race-based diasporic consciousness.[55] Yet more than foregrounding race-based diaspora, the novel's final section articulates Tea Cake's and Janie's diverging senses of planetary consciousness, which helps further crystallize Janie's figuration of archipelagic diaspora.

When the hurricane routs the muck community from its base at Lake Okeechobee's levee, Janie and Tea Cake join an exodus that swims and scrambles toward refuge in Palm Beach, a coastal city comprising insular and continental spaces. After they arrive, Tea Cake worries about the dangers of a strange city. Twice he repeats, "Us got tuh git . . . outa dis man's town" (168, 171), and he explains to Janie:

> "Every white man think he know all de GOOD darkies already. He don't need tuh know no mo'. So far as he's concerned, all dem he don't know oughta be tried and sentenced tuh six months behind de United States privy house at hard smellin.'"
>
> "How come de United States privy house, Tea Cake?"
>
> "Well, you know Old Uncle Sam always do have de biggest and de best uh everything." (172)

Here Tea Cake's signifying on the United States' claim to "de biggest and de best" hinges on one of US America's founding geographic forms—the form of the continent, whose massive size was taken by the US founders as a physical property attesting to material geography's underwriting of their revolution. From the Continental Congresses to the Continental Army, the continent's vastness bore a naturalized conflation with the ethical best. And this ethical best was generated in opposition to another ethical position—British insularity's smallness as constitutive of ethical inferiority. As discussed previously, Thomas Paine was among the revolutionary voices that invoked a distinction between (British) island and (American) continent. "Small islands," he argued, are proper "for kingdoms to take under their care; but there is something very absurd, in supposing a continent to be perpetually governed by an island."[56] Ontological distinctions among geographic forms helped create the revolution's grounding in political common sense. As power-constituted material topographies rationalizing US sovereignty, island and continent emerged as geographic things whose formal properties issued scripts calling on people and states to move.

Tea Cake's description of Uncle Sam's water closet may be no more aware of its geographic debts than Nanny's perhaps dramatically ironic reference to Haiti. But as Tea Cake specifies "biggest" as the United States' penchant, his description rests on a geographic substrate indebted to a formal distinction between island and continent. This distinction has reinforced—and taken reinforcement from—the country's founding democratic logic, which asks the largest portion of the population to decide what is best. Indeed, since the United States' founding, democracy and geography have wrought twin tyrannies: what Alexis de Tocqueville famously called "the tyranny of the majority" and what I call the tyranny of the continent.[57] Where the former looks within the United States to code the demographic minority as politically moot, the latter fetishizes continental vastness and codes insularity as inferior (fixed, parochial, self-enclosed). Where the former has rationalized the sovereignty of the US majority and the maintenance of smaller racialized populations as internal colonials, the latter has rationalized the sovereignty of the continental US nation-state and imperialism beyond the continent's shores.

As the setting for *Their Eyes'* concluding section, the Palm Beach County of the 1920s and 1930s offers a microcosmic rewriting of US America's founding distinctions between island and continent, minority and majority. This rewriting reveals a United States that would reject the founding continental logic of its sovereignty before embracing a logic, advanced from the outset by Phillis Wheatley and others, that yoked America's political liberty to liberty for a racial minority group.[58] In a town other than Palm Beach, Tea Cake's refrain "Us got tuh git . . . outa dis man's town" might express an animus toward a vague town spirit. But in early twentieth-century Palm Beach County, the phrase *this man's town* inevitably recalled that business and railroad tycoon Henry Flagler had founded insular Palm Beach as a resort in the 1890s, while originally establishing continental (or West) Palm Beach "merely as an adjunct to his fashionable colony."[59] As a 1926 tourist booklet explained, "West Palm Beach grew up on the mainland" to serve "the need . . . of society leaders" whose hotels graced Palm Beach.[60] The tourist booklet versified West Palm Beach's status as Palm Beach's continental supplement:

> The Palm Beaches are a world renowned,
>   Contrasting, close linked pair:
>   For while West Palm grows big and strong,
>   Palm Beach itself grows fair.[61]

This celebration of continental Palm Beach's supplementary relationship to insular Palm Beach constitutes a blithe disregard for the geoformal configurations that Paine alleged as a rationale for US sovereignty.

Yet while the Palm Beaches are unfaithful to the continental tyranny that rationalized US independence, the Palm Beach city and county spaces are nonetheless faithful to the tyranny of the (racial) majority. Unsurprisingly, Palm Beach County's racial logic corresponded to what

Toni Morrison discusses as US liberty's founding reliance on Blackness to create and highlight itself. If (as the tourist booklet versified) insular Palm Beach grew fair, it did so through what Morrison describes as "the thunderous ... presence of black surrogacy."[62] This surrogacy becomes apparent in the Federal Writers' Project publication *Florida: A Guide to the Southernmost State* (1939), which Hurston herself aided in writing.[63] Describing Palm Beach as "an exclusive resort" on "an 18-mile island," the guide noted that this "patch of South Sea loveliness" "has no Negro settlement, and Negroes are not allowed on the streets after dark unless actively employed in the city."[64] Indicating the material effects of producing and maintaining Palm Beach's fairness, the NAACP (National Association for the Advancement of Colored People) reported the 1923 lynching of Henry Simmons on "*Palm Beach Island*."[65] Symptomatic of the insular metropole's larger relationship to a continental county space extending from West Palm Beach to the black soil of the 'Glades, Black diasporan labor (disciplined by the racial terrorism of lynching culture) permitted Palm Beach to grow fair. Of course, the cultivation of fairness through Black exclusion is not unique to Palm Beach County. It has been a US American status quo, described in *Their Eyes* by Eatonville's Amos Hicks as "common sense" (39). But Palm Beach's perpetuation of this racialized common sense—even as the county's power configurations inverted Paine's geographically ontologized common sense—brings to the fore the incoherence of what Tea Cake identifies as the United States' founding conflation of the biggest and the best. Tellingly, and indicative of his grounding in the known world, Tea Cake wants to return to the 'Glades, the continental heart of Palm Beach County. This is a county space enthralled by the Palm Beaches' racial and geographic dissonances. During Janie and Tea Cake's previous life in the 'Glades, it was a Palm Beach vendor who sold them the gun they used to shoot alligators, whose teeth and hides could then be sold in support of the Palm Beaches' tourist industry (130–31). And it was in the 'Glades that Tea Cake famously and pivotally struck Janie in a way that, as his friend Sop-de-Bottom suggested, would cause "mah woman" to "spread her lungs all over Palm Beach County" (148). County space's participation in Palm Beach's fetishization of fairness is reflected in Sop's admiring observation that Janie's skin is so light a "person can see every place you hit her" (147).[66] Tea Cake's is a horizon of the known world, a horizon within which Black diasporan labor in the 'Glades unwittingly functions to support Palm Beach's fairness. This horizon maintains the intersecting race and gender codes that even known-world Nanny hoped Janie would escape.

Janie herself may not travel farther south than Palm Beach County, but the enormous hurricane permits her to experience an alternative and archipelagic configuration of space and human life that is of a piece with the planet. Janie's nearest access to her antipodal and hypothetical island space arrives through the novel's dedication to the type of geographically scalar play that earlier permitted her to look at a mud puddle and see an ocean with ships. Now, as the hurricane remaps Palm Beach County, the storm offers an impetus for the explicit vision of archipelagic diaspora that Janie advances in the novel's concluding pages.

Analogous to the tempest in *Miss Ulysses* that washes away a US American continental mythos that has been superimposed on Anchorage Island, the hurricane in *Their Eyes* turns Palm Beach County's continental heart into a seascape, reminding us, as Michele Currie Navakas has observed, that Florida has been a "liquid landscape," offering a "provocation to think beyond more familiar ideals of land and boundaries that made it possible to imagine the United States as settler nation and empire in the first place."[67] In the novel, county space attains a planetary compass as the narrator describes the night of the storm as carrying "the whole round world in his hands" (158). Lake Okeechobee breaks not its levee but its "seawalls" (158), and it floods continental space as "the sea . . . walking the earth" (162). As continent becomes seascape, "stray fish swim . . . in the yard" (160) in water "knee deep" (161). Janie and Tea Cake wade in "water almost to their buttocks" (161). A "slight rise" becomes a place to make headway against the flood, and a "tall house on a hump of ground" becomes an island of refuge (162). Soon Janie and Tea Cake fear the contingency of their high ground in the rising Okeechobee Sea. They "swim a distance" (164) until an underwater ridge permits them to begin wading toward the Palm Beach Road, which is built on a fill and has become a peninsula that has, on either side, water "as far as the eye could reach" (165). In this world, a "hummock" becomes an island on which a person and animals congregate (164). Another elevated place becomes a "tiny island" where man and rattlesnake seek refuge (164–65). Yet these spaces of "comparatively dry land" (161) are always contingent. As Tea Cake states, "Lake Okeechobee is forty miles wide and sixty miles long. . . . Dis house [on a hump of ground] ain't nothin' tuh swaller" (163). For the moment, the road to Palm Beach may be a peninsula, but the narrator explains that a current shoreline is "no guarantee" of a future shoreline and that an elevated site may be, at best, "high and safe perhaps" (164). Conventionally, the economy of elevation takes sea level as its gold standard, but the narrator's *perhaps* underscores this standard's radical flux not just on geologic timescales but, in an immediate way, on human timescales. The hurricane's revisions of land and water space permit *Their Eyes* to supplant the continent with islands and near-islands (*pen*insulas and shoals), undercutting the sense of ontological stability produced by supposedly immovable continental shorelines (as discussed further in chapter 4) and thereby offering a counterpressure to a US sovereignty equating the biggest with the best. Against continent-based declarations of US American sovereignty, the hurricane turns Palm Beach County into an archipelagic complex constituted by interactions between what Sylvia Wynter has called *demonic ground* and what I would describe as *demonic waters*, in which *demonic*, following the disciplines of mathematics, physics, and computer science, "connotes a working system that cannot have a determined, or knowable, outcome."[68] These demonic grounds and demonic waters form an archipelago that, as I outline subsequently in discussing the novel's conclusion, complements and exceeds Wynter's urgent and oft-invoked archipelagoes of poverty and hunger with an unforecasted and planet-shifting archipelago of love.

In the waters off the Palm Beach Road peninsula, Tea Cake contracts rabies while rescuing Janie from a rabid dog perched on a swimming cow (166). This disease leads to his death, as it eventually prompts Janie to shoot him in self-defense (184). Finally, Janie returns to Eatonville, where she contemplates her experiences, and human experiences generally, in terms resembling the floods and islandized elevations she saw in the hurricane. She says, "Love is lak de sea. It's uh movin' thing, but still and all, it takes its shape from de shore it meets, and it's different with every shore" (191). In this archipelagic and diasporic image, Janie and Tea Cake (though at odds in terms of their desires and planetary outlooks) are two islands among a proliferating chain of human islands washed by a common planetary ocean of love, in which Janie's ocean converges in certain ways with Epeli Hau'ofa's ocean, which has "a big heart" that "adopts anyone who loves" it and makes it "their home."[69] The ocean connects them all, but this connection is of a piece with the archipelago's loose logic of asyndeton. Explicit conjunctions such as *and*s, physical contiguity, and visible terrain are replaced by the ellipses of the less assuming: commas, water space, subaqueous terrain.[70] In the novel's closing vision of archipelagic diaspora, as the contours of the island stand in for the contours of individual humans, the precipitating logic of Hurston's phenomenological encounter with La Gonâve is showcased. Human islands find connection through a geographic thing (for example, the sea), even as human beings and material geography reconstitute each other like islands interacting with water along shorelines that are unrelentingly remade by forces ranging from daily waves and tides to longer-term shifts in sea level and tectonic plates. Janie's image offers a sweeping vision of human islands that are not fixed but in flux with moving waves, not isolated but interconnected by the global ocean, and not parochial but diasporic in the mode of a planetary continuum constituted by a series of nodes, which, because they repeat across a roughly spherical surface, arc toward each other even as they arc away. Here, within the strivings of the novel, Man (of Tea Cake's "dis man's town" and of Western would-be Universal continental thought) subsides in the face of another genre, that of multitudinous archipelagic humans—anti-Universals with claims to specificities, ranging across what Wynter has described as "shantytown archipelagoes" and the "ex-slave-labor archipelago" and yet simultaneously across, in Hurston's final striving articulation, a demonic sea of love washing up against islands of demonic ground.[71] This theorization of humankind's archipelagic diaspora across the planet finds an unanticipated correspondence in the work of Richard Wright, who is often viewed as antipodal to Hurston owing to his acerbic dismissal of *Their Eyes*.[72] During a 1950 trip to Haiti, Wright set out to describe Haitians in terms of their "emotional landscapes": the Haitians' "color" became ancillary in the face of the "startling" and "miraculous similarity which links life on its deepest levels into one vast reservoir of human consciousness and experience."[73] Linked to Hurston through a parallax engagement with Caribbean topography, Wright arrived at a converging vision of humans as figurative land spaces connected by a reservoir of liquid consciousness and underwater terrains of the deepest level.

Desert-Island Scenario

During the early years of Hurston's recovery from obscurity, the novelist Alice Walker looked to *Their Eyes* and exclaimed, "*There is no book more important to me than this one.*"[74] Since it first appeared in 1977, Walker's emphatic quote has found a perennial home in Hurston criticism while also appearing prominently on the covers of a train of HarperPerennial editions of *Their Eyes*. Yet for all the quote's fame in marketing and criticism, the pivotal role of the island in helping Walker articulate her admiration for *Their Eyes* has gone unremarked. When she first advanced this quotation in her essay "Zora Neale Hurston—A Cautionary Tale and a Partisan View," Walker made recourse to a desert-island scenario:

> Condemned to a deserted island for life, with an allotment of ten books to see me through, I would choose, unhesitatingly, two of Zora's: *Mules and Men*, because I would need to be able to pass on to younger generations the life of American blacks as legend and myth, and *Their Eyes Were Watching God*, because I would want to enjoy myself while identifying with the black heroine, Janie Crawford, as she acted out many roles in a variety of settings, and functioned (with spectacular results!) in romantic and sensual love. *There is no book more important to me than this one.*[75]

As Walker reached for a means of figuring her admiration, she arrived at what Nanny dismisses as "some place way off in de ocean." This is an iteration of *Their Eyes*' antipodal and hypothetical island, the absent geographic thing that structures Janie's desire and shapes the novel's investments in archipelagic diaspora.

Walker's desert-island scenario is especially important because of its potential to prompt reflection on the reading practices through which *Their Eyes* has been engaged since its recovery. Significantly, in articulating her love for the novel, Walker imagines herself as the heroine in a rewriting of the historically persistent genre of the Robinsonade. Emerging from a maritime modernity preoccupied with exploration and shipwreck, the Robinsonade has its locus classicus in Daniel Defoe's novel *Robinson Crusoe* (1719) but manifests itself in texts ranging from Shakespeare's *The Tempest* (ca. 1611) to Robert Zemeckis's film *Cast Away* (2000). Elizabeth M. DeLoughrey has discussed the genre's center of gravity as the "self-made male who accidentally colonizes a desert isle" by means of shipwreck. According to convention, the island "provides a *tabula rasa*" for "the birth of a new social order."[76] Recognizing the popular desert-island scenario as generically undergirded by the Robinsonade permits the scenario's desert island to emerge as more than an imagined topographical occasion to offer a list of favorites; within the scenario, operating at the level of figuration, the island becomes an absent geographic thing that brings formal exigencies to bear on the list's contents. Certainly, Walker's Robinsonade is overtly attentive to some of these exigencies as it gravitates toward *Mules* and *Their Eyes*, explaining that these two textual-material things would be well positioned to provide a new racial mythos and sexual economy for the new social order that the island scenario demands.

More implicit in Walker's desert-island scenario are other exigencies associated with the form of the island. These exigencies pertain to the project of rereading, as this project is imagined by many readers both inside and outside of the academy. Being marooned on an island with only a few books demands, as Jonathan Culler observes, that the projected castaway choose texts that can be reread "without fatigue."[77] In a similar vein, Marjorie Perloff remarks that desert islands permit reading at the right tempo: "desert-island time" invites us to contemplate the "big difference" produced by "what words we emphasize and how slowly and deliberately we read them." Perloff asks, "Where else but on a desert island can this luxury become a reality?"[78] If the capacity to sustain slow, deliberate, and nearly indefatigable rereadings is a textual attribute summoned by the Robinsonade's lonely island, then the inclination to grant Hurston two places on a ten-book list creates Walker's island as allegorical in relation to the critical and curricular ascendancy that Walker's own important recovery of Hurston's work helped precipitate. Strictly speaking, we are not confined to Walker's island: we as critics remain far from a geoformally determined canon that has Hurston providing two of ten options for a lifetime of rereading. Yet the notion of a desert-island reading list bears a striking resemblance to what Jonathan Arac, in defining the notion of hypercanonization, has described as a situation in which "a very few individual works monopolize curricular and critical attention."[79] In light of *Their Eyes*' significant play in a variety of courses and academic publications over the past four decades, it is fair to suggest that Walker's Hurston-oriented island has drawn nearer to reality—and drawn a larger community of castaways/rereaders—than Walker might have anticipated in the 1970s.

Walker's Robinsonade offers a useful template for contemplating the intense rereadings that *Their Eyes* receives in fields including US literature, modernism, the Atlantic world, women's studies, the Black diaspora, and the circum-Caribbean and Global South. Undoubtedly, this Hurston-oriented Robinsonade has afforded critics (myself included) the luxury of reading and rereading *Their Eyes*, approaching it with a tempo that repays deliberation over pauses and points of emphasis. As a desert-island text,

Their Eyes has sustained rereadings with only limited signs of fatigue. But from within the circumscribing space of this Robinsonade, we do well to ask about the events that might follow the era of deliberative rereading that has helped give rise to an altered (possibly new) literary-critical order.[80] This question finds something of an answer in the narratological exigencies of the figurative island space on which we currently reread. According to the Robinsonade's generic conventions, as DeLoughrey observes, the prototypical castaway eventually escapes the island and returns to the metropole.[81] Also recognizing the genre as prescribing the castaway's efforts at escape from the island, N. Katherine Hayles has proposed that the best book to take to a desert island could be a book whose rereading would precipitate that escape. But Hayles rewrites the logic of the escape, describing a book that would inspire her to prepare a raft, not necessarily as a means of escape from the island to the metropole but as a means of escape from Eurocentric assumptions about space and travel by aligning her cognition with the archipelagic "mindset of . . . Micronesian navigators," alluding to what Vicente M. Diaz has drawn attention to as Indigenous navigational techniques, including the perception of *etak* ("moving islands") and *pookof* ("the inventory of creatures indigenous to a given island").[82] Now the island is nothing to escape but is rather a facilitator and indeed animate collaborator in navigational pursuits. Similarly, Caribbean poet Derek Walcott undercuts the Robinsonade's lonely island: he imagines a desert-island scenario in which he takes with him James Joyce's *Ulysses*, a text supplanting the lone island by structuring itself on Odysseus's archipelagic travels throughout Hellas.[83] Analogous to Hayles's and Walcott's chosen texts, *Their Eyes* is a novel whose rereading precipitates escape not from the island but from the generic literary-critical Robinsonade prefigured by Walker. With its drive toward archipelagic diaspora, *Their Eyes* asks rereaders to look up from the novel's pages, toward a horizon within which the present site of rereading is, to borrow a phrase from the Barbadian writer George Lamming, "one island only" within a vast archipelago.[84] This archipelagic horizon promises a diaspora of textual-material things, people(s), and, importantly, geographic forms.

If the new formalism that has surfaced in literary studies during the past two decades has looked toward culture-dominated historicist and ideological critique and sought to recover the oft-forgotten formal debts of these literary-critical modes, then tracing the island-oriented quality of

Their Eyes' geoformal engagements underscores an analogous need for a new critical accountability to the formal features that undergird and remain largely unacknowledged in literary geographies and critical deployments of geography as interpretive frame and method.[85] Traditionally, the island has been taken as the world writ small, with its circumscribing shoreline evoking a sense of autonomy, a sense of isolation that creates it as the ideal natural laboratory for controlled experiments.[86] This trope of the isolated island—a colonial trope whose legacy is the persistent conflation of the insular with the self-enclosed, fixed, and parochial—brings the putatively natural object of the island into homology with aesthetic formalism's art object, which has traditionally and abidingly been framed as coherent, autonomous, and ontologically isolated.[87] The shoreline's seemingly incontrovertible natural existence creates a ready-made finite boundary, a circumscribing line analogous to what Jim Hansen has described as formal analysis's tendency to "always point ... towards boundaries" as a means of demarcating what may be addressed as immanent to the object under investigation.[88]

Yet because islands defy conventional and uninterrogated perceptions of their formal self-enclosure, a geoformally attentive criticism may well find in the island a crucial starting place.[89] The island's circumscribing shoreline may seem self-evident and natural, but Walcott has emphasized the sublime challenge of commenting on that nature: "There was a phrase from a Latin text at school. Quales est natura insulae? What is the nature of the island? ... I do not know if I am ready to answer it."[90] Rather than answering the question, theorists of islands have emphasized the island's seemingly natural formal qualities—size, shoreline, isolation, autonomy—as culturally imposed and phenomenologically shifting frames. Undercutting size-based distinctions among landmasses, DeLoughrey marks up the "often arbitrary division between islands and continents."[91] Edward Kamau Brathwaite describes the island's connectedness vis-à-vis geographies that far exceed the culturally fetishized shoreline: "The unity," he asserts, "is submarine."[92] In a similar vein, John R. Kukeakalani Clark has commented that for Native Hawaiians "the ocean is ... an extension of the land, it just happens to have some water on it.... It's all 'āina ... just 'āina with water on it."[93] Deleuze names the island's geo-ontological undecidability: "It is an island or a mountain, or both at once: the island is a mountain under water, and the mountain, an island that is still dry."[94] And in this he converges with Māori poet Vernice Wineera, whose poem "This Island" reminds us,

> All these islands are mountains,
> submerged,
> and we live on the tips
> like germs on the heads of pins.[95]

Hurston adds to this undecidability and estrangement, as her mode of archipelagic diaspora relies on phenomenological identifications among—and formal (con)fusions of—humans, islands, and other geographies. Benefiting from island theorists' convincing arguments against the autonomy of this most famously autonomous geographic form, a new and more general critical attentiveness to the planet's variegated formal features would, from the outset, treat form itself as merely one of the semiotically charged cultural presences with which material geography is shot through.

While heightened attention to geographic form facilitates the close reading of specific literary texts and cultural formations, it also calls for a concomitant mode of Glissantian distant reading that figures "the individual island (any individual island) as a participant within a world genre of islands, which, in their insular interlinkings, emerge as a planet-spanning archipelagic assemblage." Not "about *island interchangeability*" but rather "about *island interchange*," this mode of archipelagic distant reading opens onto other material and formal geographies, inviting critics to look toward cultural geographies (nation-state, Global South, diaspora) and recognize the formal geographies (mountain, river, archipelago) that through their planetary repetitions forge interlinkings of the planet's disparate cultural regions and traditions.[96] Long-durational analogies and (mis)recognitions between antipodal island spaces (such as the East Indies and West Indies, Haiti and Tahiti, Caledonia and New Caledonia, Nassau of *Their Eyes'* Bahamian "Saws" and Nassau of Johnny Frisbie's Northern Cook Islands) emerge as island-oriented subsets of geographic form's broader work in transhemispheric cultural mediation. The subset directs attention to similar geoformal correspondences, such as the Alps' antipodal relation to the lofty alpine spaces that repeat rhizomatically across a planet of interactive tectonic plates and cultures. Of course, recalling the contingency of the earth's formal features reminds us that some alpine spaces may yet become islands, while other mountains are already washed by the sea, with their series of protruding peaks traditionally mapped in reference to the form of the archipelago. If the wider critical disavowal of form during earlier decades has left literary studies "methodologically impoverished," and cultural studies "at sea," then critics oriented toward cultural geography might be described as poor seafarers who bear a structural resemblance to Janie and Tea Cake swimming through the Okeechobee Sea.[97] Here the island emerges as an ephemeral spot of raised ground promising to help us gain our bearings in relation to a wider compass of the planet's formal and material geographies.

CHAPTER THREE

Borderwaters and Geometries of Being Amid

Huck and Jim on the Rio Grande

Looking back at Gloria Anzaldúa's influential 1987 book *Borderlands/La Frontera: The New Mestiza*, John Alba Cutler has recently summarized the border/borderlands complex this way: "Although borders appear as lines on a map, having no mass or volume, the history of borders often creates border*lands*, zones of ongoing, agonistic contact between cultures, and often the evolution of entirely new cultural forms."[1] Borderlines have their attendant border*lands*. The italics are Cutler's, and his emphasis on the terrestrial or landed quality of the space surrounding borderlines is an accurate reflection of Anzaldúa's work, even as it should prompt questions about border-affiliated spaces that may not be land based or land dominated. How to imagine the borderlands' watery analogue, the border*waters*? And to what degree might borderlands and borderwaters be theorized as convergent or divergent frameworks, particularly in light of the variegated materialities and phenomenological traditions that have mediated human and interspecies interactions with land, water, and shoreline? Such questions, I would submit, are urgent vis-à-vis large swaths of US and broader American cultural, literary, and historical studies, which in recent decades have seen a universalization of the border/borderlands complex, such that, as historians Pekka Hämäläinen and Samuel Truett have observed, the borderlands have emerged as "a metaphor for cultural encounters" applicable "to countless places and eras."[2] This was the case in Shelley Fisher Fishkin's galvanizing presidential address at the 2004 American Studies Association convention, which Fishkin dedicated "to the memory of Gloria Anzaldúa" and in which Fishkin took Anzaldúa's famous work on the US-Mexico borderlands as emblematic of American studies' "transnational turn."[3]

In the wake of widespread impulses toward universalizing the borderlands in Americanist thought, a borderwaters framework asks whether the trope of border*lands* is our best conceptual alternative for grappling with specific sites, and immense swaths of the planet more generally, that are not geocentric but aquacentric. How to understand the human and interspecies relations that cut and flow through (above, below, within, and with various and fractal currents) the planet's aqueous and terraqueous spaces? When and where does border and borderlands theory open onto the water? And how do these openings admit dialogue with nonlanded and terraqueous epistemologies of watery borders and borderwaters?

One starting place for contemplating these questions is José E. Limón's generative borderlands study *American Encounters: Greater Mexico, the United States, and the Erotics of Culture* (1998). In his book's introduction, Limón recalls growing up "between Mexico and the United States in the border town of Laredo." Because he lived north of the Rio Grande, he was among the "*mexicanos de este lado*" (Mexicans from this side), while those who lived south of the river were "*mexicanos del otro lado*" (Mexicans from the other side). Mexican children from the two sides played by and in the river: "So there we would play, between Mexico and the United States, in the early 1950s, and sometimes sit together on a makeshift raft and fish and swim in commonality and difference—our Huck to their Jim. . . . But . . . all of us Mexican children recognized other differences, as did Huck and Jim, between the realm of the raft—the in between—and the shores on either side."[4] This metaphor—in which *Adventures of Huckleberry Finn* becomes the hinge for a geoformal comparison between Limón's Rio Grande and Mark Twain's Mississippi—can do much more than advance water space as offering a hiatus from the material and epistemic violence of an imaginary land-oriented border.

Rather, Limón's metaphor is critically productive in ways that exceed those he may have anticipated. Consider, for instance, that Twain's commentary on the Mississippi underscores the way in which water moves borders. In his 1883 memoir *Life on the Mississippi*, Twain tells stories of the way the river "has sorely perplexed the laws of men." At the riverine border between Arkansas and Mississippi, for instance, the Arkansas charter claimed territory "'to the centre of the river'—a most unstable line," while Mississippi "claimed 'to the channel'—another shifty and unstable line." Eventually, the river "threw [a] big island out of Arkansas, and yet not *within* Mississippi," creating an "exceedingly valuable island of four thousand acres" that "pay[s] taxes to neither, owing allegiance to neither."[5] Twain's stories of the Mississippi—combined with the case of, say, Cordova Island and the Chamizal dispute along the Rio Grande's El Paso–Ciudad Juárez border—are reminders of the way nonhuman sovereignties inherent in land-water shoreline dynamics may intertwine themselves in unexpected ways with human-scaled political sovereignties encoded in notions of *este lado* and *el otro lado*.[6] Just as urgently, we should read Limón's metaphor in conjunction with the archipelagic thought that permits Huck, as he appears in chapter 1 of this study, to recognize one night in the fog that he has not crashed into either of the continental lados but has crashed into an island, a node within a riverine archipelago that sprawls out into the Gulf of Mexico.[7] Thus, we are directed to look toward the borderwaters, toward the oceanic and archipelagic spaces that form an assemblage within which rivers, and all the branching capillaries of their watersheds, function as participants.

Though often obscured by the overtly landed quality of the borderlands framework, the impulse to look toward the waters has been persistent within border/borderlands scholarship even as it awaits fuller theorization. Discussions of the borderlands have dripped with oceanic and archipelagic tangents and eddies. Recall that the foundational Greater Mexico and borderlands theorist Américo Paredes opens his poetry collection *Between Two Worlds* with a poem titled "The Rio Grande" (originally published in 1934), which addresses the river and follows its "swirls and counter-currents" to "the margin of the sea."[8] Or recall that *Borderlands/ La Frontera* begins with a poem set in Border Field State Park, showcasing the US-Mexico border fence running up out of the Pacific, "rippling from the sea where Tijuana touches San Diego." Anzaldúa states, "*Miro el mar atacar / la cerca en* Border Field Park" (I watch the sea attack / the fence in Border Field Park). She avers, "The sea cannot be fenced, / *el mar* does not stop at borders."[9] Elsewhere, the career of Renato Rosaldo has placed US southwestern borderlands theory in dialogue with the archipelagic states of Indonesia and the Philippines, while José David Saldívar's *Trans-Americanity: Subaltern Modernities, Global Coloniality, and the Cultures of Greater Mexico* (2012) leavens "land-based" arenas with "intercultural contact zones" that "are notably oceanic."[10] Within other iterations of border/borderlands approaches, we have seen Andrew Lipman's discussions of the "American coast" in term of a "landless borderland" and, as alluded to in this study's introduction, Walter D. Mignolo's description of Edward Kamau Brathwaite "skipping a pebble on the ocean."[11]

I follow these oceanic and archipelagic impulses in advancing this chapter's elaborations on a borderwaters framework. Generally speaking, within Latinx scholarship, the borderlands have been evoked and imagined as encompassing the organic and landed affective processes of human culture as it undergoes the seemingly natural processes of contesting, mourning, and grappling with the melancholia evoked by a border that is superimposed by a state apparatus; the border is a line "having no mass or volume"—it is "artificial" and "unnatural."[12] To describe this border/borderlands complex in other terms: the one-dimensional and unnatural border and its epiphenomenal borderlands depend on a governmentally imposed Euclidean edict (a line) regarding spatial perception, and this governmentally imposed mode of spatial perception is attended by a seemingly organic cultural recoiling and set of land-based contestations growing out of cultural formations that exceed and direct their energies against the state's superimposed geometric idealizations of geography. In complement and contradistinction to a borderlands model that depends on an *unnatural* line, the present chapter frames borderwaters as spaces that arise along *natural* lines, or, better, as spaces that arise in relation to natural-cultural tangles that are attendant to human-ocean-archipelago interactions and negotiations. These interactions and negotiations attain different modes of relevance at different times and places, and among different national and nonnational cultures, but a general distinction between the border/borderlands complex and the borderwaters might be said to depend not only on the difference between land and water but also on a distinction between Euclidean and non-Euclidean geometry. The former (with its conceptualizations of nondimensional points, one-dimensional lines, two-dimensional planes, and smoothly surfaced three-dimensional solids) idealizes the unceasing roughness of the material world and is tethered to an imagination of the border as a one-dimensional line. This is a line that Anzaldúa called an "unnatural boundary" and that, more recently, Thomas Nail has insightfully discussed as requiring the state to actively "create a smooth and stable foundation for the border," working to instantiate the imagined line as Euclidean by using construction equipment to fight against and fill in water's erosion of ditches, gulches, valleys, gorges, dells, hollows, and other rough formations.[13] Within a borderwaters framework, meanwhile, we move away from an image of the state's Euclideanist fight against fluidity and toward a foregrounding of state and more broadly human *collaborations* and *experiments* with non-Euclidean geometries that recognize the roughness of the geologic and hydrologic and governmental, evoking tangled natural-cultural boundaries and flows.[14] The planet's watery borders and interactive borderwaters would of course involve the oceans (on undulating surfaces, suspended in blue depths, and on submerged or benthic grounds) but also shorelines and the farthest-reaching of minute rills and capillaries that fractally branch into—and indeed shape—the very surfaces of land-based watersheds, ranging from asphalt served by storm drains, to estuaries and bayous, to jagged and mountainous continental divides. If the borderwaters are, to draw on Omise'eke Natasha Tinsley, an arena in which thinking about "the materiality of water" may make our more conventional "watery metaphors" take on meanings of greater complexity, then the borderwaters are also an arena in which the ground—an ostensibly nonwatery materiality and metaphor for certainty—becomes soggy, sodden, not smoothed to accommodate borderlines but striated with rivulets and rivers, the interlapping of land and water.[15]

In describing some of the borderwaters that have constituted and interfaced with the archipelagic states of America, I turn toward the oceanic and archipelagic work of the Greater Mexican visual artist Miguel Covarrubias, whose mid-twentieth-century representations of Indonesia, the United States' Trust Territory of the Pacific Islands (TTPI), and the Caribbean help contextualize state, Indigenous, and nonhuman cultures as they have converged and diverged across non-Euclidean modes of imagining boundaries, nonboundaries, and spatial area on a terraqueous planet. At various moments throughout the chapter, I understand Covarrubias's visualizations and discussions as instances of archipelagic theorizing in and of themselves. But, more important, Covarrubias's images are metonymic, in ways that exceed his own set of aesthetic and conceptual concerns, of important governmental and more broadly cultural iterations of the borderwaters as they attained influence during the twentieth century and as they continue to have purchase today. Hence, without endorsing what others have pointed toward as the complex and sometimes vexed racial, colonial, and gender politics of Covarrubias's work, this chapter examines a set of Covarrubias's visual and written images within their broader oceanic and archipelagic ecologies, thereby permitting these images to serve as windows into several distinct, if complex and often vexed, iterations of borderwaters thought and practice that have lives beyond Covarrubias's thought and practice.[16] Appearing after the present introduction, this chapter's first section traces how Covarrubias's 1930s representations of Greater Indonesia and Greater Malaysia open onto a set of borderwaters that exist apart from and to the side of colonialism. Here waters and lands are simultaneously nodes and links, while borders are not lines but conduits, and water, like land, becomes a place to *be from*. In the second section, the chapter discusses how Covarrubias's illustrations of Indonesia—as conveyed in an early 1950s pamphlet commissioned by an Indonesian diplomatic office in the United States—conduce toward views of two competing modes of conceptualizing watery borders and their borderwaters: a Western model of the borderwaters in which states interact on terms set by the shoreline's fractal churnings and the postcolonial borderwaters of Indonesia as an archipelagic state seeking to politically mythologize Indigenous archipelagic practice. A subsequent section points toward Covarrubias's 1949 illustration of the TTPI for *Life* magazine. This illustration of the TTPI opens onto discussions of two other diverging iterations of the borderwaters. One was advanced by a United States intent on buoying up the notion of mare liberum, or the freedom of the seas, by venturing into the geometrically absurd, and another iteration operated along the non-Euclidean lines of Indonesian and Indigenous Marshallese geometries, characterized by multispecies relations in which state and human sovereignties meld with the sovereignty of the sea. The conclusion looks toward Covarrubias's 1950s theories and illustrations of Indigenous transpacific migration to underscore some trans-Indigenous ways in which the borderwaters and the borderlands interlap with one another.

The iterations of the borderwaters discussed here—in the present chapter and the larger study—are far from exhaustive. But this chapter's anatomy of certain modes of conceptualizing the borderwaters, as routed through Covarrubias's images, serves to illustrate some of the urgent ways in which a borderwaters paradigm speaks to fundamental practical issues, ranging from the very notion of a border, to the question of what we talk about when we talk about US American territory, to historical and mythological mechanisms for forging decolonial Indigenous solidarities, to accountability and justice vis-à-vis the ongoing ecological and human costs of nuclear testing. In the context of these crucial questions, a borderwaters paradigm is not primarily invested in destabilizing borders—the unstable border may be more of a fait accompli than is often recognized, given that nearly every country in the world is currently involved in border disputes and contestations.[17] Rather, to contemplate the rough geometries of borderwaters and watery borders is to assume a mode of thinking that corresponds to a planetary and geopolitical materiality that has never succumbed to Euclid's idealizations.

Greater Mexico, Greater Indonesia, and a Borderwaters *Archipiélado*

In December 1934 Zora Neale Hurston wrote to her mentor, the famed Columbia University anthropologist Franz Boas, "Do you remember ... the Mexican artist that you met one Sunday night with me ... ? He has just returned from ... study in Bali and is to do the illustrations for MULES AND MEN."[18] Hurston was referring to Miguel Covarrubias, who was born in Mexico City in 1904 and relocated to New York City in 1924, where he emerged as a major figure and force in US visual culture. As a denizen of New York for about fifteen years before returning permanently to Mexico in 1940, Covarrubias exhibited artwork in various galleries and published illustrations in magazines including *Vanity Fair*, *Time*, *Life*, *Vogue*, *Fortune*, and the *New Yorker*. During this time he also circulated among figures of the Harlem Renaissance, illustrating not only *Mules and Men* (Hurston's 1935 folklore collection) but also the dustjacket for Langston Hughes's poetry collection *The Weary Blues* (1926) as well as his own Harlem-oriented collection, *Negro Drawings* (1927).[19] Through these and other involvements in the United States, Covarrubias emerged, according to Limón, as a figure who "shaped modernist culture between the United States and ... 'Greater Mexico.'"[20] And yet he was also, as Hurston noted to Boas, a student of the culture of the Indonesian island of Bali, living there twice in the 1930s and publishing *Island of Bali* (1937), an illustrated anthropological volume that has remained a touchstone in the study of Bali and has become "his most famous work."[21] Hence, while in 1934 Paredes (born on este lado) was imagining the Rio Grande drawing him to "the margin of the sea," the island of Bali was drawing Covarrubias (born on el otro lado) beyond the margin, beyond the este lado/otro lado divide, and out into the sea. Here archipelagic and oceanic spaces did not become simply part of a complex of *greater borderlands* (as some have discussed Guam, Hawai'i, the Philippines, and the Caribbean)

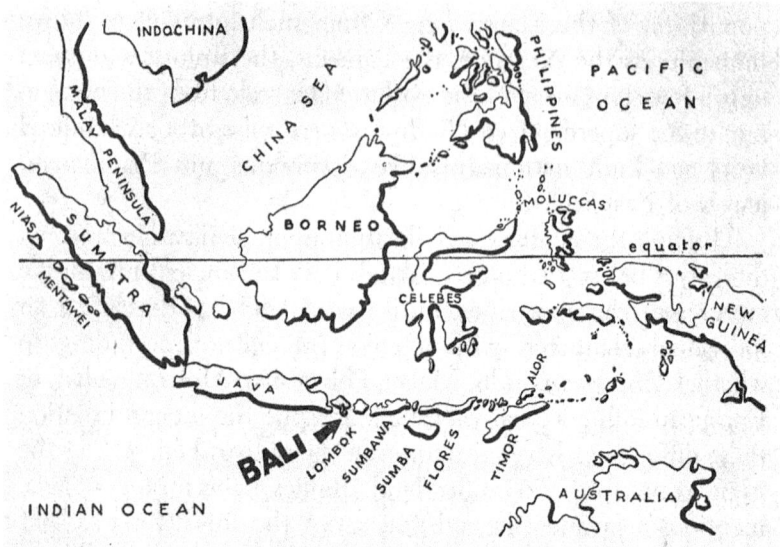

FIGURE 3.1 — "The Malay Archipelago." Miguel Covarrubias's map illustrates Bali's place in the larger archipelago. From Miguel Covarrubias, *Island of Bali* (New York: Alfred K. Knopf, 1937), 3. Courtesy of María Elena Rico Covarrubias.

but rather drew Covarrubias into the waters of figuration, into a position from which he offered visual images that figured—and that persist as important springboards for present-day theorizing of—modernity's complex of watery borders and borderwaters.[22]

Writing and illustrating *Island of Bali* set Covarrubias on a course that drew him into these arenas of figuration. The book itself does not focus on the people of Bali's interface with the sea but rather begins with a sort of apology for its lack of engagement with the sea. Chapter 1 observes that with the exception of some "small settlements of fishermen," the Balinese "rarely venture into the sea."[23] Still, Covarrubias framed Bali within a larger archipelagic context, as a component of "the Malay Archipelago," a "great chain of islands" that lies "like the backbone of some restless, formidable antediluvian monster" (see fig. 3.1).[24] And indeed, in a move that is both exoticizing and attentive to Indonesia's larger watery structures and components, Covarrubias viewed the allegedly hydrophobic Balinese in ways that are, contradictorily, hydrophilic. Chapter 2, titled "The People," opens with the following sentence: "Like a continual undersea ballet, the pulse of life in Bali moves with a measured rhythm reminiscent of the sway of marine plants and the flowing motion of octopus and jellyfish under the sweep of a submarine current."[25] If such a metaphor does not comport with his larger description of a hydrophobic Balinese culture, it was likely inspired by his own interests in the waters off Bali, which at one point led him to board a small boat and use a "wooden box with a glass bottom" to view and draw "fascinating strange sea animals... weird shapes of corals, fish, anemones, holothurians [sea cucumbers], and all kinds of floating creatures."[26]

Covarrubias's time in Indonesia, as Nancy C. Lutkehaus observes, "was formative for him in terms of helping him to develop his understanding of the interconnectedness of cultures around the Pacific Rim." Indeed, within a few months of publishing *Island of Bali*, he was invited to create a series of murals for the Golden Gate International Exposition (1939–40), a world's fair to be held on Treasure Island, an artificial island dredged up out of San Francisco Bay for the occasion.[27] The fair's theme was "a Pageant of the Pacific," and it included a building called Pacific House that functioned as the "heart of the family of nations on Treasure Island."[28] For central display in Pacific House, Covarrubias created six large murals, four of them fifteen by twenty-four feet and two of them nine by thirteen feet. These murals were maps of human and nonhuman geographies, titled *Peoples of the Pacific, Economy of the Pacific, The Fauna and Flora of the Pacific, Art Forms of the Pacific Area, Native Dwellings of the Pacific Area*, and *Native Means of Transportation in the Pacific Area* (fig. 3.2). Pacific House's stakeholders regarded the maps as symbolic of San Francisco's status as "a center for the mingling of [Pacific] peoples, of their trade and cultures of both sides of the North and South Pacific."[29] Indeed, as stated by Covarrubias in a pamphlet accompanying lithographed versions of the murals sold by Pacific House, "these maps include the three continents that rim the Pacific—Asia, America and Australia, as well as the countless islands and archipelagos that adorn it—Malaysia, Melanesia, Polynesia and Micronesia."[30]

Even as Covarrubias and Pacific House used language (e.g., "rim" and "trade") that today would position the murals as leaning toward a fraught Pacific "Rimspeak," Covarrubias also made it clear that the maps aspired to disrupt common misperceptions, noting that "because of... prejudice" against "peoples and cultures other than those of European... origin, the Pacific Ocean has come to be regarded in the popular mind as a vast expanse of water bordered by and dotted with remote, exotic peoples, and as a barrier rather than the link that it is, between peoples, cultures and economy of the countries of the Pacific Area."[31] Thus, Covarrubias's words on

FIGURE 3.2 — Lithograph of Miguel Covarrubias's mural *Native Means of Transportation in the Pacific Area*, one of six large murals on display in Pacific House during the Golden Gate International Exposition of 1939–40. From American Geographical Society Library Digital Map Collection, University of Wisconsin–Milwaukee. Courtesy of María Elena Rico Covarrubias.

colonial imaginations of the Pacific presaged Epeli Hau'ofa's commentary in the 1990s: "It was continental men, namely Europeans, on entering the Pacific after crossing huge expanses of ocean, who introduced the view" that "the islands are tiny, isolated dots in a vast ocean. Later on it was continental men, Europeans and Americans, who drew imaginary lines across the sea, making the colonial boundaries that, for the first time, confined ocean peoples to tiny spaces."[32] Simultaneously, Covarrubias's commentary on ocean space was a prewriting of a centerpiece within postcolonial Indonesia's notion of *Wawasan Nusantara* (often translated as "Archipelagic Outlook"), which takes the sea "tidak lagi sebagai pemisah, tetapi sebagai penghubung" (not as a divider but as something that links).[33]

Indeed, Covarrubias's Pacific House mappings of the Indonesian archipelago, mappings in which cultures do not stop at apparent boundaries, resembles Paredes's borderlands notion of "Greater Mexico," which "refers to all the areas inhabited by people of Mexican culture—not only within the present limits of the Republic of Mexico but in the United States as well—in a cultural rather than a political sense."[34] But within Covarrubias's mappings, the putative boundary that could not stop cultural flows was, rather than Paredes's porous border, the sea. Preparing his murals more than half a decade before Indonesia's August 17, 1945, declaration of independence, Covarrubias explained that within his mural *Peoples of the Pacific*, the "*bright green ground*" "covers Malaysia, the part of the Malay Archipelago where the Mongoloid Malaysians live" (see fig. 3.3).[35]

Addressing this same archipelagic space in his map *Art Forms of the Pacific Area*, Covarrubias used another term to describe what he elsewhere referred to as the Malaysians' geographic domain, here using the heading "INDONESIA" as a designation encompassing ethnicities hailing from what are now the postcolonial states of Indonesia and the Philippines.[36] Hence, for Covarrubias, in a manner homologous with Paredes's Greater Mexico, Indonesia became the area inhabited by people who, though ostensibly isolated from each other by the putative boundaries imposed by the sea, shared "Malaysian" or "Indonesian" cultural descent. In fact, Covarrubias's bivalent terminology—vacillating between "Malaysia" and "Indonesia" as a means of naming the archipelago—is reflective of two terms that were attaining currency as some of the colonized peoples of the region looked toward hypothetical postcolonial modes of political existence: Indonesia Raya and Melayu Raya, respectively translated as "Greater Indonesia" and "Greater Malaysia" but both imagining approximately the same ethnically evoked postcolonial territory.[37]

On a human level, as illustrated in Covarrubias's *Native Means of Transportation in the Pacific Area* (see fig. 3.2), the seas linked rather than divided the islands, not only giving rise to an archipelagic Greater Indonesia but also situating this archipelagic complex within an interlaced region that was still greater, the "Pacific Area," which, as Covarrubias explained, "boasts some of the most accomplished navigators in the world." Among these maritime navigators he named the Chinese, the Moros of the Philippines, the Malay seamen of Java and Madura, the Burmese of the Irrawaddy River, the Sinhalese of Sri Lanka, the Balinese, the Fijians, the Solomon Islanders, the Papuans, and the Aboriginal Australians. However, he wrote, "the greatest navigators of all, considering the level of their material culture, are perhaps the Polynesians who traveled thousands of miles from island to island, guided only by their unfailing instinct and crude charts of the islands and of the stars to be able to navigate at night."[38]

Covarrubias's representation of Pacific vessels sets Greater Indonesia within this chapter's first iteration of the borderwaters. In this iteration, which largely looks toward Indigenous cultures' present and past connections while sidelining or bracketing colonialism, Hauʻofa's "continental

FIGURE 3.3 — Detail from lithograph of Miguel Covarrubias's mural *Peoples of the Pacific*, illustrating Greater Malaysia/Greater Indonesia in green. On the lithograph, the green ground appears on the Malay Peninsula and down to Singapore. It further extends into most of the islands of what would later become the postcolonial Republic of Indonesia, including the entire island of Borneo (which today also includes the nation of Brunei and part of Malaysia) as well as the island of Timor (which today also includes the nation of East Timor). It excludes islands in the vicinity of New Guinea and eastward, classifying them as part of Melanesia, but Covarrubias's Greater Malaysia/Greater Indonesia extends north throughout all the islands of the then-US Commonwealth of the Philippines, nearly arriving at Taiwan. From American Geographical Society Library Digital Map Collection, University of Wisconsin–Milwaukee. Courtesy of María Elena Rico Covarrubias.

men" have not drawn "imaginary lines across the sea," and the Indonesian state's later ideology of Wawasan Nusantara exists as prestate praxis, as individuals and communities take the sea not as a divider but as something that links. This iteration of the borderwaters is not a mirror image of the borderline and the border*land*—that is, it does not involve a watery border and concomitant borderwaters. Rather, this iteration aligns with Édouard Glissant's commentary, in his 2009 *Philosophie de la Relation*, that "borders between places that are constituted by archipelagoes do not assume the form of walls, but rather of passages, of pathways."[39] These borderwaters are *waters that are borders*, and these borders among archipelagic islands invert traditional understandings of borders, as they become not barriers but passageways. They stretch from riverine waters and move not toward the land on either side of the river but rather out into the seas of Greater Indonesia and into the Pacific regional designations of Melanesia, Micronesia, and Polynesia. Amid this vast set of islands and waters, the este lado/otro lado distinction collapses with the proliferation of archipelagic spaces, where islands' relationality is not a land-to-land binary of lados simply linked by water but is rather a multifarious and multidirectional land-water relationality, a system of archipe-*lados*, a coinage I hazard because of the useful way in which -*pelago* ("sea") melds with -*lado* ("side"), reframing the sea itself as a lado—a place to be from, a place of existence—rather than simply a medium by which one may transit from one land-based lado to another.[40] Within the archipe-lado (or, Hispanicized, *archipiélado*), the binary *between* is replaced by the multicircuited and polyrelational *among* or *amid*. In this way, the coinage *archipiélado* calls into question the default notion of a terraqueous network in which the project of "cross[ing] oceans" is the project of crossing "links between disconnected nodes" of land.[41] This mode of thinking through the borderwaters first asks, Why not take the waters as the privileged nodes and the lands as the networking links? It then asks, Could both waters and lands, without affording priority to either, exist simultaneously as nodes and links?

Borderwaters, through and beyond the Sinuosities of the Coast

No doubt owing to his visibility as the writer and illustrator of *Island of Bali*, the Information Office of the Republic of Indonesia in New York City commissioned Covarrubias, at the beginning of the 1950s, to illustrate a pamphlet titled *Republic of Indonesia: New Nation of the World* (see fig. 3.4).[42] When Covarrubias lived in Bali during the 1930s, that island had been part of what was known as the Dutch East Indies. But now—after three and a half centuries of occupation by Dutch colonizers, three and a half years of occupation by the Japanese during World War II, and a postwar period during which the Netherlands unsuccessfully fought to regain a colonial possession that had declared its independence in 1945—Indonesia had emerged as a sovereign and unified nation under President Sukarno on August 17, 1950.[43] In the wake of independence, even as many Indonesians were "very suspicious" of US "neoimperialism," the new postcolonial nation was intent on introducing itself within the United States.[44] Thus, Indonesia's US-based Information Office published the Covarrubias pamphlet, providing readers with the following

FIGURE 3.4 — Front cover of *Republic of Indonesia: New Nation of the World*, a pamphlet illustrated by Miguel Covarrubias and published by the Information Office of the Republic of Indonesia in New York City. From Adriana and Tom Williams Collection of Miguel Covarrubias, Harry Ransom Center, University of Texas at Austin. Courtesy of María Elena Rico Covarrubias.

geographic information on Indonesia: "The 78 million citizens of the Republic of Indonesia live on a chain of three thousand [inhabited] islands extending for more than three thousand miles, from the Indian Ocean to the Pacific. To the east, Indonesia comes within 30 miles of Malaya. To the south, less than 250 miles from Australia. To the northeast, approximately 50 miles from the Philippines. Indonesia's islands have a land area of 735,000 square miles, about one quarter the area of [the] continental United States."

The pamphlet's statistics on Indonesia's territory (specifically noting the size of its land territory and measuring distances between countries based on the proximity of landmasses) are notably indebted to land-oriented views of national territory routed through seventeenth-century disputes that involved the Netherlands and Spain, colonizers of Indonesia and Covarrubias's Mexico respectively. Against Spanish and Portuguese claims to vast sea territories (Spain claimed the Gulf of Mexico and the Pacific Ocean, while Portugal claimed the Indian Ocean and the Atlantic south of Morocco), the Dutch lawyer Hugo Grotius, on behalf of the newly founded Dutch East India Company, published *The Freedom of the Seas; or, The Right Which Belongs to the Dutch to Take Part in the East Indian Trade* (1609). Disputing Spanish and Portuguese assertions of mare clausum (ocean space as closed and territorialized), Grotius paved the way for centuries of Dutch trade and colonization in the East Indies, arguing for what would become a staple of the European and eventually world system, mare liberum, or an open and unterritorializable sea. For Grotius, the sea was by nature like "air": "not susceptible of occupation; and . . . its common use . . . destined for all men." He argued that "the ocean . . . can be neither seized nor inclosed" for it "possesses the earth [rather] than is by it possessed."[45] Most immediately, in the twentieth century, Indonesia inherited mare liberum through the Netherlands' Territoriale Zee en Maritieme Kringen Ordonnantie 1939 (Territorial Sea and Maritime Districts Ordinance 1939), which took "Netherlands Indies territory" to encompass the land, namely, "islands . . . or parts of islands," while, consistent with Grotius's treatise, the ocean space between the islands was mare liberum where foreign vessels were free to sail.[46] Over the years, however, a small exception to mare liberum had found acceptance in maritime law. During the seventeenth and eighteenth centuries, in part based on the distance a cannon could fire seaward from the coast, European nations had come to agree that a nation could claim sea space within three miles of its land territory.[47] Hence, the Dutch ordinance of 1939 specified that the "*Netherlands Indies territorial sea*" referred to "the sea area extending . . . seaward to a distance of three nautical miles from the low-water [i.e., low-tide] mark of the islands, or parts of islands."[48] The Hague Tribunal in September 1910 had pointed to the traditional stance that "the 3 marine miles are to be measured following the sinuosities of the coast."[49]

In affixing water-based borders to the "sinuosities" of the coast, the international norm to which Indonesia was subject was a far cry from the land-based border*line*, which as Anzaldúa and Nail have pointed out seeks a Euclidean geometry that works at cross-purposes with water. Indeed, in projecting a watery border three miles seaward from the coast's sinuosities, states were in effect engaging in natural-cultural, water-human collaborations regarding their territorial boundaries, wading into questions that were geometrically grotesque (see fig. 3.5). The United States and Britain, in determining the boundary between Alaska and Canada in 1903, had engaged in discussions that examined "irregularities of the coast" such as bays and inlets and wondered, "Which do you call sinuosities, and which do you call not sinuosities?" Representatives of the two countries had debated whether it was "theoretically impossible" or merely practically impossible to follow the coast's sinuosities and create a "parallel line" in the ocean. One particularly vivid example was put forth: "Take your pair of compasses with a pencil at one end of them and proceed to draw a line of that sort; you will find the most intricate convolutions crossing one another, and that the whole thing, in fact, is impossible to carry out." The discussion raised the question whether "any power is given to the Commission to settle what is a sinuosity and what is an inlet."[50] A border logic based on coastal sinuosities evoked what Elizabeth R. Johnson and Irus Braverman have referred to as the ocean's "turbulent boundaries," creating "governance of the ocean [as] a wicked problem."[51]

Geometrically grotesque questions regarding coastal irregularities such as inlets, sinuosities, and bays mark the locus classicus of what mathematician Benoit Mandelbrot has termed *fractal geometry*, a field of mathematics that was founded on a seemingly simple question. This question, as showcased in the title of Mandelbrot's foundational 1967 article, trained its focus on the nature of an island's coastline: "How Long Is the Coast of Britain?"[52] Answering the question is not simple, as the frustrated US-British boundary commission knew and as Mandelbrot later explained: "Classical mathematics had its roots in the regular geometric structures of Euclid," but a "great revolution of ideas separates the classical mathematics

FIGURE 3.5 — The complex Gulf of Mexico shoreline produced by the Mississippi River Delta (May 24, 2001), which illustrates the difficulty of using a sinuous coast as the baseline for projecting a border three miles out into the ocean. From NASA/GSFC/METI/ERSDAC/JAROS and US/Japan ASTER Science Team, https://www.jpl.nasa.gov/spaceimages/details.php?id=PIA03497.

of the 19th century from the modern mathematics of the 20th"; "the revolution was forced by the discovery of mathematical structures that did not fit the patterns of Euclid.... These new structures were regarded ... as 'pathological,' ... as a 'gallery of monsters,' kin to the cubist painting ... that [was] upsetting established standards of taste in the arts at about the same time."[53] Mandelbrot's fractal geometry, then, seeks to recover these "patterns of Nature" that are "so irregular and fragmented" that "Euclid leaves [them] aside as being 'formless.'"[54] This new geometry emerges as a means of approaching the structures of nature's non-Euclidean materiality: "shapes they had to call *grainy, hydralike, in between, pimply, pocky, ramified, seaweedy, strange, tangled, tortuous, wiggly, wispy, wrinkled*, and the like."[55]

In these epithets one sees shades of the frustrated surveyor with a pair of compasses wrapped up in the most intricate convolutions, and hence it is unsurprising that for Mandelbrot the coastline became the original test case for fractal geometry. Responding to his own iconic question "How Long Is the Coast of Britain?" Mandelbrot answered, "It is evident that [the coast's] length is at least equal to the distance measured along a straight line.... However, the typical coastline is irregular and winding, and there is no question it is much longer than the straight line."[56] Mandelbrot elaborates, "When a bay or peninsula noticed on a map scaled to 1/100,000 is reexamined on a map at 1/10,000, subbays and subpeninsulas become visible. On a 1/1,000 scale map, sub-subbays and sub-subpeninsulas appear, and so forth. Each adds to the measured length."[57] As the scale or unit of measurement becomes "smaller and smaller," the measured length of the coastline "tends to increase steadily without bound" (see fig. 3.6).[58] Offering an illustration of the coastline's non-Euclidean existence, Mandelbrot addressed his readers: "Imagine a man walking along the coastline, taking the shortest path." When "the tide is low and the waves are negligible," this man may follow the coastline's tortuous shape "down to finer details by harnessing a mouse, then an ant, and so forth. Again, as our walker stays increasingly closer to the coastline, the distance to be covered continues to increase with no limit."[59]

The watery borders of the territorial sea, then, as they became functions of a shore whose sinuosities and inwardly capillaried watersheds were impossible to distinguish from one another, emerged as fractal spatial configurations projected three miles out from the coastlines. These seaward projections were anchored not to any stable coastline but rather to a coast that is "infinitely complex and intricately entangled with the surrounding sea," such that though we may wish to grasp "where the sea starts and where the island stops," "the border between fractal island and ocean ... can only be

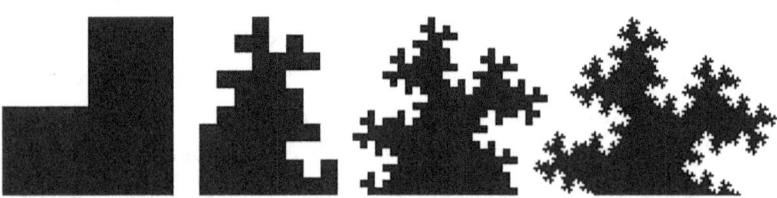

FIGURE 3.6 — Four iterations of a mathematically generated Koch Island peninsula, inspired by Benoit Mandelbrot's "Koch Island" sequence in *The Fractal Geometry of Nature* (plate 51). This series is suggestive of an island's lengthening coastline when its shores are measured at increasingly finer levels of resolution. Koch Island iterations generated by David Penry; peninsula arrangement by Christine Riggio.

approximated—never located in an exact mathematical sense."[60] Hence, the fractal coastline produces non-Euclidean borders that are projected to exist at a distance from the land out in the ocean, with their tangled and tortuous shapes anchored to a non-Euclidean shore that is in constant spatiotemporal flux as waves crash and recede, and as currents erode and deposit, producing a fractal and infinite array of temporally provisional coastlines attendant to a littoral materiality whose fractal sinuosities and inlets evoke an infinite spatial length. This was not simply theoretical but was practically acknowledged, as, over half a century after the US-British boundary meetings of 1903, the United States of the 1960s and 1970s was still acknowledging the fuzziness of distinguishing between a sinuosity and an inlet, citing an International Court of Justice decision holding "that there are no rules of a 'technically precise character' by which the validity of a nation's seaward boundary under international law could be measured."[61] Today the United States acknowledges that its shoreline-set maritime boundaries "are ambulatory and subject to changes as the coastline accretes and erodes."[62]

Here the water-based and coastline-set border is a far cry from imaginations of the land-oriented border, which governmentality advances as an unnatural Euclidean line working against natural flows of water and culture. Instead, and allied with what Twain or Limón might observe about borders set by rivers, the watery border exists as a natural-cultural collaboration between water and governmentality.[63] To take Mandelbrot's comparison between non-Euclidean geometry and modernist painting as a conceit, the coast-dependent watery border is twentieth-century cubism to the land-based Euclidean border's nineteenth-century realism. And, paradoxically, this cubist *border* in the water comes to resemble Anzaldúa's notion of the *borderland*, "a vague and undetermined place . . . in a constant state of transition."[64] Meanwhile, within this iteration of the borderwaters, the watery borders' attendant borderwaters become places where humans agree to interact with other humans on terms set by nonhuman and fractal earth-water dynamics. This Western iteration of the borderwaters constituted some of the baggage carried by the Indonesian Information Office when it, in the Covarrubias pamphlet, discussed Indonesian territory in terms that recognized islands as territory while water, except for a fractal three-mile band, remained high seas.

Yet from Indonesia's beginnings as a postcolonial state, there was a sense that the islands and their sinuosity-set seaward borders did not equal the sum total of Indonesian territorial sovereignty. As the Indonesian diplomat Arif Havas Oegroseno has written, it has long seemed starkly inadequate to envision Indonesia as "a collection of island enclaves in the midst of the high seas rather than [as] an island nation unified by the sea."[65] Against the West's island-enclave conceptualization, the Indonesian Constitution of 1945 laid claim to "the land, the waters and the natural riches contained therein," and one member of Indonesia's Committee for the Investigation of Independence had argued that "the seas between the terrestrial components of Indonesia were as much a part of Indonesia as the land and that the principle of the freedom of the seas threatened Indonesia's sovereignty and security."[66] But Indonesia did not formally upend the land-oriented Dutch territorial claims until 1957, when, governmentalizing what this chapter's first section discusses as an archipiélado model of the borderwaters, the postcolonial nation issued what has come to be known as the Djuanda Declaration, announcing that "the Government declares all waters around, between and those connecting the islands as included in the State of Indonesia, . . . under the indisputable sovereignty of Indonesia." According to the declaration, these "internal waters" (a term asserting a topological correspondence between Indonesia's seas and a land-oriented country's rivers and lakes) were circumscribed by "the line connecting the outermost points of the islands of the State of Indonesia," and beyond that line Indonesia claimed a "territorial sea" with a "breadth of . . . 12 miles" rather than three miles.[67]

While having none of the diplomatic gravity of Indonesia's Djuanda Declaration, Covarrubias's early 1950s map for the Indonesian Information Office offers a visual representation of Indonesia that highlights Indigenous presences upon the waters, gesturing toward maritime practices in which lands and waters function simultaneously as links and nodes (see fig. 3.7). The larger map also contains an inset map in the lower left corner (see fig. 3.8). This is a map of the continental United States, dropped into the ocean as if it were an island in the waters southwest of Sumatra and Java, with a smaller-scaled image of Indonesia's archipelagic territory superimposed on it. In this way, Covarrubias's illustration reenvisions the pamphlet's statistic on Indonesia as a quarter the size of the United States, reminding us that if the phrase "from sea to shining sea" is a traditional index of US continental vastness, Indonesia's own west-east measurement from sea to shining sea surpasses that of the United States. Further, Indonesia's superimposition on the United States imagines the postcolonial nation's lands and waters as set within borders (borders that happen to assume the size and shape of the continental United States), such that the

FIGURE 3.7 — Miguel Covarrubias's map of Indonesia, from *Republic of Indonesia: New Nation of the World*. The map includes four seagoing vessels: a Balinese prau in the waters amid Australia to the south and the islands of Java, Bali, and the Lesser Sunda Islands to the north; a Madurese prau plying the waters amid Sulawesi, Borneo, and the Lesser Sunda Islands; a *vinta* (traditional vessel of the Sama-laut, or "sea people") sailing the waters amid the islands of Indonesia and the Philippines; and a cargo ship (nodding toward postcolonial Indonesia's imbrications with oceanic modernity). Identification of these vessels is based on comparison with *Native Means of Transportation in the Pacific Area* and the key Covarrubias provides in *Pageant of the Pacific* (22). From Adriana and Tom Williams Collection of Miguel Covarrubias, Harry Ransom Center, University of Texas at Austin. Courtesy of María Elena Rico Covarrubias.

map figures an Indonesia that is not a quarter the size of the United States but roughly equal to it.

Covarrubias's visual image thus aligns with the vision of Mochtar Lubis, the Indonesian novelist and newspaper editor who hosted the US writer Richard Wright during his three-week visit to Indonesia for the 1955 postcolonial Asian-African Conference held in Bandung. According to Wright's travelogue *The Color Curtain: A Report on the Bandung Conference* (1956), during this visit Wright asked, "Say, just how many islands are there in this archipelago?" Mochtar replied, "About fifteen thousand; but only about three thousand are inhabited." Wright queried, "And how large in area is the space covered by these islands?" Although this conversation took place before the 1957 Djuanda Declaration, Mochtar's answer was distinct from the land-oriented text within the Information Office's pamphlet but very much resembled Covarrubias's accompanying inset map. Referring to Indonesia's territory as encompassing both land and ocean space, Mochtar answered that Indonesia was, "roughly, . . . the size of the United States."[68] Even before the 1957 declaration, notions of

BORDERWATERS · 131

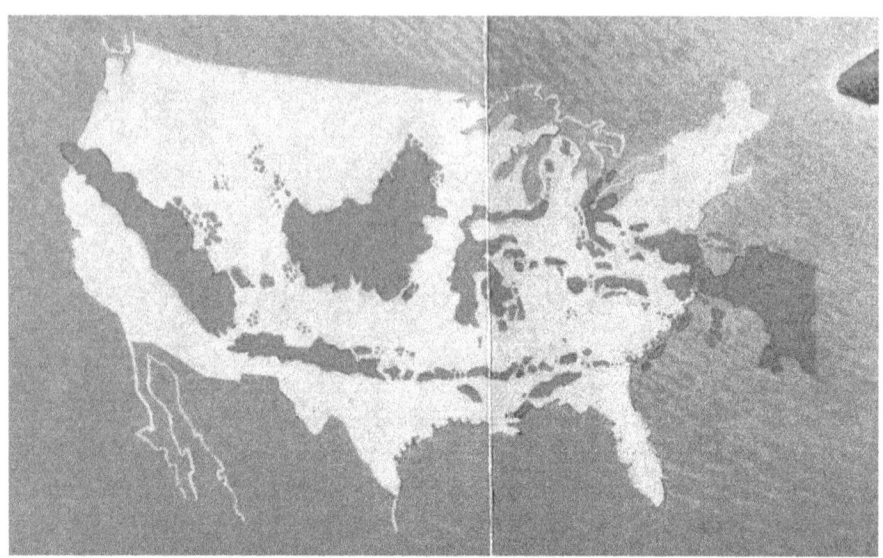

FIGURE 3.8 — Detail of the inset map included on Covarrubias's larger map of Indonesia in *Republic of Indonesia: New Nation of the World*. Courtesy of María Elena Rico Covarrubias. ☙ At its most basic level, the image of Indonesia superimposed on the United States is aimed at facilitating a size comparison. The comparison reveals Indonesia as more geographically expansive than many in the United States might suppose. Sumatra juts out into the Pacific Ocean off the California-Oregon coast. Java spans across the borderlands of Arizona, New Mexico, and Texas. Bali sits atop Dallas. Kalimantan (the Indonesian portion of Borneo) covers much of the US Midwest. Sulawesi floats just south of Lake Michigan. And the Maluku Islands (the fabled Spice Islands) span from Canada's portion of Lake Huron down across Appalachia and into the waters just off the Carolinas. Finally, the US eastern seaboard comes nowhere close to containing Indonesia as the Indonesian half of New Guinea stretches nearly to Bermuda (not pictured) in the North Atlantic. For twenty-first-century US readers, the map's illustration of Indonesia's unexpected expansiveness might be supplemented with reminders that Indonesia today has the fourth-largest population among nation-states (the United States has the third-largest population). Meanwhile, by 2050 Indonesia is predicted to have the fourth-largest economy in the world (the US economy is predicted to be the third largest). See PWC, "The World in 2050: Will the Shift in Global Economic Power Continue?," February 2015, https://www.pwc.com/gx/en/issues/the-economy/assets/world-in-2050-february-2015.pdf.

a land- *and* water-oriented "homeland" were common sense among many Indonesians. In fact, the Indonesian-language phrase that is commonly translated into English as "homeland" is *tanah air*, a term made up of two components: *tanah* (land) and *air* (water), such that nondomesticating English translations for the term could be "water land," "watery land," "land of water," or "land and water."[69] Indeed, the term *tanah air* has been canonized via a founding event within postcolonial Indonesian mythology, the Sumpah Pemuda (Youth Pledge) of 1928, which was a set of three principles adopted in the city of Batavia (renamed Jakarta in the 1940s) by a group of young, high-status Indonesian nationalists hailing from several regions and islands of the Dutch East Indies. As the Sumpah Pemuda has been adapted to Indonesian archipelagic nationalism, its first principle has since the late 1940s involved an affirmation of fidelity to "Tanah Air Indonesia," or the terraqueous patria of Indonesia.[70]

It was the task of another man named Mochtar, the Yale-trained Indonesian legal scholar and diplomat Mochtar Kusumaatmadja, to make this archipelagic structure of feeling intelligible within the realm of international law and relations. Mochtar wanted the world to radically rethink archipelagic space in ways unbeholden to Euro-American continentalism—he wished to think not like a "humdrum" "plumber or . . . carpenter" but like "a master . . . architect with a mission to build a new and better world."[71] His work as a master architect of worldwide archipelagic thought began in earnest in 1957, when, after being asked to legalistically reimagine the Java Sea as an "internal sea," he "drew straight baselines between the outermost points of the outermost islands on a map of Indonesia," so that "the waters within these baselines—the Java, Flores, and Banda seas and much else as well—would become Indonesia's internal waters."[72]

This move facilitated the Djuanda Declaration later that year, inspiring a decades-long struggle on Indonesia's part (with Mochtar among those at the helm) to gain international recognition for the declaration and to integrate an archipelago principle into the United Nations Convention on the Law of the Sea (UNCLOS).[73] Mochtar's success in this cause is reflected in the official text of UNCLOS as agreed upon in 1982: an "archipelagic State" became recognized as "a State constituted wholly by one or more archipelagos and may include other islands," wherein *archipelago* meant "a group of islands, including parts of islands, *interconnecting waters* and other natural features which are so closely interrelated that such islands, *waters* and other natural features form an intrinsic geographical, economic and political entity, or which historically have been regarded as such." On the question of how to determine which waters were part of an archipelagic state, the 1982 treaty made recourse to the approach that Mochtar himself had used in 1957: "An archipelagic State may draw straight archipelagic baselines joining the outermost points of the outermost islands and drying reefs of the archipelago" (see fig. 3.9).[74]

Yet for Mochtar, these straight Euclidean lines were not the essence of Indonesia's decolonial archipelagic perspective—rather, the straight lines were a medium for that perspective to interface with an international world of twentieth-century nation-states that were imagined, according to the Westphalian myth, to possess unequivocal sovereignty and the right to noninterference from other nation-states.[75] As he explained during a 1972 talk at the University of Rhode Island's Law of the Sea Institute, "In our language, as in many languages, we have a word for 'native country.' The French word is 'patrie,' the German word 'das heimat'; in Indonesia, it is 'tanah air,' which means 'land and water.' . . . This is a word not coined by lawyers . . . but . . . that comes from the people who have lived in these islands and these archipelagoes, and they feel it is part of them. . . . If a simple man says 'tanah air' (i.e., land and water), then I think he *means* it."[76] Hence, the model of the archipelagic state could project an outward-

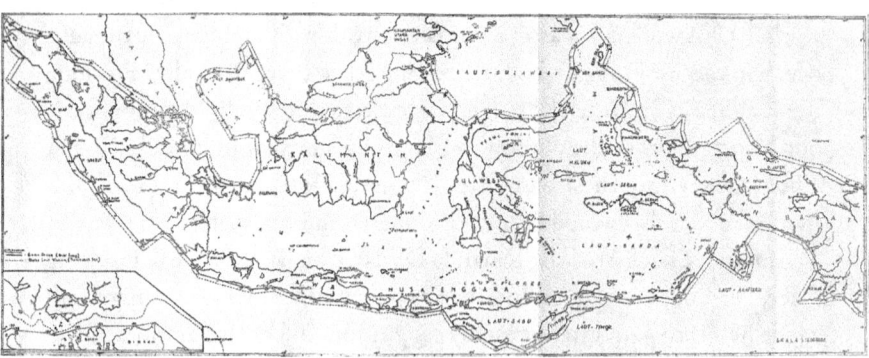

FIGURE 3.9 — Map of Indonesia's archipelagic baselines distributed by Indonesia in 1960. Waters enclosed by these baselines were claimed as sovereign territory. The map shows what appear to be double lines around Indonesian waters. The inner lines are the archipelagic baselines, like those that Mochtar Kusumaatmadja drew around Indonesia's outermost islands. Meanwhile, the band between the inner lines and outer lines marks the extent of Indonesia's claim to a twelve-mile territorial sea beyond the archipelagic baselines. From Sumitro Lono Sedewo Danuredjo, *Hukum Internasional Laut Indonesia: Suatu Usaha untuk Mempertahankan Deklarasi 1957*, vol. 2 (Jakarta: Bhratara, 1971).

facing Westphalianism that was simultaneously an inward-facing move that would permit the archipelagic baselines to provide a space in which Indonesia's tanah air could exist in its "wholeness of National Territory with all of its contents and wealth forms."[77] The archipelagic baselines could facilitate a governmentalized acknowledgment of and commitment to Indonesia's archipiélado of borderwaters, as lived by Mochtar's "simple man," whose idea of tanah air might have resonated with the description offered by the Malaysian geographer Zaharah binti Haji Mahmud: "The *air* in the term *tanah air* refers in equal parts to the maritime waters of the oceans and inland seas and the waters of the major river systems that drain into them in perpetuity," ranging from the sea to the rivers' "extensive network of tributary valleys," "alluvial hollows and pockets," and "rice fields."[78] Here the archipiélado of tanah air converges with some of Glissant's commentary on "archipelagic thought," whose thinkers follow the fractal coast and come "to know the rocks of the rivers, assuredly the smallest of both the rocks and the rivers," imagining even "the dark holes that they cover and recover" (see fig. 3.10).[79] Indeed, Indonesia's triumph in introducing tanah air (water-land) as a structure of feeling involving a land-water patria into UNCLOS's international definition of the "archipelagic State" might be considered an instantiation, on the world stage, of one of Glissant's coinages in *Poétique de la Relation* (1990).[80] Betsy Wing has straightforwardly translated Glissant's term *terre-mer* as "land-sea," while J. Michael Dash has observed that it is a play on words, a pun that rewrites the term *terre-mere* ("motherland") "not [as] mother*land* but [as] a marine habitat, neither land nor sea, that propels the subject into the 'chaos-monde,' that roaring global (dis)order in which everything imaginable exists in a glorious cacophony."[81]

In this iteration of the borderwaters, we see Indonesia establishing a territorialized terraqueous space inside of which mare liberum, the very doctrine that set the stage for the archipelago's colonization by the Dutch, is suspended. Meanwhile, the watery borders that exist as three-mile projections of the fractal shoreline are supplanted by borders projected twelve miles out from Indonesia's Euclideanized archipelagic baselines. But this Euclideanization of the watery border seems to be a means of keeping the world of Westphalian nation-states at bay, while on the inside the borderwaters would seem to evoke an archipelagic world that may ignore the continental world. This cordoned-off world is a place where Indonesia's borderwaters archipiélado exists in its non-Euclidean cacophony, a place where the Indonesian state's outward-facing Westphalianism might permit

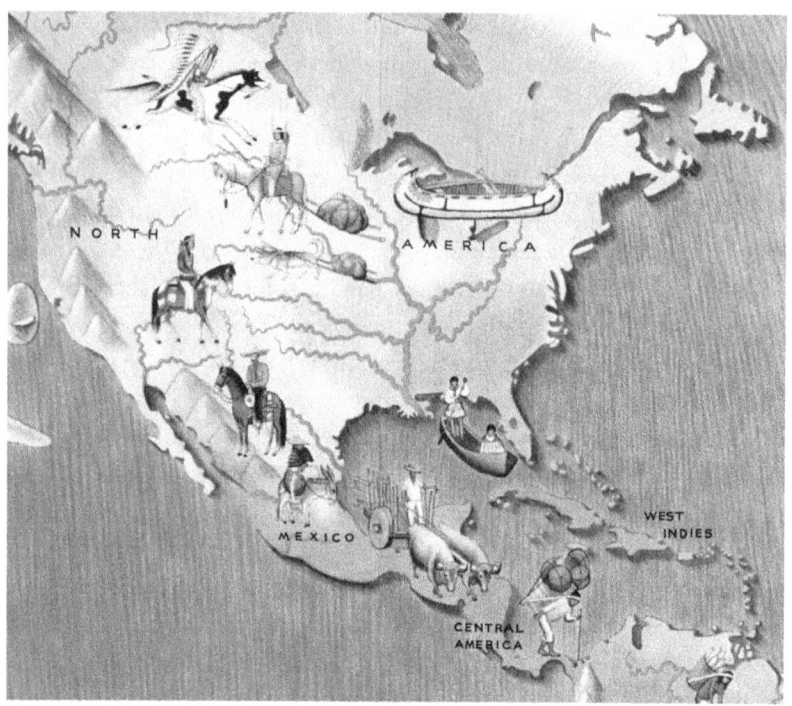

FIGURE 3.10 — Detail from the lithograph of Miguel Covarrubias's *Native Means of Transportation in the Pacific Area*. In this detail we see hints at an archipelagic perspective, which thrives amid the inlets rather than disputing their status as sinuosities. In Covarrubias's representation of North America, Indigenous canoe technology spans from the Gulf of Mexico to some of the Mississippi River's branching headwaters near the Great Lakes. From American Geographical Society Library Digital Map Collection, University of Wisconsin–Milwaukee. Courtesy of María Elena Rico Covarrubias.

an inward-facing "decolonising [of] governance," which Paul Carter has recently suggested "archipelagic thinking" may precipitate.[82]

But the inward cacophony of tanah air is far from glorious, for instance, in the account of Pramoedya Ananta Toer, an internationally honored Indonesian author and longtime political prisoner under the US-supported regime of Suharto, who as a military general oversaw the 1965–66 mass killings and imprisonments of alleged Indonesian communists and who became the country's second president in 1968.[83] Pramoedya skewered the Republic of Indonesia's archipelagic pretensions in an unsent 1969 letter detailing his transport, together with some eight hundred other political prisoners, to the prison island of Buru:

We are sailing off like our ancestors did during the age of migration, in search of land and a new life. But now we have come to a realization that we are amid the waters of our own tanah air, a maritime nation with thirteen thousand islands. It's said that everything amid the islands is also our domain, including every cup of water between two oceans, the Indian and the Pacific. This is a classic line they teach us in school.... [But we on the ship are] like the kidnapped and ship-bound Chinese prisoners who become Michener's characters en route to Hawaii; our fate is similar to that of the four million Africans held in English and American ships, carried across the Atlantic to a new continent.... Too many of us have never before ventured from our villages, never before seen the ocean. We are citizens of this maritime nation! Do you hear me? Citizens who in grade school were informed that we are descendants of a nautical people who explored the seas.[84]

Pramoedya continued, describing a journey that took him from Nusakambangan Prison (off the coast of Java) to Buru Island (among Indonesia's storied Spice Islands), a maritime excursion that corresponds (if we take Covarrubias's inset Information Office map as a guide) to a journey from the Trinity nuclear test site in New Mexico to Lexington, Kentucky: "Sometimes we break down and slow to a stop, becoming a toy bobbing in the waves in the middle of the sea—this is our ship, a ship owned by the largest archipelagic nation on the face of the earth!"[85]

Pramoedya's critique of the Indonesian state's governmentalization of historical and everyday archipelagic thought and practice is scathing and multilayered, both with intended meaning and with critical implications. First, his gesture toward a landlocked mindset among many inland Indonesians ("Too many of us have ... never before seen the ocean") corroborates Covarrubias's assessment of Balinese culture as generally hydrophobic. Thus, Pramoedya seems to imply that the Republic of Indonesia's archipelagic perspective was to a large degree a mythology. It was simultaneously outward facing, geared toward the power-motivated evocation of a new mare clausum, and inward facing, taught at schools to inland children to instill a sense of nationalism across island populations that would, in the absence of archipelagic inculcation, remain culturally incoherent.[86] Pramoedya's case in point: a genuine, rather than mythologized, archipelagic entity would have a ship that could travel its own breadth without breaking down.

Second, Pramoedya underscores the contrast between a mythologized age of migration, when ancestral Indonesians spread throughout the islands, and his present journey to a political prison, during which he and his fellow prisoners are abject, existing in conditions comparable to those described in James Michener's account of transpacific coolieism involving Chinese prisoners confined to ships amid "a mixture of urine, sweat, bowel movements and seasickness."[87] As well, he views the conditions as comparable to a slave ship's hold, of which we have Olaudah Equiano's account, involving "the groans of the dying, [which] rendered it a scene of horror almost inconceivable."[88] Notably, as Pramoedya certainly knows, both of the abject groups to whom he compares his cohort of destitute prisoners were on their way to what was—or was becoming—America: on their way to the "continent," or on their way to an archipelagic state of America (Hawai'i became the fiftieth US state in 1959, the year Michener published his historical novel *Hawaii*). The racialized abjection of Chinese and African labor—whether bound for the continent or bound for the archipelago—suggests that under what Aníbal Quijano has called America's founding dynamic of the "coloniality of power," the geographic form of the archipelago is no heaven to the continent's hell.[89] The coloniality of power, with what has been described as the racialized Americanity of the world system, has assured that both continent and archipelago have been hell, in many circumstances, for Indigenous and other racialized minority populations.[90] Indeed, the Puerto Rican poet and critic Juan Carlos Quintero Herencia has written, "The archipelagic doesn't save, nor vindicate, nor redeem anything."[91] And yet, given that Pramoedya is clearly measuring the "the largest archipelagic nation on the face of the earth" against its own decolonial ideals of archipelagic thought and practice, he seems to still see promise in the archipelago as a geoformal thought template toward decolonizing governance, even if that archipelagic decolonization may be uncrystallizable, as Quintero Herencia suggests, in "any existing or future State."[92] The borderwaters archipiélado—this tanah air, terre-mer, land-sea archipelago—has and may yet offer something other than the world system's coloniality of power.

Borderwaters in Which Lines Are Not to Be Interpreted as Boundaries

For most people who think about US geography, few countries will seem farther afield from the United States than Indonesia. Hence, it would at first seem surprising to read Covarrubias's work as plotting a set of borderwaters between the two countries, or to read Pramoedya's commentary as placing Buru-bound prisoners and America-bound prisoners in different ships that each leave what might be seen as, following Christina Sharpe, a similar "wake," as keels of racial and political abjection slice the ocean water from the West Indies to the East Indies.[93] And yet the United States and the Indonesian archipelago bordered each other throughout most of the twentieth century.[94] Indeed, if Covarrubias's Information Office map may be said to offer a thought experiment in which the continental United States is sopping wet as an island adjacent to Indonesia's tanah air, then his 1949 map of the US-administered Trust Territory of the Pacific Islands (TTPI) reminds us that the United States, literally in terms of its national geography, has mixed in the borderwaters of Indonesia's northeast (see fig. 3.11). The United States, we are reminded, has been the northern neighbor of both Covarrubias's Mexico and Indonesia.

Covarrubias's map of the TTPI is the lead illustration for an April 25, 1949, *Life* magazine article titled "The Trust Territory: Its 2,130 Islands Form a New U.S. Domain in the Pacific," which announces that the TTPI is "a great sweep of islands running west and north across three million square miles of ocean. . . . Although they are officially held in trust for the United Nations, they have been declared a strategic area in the custody of the U.S. and it can close them to other nations at will. They are not the property of the U.S., but for practical purposes they form a new 'American empire' in the Pacific."[95] Contemporary with this article in *Life* was the more technical explanation offered by Eugene F. Bogan, a former US naval officer who during World War II had established and administered the US military government in part of the region that would become the TTPI. Bogan explained that on April 2, 1947, the United Nations Security Council "approved a trusteeship agreement designating the United States as the administering authority for these former Japanese island areas," a territory that "represents a great zone of thousands of small islands scattered over 5,000,000 square miles of sea."[96] Describing the inhabitants as "part of the American family," Bogan remarked that the TTPI was "in a *de facto* (but not a *de jure*) sense . . . as much a part of the United States as Puerto Rico or the Virgin Islands."[97] Covarrubias's map situates these islands of the American family north of the Solomons and New Guinea, with the TTPI's southwestern district of Palau mingling in the water with Indonesia's easternmost claims, including claims to the western half of the island of New Guinea.

BORDERWATERS · 139

FIGURE 3.11 — Miguel Covarrubias's map of the Trust Territory of the Pacific Islands. From *Life*, April 25, 1949, p. 96. Courtesy of María Elena Rico Covarrubias.

Notably, Covarrubias's 1949 illustration for *Life* was the middle panel within a triptych of illustrations that unfolded over the course of more than a decade. The 1949 illustration offers iconic representations of a turtle (above Bikini), a shark (north of the Solomons), and a coconut crab (amid the waters of the Marshall Islands and Gilbert Islands). Each of these images had appeared a decade earlier in Covarrubias's mural *The Fauna and Flora of the Pacific*, with the turtle migrating from the waters off of Mexico, the shark moving to Micronesia from the waters of central Polynesia, and the coconut crab moving from an iconically rendered atoll of central Polynesia. And then in 1950 Covarrubias's images reappeared, with the shark and coconut crab having moved again, this time copied from the *Life* illustration by an anonymous and less accomplished hand, in a US Naval Civil Administration pamphlet provided to US personnel and dependents stationed in the TTPI's Marshall Islands district (see fig. 3.12).[98] In contemplating the movement that unfolds across a Covarrubias triptych whose final panel was created by the US Navy for its own purposes, we find something of a natural-cultural allegory regarding a US commitment to mare liberum. From the beginning, Grotius had advanced mare liberum as "a law derived from nature," and now as we watch Covarrubias's representations of multispecies actants move across mapped regions, they may remind us of certain freedoms of navigation exhibited by sea life (whether as individual organisms or as species), an ability to circulate that bespeaks a set of multispecies sovereignties that can exist apart from the sovereignties of nation-states.[99] Aligned with Anzaldúa's fence-attacking ocean, their movements seem to offer a natural logic supporting the cultural logic that has enshrined the notion of mare liberum, as if the United States were merely defending an edict of nature when it protested Indonesia's 1957 declaration that the sea could be fenced, that its tanah air was mare clausum.[100]

The United States' dedication to mare liberum was staunch, and it was not concerned—and even embraced the fact—that this approach to the ocean created its own and other nation-states' borders as a gallery of monsters, as cubist boundaries churning fractally through the sea. As the US Navy affirmed in 1952, the US geometric stance with regard to ocean borders followed in the tradition of Grotius: "The United States has always been one of the world's foremost advocates of freedom of the seas.... Because of this the Navy has always advocated the 3-mile limit of territorial waters delimited in such way that the outer limits thereof closely follow the sinuousities [*sic*] of the coast line.... The time-honored position

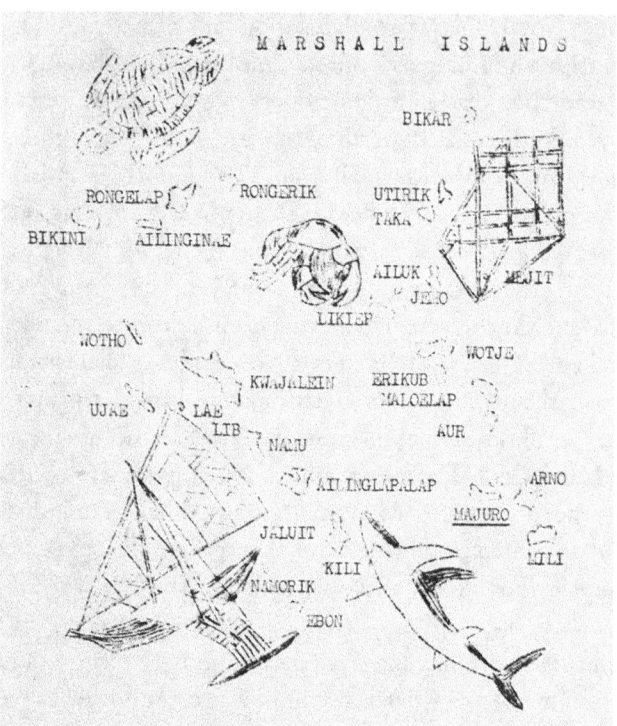

FIGURE 3.12 — Map from the 1950 pamphlet *Roster of Officers, Enlisted Men, Civilians and Dependents*, published by the US Naval Civil Administration Unit, Marshall Islands. The turtle, shark, coconut crab, stick chart, and outrigger canoe are roughly copied from Miguel Covarrubias's 1949 illustration for *Life*. Compared to the 1949 *Life* illustration, the turtle has remained almost stationary while the coconut crab has moved from the southern Marshall Islands to the waters of the northern Marshalls. Elsewhere, the shark has moved from immediately north of the Solomons to the waters amid the southern Marshall Islands.

of the Navy is that the greater the freedom and range of its warships and aircraft, the better protected are the security interests of the United States because greater utilization can be made of warships and military aircraft."[101] Thus, the United States had been careful to maintain the stance of mare liberum when it took the Philippines from Spain, designating a box of ocean space around this section of what Covarrubias framed as Greater Indonesia and claiming not the enclosed ocean but rather "the islands lying within the . . . line" (see fig. 1.7).[102] The move created a gallery of fractal US borders, projected three miles off the coast of each of the over 7,000 Philippine islands—but crucially, for the United States, it maintained mare liberum. Further geometric disruption prevailed a half century later, when President Harry S. Truman in 1945 issued a proclamation laying claim to the submerged lands of "the continental shelf off the coasts of the United States of America," declaring US "jurisdiction over the natural resources of the subsoil and sea bed . . . since the continental shelf may be regarded as an extension of the land-mass of the coast nation and thus naturally appurtenant to it." However, Truman affirmed that in spite of this US claim to jurisdiction over the adjacent seafloor, "the character as high seas of the waters above the continental shelf and the right to their free and unimpeded navigation are in no way . . . affected."[103] With the seabed claimed but the superadjacent waters remaining mare liberum, the US border became not a one-dimensional Euclidean line but the fractal and largely unknown three-dimensional topography of the benthic zone.

At the same time, as part of the spoils of World War II, the United States took control of the TTPI, which, as with the Philippines, involved a set of islands within a box of ocean space.[104] In its 1948 report to the United Nations on the TTPI, the US Navy included a map with the latitude- and longitude-set lines that marked the boundaries of the "TRUST TERRITORY OF THE PACIFIC ISLANDS" and stated that the TTPI "covers an area of some 3 million square miles in the western Pacific Ocean north of the equator."[105] Yet shortly thereafter, the US Navy issued a 1950 report to the United Nations that was more consistent with US dedication to mare liberum, even if mare liberum conduced toward embracing a notion of borders that was not only non-Euclidean but also geometrically nonsensical. The 1950 map continued to assert that the TTPI covered an "OCEAN AREA [OF] APPROX 3,000,000 SQ MILES," but the map also stated that "LINES INDICATE TERRITORIAL AREA, AND DISTRICTS OF JURISDICTION AND ARE NOT TO BE INTERPRETED AS BOUNDARIES" (see fig. 3.13).[106] These twin assertions, which became a staple of US figurations of the TTPI through the 1970s, were absurd within the realm of Euclidean geometry.[107] How can a figure's area be calculated if the very lines used in making said calculations are disavowed as the figure's boundaries?[108] Even Mandelbrot, notwithstanding his inclinations toward the grotesque forms that Euclid left behind, would have been stumped.

This was a disavowal of boundaries but strangely not of the area encompassed by the nonboundary lines; it was the geometric analogue of the political legerdemain that asserted US custody, jurisdiction, empire, administering authority, and dominion over the TTPI, and indeed discussed the TTPI as "territory of the United States," while disavowing, in

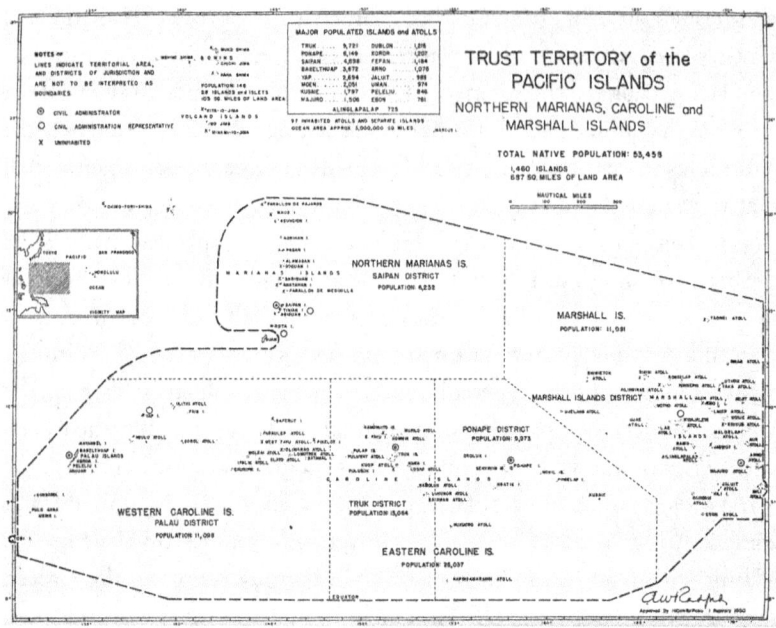

FIGURE 3.13 — Map of the TTPI published in 1950 by the Office of the Chief of Naval Operations. The map's legend indicates that the TTPI covers about three million square miles of ocean space, even as it denies the boundary status of the lines it uses to calculate the TTPI's area. From Department of the Navy, Office of the Chief of Naval Operations, *Report on the Administration of the Trust Territory of the Pacific Islands for the Period July 1, 1949, to June 30, 1950, Transmitted by the United States to the United Nations Pursuant to Article 88 of the Charter of the United Nations* (Washington, DC: Government Printing Office, 1950), vi.

the last instance, US ownership.[109] This non-Euclidean geometric stance evoked a de facto ocean territory of three million square miles while, in a de jure way, seeking to perpetuate the three-mile rule, which an assistant legal adviser to the US State Department had reaffirmed on January 2, 1947, as the United States moved toward assuming jurisdiction over the TTPI: "It would seem that, with possible minor exceptions, the territorial waters of islands however situated comprise a band three miles wide around each individual island. Thus the treatment of islands and groups of islands, with respect to territorial waters, is approximately the same as the treatment of large land masses such as continents."[110] The legal adviser's provisos ("It would seem that" and "with possible minor exceptions") might be thought of mathematically vis-à-vis Deleuze's set theory–inspired discussion of *sets, the whole,* and *Relation*: "If one had to define the whole, it would be defined by Relation.... The whole is not a closed set, but on the contrary [is] that by virtue of which the set is never absolutely closed, never completely sheltered, that which keeps it open somewhere as if by the finest thread which attaches it to the rest of the universe."[111] The provisos, then, become the finest thread that opens the set of the three-mile bands to the much larger set of the three million square miles of ocean territory. But even as the nonboundary status of the TTPI's lines seeks reconciliation with the three-mile bands, that same nonboundary status—evoking the TTPI's outer limits specifically as *nonboundaries*—becomes the finest thread linking the three-million-square-mile set to what Glissant (inspired by Deleuzian discussions such as this) figured as the "unfenced archipelago of the world totality."[112] Resembling but rechurning Anzaldúa's fence-attacking ocean, this unfenced archipelago of world totality is a whole within which an archipelagic United States and an archipelagic Indonesia become subsets, illustrated by Covarrubias as interlapping within the borderwaters, where Indonesia's Indigenous geometry of tanah air and the United States' geometrically absurd assertions of terraqueous territory grate asymmetrically against each other.

This asymmetrical grating is a key attribute of what I would see as a US iteration of the borderwaters. To borrow a dichotomy and some language from Amitav Ghosh, these borderwaters do not hinge on pitting the peopled "landscape and its topography" against governmentality's border magic, "the magic of Euclidean geometry."[113] This is not a question of governmental culture (the borderline) against human nature (the borderland). Rather, the aquaterritorial borders embraced by the United States are a set of moving nature-cultures of human and watershed, shoreline and governmentality, tide and international law, benthic zone and military—all geared toward preserving mare liberum. Within mare liberum's differently torqued version of Glissant's unfenced archipelago of world totality, all of the ocean, except for the portion contained inside a set of fractal borders that are prone to confusion between inlets and sinuosities, becomes the *de jure borderwaters* of every country on the planet and the *de facto domain* of the United States as the planet's dominant naval power. Thus, we see that radically different border grammars may exist between the realms of the borderlands and the borderwaters. Whereas Anzaldúa's assertion that "the sea cannot be fenced" takes the sea as a counterhegemonic metaphor for the borderlands' insurgency against land-based borders, that same statement—when made in reference to the material sea of the borderwaters—may function as the crux of the virtually borderless ocean on which US planetary hegemony depends.[114]

But in these post–World War II borderwaters of a newly nuclear (and for a time uniquely nuclear) United States, actions taken under the auspices of nation-state sovereignty and mare liberum merged with the nonhuman sovereignties of currents and circulating animal and plant life to produce frightening, appalling, and devastating results. If human-scaled mare liberum could look toward circulating nature for its cultural logic, the nonhuman world's sovereignties reflected back on the human world, rendering porous not just the borders but the very sovereignties of nation-states. As the leader of the largest self-consciously archipelagic state on the planet, a country whose borderwaters mingled with those of the United States, Indonesia's President Sukarno saw this danger. Referring to the "unknown horror" of nuclear testing during his opening speech for the 1955 Bandung Conference, he counseled his Asian-African guests: "Do not think that the oceans and the seas will protect us. The food that we eat, the water that we drink, yes, even the very air that we breathe can be contaminated by poisons originating from thousands of miles away. And it could be that, even if we ourselves escaped lightly, the unborn generations of our children would bear on their distorted bodies the marks of our failure to control the forces which have been released on the world."[115] Such a statement evinces a perception of Indonesia's tanah air as mingling with the waters of the TTPI, where the United States, with a United Nations mandate that included the charge to "promote the [social and] educational advancement of the [TTPI] inhabitants," was testing nuclear weapons, with especially devastating results for the atolls near which the US Navy version of Covarrubias's turtle was hovering: Bikini, Ailinginae, Rongelap, and Rongerik (see figs. 3.12 and 3.14).[116]

On one hand, there is no doubt that Sukarno was an advocate for the postcolonial Asian-African nations' integration into a system of Westphalian nation-states with unequivocal sovereignty and the right of noninterference from other governments, but I want to frame Sukarno's injunction to "not think that the oceans and the seas will protect us" as an archipelagic countercurrent to Bandung's broader postcolonial embrace of the modern nation-state.[117] Here Sukarno sees that human actions undertaken within the governmentally defined borders of one state may merge with the sovereign actants of the sea and its associated water and air currents, such that a nuclear weapon detonated on Bikini Atoll might exact a human toll within Indonesia that would have an outcome similar to the

FIGURE 3.14 — US government photograph taken as 167 Bikini Islanders boarded LST 1108, departing Bikini. During the previous month, the US military governor of the Marshall Islands had traveled to Bikini and held a Sunday meeting after church, asking the Bikinians whether they would be willing to temporarily leave the atoll so the United States could use it to test bombs "for the good of mankind and to end all world wars." After deliberations, the Bikinian leader, King Juda, told the US military governor, "We will go believing that everything is in the hands of God" (Niedenthal, *For the Good of Mankind*, 2). The Bikinians were relocated to Rongerik, where they nearly starved during their two-year residence on that atoll. From there, Bikini Islanders moved among various atolls and islands in the Marshall Islands. They have not been able to safely return to Bikini owing to their home atoll's continued radiation contamination. Niedenthal, *For the Good of Mankind*, 1–11. Photograph from https://commons.wikimedia.org/wiki/File:Leaving-bikini.jpg.

effect if, for instance, the US Navy physically entered Indonesia's tanah air and poisoned its populations. Sukarno's discussion of "our failure to control the forces which have been released on the world" situates nation-states as having an obligation to control what occurs within the borders of other nation-states, as the thingly sovereignty of the sea produces the interlapping sovereignties of nations. Pramoedya may have excoriated the Indonesian state's betrayal of archipelagic thought and practice, but the countercurrent in Sukarno's speech carries with it a multispecies ethos similar to Glissant's mythic narrative of the originary opening of archipelagic thought in the Caribbean, as "the birds carried on their wings" this mode of thought's "fragile aggregation."[118]

In the context of this countercurrent in Sukarno's speech, the notion of archipelagic sovereignty as fragile aggregation resonates with Yarimar Bonilla's work on the Caribbean's "non-sovereign politics" as a challenge to "the modernist premise of absolute sovereignty," and with Adom Getachew's framing of "anticolonial nationalism" as geared not simply toward the evocation of "nation-states" but toward postimperial and coalitional "worldmaking." Here Sukarno's natural-cultural view of sovereignty, in which archipelagic governance of the nation and the planet is characterized less by coherence than by fragile aggregation, would see incomplete and interlapping sovereignties, with lines that are to be interpreted not as boundaries but as multispecies entanglements, in every claim to sovereignty and self-determination.[119]

We find a story of these entanglements—of sovereignty and nuclear contamination and archipelagic currents of water and air—in another thread that runs from the 1939 *Pageant of the Pacific* murals, to the 1949 *Life* illustration, and to the US Navy's pirated version of Covarrubias in 1950. The story begins with Covarrubias's reference, in his *Pageant of the Pacific* pamphlet, to Pacific Islanders' navigation by means of "crude charts."[120] It was a strange reference even at the time, given that a few pages before this quotation Covarrubias had stated that terms such as "crude, primitive, savage, . . . are more and more losing favor with those who are sincerely interested in understanding the inhabitants of other lands."[121] And just a few years after the pamphlet's 1939 publication, Covarrubias would have learned that the charts were quite geometrically complex. He included a version of one of these charts in his TTPI map for *Life*, with a side caption explaining that "the outrigger canoe . . . is often navigated with the aid of the stick compass."[122] (The stick chart appears in figure 3.11, east of the turtle and Bikini.) In his research when preparing his TTPI map, Covarrubias had been drawn toward a spatial mapping technology that in English has been discussed as the Marshall Islands stick chart. Constructed of sticks representing wave or swell patterns, and with shells or bits of coral representing islands or sometimes major intersections between swells, the stick charts are of three main types: *rebbelib* (which represent large areas of ocean and island space), *meddo* (which represent more localized areas), and *mattang* (general instruction charts that one group of Marshall Islands navigators claimed would be applicable to "some island in another part of the world, one they had never seen").[123] Covarrubias evidently based his stick chart illustration on a meddo collected by Captain Winkler of the German Navy during the late nineteenth century, deposited in the Museum für Völkerkunde in Berlin and discussed and illustrated by Winkler as "Chart III" in his 1898 article on the charts (see fig. 3.15).[124] This meddo represents waters and atolls spanning from Ailinglaplap in the north to Ebon in the south and from Namorik in the west to Mili in the east, with the sticks or lines representing ocean swells and their refractions/reflections/diffractions in relation to islands and varying ocean depths.[125]

If Covarrubias had earlier described Pacific navigational charts as "crude," one wonders what he may have thought upon encountering Winkler's complex explications of general principles illustrated by the mattang as well as these principles' implications for the meanings of the lines and shells present on the meddo on which the 1949 *Life* illustration is based. Certainly, the explanations that Winkler arrived at by means of extensive discussions with Marshall Islanders constitute formidable lessons in non-Euclidean geometry.[126] Whatever Covarrubias may have thought of these lessons, Marshall Islands navigational geometry proved more complex than he took the time to comprehend, given that his illustration alters the meddo's quantity of islands (shells) from six to at least twenty-five and erases some islands from their places, which in turn creates a map that, absurdly, has swells (sticks) changing direction without cause, while at other points the swells travel forward when according to the charts' geometries of island-swell interaction they ought to change directions (see fig. 3.16). To put it in terms that those acquainted with continental US geography would understand, to a Marshall Islands navigator Covarrubias's meddo might look as strange as a map of the continental United States that places New York City in the Mojave Desert, erases California and New England, and spangles Nebraska with a dozen cities of over ten million inhabitants.

The absurdity was compounded, ominously, when the US Naval Civil Administration's pamphlet of 1950 included its own version of the chart, haphazardly copied from Covarrubias's chart and now apparently including only one island/atoll (shell) (see fig. 3.17). Here Covarrubias's randomly strewn confetti of atolls is supplanted by a solitary and misplaced Marshall Island, standing in place of atolls and islands that are, to borrow from Cutler in the context of the borderlands, "*disappeared*, . . . removed from their . . . worlds by state violence and material oppression beyond their control."[127] In contemplating these disappeared islands and atolls of

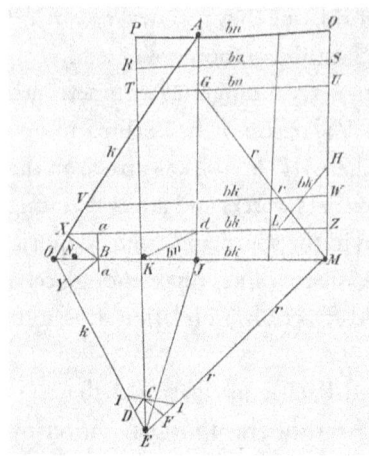 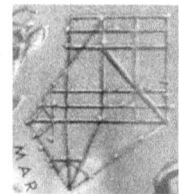 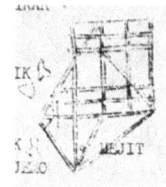

FIGURE 3.15 — (*left*) Chart III from Captain Winkler's 1898 article. Miguel Covarrubias's rendering of the Marshallese stick chart in *Life* was apparently based on this image. Winkler explains that within his drawing nearly every "point" represents a "shell" on the original meddo, which in turn represents an island/atoll: J stands for Jaluit, E for Ebon, N for Namorik, K for Kili, M for Mili, and A for Ailinglaplap. Within the stick chart's geometry, the shells are not dimensionless Euclidean points, nor are the "lines" one-dimensional; rather, the lines signify swell patterns that take place in three-dimensional space through a fourth, temporal dimension. Winkler's explanations of this chart's geometric work are more complex than Covarrubias may have taken time to absorb. From Captain Winkler, "On Sea Charts Formerly Used in the Marshall Islands, with Notices on the Navigation of These Islanders in General" (1898), in *Annual Report of the Board of Regents of the Smithsonian Institution, Showing the Operations, Expenditures, and Conditions of the Institution for the Year Ending June 30, 1899* (Washington, DC: Government Printing Office, 1901), 499.

FIGURE 3.16 — (*center*) Detail of Covarrubias's rendering of a Marshallese stick chart, from his 1949 map for *Life*. Covarrubias added numerous islands/atolls (shells) to the chart as compared to Winkler's illustration of the original in figure 3.15. Courtesy of María Elena Rico Covarrubias.

FIGURE 3.17 — (*right*) Detail of the Marshallese stick chart from *Roster of Officers, Enlisted Men, Civilians and Dependents* (1950), published by the US Naval Civil Administration Unit, Marshall Islands. Whether owing to the limitations of mimeograph technology or inattention on the illustrator's part, this version of the chart reduces the number of islands/atolls to one. This lone Marshall Island (to the left of the word *Mejit*) exerts no apparent influence on the swell patterns between the disappeared atolls of Ebon and Jaluit and no apparent influence on the swell patterns within the ocean space of the other disappeared atolls/islands charted by the original meddo: Namdrik/Namorik, Kili, Mili, and Ailinglaplap.

the archipelagic states of America, it is difficult to avoid seeing the navy's chart as explanatory vis-à-vis the larger TTPI, reflecting the same disregard for Micronesian islands and Indigenous epistemologies and people, especially as related to the nuclear testing that was contemporaneous with the Covarrubias and navy illustrations. The chart's solitary Marshall Island is a reminder that, as Elizabeth M. DeLoughrey has observed, "in nuclear discourse, islands are never understood relationally . . . [as] connected to other atolls and archipelagoes."[128] Now the absurdity depends not on geometry but on basic arithmetic involving human lives. If there is only one island, then there are zero islands, or if the population is only ninety thousand, then the population is disappeared. Those familiar with the history of nuclear testing and US militarization in the TTPI will recall the brutal arithmetic performed by US national security adviser Henry Kissinger regarding the TTPI: "There are only 90,000 people out there. Who gives a damn?"[129]

Writing of the disappeared islands of TTPI geometry, of "the land we lost" to US nuclear detonations and experiments in the mid-twentieth-century archipelagic states of America, the Marshallese poet and environmental activist Kathy Jetñil-Kijiner has offered testimony on the occasion of Nuclear Survivors' Day. She has detailed the material, bodily, and genetic instantiations of the nightmare of nuclear contamination discussed by Indonesia's Sukarno at the Asian-African Conference of 1955. Because Jetñil-Kijiner's testimony is urgent and will be enhanced by no concluding explication from me, I am letting it stand without further comment at the end of the present discussion of borderwaters in which lines are not to be taken as boundaries—in which governmental and cultural advocacy for freedom *of* the sea can never be attended by freedom *from* the sea, in which the sovereignties of the sea, compellingly accessed through Indigenous geometries as seen in the stick charts, inevitably meld with the nation-state sovereignties whose Euclidean and fractal boundaries are porous to nonhuman sovereignties. On March 1, 2013, thirty-four years after the United States recognized the independent Republic of the Marshall Islands and twenty-seven years after the Marshall Islands entered into a compact of free association with the United States, Jetñil-Kijiner marked Nuclear Survivors' Day with the following words:

> From 1946 to 1958, the United States conducted 67 nuclear tests in my home, the Marshall Islands. . . . The most powerful of those tests was the "Bravo" shot, a 15 megaton device detonated on March 1, 1954, at Bikini atoll—which

was 1,000 times the power of the Hiroshima bomb. Since then, the US has continued to deny responsibility while many Marshallese continue to die due to cancer and other radiation related illnesses. In my own family both my grandparents passed away before I was born due to cancer and just two years ago I lost my ten year old niece Bianca to leukaemia. Radiation related illnesses endure into today, and many more of our family members continue to battle with the effects of those tests which took place over 50 years ago.

We Marshallese grow up with this history and these stories.... Not just stories of cancer, but also stories of babies born with no limbs, of stillbirths and thyroid problems, of families starving on outer atolls after being displaced from their own homes, stories of ash that fell from the sky that looked like snow. And then there are the stories of the land we lost—the beautiful bountiful Bikini atoll.

... Despite all of these trials, however, our people have survived. And we continue to resist.

... I look forward to remembering the legacy of those who've not only survived but also resisted. I am proud to say I come from a line of activists who have fought against these atrocities.[130]

Taking up related themes, her Nuclear Survivors' Day testimony in March 2016 appeared as follows, highlighting ongoing disagreements regarding basic arithmetic and human life and featuring what she has on another occasion referred to as "complex narratives of disappearing islands":

At the ceremony yesterday the US Ambassador stated in his speech that, "full and final compensation has been paid." This is untrue. According to the Nuclear Claims Tribunal over $2 billion ... are still owed to the Marshallese people. Justice has not been served. But even if it was, at least in the form of monetary payment—would it be enough? Would it be enough now that we are without our islands? With climate change we ask the same questions—how much money will they shove at us to keep us quiet—to convince the world there never was a Marshall Islands?[131]

Caribbean-Pacific Islanders on the Mississippi, Remembering Los Alamos

In 1925 the US American illustrator Ralph Barton discussed Covarrubias's work as a caricaturist of US life: "Covarrubias arrived in New York a little over two years ago.... He began at once to giggle at us.... To be seen through so easily by a boy of twenty, and by a Mexican, . . . an outlander and a heathen, was a bitter but corrective pill."[132] If to Barton a Mexican was an outlander and a heathen, what did it mean to be Mexican in Covarrubias's eyes? As he later indicated in the key to his *Peoples of the Pacific* mural, the "*Mexican* [is] typified by a mestizo (Spanish and Indian)" as embodied by "the Agrarian Revolutionary hero Emiliano Zapata."[133] Indeed, in the wake of the Mexican Revolution and before moving to the United States, the young Covarrubias had participated in the cultural ferment promoted by Mexican minister of education José Vasconcelos, who wanted Mexico to "find its essential personality" by "reacquainting itself with the Mexican Indian"; Covarrubias became part of the "brigade of painters who volunteered as teachers" at "open-air schools, whose emphasis [had been expanded] to include the line drawing and color appreciation employed by Mexico's primitive artists."[134] Covarrubias, then, developed his early sense of Mexicanity in dialogue with the cultural galvanization promoted by Vasconcelos, who at the time was working out the thoughts he would shortly thereafter publish in his famous 1925 essay "La raza cósmica" (The cosmic race), which indefatigably discusses conditions on the American "continent" and endorses mestizaje, or racial mixture, as key to bringing about the existence of a "new humanity," key to "the creation of . . . the ultimate race, the cosmic race."[135] On these points, Vasconcelos was a direct inspiration for Anzaldúa's *Borderlands/La Frontera*, which riffs on "La raza cósmica" for its subtitle, *The New Mestiza*, while the terrestrial quality of its border*lands* paradigm aligns with Vasconcelos's overwhelmingly continental analysis. Directly citing Vasconcelos's "La raza cósmica" as offering a "theory . . . of inclusivity" involving "racial, ideological, cultural and biological cross-pollinization," Anzaldúa asserts that the "new *mestiza* consciousness . . . is a consciousness of the Borderlands."[136]

If Covarrubias and Anzaldúa shared Vasconcelos as an influence, however, Covarrubias did not share in Anzaldúa's land-oriented view of Mexicanity, nor did he share Vasconcelos's belief, earnestly reiterated throughout "La raza cósmica," that the Indigenous peoples of Latin America were a remnant of the lost continent of Atlantis.[137] Rather, Covarrubias should be understood as a figure of Mexicanity's border*waters*, borderwaters in which borders become the passageways of a transhemispheric and trans-Indigenous archipiélado.[138] Aligned with Te Rangihiroa and Florence "Johnny" Frisbie's narratives of trans-Indigenous contact between the Pacific and the Americas, Covarrubias in his 1954 book *The Eagle, the Jaguar, and the Serpent: Indian Art of the Americas—North America:*

Alaska, Canada, the United States asserted that many of the Americas' first peoples had contact with and indeed descended from people who arrived from the Pacific by boat. Breaking from what DeLoughrey has referred to as the larger scientific community's "refusal to recognize the maritime technologies of non-European peoples" and this refusal's consequent failure to "recogniz[e] . . . the intentional settlement of the Americas by sea rather than by the Bering Strait," Covarrubias suggested that "Melanesians, always extraordinary seamen, . . . came in waves across the ocean and landed at various places on the Pacific shores of the Americas."[139] "These seemingly fantastic theories," he stated, "are well backed by persuasive [ethnographical] arguments."[140]

Complementing these theories of American settlement from a region overlapping with the eastern reaches of Indonesia, Covarrubias gave credence to what he referred to as the "ingenious theory" of anthropologist and archaeologist Harold Sterling Gladwin, who held that the Americas had been settled in waves. As Covarrubias summarized: "The sixth and last migration, between 300 B.C. and A.D. 500, coming directly by boats across the Pacific, consisted supposedly of 'Melanesians who later turned out to be Caribs, and Polynesians who later turned out to be Arawaks.' They landed on the Pacific coast from Mexico to Peru, crossed the Isthmus of Panama, and spread to the Antilles and Florida, as well as along the coasts of Venezuela and the Guianas."[141] Drawing on Te Rangihiroa's work on Pacific-American contact, Gladwin's account had suggested that "the transpacific voyagers . . . beached their canoes in the Gulf of Tehuantepec"—some remained there and spread to other parts of the Americas by land, while "the largest and most important group" crossed the isthmus, "rebuilt their canoes and coasted northward through the eastern waters of the Gulf of Mexico."[142] Covarrubias followed Gladwin in believing that some traits "of the Mexican (Middle American) and Andean cultures are traceable to Polynesia [and] Melanesia."[143] Given that Covarrubias saw little distinction between Polynesians and Micronesians, his embrace of Gladwin's narrative in effect took Mexico as a place of sojourn and transit for Pacific Islanders, as Melanesians became Caribs and Polynesians/Micronesians became Arawaks, many of whom experienced a subsequent archipelagic renaissance amid the Caribbean islands and waters.[144] Within this iteration of the borderwaters, the ocean spaces on either side of continental Mexico become nodes (places to be from), while the isthmian portion of the continent becomes a link, transforming a conventional sense of being Mexican "de este lado" (from the borderlands north of the US-Mexican border) into a model of archipelagic Greater Mexicanity that takes Mexicans and major Indigenous Caribbean groups as Pacific Islanders "de este archipiélado"—Pacific Islanders of a Greater Mexico constituted by the borderwaters, archipelagic in its routes of Pacific descent and subsequent Caribbean settlement.

Though not as avowedly fringe as Vasconcelos's assertion that Native Americans are descended from Atlantis, Covarrubias's creolized trans-Indigenous vision of an archipelagic Mexico will sound far-fetched to many twenty-first-century ears, and I am not aware that this Melanesian-Carib and Polynesian-Arawak thesis currently finds credence among any group, scholarly or otherwise. And yet, if we bracket questions of the thesis's material history, Covarrubias's stance constitutes a forerunner to the archipelagic thought of other creolized Caribbean-Pacific trans-Indigeneities, such as the 1993 collection *A New Oceania*'s use of Derek Walcott for an epigraph, or the multidecade antimilitarization collaborations between Hawai'i and Puerto Rico, or Glissant's posited correspondence between "the reality of archipelagos in the Caribbean or the Pacific" in his creole-centric outlinings of Relation.[145] Covarrubias's notion of an archipelagic Greater Mexico imagines the Caribbean and the Pacific as corresponding archipiélados, a reminder that what Yolanda Martínez-San Miguel has discussed as "archipelagic Mexico" need not be considered solely a formation of European colonialism in the Caribbean.[146] Archipelagic Mexico may also gain worldmaking critical purchase via an artist whom Limón has named an important figure of Greater Mexico, at the intersection of Caribbean and Pacific creolite and Indigeneity.

Within this version of archipelagic Mexico, Covarrubias sent the Pacific Islanders of the Caribbean "paddl[ing] their way up the Mississippi" (see fig. 3.18).[147] They landed on North America's shore and traced the impossible sinuosities of the Mississippi's delta up into the river's infinitely branching watershed. And thus the Indigenous geometries of Marshall Islands stick charts melded into the Caribbean's fractal geometries, as discussed by Glissant, who insisted that "the archipelago ... is fractal," a place where a dedication to "archipelagic thought" takes us up into the fractal inlets and into the rivers, where we come "to know the rocks of the rivers, assuredly the smallest of both the rocks and the rivers."[148] Indeed, the map of Indigenous American cultural currents that Covarrubias created for *The Eagle, the Jaguar, and the Serpent* is consistent with this narrative, taking the Pacific Islanders of the Caribbean past the Rio Grande's sandy delta ("the margin of the sea" as imagined by Paredes) and up into

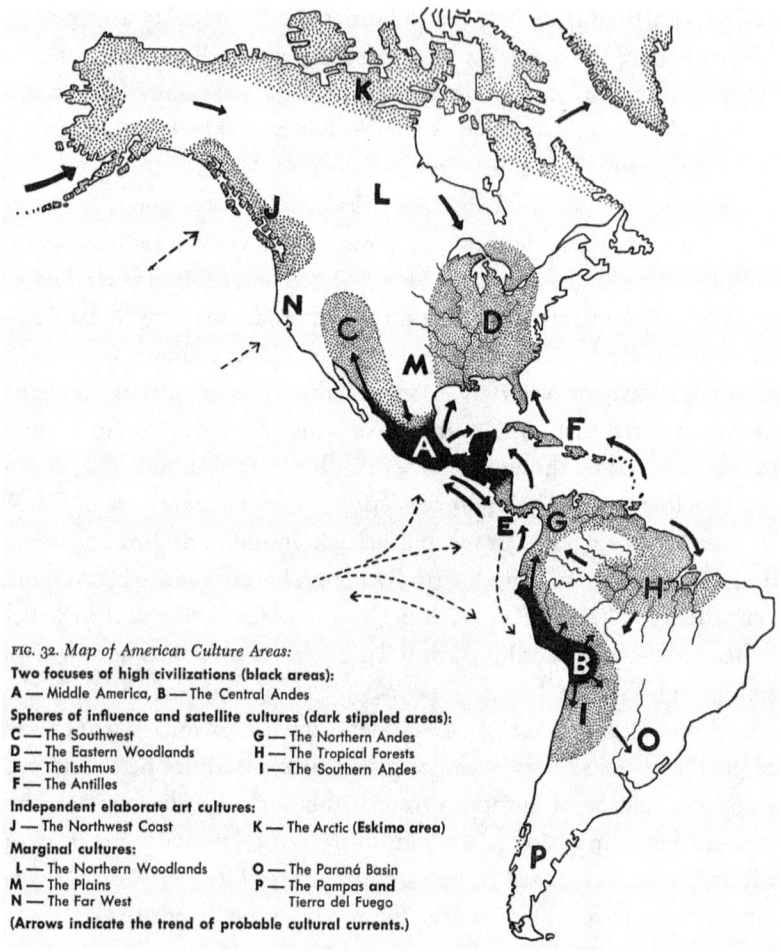

FIG. 32. *Map of American Culture Areas:*
Two focuses of high civilizations (black areas):
A — Middle America, B — The Central Andes
Spheres of influence and satellite cultures (dark stippled areas):
C — The Southwest
D — The Eastern Woodlands
E — The Isthmus
F — The Antilles
G — The Northern Andes
H — The Tropical Forests
I — The Southern Andes
Independent elaborate art cultures:
J — The Northwest Coast
K — The Arctic (**Eskimo** area)
Marginal cultures:
L — The Northern Woodlands
M — The Plains
N — The Far West
O — The Paraná Basin
P — The Pampas **and** Tierra del Fuego
(Arrows indicate the trend of probable cultural currents.)

FIGURE 3.18 — Miguel Covarrubias's "Map of American Culture Areas." Arrows on the map indicate Covarrubias's belief that portions of Mexico and South America were settled from the Pacific, with derivative populations launching into the Gulf of Mexico and Caribbean and from there traveling to Florida as well as up the Mississippi River. These aspects of Covarrubias's map are based on a map in Harold Sterling Gladwin's *Men out of Asia* (252). Gladwin wrote that "some of these Polynesian-Arawaks," after crossing the isthmus, "coasted along the shores of Colombia and Venezuela and . . . settled in the Amazon basin. Others circled up through the Lesser Antilles and so to Puerto Rico, Santo Domingo and Cuba, while still others reached the southern coasts of North America and the east coast of Mexico," with some of "these voyagers to the United States from the Antilles . . . paddl[ing] their way up the Mississippi" (317, 320). Unlike Covarrubias's map, Gladwin's map has an arrow suggesting that in addition to paddling up the Mississippi, these travelers may have paddled up the Rio Grande. From Miguel Covarrubias, *The Eagle, the Jaguar, and the Serpent: Indian Art of the Americas—North America: Alaska, Canada, the United States* (1954; repr., New York: Alfred A. Knopf, 1967), 71. Courtesy of María Elena Rico Covarrubias.

the Mississippi River, where they remain experts in the swell-island geometries of the river's fractal currents, with their navigational knowledge applicable to islands and currents they had never before seen. Here on the Mississippi they become fellow travelers with, and to my knowledge no less fictional than, Huck and Jim, whose mythic status on the river has mediated Limón's imagination of an este lado/otro lado US-Mexico borderland along the Rio Grande. Analogous to Limón's mythic Huck and Jim on the Rio Grande, Covarrubias's Caribbean-Pacific Islanders on the Mississippi might be taken as mythic, attaining symbolic and explanatory power regarding the interlap of borderlands and borderwaters, symbolic and explanatory vis-à-vis a sense of finding the archipelagic in strange, landed places.[149]

To access one such strange place, and as a mirror image of Limón's critically useful transportation of Huck and Jim from the Mississippi to the Rio Grande, we might permit Covarrubias's Caribbean-Pacific Islanders of the Mississippi, as they mythologize the interlap between borderlands and borderwaters, to point us toward a site adjacent to the Rio Grande: Los Alamos, New Mexico, a city on the Pajarito Plateau. The area was Tewa before it was Mexican, and Mexican before it was US American, even as it continues to be all of these at once.[150] One of Los Alamos's main thoroughfares is Trinity Drive, a name that fits with Greater Mexican Catholicism throughout the US Southwest. But Los Alamos's Trinity Drive is a two-minute drive from the east entrance checkpoint for the main campus of Los Alamos National Laboratory (LANL), which produced Trinity Drive's namesake, the bomb for the first-ever nuclear explosion, code-named Trinity and detonated in the New Mexican desert in July 1945.[151] From the checkpoint, it is another two minutes to a street that, unlike Trinity Drive, would feel like a non sequitur in any other borderland town: Bikini Atoll Road, where LANL's main general warehouse is located and which received its name by virtue of LANL's role in turning Bikini into a disappeared atoll, giving rise to stories and lives in which babies are born without limbs and radioactive ash falls like snow.[152] Does the appearance of the term *Bikini* on this street sign memorialize Marshall Islanders' stories? Or does the street sign's quotidian reference to the atoll constitute what Teresia K. Teaiwa once called "a celebration and a forgetting of the nuclear power that strategically and materially marginalizes and erases the living history of Pacific Islanders"?[153] Whatever the case, it is here that the borderlands and the borderwaters interlap, as Jetñil-Kijiner's testimony converges with the *testimonio* of Myrriah Gómez, a

Nuevomexicana scholar and activist who was born and raised in northern New Mexico's Pojoaque Valley, a place with many residents who commute across the Rio Grande to work at LANL.[154] Gómez tells that in 1942 her paternal great-grandparents were evicted from their ranch to make way for the lab. She tells that her cousin, a lifelong LANL employee, was the "victim of a nuclear spill" and was buried at age forty-one.[155] She tells that her "grandpa cleaned the tools that were used on plutonium and uranium and, consequently, died of colon cancer."[156] If borderlands activists and thinkers have sought to decolonize the phrase *Remember the Alamo*, then I would take Gómez's important work, which effectively directs readers to *remember Los Alamos*, as going beyond even her own framing of Los Alamos as "a borderlands region based on atomic science."[157] Gómez's work to remember Los Alamos takes us to a site of interlapping borderwaters and borderlands. Here we see entanglements across thousands of miles and, at the atomic level, between the radioactive borderwaters of Bikini Atoll and the nuclear borderlands of Trinity fame. Here we see an archipelagic world in which the oceans and seas will connect us and, as such, as Sukarno warned at Bandung, an archipelagic world in which "the oceans and the seas will [not] protect us." The entangled and entangling lines between the borderlands and borderwaters are fractal, natural-cultural. They are lines of trans-Indigenous survivance and resistance. They are geoformally analogous tracks through the water, wakes tracing a land-water archipiélado. These lines between borderwaters and borderlands are not to be interpreted as boundaries.

CHAPTER FOUR

Fractal Temporality on Vulnerable Foreshores

When Are You From? . . . No, When Are You *Really* From?

While Miguel Covarrubias's *Pageant of the Pacific* murals were on central display at Pacific House during the Golden Gate International Exposition, his friend and fellow Mexican muralist Diego Rivera worked elsewhere on Treasure Island, in the Palace of Fine and Decorative Arts near the island's southwest corner, as part of the world's fair's *Art in Action* exhibition. Before the eyes of interested fairgoers, Rivera was painting an immense mural titled *Pan American Unity*. As Rivera painted, standing high up on a scaffold, the Berkeley-educated US American artist Miné Okubo had a role as staff for the project, standing "down below, near the bottom demonstrating and answering questions of the spectators."[1] Meanwhile, as Okubo stood below Rivera's ongoing work on the transnational and transspatial conjoining of what he called "the North and . . . the South on this continent," the ground below Okubo—the island—was still lower, an entity whose creation spoke less of transspatial visions and more to questions of the transtemporal.[2]

In 1940, as Okubo worked on Treasure Island, she was standing on ground that had not existed before 1936, when the US Army Corps of Engineers began the project of dredging the island up out of San Francisco Bay, transforming Yerba Buena Shoals "from its age-old depth of 2 to 26 feet below sea level to an elevation of 13 feet above mean low water."[3] In giving rise to the four-hundred-acre island on which the fair took place, the corps spent over a year and a half using a total of eleven dredges as they pumped twenty million cubic feet of sand from the bottom of the bay into the seawalls that had been constructed to contain the island. And yet, as one contemporaneous account offered, "more than black sand spurted from the ... discharge pipes, for the dredge cutters were disturbing quiet depths that had rested inviolate through geological ages. Teeth and tusks of extinct and fearsome mammoths, more than 250,000 and perhaps a million years lost in antiquity, came through. Fossilized vegetable remains, peat ... fish and shell-fish by the million gushed into the fill; the seagulls made short work of the edibles."[4]

Okubo, then, was standing on ground that did not exist as orderly layers of geologic strata laid down in diachronic procession over the course of aeons, as, for instance, the cutting of the Colorado River has made visible in the Grand Canyon. Rather, the ground of Treasure Island existed as a dredged-up shuffling of times, a polychronic stew of geologic ages in which deep and shallow temporalities converged as fossilized mammoth bones of the Pliocene or Pleistocene settled beside fossilized vegetable remains of uncertain age as well as the remains of contemporary shellfish and fish that were killed in the process of dredging, all mixed with sand rich with microfossils of benthic (bottom-dwelling) diatoms and foraminifers, as well as alluvial deposits from rivers.[5] Okubo, looking up, answered questions about an in-progress mural dedicated to transspatial conjunction across nations and continents, but the polychronic ground on which she stood, a site of trans*temporal* conjunction, apparently called forth no questions from the spectators nor answers from Okubo.

This attentiveness to the transnational over the transtemporal is evocative of recent commentary from Rita Felski, who has noted "the rich resources available" to literary and cultural critics "for conceptualizing space," as contrasted with the "flimsiness of our temporal frameworks." Felski has pointed toward the ways in which transnational spatial heuristics have "challeng[ed] notions of the discrete, self-contained spaces of nation" but has wondered whether "similar models might help us explore the mystery of transmission across time."[6] Of course, inasmuch as the nation-state has never been an atemporal spatial unit, neither has literary and cultural criticism's suite of transnational heuristics functioned in the absence of temporal considerations.[7] And yet transnational critical impulses have frequently given rise to "alternate geographies" (e.g., the transatlantic, the hemispheric, the transpacific, the circum-Caribbean, the borderlands) that may privilege the spatial while giving shorter shrift to or even bracketing the temporal in their work to dislodge the nation from its "default position" within modes of critical analysis.[8] Against this tendency to bracket the temporal, recent years have seen what Mark McGurl calls a "new cultural geology," by which he means "a range of theoretical and other initiatives that position culture in a time-frame large enough to crack open the carapace of human self-concern, exposing it to the idea, and maybe even the fact, of its external ontological preconditions, its ground."[9]

For those who have thought with and about archipelagic and oceanic spaces, the watery and shifting quasi-ground of the shoreline has been a temporal pressure point. On one hand, Benoit Mandelbrot, in his island- and shoreline-oriented innovations of fractal geometry, proceeded in ways that bracketed the question of time. Recall that Mandelbrot's projected measurement of the fractal and infinite coastline hinges on the coast's observation "when the tide is low and the waves are negligible," a suspension of the waves' and tides' temporal cycles that permits the human to follow the coast "down to finer details by harnessing a mouse, then an ant, and so forth," revealing that on an atemporal coast "the distance to be covered continues to increase with no limit."[10] In imagining a scenario in which the human may harness infinitely smaller critters to trace the spatiality of a coast's fractal subbays and subpeninsulas to the nth degree, Mandelbrot brackets the coastline's equally fractal temporalities, its repetitive and multiscalar variations across time via the terrain's recurrent interactions with liquidity's self-similar ripples, waves, tides, floods, and (on geotemporal scales) glacial and tectonic sea-level changes. And yet on the other hand, working contrary to Mandelbrot's inclination to suspend the question of temporality as it relates to the coast, the coastline's fractal temporalities have found uptake throughout this study, as Florence "Johnny" Frisbie has imagined a North American continent submerged, as Zora Neale Hurston and Gilles Deleuze have envisioned hills and mountains as islands that are only provisionally dry, and as I have discussed borderwaters as existing vis-à-vis the shore's temporally fractal geometry. These same temporo-fractal qualities of the shore have been fundamental to theoretical models of human history as well as to models of post- and nonhuman being. Such models range from Michel Foucault's famous narrative of "man [as] a recent [nineteenth-century] invention" and his projection that "man would be erased, like a face drawn in sand at the edge of the sea," to John R. Gillis's narrative of a "human shore" spanning the 200,000-year existence of the species *Homo sapiens*, to Edward Kamau Brathwaite's coastal revision of Hegelian dialectical history as "tidalectics," to Ian Bogost's narrative of "speculative realism" as the name for "a moment when the epistemological tide [of Kantian correlationism] ebbed, revealing the iridescent shells of realism," the luminous shells of being that exists independent of "human access."[11] Archipelagic thinking's borderwaters framework, then, is chronotopic, "temporally shifting and spatially splayed"—that is, it constitutes equally, and in interdependent ways, a critical geography *and* a mode of thinking through critical temporalities.[12]

Although questions about Rivera apparently invited Okubo to look up toward the mural's transnational view of the Americas, another set of questions from the onlookers invited Okubo to look down, ultimately toward polychronic transtemporalities similar to those instantiated by Treasure Island. According to the accounts of two different interviewers who spoke with Okubo about her work on Treasure Island, "many spectators asked her what nationality she was. To alleviate the boredom she occasionally palmed herself off as [Rivera's] fifth child by a third marriage, or made up some similar story."[13] Okubo was US American—born a citizen of the United States in 1912 in Riverside, California—but in the eyes of the US government, her status as nisei (a child born in the Americas to Japanese immigrants, or issei) canceled the constitutional rights entailed by her citizenship in the wake of Japan's December 7, 1941, attack on Pearl Harbor.[14] President Franklin Delano Roosevelt's February 1942 Executive Order 9066 resulted in the imprisonment of some 110,000 US residents of Japanese descent, about two-thirds of whom were US citizens by virtue of being born in the United States, and about one third of whom were ineligible for citizenship due to US laws that discriminated against immigrants from Asia.[15] Okubo's imprisonment took her from her home in the San Francisco Bay area to a temporary internment camp at the nearby Tanforan Racetrack and finally to the more permanent Topaz internment camp in central Utah (euphemistically called the Central Utah Relocation Center). Executive Order 9066 was intent on removing people of Japanese descent from the West Coast, and indeed it removed Okubo from the twentieth century's seaward coastlines—even removing her from rivers that flowed into the sea, given the internment camp's situation within what is known as the Great Basin, an area whose watersheds and rivers have been landlocked or endorheic for tens of thousands of years.[16] The fairgoers' question (*Where are you from?*), combined with Roosevelt's loaded and cutting follow-up question (*No, where are you* really *from?*), took Okubo into the Great Basin, into that geologically rich basin of the 1981 book *Basin and Range*. In this book, and while writing of this basin, John McPhee coined the now critically popular term *deep time*, of which he explained, "Numbers do not seem to work well with regard to deep time. Any number above a couple of thousand years—fifty thousand, fifty million—will with nearly equal effect awe the imagination to the point of paralysis."[17] If in the eyes of the US government, the race-based forced removal of Okubo and her fellow prisoners was designed to take people of Japanese descent far from the Pacific Basin, the Topaz internment camp's situation within the basin of deep-time fame relocated them to polychronic coasts and waterways of fractal temporalities, where new questions arose, shared among desert terrain, alluvial dust particles, fossilized seabeds, mountains that were once islands, grating tectonic plates, imprisoned humans, trilobite fossils, and alkali-preserved mollusk shells. These new questions were, *When are you from?* and *No, when are you really from?*

In Topaz, after a stint working for the camp newspaper, the *Topaz Times*, Okubo joined the prisoner collective that founded *Trek*, an art and literary magazine they published under the Reports Division of the Central Utah Relocation Project.[18] *Trek* had a run of three issues (December 1942, February 1943, and June 1943), becoming the forerunner of internment camp magazines published subsequently, including *All Aboard!* (later published in Topaz), *Tulean Dispatch Magazine* (published in Tule Lake, northern California), and *The Pen* (published in Rohwer, Arkansas).[19] The editorial collective disbanded, as many of its young members successfully relocated, finding employment outside of the camp, while the majority of prisoners—especially the elderly and families with younger children—remained at Topaz throughout the war years.[20]

Although it lasted only seven months by the calendar, *Trek* exhibited sustained interest in deep and exotic temporalities, ancient landscapes, and cyclic waterscapes whose contemplation would make a longer print run, of, say, seven years or seven decades or seven centuries, seem equally blip-like. Indeed, just as much as it was a literary and artistic magazine, *Trek* was a magazine dedicated to narrating Topaz's place within geologic time, remarkable as a key to the transtemporal preoccupations exhibited by many aesthetic and expressive items produced by Topaz's prisoners, which have today become components of collections, including at the Topaz Museum, located in the town of Delta, sixteen miles from the Topaz site. Together with these items, *Trek* is also a key to a *postcontinental* engagement with the new cultural geology, a designation within which McGurl includes the intertwined threads of speculative realism and object-oriented ontology (OOO), whose preoccupations have been to a large degree extensions of Eurocentric conversations in *continental* philosophy.[21] Indeed, *Trek*'s work in thinking through and with material temporalities positions it as engaging in what the decolonial thinker Nelson Maldonado-Torres has called a "post-continental" philosophical mode, or a mode that distances itself from continental philosophy's "commitment with European continentality as a project as well as Eurocentric conceptions of space and time." Taking *philosophy* to "refer . . . to an activity that humans do when they face their environment with a theoretical attitude, and not only to the legacy of a particular culture," postcontinental philosophy permits "a new set of metaphors and lived realities . . . to acquire existential and epistemological significance, such as the border, the archipelago and the sea."[22] Within a postcontinental approach that takes Topaz and *Trek* as part of the borderwaters, cyclic archipelagic and aquatic temporalities become inundations and desiccations of ontological and epistemological grounds, while thinking and experiencing and being and becoming within geologic and hydrologic time and materiality emerge as modes of philosophizing regarding, to borrow language from the first issue of *Trek*, "the vulnerability to which man becomes heir in the very act of trying to fashion invulnerability for himself."[23] *Trek* and Topaz's many aesthetically minded prisoners engaged the materiality of geologic time in a mode that Wai Chee Dimock might call "weak theory," characterized by the "leakiness" of humbler and contingent generalizations that do "not aspire to full occupancy in the analytic field."[24]

In describing these Topazans' noncontinental work in weak theorizing, this chapter brings specific focus to what archipelagic thought offers as a means of approaching transtemporal dimensions, not only of human cultures across time but of human cultures' imbrications—and humankind's place—within geologic timescales that range from the relatively recent Pleistocene of about twelve thousand years ago to the much more distant Cambrian of about half a billion years ago. Indeed, as this chapter's two main sections outline, if *Trek* emplotted Topazans as living during the "age of man," the camp's writers and artists engaged in beachcombing tens of thousands of years, and even hundreds of millions of years, after the fact, using mollusk shells from a Pleistocene lake and trilobite fossils from the Cambrian ocean to devise expressive forms—ranging from poetry to brooches to carved stones—that emplotted Japanese American imprisonment in relation to pasts of a geologically longue durée.[25] Contemplating such emplotments conduced toward urgent questions of human vulnerability, ranging from the problem of human vulnerability within a country whose racist mythologies had trumped its Constitution to the problem of humankind's vulnerability and indeed apparent nothingness within the expanse of geologic time.[26] In addressing these problems, and particularly in finding human and perhaps metaphysical meaning in what otherwise might devolve into a nihilistic human response to governmental and geologic oblivion, Topaz's writers and artists produced works that showcase philosophical engagements with foreshores (areas between high and low tide) on which iridescent shells (whether of mollusks, trilobites, or human philosophy) afford access to multilayered and fractal temporalities. Within the repetitions and multiscalar mise en abymes of these temporalities, the camp's suite of artistic productions constituted a collaborative philosophical inquiry among strangers from different shores—the shores of the Pleistocene, the Cambrian, and the archipelagic states of America.[27]

Examining such collaborative artistic productions in terms of foreshores and their attendant fractal temporalities and iridescent qualities does more than highlight the way temporally torqued archipelagic thought can afford visibility to the borderwaters' presence in unexpected and seemingly fixedly continental places. It does more than emphasize the way archipelagic thought has purchase within urgent discussions of human vulnerability vis-à-vis governments and very deep geologic timelines. It reveals, as highlighted in this chapter's conclusion, the ways in which, analogous to the rough edges of the spatial dimension's putatively small island, the rough edges of seemingly small temporal moments (such as three years of unconstitutional imprisonment) may unravel in infinite ways against the rough edges of geologic aeons.

Strangers on the Foreshore

In her book *Citizen 13660*, Okubo describes the setting of Topaz as a "greasewood-covered desert," a "flat, dry land which extended for miles in all directions," upon which the camp sat as a "desolate scene": "Hundreds of low black barracks covered with tarred paper ... lined up row after row."[28] It was a place where the wind whipped "the soft alkaline dirt" so that it could be "impossible to see anything through the dust."[29] From within this mise-en-scène, the first issue of *Trek* framed Topaz's present as entangled with distant geologic pasts and futurities. In the December 1942 issue's opening article, the magazine's associate editor, Taro Katayama, explained that "upon this desert-edged tract of land, Topaz as a tangible physical thing began to materialize on July 6 of this year. On that day, the first ground was broken," and "dust was the principal, the most ubiquitous, ingredient of community existence at the beginning."[30] For Katayama, it was the dust—this fundamental ingredient of existence—that could eventually sweep Topaz out of human time and back into geologic time: "A Topaz emptied of its human component would soon be reclaimed by the barrenness from which it is just beginning to emerge."[31] Yet in the same issue of *Trek* an article by Toshio Mori (a regular *Trek* contributor who went on to publish the 1949 short story collection *Yokohama, California*) averred that Topaz was more than a blip within the area's deep geologic time. Rather, Topaz was possessed of a type of metaphysical, transtemporal existence, perhaps analogous to the topaz stones found at the nearby Topaz Mountain, for which the camp was named: "Topaz is here to stay, there will be no changes on the map. Before the Japanese came there was Topaz, and there always will be a place called Topaz."[32] When was Topaz from? Was it a human blip within the Great Basin's deep time, as Katayama suggested? Was it from the beginning of existence to the end of existence, with the perduring—though still geologically transient—materiality of topaz stone as its best metaphor? What meaning could Topaz—as a place and a suite of temporalities—have for its prisoners? During its existence *Trek* was persistently dedicated to asking these questions, dedicated to looking down, looking toward stones and other lithic forms, toward what Jeffrey Jerome Cohen has called humankind's "ancient allies in knowledge making": "A rock discovered at the shoreline opens an adventure in deep time and inhuman forces: slow sedimentation of alluvium and volcanic ash, grinding tectonic shift, crushing mass and epochal compaction, infernal heat, relentless turbidity of the sea."[33] Topaz was a rock discovered on the shoreline, as *Trek* knew, as *Trek* traced.

In tracing Topaz's shorelines, *Trek* found an ally and regular contributor in Frank Beckwith, an amateur geologist and, from 1919 to 1951, the editor of the *Millard County Chronicle*, the local newspaper in Delta, Utah.[34] As *Trek* explained in introducing Beckwith, "[He] has lived in Delta for almost 30 years and probably knows more about this region than any other man around. Between issues of his paper, he has roamed this territory, collecting fossils and Indian lore. The Smithsonian Institute gave a fossil Merostome the name of *Beckwithia typa* in his honor. Many visitors to Delta from Topaz have seen his collection of minerals."[35] During its three-issue run, *Trek* published two articles in which Beckwith focused on geology: "Landmarks of Pahvant Valley" (December 1942) and "Trilobite Fossils of Antelope Springs" (June 1943).[36] These articles, together with a piece by Jim Yamada titled "Lake Bonneville" (February 1943), constitute the magazine's most prominent work in offering an etiology, or ascription of causation, for the geologic present that characterized and dominated life in Topaz: the dust, the desert, the dust, the fossils, the dust, the stones, the dust, the mountains, the dust, the shells.

Beckwith offered a survey of the area's geology in *Trek*'s first issue: "Topaz is located on the bed of former Lake Bonneville, a lake that formed in Pleistocene times (glacial period), and at that time connected with Great Salt Lake." He continued, "The entire soil of this large valley is an alluvial deposit from and in the waters of Lake Bonneville. . . . Being laid down in water accounts for the remarkable flatness of the valley." Beckwith explained that Topaz's name derived from the nearby Topaz Mountain, while the mountains closest to the camp were known as the Drum Mountains because a still-active "double geological fault" gave "rise to movement, accompanied by noise"—something "Topaz residents will hear," a "phenomenon called 'The Rumbling of the Mountains.' . . . The sound resembles heavy rocks clashing, sometimes a sharp sound, and sometimes a very dull one, like hitting rocks under water."[37] It was as if Topaz residents could anticipate an acoustic restaging of what it might have sounded like to live on Bonneville's lake bed when it was flooded rather than desiccated. Beckwith explained that elsewhere in the valley, ten miles from Topaz, was a "lava core, which still contains residual heat and joins the heated interior of the earth," while Pahvant Butte was the "large, sharp mountain to the southeast of Topaz"—formerly "an active volcano," the mountain "bears upon its sides water terraces" from ancient Lake Bonneville's fluctuating shorelines.[38] Thus, in tandem with current geologic activity that the prisoners could perceive firsthand, the valley evinced a geologic past that could be known through traces—an inactive volcano with water-formed terraces that attested to its erstwhile status as a volcanic island ("it is an island or a mountain, or both at once," in Deleuze's words) and sediment that was water-conduced alluvium or air-driven dust or both at once.[39]

In *Trek*'s February 1943 issue, editor Jim Yamada published an article offering much more extensive information on Lake Bonneville. His remarks moved from playful to informative:

The publicity on Lake Bonneville ... has been notably meager. As far as the records show, no Pleistocene news-hawk pounded out a word of copy about it. What we know of the history of Lake Bonneville today is based on the evidence of deltas, shore terraces, sedimentation, and other geological factors. But even without an eyewitness account, the ups and downs of the lake make a fascinating story.

To picture the extent of Lake Bonneville during its prime, imagine the level of Great Salt Lake rising 1000 feet. Most of Utah would be submerged: Topaz would be under 600 feet of water; the Mormon Temple in Salt Lake City, under 850 feet.

The [north-south] length of this vast Pleistocene lake extended ... a distance of 346 miles. Its extreme width ... measured 145 miles. Its coastline, exclusive of islands, was 2550 miles; and its surface area was 19,750 square miles—only a few hundred miles less than Lake Michigan.

At this level, 1000 feet above Great Salt Lake and 5200 feet above sea level, the Bonneville waves cut terraces into the surrounding cliffs. During the time the waves were carving the shoreline, the level of the lake was relatively stable, remaining within a vertical range of 20 feet. Though it oscillated close to a pass in the rim of the basin, there was no danger of overflow so long as the inflow and the evaporation were nearly equal.

But one season they weren't equal. The tributary streams brought in far more water than evaporation could accommodate, and gradually the level of the lake rose. A trickle of water overflowed through Red Rock Pass, in the northern end of Cache Valley [in what would later become Idaho].[40]

Once the trickle began, Yamada reports, it eroded the pass and "soon a torrent was racing out of the basin," flowing eventually "to the valley of the Snake River, and from there to the Pacific."[41] Owing to this outflow, Lake Bonneville dropped by 375 feet, to what is called the "Provo" level, and "the water lingered here several times longer" than it did at the previous level, with the higher terrace presently called the Bonneville shoreline and the second terrace called the Provo shoreline. From there, the lake slowly evaporated, with the Great Salt Lake as "the outstanding remnant" (see fig. 4.1). At the same time as he offered this deep-temporal geologic narrative of Bonneville's "ups and downs," of its contraction from a rival of Lake Michigan to a saline lake with less than a tenth of the surface area, he also let readers know that this was only a small portion of the geologic story: "Examination of the sediments reveals ... [that] Lake Bonneville ... was the second of two great lakes which existed in the Bonneville Basin," the

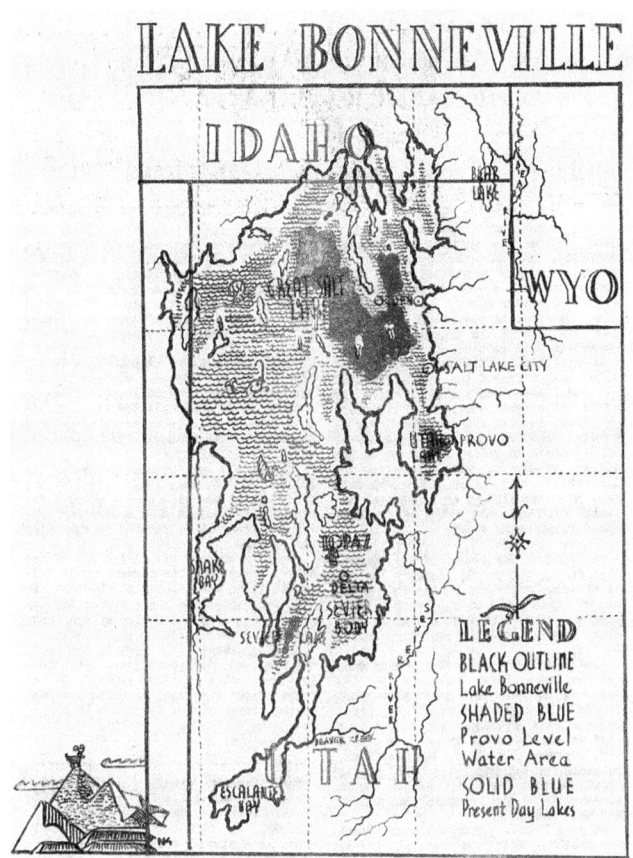

FIGURE 4.1 — The outline of Lake Bonneville at its greatest extent, as well as the Provo water level and the water level of the Great Salt Lake. The Provo water level is shaded blue (shaded gray as reproduced here), and the Great Salt Lake appears in solid blue (solid gray as reproduced here). This illustration accompanied Jim Yamada's article "Lake Bonneville." Signed NK, it was likely drawn by Nobuo Kitagaki, listed in this issue of *Trek* as an assistant on the magazine's staff. *Trek*, February 1943, 36.

prior lake "last[ing] five times longer" than the lake whose history he had just narrated.[42]

Yamada's narrative of Lake Bonneville, including its multiple shorelines and the ancestral lake that preceded it, embeds Topaz—whether as a blip or as eternal—within what I think of as the fractal temporality of the foreshore. The term *foreshore* is a name for that part of the shore "which lies between the high- and low-water marks," traditionally a reference to the area that exists between the temporal intervals of high and low tide.[43] The

FRACTAL TEMPORALITY · 169

foreshore, then, has been defined by the very temporal flux that Mandelbrot abandoned when he sought to calm the sea, so to speak, long enough for the human to harness an ant to trace the coast's fractal geometry. And yet, in terms of what I am discussing as fractal temporality, the foreshore that Mandelbrot bracketed is the crux. Attentive to fractal temporalities, a multiscalar reading of the foreshore reconsiders the traditional attachment to defining the foreshore specifically in reference to a moon-linked tide that waxes and wanes and instead generalizes the foreshore as existing anytime water waxes and wanes according to cyclic temporalities. Fractal in their self-similar repetitions and multiscalar relation to each other, foreshores would exist vis-à-vis the temporal intervals seen in ripples' blink-like blips on a pebble, chreodic interactions of water with the roughness of larger stones, waves' surgings and recedings on the rocks, and the interval between high and low tide, of course—but also up through longer temporal cycles such as, in different times and places, tsunamis, storm surges, and sea-level changes based on glacial cycles and tectonics as well as climate change and other human and inhuman factors.[44]

Within the Great Basin, and by means of Yamada's adumbration of an ancient lake that existed before Bonneville, the entirety of the basin, ranging from the mid-twentieth-century shoreline of the Great Salt Lake to the Pleistocene shoreline of Lake Bonneville, becomes a foreshore calibrated to millennia and even millions of years, as readers may imaginatively retroject a succession of massive lakes filling and evaporating before Bonneville, even while projecting the succession of lakes that will come after Bonneville within the basin. Other writers familiar with the basin have spoken of Bonneville as "just one in the succession of bodies of water to inhabit the Bonneville Basin over the last fifteen million years" or have imagined the basin inundated again by "the floodwaters of a resurgent Lake Bonneville," interlaced now with ferries and ships traversing a future inland sea that has submerged older human impresses on a basin that has now become a seabed.[45] The Great Salt Lake is Bonneville's name at low tide, and Bonneville is the Great Salt Lake's name at high tide—meanwhile, all of human history within the Bonneville basin would seem to exist precariously, vulnerably, within the cyclic temporality of the foreshore between the high and low water levels. Bonneville's multimillennial foreshore resonates with Ezra Pound's 1920 description of standard intertidal "fore-shores" as "washed in the cobalt of oblivions."[46] But now, rather than Pound's tawny sand, it is human-scaled history, tumbling with the dust and everything else, that finds itself awash in oblivion's cobalt waters.

This sense of the foreshore's oblivion has a certain poetics, of course, in critical and more generally human encounters with both of the foreshore's material components, the sea and the lithic. The spatially vast sea features, for instance, at the beginning of Sigmund Freud's *Civilization and Its Discontents* as a catachresis for "the true source of religious sentiments," a "sensation of 'eternity', a feeling as of something limitless, unbounded—as it were, 'oceanic.'"[47] The cultural availability of the ocean for such deployments hinges on what Patricia Yaeger once discussed as human figurations of "the boundless sea or the oceanic sublime."[48] Meanwhile, as for the temporally vast lithic component of the foreshore, Cohen writes of the "vertiginous perspective"—hinging on an "ontological vertigo"—evoked by thinking about stone as an emissary of "geological time," a perspective that tends toward "reducing the human to its vanishing point."[49] Traditionally unbounded and vertiginous, the aqueous and the lithic come together, under the auspices of the cyclically temporal, to evoke the foreshore. And whereas either the aqueous or the lithic alone (as representative of sublime spatial or temporal expanse, respectively) might reduce human concern to oblivion or a vanishing point, the aqueous and the lithic as choreographed by and mediated through the cyclic temporalities of the foreshore admit something like a human cognizance—rather than a human annihilation—within oblivion.

On this cognizance, consider a scene I have referenced earlier in this chapter: Bogost's image of the beachcomber, representative of a suite of speculative realists and OOO thinkers, walking the intertidal foreshore and stooping at low tide to retrieve "the iridescent shells of realism," stooping to retrieve access to what the speculative realist philosopher Quentin Meillassoux (in an essay that bid the tide go out) calls "the *great outdoors*" of philosophy, "that outside which [is] not relative to us, . . . existing in itself regardless of whether we are thinking of it or not."[50] Here, in Bogost's rendering, the objects that have been central to speculative realist and OOO thought are manifest as seashells, an apt inwardly spiraling metaphor in light of Bogost's (and other OOO thinkers') drive to "take seriously the idea that all objects recede interminably into themselves."[51] And yet during this philosophical-geologic event when the high tide of correlationism has receded—when Meillassoux has cast doubt on the *correlation* between subject and object that would frame objects as existing only within the perception of a subject and subjects as existing only in their perception of objects—the shells of this noncorrelational realism are described as "iridescent."[52] On one level—and this is most likely what

Bogost intended—we might take the shells' iridescence as synonymous with what object-oriented thinkers often refer to as *the weird*, wherein *weirdness* alludes to objects' existence not in any commonsense way but in a dark and ambiguous way that "bear[s] little resemblance to the presuppositions of everyday life."[53] Rebekah Sheldon has gone so far as to describe this reliance on the category of the weird as OOO's recourse to a mode of "mysticism."[54] If so, then the philosophers in Bogost's intertidal parable have followed Indigenous and other modes of thought in taking "shells' natural pearly iridescence" as evocative of things "eerie [and] otherworldly," such that iridescence attains a "sacred" function, emerging as something like materiality's unanticipated existential or even metaphysical warrant.[55]

Metaphysical or not, iridescence is of necessity correlational, and without wishing to critique Bogost for recurring to correlation on the very beach from which the correlationist tide has ostensibly receded, I find it useful to trace iridescence's imbrications with correlation as a means of thinking through an account of some ways humans may experience temporal materiality, particularly in a postcontinental and archipelagic vein. Clearly, iridescence is an attribute that Meillassoux would refer to as a *secondary quality* (which is correlational and exists only "in my subjective relation to" the thing itself) rather than a noncorrelational *primary quality* ("existing in itself regardless of whether we are thinking of it or not").[56] If, as Meillassoux has reiterated, color is a secondary quality while wavelength is a primary quality, then iridescence, defined as "the change in hue of the colour of an object as the observer changes position, or [as] the object changes position in relation to the viewer," is a secondary quality that unfolds *through time* as correlation shimmers between the subject and the object.[57] To elucidate: consider a shell that has come into existence and grown layer by layer by means of the successive accretions of nacre (or mother-of-pearl) produced by a soft-bodied abalone; the many accretions that make up such shells create a *multilayer stack*, or a structure composed of multiple superimposed films that (multiplying many times over the effect of a single film of oil on water) function to modulate the wavelength of the light they reflect.[58] Viewing the shell, the subject perceives the multilayer stack's reflected light as color, but the color does not become iridescent until the subject and the shell move in relation to one another across time, with movement through the temporal dimension serving to multiply the subject's angles of perception and thereby producing the characteristic shimmer of iridescence.

I join with Bogost and others in retrieving this shell from the foreshore, but I am picking it up for a different reason. Picking up the iridescent shell permits a better view, within the arena of the new cultural geology, of the way archipelagic thought facilitates and may become key to transtemporal discussions. This view comes into focus in *Trek* and the work of several Topaz artists as what I call *geotemporal iridescence*, an effect that is, consistent with Paul Giles's reference to archipelagic thought's tendency toward "temporal accretion," produced as present-day viewers access places or objects via multiple geotemporal layers or accretions, an experience that becomes particularly vivid in relation to the modulating shallow and deep temporal cycles of the foreshore.[59] As with the iridescence that enchants Bogost's object-oriented beachcomber, geotemporal iridescence tends to attain, if not a full-blown metaphysics, a metaphysical effect that, even as deep time radically deflates perceptions of human grandeur, converts that deflation into human understanding and even meaning. In picking up this iridescent shell, I am not suggesting that the prisoners at Topaz were theorizing temporality in ways that systematically or formally engaged with philosophy as traditionally defined. However, one need not be engaged with continental philosophy (either Kantian correlationism or postcorrelationist thought) to engage in archipelagic theorizing that has implications for how we understand modes of accessing geologic relationalities among humans and nonhumans across vast spans of time. If the US Virgin Islands scholar Barbara Christian has classically written of a Black and noncontinental "theorizing... in narrative forms, in... stories..., in riddles and proverbs, in the play with language," then I would suggest that *Trek* and Topaz's aesthetically minded prisoners theorized, analogously, by means of poems and stones, mollusk shells and multimillennial and aeonic foreshores, fossils and island-spangled oceans.[60]

In *Trek*'s first issue, Taro Katayama published a poem titled "Nightmare," which, in evoking a poetic setting that mimics the transtemporal situation of Topaz on the bottom of Lake Bonneville, arrives at a quality of geotemporal iridescence.[61] "Nightmare" recounts a dreamscape in which an unnamed persona "saw familiar sunlit skies / Darken with sudden argosies [or ships] that made / A screaming hell of all the plain below." Arriving from the "red horizon's rim," the unnamed "foe [is] approaching" in "wave on ominous wave." Here, as the ships proceed from the rim of the basin across the sky, they glide high across Bonneville's water level within the basin, prescient of and perhaps an inspiration for a scene in Julie Otsuka's 2002 novel of imprisonment at Topaz, in which a character dreams of looking up and seeing the surface of "the ancient . . . lake floating above the floor of the desert."⁶² This is not a re-creation of the sky as the surface of Lake Bonneville—rather, it is an evocation of what I in chapter 2 referred to as ontological undecidability. It is a sky or a water level or both at once. It is wind-driven dust or water-deposited alluvium or both at once. Topaz is situated on a flat plain or a benthic zone or both at once. And yet the very props—the ships—that evoke what may feel like the ontological anachronism of Topaz as located on a flat valley floor or a lake bed or both at once would also seem to be anachronistic, layering anachronism upon anachronism. Just as (to borrow from Yamada) no "Pleistocene news-hawk" wrote a word about Lake Bonneville, Bonneville's Pleistocene existence presumably saw no human-made ships plying its waves—more likely, any ships on a lake in this basin would be at home on a future and resurgent Bonneville. But this is a dream—of the future or of the past or of both at once. These proliferating temporal layers—transparent and stacked in a way that conveys attributes of what we might call pasts, presents, and futures—appear anachronistic to the degree that we accede to "a notion of 'wrong time'" that hinges on perceiving "time as sequential and forward moving" according to "a Western, Enlightenment conceptualization of history as empty, homogenous, and linear."⁶³ Depending on time's apprehension as tidalectical (rather than dialectical), however, this filmy multilayer material engagement with time produces not anachronism but geotemporal iridescence—offering, with its shimmering temporalities, what seems to function as an existential warrant for human meaning amid the simultaneity of viewable pasts, presents, and futures.

In "Nightmare," Katayama's persona sees the ships arriving and leaves his friends on the plain to fight and die while he himself gains "a trembling refuge in the hills," watching "from havening hill . . . while slaughter grew / Below him on the plain." The nearby hills, if one looks at the map accompanying Yamada's article on Lake Bonneville, were instantiations of Deleuze's temporally iridescent island or mountain or both at once (see fig. 4.1). Topaz the town lies at the bottom of Lake Bonneville, south of Keg Mountain/Keg Island and east of a long north-south-running island that is a composite of the Drum Mountains in the south and Topaz Mountain in the north. In fact, as Katayama noted in the lead article in the issue of *Trek* in which "Nightmare" appears, these hills/islands had only recently been the site of "a dramatic and successful search for a resident lost in the mountains," a reference to the three-day search for the

Topaz prisoner Kozo Fukagai, who became lost during an administration-approved expedition "to Mt. Topaz, 36 miles northwest of the City, to gather Christmas materials."[64]

Whatever the "Christmas materials" might have been, such an expedition, it would seem, would have been noniridescent—that is, the expedition would have been to Topaz Mountain rather than to both Topaz Mountain and Topaz Island at once. And yet such treks to the hills could be treks to specific foreshores, treks to places where prisoners could engage in beachcombing—not searching the foreshore between waves or tides but rather combing the foreshore between the Bonneville basin's massive inundations, searching for the shells of Bonneville's and other ecologies. In 1968, with both benevolent and racialized overtones, longtime Delta resident and short-story writer Dee S. Sanford remembered the internment years: "During this time there were interned eight thousand seven hundred and seventy-eight Japanese. They covered the valley like small dark ants, creeping everywhere, hunting for something to occupy their time and talents. They uncovered the sea shells in the mountains of Swazy [Swasey], Drum and Topaz. . . . Of these they fashioned jewelry to sell."[65] As later recalled by former Topaz detainee Tsuyako "Sox" Kitashima during an oral history project in the 1980s, the prisoners "found shells in the ground and bleached them. They used nail polish to tint them, and they made different kinds of jewelry with it."[66] In 1945 the *Salt Lake Tribune* offered a contemporaneous account of the prisoners' dedication to beachcombing, now on the lake bed rather than the mountains/islands:

> Where Topaz is located once was the bottom of a huge lake—and in the sands are tiny shells which patient workers sift out, much as placer miners searched for gold. At times a mile-long stretch of toilers may be seen at dawn making its way three miles north of Topaz, where the best of those shells are found. Axes, . . . sieves and odd headgear are in the line.
>
> The shells, mussel and water snail, have been preserved in the alkaline soil for thousands of years. They are washed, bleached, sorted and tinted before being made into delicate ornaments and find a ready market.

The *Tribune* explained that one of the prisoners' "thriving industries [was] that of shell jewelry—lapel ornaments, pins, etc., of very delicate workmanship, made of infinitesimal sized shells which they harvest from the desert."[67] Speaking of some of the smallest shells, one contemporary observer stated that "oftentimes the numerous ants in the vicinity very accommodatingly brought desirable tiny shells to the surface."[68]

Similar to Katayama's persona—for whom Bonneville became a temporal overlay through a dream of ships—the prisoners understood themselves as "situated on a lake bottom" and experienced the temporal overlay, the iridescence, in the mountains/islands and plain/lake bed via the tangibility of shells.[69] These shells, which may have been deposited twenty-four millennia before Topaz's construction, were as immediately present, or "tangible for human hands," within Topaz's ecology as if they had been deposited within the past twenty-four hours by the tide or the past twenty-four seconds by a wave.[70] Certainly, the shells of Lake Bonneville were as readily made into crafts, and as readily displayed in camp hobby shows, as were the seashells of the Pacific brought to Topaz by a group of prisoners who had previously lived in a detention center in Hawaiʻi.[71] How to understand the iridescence of shells that were immediately present but also Pleistocene emissaries? In an article in *Trek*'s second issue, Katayama wrote that "modern war has, by the very vastness of its encroachments, largely dispersed the aura of wonder and mystery that used to hover over the seemingly inviolate places of the earth. The southwest Pacific was certainly one of these sanctuaries of man's yearning for the far-off and the strange. Its very place-names echoed in our minds like a litany of romance—Timor, Surabaya, Java, Samburan, Papua, Macassar, Celebes, the Coral Sea." With modern warfare—which had reframed these "place-names [as] merely points . . . in communiques"—"the spell is broken."[72] These largely Indonesian archipelagic spaces no longer seemed exotic but commonplace. Likewise, modern warfare—which had seen the proliferation of concentration camps, set up by the Empire of Japan in Indonesia and the Philippines, by the Nazis in Germany, and by Roosevelt's America largely in the western United States—had brought Topaz's prisoners, most of whom were US citizens, into the presence of strange temporalities and had disrupted those temporalities' inviolate status by means of tangible and iridescent presence—the alluvium/dust in the eye, the island/mountain in the distance, the plain/lake bed of existence, the Pleistocene shell in the hand.[73] Here the smallest Pleistocene shell could be delivered by an ant, as if somehow the shell's presence could point toward a fractal temporal apprehension analogous to Mandelbrot's ant-delivered spatial insight on the fractal shoreline.

An expert shell worker at Topaz, the issei prisoner Komaye Inouye, provided classes on shellcraft, at one point "teaching the craft to a class of fifty pupils," while at another point the class was taught by Yuriko Noda (a graduate of Tokyo Women's Art School), with prisoners using Bonneville's shells to make birds, butterflies, and cartoon characters as well as picture frames, necklaces, bracelets, earrings, and brooches that repurposed the shells as flowers and flower petals.[74] One such item became a keepsake treasured by *Trek* writer Toyo Suyemoto, who in a late-life essay pointed to a shellcraft brooch from Topaz as having "deep personal significance for me" (see fig. 4.2).[75] While she was teaching Basic English classes at the camp, an issei man approached her and whispered, "For you, *Sensei* [teacher]." Suyemoto recalled:

> I marveled at the brooch, no larger than two and three-quarters inches by two inches. It was a lapel pin he had made by twisting navy blue crepe paper into a fine strand and then weaving a miniature basket filled with small flowers composed of tiny shells gathered from the sand of our Topaz camp. Topaz was located in Utah on the dried-up bed of Lake Bonneville, once a large body of water formed in the glacial period, and the shells dug up by the camp residents were mute reminders of life that had existed centuries ago. The tinted shell flowers formed a graceful arrangement, depicting even lilies-of-the-valley fashioned from minute shells the size of pinheads.[76]

FIGURE 4.2 — The shellcraft brooch given to Toyo Suyemoto by a Basic English student, as described in her memoir. From the Toyo Suyemoto Estate, donated by James Bailey to the Topaz Museum, Delta, Utah (2005.06.13). Photograph by D. Ross Storey.

FRACTAL TEMPORALITY · 177

Later, a photograph of this brooch appeared on the cover of Suyemoto's posthumously published memoir, *I Call to Remembrance: Toyo Suyemoto's Years of Internment* (2007), marking the shells'/flowers' importance to the scene in which Suyemoto finally prepares to leave Topaz: "In [a] small box I placed part of Topaz, the shell brooch from my adult student, and the sight of the shells made me muse on the lacustrine creatures that once lived shielded in these brittle casings. The lake between the mountains had evaporated centuries ago and become this desolate place of sage and wind and dust."[77]

The brooch was constituted by flowers different from those that Suyemoto might have anticipated in her poem "Gain," the first in a series of poems she published over the course of *Trek*'s three issues:

> I sought to seed the barren earth
>   And make wild beauty take
> Firm root, but how could I have known
>   The waiting long would shake
>
> Me inwardly, until I dared
>   Not say what would be gain
> From such untimely planting, or
>   What flower worth the pain?[78]

Suyemoto at one point in her memoir invites direct comparison between the brooch and this poem, telling readers that "the earth was not as barren as my poem stated" and explaining that "even the lifeless ground yielded hidden treasures to the seekers," before illustrating this explanation by retelling the story of the "brooch made from ... shells in the form of a tiny basket holding a bouquet of flowers."[79] As shells assumed the form of flowers, the combined labor of Pleistocene mollusks and twentieth-century humans assumed the form of the green fuse that traditionally, though not in "Gain," drives the flower. And the iridescent shells/flowers became an unanticipated lithic answer—or at least a stand-in for an answer—to the poem's closing ontological and existential question regarding the type of flower that would be required to make "waiting long ... worth the pain." These lithic flowers, which Suyemoto indeed understood as the brittle casings that once shielded some of Bonneville's creatures, spoke (if mutely) a reminder of life. And even as prisoners made the shells into floral assemblages, the shells reciprocally made Suyemoto think deeply (or muse). After Roosevelt declared that US residents and citizens of Japanese ancestry would be imprisoned but before Suyemoto was imprisoned, she had engaged in thinking with the flower "petals" that grew during the spring of 1942, which to her were ephemeral and represented "delicate moments."[80] But now, in Topaz, Suyemoto engaged in thinking with flower petals that were lithic and multimillennial, emissaries between the Pleistocene mollusks that accreted these mineral casings and the twentieth-century humans who arranged and viewed the shell assemblages, equally present to both, iridescent, and somehow of existential or even metaphysical import owing to this transtemporal copresence.

Although the prisoners' co-op looked into monetizing camp hobbies through sales outside of Topaz, and although Sanford's account suggests that Topaz shellcraft was produced to sell, more reflective accounts of internment arts and crafts have framed these pursuits as activities with existential import, such that craft objects became "a physical manifestation of the art of *gaman*" (accepting "what is with patience and dignity") or a mode of creating and sustaining "a myriad of intricate and layered connections" among prisoners themselves as well as between prisoners and friends beyond the camps.[81] Adding a deep temporal dimension to these accounts, and taking seriously Suyemoto's narrative of the brooch, an understanding of shellcraft as assembled on Bonneville's foreshore with materials from that foreshore moves the shells/flowers from the arena of "what is" to the arena of what was/is/will be, from synchronic connections that are "layered" and interpersonal to anachronic connections that are also layered, accretive in ways analogous to the mollusks' creation of the shells themselves or the prisoners' assembly of shellcraft flowers.[82] The shells/flowers become material answers to Suyemoto's question regarding the type of flower that would merit a long wait—that is, a flower with petals made of shells that may be two dozen millennia old and that may last another two dozen millennia or even two dozen times longer. Suyemoto's poetry, memoir, and interactions with the ancient mollusks of Bonneville's foreshore may constitute something like what Stacy Alaimo has referred to as "thinking with sea creatures" or "thinking with marine life," an activity "in which—for humans as well as for pelagic and benthic creatures—there is, ultimately, no firm divide between mind and matter, organism and environment, self and world."[83] With regard to making and apprehending shellcraft as a mode of "thinking with" the creatures of an ancient inland sea, I would suggest that the tiny sea creature—whose accreted shell may constitute a lithic writing of its thought—is fractal temporality's answer to the harnessed ant of Mandelbrot's fractal geometry. If for Suyemoto the shells can speak (albeit mutely) a reminder of ancient life, then the accreted materiality of the shells is the lithic thought (albeit nonphenomenological thought) with which Suyemoto collaborates when she engages in the process of *thinking with*.[84] In this mode of thinking with, there is no firm divide among was, is, and will be.

Three Years of Imprisonment, Give or Take Tens of Millions of Years

Accompanying Yamada's article on Lake Bonneville are two illustrations by Okubo. One of them, centered on the basin's twentieth-century conditions, illustrates the area's mountains and the terraces cut by the lake's various Pleistocene shorelines (see fig. 4.3). Here the ground is covered by the dust/alluvium that the prisoners knew well. The other drawing, for which the article's title functions as a sort of caption, imagines the ancient watery world that gave rise to the basin's conditions during the 1940s (see fig. 4.4). In this illustration the plain/lake bed on which Topaz exists is covered by Bonneville's waters, which lap up onto the higher elevations so that one sees, to the right, what looks to be a chain of islands receding toward the horizon. In this world the water level that we now see is the sky on which ships sail in Katayama's poem "Nightmare." Meanwhile, the hills amid which the poem's persona sought refuge have become an archipelago. Clearly, the scenes are temporally iridescent in the mode of Suyemoto's shell/flower brooch. But what makes Okubo's diptych perhaps more notable is her decision to place a dinosaur—an iconically rendered brontosaurus—in the foreground of the Bonneville illustration.

The dinosaur pushes the temporal frame of Okubo's illustration—and hence the frame of Bonneville and Topaz—from a matter of tens of thousands of years to a matter of tens of millions of years. One of the sources most likely consulted by Yamada would have framed Bonneville as lasting for about 25,000 years and having receded at the end of the Pleistocene (roughly 12,000 years ago), but in the presence of a brontosaurus, Topaz attains a further iridescent overlay with the Cretaceous, which during the mid-twentieth century was held to have occurred during the period from 130 to 60 million years ago.[85] And here the foreshore of Topaz's existence opens onto the global ocean, for during the late Cretaceous period, the place now referred to as Utah was part of the shoreline for what has been termed the Western Interior Seaway (see fig. 4.5).[86] Is Okubo's dinosaur, then, look-

FIGURE 4.3 — Miné Okubo's illustration of the present-day terraces created by Lake Bonneville's ancient shorelines. *Trek*, February 1943, 37.

FIGURE 4.4 — Miné Okubo's illustration of Lake Bonneville in the process of carving the present-day terraces. *Trek*, February 1943, 35.

ing out onto the islands of Bonneville or onto the islands of the Western Interior Seaway or both at once? Is the brontosaurus walking the shoreline of Bonneville's rim or that of the continent of Laramidia or both at once?

Of course, one might caution that Okubo's dinosaur should not be taken literally—that is, should not be taken as indexing a temporal frame that comports with a scientific understanding of the geography of past geologic ages. After all, while we know the *Trek* editors and other prisoners were thinking about Bonneville and their relation to its shorelines, we have no evidence that the editors thought in scientific terms specifically regarding the Cretaceous, much less of geographic entities called Laramidia and the Western Interior Seaway, terms that were not coined until after Topaz functioned as a prison. Perhaps it was the case for Okubo that, as we see in the McPhee quotation earlier in this chapter, "any number above a

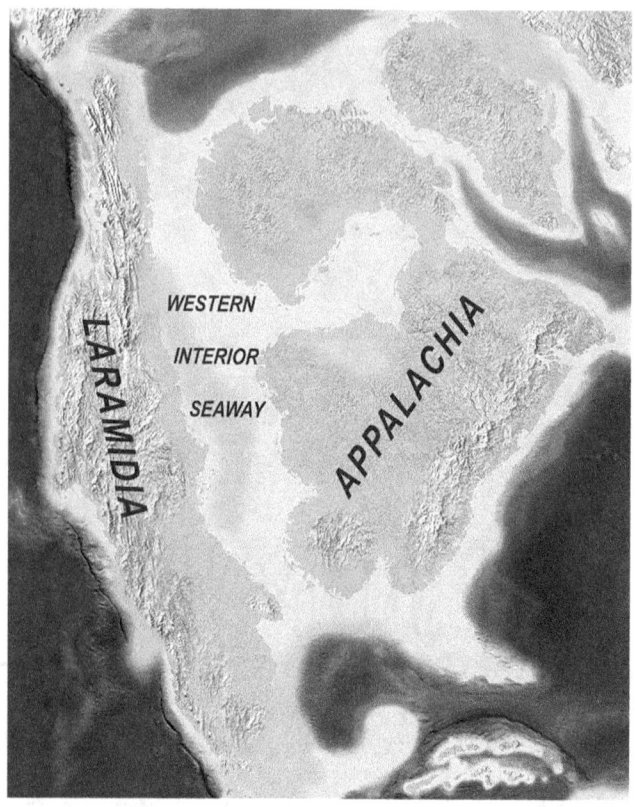

FIGURE 4.5 — Map illustrating the Western Interior Seaway, which separated the continents of Laramidia and Appalachia. From Scott D. Sampson, Mark A. Loewen, Andrew A. Farke, Eric M. Roberts, Catherine A. Forster, Joshua A. Smith, and Alan L. Titus, "New Horned Dinosaurs from Utah Provide Evidence for Intracontinental Dinosaur Endemism," *PLOS One* 5, no. 9 (September 2010).

couple of thousand years—fifty thousand, fifty million—will with nearly equal effect awe the imagination." Certainly, McPhee's observation on many humans' confusion of vast (but not equally vast) diachronic eras is borne out in Suyemoto's description of the shells/flowers as reminders of life and a lake that existed "centuries ago" rather than (more correctly) millennia ago. In a scalar way vis-à-vis Suyemoto's confusion between centuries and millennia, Bonneville's millennia might function interchangeably with the Cretaceous's tens of millions of years. But perhaps more immediately, the presence of Okubo's dinosaur could well be explained by her interest in comics, as reported in the previous issue of *Trek* by Yamada himself. During her internment, Okubo "shifted her allegiance overwhelmingly" to the comics, telling Yamada, "I feel sorry for people who don't like the funnies."[87] For decades before her internment, dinosaurs—and particularly the brontosaurus—had simply stood as a marker of that which is prehistoric. Indeed, *Trek*'s companion publication, the *Topaz Times*, was not above flattening out and caricaturing multiple deep temporalities with apparently anachronistic images of times "when the world was young" and "a man" could "kill a dinosaur" and "steal a wife."[88]

Whatever the case with the dinosaur, *Trek* editors were without a doubt thinking directly of geologic ages during which Topaz was covered not only by Bonneville but also by the ocean. In the June 1943 issue of *Trek*, the editors published an article by Beckwith titled "Trilobite Fossils of Antelope Springs," which opens as follows:

> By traveling about 50 miles westward from Topaz to Antelope Springs in the House Range, it is possible, in a manner of speaking, to go backward some 400 million years in geologic time—to go from the present age of man almost to the very dawn of evolving life on earth. For in the Cambrian period rock deposits of that locality, estimated to have been laid down at least that many millions of years ago, are to be found the fossilized remains of some of the very earliest forms of differentiated animal life known to science, notably the trilobites [see fig. 4.6].
>
> Some 400 million years ago, the Pacific Ocean covered many parts of what is now Utah, and the Antelope Springs area was under water. In that remote antiquity, even fishes had not yet evolved, and the age of reptiles, the mighty dinosaurs, was still far, far in the future. But in the shallow salt water coves of the Antelope Springs locality there lived small bug-like creatures which swam among the stalks of sea grasses, nibbling or sucking their food from the growing stems. These were the trilobites.[89]

Pointing Topaz's prisoners toward a fossil-rich area that would later attract Niles Eldredge during the same decade in which he published, with Stephen Jay Gould, the landmark evolutionary theory of "punctuated equilibria," Beckwith's description permitted the Pacific's aeonic foreshore to bring the "age of man" and Cambrian ocean ecology into a relation of geotemporal iridescence.[90] Beckwith continued, "The Antelope Springs area at that time was, as we have said, under ocean water. Limestone was forming and deposits were being washed in. Creatures died. Their remains fell upon the mud ooze of their habitat, were covered by the deposit of the next freshet, preserving them from bacteria and rot, and so became fossilized. These fossilized corpses of once living animals constitute a sort of

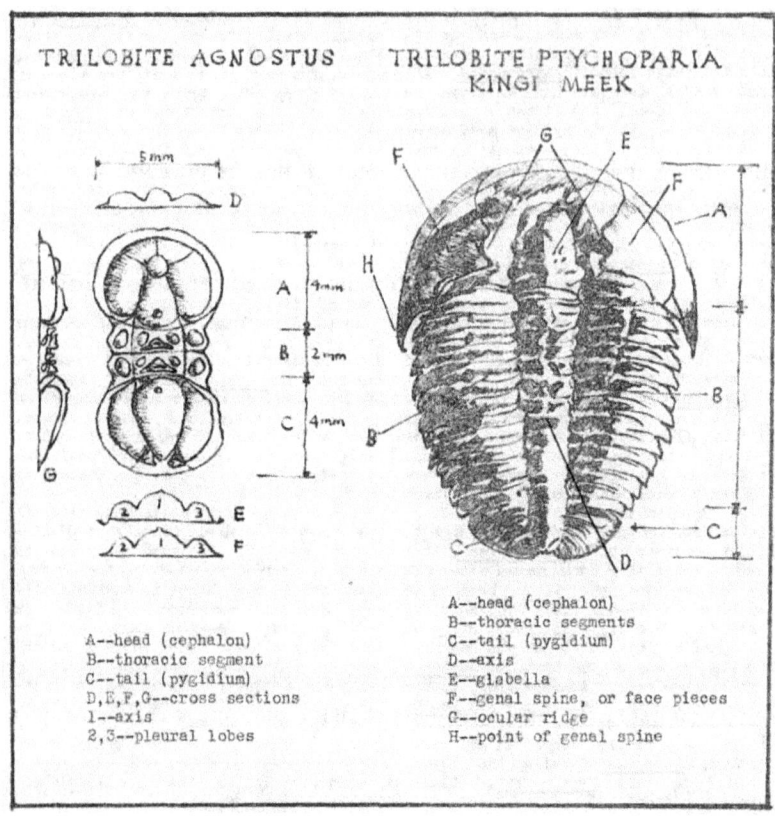

FIGURE 4.6 — Illustration accompanying Frank Beckwith's article on trilobites, diagramming two types of trilobite fossils commonly found near Antelope Springs, with *Elrathia kingii* (right) existing in large quantities. *Trek*, June 1943, 15.

marginal notation made by Nature in the process of building up and tearing down continents. They serve as time markers of early periods in the evolution of life forms."[91] Framing Antelope Springs as offering a window into "that almost inconceivably remote past," Beckwith concluded, "There is no more fascinating study in the range of sciences than that of historical geology. And nowhere in Utah is the whole varied range of geology better exemplified than here in isolated Millard County. Residents of Topaz, in their proximity to such points as Antelope Springs, have open to them an extremely rich and rewarding field of study and activity which may help relieve the relative drabness of their lives and surroundings."[92]

Prisoners at Topaz indeed made treks to Antelope Springs. The month that *Trek* published its article on trilobites, Topaz residents arranged to open a camp at Antelope Springs, which hosted scores of young people week by week during the summer of 1943, including expeditions to the trilobite field discussed by Beckwith.[93] And that winter a group of prisoners founded the Topaz Slate Club—furnished with a workspace, an electric grindstone, cutting tools, and other equipment—which was dedicated to making "such articles as ash trays, book ends, ink stands and suzuri [inkstones] . . . from the slate found near Antelope Springs."[94] Into 1944 the *Topaz Times* mentions day trips to the area.[95] According to *Beauty behind Barbed Wire: The Arts of the Japanese in Our War Relocation Camps* (published in 1952 by handicraft researcher Allen H. Eaton based on visits to the internment camps), "the slate from near Topaz had a special appeal for the residents, because of the interesting fossils often found imbedded in the stone—fossils of both animal and plant forms. . . . One of the favorite experiments with the slate cutters of Topaz was to locate a fossil and split a piece of the slate in two so that the fossil would remain unbroken but imbedded in one of the pieces." As Eaton explained, the fossils might then be showcased as components of *suzuri*, or inkstones, which are stone mortars used for grinding and mixing ink, traditionally associated with East Asian writers' and artists' work.[96]

One such inkstone was shaped and carved by Shigematsu Ishizaki, an issei man who had arrived in the United States in 1907 and operated the Menlo Fruit Company in Menlo Park, California, before being imprisoned at Topaz with his wife, a teenage son, and two adult sons.[97] Ishizaki's inkstone showcases two trilobite fossils and speaks directly to these fossils', and this petrified seabed's, relation to what Beckwith called the "age of man": within a shallow circle that is ground into the stone, Ishizaki etched the phrase "480,000,000 YEARS," and to the right of this circle he etched into the raw stone, "四億八千萬年," a kanji version of the same phrase (see fig. 4.7).[98] Without a doubt, in carving the stone so as to showcase and comment on the fossils of these Cambrian-era trilobites, Ishizaki was emplotting the present (Topaz's present, his family's present, his present) within the foreshore of the area's deep and oceanic past, even if his bald numerical approach seems to draw a straight and even Euclidean line of nearly half a billion years from the Cambrian to the age of man. And yet Ishizaki, who wrote and spoke both Japanese and English, etched the number of years elapsed between the trilobites and Topaz in both Arabic and kanji numerals.[99] From a certain rather standard perspective, one would think that no two phrases—though rendered in different languages or scripts—could be more perfect translational equivalents

FIGURE 4.7 — Inkstone carved by Shigematsu Ishizaki. One fossilized trilobite swims above the kanji characters. The other fossil (showcasing a portion of a larger trilobite's thorax) floats to the left of the ink reservoir. Topaz Museum, Delta, Utah (2017.21.01). Photograph by D. Ross Storey.

than two phrases purporting to represent the same number. Certainly, the transcultural and transhistorical quality of mathematics and numerals (as descriptors for the primary qualities of objects) is Meillassoux's basis for his notion of access to the great outdoors of philosophy, access to that which exists beyond correlation whether we think it or not.[100] And yet if the number 480,000,000 exists as an ideal bridge of incontrovertible equivalency between Arabic and kanji numerals, why write the number in both? To showcase one's ability to write in two languages? To make the fossilized trilobites' presence—and meaning within geologic time— legible to audiences of both issei (more likely to read kanji numerals) and nisei (more likely to read Arabic numerals)?

The decision was likely as surface-level as that, and yet these three questions alone have implications for how we might understand numerals' transcultural and transtemporal equivalencies in other contexts within the camp. As a speaker and writer of both languages, and as someone seeking to convey the trilobites' deep temporal presence, Ishizaki would have been well aware, as was directly discussed by one of *Trek*'s writers in the December 1942 issue, that the term *issei* (derived from 一世, in which 一 would seem to be the incontrovertible equivalent of the number 1) did not mean "first generation" in English but rather "immigrant," while the term *nisei* (derived from 二世, in which 二 would seem to be the incontrovertible equivalent of the number 2) did not mean "second generation" in English but rather "first generation."[101] In other words, and cutting to the center of ways Japanese Americans were perceived generationally and in terms of citizenship eligibility, the Japanese 一 (or 1) had its equivalent in the English 0, while the Japanese 二 (or 2) equaled the English 1. As *Trek* contributor Globularius Schraubi (said to be the pen name of Jim Oki) stated regarding the mismatch between Arabic and kanji numerals in the question of Japanese American generations, "This is a non-Euclidian proposition." In the same essay, he took up the question of numerals' relation to uneven temporal measurement, reminding readers that "Robinson Crusoe made a calendar for himself while in exile by making notches on a piece of wood." "Likewise," explained Schraubi as he framed the camp as analogous to Crusoe's island, some of Topaz's prisoners "spend their days making notches on a piece of [wood]. Sometimes they make wooden clogs as by-products."[102] Here the notch/numeral—as a way to mark or pass the time—may result in a calendar or a craft or both at once.

Indeed, within the camp, as discussed in the June 1943 issue of *Trek*, numbers (seemingly stable and predictable enough to hang our perception of reality on) worked in multiscalar and fractal temporal modes analogous to the "abnormal, non-Euclidean" geometric world evoked in H. P. Lovecraft's 1928 story "The Call of Cthulhu," so intriguing to recent thinkers for its depiction of a Pacific island (or a "mountain top" emerging from the sea) with "surfaces too great to belong to any thing right or proper for this earth," where "dimensions apart from ours" manifest when, for instance, "an angle which [is] acute . . . behave[s] as if it were obtuse."[103] Describing abnormal time rather than abnormal space, Katayama wrote that if he were to "ever attempt a volume of reminiscences about our life since evacuation," he would call it "Our Days Were Numbered," because "ever since that already incredibly remote day, a little over a year ago, when the WCCA (Wartime Civil Control Administration . . .) slapped on our first . . . Arabic tags—family and ID numbers—our existence has been a numerologist's opium dream." Katayama listed a stream of numerals that were non sequiturs in relation to each other: "Bed number, stall number, barrack number, train group number, block number, apartment number, resident identification number—in that procession of digital combinations lies the whole story of our career as an evacuee."[104] In tandem with Katayama's conceptualization of the prisoners' days as stacked non sequiturs of digital combinations, note the resemblance between his description of the temporal lapse since imprisonment ("that already incredibly remote day, a little over a year ago") and Beckwith's description of the temporal lapse since the Cambrian ocean world ("that almost inconceivably remote past," "some 400 million years ago"). That they appeared in the same issue of *Trek*—a journal for which Katayama had been associate editor, editor, and contributor—suggests that Katayama, in the wake of his poetry's reliance on Lake Bonneville's Pleistocene deep time, was now understanding imprisonment at Topaz in terms of a Cambrian ocean world whose temporality was deeper than Bonneville's by about half a billion years.

Of course, even thinking about timescales this vast introduced margins of error that involved tens of millions of years. Beckwith reported that the Antelope Springs trilobites were found in Cambrian rock that was "some 400 million years" old, while Rachel L. Carson less than a decade later listed the Cambrian as lasting from about 520 million years ago to 440 million years ago, and Ishizaki's inkstone presents the trilobites as hailing from 480 million years ago. Thinking within timescales like this, where even the margin of error would afford enough time for the entire Bonneville basin to fill and desiccate dozens of times over, would seem to require humans to count a year (or a thousand years) of imprisonment as zero. For instance, if Ishizaki were to have carved his inkstone in January 1944 (the month the Topaz Slate Club was founded), then at the Slate Club's first anniversary he could not responsibly or reasonably claim that the fossils were now 480,000,001 years old. Indeed, one would think that the entirety of Topaz's existence as an operating internment camp—from September 1942 to October 1945—ought to be tallied as zero according to the time frame adumbrated by Ishizaki's inkstone. Yet Katayama's description of imprisonment as beginning during "that already incredibly remote day," juxtaposed with Beckwith's description in the same *Trek* issue of trilobites living during "that almost inconceivably remote past," suggests that a one-year time lapse that *ought* to be counted as zero within the aeonic time lapse since the Cambrian era was *somehow* commensurate with the very aeonic lapse that would putatively negate a single year's significance. Setting Topaz's existence within the time lapse since the Cambrian was a temporal mise en abyme in which the temporal thing (the year) that was placed into the temporal abyss (400,000,000 years, give or take a few tens of millions of years) was comparable to the very abyss into which it was placed. Or, to put it in terms of the fractal foreshore, the blip-like ripple that hits and for an instant submerges the pebble is somehow commensurate with what Beckwith discussed as the ocean's aeonic "process of building up and tearing down continents." This mode of fractal temporality surfaces in the concluding paragraph of the internment account that perhaps comes closest to Katayama's imagined numerological memoir, Okubo's numerologically titled book *Citizen 13660*, which has Okubo on a bus, making her final departure from Topaz in early 1944 and reliving, *in a moment's time*, "the sorrows and the joys of my whole evacuation experience, until the barracks faded away into the distance. There was only the desert now. My thoughts shifted from the past to the future."[105]

Around the time that Okubo was leaving Topaz, relocating to New York City to work on a special issue of *Fortune* magazine, the Topaz Slate Club came into existence.[106] Emerging from the group of Topaz slate carvers, Ishizaki's inkstone offers a much more vivid view, in a different medium, of the foreshore's fractal temporality, hinted at by the inequivalency between the number 480,000,000 in Arabic and kanji numerals. The inkstone constitutes a tableau in which the stone trilobites swim in an ancient stone ocean; meanwhile, set as a mise en abyme within the stone ocean is the rectangular reservoir in which the ink is ground and mixed, called the *ink pond* (*bokuchi*, or 墨池) or the *ocean* (*umi*, or 海). Setting the ink ocean into the Cambrian ocean was a visual and verbal pun that hinged on the equivalency between the term for the body of water in which the trilobites swam and the term for the reservoir of ink from which the inkstone's user would draw. Analogous to Katayama's equivalency between the remote past of the beginning of imprisonment and the remote past of the Cambrian ocean world, Ishizaki's pun transformed an ink ocean carved at Topaz into a transtemporal portal to a trilobite sea, a challenge to what Dipesh Chakrabarty has framed as the conventional view that "geological time and the chronology of human histories remain ... unrelated."[107] Indeed, Ishizaki's inkstone evokes a version of Topaz and the world in which the future calligrapher writes with—and thinks with—ink in which trilobites have scuttled. On the foreshore of the ink ocean, inset among the accreted and iridescent shells of the trilobites, the water/ink of the Cambrian ocean became the future of Topaz, and Topaz the history of Cambrian ink.

On the question of the Topaz slate carvers' interest in arranging visual puns as sites of temporal entanglement between the Cambrian ocean and the ink oceans they themselves carved, consider a second inkstone carved at Topaz, by Toranosuke Mifune, which showcases a frog seemingly standing on some rocks in a pond while hungrily eying a flying insect (see fig. 4.8).[108] The frog is poised to draw the insect from the air above the pond into the ink pond, which functions in the carving as the frog's gut. These visual puns (the ink pond as the frog's gut, the ink pond within the pond) attain further accretions when we recognize the fundamental pun around which the entire carving is based: the putative insect within the carving was not carved by Mifune but is rather a trilobite fossil, reminiscent of Beckwith's description of trilobites as "small bug-like creatures." Opening into an oceanic realm of meaning that runs parallel with the inkstone's pond-oriented significations, the trilobite's emplotment as

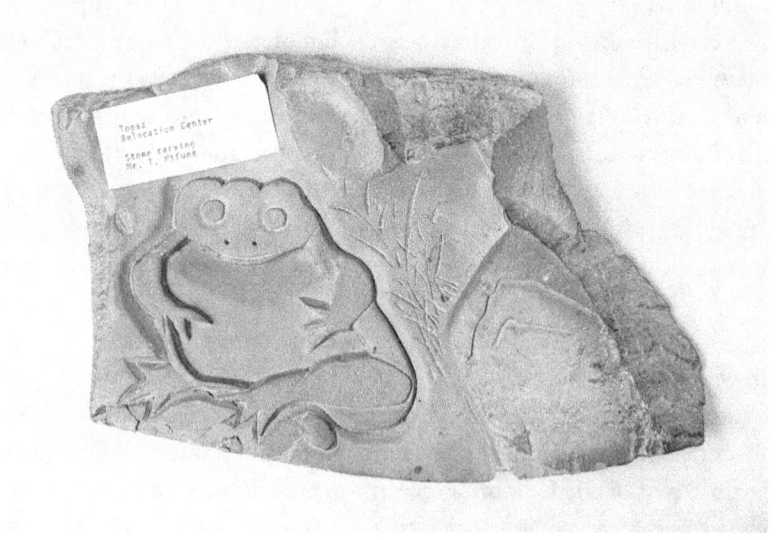

FIGURE 4.8 — Inkstone carved by Toranosuke Mifune. The trilobite/insect hovers to the left of the frog, at about eye level. In this inkstone the fossil is a casting left by the trilobite rather than the fossilized trilobite itself. Gift of Yukiyo Hayashi to the Japanese American National Museum, Los Angeles, California (2001.345.9). Photograph by Evan Kodani.

the frog's prey frames the amphibian as standing on a rocky island within a half-billion-year-old ocean, eyeing an ancient sea creature and poised to draw it from the Cambrian ocean into its gut, an ink ocean carved at Topaz. But what writing might emerge from such ancient ponds, such primordial oceans, as were carved by Ishizaki and Mifune?

A third inkstone, likely carved by Topaz prisoner Homei Iseyama, appears in Eaton's *Beauty behind Barbed Wire*, where Eaton describes it as containing "imbedded fossils"; this inkstone, says Eaton, showcases "how skillfully the fossil was handled" by the slate carvers (see fig. 4.9).[109] At first glance, one might look at the photograph and find that the fossil Eaton references is not readily apparent. What is readily apparent is that the tableau shows an inkstone with its stone lid propped to the left side. On the lid, a carved frog jumps toward the ink pond, while to the left of the lid is a rendering (presumably with ink from the stone) of the luminary seventeenth-century Japanese poet Matsuo Bashō's most famous haiku: 古池や / 蛙飛び込む / 水の音, which is often referred to as "Old Pond" or "Ancient

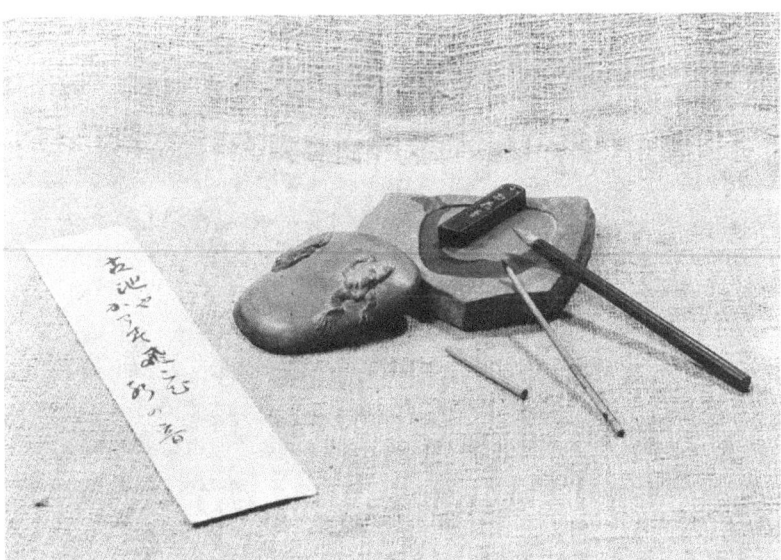

FIGURE 4.9 — Inkstone likely carved by Homei Iseyama. This photograph was reproduced in Allen H. Eaton's *Beauty behind Barbed Wire* (49). In the caption, Eaton explains, "A little water is placed in the well, the . . . ink stick moistened and rubbed against the stone until a liquid of the right consistency is produced." For more information on the photograph, see note 109. Photograph held by the Japanese American National Museum, Los Angeles, California (2015.100.156).

Pond" and may be translated as "Into an ancient pond a frog springs, water sounds."[110] The pun that remains implicit in Ishizaki's and Mifune's inkstones becomes overt in this inkstone: the "ancient pond" into which the frog jumps is the ink pond carved within the ancient seabed, with the character 池 (pond) appearing in both Bashō's poem and the kanji term for the ink reservoir. A standard interpretation of "Ancient Pond" suggests that the haiku captures "at once the eternal and the momentary. The ancient pond is eternal, but in order for us to become aware of its eternity there must be some momentary disruption. The leap of the frog, suggested by the splash of the water, is the 'now' . . . ; but the pond immediately relapses into timelessness."[111] Here, according to Yoshinobu Hakutani, we see a Zen-inspired "fusion of humanity and nature" in which the frog is not humanity but becomes analogous to humanity, having "brought himself to the deepest level of nature, where all sounds lapse into the world of silence and infinity."[112] Hence, within the economy of the tableau, the ink on the paper becomes the splash produced as an ephemeral life meets the silence of infinity and timelessness. Yet what message is conveyed by the splash of ink produced by the frog jumping into the ancient pond? The ink splashes onto the paper only to form a poem that constitutes a description of a frog jumping into an ancient pond followed by a splash. In many ways, the tableau's tautology reflects "the art of *gaman*," or "accept[ing] what is with patience and dignity": the tableau's tautology between stone and writing suggests that what is *is* what is.[113] Within this framing, human hardship—difficult as that hardship may be—becomes a blip-like ripple, a feature that counts as nothing within the ocean of eternity. Such framing may afford something like a meeting between Zen and what McGurl (as quoted earlier in this chapter) has called the new cultural geology's positioning of "culture in a time-frame large enough to crack open the carapace of human self-concern, exposing it to the idea, and maybe even the fact, of its external ontological preconditions."[114] After all, as McPhee stated, inspired by the very basin from which the Topaz slate carvers quarried their stones, if a human stands "arms spread wide . . . to represent all time on earth," then "in a single stroke with a medium-grained nail file you could eradicate human history."[115]

Yet the model offered by the inkstone is layered with another pun that pushes the tableau further than the rather predictable view that would hold human life as an insignificant drop in the ocean of deep time or eternity. Looking more closely at the carving, we may return to the question of the fossil mentioned by Eaton. As Eaton informs us, a dexterously handled fossil is incorporated into the carving, and indeed the frog's body (facing away from the viewer) appears to incorporate the fossilized carapace of a trilobite (facing the viewer).[116] Here, as the slate carver has metamorphosed the Cambrian trilobite into a frog/human of the "age of man," the well-known short-term process of a tadpole's metamorphosis into a frog becomes a vehicle for thinking about evolution, for thinking about what Beckwith in his *Trek* article on trilobites refers to as the story of "evolving life on earth," particularly as this story relates to aeonic foreshores and the ocean's "building up and tearing down [of] continents." Leaning on and recontextualizing Zen scholar-practitioner Daisetz T. Suzuki's transontological interpretation of "Ancient Pond" as the human poet's melding with the frog and the pond to showcase "all in one and one in all," we might say that within the inkstone's tableau, human life (the frog) has emerged from the ocean (as depicted in its metamorphosis from a Cambrian sea creature), but now, participating in the cyclicity of the foreshore, human life is making its way back (via the jump) into the ocean (ink ocean).[117] The splash (of ink) resulting from the frog/human/trilobite's return to the pond/ocean from which it emerged reinflects the Bashō poem with a prehistory of the ancient pond/ocean—namely, that if the life of an individual or even of a species is a blip-like ripple in the pond/ocean, then the pond/ocean has nonetheless seethed with the genre of life for time periods that might put the very stones to shame. Has the stone from which the inkstone is carved existed for 480 million years? No matter. Life (a continuous set of generic processes that over the longue durée of foreshores gives rise to archipelagically interrelated trilobites, amphibians, and humans) predates the stone, as evidenced by the fossilized trilobite contained in the stone and as suggested by the mid-twentieth-century scientific consensus placing life's genesis at more than one billion and possibly more than two billion years before the present.[118] (The current scientific consensus would date the beginning of life to about 3.5 billion years ago, significantly older than the approximately 2-billion-year-old stone that has been excavated by the Colorado River at the very bottom of the Grand Canyon.) This is a markedly different version of life than we have, for instance, in early twentieth-century writer James Weldon Johnson's short poem "Life," which frames life thus: "Out of the infinite sea of eternity / To climb, and for an instant stand / Upon an island speck of time."[119] The inkstone moves away from viewing humanity as a speck-like temporal island within an infinite sea and rather views the human species as a node within a temporal archipelago of life that extends not only transspatially

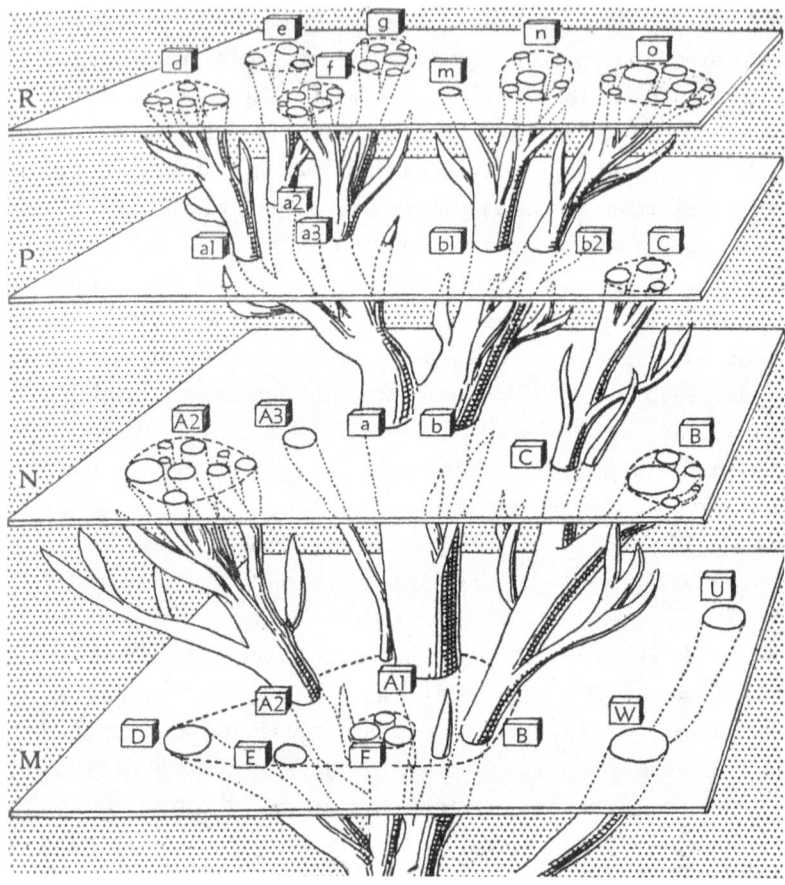

(as seen in Charles Darwin's famous archipelago-facilitated commentary on finch speciation) but also as a transtemporal archipelago of species interlinked from the "age of man" to the Cambrian and even to ages before and after that (see fig. 4.10).[120]

Consider these accretions of thought on existence, as instantiated by the inkstone, vis-à-vis the perspectives offered by process philosopher Alfred North Whitehead—whose critical futures have recently risen with several modes of new geologic criticism—during a 1927 lecture at the University of Virginia.[121] Whitehead understood "a rock [as] nothing else than a society of molecules, indulging in every species of activity open to molecules." He explained:

> I draw attention to this lowly form of society in order to dispel the notion that social life is a peculiarity of the higher organisms. The contrary is the

FIGURE 4.10 — (*opposite*) Illustration of a "small portion of the 'tree of life,'" representing "a few main branches and numerous lesser ones, which correspond to zoological taxonomic categories called phyla, classes, orders, families, genera, and species," as explained by the diagram's original caption. This illustration appeared in a biology textbook that began preparation in 1948 and was published in 1952. The four cross sections—M, N, P, and R—represent different "moments of geologic time," revealing that while, at any given geologic moment, different species may look like separate biotic islands, they are also archipelagically interconnected below the surface; here the islands of speciated life communities—even if these islands are situated at vastly different moments in geologic time—resemble Edward Kamau Brathwaite's famous dictum on islands' subaqueous and archipelagic interrelations: "The unity is submarine" (*Contradictory Omens*, 64). Inspired by Brathwaite, the Japanese anthropologist and cultural critic Ryuta Imafuku makes the following observation in his book *Guntō-SekaiRon* (Archipelago-World): "Once you take notice of the world's submarine interconnectedness, the land of your home will scatter on the sea like the seeds fallen from the trees and will flow into the world's countless shores" (quoted in Gabrakova, *Unnamable Archipelago*, 24). At Topaz, the iridescent inkstones of Ishizaki, Mifune, and Iseyama were archipelagic in ways that permitted submarine connections to move from Brathwaite and Imafuku's spatial dimension to the temporal dimension, as iridescent shells from the temporal islands of the 1940s and the Cambrian scattered onto geologic and evolutionary time's countless foreshores. From Raymond C. Moore, Cecil G. Lalicker, and Alfred G. Fischer, *Invertebrate Fossils* (New York: McGraw-Hill, 1952), 15.

case. So far as survival value is concerned, a piece of rock, with its past history of some eight hundred millions of years, far outstrips the short span attained by any nation. The emergence of [biological] life is better conceived as a bid for freedom on the part of organisms, a bid for a certain independence of individuality with self-interests.... The immediate effect of this emergence of sensitive individuality has been to reduce the term of life for societies from hundreds of millions of years to hundreds of years, or even to scores of years.[122]

Whereas Whitehead spoke of stones as engaging in social life without biological life and highlighted the way in which biological life traded the stone's relative invulnerability for a shot at ephemeral and vulnerable individuality, the trilobite-frog-ocean-haiku tableau produced by the inkstone reminds us that biological life (extending from a multibillion-year-before-the-present genesis mythologized by the Cambrian trilobite to a humankind emblematized by the frog) is older than many stones. Consider the come-lately 480,000,000-year-old stone that formed *in the wake of* and preserved the trilobite. Within the old pond or ancient ocean of temporalities that usually remain unfathomable to humans, life and minerals have not been each other's inaccessible great outdoors but have been transcorporeal collaborators.[123] We see this as the biotic matter of the trilobite invites ocean water and dissolved minerals to replace it with a three-dimensional stone photocopy of a trilobite (a fossil), or as a fossilized trilobite invites a slate carver to produce a visual and iridescent pun (an inkstone) that profoundly rewrites a famous haiku's commentary on the relation of the blip-like ripple to the aeonic foreshore's oceanic transtemporality.[124] The human, metamorphosing from an ocean-dwelling trilobite and climbing out onto the land, does not exist on a plane above the trilobite. Rather, relocating itself in a leap to within the ancient pond/ocean from which it emerged, it showcases itself as an amphibian; taking the frog as its amphibious vehicle, the human becomes an *ontological amphibian*, "moving among worlds," shifting on the question of "which ontology . . . to inhabit," acting in evolutionary and deep-temporal dialogue with the cyclic repetitions of the foreshore.[125] The inkstone's theorizations have commerce with some of the *Trek* editors' commentary in the journal issue that included Beckwith's article on trilobites: "The history of the world may be summed up as a series of constantly recurring relocations. . . . Relocation means moving, and everything moves."[126] Looking for a path away from the short-term view that would perceive relocation as a wartime tragedy and exception, yet simultaneously away from a geologically nihilistic view that would see wartime relocation as meaningless against "the long yardsticks of geology and evolution," the editors were framing relocation—fractal in its multiscalar and reciprocally nested cycles—as the engine of world history.[127] Within this model of world history, within this iridescent geotemporality, Topaz's inkstones give lithic heft to human-historical relocation as fractally commensurate with relocation that transpires within prehistory and other more-than-human histories. Here processes of relation take place on the foreshores of the Cambrian or the foreshores of an ink ocean, situated on the foreshores of Bonneville, carved at a site of entanglement between ages of prehistory and the age of man. And they prospectively endure via their stone medium into ages after the Anthropocene.

Vulnerable Temporalities: Flimsy Anachrony and Filmy Iridescence

To point out a connection that is both transpacific and transtemporal between the twentieth and the thirteenth centuries, the *Trek* writers and Topaz slate carvers were in many ways taking up questions of human vulnerability or impermanence within deep geologic time that were similar to those outlined in the Japanese writer Kamo no Chōmei's famous thirteenth-century *Hōjōki*. With an English title sometimes rendered as *The Ten Foot Square Hut*, Chōmei's essay orients itself around the "fleeting evanescent nature of man and his habitation" in the face of the earth's climate and geology—its typhoons, sea surges, floods, fires, and earthquakes.[128] As Chōmei states, "Like the dew on the morning glory are man and his house . . . who knows which will survive the other? The dew may fall and the flower remain, but only to wither in the morning sun, or the dew may stay on the withered flower, but it will not see another evening"; meanwhile, aeonic temporalities that far exceed either the dew (the human) or the flower (the house) march on unrelentingly.[129] Concluding that "if you have a lot of property you have many cares," Chōmei's essay underlines the futility of human cares, an apprehension that ultimately causes him to decide to "spend . . . [his] dew-like existence" in a shelter "a tenth of the size of [his] former home."[130] He explains, "The hermit-crab chooses a small shell and that is because he well knows the needs of his own body. The fishing-eagle chooses a rough beach because he does not want man's competition. Just so am I. If one knows himself and knows what the world is he will merely wish for quiet and be pleased when he has nothing to grieve about, wanting nothing and caring for nobody."[131] And yet at Topaz Chōmei's imagination of life in terms of ephemeral petals is metamorphosed into Suyemoto's view of long-durational life networks forged by existentially meaningful kinship between herself and Pleistocene mollusks, with multimillennial shells-as-flower-petals emerging as an enduring lithic answer to Chōmei's fast-fading morning glory, while his hermit crab shell of human evanescence is metamorphosed into shells of deep temporal iridescence. At Topaz, the fishing eagle's rough beach is metamorphosed into geotemporal foreshores whereon fossilized trilobites become keys not to geologic nihilism but to an existentially meaningful communion of contingent commensurabilities between the cycles of blip-like ripples and aeonic changes in sea level, keys to entanglements between the Cambrian ocean world and worlds evoked by ink from an ink ocean carved during imprisonment in the 1940s.

Further advancing thoughts on human vulnerability that might be taken as an answer, eight hundred years after the fact, to Chōmei's commentary on human vulnerability within geologic time, Katayama at one point mused in *Trek* on the existential meaning of his broken radio, which could do nothing except "confront [him] with its soundless, ivory plastic i[m]becility." As if riffing on Chōmei's assertions regarding the tyranny of a large home, Katayama wrote of "the tyranny of modern conveniences": "The lesson is plain to us. Man, who glories in the belief that he is progressively freeing himself by his ingenuity from the limitations of his original untrammeled state, is only delivering himself to a more inexorable bondage—the bondage of utter dependence on his own inventions." In decrying humankind's "trust in the machine," Katayama pointed to "the whole list of [man's] more ingenious inventions" as constituting "examples of the vulnerability to which man becomes heir in the very act of trying to fashion invulnerability for himself."[132] In its paradoxical articulation of vulnerability, Katayama's 1942 statement resembles Benjamin Franklin's eighteenth-century commentary on the paradoxical entanglements of humility and pride: "I cannot boast of much Success in acquiring the *Reality* of [humility]. . . . For even if I could conceive that I had completely overcome [pride], I should probably be proud of my Humility."[133] Likewise with Katayama's stance on the entanglements between vulnerability and invulnerability: if we take on increased vulnerability as we seek invulnerability, then does ceasing to strive for invulnerability (so as to avoid the attendant vulnerability) constitute yet another striving for invulnerability that would lead to vulnerability?

On questions of geographic space, archipelagic thinking has needed to navigate an analogous and indeed interrelated paradox. If the magnitude-loving logic of continental exceptionalism has consistently devalued island spaces, framing them as vulnerable for their smallness, then in offering a reminder of islands as archipelagic (that is, islands as components of sprawling networks and constellations that include vast swaths of ocean) are we seeking island invulnerability by acquiescing to the very magnitude-loving logic that has framed islands as inconsequential and hence vulnerable in the first place? And does such a magnitude-based argument for islands' importance reaffirm the very valorization of magnitude that ineluctably leads toward the belittlement and vulnerability of islands?[134] My own favored answer to this vexed question of engaging in a contest of comparative magnitude with the continent has been to turn toward fractal geometry's infinite island, mediated by the Mandelbrotean ant tracing the island's shoreline. Making recourse to the infinite island is not to say, *If you have the vast continent, we have the infinite island (and the still larger sublime ocean and sprawling archipelago)*. Rather, the infinite island offers a way beyond the comparative (in)vulnerabilities at stake in a comparative magnitude debate: there can be no back-and-forth about whether a continent or an island (or ocean or archipelago) is *more* infinite, because of course four hundred or four thousand or four million times infinity is still infinity.[135]

In an analogous way, but now in the realm of time, the Topaz writers and slate carvers whom I have been discussing were undertaking philosophical and aesthetic work that was, in its overarching attentiveness to the multiscalar ebbs and flows of the aeonic and immediate foreshores, engaged in archipelagically theorizing what I have been referring to as fractal temporality. Participants in and thinkers of what Maldonado-Torres has called postcontinental philosophy, these Topazans produced aesthetic work in fractal temporality which laid siege to linear, Euclidean timelines in a way that obliterated questions of comparative temporal duration and concomitant vulnerability during what was crystallizing as the "age of man." This Topazan fractal temporality has a certain commerce with what Benjamin Norris has discussed as "the fractal temporality of the unconscious" (and I might add conscious) mind.[136] But beyond simply finding an emblem in Okubo's experience on the bus (having a flashback of her entire life at Topaz in a matter of seconds), this approach to the texture of *materialities* (the iridescent shells of the Pleistocene and the Cambrian, for instance) constituted engagements with what Mark Rifkin has in another context referred to as "the texture of . . . *temporalities*," wherein repeating textural temporalities—textures that might be called grainy, hydralike, in between, pimply, pocky, ramified, seaweedy, strange, tangled, tortuous, wiggly, wispy, wrinkled—are not beholden to a linear temporal perception that would see fractal repetition as an anachronistic mode in which "the future will move backwards."[137]

Here, rather, Timothy Morton's reimagination of the Mandelbrotean ant becomes relevant to the fractal temporality theorized by the Topazans. Morton has projected that the ant's coastline wanderings might lead it to another island, equally infinite to the first: "Imagine her crawling around the surface of a rock on the seashore in a tidal pool."[138] Though Morton has other conceptual reasons for imagining the ant apparently getting stranded on this offshore rock, it is notable that whereas Mandelbrot bracketed the temporality of waves and tide, Morton's reimagination of the ant fully admits the foreshore's tidal temporality, its "rippling with time"—after all, the rock is in a *tidal* pool, and the backstory for the walking (not swimming) ant's arrival on the islandized rock would need to involve a tidal shift such that rising waters around a small *pen*insula on which the ant was walking caused that piece of land to become a fully islandized *insula*.[139] And here—as in Topaz when the ants sometimes brought desirable shells to the surface—this reimagined Mandelbrotean ant, walking circles on an islandized rock on the foreshore, delivers the iridescent shell to us, so to speak, aiding us in seeing, in an inkstone carved on a three-year island of time at Topaz, an exoskeletal trilobite shell that swims, crawls, and jumps across an archipelago of temporalities as an ontological amphibian, as an alternatingly biotic/mineral/aesthetic trilobite-pollywog-frog-human that is, with a Bashōean leap, recycling back through its series of beings, its series of, in Elizabeth A. Povinelli's term, "object-events."[140] Like the reimagined ant on the islandized rock, this shell's temporo-fractal existence reminds us that the three-year island of Topaz is as infinite as any spatial island whose coast Mandelbrot's ant might trace. Whether it is three seconds between ripples, thirty seconds between waves, three years of imprisonment, thirty thousand years between lacustrine inundations, or half a billion years since the trilobite scuttled, it is infinite. To advance the figure of an infinite island of fractal temporality is not to enter into a contest of comparative temporal duration with the continentally scaled geologic ages, aeons, and still vaster durations. It is not to say, *If you have the half-billion-year aeon, we may look toward the infinite three years of imprisonment in Topaz; if you have the Pleistocene lake that evaporated some twelve thousand years ago, then the Topazans collectively spent over twice that long on the lake bed (imagine the tally marks of days on Crusoe's island, mentioned by Schraubi, undertaken by Topaz's several thousand residents over the course of three years).* It is not to say, *If you can point toward a universe that has existed for about 13.8 billion years, then the collective synchronic consciousness of humankind during any two-year period of the 2010s exceeded the duration of the universe and all known diachronic temporality to this point.*[141] Rather, to put forth a fractal temporal view that has the broad synchronic present (any present at any moment) balancing out with deep diachronic time is to seek an end to arguments of comparative magnitude (and hence comparative vulnerability) between islandized moments and continentalized ages. Is anachronic time the result? Such an end leads to a view that some, leaning on Felski's observation regarding the "flimsiness" of our temporal approaches, might critique as flimsy—untenable, nonsensical, as, say, the Cambrian becoming the future of Topaz while Topaz becomes the history of Cambrian ink. Is this anachronic stew—emblematized by the dredged-up ground on which Okubo stood on Treasure Island—simply a geologic version of the "pile of debris" seen by Walter Benjamin's famous backward-flying "angel of history"?[142] But another flying being offers a different view, metamorphosing flimsy anachrony into filmy iridescence before our eyes, connecting temporal moments (they're all moments) into an archipelago of temporalities: an amphibious human/frog/trilobite/stone glides through the air with an iridescent trajectory that has 1940s Topaz as a past and the Cambrian as a future.

CHAPTER FIVE

Spiraling Futures of the Archipelagic States of America

History, Really Beginning

For the prisoners at Topaz, Lake Bonneville's foreshore became a medium for human engagement with remote and iridescent geologic times. And a few decades after their release, it was on this very Bonnevillean foreshore that the New York–based artist Robert Smithson in 1970 produced his most famous work, *Spiral Jetty*. Creating this icon of 1960s and 1970s earth art just fifteen miles south of the Golden Spike National Historic Site that marked the completion of the transcontinental railroad, Smithson moved mud and rocks with construction equipment to create a jetty that extended from the Great Salt Lake's shoreline into its algae-pink and deeply saline waters. If a jetty is a structure that traditionally projects into the water to protect a harbor, beach, or stretch of coast from waves and currents, Smithson's jetty departs from the conventional and utilitarian jetty's straight-line projection and instead spirals into the water, fifteen feet wide and 1,500 feet long (see fig. 5.1).[1] Like the prisoners at Topaz, Smithson was deeply cognizant of his work's situation on the foreshore between the basin's low tide (the Great Salt Lake) and its high tide (Lake Bonneville). Indeed, toward the beginning of his 1970 film on *Spiral Jetty*, we hear a metronome tick while the camera pans in on a map that marks Bonneville's and the Great Salt Lake's different positions on the same geotemporal

FIGURE 5.1 — Aerial photograph of Robert Smithson's *Spiral Jetty* (1970), taken by Hikmet Sidney Loe on August 9, 2005. White salt crystals encrust the shoreline and the jetty as it spirals into the pink water of the Great Salt Lake. The presence of an unpaved road (right) offers perspective on the jetty's scale. Photograph courtesy of Hikmet Sidney Loe. © 2020 Holt/Smithson Foundation and Dia Art Foundation / Licensed by VAGA at Artists Rights Society (ARS), NY.

foreshore. This scene's engagement with geologic time—particularly as it implies that the Bonneville basin's future may spiral back to look like its past—is consistent with a statement Smithson made the year before *Spiral Jetty*'s construction: "The future ... is the obsolete in reverse. The future is always going backwards. Our future tends to be prehistoric."[2]

Here at *Spiral Jetty*, then, we find an apropos site to take up future-oriented questions that have arisen in literary and cultural discussions surrounding deep time, and particularly surrounding distant futurities. Underscoring existential implications that he believes Wai Chee Dimock left unaddressed in *Through Other Continents: American Literature across Deep Time*, Mark McGurl has discussed deep time as a concept that opens onto "the posthuman comedy," a term by which he refers to works in which "spatiotemporal vastness" becomes "an existential problem," comedic to the degree that humans perceive any values at all in a cosmos whose indifference makes a jest of human concerns.[3] As McGurl posits, humanity's gravest strife might well be seen as a comedic pratfall when contextualized with the fact that, as science assures us, Earth is ineluctably moving toward incineration by a blazing Sun 4.5 billion years in the future.[4] Dimock, for her part, has responded to McGurl by acknowledging that "most of us, and most works of literature, have indeed been blind" to this "spectacular heat-death . . . slated to happen some 4.5 thousand million years from now," this "catastrophe projected far into the future, but guaranteed to happen." Still, she remarks, "While the outcome is not in doubt, the routes to it are likely to be numerous, and the content of any particular slice of time, on that long run of 4.5 thousand million years, is anyone's guess. . . . That endpoint neither dictates nor even unduly restricts the range of possibilities emerging at every stage."[5]

Smithson's 1970 film on *Spiral Jetty* speaks to the major vectors of McGurl and Dimock's exchange, particularly as we approach the question of the times and possibilities that will transpire between the present and the Earth's future "heat death" in the nuclear fusion of a rioting red giant Sun.[6] Indeed, the film begins on the surface of the Sun, as Earth's local star expels solar flares. And the film concludes with the Sun, as the last scenes use footage shot from a helicopter's aerial perspective, centering the Sun's glare onto the jetty's coils and then zooming in until, as Smithson's notes call for, the jetty's center "burns into bright light" (see fig. 5.2).[7] Between the beginning in the Sun and the end in the Sun, Smithson at one point appears in a pivotal scene that has him running along the jetty toward the center, taking "that long run" (to echo Dimock) toward the ultimate point on the timeline where everything will finally burn into bright light. In this scene of Smithson running on a jetty that he once described as analogous to "a road that goes forward and backward," we have a sense of geologic time moving forward and yet backward, as if Smithson were moving forward into the distant future and yet simultaneously traveling what in the 1970s became known as "The Geologic Time Spiral" (see fig. 5.3) back to Earth's accretion 4.5 billion years ago, instantiating a way in which the posthuman future may look like prehuman prehistory.[8]

Upon reaching the center, this prehistoric future in which Earth will end in a burning Sun, Smithson stops for a moment and then begins walking back. Later, when asked about his feelings upon reaching the end of the jetty, Smithson said, "I had no feelings. It was just like there you were, and then you just walked back. There were no discoveries."[9] No discoveries. It was simple—Earth began with the Sun, and it will end, unremarkably, with the Sun. But with Smithson's decision to turn and walk away

FIGURE 5.2 — The Sun burning brightly in the center of *Spiral Jetty*, from Robert Smithson's 1970 film *Spiral Jetty*. © 2020 Holt/Smithson Foundation / Licensed by VAGA at Artists Rights Society (ARS), New York.

from the center—to turn back from what we might read as the far-future event of Earth's final incineration—he plays the role of a Mandelbrotean ant walking through fractal time rather than fractal space, and hence his diachronic journey to the end of the jetty becomes no more sublime than any one of the peninsular or subpeninsular temporal tendrils along the synchronic shorelines of the temporal jetty that juts into the 4.5 billion years of Earth's diachronic future.

In fact, the shoreline of the jetty along which Smithson walks back is populated, as planned by Smithson himself, with fractal repetitions of the jetty's temporal shape; having researched crystal formation, Smithson anticipated that the jetty's rocks would be encrusted with salt crystals, each of which would, at the level of interactions among atoms, "actually wind itself into a spiral during growth," so that "the Spiral Jetty could be considered one layer within the spiraling crystal lattice, magnified trillions of times."[10] Such an image—of a spiraling jetty of geologic time made up of rocks encrusted with innumerable temporal spirals along the way—takes spatiality as a metaphor for temporality, directing our minds toward the infinitely spiraling synchronic futures that collectively dwarf the diachronic spiral

SPIRALING FUTURES · 205

FIGURE 5.3 — "The Geologic Time Spiral." The US Geological Survey used the phrase "geologic time spiral" to describe an illustration that appeared in a 1974 publication on Utah's Canyonlands National Park. A few years prior, in 1972, Robert Smithson conceived of *Spiral Jetty* in Utah as a geologic and evolutionary time spiral: "Following the spiral steps we return to our origins, back to some pulpy protoplasm, a floating eye adrift in an antediluvian ocean." Smithson, "Spiral Jetty," 17. For the 1974 quotation and version of the illustration, see Lohman, *Geology of Canyonlands*, ix, 110–11. Image from Joseph Graham, William Newman, and John Stacy, "The Geologic Time Spiral—A Path to the Past," U.S. Geological Survey General Information Product 58 (2008), https://pubs.usgs.gov/gip/2008/58/.

that would conduce directly toward heat death. Here another statement by Smithson attains purchase: "If time is a place, then innumerable places [and hence times] are possible.... Time breaks down into many times."[11] Mapping McGurl and Dimock's exchange onto this temporal reading of Smithson's *Spiral Jetty*, we might say that whereas McGurl seeks to remind us of the existential dangers of deep-temporal thought by running us quickly down the middle of the jetty to the determinate and seemingly deflating end of Earth's history at the spiral's incinerating center, Dimock asks us to be deflated not by the notion of a final incineration but rather by the lack of punch that the incineration actually offers, compared with the ways of being in time that will exist between the present and the end.[12] Yet if Dimock litotically speculates that these ways are "likely to be numerous," *Spiral Jetty* would frame them as mind-boggling, ranging from geologic time's macrospiral all the way down to spiraling formations at the atomic level. Certainly, *Spiral Jetty* has been a place that illustrates multifarious ways of being in time, as it has sometimes been submerged and sometimes left dry and at other times has become an archipelago of rocks/islands that spiral out into the Great Salt Lake (see fig. 5.4).[13]

If, as Édouard Glissant says, "archipelagic thought" does not seek a "single imperious direction" but rather "bursts upon all horizons," then *Spiral Jetty* is an instantiation of archipelagized thought regarding outward-bursting and innumerable futures.[14] *Spiral Jetty*, in other words, offers a vision of futurities that is radically different from the vision of the future we see enshrined by its neighboring monument. Over the decades, the nearby Golden Spike National Historic Site (as of 2019 redesignated as a historical park) has taken the completion of the transcontinental railroad as "a prophecy, a portent of things to come," involving the triumph of colonial modernity's version of progress, traced in a straight and imperious line culminating in "the completion of a Republic that is continental."[15] Thus, the continent is the central hero in a progressive story of the uniting of, as is inscribed on the golden spike itself, "two great oceans."[16] With *Spiral Jetty*, however, the notion of a progressivist future collapses, not only in the heat death of the diachronic future but in the synchronic futurities—the spirals upon spirals, the turnings and turnings back—of the jetty's rocks in the brine and the salt crystals that form fractally in relation to the larger work.

In this way, *Spiral Jetty* archipelagically deflates the mythic site that is supposed to have turned the United States into a truly continental republic; it emerges as geoformally aligned with rocky saltwater shorelines on

FIGURE 5.4 — *Spiral Jetty* as a spiral archipelago. This photograph was taken on August 31, 2012, when the lake level was at 4,196 feet above sea level. Photograph courtesy of Joseph Kraft. © 2020 Holt/Smithson Foundation and Dia Art Foundation / Licensed by VAGA at Artists Rights Society (ARS), NY.

all horizons, including those of Pacific and Caribbean futurities. These are geoformal connections that *Spiral Jetty* does not create (again, it is not the hero) but in which it participates. Recall, as I have mentioned previously, that in 1993 at the University of the South Pacific, Eric Waddell, Vijay Naidu, and Epeli Hauʻofa used excerpts from the Saint Lucian poet Derek Walcott's 1979 poem "The Sea Is History" as the epigraph for their collection *A New Oceania: Rediscovering Our Sea of Islands*. According to this epigraph, we see "History, really beginning" in "the salt chuckle of rocks / with their sea pools."[17] Thus, *Spiral Jetty*—in its meditations on future histories via the salt chuckle of rocks in a salty inland sea—joins with Caribbean and Pacific thinkers in contemplating histories and futures that answer such enduring models of continental-progressivist history as have been advanced in Georg Wilhelm Friedrich Hegel's nineteenth-century *Lectures on the Philosophy of World History*. Here Hegel specifically identified continents as the true stages of history while disqualifying islands in general ("we must not imagine that [history] can occur on a desert island"). It was also here that Hegel afforded the Caribbean and Pacific their own case-specific disqualifications from history: if "the natives of the

West Indian islands have died out altogether," then "the [Pacific] archipelago between South America and Asia" displays "physical immaturity even in respect of its origin; for most of the islands are based on coral, and are so constituted as to be, so to speak, merely a superficial covering for rocks which rise up out of the bottomless depths and bear the marks of relatively recent origin."[18] But within the Caribbean-Pacific epigraph of *A New Oceania*, and with *Spiral Jetty* as a collaborator hitting against the very heart of what Manu Karuka has recently described as the transcontinental railroad's "continental imperialism," the rocks that Hegel rejected now become the chief cornerstones of future history, with futurities proliferating over and over again and without end in each chuckle—or each clicking and clacking together—of innumerable stones in a surf of spiraling waves.[19] These futures become nether-dimensional in relation to US American continentalist histories and futures of railroad ties and golden spikes; *that was not history,* say the archipelagic futures—*these salt chuckles in the spiraling waves are history, really beginning.*

Thus, *Spiral Jetty* is aligned with oceanic shorelines across the planet via the salt chuckle of rocks. It is also aligned via the spiral's transcultural currency as a marker of interconnection and nonlinear temporalities—as we see among the Haitian literary Spiralists, who have viewed the shape as disrupting "the idea of time's unfettered linear passage," and as we see to the degree that the spiral has, among several Pacific writers, represented pan-Polynesian solidarity as a "structure [that] confronts and defies the Western linear hierarchical way of thinking" because the spiral "'looks' back even as it progresses."[20] Making recourse to a temporally spiraling archipelago and its constituent salt-chuckling rocks, this chapter is dedicated to decontinentalizing US American and post-US futurity.[21] Thus, it brushes the future against the continentalist grain. After running out to the heat death of the universe, this chapter walks back along the chuckling rocks of spiraling futures, bringing specific focus to three projected future moments through which we see history, really beginning. The first moment is in a mind-bogglingly distant future, during which human brains and thinking islands flicker into existence in the vacuum of space, with spirals of recurrence providing a window into what it looks like for the humanities to give attention to truly deep time, thereby, by means of an argument ad absurdum, offering insight into ways archipelagic thinking might revise and refine some of its own premises. The second moment looks toward a future ranging from five centuries from now to perhaps a million years from now, during which posthuman scientists examine albatross-curated plastic archives of our Anthropocene present, looking at plastic that the birds have gathered from the spiraling gyres of today's Great Pacific Garbage Patch. The third moment takes place perhaps a century from now, when spacefaring archipelagic humans undercut US notions of existing "in perpetuity," pulling a new form of life out of a spiral of stones floating above a near-Mars asteroid. In approaching these futurities, which are conceived at temporal scales alien not only to present-day humans but also to each other, I draw on three early twenty-first-century short stories: US Virgin Islands writer Tiphanie Yanique's "The Bridge Stories," British writer A. S. Byatt's "Sea Story," and Filipino writer Timothy James M. Dimacali's "Sky Gypsies." The form of the short story—brief but layered with meaning—might well be taken as a reflection on humankind's place, balanced between geologic nothingness and species narcissism, within spiraling futures that may forget us but never be fully without us.[22]

Can an Archipelago Think? A Boltzmann Brain in the Caribbean Sea

In the conclusion to his important study *Think Like an Archipelago: Paradox in the Work of Édouard Glissant* (2018), Michael Wiedorn begins with an assertion that is both punchy and incontestably commonsensical: "Archipelagoes, need it be recalled, are themselves quite incapable of thought." He then elucidates, explaining that although Glissant's writings speak of *pensée archipélique*, or "archipelagic thought," the term does not refer to thought as performed by archipelagoes but rather to human "thought that emanates from the Caribbean archipelago and that somehow resembles it."[23] Indeed, there can be little doubt that Wiedorn is correct. Glissant's archipelagic thought would not be thinking that is thought by archipelagoes—it would rather be thinking that is thought by humans who are thinking about archipelagoes, or by humans who are thinking with archipelagoes (as we might think with an abacus), or by humans who are thinking about how archipelagoes would think if archipelagoes *could* think. And yet the question of decontinentalized futurity—with its attendant openness to the multifarious ways of being in future times—affords us a chance to question Wiedorn's assertion that archipelagoes are incapable of thought. In taking up this question, I want to push beyond the notion of objects engaging in nonphenomenological thought (as assumed regarding the mollusk shells in the previous chapter) and into the question of objects exhibiting phenomenological thought.

Smithson, McGurl, and Dimock point toward an ultimate temporal horizon in which Earth will be incinerated by the Sun about 4.5 billion years from now, pushing to the apparent limit of Dipesh Chakrabarty's influential 2009 suggestion that the Anthropocene's classification of humans as a geologic force requires that we place human history into dialogue with geologic time spans.[24] But even at temporal scales like these, humanists have only dipped a toe, or much less than a toe, into the waters of science's deep time. For the sake of argument (that is, for the sake of not arbitrarily privileging geology and climate science over cosmology and theoretical physics), we might hazard a glance at the Wikipedia page titled "Timeline of the Far Future," which describes itself as being "about the far future postulated by science" and takes us much farther than 4.5 billion years beyond the present, permitting us to continue walking the jetty's coils into times that are inconceivably more distant, populated with future events that have been projected in sources drawn from peer-reviewed scientific journals.[25] Within this publicly curated timeline of peer-reviewed scientific findings, humanity is a blip on the way. In fact, the entire 4.5-billion-year history of Earth is a blip on the way. Or better, compared with the unimaginably distant futurities we are talking about now, the entire 13.8-billion-year history of the universe is a blip on the way. Or not even a blip. Recall, from the previous chapter, John McPhee's vertigo-inducing visualization of human history as compared to deep geologic time: if a human stands "arms spread wide . . . to represent all time on earth," then "in a single stroke with a medium-grained nail file you could eradicate human history."[26] Here is a follow-up visualization for thinking about the 13.8-billion-year history of the universe compared to its incredibly distant futures: if a human were to stand with arms spread wide to represent time from the beginning of the universe (the big bang) to the end (as marked by the predicted triumph of entropy), a single stroke with a medium-grained nail file would eradicate all of (and mind-bogglingly more than) the universe's 13.8-billion-year history to this point. In fact, the futurities we are discussing are so distant that removing a single atom from the tip of the human's fingernail would *also* eradicate all of (and mind-bogglingly more than) the universe's 13.8-billion-year history to this point. Finally, the best heuristic might be to visualize the universe as not even having started yet. In other words, with nearly 14 billion years behind us, we are still looking forward to history, really beginning.[27]

In reading through "Timeline of the Far Future," let us begin with some very short-term projections that will feel familiar enough to scholars in the humanities who have been accustomed to taking science seriously on timescales calibrated to the Anthropocene.[28] According to the Australian theoretical physicist Brandon Carter, humans have a 95 percent chance of being extinct 10,000 years from now (yfn), or we might trust in Princeton astrophysicist J. Richard Gott's more sanguine prediction that our 95 percent likelihood of extinction will not arrive until 7.8 million yfn. In any case, assuming with Carter that humans will be extinct 10,000 yfn, we will miss the recovery of the planet's coral reef ecosystems, in the wake of human-caused ocean acidification. Or, assuming with Gott that humans will be extinct in 7.8 million years, we will miss seeing Hawai'i Island (the youngest and largest of the current Hawaiian Islands) erode into the ocean 80 million yfn.

From here, as we proceed down this "Timeline of the Far Future," we move quickly from the very short term toward the inconceivably longer—that is, from the comparatively puny deep times of the Anthropocene and Earth to the deepest of deep times as discussed in cosmology and theoretical physics. Owing to the Sun's intensifying heat, conditions for life on Earth will decline rapidly beginning about 500 million yfn, so that by 700–800 million yfn, "plants and animals would primarily be found in the oceans." And assuming Earth is not ejected from the solar system owing to an enormous collision with another object, it will be destroyed in the Sun 7.9 billion yfn, while at 100–150 billion yfn, the universe's expansion will cause nearly all galaxies to move beyond the Milky Way's observable universe. At a quadrillion yfn, the Sun will have cooled to 5 degrees above absolute zero, that is, 5 degrees above −273.15 Celsius. From a human perspective, things are looking rather bleak now, as they have for the past several hundreds of trillions of years and as they will, it would seem, for mind-bogglingly longer. Stars as we know them are gone. We might take consolation from the familiar notion of a black hole, but then at 1.7×10^{106} yfn, we are hit with "the end of the Black Hole Era" and a gradual "winding down to . . . the heat death of the universe" (or thermal equilibrium of the universe), which is estimated to occur at $10^{10^{120}}$ yfn.[29] (For context, the volume of the entire observable universe would be insufficient—a figurative nail shaving's worth of volume—compared to the space required to contain the number of books it would take to write out the zeros in the number $10^{10^{120}}$.)[30] Around the time the final black holes are disappearing, the article's editors add the following note: "Although listed in years for convenience, the numbers beyond this point are so vast that their digits would remain unchanged regardless of which conventional units they were listed in, be they nanoseconds or star lifespans." This is the scene at the end of scientific time's jetty of entropy.

In running out to the end of this jetty, we have been consistent with what Glissant calls continental thought's urge to see "all-at-once," arriving at what Donna J. Haraway famously described as science's "conquering gaze from nowhere."[31] The view from the impossible masthead of this poststarship might be considered the reductio ad absurdum of what Jared Hickman once described as "cosmic American studies," involving "a historical ontology in which we can observe the succession of 'worlds.'"[32] It all seems very post-Earth, post–Milky Way, poststar, post–black hole, and postenergy—certainly, it would seem, postocean, postcontinent, and postarchipelago.[33] But, surprisingly, science might suggest that it is not fully posthuman. It is not that human-made plastic, so often mythologized as infinite, has remained—this technofossil was gone long before stars ceased to exist. Rather, as we float in our poststarship during an era when the difference between the nanosecond and the lifetime of a star is negligible, we bump into a curious event on the "Timeline of the Far Future." This event is sandwiched between two apparently competing estimates for when all black holes will have evaporated into subatomic particles. At $10^{10^{50}}$ yfn, we read, "Estimated time for a Boltzmann brain to appear in the vacuum via a spontaneous entropy decrease." By following a note that has been appended to this event, we learn that the numerical figure "represents the time by which the event will most probably have happened," though "it may occur randomly at any time from the present." What is this event of the inconceivably far future, or rather this event that could occur at any point between the present and the inconceivably distant future? Strange as it all may seem to traditional modes of humanistic thought, looking into it is logically necessary to the degree that we in the humanities are dedicated to talking about human positionality within science's notion of deep time in a way that is actually accountable to the deepest of times. Further, the Boltzmann brain's relation to the infinite causes it to link up with archipelagic thought, with particular implications for a non-Glissantian mode of archipelagic thought involving thinking that is undertaken by islands themselves. Getting there requires a dive into the peer-reviewed literature and related sources.

Since the early 2000s, a certain set of theoretical physicists and cosmologists have been discussing what is called the *Boltzmann brain paradox*. This paradox has roots in the late nineteenth-century thought of the luminary Austrian physicist Ludwig Boltzmann. Boltzmann's work on the second law of thermodynamics (which predicts the ever-increasing entropy or disorder that prefigures the heat death of the universe) led him to look out into the highly ordered cosmos and suggest that Earth along with every other visible feature must exist as a random thermal fluctuation (or a random increase in order) within a generally chaotic or entropic universe.[34] Given the extremely high level of orderliness that he saw in the cosmos, Boltzmann conceded that it would seem unimaginably improbable for the entire visible universe to randomly fluctuate into existence. But, he countered, if our visible and highly ordered universe is understood to be an infinitesimally "small... part of the whole [disordered] universe," then as the amounts of time and space under consideration approach infinity, "the probability [is] great" that a highly ordered place like our universe would randomly fluctuate into existence.[35] This thought process resembles Jorge Luis Borges's famous 1941 story "The Library of Babel," which imagines an infinite library containing endless books containing each possible combination of letters and punctuation, with, as the narrator believes, each book eventually repeating itself infinitely as the library extends eternally. Such a library would promise to contain everything, including a book offering the true and "detailed history of the future." But "the formless and chaotic nature of virtually all books" in the library is overwhelming, such that "for every rational line or forthright statement there are leagues of senseless cacophony, verbal nonsense, and incoherency."[36] To frame Boltzmann's cosmic claim in terms of the Library of Babel: Boltzmann believed that by random chance, he happened to be in a portion of the library that astoundingly happened to contain not simply one single coherent book but millions of coherent books all in a row. Still, if the universe's library of features was infinite, such a section of the library was certain to exist.[37]

Boltzmann's late nineteenth-century observation began to condense into the notion of the Boltzmann brain about a century later, when in 1997 the British cosmologist and astrophysicist Martin Rees observed that the second law of thermodynamics predicts that smaller fluctuations in entropy will be vastly more likely than larger fluctuations—that is, if a randomly fluctuated planet will be extremely unlikely, "everything within range of our telescopes" will be mind-bogglingly more unlikely. Hence, according to Rees, Boltzmann should have considered the incredible odds against very large fluctuations and sought to explain existence by recourse to the smallest and hence most likely random fluctuation that would be consistent with what he saw in the cosmos—namely, Boltzmann "should have concluded that his brain" alone (so much smaller and hence more likely to fluctuate into existence than the entire cosmos) had randomly fluctuated into existence and was "receiving... stimuli that gave the illusion of a coherent external world which didn't actually exist."[38] During the ensuing decade, the Boltzmann brain paradox truly crystallized, with theoretical physicists and cosmologists recognizing that leading theories of the origin, nature, and future of the universe indeed predict that although the probability of a human brain (or any other object) fluctuating into existence in the vacuum of space at any given moment is incredibly low, it is nonetheless not zero, and hence, in a universe that has space existing eternally (even after the heat death at $10^{10^{120}}$ yfn) and that may be inflating eternally, an infinite number of human brains (i.e., Boltzmann brains) would be predicted to randomly flicker in and out of conscious existence in the vacuum of space.[39] Although human brains are not special in being predicted to flicker in and out of existence (an infinity of Boltzmann toasters, oak trees, obsidian shards, iPhones, etc. are also predicted to flicker in and out of existence), the prediction of infinite Boltzmann brains has presented physicists and cosmologists with a startling likelihood or even a near certainty.[40] In light of the Copernican principle, which "states that it is unlikely for your location in the universe to be special," we must grant the following: if randomly fluctuated Boltzmann brains "outnumber ordinary observers like us [i.e., biologically evolved humans] by an infinite factor," we should assume that it is incredibly unlikely for us to be biologically evolved humans but instead that we are almost certainly Boltzmann brains, "complete with 'memories'" of pasts that we haven't materially experienced, "fluctuating briefly out of chaos and then immediately equilibrating back into chaos again."[41]

If the idea of being a Boltzmann brain sounds absurd to nonphysicists and noncosmologists, it also sounds absurd to many of the physicists and cosmologists who have been participating in these arguments. In 2017, for instance, Sean Carroll (a theoretical physicist at the California Institute of Technology) suggested that theories of the universe that predict that we ourselves are Boltzmann brains are "cognitively unstable" because they have us using data collected through "the evidence of our senses" to arrive at an understanding of the universe that then predicts "that our sense data are completely unreliable."[42] Or, as elaborated by Jason Pollack (a coauthor with Carroll on Boltzmann brains), if the scientists who study Boltzmann brains are themselves Boltzmann brains, they have almost no reason to suspect that they have anything like an accurate understanding of the physical laws that they project would give rise to Boltzmann brains: "Most possible Boltzmann brains will be hopelessly deluded in their understanding of the laws of physics, and if we are indeed a Boltzmann brain the probability is overwhelming that we're one of these poor souls."[43] Why, then, discuss Boltzmann brains at all? Because their predicted existence seems to undermine science's leading theories regarding the nature (past, present, and future) of the universe. Indeed, as one team of scientists has reminded: "It is useful to keep in mind that Boltzmann Brains are a difficulty, not a desirable feature, of a given cosmological model."[44] Hence, the Boltzmann brain problem becomes an argument ad absurdum, a goad to either throw out the prevailing understanding of the universe or revise it so it no longer predicts that we are almost certainly brains randomly fluctuating briefly into existence within the vacuum of space.[45]

The cognitively unstable implications of imagining a universe characterized by infinitely existing space and possibly infinite inflation may seem quite far from islands and oceans and archipelagoes and shorelines, until we recall that archipelagic thought has leaned heavily—and even depended—on the notion of the infinite. As Wiedorn reminds us, Glissant's "archipelagic thought is aligned with particularity (the rivers' rocks . . .), and above all with focusing on and preserving the infinite quantity of all particularities."[46] If Glissant relied in part on Benoit Mandelbrot's fractal geometry to arrive at archipelagic thinking's infinitely granulated view of the universe, Michelle Ann Stephens and I have also recurred to Mandelbrot to reframe one of the archipelago's major components, the island, as infinite both in the circumference of its unceasingly jagged shoreline and in the area produced by its unending corrugations.[47] Similarly, within the realm of object-oriented ontology and speculative realism, which would have us push toward an infinitude beyond human finitude by means of taking "seriously the idea that all objects recede *interminably* into themselves," the island becomes the chief metaphor for all objects, according to Timothy Morton, who reminds us of fractal "circumstances—ways of measuring [the] island—that cause its circumference to be infinite," such that "one ends up with a shape that is bounded yet infinite."[48] Is the island's fractal infinitude analogous to the infinitude of the universe's proposed infinite space and possible infinite inflation? If so, then within the maelstrom of a single island's corrugations, there is a chance that, at any point between the present and the inconceivably distant future, an island-nested Boltzmann brain may flicker into existence, a cosmologically instantiated version of Gilles Deleuze's mid-twentieth-century prediction of a "human being" who would "be the deserted island itself," of "humans [who would be] the pure consciousness of the island."[49] But it is extremely unlikely that this island-nested brain, or Boltzmann island, would flicker into existence on Earth, because Earth will not last long enough to make this statistically probable. Still, theoretical physics provides a work-around for this problem: again, it is not only thinking human brains that are predicted to fluctuate into existence in the vacuum but also every other possible configuration of particles, which would include toasters, obsidian shards, and a set of stapled pages containing an Indonesian translation of Borges's story "The Library of Babel"—as well as islands, including islands that happen to function, based on their configuration at a certain point in their fractal churnings, like human brains.[50]

Integrating the notion of the Boltzmann brain with archipelagic thinking's infinite island and then adding the Copernican principle, which asserts that we do not inhabit a unique situation in the universe, presents us with the problem that we (let *we* denote this book's readers and its writer) may not be biologically evolved humans. We may not even be randomly fluctuated Boltzmann brains. Rather, we may be Boltzmann islands whose fractal churnings have arrived at configurations that temporarily mimic the function of a brain with human intelligence. To proceed, let us bracket the question of whether we ourselves are such islands, turning our attention instead to the fact that a Boltzmann island—or at least a literary representation of an entity that could pass a Turing test for being such an island—has already flickered into existence. This random fluctuation occurs in US Virgin Islands writer Tiphanie Yanique's Pushcart-winning short story "The Bridge Stories: A Short Collection," published in her 2010 collection *How to Escape from a Leper Colony: A Novella and Stories*.[51] As the title suggests, Yanique's short story contains a series of even shorter stories—each of them told from a different perspective and each interlaced in narrating the collapse of a US-financed and Caribbean-made set of bridges that have been built to connect all the islands of the Caribbean archipelago. The second story is recounted "by a Catholic Lady," the third story "by someone's grandfather," and the fourth "by a seventeen-year-old schoolgirl."[52] The first story, however, has an island for its narrator: it is told "by an Island that is between things."[53]

Yanique's speaking island is a literary representation of a Boltzmann island that will, according to cosmology's best current models of the universe, fluctuate into existence sometime, and an infinite number of times, between the present and the mind-bogglingly distant future. We may well consider this to be the case whether or not Yanique wrote her story with the Boltzmann brain scenario in mind at all. After all, current cosmological models and archipelagic infinitude combine to produce a statistical certainty that such an island as appears in Yanique's story *will* exist physically at some point and at an infinite number of points.[54] If the island we have in Yanique's story is not *the* actual material island floating in an ocean that is in turn floating in the vacuum of space, then it might be considered a representation of that future island, a true memory of the future recorded in literary writing in the early twenty-first century. Indeed, if we take seriously the claims of deep time and the infinite island, then reading Yanique's story as a true history of an actual future Boltzmann island is the least eccentric of interpretations. Could this thinking and storytelling Boltzmann island be a mode of arriving at the true object of nissology, which Grant McCall in 1994 defined as "the study of islands on their own terms ... and the promotion of international cooperation and networking amongst islands"?[55] In the 1990s McCall intended for his term *island* to be a stand-in for islanders, or people who live on islands; he was not suggesting that scholars should attempt to fathom the existence of islands as actual beings. But in the wake of cosmology's subsequent Boltzmann brain paradox and contemporary philosophy's object-oriented insistence that we speculate on how to "understand [a thing] on its own terms," we may now entertain the idea that Yanique's story represents an actual thinking Boltzmann island of the future and hence an opportunity to understand something about a thing—the island—that usually does not communicate itself to us on its own terms.[56]

In narrating its page-long microstory, the Boltzmann island (apparently a Boltzmann version of one of the US Virgin Islands) tells readers of a human "bridge maker" who formerly lived on it—that is, who formerly lived on the island who is narrating the story. The bridge maker made "tiny little bridges" that functioned as jewelry, and "the people" who lived on the narrator "wore [these] little bridges around their necks." But before the bridge maker died, "his living family insisted that he leave a real legacy. He was famous for small things. They wanted him to be known for big things. So he built a real bridge. Paid for by the Yankees—not to honor his memory, but really for their own convenience.... Huge and stretching from Guyana—the place in the world most south—to Miami—the place in the world most north."[57] However, the bridge maker had previously made only jewelry-sized bridges, and now he made this pan-Caribbean bridge the same way, "delicate and pretty," so that at the bridge's dedication, a camera flashed and "the bridge fell apart. And not only in that spot but in places all over the Caribbean, so that the many families who had gathered to take pictures . . . also went into the ocean. And though they were surrounded by the sea no one in any of the communities had bothered to learn to swim. The water never seemed as important as the land."[58] The Boltzmann island's story, then, is a cautionary one. The Boltzmann island draws on its insight as an island to underscore the miscalculations of the Caribbean's human population, who, lured by the logic of the Yankee humans' continental exceptionalism, are not satisfied with "small things" (like small bridges or islands) and instead want "big things" (like big bridges or continents). Further, the Boltzmann island critiques the people of this version of the Caribbean for being land-centric rather than water-centric, for not recognizing that water is equally important to land. On this point, the people's drowning emerges as the ultimate comeuppance for their failure to recognize swimming as a necessity for *human beings* who are, like *island beings*, "surrounded by the sea" but who are, unlike island beings, prone not toward archipelagic connections that are subaqueous (as Brathwaite valorizes) but rather toward superaqueous connections like bridges (as the continentalist Yankees valorize). And if "the people" of the Caribbean take their cues from Yankee continentalism, the Boltzmann island of the archipelagic states of America speaks from an archipelagic view, with its description of a terraqueous world existing from continental coast to continental coast, from Guyana in the south to Miami in the north. This vision of a terraqueous span from continent to continent becomes the Boltzmann island's archipelagic answer to US continentalism's dictum "from sea to shining sea," wherein the seas on either side of the continent are nonspaces. Now, a Boltzmann US Virgin Island in the Caribbean Sea inverts the image so that the continents on either side of the sea are the nonspaces.

All of this is a literary representation not of the past nor of the present but of the future, as it is statistically predicted to fluctuate into existence at any moment—and at many moments—on the timeline between the early twenty-first century and space's projected infinite temporal horizon. If, as McGurl has suggested, the sciences of geology and short-range astronomy point toward a posthuman comedy on the temporal scale calibrated to Earth and a red giant Sun, then wait long enough and the sciences of theoretical physics and cosmology reframe this trip to the theater. It is no longer a full-length play but just the first nanosecond (or a nanosecond divided by infinity) within temporalities that spiral beyond the posthuman, temporalities that give rise to spirals of recurring Boltzmann brains and repeating Boltzmann islands with the ability to think on par with humans. Throughout a universe that is like a spiraling and infinitely chambered nautilus (with apologies to Oliver Wendell Holmes Sr.), we may be confident that this storytelling US Virgin Island's terraqueous commentaries and archipelagic redescriptions will reverberate as our universe-sized shell tumbles in the "unresting sea" of cosmological existence.[59] Yanique has evoked a future of archipelagic thinking (that is, *archipelagoes actually thinking*) beyond finitude.[60]

And yet if the Boltzmann brain paradox is an argument ad absurdum for theoretical physicists and cosmologists, goading them to revise or abandon their cosmological models, could Yanique's Boltzmann island also be a goad to the island's and archipelago's interlocutors—ranging from Glissant, to archipelagic Americanists, to object-oriented ontologists and speculative realists—to also revise and refine our operating theories regarding islands and the universe? How might the extreme weirdness of loitering so far out on time's jetty invite us to reject, qualify, or illuminate some of our present understandings?

The place of the infinite in archipelagic thinking might be a starting point, given that it is this notion of the infinite island or the infinitude of archipelagic relationality that has linked us up with exotic temporalities that seem statistically sure to give rise to Boltzmann islands. The infinite island seems to have been Mandelbrot's stance across at least three decades, ranging from his 1967 article "How Long Is the Coast of Britain? Statistical Self-Similarity and Fractal Dimension" to his 1982 book *The Fractal Geometry of Nature*. This trajectory within Mandelbrot's work has inspired thinkers ranging from Glissant to archipelagic Americanists to object-oriented ontologists. However, when Mandelbrot was in his late seventies, the notion of "nature" in his 1982 book title caught up with him, causing him to revise his stance on the purview of natural fractals, now reframed as physically incapable of attaining the theoretically infinite resolutions he had earlier asserted. We read in later Mandelbrot, in the 2004 study *The (Mis)Behavior of Markets: A Fractal View of Financial Turbulence*, that a distinction must be made between "real, as opposed to theoretical, fractal data":

> Consider a real [or natural] fractal: the way air passages in the lungs branch from the main bronchial tubes to the millions of tiny bronchi feeding individual

alveoli cells. There is a physical limit to how many and how tiny these fractal tubes can be, or need to be, for the support of life. Tubes above and below a certain size ... *simply do not occur in nature*. Likewise ... [fractal] scaling works in the broad, macroscopic middle of the spectrum; but at the far ends, in what you might call the quantum and cosmic zones, new laws ... apply.[61]

Theoretically, then, in terms of mathematics, an island is infinite in the way an infinite number of points can fill any space, but on the level of *the actual fractal geometry of actual nature*, the island is finite, and its corrugations, though still mind-bogglingly intricate on a human scale, do not resolve infinitely into incessantly more intricate corrugations—instead, their constitution by actual particles that exist in actual nature causes them to meet a physical limit beyond which the corrugations cannot plummet. Having arrived at this qualification on the island's infinitude, have we also arrived at a place where the most likely interpretation of Yanique's story is no longer that it is a true and accurate history of a future Boltzmann island? Not necessarily. Cosmology and theoretical physics' predictions of Boltzmann brains (and Boltzmann islands) are also subject to the same qualifications of "nature" that Mandelbrot's quotation places on fractal things like islands. Hence, the Boltzmann island problem prompts an important qualification on archipelagic thinking's notion of infinity, but Boltzmann islands are still predicted to proliferate infinitely in the future, and hence interpreting Yanique's story as spoken by a Boltzmann island is still the least eccentric of interpretations.

But it is on this question of centricity and eccentricity vis-à-vis Boltzmann brains/Boltzmann islands that a second archipelagic illumination depends. Recall that if there exists only a finite number of biologically evolved human consciousnesses but an infinite quantity of Boltzmann brain or island consciousnesses, then the Copernican principle (which is based on Copernicus's antigeocentric observation that the Earth revolves around the Sun and which by extension affirms that we are not central or special in the universe) tells us that we ourselves are almost certainly Boltzmann brains or Boltzmann islands. Now it is one thing (albeit a very strange thing) for humanists to entertain the idea that a short story's best interpretation involves reading the narrator as speaking the true words of an actual Boltzmann island that will exist in the future. But it is much more difficult to convince humans that their own best interpretation of themselves should be that they themselves *are* Boltzmann brains/islands who live under the delusion that they are humans—and this, extrapolated from Copernicus's conviction that the Earth revolves around the Sun rather than that the Sun revolves around the Earth! Most humans besides a perverse few (and you know who you are) would sooner accept geocentrism than the idea that their memories of everything they have ever experienced are illusions and that they are consciousnesses having fluctuated into existence a moment ago within the vacuum of space. But archipelagic Americanist thought has something to say on this Boltzmann brain–inspired cosmological vision of what comes after the posthuman, because it is the question of *what revolves around what* that has been at the very root of the US founding's continental exceptionalism. As quoted previously in this study, in 1776 Thomas Paine argued, "Small islands not capable of protecting themselves, are the proper objects for kingdoms to take under their care; but there is something very absurd, in supposing a continent to be perpetually governed by an island." In the sentence that immediately follows this island-continent rationale for US sovereignty, Paine metaphorized island-continent relationality in terms of spiraling planets, satellites, and orbits: "In no instance hath nature made the satellite larger than its primary planet, and as England and America, with respect to each other, reverses the common order of nature, it is evident they belong to different systems: England to Europe, America to itself."[62]

Hence, from the beginning, continental exceptionalism has relied on Copernican questions of gravitationally determined centricity and eccentricity to argue that the larger US American continental union does not orbit (and hence cannot be controlled by) the small island of England; rather, the small island of England is the satellite of a larger continental Europe, while the US American continental union stands apart as the center of another system entirely, vast enough that it can be a satellite to no entity and structurally poised, because it is so vast, to capture any number of satellites in the form of small islands.[63] Thus, even as on the cosmic level the Copernican principle removes Earth and humanity from the center of the universe, it at the same time, Janus-faced and consistent with Hegel's continent-centered historical model, places the US American and other continents at the center of world history. Archipelagic thinking, however, offers other models, emerging from multiple arenas, that admit contingently centered eccentricities as the standard. Antonio Benítez-Rojo has described the "meta-archipelago" as "having neither a boundary nor a center," a model that peels spatial reference away from the notions of massiveness and concomitant gravity on which continental exceptionalism depends.[64] Rather, this meta-archipelagic view, in declining to privilege any center, comes to resemble Borges's description of the universe as it surfaces in "The Library of Babel": "*The Library* [i.e., the Universe] *is a sphere whose exact center is any* [point] *and whose circumference is unattainable.*"[65] Within this archipelagic universe, where no point is the central frame of reference but any point may be provisionally taken as such, we attain such radical relations to space-time as are undertaken by Micronesian navigators, whose intellectual technology of etak is a model in which they do not navigate an archipelago by moving across the ocean; rather, "for the navigator, the canoe remains stationary and the islands zip by," the massive planet moving in relation to the small canoe, rather than vice versa.[66] This is the noncentered and particular archipelagic ethos of Yanique's narrator, who is "an Island that is between things," as if the island itself were what Borges at one point describes as a "terraqueous world placed between two mirrors that multiplied it endlessly," with any of the terraqueous globes amid the unceasing reflectional chain potentially taken as a contingent and noncentering center.[67]

What are the upshots of this archipelagic and non-Copernican model? It means that although cosmology's current version of the future will see an infinite number of thinking Boltzmann islands speaking the exact words of Yanique's narrator, we today have all the latitude in the terraqueous world to interpret the story otherwise, as something particular to the early twenty-first century rather than as a true memory of the future as it is statistically predicted to come into existence between the present and $10^{10^{50}}$ yfn. It also means that although an infinite number of thinking Boltzmann entities are predicted to come into existence in the future, the gravity of that infinity of consciousnesses need have no determinative relation to our own noncentered ontologies. And therefore you, gentle reader in your twenty-first-century particularity, need not believe that you are a Boltzmann island.

National Monuments and Albatross-Curated Archives of the Anthropocene

In chapter 58 of Herman Melville's 1851 novel *Moby-Dick*, the narrator, Ishmael, contrasts the sublime and churning ocean with the puniness of Western/colonial modernity's most august endeavors: "Though we know the sea to be an everlasting terra incognita, so that Columbus sailed over numberless unknown worlds to discover his one superficial western one . . . ; though but a moment's consideration will teach, that however baby man may brag of his science and skill, and however much, in a flattering future, that science and skill may augment; yet for ever and for ever, to the crack of doom, the sea will insult and murder him."[68] But we have reason to believe that Earth's ocean will dry up long before forever and forever. Astronomy and biology project that before the ocean dries up, the sea will be life's last refuge on an Earth besieged by a red giant Sun, and cosmology has explained that then, after the ocean's desiccation and the Earth's final incineration, time will take the very long run out toward the heat death of the universe, followed still by entropic space that continues existing, at least according to current scientific models, forever and forever.

In the *much* shorter term, contemporary climate science elaborates on Ishmael's projection regarding humankind's destiny as a permanent plaything of the cruel ocean. Escalating in popularity since its articulation in 2000, the notion of the Anthropocene has generated great interest as a description of "the central role of mankind in geology and ecology."[69] As the environmental scientists Paul J. Crutzen and Eugene F. Stoermer have observed, since the Industrial Revolution of the late eighteenth century and possibly since the end of the Pleistocene about ten to twelve thousand years ago, "mankind" has become "a major geological force" and may "remain [so] for many millennia, maybe millions of years, to come."[70] No longer a bobbing dinghy destined to capsize on the cruel waves of Ishmael's murderous ocean, humankind, by means of extractive capitalism and carbon economies and plastic production and nuclear weapons, has apparently switched places with the sea, now emerging not as the ocean's murder victim but as its murderer. One need only consider ocean acidification due to human carbon dioxide emissions, unprecedented coral reef die-offs, the collapse of fisheries that formerly seemed limitless, plastic pollution that swirls for centuries in oceanic gyres, undersea mining that obliterates unknown ecosystems, and oceanic dead zones caused by fertilizer runoff.[71] But will the ocean remain pacific, placid in the face of human abuse? Not so, say several commentators. As the poet and environmental activist Kathy Jetñil-Kijiner has pointed out, in seeking economic and nationalist invulnerability (as seen in ExxonMobil's decades-long funding of climate change deniers, for instance), "the human race" may be "funding the world [including the human world] to be washed into the sea."[72] Similarly, James Lovelock has projected an Earth that is not beaten into submission by human industry but that rather takes revenge, "the revenge of Gaia," answering some humans' misguided aspirations toward techno-invulnerability with geologic reminders of humankind's final vulnerability; as "the ocean rises to repossess" the land, we may anticipate not simply a steady sea-level rise but "sudden and wholly unpredicted discontinuities" in ocean levels.[73] If, as Ishmael says, "Columbus sailed over numberless [oceanic] worlds to [encounter] his one superficial western one," then those numberless oceanic worlds of the deep will take revenge on and outlast the Western world—and broader human worlds—of the surface. Indeed, we have moved into what Ishmael calls a "flattering future" of augmented "science and skill," or what climate scientists call the Anthropocene's "Great Acceleration," when the "human imprint on the Earth System" has attained an "exponential character."[74] But during this era of the ocean's exponential abuse by human science and skill, the ocean is projected to fight back.

It has been during the Great Acceleration's assault on the ocean that most nation-states of the world have emerged as less *superficial*, to use Ishmael's term—that is, they have become nations no longer constituted simply by land *surfaces*. More specifically, through the 1982 United Nations Convention on the Law of the Sea (UNCLOS), nation-states have used the notion of an exclusive economic zone (EEZ) to become more oceanic, making claims to the numberless oceanic worlds of the deep.[75] Especially during the first few decades of the twenty-first century, self-reflexivity regarding this transition from a land-based superficial nation to a terraqueous nation that includes oceanic depths has found emphasis among some contingents within the nonmonolithic US government. The National Oceanic and Atmospheric Administration (NOAA) and the National Science and Technology Council have framed the United States as "an Ocean Nation," a nation with "the largest Exclusive Economic Zone (EEZ) of any nation."[76] Based on this oceanic and archipelagic perception, politicians and governmental administrators have sometimes sought to reroute the future, moving the United States and perhaps the planet into what Crutzen and colleagues have imagined as a subsequent stage of the Anthropocene in which humans become "stewards of the Earth system," seeking something like a truce and even an alliance between humankind and the ocean.[77] To this end, in 2010 President Barack Obama signed Executive Order 13547, titled "Stewardship of the Ocean, Our Coasts, and the Great Lakes," which seeks "to achieve an America whose stewardship ensures that the ocean, our coasts, and the Great Lakes are healthy and resilient, safe and productive, and understood and treasured so as to promote the well-being, prosperity, and security of present and future generations."[78] Consistent with this ideal of oceanic stewardship, President Obama and his predecessor, President George W. Bush, designated a set of vast marine national monuments within the US EEZ. In 2006 President Bush created the first of these in the waters around the Northwestern Hawaiian Islands; this monument, the Papahānaumokuākea Marine National Monument, originally protected an area of 140,000 square miles (about the size of North and South Dakota combined) and was expanded in 2016 by President Obama to 582,578 square miles (about the size of Alaska, New Hampshire, and Massachusetts combined; see fig. 5.5).[79] Bush established another three oceanic monuments immediately before leaving office in 2009: the Marianas Trench Marine National Monument (95,216 square miles, about the size of Oregon), Rose Atoll Marine National Monument (13,451 square miles, about the size of Maryland, Delaware, and Rhode Island combined), and the Pacific Remote Islands Marine National Monument (initially 83,000 square miles, expanded by Obama in 2014 to 490,000 square miles, about the size of Texas, California, and Missouri combined).[80] In 2016 Obama designated the Northeast Canyons and Seamounts Marine National Monument (4,913 square miles, roughly the size of Connecticut), the first national monument in the Atlantic.[81] Together, these five little-known US national monuments cover an oceanic area roughly equal to a third of the land area of the United States. These marine national monuments could contain Yellowstone National Park, the crown jewel of the US national parks system and emblem of US America's vast continental frontier, about 340 times over.

Analogous to national parks but not created in perpetuity by an act of Congress, national monuments are established by presidential proclamation under the auspices of the 1906 Antiquities Act, which states that "the President of the United States is hereby authorized . . . to declare by public proclamation historic landmarks, historic and prehistoric structures, and other objects of historic or scientific interest that are situated upon the lands owned or controlled by the Government of the United States."[82] Applying the land-oriented Antiquities Act rather creatively to the oceanic surroundings of these islands, atolls, and archipelagoes, Bush's and Obama's proclamations looked implicitly toward the Submerged Lands Act and the Outer Continental Shelf Lands Act, both from 1953, which laid claim to underwater "lands" within the United States' three-mile band of territorial sea or areas of the continental shelf it had claimed.[83] Over half a century later, Bush and Obama were making proclamations that

FIGURE 5.5 — The Papahānaumokuākea Marine National Monument, which was expanded in 2016 to 582,578 square miles. It is the largest marine protected area held by any nation-state. For a map of all US marine national monuments in the Pacific, see figure 1.11. From Papahānaumokuākea Marine National Monument, accessed August 29, 2020, https://www.papahanaumokuakea.gov/.

set apart, for scientific and cultural purposes, the submerged lands and superadjacent waters of the United States' largely archipelago-anchored EEZ. The seabird biologist Mark J. Rauzon has stated that in creating the marine national monuments, the Bush administration undertook "an environmental act so audacious that with the stroke of a pen Bush became one of the 'greenest' presidents."[84] These monuments, as articulated in Obama's ethics regarding the ocean, seek environmental stewardship now for the benefit of future generations.

Craig Santos Perez, however, has questioned the monuments' commitment to the future, underscoring the ongoing problem of plastic pollution in Papahānaumokuākea in particular. On this latter topic, Perez published a 2013 editorial titled "Our Sea of Plastic," which begins with a quotation from Hauʻofa: "The sea is our pathway to each other and to everyone else, the sea is our endless saga."[85] Perez subsequently highlights the ramifications of the sea, and specifically the ocean current, as a pathway by stating, "In the North Pacific Ocean, currents gather marine debris from the Western coast of North America to the eastern coast of Asia. Wind and surface currents trap the floating waste towards the center of the gyre. Turning. And turning as it widens." Perez was describing a trash spiral in

SPIRALING FUTURES · 227

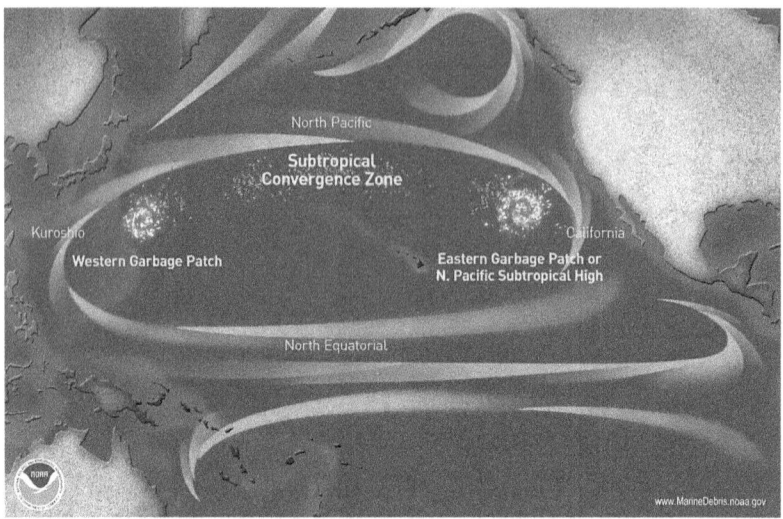

FIGURE 5.6 — The Great Pacific Garbage Patch, with a western patch in the water southeast of Japan and an eastern patch between California and Hawai'i. The subtropical convergence zone spans between the two gyres, intersecting with the Northwestern Hawaiian Islands. The Great Pacific Garbage Patch is not a discrete entity with an easily defined border; hence, determining its area is difficult and depends on the minimum concentration of plastic that any given person may determine is necessary for a particular portion of the sea to be considered part of the patch. From "Garbage Patches: What and Where Are Garbage Patches?," NOAA Marine Debris Program, Office of Response and Restoration, accessed August 21, 2020, https://marinedebris.noaa.gov/info/patch .html.

the ocean, the Great Pacific Garbage Patch (see fig. 5.6), which according to his 2013 editorial had attained "twice the area of the continental US": "As plastic floats, the sun breaks it down. Down into smaller and smaller pieces, which will take centuries to fully decompose. These particulates remain suspended on the surface, or right below the surface, of the ocean. Oceania is vast, Oceania is plastic soup." Perez vividly describes the scene on an atoll amid this plastic soup. On Pihemanu, or Midway Atoll, which is "part of the Papahānaumoku[ākea] Marine National Monument," Mōlī or Laysan albatrosses nest: "When they hunt, sometimes a piece of plastic is tangled in their food, and sometimes they mistake the plastic for food. Adult birds feed their chicks the plastic. The birds swallow and feel full. Their food and water intake reduce, causing dehydration and starvation. Sometimes, the plastic tears their digestive tracts." He continues, "If you take a picture of this post-island paradise, as others have, you will capture birds strewn across the landscape: dead. Their bodies decomposing. Their bodies filled with plastic. Plastic will outlast bird bones."

Within the editorial, Perez includes a photograph by the US artist and photographer Chris Jordan, whose project *Midway: Message from the Gyre* is a series of photographs of resilient plastic objects (cigarette lighters, plastic bottle caps, swaths of fishing net, soap-dispenser valves, shards of unidentifiable plastic, and microplastic confetti that has broken down from larger shards) surrounded by the remaining feathers, bones, and beaks of the juvenile albatrosses that have been killed by these plastic objects (see fig. 5.7).[86] On his website Jordan marvels that among "islands more than 2000 miles from the nearest continent, the detritus of our mass consumption surfaces in an astonishing place: inside the stomachs of thousands of dead baby albatrosses," reflecting back to us "an appallingly emblematic result of the collective trance of our consumerism and runaway industrial growth."[87] Over two-thirds of all Laysan albatrosses breed at Midway, and according to one estimate, about one-third of Midway's albatross chicks die, "many as the result of being mistakenly fed plastic by their parents."[88] Midway's scenes of plastic beaches and plastic deaths are repeated throughout the Northwestern Hawaiian Islands and atolls.[89] Thus, we have Benítez-Rojo's repeating island as the site of castaway plastic that has ridden the currents of a plastic-soup version of Hauʻofa's ocean, a pathway between human hands and nonhuman entrails, between the profit models of human corporations and the corporeal puncturing of oceanic life from the inside. Indeed, the ocean—working in conjunction with humankind's plastic-laden rivers and watersheds—is a pathway between the throwaway cultures of the Pacific Rim and the United States' largest and supposedly remotest wildlife sanctuary. Further, choices made today and in the future—by governments, corporations, and individuals—are pathways between the US American present and the US American future, with ramifications for post-US futurities.

One way of attending to these futurities surfaces in English writer A. S. Byatt's 2013 short story "Sea Story," which in just over two thousand words manages to have a temporal setting that spans from the early twenty-first century to a posthuman swim in the spiral of oceanic time.[90] The story begins on the coast of Britain. Its central character is Harold, son of an oceanographer and grandson of an oceanographer. Harold loves the ocean: he experiences "a moment of pure glee" when he reads "for the first time chapter 58 of *Moby Dick*," and "the space inside his skull" is made of sand, crashing waves, and the "huge curve of the horizon." Fittingly, then,

FIGURE 5.7 — The plastic stomach contents that remain as a dead albatross chick decays on Midway Atoll in Papahānaumokuākea Marine National Monument. Taken by Chris Jordan in 2009 and available through the US Fish and Wildlife Service Headquarters' Flickr photostream, this photograph also appears as the lead image in Jordan's *Midway: Message from the Gyre*. "Albatross at Midway Atoll Refuge," U.S. Fish and Wildlife Service Headquarters Flickr photostream, accessed August 29, 2020, https://www.flickr.com /photos/usfwshq/8080507529/in/album-72157631753678584/.

he falls in love at first sight with a marine biologist, Laura, who sidles up next to his boat in a wetsuit. He talks with her just twice (while she swims near his boat and later that evening at a pub) because she is leaving to take her "dream job" as "part of a team studying the life-cycle of eels" in the Caribbean. After she leaves for the Caribbean, Harold's letters and emails fail to reach her, so he sends a letter via Hauʻofa's pathway of the sea, adding his bit to the ocean's plastic soup: he puts a message in a bottle and rows out into the ocean to a place "where he [knows], from his grandfather's work [in oceanography], that the currents could possibly take the message as far as the Sargasso Sea." Here he drops the "Perrier bottle" made of "green plastic" into "the water where it move[s], apparently purposefully, away." The bottle, which he has selected because Perrier was Laura's drink of choice at the pub, travels the ocean currents as planned. It moves down the coast of England. It then gets caught in a current that takes it past the Netherlands and Denmark and Norway and into an Arctic gyre. It moves into a current that takes it down the coast of Greenland and past Newfoundland and Nova Scotia and Massachusetts. Here a cold current takes it right down the North American coast, "south into the Caribbean."

Now the bottle is caught in "the Atlantic Gyre or the Caribbean Trash Vortex, ... said to be the size of Texas." The bottle begins breaking up among plastics of "all shapes and sizes," some of them of "jewelled colours, emerald, opal, crimson, cobalt, ultramarine." A seagull "carri[es] away a smeared strip to feed to its chicks, who would die with bellies distended by this stuff." Meanwhile, the cap is eaten by a green sea turtle, which chokes and dies, and then another turtle eats the cap and also dies. Harold's love note is eaten and excreted by an eel, while the bottle's shreds harm squid, fish, and birds "whose guts were already swollen with [plastic] waste." Eventually, the bottle's resilient pieces are "washed and rubbed into nurdles which join ... the mass of other pale [plastic] beads": "Parts of this mess did in fact reach their intended destination, ... caught in vast trailing micronets [that were] ... part of a long and painstaking experiment to examine the bulk of [plastic] nurdles and the diminishing bulk of the plankton. There she was, Laura, ... gathering in ... the [plastic] beads. ... She looked at them in a glass dish under a strong microscope. The message she read was the human occupation and corruption of the masterless ocean."

In the final paragraph, Harold and Laura die. These deaths are followed by the story's closing two sentences, which run us down a spiraling jetty to the forever and forever of plastic: "Fires raged and floods drove through streets and houses as the planet became more and more inimical to human life. The sempiternal nurdles, indestructible, swayed on and under the surface of the sea."

On one level, "Sea Story" offers a parable of history, really beginning, that operates at a personal level in relation to the ocean. When Laura drinks from a plastic bottle in the pub, she may imagine it will be recycled, and it may be.[91] But the unintended consequence of her drinking from the single-use plastic bottle in the first place is that someone else—a stranger, really—places a plastic bottle in the ocean, and its plastic harms the marine life that she dedicates her life to studying. The plastic bottle in the pub, used by a human for half an hour, is not history but prologue to a plastic history really beginning. Thus, "Sea Story" points to any number of sempiternal single-use plastic items that may seem like mere blips in the lives of Byatt's readers. Highly relevant to this consumer illusion of plastic as ephemeral is the way Harold loves the sea. Harold loves it in a way mediated by chapter 58 of *Moby-Dick*, which frames the sea as indestructible and concludes as follows: "For as this appalling ocean surrounds the verdant land, so in the soul of man there lies one insular Tahiti, full of peace and joy, but encompassed by all the horrors of the half known life. God keep thee! Push not off from that isle, thou canst never return!"[92] In their use of plastic, Harold and Laura follow Ishmael's imperative, holding fast to "that isle" of human time, refusing to push off, with their plastic, into an ocean of half-known life, declining to think beyond the thirty-minute use of a plastic bottle or the ten-second use of a plastic flosser, declining to consider how these quotidian temporal increments are prologue to an oceanic and epic future history in which, five hundred years from now, the *unrecyclable* cap of even a *recycled* bottle will have killed or otherwise affected untold generations of sea life.[93] Against this confinement to the island of human time (an island that disposable consumerism invites us to regard as infinite and act accordingly), Byatt's story insists that readers push off from the isle and into an accurate understanding of the oceanic temporality of plastic. Further, the story seems to hope that Melville is correct, that upon seeing the bottle's shredded existence spiraling in an oceanic gyre until the crack of doom, readers will never be able to return to the happy isle. Pushing out into the plastic-soup ocean, we see that every seemingly happy isle of human-scaled plastic use is a repeating Midway Atoll, littered with clumps of sempiternal plastic boluses, albatross-curated archives of humans' disposable lifeways.

Beyond having implications for how individual humans may decide to alter future centuries in the various gyres of the global ocean, "Sea Story," when read in dialogue with the presidential directives contained in the proclamation creating the Papahānaumokuākea Marine National Monument, points toward a US obligation to curb the use of plastic not only within its borders but worldwide as well, given the way ocean currents evoke US borderwaters that are thousands of miles outside of the United States' watery borders. In using the ocean to convey a love letter to Laura, Harold drops his plastic Perrier bottle "into the water where it move[s], apparently purposefully, away." With its seemingly purposeful plastic bottle, the scene resembles certain aspects of Jane Bennett's thinking on "thing-power," which sees an intentional vitality in "bodies inorganic as well as organic," with this vitality becoming especially visible to humans when a thing, like a plastic bottle cap or a tsunami or a crystal or a power grid, "inexplicably choose[s] one path of development rather than another."[94] I agree with Bennett that in the context of present-day consumerism, "the sheer volume of commodities, and the hyperconsumptive necessity of junking them to make room for new ones, conceals the vitality of matter."[95] To be sure, the plastic bottle's thirty-minute life in the pub is a prologue to its half-millennium life in the ocean. But the governmental answer to the ocean's plastic soup will not finally reside in recuperating plastic's vitality.

In fact, corporate recuperations of this vibrancy are currently working to deflate the government's and consumers' will to regulate disposable plastic. Since 1953 the industry-funded nonprofit organization Keep America Beautiful has deliberately sought to assuage consumer and governmental unease regarding the massive litter and landfill plagues produced by corporations' move toward ever more disposable packaging.[96] Founded and funded by corporations (including Alcoa, Anheuser-Busch, Coca-Cola, Dow Chemical, the Dixie Cup Company, McDonald's, PepsiCo, and many others) that have purposefully made disposability a cornerstone of their profit models, Keep America Beautiful and its corporate sponsors have consistently lobbied to defeat government- and consumer-driven legislation that seeks to promote reusable packaging.[97] Having helped shepherd the United States from an era of reusable containers to an era of single-use containers (e.g., 100 percent of soft drink containers were reusable in 1947, compared with 0.4 percent in 1998), Keep America Beautiful in the 2010s advanced an ad campaign titled "I Want to Be Recycled," targeting the two-thirds of US Americans who have not regularly been recycling the disposable packaging that the nonprofit's corporate sponsors have been profiting from.[98] The ad campaign's premise: "Imagine a plastic bottle that dreams of becoming a pair of jeans, a steel food can that wants to breeze by as a bicycle, or a shampoo bottle that continues to bring smiles to the beautiful faces of children as a hairbrush. Would you help to make their dreams come true if you could?"[99] Featured on television, radio, and billboards, as well as in print sources, these ads often star a vibrant plastic bottle who is thinking about the future, standing in the grass next to a park bench, saying, "I want to be a bench. Recycle me," or standing on a sidewalk near some clothed human legs, saying, "I want to be a pair of jeans. Recycle me."[100]

One of the television ads, a thirty-second spot titled "Journey 30" (2013), begins on a city street lined with trash cans. Out of one of the cans pops a plastic bottle. This bottle is vibrant, speaking with a voice that presents as a human female apparently hailing from a landlocked midwestern US state. As she rolls west across the United States' continental frontier (the prairie, the Rockies, the railway, a desert), she explains, "Everybody has a dream. Mine was to see the ocean. And with a little help, I made it." The ad concludes with a man randomly picking her up and recycling her, which permits her to become a bench poised picturesquely above a rocky West Coast shoreline.[101] This spot seems like a corporate answer to US director Ramin Bahrani's 2009 short film "Plastic Bag," which also stars a vibrant piece of plastic, a grocery bag voiced by Werner Herzog, on its way to the Great Pacific Garbage Patch. Whereas Keep America Beautiful seeks to obviate governmental regulation by suggesting that random city dwellers may simply practice random acts of ecological kindness to reroute any given piece of disposable plastic on its way to the ocean, Herzog, as a plastic bag spiraling in an oceanic gyre for untold centuries, comes closer to accusing the corporations that created him, telling viewers what he would say to his maker if he could say just one thing: "I wish you had created me so that I could die."[102] Herzog's haunting closing line assures us that we do not need plastic that is vibrant—we need plastic that dies or, better, plastic that was never born.

But of course, readers of Byatt's story know that the Perrier bottle does not go to the ocean because it dreams of doing so. And they know this piece of green plastic, when dropped into the water, does not move away owing to any purpose of the bottle itself. They know that Harold is the grandson of an oceanographer, and when the bottle moves away, it is because Harold has knowingly released it into a current that has a statistical likelihood of carrying it to the Caribbean. Harold's calculated use of currents in the Atlantic and Caribbean moves us toward thinking through ways in which the very existence of the Papahānaumokuākea Marine National Monument restructures agency and accountability vis-à-vis the repeating plastic islands of the Northwestern Hawaiian Islands. Plastic pollution that makes its way to the patch, and that consequently injures Papahānaumokuākea, arrives from countries all around the Pacific Rim, traveling on predicable oceanic pathways analogous to the current into which Harold drops the Perrier bottle. In spite (or because) of decades of Keep America Beautiful ads sponsored by companies that are dedicated to increasing the use of plastic packaging while assuaging consumers' discomfort with single-use packaging, one recent estimate suggests that US coastal populations create more plastic litter than the coastal populations of any other country—275,425 tons in 2010, compared to China's 231,157 tons, Indonesia's 77,822 tons, and India's 13,728 tons. Produced within fifty kilometers of the coasts, this is "plastic waste with high risk of polluting surrounding rivers" and hence of entering the ocean, rather than becoming a bench overlooking the ocean.[103] By another estimate, "each year the Los Angeles River alone carries enough trash to the ocean to fill the inside of the Rose Bowl between twenty feet and thirty-four feet high."[104] It is impossible to predict exactly where each piece of plastic litter will go: during a three-day sampling period in the early 2000s, the Los Angeles and San Gabriel Rivers were found to have transported over 2.3 billion pieces of plastic into the sea.[105] But it is certain—based on what we know of oceanic currents—that a portion of this plastic litter will enter and injure the ecosystem of Papahānaumokuākea.[106]

This certainty runs counter to Bush's proclamation creating the monument, which states that the secretary of commerce and the secretary of the interior "shall prohibit any person" not only from "discharging or depositing any material or other matter into the monument" but also from "discharging or depositing any material or other matter *outside of the monument* that subsequently enters the monument and injures any resources of the monument."[107] Typically, it would seem, this duty of the secretaries of commerce and the interior might be viewed as relevant to marine vessels immediately outside the monument's watery borders, but Harold's use of scientifically knowable and predictable currents reminds us that the secretaries have an obligation to prohibit plastic pollution from entering the ocean and injuring Papahānaumokuākea via US rivers. And of course, given that decades of antilittering and pro-recycling ads by Keep America Beautiful have succeeded in making consumers feel good about increasing their consumption of single-use plastic bottles but have failed to prevent US consumers from becoming the world's top-ranked sea-facing litterbugs, it is time—and past time—for the secretaries to take measures to stop the plastic pollution at its source, which is neither the consumer's hand nor the river's mouth but is the manufacturer of single-use plastic.[108] According to Papahānaumokuākea's founding document, this is an obligation that the secretaries of commerce and the interior have toward actions that take place outside the borders of the monument but inside the borders of the United States.

Still, as anyone who studies oceanic plastic pollution knows, the United States may be the top contributor of ocean-bound litter, but it is not the top contributor of oceanic plastic more generally. According to one 2015 estimate, the United States contributes 0.04–0.11 million metric tons of plastic marine debris per year, compared with 1.32–3.53 million metric tons for China, such that China, as the worst plastic polluter in the world, contributes at least twelve times as much plastic to the ocean.[109] Elsewhere, on the topic of annual global plastic inputs from rivers into the ocean, we see that as of 2015 Asia was estimated to contribute 86 percent of global river plastic input to the ocean, followed by Africa at 7.8 percent, South America at 4.8 percent, Central and North America at 0.95 percent, Europe at 0.28 percent, and Australia and the Pacific Islands at 0.02 percent. Among the top twenty highest-ranking rivers for oceanic plastic pollution, six are in China, and four are in Indonesia, while none are in the United States (see fig. 5.8).[110] The scale of the problem, as it slides across

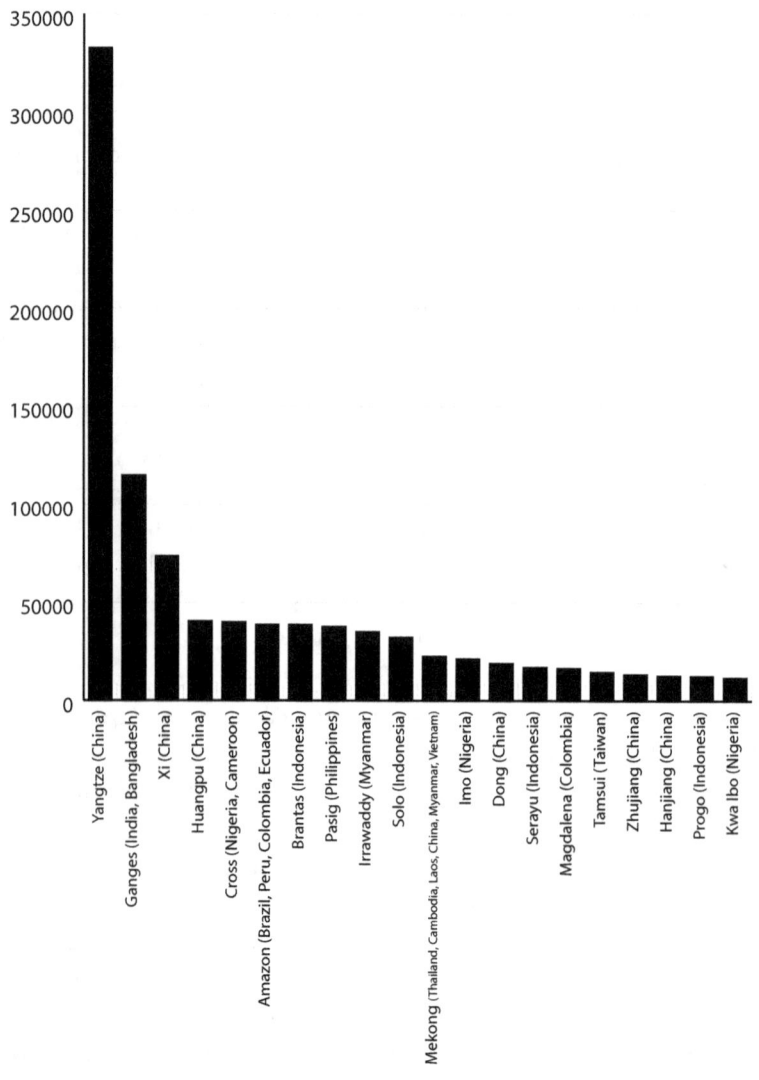

geography, makes the Rose Bowl look like a fingernail clipping. Meanwhile, the amount of plastic in the Great Pacific Garbage Patch is increasing exponentially.[111]

One mode of thinking about borders might lead us to suppose that the United States has no purview over the massive influx of non-US plastic into the Papahānaumokuākea Marine National Monument, but this is not what President Bush's proclamation says. If the sea with its currents cannot be fenced, as Gloria Anzaldúa remarks, then Bush's proclamation, perhaps surprisingly aligned with Sukarno's Bandung Conference warnings against nuclear testing, insists on another mechanism to protect the marine national monument from injurious "material or other matter" released in watersheds that are outside of US borders but that nonetheless constitute highly consequential US borderwaters: "The Secretary of State, in consultation with the Secretaries [of Commerce and the Interior], shall take appropriate action to *enter into negotiations with other governments* to make necessary arrangements for the protection of the monument.... The Secretary of State, in consultation with the Secretaries, *shall seek the cooperation of other governments* and international organizations in furtherance of the purposes of this proclamation."[112]

It is strange, then, that at the end of the second decade of the twenty-first century the United States was not leading the fight against plastic pollution. Instead, as seen at a United Nations conference in March 2019, it broke with an overwhelming international consensus among the United

FIGURE 5.8 — (*opposite*) Oceanic plastic emissions (in metric tons) by the world's top-twenty most polluting rivers in 2015. Data visualization by Lalitree Darnielle, based on data reported in Lebreton et al., "River Plastic Emissions." None of the top-twenty polluting rivers is in the United States, but recycled US plastic may nonetheless make its way to the ocean via some of the top-twenty rivers. Asia has long been a prime destination for US recycling waste. Until 2018 the United States shipped much of its plastic recycling to China, where the plastic could find its way into Chinese rivers and subsequently the ocean. In 2019 a media spotlight fell on the Indonesian village of Bangun as a destination for plastic from the United States and other countries. Bangun is located on the Brantas River, ranked first in Indonesia and sixth or seventh in the world for plastic discharge into the ocean. Mike Ives, "Recyclers Cringe as Southeast Asia Says It's Sick of the West's Trash," *New York Times*, June 7, 2019, https://www.nytimes.com/2019/06/07/world/asia/asia-trash.html; and Shashank Bengali, "Your Trash Is Suffocating This Indonesian Village," *Los Angeles Times*, October 25, 2019, https://www.latimes.com/world-nation/story/2019-10-25/plastic-pollution-waste-recycling-indonesia.

Nations Environment Assembly, *working against rather than seeking legally binding proposals that would strengthen international cooperation against marine plastic and phase out single-use plastics worldwide*.[113]

One wonders how far out onto time's jetty it will be—or how far into the sempiternal spirals of Byatt's shredded Perrier bottle—before the US government may begin prioritizing the stewardship of its own marine national monuments rather than permitting them to function as the tragic commons of designing corporations and consumers whose complacency is partially produced by the nostrums of corporate antilittering and pro-recycling public service announcements. A common trope in discussions of the Anthropocene involves imagining a future after the end of the world as we know it, a future that includes posthuman or nonhuman analogues to present-day scientists. We may be asked to imagine a "field geologist living say 10,000 years from now" who identifies "the onset of the Anthropocene" in "an assemblage of numerous high-tech artifacts in a highly compacted sedimentary layer," or "extraterrestrial visitors" some hundred million years from now whose scientists identify Earth's "Human Period," "a brief geological instant that will seem lost among many millions of other such instants."[114] Along these lines, Alexis Pauline Gumbs's *M Archive: After the End of the World* (2018) imagines a distant posthuman future in which it will perhaps be "critical black oceanographers" or "critical black marine biologists," looking back on our present and nearer-term human future, who find evidence that people (us and our human descendants) began believing "they were 60 percent cola" rather than 60 percent water.[115] Further, these posthuman Black scientists, as they study the ancient ocean of today with the retrospect of millennia, are able to identify a principle of "water debt" incurred by corporations, including "cola producers," discovering through their research that the corporations owed the humans so much in water debt that "Coca-Cola alone would have [had] to invent a free purification system, build spaceships fast enough to go to the next solar system and import stolen water from elsewhere in the galaxy to even touch a tenth of what they had done."[116] *M Archive* is not clear on the precise nature of the geologic or paleontological data on which these far-future Black oceanographers and marine biologists might rely. But one imagines that just as present-day human scientists have been able to use island-preserved fossils to trace the evolutionary emergence of the albatross, Gumbs's far-future posthuman scientists might find evidence of corporate water debt in albatross-curated archives of plastic technofossils. Taking the shape and size of juvenile albatross stomachs, these fossilized assemblages of plastic bottle caps, cigarette lighters, flossers, nurdles, and shards of Perrier and Coke packaging (perhaps coalesced into something like the recently described lithic form of the "plastiglomerate") may offer traces of the corporate-sponsored plastic ocean that spiraled amid the lands and waters of what an ancient archipelagic empire of the early twenty-first-century once claimed to control, but then declined to protect, as the largest nationally held marine protected area on the planet.[117]

This Isn't America: Seafaring and Spacefaring across Temporal Borders

In the late 1980s the US American ethnobotanist and environmentalist Paul Alan Cox was in the independent country of Western Samoa (now the Independent State of Samoa), in the village of Falealupo, on the west end of the island of Savai'i. He was negotiating with thirty village chiefs to establish what has now become the Falealupo Rainforest Preserve. Working with a consortium of private and corporate donors, Cox was seeking to collaborate with the village to stymie logging interests and establish a Samoan national park geared toward protecting the rain forest's "indigenous flora and fauna" while still permitting "limited cultural uses of the forests" involving "traditional techniques and tools."[118] He had drafted a Samoan-language covenant that he hoped the chiefs would agree to, with the stated "purpose of preserving forever the rain forests of the Falealupo peninsula."[119] As narrated in his 1999 environmental memoir, *Nafanua: Saving the Samoan Rain Forest*, Cox sat with the chiefs and began reading the covenant draft as he had written it but was interrupted, when he arrived at the word "forever," by a chief named A'eau. "I have a problem with that word," said A'eau. "Only God is forever. Man is limited in time." Cox responded, "Yes, but the intent of a national park is to preserve it forever. All of the American national parks are preserved forever." In answer to Cox's analogy, another chief, Fuiono Senio, "sternly interjected": "This isn't America.... This is Samoa. We can't guarantee what will happen in the distant future. We can only guarantee what will happen in our own lifetimes." Recalling his own thoughts at this juncture in the negotiations, Cox writes, "My mind reeled. All of the national parks I had heard of had been established in perpetuity. None had time limits on them." But "the chiefs seemed insistent," so Cox suggested a 100-year period of protection, to which Fuiono Senio replied, "There isn't a person in this room who will be alive a hundred years from now.... In Samoa, we can't control from the grave what future generations will do. Can you do any better?" They finally agreed on fifty years.[120]

Although Cox and Fuiono Senio shared the 1997 Goldman Environmental Prize for collaborating to preserve the Falealupo rain forests, the scalar difference between their perceptions of futurity marks what might be thought of as a temporal megalomania on the part of the United States.[121] No doubt the short-term actions of the geologically ephemeral United States are capable of *destroying* or otherwise affecting forests and oceans and ecosystems and stones for millions of years into the future. But the United States is not capable of actively *protecting* these things for millions of years into the future, much less "in perpetuity," given that the timelines of undisturbed forests and oceans and ecosystems and stones tend *to dwarf rather than fit within* the timelines of nation-states and empires. In the US aspiration to preserve *in perpetuity*, we see the time-oriented face of continental exceptionalism's manifest destiny, in which the United States covets the distant futurity encoded in the term *destiny*, such that, to riff on a famous axiom attributed to Fredric Jameson, it is easier to imagine the end of the world—the end of the stones, the oceans, the ecosystems—than the end of the United States of America.[122] Hence, concomitant with the highly visible preservation effect produced by the US national parks' dedication to spatial management is the national parks' project of temporal management, which advances a vision of a United States whose temporal borders have no expiration date but unspool unceasingly, in perpetuity, into the future. In the face of forever, might Fuiono Senio's humbler vision of temporal management represent one mode of archipelagic temporality, an engagement in which temporal units, if they were mapped onto space, would more closely resemble the granularity of the rocks of the rivers than they would the megalithic continent?

Whatever the case, at around the same time as Cox was negotiating with the chiefs of Faleolupo in Western Samoa, he was aiding in negotiations that would culminate in a US national park in American Samoa. Called the National Park of American Samoa, this park, like the Falealupo Rainforest Preserve, is not established in perpetuity but rather involves only a fifty-year lease of the protected areas, with the lease negotiations concluded in September 1993 between the governor of American Samoa (acting on behalf of village landowners) and the US National Park Service.[123] Somewhat remarkably, in *American* Samoa, the negotiations required an attentiveness to the ideal behind what Cox encountered in his negotiations in Western Samoa. Cox and a colleague report that in American Samoa, the Samoan chiefs made it clear that, "given their responsibilities to both their ancestors and to unborn generations, they did not regard it as prudent to surrender control of their forests to a country such as the US which has been in existence 'scarcely more than 200 years.'"[124] The Samoan chiefs' words ("scarcely more than 200 years" and "This isn't America.... This is Samoa") reverberate within lands and waters claimed by the United States. Indeed, the National Park of American Samoa's fifty-year lease constitutes a compromise, a US acquiescence to a mode of temporal thought that is humbler and certainly more accurate than a traditional US view in which manifest destiny melds with temporal infinity. Relatedly, the fifty-year lease in American Samoa is a de facto acknowledgment that this isn't simply the United States of America—this is at the same time Samoa, and this will, during the long walk down perpetuity's spiral, become something utterly unrecognizable to humans living on Earth during the late twentieth and early twenty-first centuries.[125] Against a traditional US American eternity, the fifty-year lease is a tacit acknowledgment that US sovereignty has borders that are not only spatial but, just as important, temporal.[126]

The question of US temporal borders—or the question of when US territorial claims might end—has been taken up variously by referenda, commentators, and activists in the context of US empire.[127] On the one hand, the writer Doug Mack, in his book *The Not-Quite States of America: Dispatches from the Territories and Other Far-Flung Outposts of the USA* (2017), has argued that all current nonstate territories should be organized and incorporated "so that they're really, truly part of the country, not merely possessions, and have the full and unquestioned protections of the Constitution."[128] This tack would cement the not-quite states of America into the United States, making them US states, assuring that they are (to use a term from the US Pledge of Allegiance) "indivisible" from the rest of the United States and hence heirs to a putatively perpetual US sovereignty. On the other hand, Dean Itsuji Saranillio, in his study *Unsustainable Empire: Alternative Histories of Hawai'i Statehood* (2018), denaturalizes the common US assumption that US statehood—that "highest form of U.S. governance attainable" and "the pinnacle of settler civilization"—is necessarily a perpetual status.[129] Rather than being "permanently settled," US states and their US statehood are in flux vis-à-vis "Native counterclaims," to the point that "every U.S. state has a statehood story [involving Indigenous counterclaims] to tell."[130] In this light, the fifty-year lease for the National Park of American Samoa, which is an anomalous term facilitated by a US governmental perception that the archipelago is an anomalous geographic form, erupts as a compromise between settler and Indigenous times, permitting the rubric of the archipelagic states of America to help crystallize what Mark Rifkin calls a "pluralize[d] temporality" in which "Indigenous forms of time push against the imperatives of settler sovereignty."[131]

While Indigenous pushes against the borders of US settler time may seem futile or laughable to some, a short story by the Filipino science fiction writer Timothy James M. Dimacali helps imagine some ways in which the United States of today may be very much like Fuiono Senio's Samoa, unable to guarantee what will happen beyond about half a century's time. Dimacali's story "Sky Gypsies" is set sometime after 2084, the year when, according to the history recounted by the narrator, "the United Nations opened up international mining rights" among the asteroids near "the Martian colony" so that what the United Nations apparently called "minor nations could establish their own space mining operations, lessening [Earth's] dependence on" the Mars-based facilities that were now controlled by an entity called "the Martian Union."[132] In this future, Dimacali imagines that the Sama-laut, or the so-called sea gypsies whose littoral and seafaring cultures span archipelagic Southeast Asia (including the present-day Philippines, Indonesia, Malaysia, and Brunei), have made "the transition from seafaring to spacefaring," showing "an inborn aptitude for navigation and resistance to both extreme pressure and motion sickness," as well as a resistance "against most of the cellular degradation typical of prolonged exposure to solar radiation."[133] Set a few decades after 2084, the story focuses on a father-son team of Sama-laut miners, named Mandali and Sanno respectively, aboard a small ship called the *Karumarga*.[134] They are seeking platinum-rich asteroids. During the story's main episode of asteroid mining, the *Karumarga* approaches a planetoid, and Mandali "recheck[s] his coordinates, reassuring himself that the area [has] not been previously staked by another miner." The narrator explains that such "redundancies [are] a necessary nuisance in this place," for "although mining territories [are] defined by law, the discovery of new asteroids and radical changes in the orbits of known ones . . . mean[s] that the boundaries [are] difficult, if not impossible, to enforce."[135]

Having determined that this asteroid is unclaimed, the team shoots an explosive probe at the surface and contains the resulting rubble by using a magnetic dome so that "the cloud of debris left by the probe float[s] in a tight spiral within its controlled magnetic field" (see fig. 5.9).[136] An experienced miner, Mandali jumps "into the swirling mass of rocks... below." While he weightlessly navigates the spiral of debris, seeming to swim in the vacuum of space as his Earth-based Sama-laut ancestors did in the ocean, he sees through his tech-enhanced goggles "a strangely colored speck." Having "never seen anything like this before," he "quickly pocket[s] the precious rock" and "swim[s] back to the safety of his ship."[137] However, before they can begin the return journey to their Sama-laut space settlement, a ship with the crimson markings of the Martian Union Police approaches. Two Martian Union patrolmen board to inspect the *Karumarga*'s meager cargo of marginally valuable ore, and they take one-fifth of the ore as a tax.[138] After the Martian Union Police depart, Mandali shows Sanno the strange rock, which he had kept concealed during the inspection: through the techgoggles Sanno and Mandali can see that "something [is] actively breaking down the rock and releasing oxygen into space.... A life form perhaps, similar to the tiny water plants of Earth's seas that [Mandali's] elders used to talk about?... Perhaps they could harvest it somehow, use it so that [their] people no longer needed to rely on Outsider technology for the air they breathed." The story concludes, "Mandali thanked Tuhan [God] for guiding them to these waters.... He steered the ship full on into the solar wind, and the *Karumarga* rocked gently as it sailed on its long journey home."[139]

Although this story is set only decades from now and is near-term in relation to the half-millennium lifetime of ocean plastic or the utterly exotic temporality of the Boltzmann brain, Dimacali's narrative seems to have very little to do with the United States. On one level, this is unremarkable—Dimacali is not a US American writer but rather "a third-generation Manileño, born and raised in the [Philippines'] urbanized capital."[140] But given that as of the present writing it has only been several decades since the termination of the United States' half-century claim to the Philippines as a US territory, taking for granted the United States' absence from the story runs the risk of acquiescing to a temporal version of manifest destiny that sees US sovereignty as extending in perpetuity. In other words, to note the absence of the United States—from the Philippines today and from Dimacali's spacefaring narrative of the future—is to advance a reminder that we are not presently waiting for some nearly unimaginable futurity when US boundaries will be in flux. Rather, temporal flux has abounded during recent decades, causing spatial boundaries (as in the cases of the Philippines or the Trust Territory of the Pacific Islands

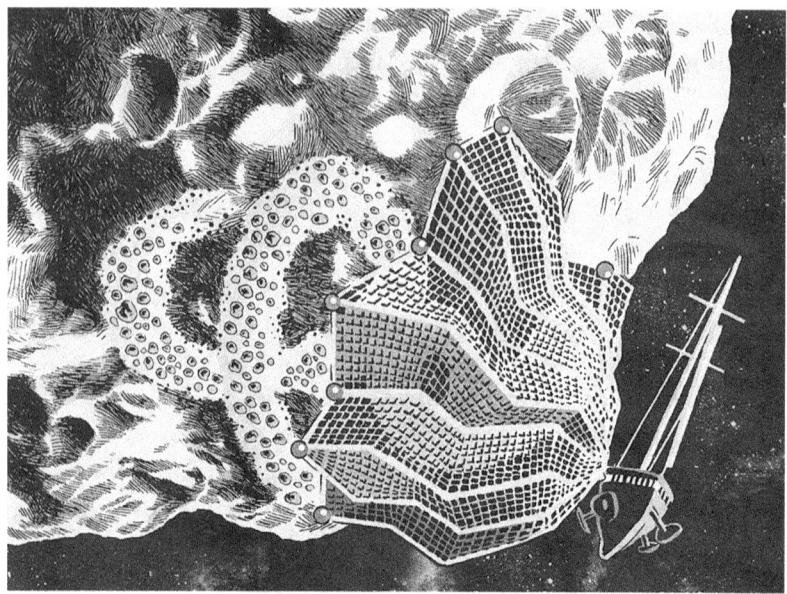

FIGURE 5.9 — A cloud of mining debris spiraling above the surface of an asteroid. Timothy James M. Dimacali has adapted his 2007 short story to the format of a comic book, illustrated by John Raymond Bumanglag and published in the first issue of the Philippine magazine *Kwentillion*, May 26, 2012. This excerpt from the comic book's front cover shows the *Karumarga* disengaging its magnetic dome, revealing the spiral of debris from which Mandali has just pulled a rock containing an unknown life-form. Courtesy of Timothy James M. Dimacali and John Raymond Bumanglag.

or the Panama Canal Zone or Pukapuka or the EEZ) to both expand and contract, coming into existence and yet, against perpetuity, having temporal expiration dates as well. Hence, to ignore the absence of the United States from Dimacali's story may be to overlook the certainty that present-day US territories—whether US nonstates or US states—will also in the future exit the temporal borders of US sovereignty. This is an absolute certainty—one need not think all the way out to the Boltzmann brains but simply to the time 80 million years from now when the last of today's Hawaiian Islands will have eroded into the ocean.

But like Dimacali, the Sama-laut of "Sky Gypsies" are descended from people who did not need to wait tens of millions of years to arrive at, and exit, the United States' temporal borders. Although never without Indigenous counterclaims, the Philippines entered US temporal borders in 1898 with the Treaty of Paris, and it exited US temporal borders on

July 4, 1946, when the United States acknowledged the independent Republic of the Philippines. If the Sama-laut, as former US nationals, hail from one of the "minor nations" mentioned by the story's narrator, we may imagine that in this future of several decades hence, some of the other post-2084 "minor nations" will have populations that are, like the Sama-laut, descended from US nationals and citizens. If the Philippines' past is US empire's prologue, then these other minor nations of Dimacali's future might include Samoa (now reunified rather than divided into the Independent State of Samoa and American Samoa), the Restored Kingdom of Hawai'i (now having its sovereignty recognized internationally but still working with the United Nations toward ending US control of the Papahānaumokuākea Marine National Monument), the Republic of Borinquen and Vieques (a twin-island country that the people of erstwhile Puerto Rico modeled after the Republic of Trinidad and Tobago), and a confederated group of reservation-shaped Indigenous nation-states that spangle the North American continent like an archipelago (including an Indian reoccupation of Alcatraz Island in San Francisco Bay, as a reminder that the confederated archipelago of North American Indigenous nation-states is a metonymy of the island, Turtle Island, that has yet to be fully decolonized).[141]

Beyond knowing that "minor nations" exist on Dimacali's Earth of several decades into the future, we see within Dimacali's solar system the emergence of an independent and powerful entity called the Martian Union, whose influence the Earth-based United Nations is seeking to undercut. This is an entity whose backstory we are left to imagine, but the backstory's broad brushstrokes may be fairly predictable if we consider the constrained number of major geopolitical and exopolitical (or off-Earth) lines that can be drawn between our early twenty-first-century present and Dimacali's imagined future. Given that as of the present writing the United States is the only nation-state to have successfully landed an operating probe on Mars, the Martian Union's backstory might have unfolded along the following lines, as told from Dimacali's future.[142] Around the mid-twenty-first century, the United States (through NASA's establishment of a science-oriented Martian colony) helped give rise to a set of private Mars-based mining corporations, which, over the course of a decade or so, joined together to become the solar system's first exopolitical entity, the Martian Union. As a cartel, the Martian Union came to dominate the space-based mining operations that the United States and other United Nations members relied on, precipitating first US and then United Nations efforts to regulate and rein in the cartel and its leaders. In response, the Martian Union cast off what it saw as superannuated political links to the United States and the United Nations. It declared independence in 2076 perhaps, with the self-consciously planetary Martian Union of the late twenty-first century becoming analogous to the self-consciously continental United States of the late eighteenth century, while the declining United States of the late twenty-first-century became analogous to what Thomas Paine in 1776 referred to as insular England with its "narrow limits of three hundred and sixty miles."[143] In fact, the line between our early twenty-first-century present and Dimacali's future Martian Union would virtually require the emergence of a late twenty-first-century Mars-based version of Paine looking back across space at the faraway United States and arguing, as Paine argued regarding the absurdity of an island governing a continent, that it is absurd to think that a mere nation-state on the old world could perpetually govern a *planetary* union on Mars.[144] Dimacali has suggested that "all good scifi, no matter how far into the future it's placed, is still a projection of contemporary problems," and he has seen his own work specifically as contesting space travel as a metaphor for "the age of Western expansionism."[145] Thus, the implied backstories of the "minor nations" and the Martian Union point toward the coming decades as bringing to pass a clearer view of US temporal borders on Earth, as newly recognized nations roll back notions of US perpetuity and as the first exopolitical entity beats the United States at its own expansionist game.

Indeed, we might take the narrator's comments on, and Mandali's facility in negotiating, boundaries in space as illuminating with regard to the watery borders and borderwaters of the archipelagic states of America, including their precolonial pasts, US American presents, and decolonial futures. Again, through the narrator's eyes, we see Mandali using ancestral seafaring navigational knowledge to adeptly negotiate "mining territories" whose boundaries shift radically with the "discovery of new asteroids and radical changes in the orbits of known ones," such that "boundaries [are] difficult, if not impossible, to enforce." This vision of complex borders shifting across time in three-dimensional orbital spaces may be taken to point toward the complexity of today's watery borders and borderwaters, in which exceedingly strange—and possibly unenforceable—versions of borders exist: a school of twenty tuna in a nation's EEZ becomes a school of twenty mobile tuna-shaped national borders; an ambulatory shoreline constituted by the constantly churning negotiations of surf and sand becomes the basis on which we project the fractal border of a territorial sea; the act of dropping a plastic bottle in the Yangtze River in Shanghai constitutes an act of future border crossing that the presidential proclamation regarding Papahānaumokuākea obligates the United States to attempt to stop; a local chief in Western Samoa says, "This isn't America," and the US National Park Service decides against perpetuity in *American* Samoa. If in Dimacali's future the spacefaring Sama-laut are able to negotiate the unenforceable borders among asteroids as they spiral around the Sun, it is because they are descendants of seafaring Sama-laut who according to late twentieth- and early twenty-first-century scholars have lived and traveled in archipelagic Southeast Asia and have been seen by nation-states at various times and places as Indonesians, Filipinos, Malaysians, Bruneians, and US nationals and yet have frequently declined to take upon themselves a national alignment.[146] Instead, they have "frustrated [land-oriented] colonial projects to order knowledge of ethnic difference," existing on "the edges of governance" as "a dispersed seafaring people of the region who do not tie their sense of ethnic collectivity to a particular place of 'origin.'"[147] Yet I would not take the archipelagic travels of the Sama-laut—either seafaring or spacefaring—as a utopian vision of archipelagic transnationalism in the spatial register. Rather, I would see their spacefaring negotiations of radically shifting boundaries as emblematic, in the temporal register, of the way the decades of the future might collaborate with ongoing Indigenous counterclaims to highlight the temporal boundaries of US sovereignty, placing current US nationals and US citizens at the edge—and even outside the edge—of governance. Within Dimacali's story, the ultimate arrival at this edge stems from a stone floating in the spiral of rocks among which he swims. What is it? We don't know. But out of this spiral he has pulled the promise of another mode of life, the promise of truly alien sovereignties that recall Earth's borderwaters.

CONCLUSION

Distant Reading the Archipelagic Gyre:
Digital Humanities Archipelagoes

DATA COLLECTION, PREPARATION, AND VISUALIZATION
BY BRIAN CROXALL, WITH ASSISTANCE FROM LORIN GROESBECK,
JEREMY BROWNE, AND LALITREE DARNIELLE

In *Borderwaters* I have been careful not to call for, or suggest that there has been, an archipelagic turn in the study of US culture. As I discuss in this conclusion, rather than an archipelagic turn, I would conceive of an archipelagic gyre—not a gyre *in* the study of US culture but a gyre whose fractal currents exist apart from and help constitute the borderwaters that interlap with the watery borders of the archipelagic states of America. To arrive at this closing image of an archipelagic gyre that churns up Americanist thought and US American geography, I here turn toward interfacing histories, presents, and futures between archipelagic thinking and digital humanities (DH). Turning toward DH is especially apropos because both DH and archipelagic thought have been interested in the tension between reading closely and reading distantly. The field of DH has often been synonymous in the broader humanities with discussions of distant reading and its relation to close reading, and *Borderwaters* has, throughout, been interested in multiscalar views of US American and planetary cultures, as viewed from close and far and the gradations in between.[1] Indeed, this study's introduction posited the archipelago as a material and conceptual layer of mediation between the macro and the micro, a thought template that may offer deeply zoomed-in resolutions while also permitting us to pan out for views of exotically vast spaces and times, between the blip of a ripple and aeonic changes in sea level. In reflecting on how and what DH and archipelagic thinking might learn from each other regarding these converging interests in the near and the far, I first trace and comment on the place of the archipelago in DH thought of the past three decades, pointing out ways in which DH generally may benefit from giving heightened attention to archipelagic work that is already taking place within DH as well as from giving further consideration to archipelagic thinkers' theorizations of archipelagic ontology and epistemology. Subsequently, and reciprocally, I use DH's hallmark machine-assisted distant reading to offer some perspective on the present study's relation to broader trends in Americanist scholarship in history, literary studies, and American studies. Throughout, these reciprocal discussions draw context and insight from figures and arguments that appear in the preceding chapters and the introduction, bringing into greater focus the ways in which this study's work in spatial and temporal scale aligns with and offers models for further grasping the tensions and scalar gradations between close and distant reading, both in DH and in Americanist thought as it interlaps with an archipelagic gyre.

What Is a DH Archipelago?

In his 1994 essay "Modern European Literature: A Geographical Sketch," which now appears as the first chapter of the book *Distant Reading* (2013), Franco Moretti asks, "Would there be Shakespeare, had England not been an island?" He does not answer this query, following it instead with a question and a speculation: "Who knows? But that the greatest novelties of tragic form should arise away from the mainland ... is quite a sign of what European literature had to gain from losing its unity."[2] What is behind Moretti's question? Why would Shakespeare's innovations be at all tied to England's existence on an island at a distance from the "mainland"? We find an answer in Moretti's 2013 introductory remarks on the essay's origins: "I had been thinking for some time about European literature—in particular, about its capacity to generate new forms, which seemed so historically unique—and in a book I had just finished reading I found the theoretical framework for the essay: it was Ernst Mayr's *Systematics and the Origin of Species*, where the concept of 'allopatric speciation' (allopatry = a homeland elsewhere) explained the genesis of new species by their movement into new spaces."[3]

Following Mayr's 1942 study in its treatment of "archipelagos ... as models of geographic speciation," Moretti explains that he came to see Europe's various formal innovations in archipelagic terms: "discontinuous, fractured, the European space functions as a sort of archipelago of (national) sub-spaces, each of them specializing in one formal variation."[4] Hence, for Moretti, "the notion of 'European literature', singular, was replaced by that of an archipelago of distinct yet close national cultures, where styles and stories moved quickly and frequently, undergoing all sorts of metamorphoses."[5]

Indeed, evolutionary theory—which, as Moretti puts it, takes the archipelago as its "geographical substratum"—is a conceptual substratum from which we have seen the edifice of "distant reading" emerge in DH and the humanities more generally.[6] Moving away from the tradition of close reading that places pressure on "exactly *this* word and *this* sentence," distant reading views from afar, harnessing a relatively vast quantity of data—drawn, for instance, from a corpus of forty-four novelistic genres over the course of 160 years—to offer "a sharper sense of their overall interconnection," involving both their repetitions and their evolutionary and archipelagizing diversifications.[7] Moretti's version of evolution's archipelago is terrestrial, land oriented: islands of land are separated by waters whose sole function is to evoke "a world made of separate spaces," thereby prompting "the *diversification* of existing forms produced by speciation."[8] For Moretti, it seems, the waters between islands are nonspaces, uncrossable according to evolutionary theory's logic. But if the waters ever are crossed, it is by recourse to what he regards as an antithetical theory, world-systems theory, in which "the long-distance trade of modern capitalism *bridges* the greatest of oceans, and subjects all societies to a single, continuous geography." For Moretti, evolution's archipelago offers a theory of "separate spaces" (the ocean as an unbridgeable nonspace), while world-systems theory antithetically offers "a theory of sameness" (the ocean as a bridged nonspace).[9] As of *Distant Reading*'s publication in 2013, and in the wake of the "heady mood of permanent exploration" associated with the large amount of quantitative data that he and others at the Stanford Literary Lab had gathered, Moretti anticipated that the future development of a "general theory of the new [big data] literary archive" would likely involve a continued "encounter of evolutionary theory and historical materialism."[10]

Moretti's terrestrial version of the archipelago, in which islands are separate spaces and water is a nonspace, stands in tension with *Borderwaters'* stance on archipelagic islands' relation to each other and to their surrounding, very material archipelagic waters. Time and again, thinkers I have engaged with, and my own thoughts in relation to those thinkers, have given rise to terraqueous archipelagic models, ranging from chapter 1's discussions of US America as set amid water, to chapter 2's treatments of flooding and the archipelagizing of continental space, to chapter 3's recourse to tanah air as a land-water patria, to chapter 4's meditations on inundations and desiccations on geotemporal foreshores. Meanwhile, chapter 5 offers a vision of a speaking island who admonishes humans for not knowing how to swim, together with contemplations of an oceanic gyre that swirls to the crack of doom and discussions of a spacefaring people whose earthling ancestors had homewaters but no homeland.

Further marking this tension, Moretti's terrestrial model of the archipelago, as of course he himself knows, is somewhat flat-footed in relation to Charles Darwin, who in *On the Origin of Species* (1859) begins the chapter in which he offers his famous discussion of Galapagos finches with the following two sentences, foregrounding aquatic rather than terrestrial life and migration: "As lakes and river-systems are separated from each other by barriers of land, it might have been thought that fresh-water [organisms] would not have ranged widely within the same country, and as the sea is apparently a still more impassible barrier, that they never would have extended to distant countries. But the case is exactly the reverse."[11] Indeed, Darwin was writing in a culture and language in which, as is attested by several eighteenth- and nineteenth-century editions of the *Encyclopaedia Britannica*, an archipelago was not a series of land spaces interrupted by the blank space of the sea but "a sea interrupted with islands," a continuous sea "studded" with islands.[12] Willard McCarty, of the Centre for Computing in the Humanities at King's College London, well understood this in the 2000s, when he overtly took the archipelago as a chief structuring metaphor for humanities computing (now seen as existing under the umbrella of DH).[13] In a 2004 plenary address, later published in a 2006 issue of *Literary and Linguistic Computing*, McCarty took the metaphor of the "'archipelago' . . . as [the] basis for imagining a structure generous enough to accommodate the kind of practice humanities computing has shown itself to be."[14] In so doing, he drew on the *Oxford English Dictionary*

(*OED*) for the etymology and history of the term, reporting on its origin as a name for a sea in the Mediterranean but explaining that "by the early 16th-century explorers had reapplied 'archipelago' to mean the many islands of that sea, or a group of islands in any sea."[15] McCarty's discussion converged with Moretti's recourse to evolution's archipelago: just as "the Age of Exploration" brought "large amounts of new evidence to the attention of European naturalists" and thereby "challenged received ways of classifying the living world," so too were digital humanists now having "a similar effect on disciplines across the humanities" owing to "our ability to command far larger amounts of evidence from computers."[16] According to McCarty's narrative, just as Europe's ship-facilitated geographic explorations of the wide world spawned Darwin's archipelagic taxonomies, distant reading's computer-facilitated engagements with what we now call *big data* spawned the archipelagic taxonomies of Moretti and others in DH.

As intriguing as these uses of the archipelago are, I want to suggest that if distant reading specifically and DH more generally are to continue with a theory and practice that take the archipelago as an implicit geographic substratum and an occasionally explicit structuring metaphor, then thinkers in these areas will do well to give heightened attention to what this book's introduction frames as one of archipelagic studies' foundational and yet surprisingly knotty questions, namely, *What is an archipelago?*[17] To be sure, Darwin, Mayr, and the *OED* have offered certain key narratives to archipelagic studies: quoting the *OED* as a definitional baseline is de rigueur, and evolution's archipelago-facilitated allopatric speciation has sometimes been an implicit model, as we see, for instance, in Vicente M. Diaz's discussions of linguistic and canoe-technology speciation among "Austronesian" groups in the Pacific and Indian Oceans.[18] But if DH's big data has sometimes been taken as the "ocean," while some patterns within that data emerge as "content islands," what might the field's "heady mood of ... exploration," modeled on Europe's "Age of Exploration," be able to learn regarding one of its founding disciplinary geographies from thinkers who have approached the archipelago from alternative intellectual and experiential genealogies?[19] Caribbean thinkers, for instance, have contemplated archipelagic ontology and epistemology in ways that have crystallized *the anti-explorer's method*: "In the explorer's world, space is mapped, before it is known, by a globe-enveloping set of bisecting lines that drive toward human efforts at discovering or knowing the portions of the grid that contain *terra incognita* and *mare incognitum*," while Caribbean engagements with chaos and fractal geometry have evoked "the anti-explorer's method, which involves looking at the putatively known world and attesting to its final unknowability."[20] To advance the figure of the anti-explorer is not to take yet another potshot at DH positivism or putative claims to objectivity—it is rather a question of considering how archipelagic thought might contribute to DH thinkers' already and increasingly attentive relation to the nonobjectivity of what computer-facilitated reading may have to say to us.

Several DH scholars have already taken up the archipelago—and the question *What is an archipelago?*—from alternative epistemological and experiential genealogies, frequently with concern for convergences between the materiality of archipelagic spaces and the networked and other logics of the digital. Strikingly relevant here is *archipelagos: a journal of Caribbean digital praxis* (issues prior to 2020 published under the journal title *sx archipelagos: a small axe platform for digital practice*), which contemplates the Caribbean and its diasporas from a position in which digital communication, including the internet, is "analogous in important ways to the Caribbean itself as a dynamic and fluid cultural space: it is generated from disparate places and by disparate peoples; it challenges fundamentally the geographical and physical barriers that disrupt or disallow connection; and it places others and elsewheres in relentless relation. Yet while we celebrate these opportunities for connectedness, we also must make certain that our work in the digital realm undermines and confronts rather than re-inscribes forms of silencing and exclusion in the Caribbean."[21]

Another collaborative project has been Te Whakakaokao, or the Ngā Upoko Tukutuku Reo Māori Working Group at the Aotearoa/New Zealand National Library, which has been intervening in settler-colonial modes of organizing knowledge by developing and maintaining Māori-language subject headings, self-consciously structuring digital search capacities and ways of knowing based on the tradition of Māori weaving and latticework called *tukutuku*.[22] Elsewhere, the Indonesian DH scholar Iskandar Zulkarnain is at work on a resonantly titled book manuscript, "'Programming' the Archipelago: Digital Visual Cultures and Nationalism in Indonesia," and has published on the ways the Indonesian historical notion of Nusantara (one of Indonesia's major narratives of archipelagic self-perception, as discussed in chapter 3 of *Borderwaters*) has given structure to *Nusantara Online*, an Indonesian-made massively multiplayer online role-playing game, which in turn is reshaping nationalism in the Indonesian archipelago today.[23] Meanwhile, Lisa Swanstrom has drawn on archipelagic studies to contemplate data and algorithmically driven art projects in the Mediterranean that "are not about mining data or harvesting Big Data or presenting data as objective slices of reality" but instead engage participants in "confronting... data in an experiential, embodied manner that cannot be dismissed as easily as abstract data dumps so readily seem to be."[24]

These projects—which foster alternative archipelagic knowledge growing out of the Caribbean, Indonesia, the Pacific, and the Mediterranean—constitute some of DH's homegrown alternatives and complements to earlier and in many ways foundational DH deployments of the archipelago as a muse for exploration. Indeed, such projects may well prompt heightened self-reflexivity among DH scholars, whose field continues to bear the impress of the archipelago, whether as structuring metaphor or geographic substratum.[25] As a prominent example, consider the Ivy- and Oxbridge-backed Linking Islands of Data project, which in 2019 announced funding from the British Arts and Humanities Research Council. It is dedicated to the study of "the Classical World" and "guidance for best practice in the use of Linked Open Data and high resolution document handling."[26] How might participants in this project's workshops at Open Context, Brown University, and the University of Cambridge's Fitzwilliam Museum benefit from considering not only archipelagic thought as it emerged in the Greco-Roman Mediterranean that their islands of data document but also modes of alt-archipelagic knowing and practice that have arisen within various island-ocean constellations to which the Mediterranean term *archipelago* has now been applied?[27]

DH Distant Reading and Archipelagic Thinking

I have never thought of myself as a digital humanist, but my work has benefited from big data and distant reading. For instance, *Borderwaters*' fifth chapter builds in part on foundations laid by the big data collected and read by computers regarding the way the universe would seem to work, the way the climate and ocean currents would seem to function, and the way Earth's orbit would seem to fit into the solar system. On a *much* humbler scale than the distant reading we see in cosmology, astronomy, and climate science, I myself undertook some distant reading in preparing the introduction for *Archipelagic American Studies*, relying on the advanced-search function in JSTOR and Project Muse to trace the number of times the term *archipelago* appeared in *American Quarterly* from its founding in 1949 through 2015.²⁸ And in *Borderwaters* I have used Google Books and other basic tools to search the monographs and essays of major Americanist thinkers for pejorative uses of the term *insular*. This is seen in chapter 2, where I note that while an Americanist trend toward pejorative use of the term is understandable in light of standard usage, it nonetheless presents an urgent question for the field: if galvanizing voices in the development of postexceptionalist US American cultural and literary studies have paired the island's defining geoformal quality with devalued categories such as the fixed, self-enclosed, nationalist, and parochial, then one must wonder to what extent the field is equipped to access the archipelagic topographies of the hemisphere and planet it takes as its extensions. I would see this albeit basic use of the digital in my own work as allied with decolonial and postcolonial currents within DH, using algorithms to highlight a troubling epistemic trend that has been unintentionally (and by incredible thinkers) carried into current Americanist discussions.²⁹ This use of algorithms to reveal such epistemic trends is the flip side of what Safiya Umoja Noble has cautioned us about regarding "algorithmic oppression," or "discrimination . . . embedded in computer code and, increasingly, in artificial intelligence technologies that we are reliant on."³⁰

Indeed, as I have contemplated *Borderwaters*' relation to big data and the ways algorithms might oppress, I have needed to consider the striking epistemological convergence between the machine reading of what Swanstrom calls "big data dumps" and what Édouard Glissant calls "continental thoughts": "continental thoughts" are "system-thoughts," making us "think that we see the world as a bloc, taken wholesale, all-at-once, as a sort of imposing synthesis, just as we can see, through the window of an airplane, the configurations of landscapes or mountainous surfaces."³¹ Concerns about a convergence between machine reading and continental thought are only amplified by the structuring metaphor of Ted Underwood's recent book *Distant Horizons: Digital Evidence and Literary Change* (2019), which describes the benefits of distant reading as we move into the 2020s: "you can drive across a continent" and "never [notice] the curvature of the earth," but distant reading offers access to the planet's curvature, to the "longer arcs of change [that] have been hidden from us by their sheer scale."³² Taking us out of the car and placing us in the very airplane of continental thought against which Glissant cautions, Underwood explains, "The curve of the horizon only becomes visible some distance above the earth."³³

Glissant's caution against aerial views notwithstanding, questions of spatial and temporal scale are foundational to *Borderwaters*' archipelagic thinking, and chapter 5 centers on temporal scales that offer views far more distant than those that reveal the curvature of the earth: we see views from the mastheads of humans' interplanetary ships, aliens' starships, and cosmologists' poststarships. So my own stance, of course, is that admiration for Glissant should not keep archipelagic thinkers out of DH airplanes. One need only recall Florence "Johnny" Frisbie of this study's first chapter, who, after a childhood spent traveling the Pacific with a ship's-eye view, wrote the following of looking down at the Pacific Ocean during her first airplane ride as a young teenager: "Through a tiny porthole I could see, ten thousand feet below me, a sheet of galvanized iron, corrugated, brand-new, and dazzling. The great Pacific rollers were ripples." Frisbie's mind immediately seized on the productive tension between distant and close, amazed to look down and see a "toy ship" and yet know that the "tiny craft" was carrying a cargo of "perhaps a hundred tons."[34] Similarly, Hau'ofa sandwiches his foundational observation that "the world of Oceania . . . is huge and growing bigger every day" between close and distant: between an on-the-spot car ride that helped him see that Hawai'i's "Big Island was growing, rising from the depths of a mighty sea," and a distant reading of the Pacific in which "thousands" of Pacific Islanders "are flying back and forth across national boundaries, the International Dateline, and the Equator, . . . cultivating their ever growing universe in their own ways."[35] On this latter image of cutting back and forth, it is easy to imagine that Hau'ofa would have welcomed data-visualization collaboration with the DH scholars associated with the In the Same Boats platform, which presents users with "interactive visualizations that trace the movements of significant cultural actors from the Caribbean and wider Americas, Africa, and Europe within the 20th century Afro-Atlantic world" (see fig. C.1).[36]

In fact, if Glissant at one point suggests that archipelagic thought does not confine itself to a "single imperious direction" but rather "bursts upon all horizons," then in pursuing DH's distant horizons I am enthusiastic about the ways in which, for instance, chapter 4's discussions of stones and shells on the fractal foreshore might converge with Underwood's prominent DH blog, *The Stone and the Shell*, with a masthead image that features a nautilus shell on a fractal shoreline where a small wave advances while a previous wave recedes via thousands of subtle capillaries that striate the beach.[37] I am also enthusiastic about the potential of *Borderwaters*' introduction, in its discussion of Donald Trump's commentary on Puerto

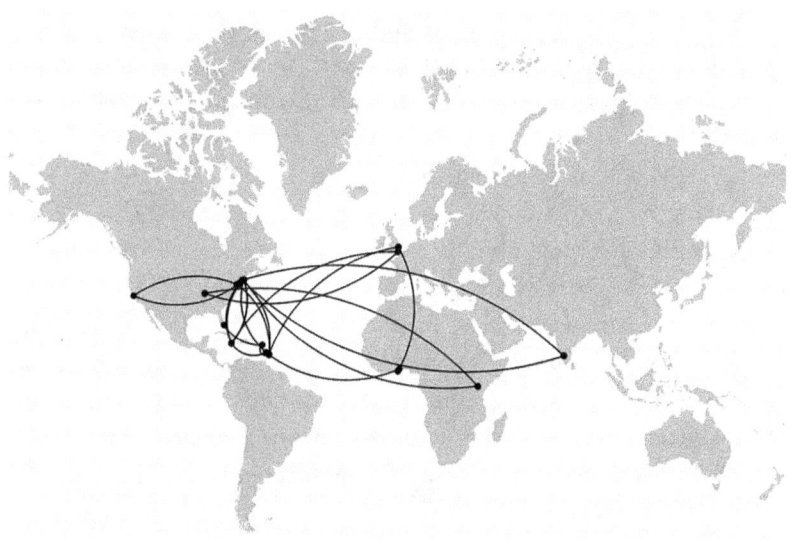

FIGURE C.1 — Map representing the travels of Edward Kamau Brathwaite between December 1949 and May 2003, created with In the Same Boats' interactive "Trajectories" visualization generator. Users of "Trajectories" may select from a list of several Caribbean and Afro-Atlantic intellectuals, mapping their overlapping travels by month and year. As stated on the project website, "the platform seeks to push back against the ways in which 'Global South' intellectual production has been balkanized in the academy, its limits and contours largely determined by imperial metropoles." It is easy to imagine that Hau'ofa would have been fascinated by a digital humanities tool similar to this, which could have helped him visualize the crisscrossing set of Pacific travel trajectories toward which he pointed.

Rico as "an island, surrounded by . . . big water," to converge with postcolonial DH in thinking through the ways Columbia University's Puerto Rico Mapathon (a DH relief effort in Hurricane Maria's wake) was grappling not only with the ongoing legacies of colonialism but also with the intersecting structures of continental exceptionalism.[38] If the postcolonial DH scholar Roopika Risam, writing of the Mapathon, has described post-Maria Puerto Ricans as "United States citizens cut off from access to food, water, shelter, and health care," one might consider how caricatural assumptions regarding islands—as showcased by Trump and Moretti and the common pejorative use of the term *insular*—have been the preconditions for the perception and treatment of islands as "cut off."[39]

All of these intersections speak to *Borderwaters*' position in relation to an island-dependent parable recently offered by Underwood, commenting on the perceived risks of distant reading. In this parable Underwood suggests that conventional humanists may tend to see digital humanists as analogous to "the scientists of *Jurassic Park*," implying that the former might be inclined to see the latter as better confined to an island away from the main humanist populations, given that they are intent on pursuing dangerous experiments like "cloning dinosaurs" or "us[ing] numbers to learn something about literary history."[40] Again, I am not a digital humanist, but neither do I identify with the conventional humanists of Underwood's parable. Rather, I have admired my friends and colleagues in DH, and when their creations have made archipelagic migrations from the DH island to the terraqueous spaces I have been more familiar with (that is, when I have learned from them), I have experienced intrigue and wonder rather than the foreboding we are invited to feel upon realizing, in *Jurassic Park*'s epilogue, that "since the dinosaurs [are] fundamentally birds," they have found a way to "migrate," escaping Isla Nublar and arriving in isthmian Costa Rica.[41]

Further, I recognize that just as I have suggested that DH scholars would benefit from giving attention to what archipelagic thinkers have had to say about terraqueous ontologies and epistemologies, the arguments in *Borderwaters* benefit from considering how computer-assisted reading may illuminate the place of the archipelago within Americanist thought. Indeed, I would suggest that the distant reading of Americanist scholarship may join with archipelagic DH currents such as the journal *archipelagos* and other work in contributing to reflections on the place of archipelagic thinking in DH. To this end, I have worked with Brian Croxall of my university's Office of Digital Humanities and Lorin Groesbeck (an American studies major and digital humanities and technology minor who has now graduated) to procure and distant read the full runs of the flagship journals in the fields of American studies, American literary studies, and American history from their founding to the end of the second decade of the twenty-first century: *American Quarterly* (1949–2019), *American Literature* (1929–2019), and the *Journal of American History* (1964–2019). In graphing and discussing several archipelagic keywords, *Borderwaters* enters the ocean of big data: the corpus includes 4,702 *American Quarterly* articles, 9,421 *American Literature* articles, and 31,341 *Journal of American History* articles.[42]

My discussion here focuses mainly on trends in searches we have done for the following keywords: *continent* and *mainland*, *ocean* and *sea*, *island* and *archipelago*. Another affiliated term, *transnational*, also appears.[43]

Unless otherwise noted, all graphs and tallies reference the number of articles containing at least one mention of a particular keyword during a particular decade (that is, generally we are not discussing the sheer number of times a term has appeared). Searching for and graphing these keywords does not permit us to find every mention of archipelagoes, islands, continents, mainlands, oceans, and seas. A scholar may mention Hawaiʻi without using any of the keywords or might use the terms *the Atlantic* and *the Caribbean* without ever appending *Ocean* or *Sea*. Or a scholar may treat the continental United States as the *main* land without ever using the term *mainland* or may take the continent as the stage of US history without mentioning the continentality of the assumed stage. What's more, use of a certain term would not necessarily imply an author's favorability toward that term, since, for instance, a scholar might use the term *island* as a means of disparaging a group of intellectual rivals or might use the term *continent* during a metageographic critique of the United States' conventional geographic self-perception. However, visualizing the terms from above (while acknowledging with Frisbie that a feature viewed from different distances may look like either an enormous wave or a ripple) offers us a set of illuminating if contingent views of the keywords' situation within a certain version of the arc of Americanist research and thought.

Across the board in the three journals, when we read for the number of articles that mention a given term, the word *continent* is used a great deal more frequently than *mainland* (see figs. C.2 and C.3). To take the decade of the 2000s as a case in point, the ratio is about 22 to 1 for *American Literature*, 7 to 1 for *American Quarterly*, and 5 to 1 for the *Journal of American History*.[44] Compared to the term *continent*, the less used term *mainland* is vexed.[45] On one hand, a scholar might use the term *continent* dozens of times without ever thinking about islands, oceans, or archipelagoes, which comports with traditional US mythologies that hold these forms to be definitionally beyond the ken of US Americanness. *Mainland*, on the other hand, immediately acknowledges noncontinental spaces as US American. In fact, in Americanist contexts, the term is most likely to be used while giving some form of direct attention to the archipelagic states of America.[46] But the acknowledgment of these spaces as US American is attended by a hierarchy. Within the dichotomy of *mainland and island*, the former is of course taken as *main*. The latter is meanwhile subordinate, something to which a series of disenfranchising US Supreme Court cases called the Insular Cases might fittingly apply, or something that, if a US federal judge were to make a ruling while living there, could become the

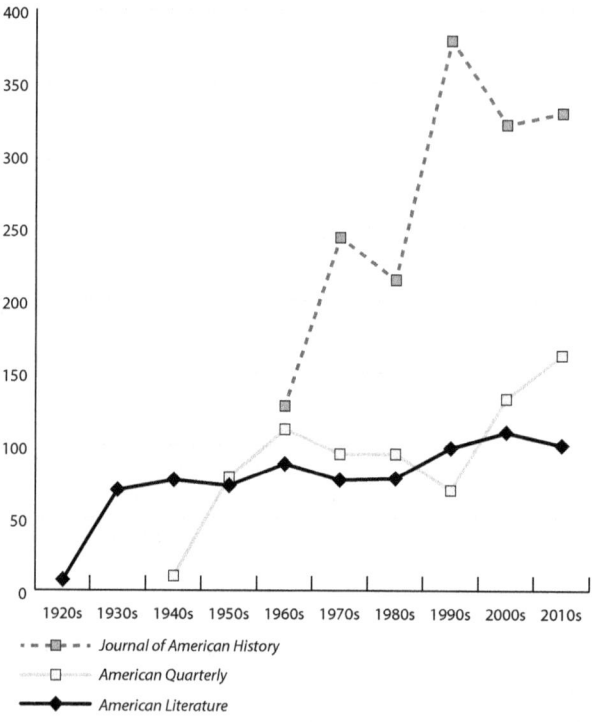

FIGURE C.2 — The number of articles that use *continent* per decade in the *Journal of American History*, *American Quarterly*, and *American Literature*. (Here and elsewhere, lower numbers for a journal's first decade may reflect its existence for only part of that decade.)

geographic pretext for the US attorney general to question the rule of law (see the introduction to this book). In light of the material and tangible effects of this hierarchy, it is no wonder that the Hawaiian poet Joseph P. Balaz in 1989 published a poem that preferred "da continent" to "da mainland" when speaking of the continental United States, concluding that "Hawai'i / is da mainland to me."[47] By comparing the *mainland* graphs to the further visualizations in the following pages, readers will see that the *Journal of American History*'s use of *mainland* appears correlated with its use of *sea* and *island*, while *American Quarterly*'s use of the term is correlated with appearances of *transnational* and *archipelago*. Paradoxically, and in what are undoubtedly unintended ways on the part of scholars, giving heightened attention to terraqueous spaces has sometimes been an occasion to reinforce the island's abject place in the chain of geographic being.

Meanwhile, *continent* may be present or absent for a variety of reasons. Again, it will tend to be used without concern for islands, oceans,

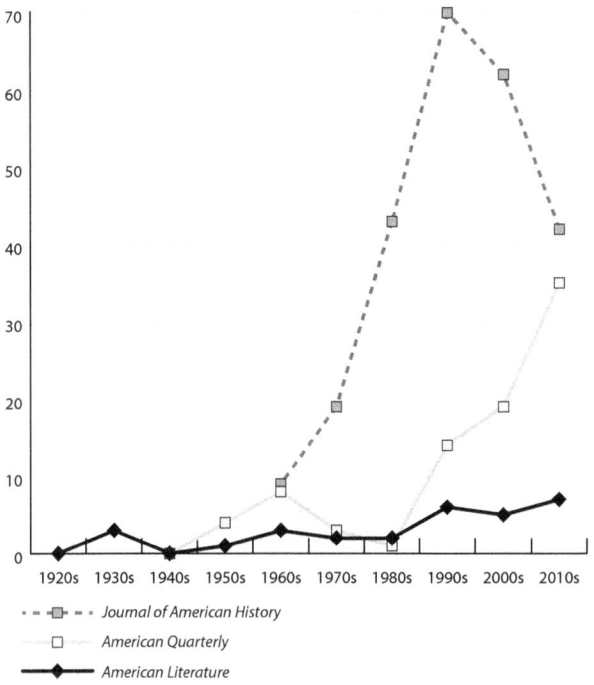

FIGURE C.3 — The number of articles that use *mainland* per decade in the *Journal of American History*, *American Quarterly*, and *American Literature*.

or archipelagoes. And in a more limited set of cases, following Balaz's logic for advancing *continent* as a preferred term, it might evince exquisite attunement to the archipelagic states of America. But in most cases we may assume that the continent is present even when the term is not mentioned. To make a brief but relevant foray out of the Americanist journals themselves, consider Moretti's own commentary on the United States, as seen in his 2019 book *Far Country: Scenes from American Culture*, which showcases five essays based on lectures he gave for the yearlong Literary History course he regularly taught at Stanford University.[48] By uploading the full text of *Far Country* into Voyant Tools, a suite of DH visualization tools created by Stéfan Sinclair and Geoffrey Rockwell, I am able to focus on the term *American* (it occurs 51 times) and see that the term's top collocates (or the words that appear in its vicinity) are *hegemony*, *western*, and *free*.[49] Voyant Tools' search tools give no indication that the continent is one of the book's major concerns. But reading the hard copy of *Far*

Country, I see how the continent, though the term is mentioned only four times in the book, is the usually unstated ground on which *American* and its major collocates are mapped. *Western* refers to western films of the US American frontier, a genre that Moretti says was key to the post-1945 moment at which "American cultural hegemony began in earnest." This genre consolidated "a vast continent of heterogeneous immigrants, coming from all corners of Europe," and then western films afforded Europe-based "European audiences" a view of the fabled US continental frontier, seducing them with "the hope of a space so incommensurably larger" than that of the nation-states that crowded the European continent.[50] I tend to agree with Moretti on the continent's relation to Euro-American consolidation, and I find compelling his reading of the western's role in evoking US hegemony (still, as *Borderwaters*' third chapter points out, the vast oceanic spaces of the Trust Territory of the Pacific Islands also played a role in the United States' post-1945 hegemony). Further, his focus on *America as the vast western frontier*, via such classic interpreters of US culture as Richard Slotkin, is absolutely consistent with the mode of US American literary history that is conventional in survey courses, as is affirmed in *Borderwaters*' first chapter.[51] All of this illustrates the way the continent is likely to be the ground for thoughts about the United States, even when it does not surface in highly visible ways that make the term *continent* legible in the context of distant reading. Even when the term itself does not appear prominently, this landmass has a gravity that keeps many thinkers (including those who have dexterously reimagined Europe as an archipelago) telling stories in which the continent is US American geography's central protagonist.

In spite of the continent's gravity, however, it seems clear that during their decades of existence, the three journals have been publishing work that regularly mentions or discusses the three keywords that name the archipelago's constituent parts: *island*, *sea*, and *ocean* (see figs. C.4–C.6). In the *Journal of American History*, *ocean*, *sea*, and *island* all saw large increases in use from the 1970s–1980s to the 1990s–2000s. And while the 2010s saw the use of *island* and *sea* decline in this journal, the term *ocean*, which experienced the largest percentage jump in the 1990s and was formerly much less popular than *sea*, had staying power after its original rise, so that during the second decade of the twenty-first century *ocean* overtook *sea* as the preferred term among Americanist historians publishing in this flagship journal.[52] In *American Literature*, the three terms have appeared at a steady clip, even as *island* and *sea* were used less frequently in the 2010s than during any other full decade, while *ocean* rose to its all-time highest usage during the 2010s. Even so, during the 2010s *sea* remained the preferred term by a ratio of about 3 to 2 among this journal's cohort of Americanist literary scholars.[53] In *American Quarterly* each of the three terms has seen a notable increase since the journal's first full decade in the 1950s. The lines we see for *island* and *sea* appear quite similar, indicating a correlation between usages of these terms, even if *island* increased by 2.5 times from the 1950s to the 2010s, while *sea* approximately doubled in frequency.[54] Elsewhere, uses of *ocean* hovered at about forty articles per decade during *American Quarterly*'s first half century, much less common than *sea*, but since the new millennium *ocean*'s use has risen rapidly, more than tripling, so that it comes closer to rivaling *sea* as the preferred term among that journal's scholars.[55] Based on searches for these three keywords in these three flagship journals, it seems that the archipelago's components have never been ignored in Americanist scholarship—interest has held more or less steady in American literary studies, spiked and then in some cases decreased in American history, and dramatically increased in American studies, but in none of the three fields has interest been absent during any decade of a journal's existence. Meanwhile, a perhaps unexpected subplot involves the strong twentieth-century preference for the term *sea* over *ocean*, followed by *sea*'s twenty-first-century decline in comparative popularity to the point that *ocean* is closing the gap in American literary studies and American studies while it has surpassed *sea* in American history.

Although the terms *island* and *sea/ocean* have been consistently discussed in the journals, and although these terms describe the constituent components of material archipelagoes, the term *archipelago* has been absent from most articles that mention islands and seas and oceans (see fig. C.7 on page 266). Indeed, *archipelago* was nearly absent from the *Journal of American History* during the 1960s–1970s, rising to four uses during the 1980s, to fifteen in both the 1990s and 2000s, and to twenty-one in the 2010s. In *American Literature*, it appeared in one to five articles per decade from the 1930s to the 1990s. In the 2000s it hit seven, and in the 2010s it hit fifteen, triple its highest point during any decade of the twentieth century, though admittedly still vanishingly small vis-à-vis the number of articles published in *American Literature* per decade. Meanwhile, during the half century from the 1950s to the 1990s, *American Quarterly* published a total of only seven articles that used the term, but then *archipelago* shot up to ten articles in the 2000s and to forty-six articles in the 2010s, so that in the most recent full decade, on a per-article basis, the term found mention in *American Quarterly* more frequently than *ocean* during any

c.4

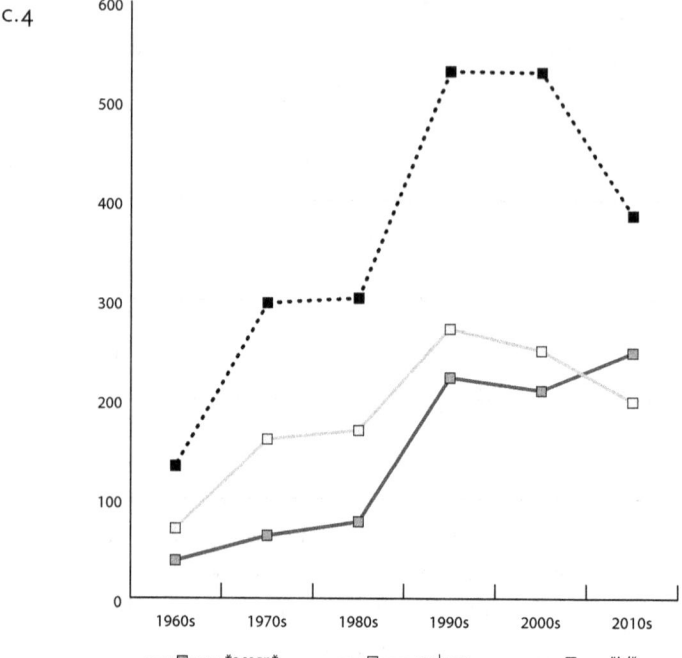

c.5

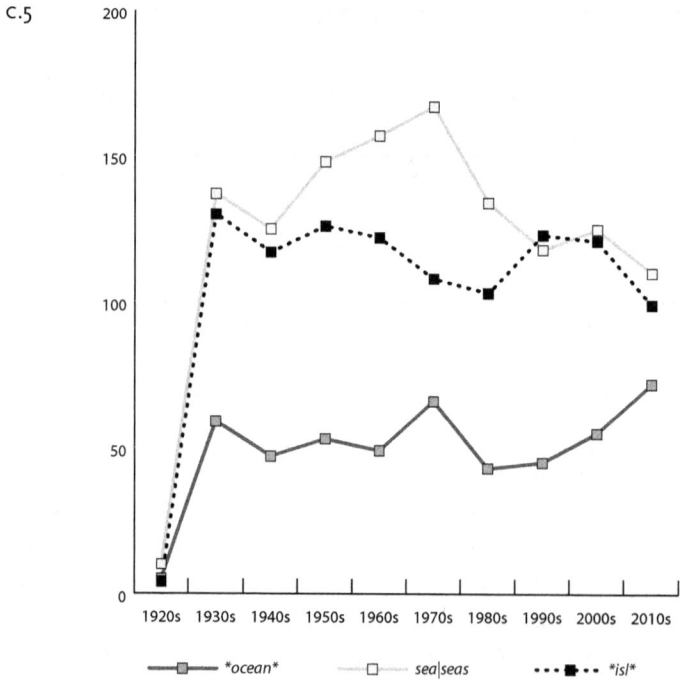

C.6

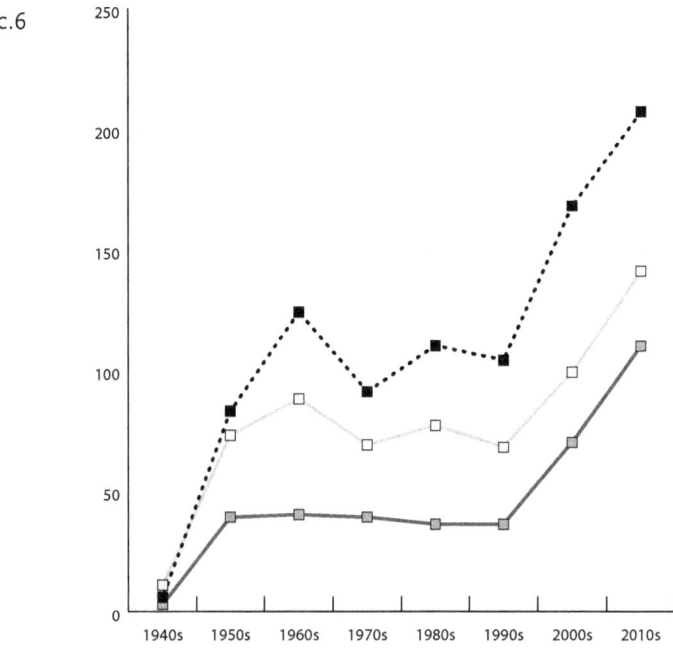

FIGURE C.4 — (*opposite, above*) The number of articles per decade that use **ocean**, *sea* or *seas*, and **isl** (including *island, isle,* and derivatives) in the *Journal of American History*.

FIGURE C.5 — (*opposite, below*) The number of articles per decade that use **ocean**, *sea* or *seas*, and **isl** (including *island, isle,* and derivatives) in *American Literature*.

FIGURE C.6 — (*above*) The number of articles per decade that use **ocean**, *sea* or *seas*, and **isl** (including *island, isle,* and derivatives) in *American Quarterly*.

given decade from the 1950s to the 1990s.[56] A story emerges here, based on the persistent interest in islands and seas and oceans in all three fields, coupled with the belated twenty-first-century rise of the term *archipelago*. This story resonates with Harrod J. Suarez's recent discussion of "the difference between studying an archipelago and studying *archipelagically*": scholars may look at islands and their watery environs without apprehending the discontinuous conjunction of the archipelago that is before their eyes, analogous to Huck Finn, as discussed in this study's first chapter, who crashes into an island and initially cannot tell what it is.[57] As for the twenty-first-century rise of *archipelago*, which is consistent if uneven across the journals, we may see a scholarly instantiation of what chapter 1

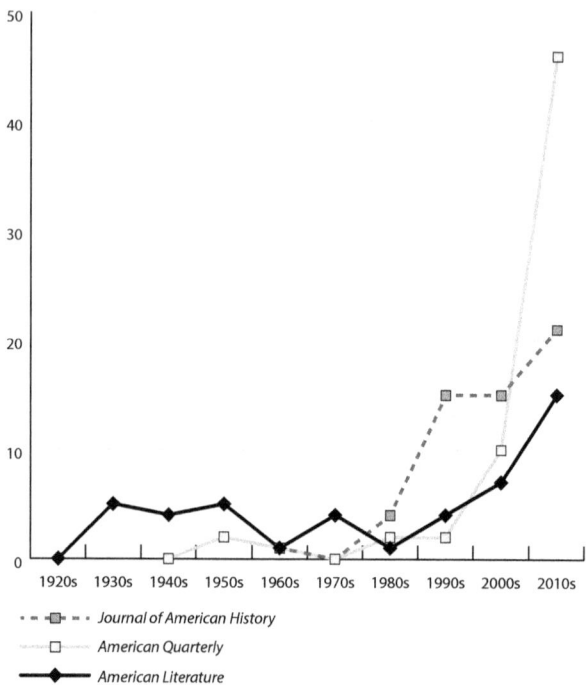

FIGURE C.7 — The number of articles that use *archipel* per decade in the *Journal of American History*, *American Quarterly*, and *American Literature*.

references as Huck's archipelagic thought, or his openness to letting go of his continental assumptions, his openness to seeing the island as an iteration of the long chain of islands that the river has previously shown him.

Of course, compared to the entire corpus of 45,464 journal articles, the number of articles that mention *archipelago*, and hence in some way evince an awareness of or willingness to think with the archipelagic form, is small. It is "vanishingly small," as one thought-provoking reviewer put it when Croxall and I submitted a proposal based on this work to the Association for Computers and the Humanities conference in 2019.[58] (Since reading this review, we have wondered how archipelagic thought's nondismissive and fractally mediated relation to putative smallness might usefully remind some of our distant reading colleagues of the way comparatively big data may be approached not for "what . . . we can track at scale" but rather for "what might be *hidden* in [the] corpus.")[59] To grasp how small these numbers are, consider the set of graphs that visualize the rise of a big term, *transnational,* central of course to the transnational turn

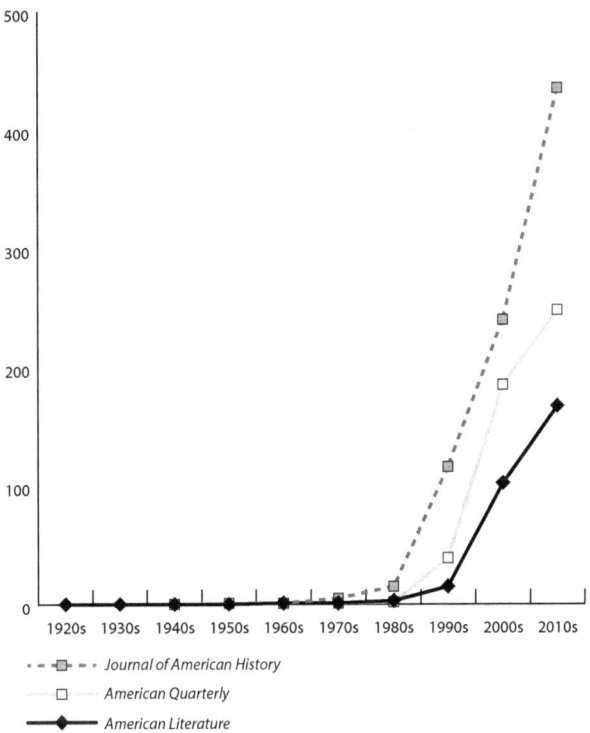

FIGURE C.8 — The number of articles that use *transnational* per decade in the *Journal of American History*, *American Quarterly*, and *American Literature*.

that altered Americanist thought beginning in the late 1990s, as discussed in chapter 1 (see fig. C.8). The term *transnational* was a nearly flat line in each of the three journals from their foundings through the 1980s. It had a bump in the 1990s (15 articles in *American Literature*, 39 in *American Quarterly*, and 116 in *Journal of American History*). Then the turn really *turned* in the 2000s, hitting 102 in *American Literature*, 185 in *American Quarterly*, and 240 in the *Journal of American History*. Indeed, the transnational saturates much of Americanist thought, with the term appearing in 7 percent of articles in the *Journal of American History*, 35 percent in *American Quarterly*, and 39 percent in *American Literature* during the 2010s.[60] By the numbers, the *transnational* covers more of the Americanist Earth than the *sea* and the *ocean*.[61]

In underlining transnationalism's ubiquitous rise, I am not calling for its toppling. I am drawing attention to a big term relative to a small term during the 2010s: in *American Literature* we saw *transnational* appear in about eleven articles for every one article that used *archipelago*, and in the *Journal of American History* it was a ratio of about twenty-one to one, while in *American Quarterly* the terms *transnational* and *archipelago* came somewhat closer to each other, with a ratio of about five to one.[62] Returning to Frisbie's fractal metaphor, the form of the transnationalist and archipelagic waves looks similar in the graphs, even if one is a great Pacific roller while the other is a ripple. Or, to scale it differently, one is a tsunami, and the other is a breaker that looks like a ripple, "vanishingly small," from the DH airplane of distant reading. But from within the airplane, it is crucial to remember what it is like to be down among the waves. From the shore, some of the individual mentions of *archipelago* indeed continue to look like ripples.[63] But giving close attention to archipelagic articles by John Levi Barnard in *American Literature* or David A. Chang in *Journal of American History* or Jodi A. Byrd in *American Quarterly* is a reminder that what looks like a ripple from the DH airplane can be, on the beach, a breaker that knocks your feet out from under you and sends you tumbling, in a good way, as the surf churns up the continentalist ground you thought was solid.[64] It is a reminder that while from a DH airplane the islands in the ocean may appear to be, in Moretti's phrase, "tiny dots in the graph," these dots are an archipelago of infinitely corrugated islands surrounded by an infinitely corrugated ocean when experienced at close range.[65] To point this out is to take seriously Caribbean thinkers' recourse to the fractal quality of an island, which acknowledges that even within a grain of sand there can be more ecological, geologic, and historical data and *being* than a human brain is able to process on its own.

Zora Neale Hurston and Édouard Glissant offer complementary images that together bring a sense of scalar gradation to dichotomies between the great wave and the ripple, between the island as a dot and the island whose every grain of sand requires an ocean of data for its explication. At the end of chapter 2, I frame Hurston's *Their Eyes Were Watching God* as a hypercanonical novel whose tireless rereading asks rereaders to look up from the novel's pages, toward a horizon within which the present site of rereading is one island only within a vast archipelago. Hurston's reader, then, is the close reader whose indefatigable work in close reading precipitates a sense of urgency regarding the distant horizons of distant reading. Meanwhile, as Glissant wrote in 1990, out on the "horizon" we find a "distant reader" driven by an urgent sense that there is "so much of the world to be uncovered." This distant reader is inclined to eschew "the man who walks" the beach engaged in apparently obsessive fractal close readings of its near infinity of ceaselessly changing features. Addressing the "distant reader," Glissant says, "look at him," look at "the man who walks" the beach: you may be "able to leave this one person alone in his [fractal close reading] outlook," "but he will not leave you," and "the shadow he throws from a distance" nearly reaches you.[66] Hence, Glissant's reader is the distant reader whose work in distant reading unceasingly asks us to look back to the unceasing granularity of the fractal beach. One imagines Hurston's close reader looking up and Glissant's distant reader looking back, their eyes meeting momentarily. In the continuum between these reciprocal gazes, we find every fractal scale and plenitude of archipelagic thinking as it engages times and spaces that exist, to borrow from chapter 4's discussion of Benoit Mandelbrot, between the cosmic and the quantum (see figs. C.9–C.12).

How to think, between the quantum and the cosmic, about what has been happening with the archipelagic? From a distance, the numbers for *archipelago* in *American Literature* aren't much to talk about. But closer up, this journal afforded me a trial run for an earlier draft of chapter 2, whose treatment of Hurston now constitutes a precondition for asking about archipelagic scales between distant and close reading.[67] Meanwhile, and indeed from a distance, something more is afoot in the *Journal of American History*, whose raw numbers for *archipelago* have increased abruptly, and especially in *American Quarterly*, where the ratio of articles containing *archipelago* to those containing *transnational* has hit a rather remarkable one to five. Although Michelle Ann Stephens and I have emphasized some important distinctions between the archipelagic and the transnational (including the archipelagic's attentiveness to geographic form and materiality), several commentators have understandably seen the archipelagic as one manifestation of transnationalism's allopatric speciation, as if the transpacific, the transatlantic, the hemispheric, the borderlands, the planetary, and the archipelagic were specialized varieties of finches that have diverged from the originary transnational finch that a big storm blew over to the archipelago from the mainland in the late 1990s.[68] An analogous and equally stormy way to think of this proposed relationality would be through the Japanese woodblock printer Hokusai's nineteenth-century *The Great Wave off Kanagawa* (see fig. C.13), wherein transnationalism might be taken as the great wave, while the smaller waves that corrugate the great wave's crest become varieties of transnationalism, fractal repetitions of the larger wave, as Mandelbrot has implied regarding Hokusai's work.[69]

C.9

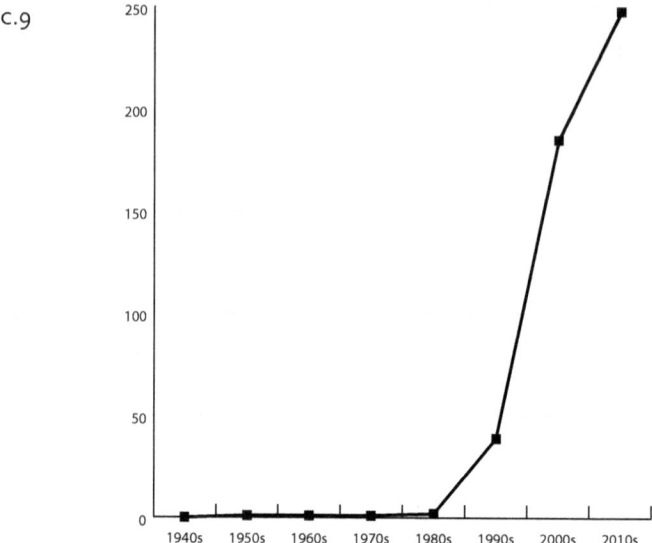

C.11

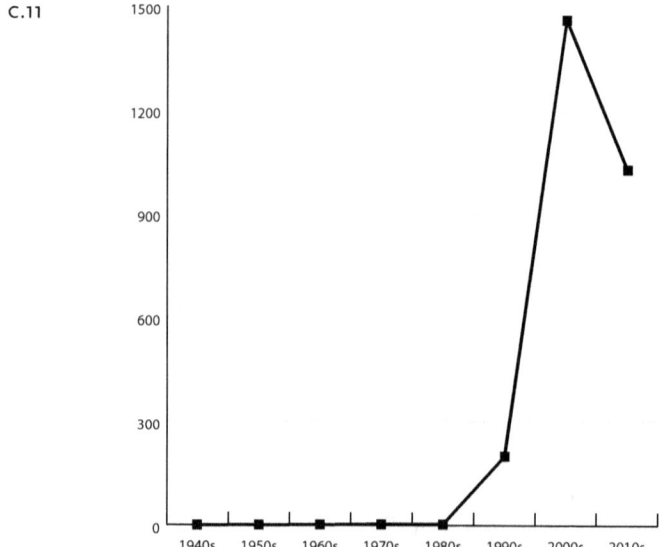

FIGURES C.9–C.12 — Four ways of graphing *"transnational"* in *American Quarterly*. These are just four of the infinite ways a term may be visualized across the run of a journal. Graph C.9 (*upper left*, showing per-decade tallies of articles that include *transnational* at least once) might be thought of as "the great wave," while graph C.10 (*upper right*, showing year-by-year tallies of articles that include *transnational* at least once) might be thought of as the great wave viewed with a level of resolution that brings its self-similar ripples into focus. In the lower row, we see an analogous wave and self-similar ripple formation, now visualizing tallies for total individual instances of *transnational*, by decade (C.11, *lower left*) and by year (C.12, *lower right*). Viewing these four graphs

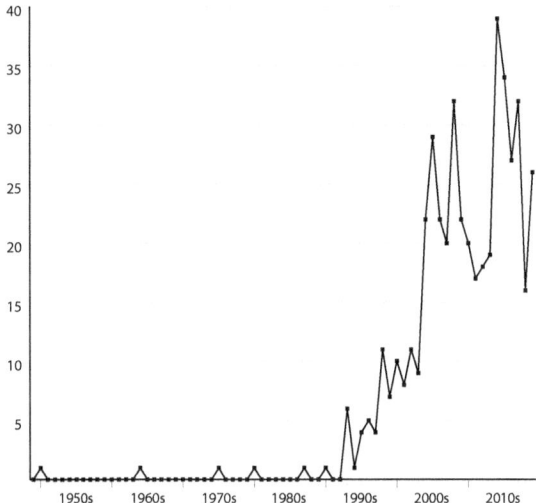

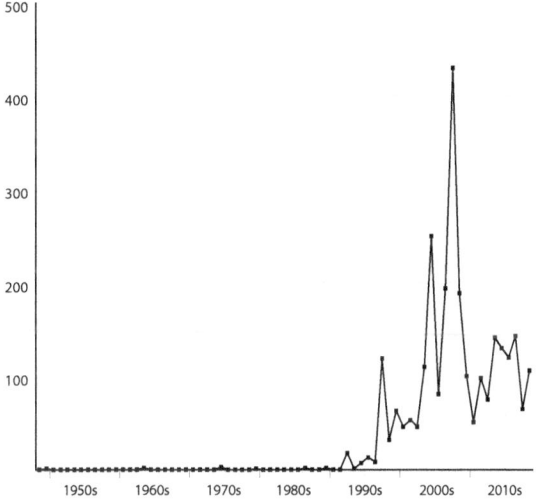

together, we see that in terms of its sheer number of repetitions, *transnational* did not appear as frequently in the 2010s as it did in the 2000s (*lower row*). But the upper row reminds us that even if *transnational* may be waning in terms of total repetitions, it may still be waxing in terms of field saturation, as it appeared in a greater number of articles in the 2010s than in the 2000s. In the infinity of ways a term's unending particularities may be visualized, between the cosmic and the quantum, we see perhaps a meeting of the minds between Édouard Glissant's archipelagic thought, which wants to see particularity right down to the very smallest rocks of the smallest rivers, and Ted Underwood's proviso on quantitative approaches: "Quantitative models are no more objective than any other historical interpretation; they are just another way to grapple with the mystery of the human past, which doesn't become less complex or less perplexing as we back up to take a wider view." Underwood, *Distant Horizons*, xix.

FIGURE C.13 — Hokusai's nineteenth-century woodblock print *Under the Wave off Kanagawa*, also known as *The Great Wave*. The image portrays the great wave corrugated with smaller waves, an attribute that drew Benoit Mandelbrot's attention in discussions of the fractal geometry of nature. From New York Metropolitan Museum of Art (JP1847).

To be sure, the transnational has played an indelible role in my own perception of archipelagic thinking as potentially relevant to Americanist scholarship, but I see myself as less immediately aligned with Donald Pease's turn-of-the-millennium endorsements of the transnational turn than with his much less visible suggestion, during a question-and-answer session at the 2009 Futures of American Studies Institute, that one of the institute's plenary speakers ought to give attention to "the ontology of geography."[70] Because I had already begun thinking about the forms and materialities of the archipelagoes (Hawai'i and Indonesia) amid which I had lived while growing up, this imperative resonated with me experientially. It also resonated with me intellectually, given that I was at the time in the process of reading the work of foundational archipelagic thinkers, who, as Alice Te Punga Somerville has emphasized, did not require any "turn" to arrive at the materiality of archipelagoes, oceans, and islands because they were already there.[71] Predating and otherwise thinking apart from the Americanist transnational turn, these foundational thinkers, who hail from terraqueous regions across the planet, helped give rise to what has crystallized into "contemporary archipelagic thinking," a set of intellectual and engaged activities that neither descend from nor depend on Americanist scholarship for their genealogy and vitality.[72] Certainly, if Croxall and I had chosen to distant read the full run of journals more aligned with these archipelagic genealogies and vitalities, our visualizations would look much different: the contrast between the flagship USS *American Literature* and *Small Axe: A Caribbean Journal of Criticism*, between the flagship USS *Journal of American History* and the *Contemporary Pacific*. In different essays, Harrod J. Suarez and Susan Gillman have insightfully pointed toward archipelagic American studies' genealogical relation to thinkers whose work has appeared more often in a Caribbean *canoa* or Pacific *waka* than in an Americanist flagship.[73]

A transnational turn? An archipelagic turn? Hester Blum observes that for Americanist scholars today, the "turn" has emerged as the most "pervasive" mode of attempting to "capture broad intellectual momentum," with "the notion of a turn mark[ing] a differentiation between what came before and what is to come, indicating routes plotted if not yet explored, imagined if not yet surveyed."[74] Given the pervasiveness of the notion of a turn, it is unsurprising that some have referenced an "archipelagic turn" in American studies, but the phrase gives me pause.[75] On one level, this pause stems from the way the transnational turn is discussed, with scholars—even scholars who are in the thick of the transnational—regularly referring to it as "the so-called transnational turn."[76] If the transnational, which has covered more of the Americanist Earth than the ocean or sea, is not assuredly a turn outright, then the archipelagic certainly isn't. It is not "the next big thing," to eschew a phrase with a contested and regretted life in DH circles.[77] Rather, I am intrigued by Paul Giles's observation on the term *archipelagic*: "It may perhaps be that the inherently oppositional nature of this term lends itself to an institutional outsideness, a perpetual spiral whereby any given object is analyzed from an always already alien position."[78] Following Giles's reference to a "perpetual spiral," rather than an archipelagic turn I would think of an archipelagic gyre, looking from a moving position that is alien to continental gravity and yet whose borderwaters include not only the oceans and seas but also the rivers and the infinity of capillaried drainages of both insular and continental watersheds. Independent from the ocean nation of the United States and yet coursing through its shifting terraqueous states, this archipelagic gyre pulls things in: epistemological shipwrecks, watery borders, skipping stones, canoes lost in the fog, Pacific cowboys, geography as form, submerged ontologies, lost non-Euclidean maps, tanah air, beachcombing a half-billion years after the fact, Boltzmann brains, plastic conceptual frames, the archive of albatross guts, flagships, canoa, waka, the salt chuckle of rocks amid the spiraling archipelago in a great salt lake. From within and without the temporal and spatial realms of the United States' fractal and watery borders, an archipelagic gyre churns up this circulating and nonutopian miscellany of the borderwaters, dropping some items into the deep benthic zone's sediments of meaning and spitting others up onto human and inhuman shores, flotsam and jetsam, metonymic of an oceanic and archipelagic US America apprehending its own geographic claims and materiality, its own grating archipelagic states of dissension, again and in some circumstances for the first time.

NOTES

Introduction

A small portion of the material in the introduction is drawn from my essay "What Is an Archipelago? On Bandung Praxis, Lingua Franca, and Archipelagic Interlapping," in *Contemporary Archipelagic Thinking: Towards New Comparative Methodologies and Disciplinary Formations*, edited by Yolanda Martínez-San Miguel and Michelle Stephens (2020), and I thank Rowman and Littlefield for permission to republish this adapted material.

1 Rafi Segal and Yonatan Cohen, "Territorial Map of the World," *openDemocracy: Free Thinking for the World*, October 7, 2013, https://www.opendemocracy.net/en/territorial-map-of-world/. More specifically, the two hundred nautical miles of the EEZ are measured "from the baselines from which the breadth of the territorial sea is measured," which itself extends twelve miles out from the shoreline. United Nations, *Law of the Sea*, 18, 3.
2 On the Caribbean as the third US border, see "Fact Sheet: Caribbean Third Border Initiative," The White House: President George W. Bush, April 21, 2001, https://georgewbush-whitehouse.archives.gov/news/releases/2001/04/20010423-5.html; and Bridget Johnson, "U.S. Vows Greater Maritime Security Collaboration in Jamaica, Colombia Meetings," *Homeland Security Today*, February 9, 2018, https://www.hstoday.us/subject-matter-areas/maritime-security/greater-maritime-security-collaboration-jamaica-colombia/.
3 "Maritime Zones and Boundaries," NOAA Office of General Counsel, accessed August 24, 2020, https://www.gc.noaa.gov/gcil_maritime.html.
4 On NOAA's "Maritime Zones and Boundaries" page, this map is hyperlinked from text that reads "Map of the U.S. Exclusive Economic Zone." The United States has not signed UNCLOS, but President Ronald Reagan adopted UNCLOS's definition of the EEZ by presidential proclamation in 1983. Dautel, "Transoceanic Trash," 191–92.
5 "The United States Is an Ocean Nation," NOAA Office of General Counsel, accessed August 24, 2020, https://www.gc.noaa.gov/documents/2011/012711_gcil_maritime_eez_map.pdf. As of August 2020, Wikipedia's article "Exclusive Economic Zone" lists the United States as having the largest EEZ in the world, at 11,351,000 square kilometers, with France listed as having the second largest, at 10,700,000 square kilometers. Wikipedia, s.v. "Exclusive Economic Zone," last modified August 24, 2020, 21:04 (UTC), https://en.wikipedia.org/wiki/Exclusive_economic_zone.

6   In recognition that the United States of America is not the only American nation-state, and because this study discusses American cultures and events affiliated with both the United States and the broader Americas, *Borderwaters* does not use the unadorned term *America* to refer to the United States, nor does it use the term *American* to refer to US citizens or nationals. Rather, when referring to the United States, I use *United States of America, United States, US,* and *US America*. In referring to the United States adjectivally, I use *US* or *US American*. The latter term may also refer to US citizens or nationals. I make exceptions to these rules. Of course, quotations remain unchanged, and I refer to academic fields according to their own standard self-reference: *American studies, American literary studies,* and *American history*. Although these fields are US focused, they often address cultures, events, and literatures produced before the United States came into existence, and while it would be convenient to simply change *American history* to *US history*, the latter term would be proleptic in reference to the pre-US but nonetheless American cultures that these fields address. Further, I follow standard practice in referring to scholars in these fields as *Americanists*; the term *US Americanist* would run the risk of suggesting my reference is to US-based scholars, while the fields of course involve vibrant contributions from non-US scholars. In referring to US ethnicities and places, I use standard terms such as *African American, Japanese American, Native American, Euro-American,* and *American Samoa*. On a few occasions, I echo other scholars or speakers in their use of the terms *America* or *American* when the repetition is clear. The phrase *archipelagic states of America* is an echo of *United States of America,* and it has a US referent, while *the archipelagic Americas* refers to archipelagic spaces in the broader Americas.

7   Matthew Klint, "All the Patriotic Quotes in Your U.S. Passport," *Live and Let's Fly* (blog), July 4, 2018, https://liveandletsfly.com/us-passport-quotes/.

8   I draw the term *seagoing manifest destiny* from Drinnon, *Facing West,* 129.

9   Roosevelt, *Strenuous Life,* 1. I borrow the term *imperial archipelago* from Thompson, *Imperial Archipelago.*

10 Roosevelt, *Strenuous Life,* 6–7.

11 Roosevelt, *Strenuous Life,* 9; and Roosevelt, *Foes of Our Own Household,* 63.

12 Minow, "Enduring Burdens," vii, viii.

13 Craig Santos Perez, "Guam, Where America's Voting Rights End," *Craig Santos Perez* (blog), August 9, 2017, https://craigsantosperez.wordpress.com/2017/08/09/guam-where-americas-voting-rights-end/.

14 "Birtherism," Trump Twitter Archive, accessed August 24, 2020, http://www.trumptwitterarchive.com/highlights/birtherism.

15 Quoted in Charlie Savage, "Jeff Sessions Dismisses Hawaii as 'an Island in the Pacific,'" *New York Times,* April 20, 2017, https://www.nytimes.com/2017/04/20/us/politics/jeff-sessions-judge-hawaii-pacific-island.html.

16 Trump is quoted in Brandon Carter, "Trump Slams Puerto Rico: 'They Want Everything to Be Done for Them,'" *Hill,* September 30, 2017, https://thehill.com/homenews/administration/353216-trump-criticizes-san-juan-mayors-poor-leadership-during

-puerto-rico; Jordan Fabian, "Trump Says Puerto Rico Relief Hampered by 'Big Water, Ocean Water,'" *Hill*, September 29, 2017, https://thehill.com/homenews/administration/353094-trump-says-puerto-rico-relief-hampered-by-big-water-ocean-water; and Philip Bump, "The 'Very Big Ocean' between Here and Puerto Rico Is Not a Perfect Excuse for a Lack of Aid," *Washington Post*, September 26, 2017, https://www.washingtonpost.com/news/politics/wp/2017/09/26/the-very-big-ocean-between-here-and-puerto-rico-is-not-a-perfect-excuse-for-a-lack-of-aid/?utm_term=.f5a8e02162df.

17 Fabiola Santiago, "Trump Didn't Do a 'Fantastic Job' in Puerto Rico. Ask the Loved Ones of the 2,975 Dead," *Miami Herald*, September 1, 2018, https://www.miamiherald.com/news/local/news-columns-blogs/fabiola-santiago/article217587305.html.

18 Tocqueville, *Democracy in America*, 180.

19 L. Lowe, *Immigrant Acts*, 28.

20 Paine, *Common Sense*, 93.

21 Mignolo and Walsh, *On Decoloniality*, 5.

22 On US demographic trends and white fears, see Dudley L. Poston Jr. and Rogelio Sáenz, "U.S. Whites Will Soon Be the Minority in Number, but Not Power," *Baltimore Sun*, August 8, 2017, http://www.baltimoresun.com/news/opinion/oped/bs-ed-op-0809-minority-majority-20170808-story.html.

23 Roberts and Stephens, "Archipelagic American Studies: Decontinentalizing," 1–4, 11.

24 Bulosan, *America Is in the Heart*, 246.

25 Roberts and Stephens, "Archipelagic American Studies: Decontinentalizing," 1.

26 These particular rhymes are words of my own choosing, based on the entries and pronunciation guidelines for "archipelagic" in the *Oxford English Dictionary* and *Merriam-Webster*. *Oxford English Dictionary*, s.v. "archipelagic," online ed., accessed August 14, 2020, https://www.oed.com/view/Entry/10386?redirectedFrom=archipelagic#eid; *Merriam-Webster*, "archipelagic," online ed., accessed August 14, 2020, https://www.merriam-webster.com/dictionary/archipelagic.

27 *Oxford English Dictionary*, 2nd ed. (1989), s.v. "archipelago"; and *Oxford English Dictionary*, s.v. "archipelago," online ed., accessed August 14, 2020, https://www.oed.com/view/Entry/10387?redirectedFrom=archipelago#eid.

28 *Oxford English Dictionary*, 1st ed. (1933), s.v. "archipelago"; and *A New English Dictionary on Historical Principles*, vol. 1 (1888), s.v. "archipelago."

29 Benjamin, *Illuminations*, 257–58.

30 Handley, *New World Poetics*, 42.

31 Glissant, *Introduction à une Poétique du Divers*, 45. On translation, islands, and archipelagoes, see Gabrakova, *Unnamable Archipelago*, 137–52.

32 Walcott, "Isla Incognita," 52.

33 *Oxford English Dictionary*, s.v. "Melanesian," online ed., accessed August 14, 2020, https://www.oed.com/view/Entry/116014?redirectedFrom=melanesian#eid.

34 McDougall, "'We Are Not American,'" 261.

35 For useful perspective on coral as analogous to humans in creating land, see Byrnes, "The Infrastructure of Coral," 32. Also on coral, see Helmreich, *Sounding the Limits of Life*, 48–61.
36 See Roberts, "What Is an Archipelago?," 95, 97.
37 Quintero Herencia, *La hoja de mar*, 25.
38 Wiedorn, *Think Like an Archipelago*, 125.
39 Glissant, "Europe and the Antilles, 256–57.
40 Glissant, *Introduction à une Poétique du Divers*, 44.
41 Along these lines, in discussing the archipelagization of Europe, Glissant looks to France and lists some of the "many islands taking shape": "the Basque country, Catalonia, Brittany, Corsica, Alsace," each of which has significant ties or interisland relations with non-French regions or cultural islands. Glissant, "Europe and the Antilles," 256.
42 Whitman, *Leaves of Grass*, 532.
43 Noudelmann, "Literature," 207.
44 United Nations, *Law of the Sea*, 39.
45 Eldredge, *Life Pulse*, 56.
46 See Moretti, *Distant Reading*.
47 Dimock, "Low Epic," 623.
48 I use the terms *archipelagic thinking* and *archipelagic thought* interchangeably throughout this study, and I see archipelagic thought/thinking as something that has emerged with different genealogies from multiple archipelagoes. See Pugh, "Island Movements."
49 For the full series of this publication, see the bibliography entries for Henry Gannett (1885, 1900, 1904), Edward M. Douglas (1923, 1930), and Franklin K. van Zandt (1966 and 1976).
50 Gannett, *Boundaries of the United States* (1885), 7.
51 Gannett, *Boundaries of the United States* (1900), 5.
52 Gannett, *Boundaries of the United States* (1904), 3.
53 Douglas, *Boundaries, Areas, Geographic Centers* (1923), iii.
54 Douglas, *Boundaries, Areas, Geographic Centers* (1930), iii.
55 Van Zandt, *Boundaries of the United States and the Several States* (1966), vii.
56 Of course, the Aleutian Islands are part of Alaska, and these initial continental claims also involved islands near the continental coasts.
57 Van Zandt, *Boundaries of the United States* (1976), 23.
58 Goldstein, "Introduction," 1.
59 Lai, "Discontiguous States of America," 3.
60 Perez, "Transterritorial Currents," 619.
61 Benítez-Rojo, *Repeating Island*, 2.
62 I greatly admire this work, even as it makes recourse to a borderlands framework in approaching terraqueous spaces: on the "American Pacific" and the borderlands, see Wilson, *Reimagining the American Pacific*, 2, 7, 38, 282–83; on Puerto Rico as a "borderland state," see Ramón E. Soto-Crespo, *Mainland Passage*, 2; on the US South as a

borderland between the US North and the Caribbean, see Guterl, *American Mediterranean*, 11; for the phrase "watery borderlands," see Allison, "Beyond It All," 6; for the phrase "littoral borderlands," see Igler, *Great Ocean*, 184; on the Strait of Gibraltar as a borderland characterized by the ocean's depths, see S. Pack, *Deepest Border*; on "the borderlands of early America" as characterized by "spaces and relationships that were . . . amphibious, archipelagic, and multifaceted," see Truett, "Settler Colonialism," 438.

63 My first published use of the term *borderwaters* appears in Roberts and Stephens, "Archipelagic American Studies: Decontinentalizing," 9. A few months prior, Tyson Reeder used this term in his "'Sovereign Lords' and 'Dependent Administrators': Artigan Privateers, Atlantic Borderwaters, and State Building in the Early Nineteenth Century." Since 2012 I have become aware of the term *borderwaters*' use in an insightful essay by Omise'eke Natasha Tinsley, "Black Atlantic, Queer Atlantic: Queer Imaginings of the Middle Passage." I draw on this usage in chapter 3 of the present study. In 2019 Kyrstin Mallon Andrews also offered an insightful description of the notion of *borderwaters* as a framework and lens for thinking about borders in the Caribbean. Andrews, "Borderwaters: Conversing with Fluidity at the Dominican Border," *Cultural Anthropology*, October 29, 2019, https://culanth.org/fieldsights/borderwaters.

64 Yaeger, "Sea Trash," 524.
65 Bolton, *Spanish Borderlands*; and Bolton, "Epic of Greater America," 473, 448, 473.
66 Adelman and Aron, "From Borderlands to Borders," 816.
67 Hämäläinen and Truett, "On Borderlands," 338, 348.
68 Anzaldúa, *Borderlands/La Frontera*, 3.
69 Brady, "Border," 36; and Cutler, "New Border," 499.
70 Cutler, "New Border," 499.
71 Mignolo, *Local Histories/Global Designs*, 11.
72 Mignolo and Tlostanova, "Theorizing from the Borders," 208.
73 Mignolo and Tlostanova, "Theorizing from the Borders," 207.
74 On the place of Du Bois's reference to "the islands of the sea" in the archipelagic study of American culture, see Roberts and Stephens, "Archipelagic American Studies: Decontinentalizing," 10.
75 Mignolo and Walsh, *On Decoloniality*, 5, 1.
76 Mignolo, *Local Histories/Global Designs*, 6, 4.
77 Mignolo and Tlostanova, "Theorizing from the Borders," 209–10.
78 Brathwaite, "Caribbean Theme," 246. In this quotation I change Brathwaite's *Guadaloupe* to the more standard *Guadeloupe*.
79 Brathwaite states, "The Caribbean, though sharing and inter-lapping, . . . does not fit into establishment African or North American notions of cultural diversity and integration." Brathwaite, *Contradictory Omens*, 5.
80 Deleuze, "Desert Islands," 9.
81 Bishop, "Map," 3.
82 Brathwaite, *History of the Voice*, 42.
83 Anzaldúa, *Borderlands/La Frontera*, 1, 3.

84 Glissant, "Unforeseeable Diversity of the World," 292.
85 Schwyzer, introduction to *Archipelagic Identities*, 4. John Kerrigan's lengthy discussion on why his archipelagic study does not extend to America is also illuminating on the ways the archipelagic may stand in tension with boundaries. Kerrigan, *Archipelagic English*, 57–59.
86 This conversation occurred after my talk "Archipelagoes, Oceans, and Visual Theorizing" for the Brigham Young University Art Department Lecture Series in March 2017.
87 Butcher and Elson, *Sovereignty and the Sea*, 52–53.
88 Quoted in Hsu, "Hierarchies of Migration Rights," 1. Thanks to Hsu for sharing the written version of this talk and for permitting me to cite it.
89 Quoted in Hsu, "Hierarchies of Migration Rights," 13–14.
90 Sawczyn, "United States Immigration Policy toward Cuba."
91 "Why Is the South China Sea Contentious?," *BBC News*, July 12, 2016, https://www.bbc.com/news/world-asia-pacific-13748349. Byrnes, "The Infrastructure of Coral."
92 Singer and Cole, *Ghost Fleet*, 3–7.
93 Geng, "Legality of Foreign Military Activities," 27; and Anthony Kuhn, "China Is Placing Underwater Sensors in the Pacific near Guam," *NPR*, February 6, 2018, https://www.npr.org/sections/parallels/2018/02/06/582390143/china-is-placing-underwater-sensors-in-the-pacific-near-guam.
94 Latour, *We Have Never Been Modern*, 7, 6. Also on the composite thinking of nature and culture, see Latour, *Facing Gaia*, 7–40.
95 Anzaldúa, *Borderlands/La Frontera*, 3.
96 Eckel, in Blum et al., roundtable review of *Archipelagic American Studies*, 5.
97 On transnational American studies as potentially an academic superstructure of globalized neoliberalism, see Bérubé, "American Studies without Exceptions." On *American studies* as the dominant institutionalized term for what is perhaps more accurately but much less frequently referred to as *critical US studies*, see Radway, "What's in a Name?"; and Aravamudan, "Rogue States and Emergent Disciplines," 18.
98 See Traister, "Object of Study."
99 For important discussions of islands and post- and decoloniality, see Nadarajah and Grydehøj, "Island Studies as a Decolonial Project"; and Gómez-Barris and Joseph, "Coloniality and Islands," 1–10.
100 See "About the Author" pages in Tsao, *Oddfits*; and Tsao, *More Known World*.
101 Tsao, *More Known World*, 144.
102 Tsao, *More Known World*, 48.
103 Tsao, *More Known World*, 125, 126, 196.
104 Walcott, "Isla Incognita," 56.
105 Du Bois, *Souls of Black Folk*, 15.

Chapter One: Interlapping Continents and Archipelagoes of American Studies

1. Baym first appeared on the editorial board for the *Norton Anthology of American Literature*'s second edition, published in 1985. She was listed as general editor of the anthology from its fifth edition (1998) to its eighth edition (2012). As of 2017, the anthology's website reported that it had been "read by more than 2.5 million students over 30 years" and described the eighth edition as featuring "a diverse and balanced variety of works." Accessed January 13, 2017, http://books.wwnorton.com/books/webad.aspx?id=23664. Though this Norton website no longer exists as of 2021, the same publisher-provided language can still be found on commercial bookselling websites for various volumes of the eighth edition.
2. Yoshihara, "Editor's Note" (March 2015), v.
3. Baym, "Melodramas of Beset Manhood," 123.
4. For the Baym quotation and for Baym on Smith and Lewis, see "Melodramas of Beset Manhood," 131. For quotations on the continent and garden from Smith and Lewis, see H. Smith, *Virgin Land*, 4; and R. Lewis, *American Adam*, 78, 165, 43, 72.
5. Baym, "Melodramas of Beset Manhood," 131.
6. Baym, "Melodramas of Beset Manhood," 132, 133.
7. Quoted in Baym, "Melodramas of Beset Manhood," 137. For Poirier's original quotation, see Poirier, *A World Elsewhere*, 3.
8. Baym et al., "Preface to the Second Edition," xxx.
9. Baym and Levine, "Preface to the Eighth Edition," xvii.
10. These exclusions are confirmed not only by attentively looking through the table of contents and biographical essays in the print copy of the *Norton Anthology of American Literature*, 9th edition, but also by using the search function in the electronic version of the same publication. See https://digital.wwnorton.com/americanlit9pre1865 and https://digital.wwnorton.com/americanlit9post1865.
11. See also Roberts, "Archipelagic American Literary History," 136. Several of the writers in the *Norton* were born on non-US islands. In addition to those born on the island of Great Britain, we see Alexander Hamilton (Nevis), José Martí (Cuba), Claude McKay (Jamaica), Li-Young Lee (Java), Jamaica Kincaid (Antigua), Edwidge Danticat (Haiti), and Junot Díaz (the Dominican Republic). R. Levine, *Norton Anthology of American Literature*.
12. See Raffety, "Nineteenth-Century American Maritime History"; and Roland, Bolster, and Keyssar, *Way of the Ship*. For a visualization of the surge in American maritime history, see this book's conclusion, especially as related to the terms *ocean* and *sea* in *Journal of American History*.
13. On a US American literature of the sea, see, for instance, Bender, *Sea Brothers*; and Blum, *View from the Masthead*. On an "oceanic turn" and "blue humanities," see Mentz and Rojas, "Introduction." See also Burnham, *Transoceanic America*.
14. See Kaplan and Pease, *Cultures of United States Imperialism*. As Alice Te Punga Somerville has stated, "Two of the dominant 'island' regions of the world—the Caribbean

and the Pacific—have produced scholars and artists who begin 'at home' with the island in an expansive, perhaps even always already archipelagic, sense." Somerville, "Great Pacific Garbage Patch," 322.

15 Okihiro, *Island World*, 2.
16 Okihiro, *Island World*, 4.
17 For a visualization and discussion of the use of *archipelago* in *American Quarterly*, see this study's conclusion.
18 Gómez-Barris and Fiol-Matta, "Introduction," 501–2.
19 Vazquez, "Learning to Live in Miami," 872; and Roberts and Stephens, "Archipelagic American Studies: Decontinentalizing," 10.
20 Perez, "Transterritorial Currents," 619; and Lyons and Tengan, "Introduction," 553.
21 Lyons and Tengan, "Introduction," 567.
22 Yoshihara, "Editor's Note" (September 2015), viii.
23 M. Cohen, "Literary Studies," 657.
24 Guterl, *American Mediterranean*, 11.
25 On the Caribbean as literally mediterranean, see Gillman, "Black Jacobins," 170; and Gillman, "Humboldt's American Mediterranean," 510. On Carpentier, see Gillman, "Black Jacobins"; on Roberts, see Gillman, "It Takes an Archipelago"; on Humboldt, see Gillman, "Humboldt's American Mediterranean." For a list of cultural historians and others who have compared the Caribbean to the Mediterranean, see Gillman, "Humboldt's American Mediterranean," 506, 526n5.
26 Glissant, *La cohée du Lamentin*, 75.
27 Twain, *Adventures of Huckleberry Finn*, 31, 32. Further references to the novel are cited in the text.
28 H. Smith, *Virgin Land*, 3; Marx, *Machine in the Garden*, 40; and Trachtenberg, *Brooklyn Bridge*, 118. According to Jonathan Arac, this initial moment of hypercanonization began in the post–World War II 1940s and continued through the mid-1960s. Arac, *Huckleberry Finn*, 6, 7.
29 Babcock, introduction to *American Frontier*, 17.
30 Liebling, *Earl of Louisiana*, 87.
31 *Oxford English Dictionary*, s.v. "Mediterranean," online ed., accessed August 15, 2020. https://www.oed.com/view/Entry/115766?redirectedFrom=mediterranean#eid.
32 On the significance of Huck's apology, see, for instance, J. McIntyre, "Three Practical Jokes," 33–34; and Barrish, *Cambridge Introduction to American Literary Realism*, 168.
33 Turner, *Frontier in American History*, 19, 1. Turner's speech "The Significance of the Frontier in American History" (1893) is published in Turner, *Frontier in American History*.
34 Turner, *Frontier in American History*, 38.
35 Cooper, *Prairie*, 14. For a useful discussion of certain nineteenth-century US continental writers' use of oceanic and archipelagic metaphors to mediate the continent, see Donahue, "Poe's Fluid, Terraqueous Landscapes."
36 Turner, *Frontier in American History*, 309. Turner's speech "The West and American Ideals" (1914) is published in Turner, *Frontier in American History*.

37 On Columbus and discovery, see Turner, *Frontier in American History*, 293; for the quotation from Tennyson, see Turner, *Frontier in American History*, 310.
38 H. Smith, *Virgin Land*, 4.
39 H. Smith, *Virgin Land*, 12.
40 Quoted in H. Smith, *Virgin Land*, 19, 20, 28.
41 Whitman, quoted in H. Smith, *Virgin Land*, 45, 46, 47.
42 Marx, *Machine in the Garden*, 34.
43 Marx, *Machine in the Garden*, 42, 66.
44 Marx, *Machine in the Garden*, 325, 326.
45 Marx, *Machine in the Garden*, 326.
46 Marx, *Machine in the Garden*, 327.
47 For comparisons between *Huckleberry Finn* and the *Odyssey*, see Solomon, "Huckleberry Finn"; and Deneen, "Was Huck Greek?" Additionally, scores of observers over the years have referred to *Huckleberry Finn* as an "American *Odyssey*."
48 Kaplan, "Call for a Truce," 144.
49 Benítez-Rojo, *Repeating Island*, 2.
50 Lipsitz, "Our America," 138.
51 On continents as perceived rather than solidly geologic facts, see M. Lewis and Wigen, *Myth of Continents*, 21–46. On the continental model as "grant[ing] Europe the priority that Europeans and their descendants overseas believed it deserved," see M. Lewis and Wigen, *Myth of Continents*, 36.
52 Dimock, *Through Other Continents*, 3.
53 Dimock, *Through Other Continents*, 3–4 (my italics).
54 For a discussion of transnational Americanists' frequent imaginations of the US American continent as insular, see chapter 2.
55 Dimock, *Through Other Continents*, 4.
56 Quoted in Dimock, *Through Other Continents*, 4.
57 Braudel, *Mediterranean*, 23.
58 Braudel, *Mediterranean*, 23.
59 Braudel, *Mediterranean*, 103, 148, 149.
60 Braudel, *Mediterranean*, 149.
61 Dimock, *Through Other Continents*, 145, 164, 165, 177, 158–63, 163.
62 Dimock, *Through Other Continents*, 142.
63 For other recent and important work that has brought the Americas into a realm of multicontinental studies, see L. Lowe, *Intimacies of Four Continents*; and Ghosh and Miller, *Thinking Literature across Continents*.
64 M. Lewis and Wigen, *Myth of Continents*, 203–4. On Puerto Rico as an anomaly in relation to the continental United States, see Soto-Crespo, *Mainland Passage*.
65 Perez, *From Unincorporated Territory [hacha]*, 7.
66 M. Lewis and Wigen, *Myth of Continents*, 21, 36.
67 Batongbacal, "Defining Archipelagic Studies," 183.
68 Latour, *We Have Never Been Modern*.
69 Glissant, *La cohée du Lamentin*, 37, 75.

70 On America as the "transatlantic continent," see Hegel, *Lectures*, 163. On Africa as "unhistorical," see Hegel, *Lectures*, 190.

71 Hegel, *Lectures*, 96. On Hegel's discussions of the Caribbean and Pacific as unhistorical, see the introduction to chapter 5 in the present study.

72 Du Bois, *Souls of Black Folk*, 15.

73 On *nissology*, defined as "the study of islands on their own terms," see McCall, "Nissology," 1–2. John R. Gillis has written persuasively on not taking islands as miniature continents in "Not Continents in Miniature: Islands as Ecotones."

74 Ralph Wiley's unproduced screenplay *Spike Lee's Huckleberry Finn* (copyright 1997) offers an alternative interpretation of this scene, such that Jim does not actually believe he has had a dream but rather understands that Huck is lying to him. Thanks to Shelley Fisher Fishkin for sharing excerpts from Wiley's screenplay. Shelley Fisher Fishkin, email message to Brian Russell Roberts, April 5, 2016.

75 The end of the novel does not seem to take Jim's interpretive projects seriously, as showcased in the comic relief constituted by Jim's late suggestion that forty dollars as compensation for an unnecessarily prolonged captivity constitutes a fulfillment of one of his earlier sign-based predictions (55, 360–61).

76 Fiedler, "Come Back," 521, 523, 525.

77 Quoted in Sumida, "Reevaluating Mark Twain's Novel," 590.

78 Sumida, "Reevaluating Mark Twain's Novel," 592. Sumida has called this unpublished and lost book "the abandoned Hawaii novel of 1884" (589). Although Twain claimed to have completed the novel and was ready to send it to press, it survives in the Bancroft Library only as three fragments from the manuscript's beginning (590–92). Sumida observes, "The quality of the [available] writing prompts . . . William M. Gibson to note that . . . 'the indications are that Clemens was right in deciding not to publish the book'" (593).

79 Mark Twain, "CHAP. I.," Sandwich Islands novel (MT 01209); courtesy of the Mark Twain Project, the Bancroft Library, University of California, Berkeley.

80 Twain, *Mark Twain's Letters*, 824.

81 Except for a few flagged references to the book's 2016 second edition, subsequent references to *Miss Ulysses* are to the first edition (1948) and are cited in the text.

82 Arac, *Huckleberry Finn*, 7.

83 Teaiwa, "What Remains to Be Seen," 731. Huck surfaces explicitly as a sort of unwilling memoirist in the novel's final paragraph (362).

84 R. Frisbie, introduction to *Miss Ulysses*, viii.

85 Thompson, *Imperial Archipelago*. The United States claimed Pukapuka from 1859 until the early 1980s, when the atoll was acknowledged to fall under the jurisdiction of the Cook Islands; see Skaggs, *Great Guano Rush*, 231; and Jagota, *Maritime Boundary*, 93. See also *Pacific Island Treaties*, 7–8, 30–33.

86 R. Frisbie, introduction to *Miss Ulysses*, vii.

87 On Johnny writing in Apia, see F. Frisbie, *Miss Ulysses*, 76. On her writing process, see 117–18.

88 Florence "Johnny" Frisbie, email message to Brian Russell Roberts, February 8, 2014.

89 Chang, *World*, vii.
90 Moretti, *Distant Reading*, 128.
91 Sigurðsson, introduction to *The Vinland Sagas*, ix–xxxviii. Discussions of Vikings as predating Columbus in America have been long-running and quite popular. Kolodny, *In Search of First Contact*. Johnny likely had direct access to such discussions via her father, who exchanged voluminous missives with fellow Pacific-based US writer James Norman Hall during the 1930s and 1940s, at points discussing Hall's travels to Iceland and difficulties writing a book about it. See Hall, *Forgotten One*, 154–246 (for the correspondence) and 199, 239 (for specific references to Iceland).
92 For the dates of the Beagleholes' research in Pukapuka, see Beaglehole and Beaglehole, *Ethnology of Pukapuka*, 4.
93 Beaglehole and Beaglehole, *Ethnology of Pukapuka*, 326.
94 Beaglehole and Beaglehole, *Ethnology of Pukapuka*, 401.
95 Beaglehole and Beaglehole, *Ethnology of Pukapuka*, 401.
96 Buck, *Vikings of the Pacific*, 4. While the 1938 edition is titled *Vikings of the Sunrise*, the 1959 edition is titled *Vikings of the Pacific*.
97 Buck, *Vikings of the Pacific*, 5.
98 Buck, *Vikings of the Pacific*, 324.
99 As Annette Kolodny explains, English-language translations of the Vinland sagas began circulating in the 1830s "in both scholarly venues and the popular press," with "Anglo-Americans . . . eagerly embrac[ing] the romantic notion of a Viking heritage and a Vinland colony located in New England," to the point that "popular nineteenth-century American literature was filled with tales of Viking adventurers in a New England Vinland." Kolodny, *In Search of First Contact*, 12, 10.
100 Cusick, *David Cusick's Sketches*, 13, 14.
101 For recent scholarly work on pre-Columbian Polynesian contact with America, see T. Jones, Storey, Matisoo-Smith, and Ramírez-Aliaga, *Polynesians in America*. On L'Anse aux Meadows, a confirmed pre-Columbian Norse site on the island of Newfoundland dating to about 1000 CE, see Ingstad, *Discovery of a Norse Settlement*.
102 Glissant, *La cohée du Lamentin*, 72; and Handley, *New World Poetics*, 54.
103 Gillis, *Islands of the Mind*, 62–63.
104 Lyons and Tengan, "Introduction," 567.
105 On the space of America as "the Indies," see M. Lewis and Wigen, *Myth of Continents*, 25. On the same space as "a vast archipelago," see Gillis, *Islands of the Mind*, 59. On America as intellectually invented, see M. Lewis and Wigen, *Myth of Continents*, 25.
106 M. Lewis and Wigen, *Myth of Continents*, 25.
107 Lionnet, "Continents and Archipelagoes," 1508, 1506.
108 Maldonado-Torres, "Post-Continental Philosophy," 3, 4; and Glissant, quoted in Dash, "Stranger by the Shore," 359.
109 H. Smith, *Virgin Land*, 6; and Deleuze and Guattari, *Thousand Plateaus*, 19.
110 Deleuze and Guattari, *Thousand Plateaus*, 8, 19.

111 For a rich set of discussions on Columbus and the discovery/invasion of America, see *Northeast Indian Quarterly*'s special issue "View from the Shore: American Indian Perspectives on the Quincentenary" (vol. 7, no. 3, 1990), edited by José Barreiro. See also Kolodny, *In Search of First Contact*, 11–12.
112 Quoted in Dash, "Stranger by the Shore," 360.
113 In using terms such as *precontinental* and *postcontinental*, I am not implying that all geographic perception can be divided, as if in a process of linear development, into precontinental, continental, and postcontinental phases. In spite of continentalism's present planetary dominance, some modes of geographic perception have never been continental.
114 Snyder, "Rediscovery of Turtle Island," 301, 304; and Couture and McGowan, *Metaphoric Mind*, 55.
115 The cowboy thematic is prominent throughout *Miss Ulysses* owing to Robert Dean Frisbie's "stories of Cowboyland," or accounts of running cattle in the Sierra Nevada. F. Frisbie, *Miss Ulysses*, 18.
116 Lippmann, *Cold War*, 11–12; and Waligora-Davis, "'Myth of the Continents,'" 195.
117 Bogost, *Alien Phenomenology*, 12.
118 For a discussion on this topic related to the Philippines, see Roberts, "Archipelagic American Literary History," 135–36; and Cruz, *Transpacific Femininities*.
119 Noodin, "Megwa Baabaamiiaayaayaang Dibaajomoyaang," 175.
120 Florence "Johnny" Frisbie and Brian Russell Roberts, conversation, Honolulu, Hawai'i, February 11, 2014.
121 Johnny also discusses Elaine's negotiation of this requirement in the second edition of her book. F. Frisbie, *Miss Ulysses* (2016), 302. During the writing of *Miss Ulysses*, Johnny viewed herself and all of her siblings as US citizens, routed through their father's US citizenship (*Miss Ulysses* [1948], 108). On the US citizenship policies to which Johnny referred during our 2014 conversation, see Orfield, "Citizenship Act of 1934."
122 For the treaty's text, see *Treaty with the Cook Islands*, 1–3.
123 This quotation from *Miss Ulysses* references the US-Japanese Battle of Tarawa, on Tarawa Atoll in the Gilbert Islands (today, the Republic of Kiribati).
124 F. Frisbie, *Miss Ulysses* (2016), 301.
125 On Robert Frisbie's death and Johnny's arrival in Hawai'i, see F. Frisbie, *Miss Ulysses* (2016), 298, 301.
126 On Elaine's birth, see F. Frisbie, *Miss Ulysses*, 7. Johnny herself was born in Tahiti (4).
127 *Treaty with the Cook Islands*, 1.
128 For the date of Johnny's arrival in Honolulu, see F. Frisbie, *Miss Ulysses* (2016), 301.
129 During a follow-up conversation in 2019, Johnny explained to me that one of her major objections to Honolulu upon her arrival in 1950 was that the hotels and other establishments pruned the coconut trees in ways geared toward appealing to tourists. She also explained that although in 2014 she was very aware of prior US claims to Pukapuka, she had not known about these claims while she was living in Pukapuka. Rather, she had only learned about them a few years prior to our first conversation in

2014. Florence "Johnny" Frisbie and Brian Russell Roberts, conversation, Honolulu, Hawai'i, November 9, 2019.
130 Quoted in Dash, "Stranger by the Shore," 360.
131 Lyons, *American Pacificism*, 4; Wilson, *Reimagining the American Pacific*, 1; Na'puti and Bevacqua, "Militarization and Resistance," 841; and Teves, *Defiant Indigeneity*.
132 With the establishment of Hinemoana of Turtle Island in the 2010s, a collective of Pacific Islander feminists residing in California and Oregon adopted a name that stages an interlapping of the archipelagic Pacific and an archipelagic version of Turtle Island, disengaged from settler-colonial teleologies of the North American continent. "About," Muliwai: Recognizing Each Other in the Indigenous Pacific and Beyond, accessed August 25, 2020, https://morethantwominutes.wordpress.com/about. On the shoal as an unstable and submerged staging ground between Indigenous and Black thought and activism, see King, *Black Shoals*.

Chapter Two: Archipelagic Diaspora and Geographic Form

1 Hurston, *Dust Tracks*, 43. Subsequent references to *Dust Tracks* are cited in the text.
2 Quoted in Boyd, *Wrapped in Rainbows*, 275–76.
3 See Carla Kaplan, ed., introduction to "The Forties," in Hurston, *Zora Neale Hurston: A Life in Letters*, 434.
4 Hurston, "Crazy for This Democracy," 946, 947.
5 Hurston, *Tell My Horse*, 135.
6 See Boyd, *Wrapped in Rainbows*, 295.
7 Carby, "Politics of Fiction," 82.
8 Pavlić, *Crossroads Modernism*, 147–243; Cartwright, "'To Walk with the Storm'"; Bone, "(Extended) South of Black Folk"; and Lamothe, *Inventing the New Negro*, 160–78.
9 Benítez-Rojo, *Repeating Island*, 2.
10 Benítez-Rojo, *Repeating Island*, 4.
11 Benítez-Rojo, *Repeating Island*, 4. On the Caribbean as key to world culture, see Glissant, *Poetics of Relation*, 5–9; and Bernabé, Chamoiseau, and Confiant, "In Praise of Creoleness," 902–3.
12 Du Bois, *Souls of Black Folk*, 15.
13 On postexceptionalist American studies, see Pease, "Re-thinking 'American Studies,'" 19, 20.
14 Curiel et al., introduction to *Post-Nationalist American Studies*, 2. Examples of scholars who have paid attention to island spaces include Kaplan, *Anarchy of Empire*; and Stephens, *Black Empire*.
15 Kaplan, "Manifest Domesticity," 583.
16 Brickhouse, "Hemispheric Jamestown," 21.
17 For the former view, see Carby, "Politics of Fiction," 87; Duck, "'*Go* There tuh *Know* There,'" 277; and Meehan, *People Get Ready*, 77.

18 Handley, "Environmental Phenomenology of Diaspora," 656.
19 Hegel, *Lectures*, 155; and Semple, *Influences of Geographic Environment*, 1.
20 McKittrick has drawn attention to "the relationship between black populations and . . . geography as space, place, and location in their physical materiality and imaginative configurations." McKittrick, *Demonic Grounds*, x. In *The Black Shoals: Offshore Formations of Black and Native Studies*, King has attended to the materiality of the offshore formation of the "shoal" as a means of theorizing Black and Native studies. Giles calls for a "geographical materialism." Giles, "Deterritorialization of American Literature," 39. See also Tilley, *Phenomenology of Landscape*; Tally, *Geocritical Explorations*; M. Cohen, "Literary Studies"; and Blum, "Prospect of Oceanic Studies."
21 My thinking on geographic form not as an immutable category but as produced through phenomenological engagement with the planet's features is inspired in part by Roland Barthes on structure as a "simulacrum" involving "intellect added to object." Barthes, *Critical Essays*, 215.
22 Giles, "Antipodean American Literature," 23.
23 Giles, "Antipodean American Literature," 23. See Pratt, *Imperial Eyes*, 6.
24 See Giles, *Antipodean America*, 39–79.
25 Duck, "'*Go* There tuh *Know* There,'" 278.
26 Hurston, *Their Eyes Were Watching God*, 11. Subsequent references to *Their Eyes* are cited in the text.
27 Lamothe, *Inventing the New Negro*, 162; and Sorensen, "Modernity on a Global Stage," 10–11.
28 Julius Scott, *Common Wind*; and B. Byrd, *Black Republic*.
29 Borrowing from Edward Kamau Brathwaite on tidal flows, Elizabeth M. DeLoughrey, among others, has usefully "destabilize[d] the myth of island isolation." DeLoughrey, *Routes and Roots*, 2.
30 Lyotard, "The Sublime and the Avant-Garde," 458; and McKittrick, "Mathematics Black Life," 22.
31 On things and subject-object relations, see Brown, "Thing Theory"; and Bernstein, "Dances with Things."
32 Bennett, *Vibrant Matter*, 9.
33 Morton, *Hyperobjects*, 1.
34 See Harper, "Empire"; and Hofmeyr, "Universalizing the Indian Ocean," 722–23.
35 On suitors and Odysseus as beggar, see Homer, *Odyssey*, xvii–xxiv.
36 Wright, *Color Curtain*, 443.
37 This sublime island is "not what [Janie] desire[s]" but is "the formal frame which confers consistency on [her] desire." Žižek, *Plague of Fantasies*, 39.
38 Stevens, *Letters of Wallace Stevens*, 268; and Federal Writers' Project, *Florida*, 198–99.
39 Standiford, *Last Train to Paradise*, 32.
40 Hurston, *Tell My Horse*, 133.
41 Hurston, *Tell My Horse*, 133.
42 Hurston, *Tell My Horse*, 134, 135.

43 Deleuze, "Desert Islands," 10, 11.
44 Sonya Posmentier's insightful reading of an earlier article version of this chapter has helped refine my discussion of archipelagic diaspora in relation to more traditional modes of thinking about diaspora. Posmentier, *Cultivation and Catastrophe*, 125–26.
45 Du Bois, "Criteria of Negro Art," 20.
46 Brubaker, "'Diaspora' Diaspora," 3.
47 Weheliye, *Habeas Viscus*, 31.
48 Glissant, *La cohée du Lamentin*, 37; Ryuta Imafuku, "Noah's Stories in Shaky Archipelagos: Martinique, Haiti, Fukushima," *openDemocracy: Free Thinking for the World*, June 8, 2012, https://www.opendemocracy.net/en/noahs-stories-in-shaky-archipelagos-martinique-haiti-fukushima/.
49 Frisbie, *Miss Ulysses*; and Turner, *Frontier in American History*, 38. On Walcott and *The Odyssey*, see, for instance, Hofmeister, "From Homer to *Omeros*."
50 Waddell, Naidu, and Hauʻofa, *New Oceania*, viii.
51 Frisbie, *Miss Ulysses*, 65.
52 Malkin, *Small Greek World*, 26, 3, 26.
53 For another discussion of convergences between tropes of diaspora and archipelago, see Cribb and Ford, "Indonesia as an Archipelago," 8.
54 Here *Their Eyes* exemplifies Barbara Christian's description of theorizing through "stories we create." Christian, "Race for Theory," 52.
55 A. Kent, *African, Native, and Jewish American Literature*, 66; and Doyle, "Atlantic Modernism at the Crossing," 116, 133–34.
56 Paine, *Common Sense*, 93. For eighteenth-century arguments similar to Paine's, see Ramsay, "Dr. Ramsay's Oration."
57 Tocqueville, *Democracy in America*, 180.
58 Wheatley, *Complete Writings*, 39–40, 88–90.
59 Federal Writers' Project, *Florida*, 315.
60 Murdock, *Palm Beach*, 68.
61 Murdock, *Palm Beach*, 4.
62 Morrison, *Playing in the Dark*, 13.
63 On Hurston's involvement, see Bordelon, "Zora Neale Hurston," 25–28.
64 Federal Writers' Project, *Florida*, 227, 230, 229.
65 NAACP, *Fourteenth Annual Report*, 18. For background on this lynching and twenty-first-century efforts to remember it, see Hannah Morse, "Why There's a Push to Never Forget the Two Men Lynched in Palm Beach County," *Palm Beach Post*, July, 12, 2019, https://www.palmbeachpost.com/news/20190712/why-theres-push-to-never-forget-two-men-lynched-in-palm-beach-county.
66 For a foundational reading of Tea Cake's physical violence against Janie, see Walker, *In Search of Our Mothers' Gardens*, 304–12.
67 Navakas, *Liquid Landscape*, 2.
68 McKittrick, *Demonic Grounds*, xxiv; see also Wynter, "Beyond Miranda's Meanings."
69 Hauʻofa, "Our Sea of Islands," 10–11.

70 On islands and asyndeton, see de Certeau, *Practice of Everyday Life*, 101.
71 In using the term *Man*, I am following Wynter in reference to the universalized notion of Western or Indo-European "Man" as the generic human; see, for instance, Wynter, "Beyond the Word of Man." On "the anti-Universal" and "the claim to specificity," see Wynter, "Beyond the Word of Man," 639. On "shantytown archipelagoes," see Wynter, "Beyond the Word of Man," 645. On the "ex-slave-labor archipelago," see Wynter and McKittrick, "Unparalleled Catastrophe for Our Species?," 41.
72 Richard Wright, "Between Laughter and Tears," *New Masses*, October 5, 1937, 22, 25.
73 Wright, quoted in Karem, *Purloined Islands*, 235.
74 Walker, "Zora Neale Hurston," xiii.
75 Walker, "Zora Neale Hurston," xiii. In her 1983 version of the 1977 publication, Walker revised the term *deserted island* to the more standard *desert island*. Walker, *In Search of Our Mothers' Gardens*, 86.
76 DeLoughrey, *Routes and Roots*, 13.
77 Culler, "Desert Island Texts," 254.
78 Perloff, "Removing the Eggshells," 276–77.
79 Arac, *Huckleberry Finn*, 133.
80 On *Their Eyes* and the new US American canon, see J. Lowe, "Materials," 7.
81 DeLoughrey, *Routes and Roots*, 14.
82 Hayles, "Cognition on a Desert Island," 338; and Diaz, "Voyaging for Anti-Colonial Recovery," 25, 27.
83 Derek Walcott, interview by Sue Lawley, *Desert Island Discs*, BBC, June 9, 1991, http://www.bbc.co.uk/programmes/p0093z3h.
84 Lamming, *Pleasures of Exile*, 154.
85 On the new formalism, see Levinson, "What Is New Formalism?," 559.
86 See Grove, *Green Imperialism*, 1–15.
87 See Ransom, "Criticism, Inc.," 598; and Levinson, "What Is New Formalism?," 561.
88 Hansen, "Formalism and Its Malcontents," 667.
89 In critically approaching geographic form, I am thinking in analogy to discussions outlining language and culture as pivotal to the analysis of literary and cultural form. See Rooney, "Form and Contentment"; Mitchell, "Commitment to Form"; and Hansen, "Formalism and Its Malcontents."
90 Walcott, "Isla Incognita," 52.
91 DeLoughrey, *Routes and Roots*, 2.
92 Brathwaite, *Contradictory Omens*, 64.
93 Quoted in Ingersoll, *Waves of Knowing*, 87.
94 Deleuze, "Desert Islands," 13.
95 Wineera, "This Island," 4.
96 For these quotations on Glissantian distant reading, see Roberts and Stephens, "Archipelagic American Studies: Decontinentalizing," 29.
97 Rooney, "Form and Contentment," 26.

Chapter Three: Borderwaters and Geometries of Being Amid

1. Cutler, "Borders and Borderland Literature," 158–59.
2. Hämäläinen and Truett, "On Borderlands," 343. For further discussion of the borderlands' universalization, see Cutler, "Borders and Borderland Literature," 163.
3. Fishkin, "Crossroads of Cultures," 17.
4. Limón, *American Encounters*, 2–3.
5. Twain, *Life on the Mississippi*, 253. See the same page for another story on the shifting river.
6. On the Chamizal dispute, see Friedman, "Political Props."
7. Twain, *Adventures of Huckleberry Finn*, 100.
8. Paredes, "Rio Grande," 15–16.
9. Anzaldúa, *Borderlands/La Frontera*, 2–3.
10. Rosaldo, *Culture and Truth*; Rosaldo, "Introduction"; and Saldívar, *Trans-Americanity*, xxvii.
11. Lipman, *Saltwater Frontier*, 85–124; and Mignolo, *Local Histories/Global Designs*, 4.
12. Cutler, "Borders and Borderland Literature," 158; Paredes, *Texas-Mexican Cancionero*, xvii; Anzaldúa, *Borderlands/La Frontera*, 3.
13. Anzaldúa, *Borderlands/La Frontera*, 3; and Nail, *Theory of the Border*, 169. On cultural flows and hydrologic flows more generally, see Nail, *Theory of the Border*, 6, 48, 155, 169–70. For references to perceptions of borders as Euclidean and one-dimensional lines, see Stern, "Nationalism on the Line," 314; Merivale, "Audible Palimpsests," 159; Evans, preface to *Borderlands*, xviii; and Price, *Dry Place*, 118–19.
14. On the United States and Mexico's Euclideanist fight against the Rio Grande to preserve a stable dividing line, see Martínez, *Troublesome Border*, 25–30; and Rebert, "Drawing the Line," 159–62. On Europeans and Euro-Americans' Euclideanist fight on two-dimensional paper against Indigenous Americans' tradition- and rock art–inscribed boundaries on the continent, see Barr and Countryman, "Introduction."
15. Tinsley, "Black Atlantic, Queer Atlantic," 212. For a study that takes seriously the archipelagic topography created not only by oceans but also by rivers, see Joseph, *Fluid New York*.
16. For comments on Covarrubias's racial, colonial, and gender representations, see Ross, *Manning the Race*, 143; Pollmann, "Margaret Mead's Balinese," 17, 18–19, 22; Mewburn, "Oil, Art, and Politics," 99; and Vickers, "Word and Image."
17. Perez, "Guam and Archipelagic American Studies," 108; and Annalisa Merelli and Quartz, "Map: Every Country in the World Involved in a Territorial Dispute," *Atlantic*, March 20, 2014, https://www.theatlantic.com/international/archive/2014/03/map-every-country-in-the-world-involved-in-a-territorial-dispute/284533/.
18. Hurston, *Zora Neale Hurston: A Life in Letters*, 327.
19. For a concise biographical timeline on Covarrubias, see de la Garza, "Covarrubias Chronology." See also A. Williams, *Covarrubias*.
20. Limón, "Greater Mexico, Modernism, and New York," 83.

21 Vickers, foreword to *Island of Bali*, xix. Covarrubias lived in Bali from late 1930 to mid-1931 and again from late 1933 to about mid-1934. A. Williams and Chong, *Covarrubias in Bali*, 10–37.

22 In pointing toward the waters of figuration, I am thinking of the question, "How do waters, as subjects of continuous sensory encounters . . . shape the emergence of language and ideas?" Chen, MacLeod, and Neimanis, "Introduction," 10. On archipelagic spaces as greater borderlands, see Cline, "Imperial Perspectives on the Borderlands," 173; Cutter, "Western Spanish Borderlands," 42; and Habell-Pallán, *Loca Motion*, 23.

23 Covarrubias, *Island of Bali*, 8. For Covarrubias's explanation on Bali and the sea, see pages 7–8.

24 Covarrubias, *Island of Bali*, 1.

25 Covarrubias, *Island of Bali*, 9.

26 Rosa Covarrubias, quoted in A. Williams and Chong, *Covarrubias in Bali*, 23.

27 Lutkehaus, "Miguel Covarrubias," 115, 117. On Covarrubias's invitation to participate in the exposition, see A. Williams, *Covarrubias*, 100–101. On Treasure Island, see James and Weller, *Treasure Island*, 17–23.

28 James and Weller, *Treasure Island*, 26, 305.

29 Pacific House, "Pageant of the Pacific," [5]. The pamphlet's pages are unnumbered; page numbers were calculated using the front cover as the first page.

30 Covarrubias, *Pageant of the Pacific*, [7]. The pamphlet's pages are unnumbered; page numbers were calculated using the front cover as the first page.

31 Covarrubias, *Pageant of the Pacific*, [7]. On "Rimspeak," see Cumings, "Rimspeak."

32 Hauʻofa, "Our Sea of Islands," 7.

33 Widodo, Anwari, and Maryanto, *Pendidikan Kewarganegaraan*, 175.

34 Paredes, *Texas-Mexican Cancionero*, xiv.

35 Covarrubias, *Pageant of the Pacific*, [9].

36 Covarrubias, *Pageant of the Pacific*, [17].

37 See A. McIntyre, "'Greater Indonesia' Idea of Nationalism"; and Kheng, *Red Star over Malaya*, 9–13. Also on ethnicity, race, and this same archipelagic space, see Okihiro, "Island Race."

38 Covarrubias, *Pageant of the Pacific*, [22].

39 Glissant, *Philosophie de la Relation*, 57.

40 With the phrase "be from," I am echoing poet Craig Santos Perez's use of the word *from* in the titles of his *From Unincorporated Territory* series, beginning with *From Unincorporated Territory [hacha]*.

41 C. Levine, *Forms*, 114.

42 *Republic of Indonesia: New Nation of the World* (undated), manuscript box 4 (uncataloged "ephemera"), Adriana and Tom Williams Collection of Miguel Covarrubias, Harry Ransom Center, University of Texas at Austin. Based on the pamphlet's content, it was likely published in 1951, which is the publication date provided in de Maria y Campos Castelló, *Covarrubias*, 33. Registered as a foreign agent in the United States, the Information Office of the Republic of Indonesia, also called the Republic of Indonesia Office, opened in New York in 1949 and operated through the mid-1950s.

See the office's periodical, ranging from *Report on Indonesia* 1, no. 1 (July 7, 1949) to *Report on Indonesia* 5, no. 15 (June 30, 1954). After this point, the periodical was published by the Indonesian Embassy in Washington, DC; *Report on Indonesia* 6, no. 1 (August–September 1954). Issues of *Report on Indonesia* available at Memorial Library, University of Wisconsin–Madison, call number AP R426 O58 I42.

43 For an overview of this history, see Vickers, *History of Modern Indonesia*, 115.
44 Lubis, *Perlawatan ke Amerika Serikat*, 13–14.
45 Grotius, *Freedom of the Seas*, 28, 37. On Spanish and Portuguese territorialization of the ocean, see James Scott, "Introductory Note," vii.
46 The quotes are from "Territorial Sea and Maritime Districts Ordinance 1939," 194. On vessels sailing freely, see Danusaputro, "Wawasan Nusantara," 62.
47 H. Kent, "Historical Origins."
48 "Territorial Sea and Maritime Districts Ordinance 1939," 194.
49 Quoted in Van Zandt, *Boundaries of the United States* (1966), 67.
50 Alaskan Boundary Tribunal, *Proceedings of the Alaskan Boundary Tribunal*, 218–19. For an intriguing and complementary discussion of the fractal ambiguities of the watery US-Canada border and the San Juan Islands, see Riquet, *Aesthetics of Island Space*, 177–244.
51 Braverman and Johnson, "Blue Legalities," 11, 19.
52 Mandelbrot, "How Long Is the Coast of Britain?"
53 Mandelbrot, *Fractal Geometry of Nature*, 3.
54 Mandelbrot, *Fractal Geometry of Nature*, 1.
55 Mandelbrot, *Fractal Geometry of Nature*, 5.
56 Mandelbrot, *Fractal Geometry of Nature*, 25.
57 Mandelbrot, *Fractal Geometry of Nature*, 26.
58 Mandelbrot, *Fractal Geometry of Nature*, 26–27.
59 Mandelbrot, *Fractal Geometry of Nature*, 26.
60 Samuel, "On Seeing and Believing," 94.
61 Van Zandt, *Boundaries of the United States* (1966), 68; and van Zandt, *Boundaries of the United States* (1976), 46. On approaches to Euclideanizing bays, see, for instance, Strohl, *International Law of Bays*, 54–55. Further, the ordinance of 1939 has a provision for drawing straight lines across bays; see "Territorial Sea and Maritime Districts Ordinance 1939," 194. See also United Nations, *Law of the Sea*, 4–5.
62 "Maritime Zones and Boundaries," NOAA Office of General Counsel, accessed August 24, 2020, https://www.gc.noaa.gov/gcil_maritime.html.
63 In spite of frequent imaginations, in the context of a borderlands model, of the border as a Euclidean dividing line, and in spite of US efforts (as discussed by Nail) to keep water from disrupting the line's Euclidean idealization, the fact that much of the US-Mexico border is set by the Rio Grande is a reminder of the shoreline's importance for considering convergences between the borderwaters and the borderlands.
64 Anzaldúa, *Borderlands/La Frontera*, 3.
65 Oegroseno, "Indonesia's Maritime Boundaries," 49.
66 Butcher and Elson, *Sovereignty and the Sea*, 47.

67　Djuanda, "Announcement," 86.
68　Wright, *Color Curtain*, 505.
69　On domesticating translation practices, see Venuti, *Translator's Invisibility*, 13–15.
70　Quoted in Foulcher, "*Sumpah Pemuda*," 385. Earlier iterations of the Sumpah Pemuda had not used "Tanah Air Indonesia" but simply "tanah Indonesia," that is, Indonesian "land" or "lands" (380). For further context on *tanah air*'s usage in nineteenth-century and nationalist contexts, see Cribb and Ford, "Indonesia as an Archipelago," 11.
71　Kusumaatmadja, "Legal Regime of Archipelagoes," 171. Based on conventions surrounding Indonesian names, it is standard for my discussion to refer to Mochtar Kusumaatmadja by the first component of his name, Mochtar. However, for consistency in citation style, notes and bibliographical references shorten and alphabetize his name by its final component, Kusumaatmadja.
72　Butcher and Elson, *Sovereignty and the Sea*, 66. Before Mochtar's use of archipelagic baselines, the concept was under discussion by the International Law Commission regarding archipelagoes that existed along a so-called mainland's coast, but there was confusion on whether such a hypothetical system would apply merely to coastal archipelagoes or also to "mid-ocean archipelagic States." O'Connell, "Mid-Ocean Archipelagos in International Law," 19.
73　Danusaputro, "International Sea System," 43. Indonesia was not the only country involved in the fight for recognition of the category of archipelagic state. The other archipelagic states that negotiated for recognition as such in the run-up to UNCLOS 1982 included Fiji, the Philippines, Mauritius, and the Bahamas. See Munavvar, *Ocean States*.
74　United Nations, *Law of the Sea*, 15 (my italics).
75　On the Westphalian myth, see Osiander, "Sovereignty."
76　Kusumaatmadja, "Supplementary Remarks," 174.
77　Danusaputro, "Wawasan Nusantara," 59.
78　Mahmud, "Malay Concept of *Tanah Air*," 6, 11.
79　Glissant, *Philosophie de la Relation*, 45. For resonant Indonesian thinking on rivers' interface with the ocean, see Danusaputro, "International Sea System," 27.
80　On tanah air as a structure of feeling within UNCLOS's notion of the archipelagic State, see Roberts, "What Is an Archipelago?"
81　Glissant, *Poétique de la Relation*, 19; Glissant, *Poetics of Relation*, 7; and Dash, "Stranger by the Shore," 359.
82　Carter, *Decolonising Governance*.
83　On Pramoedya's imprisonment in the context of the mass killing of perhaps one million people, see Samuels, introduction to *The Mute's Soliloquy*, xiii–xxii. For evidence of US support for the mass killings, see "Indonesia: US Documents Released on 1965–66 Massacres," Human Rights Watch, October 18, 2017, https://www.hrw.org/news/2017/10/18/indonesia-us-documents-released-1965-66-massacres.
84　Toer, *Nyanyi Sunyi seorang Bisu*, 2–3. Based on conventions surrounding Indonesian names, it is standard for my discussion to refer to Pramoedya Ananta Toer by the first

component of his name, Pramoedya. However, for consistency in citation style, notes and bibliographical references shorten and alphabetize his name by its final component, Toer.

85 Toer, *Nyanyi Sunyi seorang Bisu*, 6.
86 In adopting straight archipelagic baselines, Indonesia in a real sense was interested, for defense purposes, in taming the fractal geometry of the three-mile seaward borders it had inherited from the Dutch. As stated by one of Mochtar Kusumaatmadja's Indonesian coworkers in advancing the archipelagic perspective, archipelagic baselines would convert a country whose borders were a function of a "coast . . . more than three times that of the equator" into a country whose borders were "shortened [in] length . . . and greatly simplified [in] measurement." Danusaputro, "Wawasan Nusantara," 85.
87 Michener, *Hawaii*, 416.
88 Equiano, *Life of Olaudah Equiano*, 60.
89 On the "coloniality of power," "expressed in the 'racial' distribution of work" and arising specifically in the Americas, see Quijano, "Coloniality of Power," 218.
90 On Americanity and trans-Americanity, see Saldívar, *Trans-Americanity*, ix–xxviii.
91 Quintero Herencia, *La hoja de mar*, 17.
92 Quintero Herencia, *La hoja de mar*, 24.
93 Sharpe, *In the Wake*.
94 Roberts and Stephens, "Archipelagic American Studies: Decontinentalizing," 8.
95 "The Trust Territory: Its 2,130 Islands Form a New U.S. Domain in the Pacific," *Life*, April 25, 1949, 97.
96 Bogan, "Government of the Trust Territory," 164. The discrepancy between *Life*'s figure of three million square miles and Bogan's figure of five million square miles stems from Bogan's inclusion of the Bonin Islands (which also transferred from Japan to the United States after World War II) in the TTPI.
97 Bogan, "Government of the Trust Territory," 174, 165.
98 US Naval Civil Administration Unit, Marshall Islands, *Roster of Officers, Enlisted Men, Civilians and Dependents*.
99 Grotius, *Freedom of the Seas*, 5.
100 O'Connell, "Mid-Ocean Archipelagos in International Law," 39.
101 Committee on Interior and Insular Affairs, *Investigation and Study of the Seaward Boundaries*, 18.
102 Quoted in US Bureau of the Census, *Census of the Philippine Islands*, 49.
103 Truman, "Policy of the United States," 496.
104 Navy Department, *Information on the Trust Territory*, 1.
105 Navy Department, *Information on the Trust Territory*, front endpapers and 1.
106 Department of the Navy, Office of the Chief of Naval Operations, *Report on the Administration of the Trust Territory*, vi.
107 See other maps of the TTPI that use similar language: Richard, *United States Naval Administration of the Trust Territory*, front map; Meller, *Congress of Micronesia*, 12–13; *Trust Territory of the Pacific Islands*; and McHenry, *Micronesia*, front map.

108 As stated in Euclid's definitions 13 and 14: "A *boundary* is that which is an extremity of anything," and "a *figure* is that which is contained by any boundary or boundaries." Euclid, *Euclid's Elements*, 1.
109 For US use of the phrase *territory of the United States* vis-à-vis the TTPI and the islands of Palau specifically, see van Zandt, *Boundaries of the United States* (1966), 34.
110 Quoted in O'Connell, "Mid-Ocean Archipelagos in International Law," 45.
111 Deleuze, *Cinema 1*, 10. On Deleuze and set theory, see Duffy, *Deleuze and the History of Mathematics*, 155–59.
112 Glissant, "Unforeseeable Diversity of the World," 292.
113 Amitav Ghosh, "Four Corners," *Granta* 26 (May 1, 1989), https://granta.com/four-corners/.
114 For further crystallization of Anzaldúa's stance on the sea in relation to the United States and Indonesia, see Roberts, "On the Borderwaters."
115 Sukarno, "Speech by President Sukarno," 24.
116 Article 6 of the United States' Trustee Agreement with the UN, quoted in McHenry, *Micronesia*, 33. On Indonesia's concern with radioactive pollution and the ocean, see Danusaputro, *Tata Lautan Nusantara dalam Hukum dan Sejarahnya*, 100, 180.
117 The Bandung Conference's final communiqué contained a "Declaration on the Promotion of World Peace and Co-operation," whose second and third principles endorsed "respect for the sovereignty and territorial integrity of all nations" and "recognition of the equality of all races and of the equality of all nations large and small." "Final Communique," 168.
118 Glissant, *La cohée du Lamentin*, 73.
119 Bonilla, *Non-sovereign Futures*, xiv; and Getachew, *Worldmaking after Empire*, 2. On multispecies entanglements and biological and nonbiological actants, see van Dooren, Kirksey, and Münster, "Multispecies Studies."
120 Covarrubias, *Pageant of the Pacific*, [22].
121 Covarrubias, *Pageant of the Pacific*, [15].
122 "The Trust Territory," 97.
123 Feinberg et al., "'Drawing the Coral Heads,'" 245. The Marshall Islands navigators' commentary on the mattang is quoted in Ascher, *Mathematics Elsewhere*, 103.
124 Captain Winkler, "On Sea Charts," 498–500; the chart also appears in Schück, *Stabkarten der Marshall-Insulaner*, pl. 7, fig. 35. Based on Marcia Ascher's 1995 efforts to collate known stick charts and their representations in the scholarly literature, this stick chart (referred to as chart 35) has appeared only in Winkler and Schück. Ascher, "Models and Maps," 368. Given that the Winkler source is in English and given the marked resemblances between Covarrubias's and Winkler's illustrations of Marshall Islands outrigger canoes, my working assumption is that Covarrubias's source was Winkler.
125 Winkler, "On Sea Charts," 491, 493–94, 498–500.
126 Ascher has ranked Marshall Islands stick charts as highly significant to an understanding of "a global and humanistic history of mathematics." Ascher, *Mathematics Elsewhere*, ix, 3. There is no "single, universal path . . . that cultures or mathematical

ideas follow," but rather they have lives apart from Western mathematics, constituting what Ascher calls "a global mosaic" of mathematical ideas (2). In other words, these are not pre-Euclidean lives but non-Euclidean lives.

127 Cutler, *Ends of Assimilation*, 184.
128 DeLoughrey, *Allegories of the Anthropocene*, 174.
129 Quoted in Hickel, *Who Owns America?*, 208. Hickel (US interior secretary under Richard Nixon) reports that Kissinger spoke these words during a 1969 meeting in the office of US secretary of state William Rogers.
130 Kathy Jetñil-Kijiner, "Reflections on Nuclear Survivors Day," *Kathy Jetñil-Kijiner* (blog), March 1, 2013, https://jkijiner.wordpress.com/tag/nuclear-survivors-day/.
131 Kathy Jetñil-Kijiner, "Shadows of Our Past: 2016 Nuclear Day in the Marshalls," *Kathy Jetñil-Kijiner* (blog), March 25, 2016, https://www.kathyjetnilkijiner.com/shadows-of-our-past-2016-nuclear-day-in-the-marshalls/. The quotation "complex narratives of disappearing islands" is from Kathy Jetñil-Kijiner, "'Butterfly Thief' and Complex Narratives of Disappearing Islands," *Kathy Jetñil-Kijiner* (blog), April 30, 2017, https://www.kathyjetnilkijiner.com/butterfly-thief-and-complex-narratives-of-disappearing-islands/.
132 Ralph Barton, "It Is to Laugh," review of *The Prince of Wales and Other Famous Americans: A Collection of Sixty-Six Caricatures*, by Miguel Covarrubias, *New York Herald Tribune, Books*, October 25, 1925, 4.
133 Covarrubias, *Pageant of the Pacific*, [10].
134 A. Williams, *Covarrubias*, 12.
135 Vasconcelos, "La raza cósmica," 47, 78, 80.
136 Anzaldúa, *Borderlands/La Frontera*, 77.
137 Vasconcelos, "La raza cósmica," 47, 61.
138 On trans-Indigeneity, see Allen, *Trans-Indigenous*.
139 DeLoughrey, *Routes and Roots*, 16; and Covarrubias, *Eagle*, 24.
140 Covarrubias, *Eagle*, 24. Covarrubias was drawing on arguments in Rivet, *Los orígenes del hombre americano*.
141 Covarrubias, *Eagle*, 29, 28.
142 Gladwin, *Men out of Asia*, 303. For Gladwin on Te Rangihiroa (Peter Buck), see Gladwin, *Men out of Asia*, 235, 239, 246–47.
143 Covarrubias, *Eagle*, 28.
144 For his *Peoples of the Pacific* mural, Covarrubias used orange to indicate regions inhabited by either Polynesians or Micronesians, remarking in the accompanying pamphlet that "Micronesians and Polynesians" exhibit similar racial "admixtures" and reminding viewers that the archipelagic "cultures of the Pacific" "are superimposed or overlap." Covarrubias, *Pageant of the Pacific*, [11, 8, 14]. He again conflated Polynesian and Micronesian cultures by associating Polynesian navigational prowess with "charts of the islands," although research into Indigenous navigational charts of the Pacific apparently would have led him only to the Micronesian and specifically Marshallese stick charts that he illustrated for his map of the TTPI ([12]). Marshallese stick charts are said to be the "only [known] physical charts produced by local map

makers in the insular Pacific prior to Western influence." Feinberg et al., "'Drawing the Coral Heads,'" 245.

145 On collaborations between Hawaiʻi and Puerto Rico, see Garrison, "Settler Responsibility," 64–68; on Caribbean-Pacific correspondences, see Glissant, *Poetics of Relation*, 34.

146 Martínez-San Miguel uses the term *archipelagic Mexico* a handful of times in her essay "Colonial and Mexican Archipelagoes: Reimagining Colonial Caribbean Studies" (159, 160, 161, 169).

147 Gladwin, *Men Out of Asia*, 320.

148 Glissant, *Philosophie de la Relation*, 47, 45.

149 See, for instance, Sae-Saue, *Southwest Asia*.

150 On successive waves of colonization, displacement, and survivance on and around the Pajarito Plateau, see Gómez, "Nuclear Alienation," 35–71.

151 On Trinity Drive and the Trinity Test, see Martin, *Los Alamos Place Names*, 130.

152 On Bikini Atoll Road, see Martin, *Los Alamos Place Names*, 17. On the main general warehouse (SM-30), see US Department of Energy and National Nuclear Security Administration, *Draft Site-Wide Environmental Impact Statement*, J-49. Another Los Alamos street named for a Marshall Islands nuclear test site is Eniwetok Road, whose namesake is an atoll used for US nuclear testing from 1948 to 1954. Enewetak Atoll (according to the more standard spelling) is known as the site of the United States' first thermonuclear explosion in November 1952. Martin, *Los Alamos Place Names*, 50.

153 Teaiwa, "Bikinis and Other S/pacific N/oceans," 87.

154 Gómez, "Nuclear Alienation," 7.

155 Gómez, "Nuclear Alienation," 8.

156 Gómez, "Nuclear Alienation," 9.

157 Gómez, "Nuclear Alienation," 25. On the Alamo, see de Hoyos, *Chicano Poems for the Barrio*, [6, 23–24] (original is unnumbered; page numbers were calculated using the title page as the first page); Anzaldúa, *Borderlands/La Frontera*, 6–7; and Flores, *Remembering the Alamo*.

Chapter Four: Fractal Temporality on Vulnerable Foreshores

1 Okubo, quoted in Sun, *Miné Okubo*, 18. On Okubo as staff for Rivera, see Lee, *Painting on the Left*, 193, 200, 250n17. For about twenty seconds, Okubo appears at work on Rivera's mural in Orville C. Goldner's short film *Art in Action Exhibition* (1939/1940), Bay Area Television Archive, San Francisco State University, https://diva.sfsu.edu/bundles/187038.

2 Rivera, quoted in Lee, *Painting on the Left*, 209.

3 James and Weller, *Treasure Island*, 18.

4 James and Weller, *Treasure Island*, 18. For an overview of the island's creation, see James and Weller, *Treasure Island*, 17–23.

5. McGann, Sloan, and Wan, "Biostratigraphy beneath Central San Francisco Bay," 11–18.
6. Felski, *Limits of Critique*, 154–55.
7. The nation's fundamental imbrications with temporality have been foregrounded at founding moments in the study of the nation, as in Ernest Renan's "What Is a Nation?" (1882) and Benedict Anderson's notion of nation formation through emplotment in "the steady onward clocking of homogeneous, empty time." B. Anderson, *Imagined Communities*, 33. Thanks to Russ Castronovo, whose presentation "Out of Order: Criticism and Anachronism" at the 2017 American Studies Association convention (during the "Futures Past/Futures Perfect" session) was useful to me on this point and others in this chapter.
8. Dimock, "Planet and America," 3.
9. McGurl, "New Cultural Geology," 380.
10. Mandelbrot, *Fractal Geometry of Nature*, 26.
11. Foucault, *Order of Things*, 386, 387; Gillis, *Human Shore*, 1–6, 19; Brathwaite, *ConVERSations with Nathaniel Mackey*, 34; Brathwaite, "Caribbean Culture," 42–45; and Bogost, *Alien Phenomenology*, 5. For further reading on tidalectics, see DeLoughrey, *Routes and Roots*, 1–48.
12. For the quotation, see Roberts and Stephens, "Archipelagic American Studies: Decontinentalizing," 1.
13. Jim Yamada, "Portrait of an Artist," *Trek*, December 1942, 22; see also Sun, *Miné Okubo*, 18. This chapter cites Topaz's serial publications—including *Trek*, *All Aboard!*, and *Topaz Times*—via Utah State University's Topaz Japanese-American Relocation Center Digital Collection (accessed August 18, 2020, https://digital.lib.usu.edu/digital/collection/Topaz) and the University of Utah's Utah Digital Newspapers database (accessed August 18, 2020, https://digitalnewspapers.org/newspaper/?paper=Topaz+Times).
14. On Okubo's life and work, see Robinson, *Great Unknown*, 220–29.
15. For concise narratives of the United States' imprisonment of people of Japanese descent during World War II and at Topaz in particular, see Hirabayashi, "Incarceration," 133–38; and Arrington, *Price of Prejudice*. My terminology throughout this chapter (preferring the term *prisoner* over *evacuee*, and *internment camp* over *relocation center*) seeks consistency with the Topaz Museum Board's suggestions. Topaz Museum Board, "Note on Terminology."
16. The "exclusion area" included California, western Washington, western Oregon, and southern Arizona. Dembitz, "Racial Discrimination," 15.
17. McPhee, *Basin and Range*, 21.
18. See Okubo, *Citizen 13660*, 134; and page 1 of *Trek*'s three issues: December 1942, February 1943, and June 1943.
19. Robinson, "Writing the Internment," 47.
20. Okubo, *Citizen 13660*, 206–9; Robinson, "Writing the Internment," 45; and Jim Yamada, "Falderol," *Trek*, June 1943, 42.

21 For McGurl's discussion of speculative realism and OOO as part of the heterogeneous mix of posthumanist approaches he refers to as the new cultural geology, see McGurl, "New Cultural Geology," 384–85. On speculative realism and OOO's relation to continental philosophy, see Ennis, introduction to *Post-Continental Voices*, 1.

22 Maldonado-Torres, "Post-Continental Philosophy," 1, 2, 5. Maldonado-Torres's term *postcontinental philosophy* converges with John Mullarkey's titular term in *Post-Continental Philosophy: An Outline*, where he discusses the term *continental philosophy* as a "sham geo-cultural distinction," acknowledging that "there is not one philosophical theme that is exclusive to the European Continent," even as he continues to focus on philosophy (now on immanence rather than the traditional transcendence) that has emerged from the European continent (1, 2–11). In the wake of the appearance of Mullarkey's study, Lorna Burns has provocatively outlined a Deleuzian bridge between Mullarkey's Eurocentric postcontinental philosophy and the Caribbean postcontinentalism of such figures as Édouard Glissant and Antonio Benítez-Rojo. Burns, *Contemporary Caribbean Writing and Deleuze*, 1–26. In another arena, philosophy's "speculative turn" has been described as involving "varieties of continental materialism and realism" but also (as christened by the Punctum Books series Speculations) as "post-continental philosophy." Bryant, Srnicek, and Harman, "Towards a Speculative Philosophy," 7; and Punctum Books, "Speculations," accessed August 18, 2020, http://punctumbooks.com/imprints/speculations/; also, on speculative realism/OOO as postcontinental, see Ennis, *Post-Continental Voices*.

23 Taro Katayama, "Digressions," *Trek*, December 1942, 29.

24 Dimock, "Weak Theory," 736.

25 For *Trek* on the Pleistocene, see Jim Yamada, "Lake Bonneville," *Trek*, February 1943, 37; on the Cambrian and for the quotation on the "age of man," see Frank Beckwith Sr., "Trilobite Fossils of Antelope Springs," *Trek*, June 1943, 14.

26 On recent interest in taking this race-based and unconstitutional imprisonment as a template for twenty-first-century US policy, see "Trump Doubles Down on Vow to Bar Muslims," *Fox News*, December 8, 2015, https://www.foxnews.com/politics/trump-doubles-down-on-vow-to-bar-muslims. On the mass incarceration of Japanese Americans as unconstitutional, see Trump v. Hawaii, 138 S. Ct. 2392 (2018).

27 I am alluding to Ronald Takaki's foundational if contested book *Strangers from a Different Shore: A History of Asian Americans*, but the Glissantian image of "the stranger by the shore," as discussed by J. Michael Dash, is equally determinative here. Dash, "Stranger by the Shore," 367.

28 Okubo, *Citizen 13660*, 122.

29 Okubo, *Citizen 13660*, 123.

30 Taro Katayama, "State of the City," *Trek*, December 1942, 3.

31 Katayama, "State of the City," 11.

32 Toshio Mori, "Topaz Station," *Trek*, December 1942, 25.

33 J. Cohen, *Stone*, 4.

34 Biographical information drawn from "Frank Beckwith Collection," MWDL: Mountain West Digital Library, accessed August 28, 2020, https://mwdl.org/collections

/FrankBeckwithCollection.php; and "About Us," *Millard County Chronicle Progress*, September 10, 2012, http://millardccp.com/about-mccp.
35 Biographical overview appended to Frank Beckwith Sr., "Landmarks of Pahvant Valley," *Trek*, December 1942, 20.
36 For Beckwith's other *Trek* article, see Frank Beckwith Sr., "Escalante in Millard County," *Trek*, February 1943, 17–20.
37 Beckwith, "Landmarks of Pahvant Valley," 17.
38 Beckwith, "Landmarks of Pahvant Valley," 20.
39 Deleuze, "Desert Islands," 13.
40 Yamada, "Lake Bonneville," 35.
41 Yamada, "Lake Bonneville," 35.
42 Yamada, "Lake Bonneville," 37.
43 *Oxford English Dictionary*, s.v. "foreshore, n.," online ed., accessed August 18, 2020, https://www.oed.com/view/Entry/73162?redirectedFrom=foreshore#eid.
44 In thinking about chreodic ocean patterns, I have been inspired by Stephanie Strickland and Cynthia Lawson Jaramillo's introduction to their digital poem "slippingglimpse" (2007), available at http://slippingglimpse.org/.
45 T. Williams, *Refuge*, 30; and Collings, "Afterword," 229. Collings's quotation is a reference to a short story by Orson Scott Card, "Salvage," in Card, *Folk of the Fringe*, 64–82.
46 Pound, "Hugh Selwyn Mauberley," 60.
47 Freud, *Civilization and Its Discontents*, 10, 11. On the mechanics of this mode of catachresis, see Roberts and Stephens, "Archipelagic American Studies: Decontinentalizing," 30.
48 Yaeger, "Sea Trash," 535.
49 J. Cohen, *Stone*, 1, 3.
50 Bogost, *Alien Phenomenology*, 5; and Meillassoux, *After Finitude*, 7.
51 Bogost, *Alien Phenomenology*, 9; see also Bryant, Srnicek, and Harman, "Towards a Speculative Philosophy," 8.
52 Meillassoux, *After Finitude*, 5.
53 Harman, *Towards Speculative Realism*, 2. See also Harman, "On the Undermining of Objects," 24.
54 Sheldon, "Dark Correlationism," 139.
55 For the first two quotes, see Lang, "Reflections on the Iridescent One," 98; on the "sacred," see Sutton and Snow, *Iridescence*, 96.
56 Meillassoux, *After Finitude*, 2, 7.
57 On color as a secondary quality, see Meillassoux, *After Finitude*, 11–12. The definition of *iridescence* is from Sutton and Snow, *Iridescence*, 13.
58 Sutton and Snow, *Iridescence*, 14, 50.
59 Giles, "Archipelagic Accretion," 430.
60 Christian, "Race for Theory," 52.
61 Taro Katayama, "Nightmare," *Trek*, December 1942, 25.
62 Otsuka, *When the Emperor Was Divine*, 59.

63 Freeman, "Synchronic/Anachronic," 133–34.
64 Katayama, "State of the City," 11; and "Hundreds Search for Missing Nisei," *Topaz Times*, December 22, 1942, 1. See also "Missing Resident Found Alive," *Topaz Times*, December 24, 1942, 1. On the prisoners' regular excursions away from camp to gather materials for crafts, see Hill, *Chiura Obata's Topaz Moon*, 81.
65 Sanford, *Marjum Pass*, 126.
66 "Sox" Tsuyako Kitashima, San Francisco, California, tape no. 25, interview by Sandra Taylor, November 6, 1987, Topaz Oral Histories, J. Willard Marriott Library, University of Utah, accessed August 18, 2020, https://collections.lib.utah.edu/details?id=1044195.
67 "Life at Topaz . . . ," *Salt Lake Tribune*, March 4, 1945, sec. D, p. 4. Jane Beckwith, founding director of the Topaz Museum, suggests that in light of the many gallons of shells now being donated to the museum by descendants of the prisoners at Topaz, there must have been places where the shells could be scooped up by the shovelful, rather than tediously collected as is implied in the *Salt Lake Tribune*'s article. Conversation with Jane Beckwith, November 30, 2019.
68 Eaton, *Beauty behind Barbed Wire*, 44. In this discussion, Allen H. Eaton is referencing the internment camps at Topaz and Tule Lake, both of which were on or near old shell beds. In the vicinity of Topaz, I have personally seen anthills riddled with very small shells from Lake Bonneville.
69 Evelyn Kirimura, "Toppats and Co.," *All Aboard!*, Spring 1944, 9.
70 Gumbrecht, *Production of Presence*, xiii.
71 "Hawaiians' Shell Exhibit Attracts Topaz Residents," *Topaz Times*, May 18, 1943, 1; and "Co-op to Hold Hobby Show," *Co-op News*, June 2, 1944, 1. *Co-op News* is searchable as part of the *Topaz Times* through the University of Utah's Utah Digital Newspapers database.
72 Taro Katayama, "Digressions," *Trek*, February 1943, 41.
73 Huie, *Forgotten Ones*; and McCallus, *Forgotten under a Tropical Sun*, 245n16.
74 The quotation is from Eaton, *Beauty behind Barbed Wire*, 44. Eaton reports the shell worker's name as Komija Inouye, while the Japanese-American Internee Data File lists her name as Komaye Inouye. Japanese-American Internee Data File, 1942–1946, Record Group 210, National Archives, accessed March 18, 2020, https://aad.archives.gov/aad/record-detail.jsp?dt=3099&mtch=1&cat=GP21,22,23,24,44&tf=F&sc=30043,30012,30013,30014,30042,30038,30028,30040&q=Komaye+Inouye&bc=,sl,fd&rpp=10&pg=1&rid=22189. On Noda's teaching, see "Shellcraft," *Topaz Times*, June 10, 1944, 1; and "Shellcraft Class," *Topaz Times*, May 20, 1944, 2. For the list of items, see Eaton, *Beauty behind Barbed Wire*, 44; and Hirasuna, *Art of Gaman*, 52–53, 114–15.
75 Suyemoto, "Another Spring," 21.
76 Suyemoto, "Another Spring," 22. Suyemoto's memoir indicates the issei man was in her Basic English course. Suyemoto, *I Call to Remembrance*, 138.
77 Suyemoto, *I Call to Remembrance*, 201.
78 Toyo Suyemoto, "Gain," *Trek*, December 1942, 6.
79 Suyemoto, *I Call to Remembrance*, 138.

80 For the quote on "petals" as "delicate moments," see Suyemoto, *I Call to Remembrance*, 13.
81 Hirasuna, *Art of Gaman*, 7; and Dusselier, *Artifacts of Loss*, 88. On the possibility of monetizing camp hobbies, see "Co-op to Hold Hobby Show." On some prisoners' reluctance to sell their work, see Eaton, *Beauty behind Barbed Wire*, 6.
82 My thinking on the shells' "anachronic" existence converges with art historians Alexander Nagel and Christopher S. Wood's recent use of the term *anachronic* to describe "the work of art when it is late, when it repeats, when it hesitates, when it remembers, but also when it projects a future or an ideal"; Nagel and Wood, *Anachronic Renaissance*, 13.
83 Alaimo, "New Materialisms, Old Humanisms," 283.
84 I draw the notion of *nonphenomenological thought* from Steven Shaviro, who in an article titled "Non-phenomenological Thought" has argued against Meillassoux's claim that "thought cannot be grounded in physical matter" (48), suggesting instead that "thought is not ... an especially human privilege," citing biological research indicating that "something much like thinking," an "experiential sensitivity," goes on in trees, slime mold, and bacteria "even though none of these organisms have brains" (52). As for "inanimate things," Shaviro suggests that they have "dispositional properties" and "exhibit a certain *aboutness*," with salt's "power to be dissolved in water" taken as "a kind of intentional orientation" (52).
85 F. Pack, *Lake Bonneville*, 31; and Carson, *Sea around Us*, 10.
86 On Laramidia and the Western Interior Seaway, see Sampson et al., "New Horned Dinosaurs," 1. On the shoreline in Utah, see Ryder, "Oil and Gas Potential," 94.
87 Yamada, "Portrait of an Artist," 22.
88 "Education for a Changing World," *Topaz Times*, April 3, 1943, Americanization supplement, p. B. For background on a famous early cartoon drawing of a brontosaurus, see Merkl, *Dinomania*, 255–60.
89 Beckwith, "Trilobite Fossils," 14.
90 Eldredge later wrote of "the famous Wheeler Amphitheater at Antelope Springs, with its gray Wheeler Shale that has yielded countless thousands of complete trilobites." Eldredge, *Life Pulse*, 63; on the landmark theory, see Eldredge and Gould, "Punctuated Equilibria." Eldredge recalls that he went to Antelope Springs in the 1970s, after he had published the original ideas on punctuated equilibria in 1971. Niles Eldredge, email message to Brian Russell Roberts, July 7, 2018.
91 Beckwith, "Trilobite Fossils," 14.
92 Beckwith, "Trilobite Fossils," 16.
93 For mention of an expedition to the trilobite field, see Tad Fujita, "Y Camp Memories," *Topaz Times*, July 31, 1943, 6. On the camp's opening, see "Children's Summer Camp Readied for Topazans," *Topaz Times*, June 8, 1943, 2. Other *Topaz Times* articles referencing the camp appear throughout the summer of 1943.
94 "Slate Club Formed, Office at Rec 30," *Topaz Times*, January 11, 1944, 2. On the Topaz Slate Club, see also "Slate Club," *Topaz Times*, February 10, 1944, 2; and "Handicraft Show Set for Week End," *Topaz Times*, February 24, 1944, 3.

95 "Antelope Springs to Open for Day Trips," *Topaz Times*, June 10, 1944, 1. My understanding is that the name Topaz Slate Club was a misnomer, given that the area around Antelope Springs is characterized by the Wheeler shale formation and not a slate formation. However, in keeping with the group's name, I refer to them as *slate carvers*. Thanks to Niles Eldredge and Ron Harris for answering my queries on slate versus shale in the area.

96 Eaton, *Beauty behind Barbed Wire*, 48. Though the cultural context is different, see also Ko, *Social Life of Inkstones*, 1.

97 The Topaz Museum's inkstone display lists Ishizaki as this inkstone's carver. For background on Ishizaki, see the "Ishizake, Shigemat E." record in the Japanese-American Internee Data File, 1942–1946, Record Group 210, National Archives, accessed August 18, 2020, https://aad.archives.gov/aad/record-detail.jsp?dt=3099&mtch =1&cat=GP21,22,23,24,44&tf=F&sc=30043,30012,30013,30014,30042,30038,300 28,30040&q=Shigemat+E.+Ishizaki&bc=,sl,fd&rpp=10&pg=1&rid=24021; and his obituary in "Milestones," *Pacific Citizen*, April 12, 1974, 6, http://ddr.densho.org /media/ddr-pc-46/ddr-pc-46-14-mezzanine-a66d76f5be.pdf. I have drawn family information from the "Ishizaki, Edward Shigematsu" entry in War Relocation Authority, *Central Utah Final Accountability Report*, October 1945, p. 52, Topaz Japanese-American Relocation Center Digital Collection, Utah State University Digital History Collections, accessed August 18, 2020, https://digital.lib.usu .edu/digital/collection/Topaz/id/7733. Thanks to Gregory Ishizaki, grandson of Shigematsu Ishizaki, for helping confirm details on the Ishizaki family at Topaz; Gregory Ishizaki, email messages to Brian Russell Roberts, April 29 and May 16, 2020.

98 Thanks to Jack Stoneman for help with translations from kanji, here as well as in my subsequent discussion of the ink reservoir's kanji rendering as "ink pond" or "ocean."

99 On his ability to speak and write both English and Japanese, see Ishizaki's entry in the Japanese-American Internee Data File.

100 Meillassoux, *After Finitude*, 3.

101 Globularius Schraubi, "Yule Greetings, Friends!," *Trek*, December 1942, 15.

102 Schraubi, "Yule Greetings, Friends!," 15. Schraubi's original spelling of *non-Euclidian* (rather than the more standard *non-Euclidean*) has been retained. On Oki's pen name, see Robinson, "Writing the Internment," 47; and Stan Yogi, "Literature in Camp," *Densho Encyclopedia*, May 11, 2017, http://encyclopedia.densho.org /Literature_in_camp/.

103 Lovecraft, "Call of Cthulhu," 27, 26, 27, 31. For critical interest, see Harman, *Weird Realism*, 70–71; and Blacklock, *Emergence of the Fourth Dimension*, 197–98.

104 Taro Katayama, "Digressions," *Trek*, June 1943, 40. Katayama's retrospective on his year in Topaz was precipitated by his imminent entry into the US military, as signaled by his byline for this article: "Pvt. Taro Katayama."

105 Okubo, *Citizen 13660*, 209.

106 Sun, *Miné Okubo*, 41.

107 Chakrabarty, "Climate of History," 208.

108 The Japanese American National Museum lists this inkstone's creator as "Mr. T. Mifune" of Topaz. Toranosuke Mifune was the only man imprisoned at Topaz with the last name of Mifune and the first initial of T; see the "Mifune, Toranosuke" entry in War Relocation Authority, *Central Utah Final Accountability Report*, October 1945, p. 96, Topaz Japanese-American Relocation Center Digital Collection, Utah State University Digital History Collections, accessed August 18, 2020, https://digital.lib.usu.edu/digital/collection/Topaz/id/7777.

109 Eaton, *Beauty behind Barbed Wire*, 49, 48. In the photograph's caption, Eaton specifies that this inkstone "was shaped, probably, at Topaz." The photograph was taken by one of the photographers Eaton sent to Topaz and other internment camps (6). This inkstone closely matches in craftsmanship and style an inkstone attributed to Homei Iseyama on the frontispiece to Hirasuna, *Art of Gaman*. I have been unable to locate the original inkstone, but Carolyn Holden (Iseyama's granddaughter) confirms that the inkstone in the photograph looks like the work of her grandfather, and Hirasuna also feels confident this inkstone was carved by Iseyama. Carolyn Holden, email message to Brian Russell Roberts, April 4, 2018; and Delphine Hirasuna, email message to Brian Russell Roberts, June 6, 2018.

110 Thanks to Scott Miller for this original translation of a much-translated poem by Bashō.

111 Keene, *World within Walls*, 89. For allied interpretations of the poem, see Cao, "Poetry and Zen," 30; and Ueda, *Bashō and His Interpreters*, 141.

112 Hakutani, *Haiku and Modernist Poetics*, 17.

113 Hirasuna, *Art of Gaman*, 7.

114 McGurl, "New Cultural Geology," 380.

115 McPhee, *Basin and Range*, 132.

116 My identification of the fossil as a trilobite is based on comparing the contours on the frog's back (which displays an apparent axial lobe straddled by two apparent pleural lobes) with the shape of trilobites that I have seen in diagrams, photographs, museums, and fossils that family members and I have found in the vicinity of Antelope Springs. However, the original photograph's resolution is uneven, and as I mention in endnote 109, I have been unable to locate the original inkstone although I have been in contact with Hirasuna and Iseyama's family. Hence, without seeing the actual stone, I am unable to definitively state what kind of fossil Eaton referenced as embedded in the inkstone. Thus, while I move forward with the assumption that this stone, like Ishizaki's and Mifune's inkstones, incorporates a trilobite fossil, I acknowledge that future research may locate the stone itself (perhaps in an attic or a private collection), which may showcase the fossil in ways I am not seeing here. I would welcome learning more about the stone, even as I imagine the broad strokes of my subsequent analysis would remain similar regardless of the specific type of fossil that is embedded in the stone.

117 Suzuki, "Buddhist Symbolism," 38.

118 Carson, *Sea around Us*, 10–11; and Ducrocq, *Origins of Life*, 52.

119 Johnson, "Life," 49.

120 See Darwin, *On the Origin of Species*, 383–410.
121 Haraway, *Staying with the Trouble*, 12; and Harman, *Towards Speculative Realism*, 22–43.
122 Whitehead, *Symbolism*, 64–65.
123 In discussing biotic life and minerals as transcorporeal, I am adapting Alaimo's discussion of transcorporeality, an imagination of "human corporeality as trans-corporeality, in which the human is always intermeshed with the more-than-human world, underlin[ing] the extent to which the corporeal substance of the human is ultimately inseparable from 'the environment.'" Alaimo, "Trans-Corporeal Feminisms," 238.
124 For the term *stone photocopy*, see Dr. Alaka, "The Fossil Record, A History of Life," *Science* (blog), November 2, 2012, http://sciencearticlz.blogspot.com/2012/11/the-fossil-record-history-of-life.html.
125 Kirksey, *Emergent Ecologies*, 4–5.
126 "Editors Note," *Trek*, June 1943, 25.
127 The quotation is from Heise, *Imagining Extinction*, 226.
128 Chōmei, *Ten Foot Square Hut*, 11.
129 Chōmei, *Ten Foot Square Hut*, 1–2.
130 Chōmei, *Ten Foot Square Hut*, 11, 12.
131 Chōmei, *Ten Foot Square Hut*, 17–18.
132 Katayama, "Digressions," December 1942, 29.
133 Franklin, *Autobiography*, 92–93.
134 Questions of belittlement and vastness are at the center of Epeli Hau'ofa's classic essay "Our Sea of Islands." See also Kabutaulaka, "Bigness of Our Smallness"; and Ratuva, "David vs Goliath."
135 Some of the language in this paragraph resembles language in Roberts and Stephens, "Archipelagic American Studies: Decontinentalizing," 23. It is based on Roberts, "Coloring of the Sea Almond."
136 Norris, "Re-asking the Question," 37.
137 Rifkin, *Beyond Settler Time*, viii–ix (my italics); and Alaimo, "Anthropocene at Sea," 158. The list of textural attributes is from Mandelbrot, *Fractal Geometry of Nature*, 5.
138 Morton, "Molten Entities," 75.
139 For the quote on temporality as rippling, see Morton, *Hyperobjects*, 63.
140 Povinelli, *Geontologies*, 75.
141 For year-by-year information on the population of Topaz, see Arrington, *Price of Prejudice*, 43. The figure of 13.8 billion years as the age of the universe is from Planck Collaboration, "*Planck* 2015 Results."
142 Benjamin, *Illuminations*, 258, 257.

Chapter Five: Spiraling Futures of the Archipelagic States of America

1 For these dimensions see Kim Levin, "Reflections on Robert Smithson's 'Spiral Jetty,'" *Arts Magazine*, May 1978, 136.
2 Smithson, "Fragments of an Interview," 90.

3 McGurl, "Posthuman Comedy," 537, 542.
4 McGurl, "Posthuman Comedy," 538.
5 Dimock, "Low Epic," 614–15.
6 McGurl, and Dimock following him, uses the term *heat death* rather unconventionally to refer to Earth's incineration by the Sun when it enters its red giant phase and engulfs (or at least renders uninhabitable) the solar system's inner planets, including Earth. But typically the term *heat death* is a reference to the second law of thermodynamics' key concept of entropy, which looks toward a universe that in the far-distant future will have stopped moving because all heat has been equalized everywhere.
7 Loe, *Spiral Jetty Encyclo*, 137.
8 The quotation is from Smithson, "Spiral Jetty," 20. For early appearances of the geologic time spiral in 1970 and 1974, see Newman, *Geologic Time*, 18–19; and Lohman, *Geology of Canyonlands*, 110–11.
9 Quoted in Loe, "*Spiral Jetty*, The Film," 256.
10 The first quotation appears in the film *The Spiral Jetty*, directed by Smithson (1970); Smithson drew it from Verma and Krishna, *Polymorphism and Polytypism in Crystals*, 207. The second quotation is from Smithson, "Spiral Jetty," 16.
11 Smithson, "Entropy and the New Monuments," 11.
12 McGurl's thesis on a "posthuman comedy" is consistent with Smithson's assertion that "fragments of a timeless geology laugh without mirth at the time-filled hopes of ecology." Smithson, "Spiral Jetty," 20.
13 For a chart plotting the lake level in relation to *Spiral Jetty* from 1970 to 2010, see Hikmet Loe, "The Spiral Jetty: Strata of Water," *15 Bytes: Artists of Utah Ezine*, April 2010, 5, http://www.artistsofutah.org/15bytes/10apr/page5.html.
14 Glissant, *La cohée du Lamentin*, 75.
15 The two quotations in this sentence are drawn from Meyer, *The Golden Spike*, a film originally released in 1969 for the centennial of the golden spike's placement. The remastered and revised version of this film, released in 2006, resulted from a collaboration between the Golden Spike National Historic Site and the US National Park Service, and as of November 2018 it was the film shown at the historic site's visitor center. The film draws the latter of the two quotations from Bowles, *Across the Continent*, 273. As of March 12, 2019, the Golden Spike National Historic Site was redesignated as the Golden Spike National Historical Park.
16 Quoted in Matthew Klint, "All the Patriotic Quotes in Your U.S. Passport," *Live and Let's Fly* (blog), July 4, 2018, https://liveandletsfly.com/us-passport-quotes/.
17 Quoted in Waddell, Naidu, and Hauʻofa, *New Oceania*, viii.
18 Hegel, *Lectures*, 96, 163, 162.
19 Karuka, *Empire's Tracks*, 33.
20 Glover, *Haiti Unbound*, viii; and Marsh, "Theory 'versus' Pacific Islands Writing," 340. On the spiral as a pan-Polynesian symbol, see Keown, *Postcolonial Pacific Writing*, 193.
21 In using the term *futurity* in this chapter, I am pointing toward a set of future possibilities, toward a qualified openness vis-à-vis the future, and toward a sense of the ways

humans make use of notions of the future. See Muñoz, *Cruising Utopia*, 16; Eshel, *Futurity*, 4–5; and Adelson, "Futurity Now," 215.

22　In writing this chapter around three different scales of future temporality, I have been inspired by Andrea Westermann's "A Technofossil of the Anthropocene: Sliding Up and Down Temporal Scales with Plastic."

23　Wiedorn, *Think Like an Archipelago*, 113.

24　Chakrabarty, "Climate of History."

25　Wikipedia, s.v. "Timeline of the Far Future," last modified July 2, 2020, 15:21 (UTC), https://en.wikipedia.org/wiki/Timeline_of_the_far_future.

26　McPhee, *Basin and Range*, 132.

27　Thanks to Michael Roberts for helping me recognize that even an atom would be too big for this analogy. The figure of 13.8 billion years is from Planck Collaboration, "*Planck* 2015 Results"; however, as of 2019 there has been a suggestion that the universe is between 12.5 and 13 billion years old. Riess et al., "Large Magellanic Cloud Cepheid Standards"; and Seth Borenstein, "New Study Says Universe Expanding Faster and Is Younger," *AP News*, April 26, 2019, https://www.apnews.com/fac50d45a19f4239848b1712cfd22c36.

28　Wikipedia, s.v. "Timeline of the Far Future." Unless otherwise noted, descriptions and quotations that appear in this paragraph and the subsequent two paragraphs are drawn from "Timeline of the Far Future."

29　To avoid ambiguity, it is worth mentioning that in evaluating the number $10^{10^{120}}$, the 10^{120} should be evaluated first. This results in a number very much larger than if the 10^{10} were evaluated first. The same order of operations applies to $10^{10^{50}}$, which is another very large number discussed in this chapter. Thanks to Michael Roberts and Ryan Camacho for advising me on potential ambiguities regarding how some mathematicians and others might evaluate these numbers.

30　Thanks to Michael Roberts for this estimate on books and pages in comparison to the volume of the observable universe.

31　Glissant, quoted in Wiedorn, *Think Like an Archipelago*, 113. Haraway, "Situated Knowledges," 581.

32　Hickman, "Cosmic American Studies," 974. The language in this sentence intentionally echoes the title of Hester Blum's *The View from the Masthead: Maritime Imagination and Antebellum American Sea Narratives*. Blum's discussion of Melville's narrator Ishmael assuming a lookout place on the masthead, whereupon "he cannot help but consider what he calls the 'problem of the universe'" (1, 119–21) is a reminder that US American literature has been looking toward—if not espying—such universe-oriented problems as Boltzmann brains and final heat death since at least the nineteenth century.

33　With the phrase *postenergy* I am referring to the era of post–usable energy in the run-up to the heat death of the universe. But the phrase is also meant to highlight the alienness of this scene to one of the most urgent social and scientific problems of our day, as outlined in Imre Szeman and Dominic Boyer's collection *Energy Humanities: An Anthology*.

34 For a primary readership in the humanities, I am relying on the term *chaotic* as it is colloquially used, but more technically correct terms would be *probabilistic* or *stochastic*.
35 Boltzmann, "On Certain Questions," 415.
36 Borges, "Library of Babel," 115, 113, 114.
37 Although the narrator believes the library is infinite, its infinitude is neither universally agreed upon nor certain within the story. The library may be finite but unthinkably large, in which case such an ordered section of the library as is being discussed would not be *certain* to exist but rather could be *all but certain* to exist.
38 Rees, *Before the Beginning*, 221.
39 On Boltzmann brain formation within the context of cosmic inflation theory, see Albrecht and Sorbo, "Can the Universe Afford Inflation?"; and Linde, "Sinks in the Landscape."
40 The model of the universe predicting Boltzmann brains also predicts that cameras and photographs of birthday parties will fluctuate into existence. Carroll, "Why Boltzmann Brains Are Bad," 10–11
41 Gott, "Boltzmann Brains," 2; and Albrecht and Sorbo, "Can the Universe Afford Inflation?," 5. In the mid-twentieth century, H. Bondi described "what may be called the Copernican principle—that the Earth is not in a central, specially favoured position," which is "only a small step from . . . the statement that the Earth is in a *typical position*." Bondi, *Cosmology*, 13.
42 Carroll, "Why Boltzmann Brains Are Bad," 3, 2. For another discussion of Boltzmann brains as philosophically untenable, see Davenport and Olum, "Are There Boltzmann Brains in the Vacuum?," 2.
43 Jason Pollack, email message to Brian Russell Roberts, August 15, 2019.
44 Boddy, Carroll, and Pollack, "Why Boltzmann Brains Do Not Fluctuate into Existence," 238. On the Boltzmann brain problem as arising in leading scientific understandings of the universe, see Carroll, "Why Boltzmann Brains Are Bad," 2–3; and Boddy, Carroll, and Pollack, "Why Boltzmann Brains Do Not Fluctuate into Existence," 228.
45 Aside from the sources cited in the preceding, my understanding of the Boltzmann brain problem has been informed by Barrow and Tipler, *Anthropic Cosmological Principle*, 173–80; Dyson, Kleban, and Susskind, "Disturbing Implications"; Albrecht, "Cosmic Inflation"; Page, "Susskind's Challenge"; Hartle and Srednicki, "Are We Typical?"; Page, "Is Our Universe Likely to Decay?"; Dennis Overbye, "Big Brain Theory: Have Cosmologists Lost Theirs?," *New York Times*, January 15, 2008, https://www.nytimes.com/2008/01/15/science/15brain.html; Koperski, *Physics of Theism*, 58–101; and Page, "Cosmological Ontology and Epistemology."
46 Wiedorn, *Think Like an Archipelago*, 113.
47 Glissant mentions "the theories of Benoit Mandelbrot" in *Poetics of Relation* (93). For his use of Mandelbrot's term *fractal*, see, for instance, Glissant, *Philosophie de la Relation*, 47. For our reframing of the island, see Roberts and Stephens, "Archipelagic American Studies: Decontinentalizing," 24–28.

48 Bogost, *Alien Phenomenology*, 9 (my italics); and Morton, "Molten Entities," 73.
49 Deleuze, "Desert Islands," 11, 10.
50 On the prediction that not only Boltzmann brains but Boltzmann people, solar systems, galaxies, and universes will fluctuate into existence, see Carroll, "Why Boltzmann Brains Are Bad," 10.
51 My analysis here cites the story's 2010 publication. However, the story first appeared five years earlier: Tiphanie Yanique, "The Bridge," *Sonora Review* 49 (2005): 59–68. In association with the Pushcart Prize, it appeared again in 2008: Tiphanie Yanique, "The Bridge," in *Pushcart Prize XXXII: Best of the Small Presses*, ed. Bill Henderson (New York: Norton, 2008), 363–77.
52 Yanique, "Bridge Stories," 16, 22, 26.
53 Yanique, "Bridge Stories," 15.
54 In fact, the prediction is that an *infinite* number of such islands will exist, in a series of fluctuations that might be said to resemble reincarnation.
55 McCall, "Nissology," 2.
56 The quotation is from Bogost, *Alien Phenomenology*, 10.
57 Yanique, "Bridge Stories," 15.
58 Yanique, "Bridge Stories," 15–16.
59 Holmes, "Chambered Nautilus," 31–32. The "unresting sea" quotation is from Holmes but might well have been from Gott's article "Boltzmann Brains—I'd Rather See Than Be One," which imagines the future of space-time as involving an "infinitely expanding inflationary sea" wherein "an infinite number of bubble universes . . . can form" (3).
60 My thoughts on Yanique as an archipelagic writer are inspired by Martínez-San Miguel, "Colonial and Mexican Archipelagoes," 165–69; and Sherrard-Johnson, "'Perfection with a Hole in the Middle.'"
61 Mandelbrot and Hudson, *(Mis)Behavior of Markets*, 219. For correctness, I have changed Mandelbrot's *bronchii* to *bronchi*.
62 Paine, *Common Sense*, 93.
63 England of course is not an island in and of itself but is rather situated on the island of Great Britain. With the phrase *the small island of England*, I am using language that reflects Paine's framing of England.
64 Benítez-Rojo, *Repeating Island*, 4.
65 Borges, "Library of Babel," 113.
66 Diaz, "Voyaging for Anti-Colonial Recovery," 26.
67 Borges, "Aleph," 283.
68 Melville, *Moby-Dick*, 235.
69 Crutzen and Stoermer, "'Anthropocene,'" 17.
70 Crutzen and Stoermer, "'Anthropocene,'" 18; see also Crutzen, "Geology of Mankind," 23.
71 My initial sense of the urgency of these issues was prompted by Yaeger, "Sea Trash." Also influential in conveying this urgency have been chapters 5 and 6 of Alaimo, *Exposed*.

72 Jetñil-Kijiner, "'Butterfly Thief.'"
73 Lovelock, *Revenge of Gaia*, 55, 50.
74 Steffen, Crutzen, and McNeill, "Anthropocene," 618.
75 On notions of sovereignty extending beyond surface area to volume, and particularly in relation to the ocean, see Billé, "Voluminous," 1–3.
76 National Science and Technology Council, *United States as an Ocean Nation*, 24. See also the discussion of the NOAA website in this book's introduction.
77 Steffen, Crutzen, and McNeill, "Anthropocene," 618.
78 Obama, "Stewardship of the Ocean," 43023.
79 Bush, "Establishment of the Northwestern Hawaiian Islands Marine National Monument"; and Obama, "Papahānaumokuākea Marine National Monument Expansion." Size figures, in terms of square miles, for this and other marine national monuments are drawn from the relevant entries in the Marine Conservation Institute's Marine Protection Atlas, accessed December 20, 2020, http://www.mpatlas.org/.
80 Bush, "Establishment of the Marianas Trench Marine National Monument"; Bush, "Establishment of the Rose Atoll Marine National Monument"; Bush, "Establishment of the Pacific Remote Islands Marine National Monument"; and Obama, "Pacific Remote Islands Marine National Monument Expansion."
81 Obama, "Northeast Canyons and Seamounts Marine National Monument."
82 "The Antiquities Act of 1906: 16 USC 431-433," National Park Service, Legislative and Congressional Affairs, accessed August 29, 2020, https://www.nps.gov/subjects/legal/the-antiquities-act-of-1906.htm.
83 On these acts, see van Zandt, *Boundaries of the United States* (1966), 67–70; on these acts' relevance to marine national monuments, see Craig, "Law Professor Amicus Brief."
84 Rauzon, *Isles of Amnesia*, 1.
85 Craig Santos Perez, "Our Sea of Plastic," *Kenyon Review*, February 1, 2013, https://www.kenyonreview.org/2013/02/our-sea-of-plastic/. For further commentary from Perez on marine national monuments, see Craig Santos Perez, "Blue-Washing the Colonization and Militarization of Our Ocean: How U.S. Marine National Monuments Protect Environmentally Harmful U.S. Military Bases throughout the Pacific and the World," *Hawaii Independent*, June 26, 2014, republished on *Wrong Kind of Green* (blog), November 27, 2016, http://www.wrongkindofgreen.org/2016/11/27/blue-washing-the-colonization-and-militarization-of-our-ocean/.
86 Chris Jordan, *Midway: Message from the Gyre* (2009–current), Chris Jordan: Photographic Arts, http://www.chrisjordan.com/gallery/midway/#CF000313%20 18x24.
87 Chris Jordan, "About This Project" (February 2011), *Midway: Message from the Gyre*, Chris Jordan: Photographic Arts, http://www.chrisjordan.com/gallery/midway/#about.
88 Van Dooren, *Flight Ways*, 24; and "Q&A: Your Midway Questions Answered," BBC News, March 28, 2008, http://news.bbc.co.uk/2/hi/talking_point/7318837.stm.
89 Liittschwager and Middleton, *Archipelago*, 131.

90   A. S. Byatt, "Sea Story," *Guardian*, March 15, 2013, https://www.theguardian.com/books/2013/mar/15/as-byatt-short-story-sea.

91   As of the mid- to late 2010s, the United Kingdom was recycling about 46 percent of its plastic packaging, while the United States was estimated to recycle less than five percent of its plastic waste. Department for Environment, Food and Rural Affairs, "UK Statistics on Waste," Government Statistical Service, March 7, 2019, https://assets.publishing.service.gov.uk/government/uploads/system/uploads/attachment_data/file/784263/UK_Statistics_on_Waste_statistical_notice_March_2019_rev_FINAL.pdf; and Jan Dell, "U.S. Plastic Recycling Rate Projected to Drop to 4.4% in 2018," plasticpollutioncoalition, October 4, 2018, https://www.plasticpollutioncoalition.org/pft/2018/10/4/us-plastic-recycling-rate-projected-to-drop-to-44-in-2018.

92   Melville, *Moby-Dick*, 236.

93   Five centuries is often predicted as the approximate amount of time it will take for plastic to degrade in the ocean. See Dautel, "Transoceanic Trash," 183; and Hohn, "Moby-Duck," 124.

94   Bennett, *Vibrant Matter*, 6, 7. On the plastic bottle cap and the power grid, see Bennett, *Vibrant Matter*, 4, 20–28.

95   Bennett, *Vibrant Matter*, 5.

96   This paragraph's narrative on Keep America Beautiful is indebted to Rogers, *Gone Tomorrow*, 129–53.

97   On Keep America Beautiful's founders and funders, see "Our Partners," Keep America Beautiful, accessed March 8, 2019, https://www.kab.org/our-partners?field_partner_type_tid=28; and Rogers, *Gone Tomorrow*, 141–42.

98   "Refillable Glass Bottles: The Decline of Refillable Beverage Bottles in the U.S.," CRI: Container Recycling Institute, accessed August 31, 2020, http://www.container-recycling.org/index.php/refillable-glass-bottles/53-facts-a-statistics/glass/428-the-decline-of-refillable-beverage-bottles-in-the-us; and Ad Council, "'I Want to Be Recycled' Campaign to Target the Nearly Two-Thirds (62 Percent) of Americans Who Are Not Avid Recyclers, According to New Research Released Today" (press release), CISION: PR Newswire July 11, 2013, https://www.prnewswire.com/news-releases/i-want-to-be-recycled-campaign-to-target-the-nearly-two-thirds-62-percent-of-americans-who-are-not-avid-recyclers-according-to-new-research-released-today-215060381.html.

99   "I Want to Be Recycled," Keep America Beautiful, accessed August 10, 2020, https://kab.org/campaigns/i-want-to-be-recycled/.

100   On the campaign in various media, see "Go-To Guide: Tailgating Recycling Events—America Recycles Day, November 15," published July 2018, accessed August 19, 2020, https://americarecyclesday.org/wp-content/uploads/2018/07/Tailgating_Guide2015_2018.pdf.

101   Keep America Beautiful, Ad Council, and Pereira O'Dell, "Journey 30," AdForum, 2013, https://www.adforum.com/creative-work/ad/player/34497362/journey-30/keep-america-beautiful. For a reflection on how this ad campaign may promote

human identification with putatively vibrant plastic, see Dora Malech's poem "As I Gather," *New England Review* 38, no. 1 (2017): 69–70.

102 The bag uses the term *maker* to refer to the consumer who uses it, but I am assuming a viewership sophisticated enough to observe that the plastic bag has misidentified its maker. Bahrani, "Plastic Bag."

103 For 2010 figures and this quotation, see the caption and interactive map in "Plastic Waste Littered, 2010," Our World in Data, accessed August 29, 2020, https://ourworldindata.org/grapher/plastic-waste-littered.

104 Dautel, "Transoceanic Trash," 184.

105 For the number of plastic objects and fragments entering the ocean via the Los Angeles and San Gabriel Rivers, see C. J. Moore, "Synthetic Polymers in the Marine Environment," 135. On the impossibility of predicting, at the outset, where each piece of plastic will travel, see Hohn, "Moby-Duck," 79.

106 On oceanic current models and litter from California and other sites on the Pacific Rim finding its way to the Great Pacific Garbage Patch, see Ingraham and Ebbesmeyer, "Surface Current Concentration of Floating Marine Debris."

107 Bush, "Establishment of the Northwestern Hawaiian Islands Marine National Monument," 36446 (my italics).

108 On government's potential role, see Mallos, "Turning the Tide on Marine Debris," 92.

109 Jenna R. Jambeck, Roland Geyer, Chris Wilcox, Theodore R. Siegler, Miriam Perryman, Anthony Andrady, Ramani Narayan, and Kara Lavender Law, "Plastic Waste Inputs from Land into the Ocean," *Science*, February 13, 2015, 769.

110 Hannah Ritchie and Max Roser, "Plastic Pollution," Our World in Data, September 2018, https://ourworldindata.org/plastic-pollution.

111 Lebreton et al., "Evidence."

112 Bush, "Establishment of the Northwestern Hawaiian Islands Marine National Monument," 36444 (my italics).

113 "Tyranny of the Minority Slows International Progress on Addressing Plastic Pollution," Press Room, Center for International Environmental Law, March 15, 2019, https://www.ciel.org/news/tyranny-of-the-minority-slows-international-progress-on-addressing-plastic-pollution/?fbclid=IwAR01AQeCT9-W19aYM8eBZzysXFYeAneft2f-s7RojAyurArRy1—EXdscXE.

114 Howard, "Proposal," 1859; and Zalasiewicz, *Earth after Us*, 4, 5.

115 Gumbs, *M Archive*, 13, 11, 42.

116 Gumbs, *M Archive*, 40, 42, 40.

117 On albatrosses and the fossil record, see M. Jones, "Perspectives," 143. On plastiglomerate as a new form of rock with plastic inclusions, see Corcoran, Moore, and Jazvac, "Anthropogenic Marker Horizon." More broadly, in writing this section of the chapter, I have been inspired by van Dooren, *Flight Ways*, 21–43; and C. Moore, *Plastic Ocean*. The Ross Sea Region Marine Protected Area is larger than Papahānaumokuākea, but Antarctica's Ross Sea, first protected in 2017, is in international waters and has a protection window of thirty-five years. "Ross Sea Region,"

Marine Protection Atlas, accessed August 29, 2020, http://mpatlas.org/mpa/sites/9047/.
118 Cox, *Nafanua*, 159.
119 Cox, *Nafanua*, 158.
120 Cox, *Nafanua*, 160.
121 "Recipient List," Goldman Environmental Prize, accessed August 29, 2020, https://www.goldmanprize.org/recipient-list/.
122 On the Jameson quotation, see Grattan, *Hope Isn't Stupid*, 8.
123 On the National Park of American Samoa and the 1993 date for concluding negotiations for the fifty-year lease, see US Department of the Interior/National Park Service, *General Management Plan/Environmental Impact Statement*, 5, 17, 259. The origin of the idea for the fifty-year lease during negotiations is somewhat unclear; it may have arisen in Western Samoa or American Samoa. In *Nafanua*, Cox seems to point toward Western Samoa as the origin of the idea, since in that narrative he sees the Western Samoan chiefs' idea as unprecedented (160), but in the same memoir this episode does not occur until after President Ronald Reagan's October 31, 1988, signing of House Resolution 4818, which established the National Park of American Samoa (151). The final lease negotiations for this US national park were not concluded until 1993, some five years after Reagan signed House Resolution 4818, but in deference to Indigenous concern for "the communal land tenure (*matai*) system" in American Samoa, "the option of long-term leases was mentioned as a possible approach" for a national park in American Samoa as early as September 1986; and the idea for a lease of fifty-five years or less was on the table in the proposed park's negotiations at least as early as September 1987. National Park Service and American Samoa Government, *Feasibility Study*, 8, 136–38.
124 Cox and Elmqvist, "Indigenous Control of Tropical Rainforest Reserves: An Alternative Strategy for Conservation," 319.
125 Writing of the fifty-year lease of the National Park of American Samoa, Cox and Elmqvist observe that "leases explicitly recognize and legitimize indigenous land rights." Cox and Elmqvist, "Indigenous Control of Tropical Rainforest Reserves," 320.
126 On environmental colonialism in American Samoa, see Aumua Amata, "Amata Blasts Administration's 'Environmental Colonialism,'" press release, United States Congresswoman Aumua Amata Coleman Radewagen, March 19, 2015, https://radewagen.house.gov/media-center/press-releases/amata-blasts-administration-s-environmental-colonialism.
127 On some histories behind what I am discussing as US temporal borders, see Immerwahr, *How to Hide an Empire*.
128 Mack, *Not-Quite States of America*, 270.
129 Saranillio, *Unsustainable Empire*, ix.
130 Saranillio, *Unsustainable Empire*, ix, xi, xii.
131 Rifkin, *Beyond Settler Time*, ix.
132 Dimacali, "Sky Gypsies," 147, 152.

133 Dimacali, "Sky Gypsies," 147. On the Sama-laut, see Bottignolo, *Celebrations with the Sun*; and Gaynor, *Intertidal History in Island Southeast Asia*.

134 The narrator notes that the *Karumarga* is a "skyharvesting ship belonging to a third-generation *Sama Laut*," and that the Sama-laut have been mining asteroids for "three generations"; Dimacali, "Sky Gypsies," 148. Presumably, the father, Mandali, is the ship's owner, so we may assume that at least one of his grandparents was a first-generation spacefaring Sama-laut.

135 Dimacali, "Sky Gypsies," 149.

136 Dimacali, "Sky Gypsies," 150.

137 Dimacali, "Sky Gypsies," 150–51.

138 Dimacali, "Sky Gypsies," 152.

139 Dimacali, "Sky Gypsies," 153.

140 Caroline Cryonic, "Interview with Sci-Fi Author Timothy James Dimacali," *Adarna SF: A Speculative Fiction Blog for the Ebook Revolution*, August 5, 2013, https://fridafantastic.wordpress.com/2013/08/05/interview-sci-fi-timothy-james-dimacali/.

141 Here I am referencing the 1969–71 occupation of Alcatraz Island by the Indians of All Tribes, a watershed event in Native American radicalism in which Turtle Island itself was overlaid and diffracted, via the Alcatraz Proclamation, with the image of an archipelago of Indian reservations that were analogous to San Francisco Bay's Alcatraz. See P. Smith and Warrior, *Like a Hurricane*, 28–29.

142 Wikipedia, s.v. "List of Missions to Mars," last modified July 1, 2020, 23:46 (UTC), https://en.wikipedia.org/wiki/List_of_missions_to_Mars. As of the present writing, the private company SpaceX, whose business model has to a large degree depended on contracts with NASA, has aggressive plans for colonizing Mars during the coming decades. Mike Wall, "Starship and Super Heavy: SpaceX's Mars-Colonizing Transportation System," Space.com, October 9, 2019, https://www.space.com/spacex-starship-super-heavy.html. As this book was going into production, China successfully launched a probe to Mars from Hainan Island. Depending on whether this probe, Tianwen-1, becomes the first non-US probe to successfully land on Mars, my speculations on the timeline between the present and Dimacali's future might be reimagined with Chinese characteristics. Smriti Mallapaty, "China's Successful Launch of Mars Mission Seals Global Era in Deep-Space Exploration," *Nature*, July 23, 2020, https://www.nature.com/articles/d41586-020-02187-7#:~:text=A%20Chinese%20spacecraft%20is%20on,land%20on%20the%20red%20planet.

143 Paine, *Common Sense*, 88.

144 The European colonization of the continental United States has long been taken as a thought template for human colonization of space and Mars specifically. Recently Elon Musk of SpaceX has imagined his Interplanetary Transport System as analogous "to the transcontinental railroad that helped open the American West to settlement from the East and Midwest in the 19th century." Wall, "Starship and Super Heavy."

145 Cryonic, "Interview."

146 On some Sama-laut people's lack of self-perception as aligned with nation-states, see Bottignolo, *Celebrations with the Sun*, 10.
147 Gaynor, "Liquid Territory," 112, 8, 6.

Conclusion

1 As viewed from the larger humanities, distant reading has emerged as DH's most iconic approach. But as Kathleen Fitzpatrick has written, DH more broadly defined is "a nexus of fields within which scholars use computing technologies to investigate the kinds of questions that are traditional to the humanities, or . . . ask traditional kinds of humanities-oriented questions about computing technologies." Kathleen Fitzpatrick, "The Humanities, Done Digitally," *Chronicle of Higher Education*, May 8, 2011, https://www.chronicle.com/article/The-Humanities-Done-Digitally/127382.
2 Moretti, *Distant Reading*, 13.
3 Moretti, *Distant Reading*, 1. For ease of reading, I have removed the italics that offset Moretti's introductory blurbs for essays in *Distant Reading*.
4 Moretti, *Distant Reading*, 12.
5 Moretti, *Distant Reading*, 1.
6 Moretti, *Distant Reading*, 128; and Moretti, *Graphs, Maps, Trees*, 1. On Moretti's role in popularizing distant reading, see Drucker, "Why Distant Reading Isn't," 633. For an incisive discussion of distant reading in the context of the Me Too Movement, including "the many critiques that have been levied over the years at distant reading, and about how that particular field is . . . unwelcoming to women," and including future directions for distant reading, see Lauren F. Klein, "Distant Reading after Moretti," Lauren F. Klein: Digital Humanities, Data Science, and Early American Literature, January 10, 2018, https://lklein.com/digital-humanities/distant-reading-after-moretti/.
7 The quotations in this sentence are from Moretti, *Graphs, Maps, Trees*, 3 and 1. Other details and perspectives are drawn from Moretti, *Graphs, Maps, Trees*, 4, 18, 30.
8 Moretti, *Distant Reading*, 128.
9 Moretti, *Distant Reading*, 128.
10 Moretti, *Distant Reading*, 122.
11 Darwin, *On the Origin of Species*, 383.
12 The encyclopedia's fourth edition in 1810 repeated the first edition's definition of an archipelago as "a sea interrupted with islands." *Encyclopædia Britannica* (1771), s.v. "archipelago," 1:346; and *Encyclopaedia Britannica*, 4th ed. (1810), s.v. "archipelago," 2:553. The encyclopedia's eighth edition, published in 1853, nodded toward why previous editions had seen the islands as interruptions: the term had origins as the name of a sea in the Greek Mediterranean, and "the navigation of this sea is rendered difficult by the many islands and rocks with which it abounds." *Encyclopaedia Britannica*, 8th ed. (1853), s.v. "archipelago," 3:431. Around the time Darwin was publishing *On the Origin of Species*, both he and the *Encyclopaedia Britannica* were discussing islands as *studding* the sea. *Encyclopaedia Britannica*, 9th ed. (1875), s.v. "archipelago," 2:334; and Darwin, *On the Origin of Species*, 393.

13 On the relationship between humanities computing and digital humanities, which is more disciplinarily complicated than this brief parenthetical aside is able to communicate, see Kirschenbaum, "What Is Digital Humanities?"
14 McCarty, "Tree, Turf, Centre, Archipelago," 3.
15 McCarty, "Tree, Turf, Centre, Archipelago," 6.
16 McCarty, "Tree, Turf, Centre, Archipelago," 6–7.
17 See also Roberts, "What Is an Archipelago?"
18 Diaz, "Voyaging for Anti-Colonial Recovery," 23.
19 On big data as oceanic, see Stark and Hoffmann, "Data Is the New What?," 6. On "content islands," see Manovich, "Science of Culture?," 7.
20 Roberts and Stephens, "Archipelagic American Studies: Decontinentalizing," 20, 23.
21 Kaiama L. Glover and Alex Gil, "About Us," *archipelagos*, accessed August 10, 2020, http://archipelagosjournal.org/about.html.
22 "Te Whakakaokao," National Library of New Zealand, accessed August 22, 2020, https://natlib.govt.nz/about-us/friends-and-advisors/te-whakakaokao. Thanks to Miriam Posner for pointing out this project's relevance to archipelagic studies. Posner, "Data Trouble."
23 Zulkarnain, "'Playable' Nationalism"; on Zulkarnain's "'Programming' the Archipelago," see "Iskandar Zulkarnain F'14," *American Council of Learned Societies*, accessed August 13, 2020, https://www.acls.org/research/fellow.aspx?cid=25AE2BC6-50CA-E311-9BEC-000C29A3451A.
24 Swanstrom, "Digital Currents," 205.
25 As imported into DH by figures including Moretti and McCarty, the structuring metaphors of evolution and exploration have the archipelago as their geographic substratum, whether overtly or implicitly; see Jackson et al., "Building Bridges"; S. Anderson and Blanke, "Taking the Long View"; and Milligan, *History in the Age of Abundance?*, 54–58. Elsewhere, we see the archipelago invoked as a metaphor for collaborative human and digital networks. See Underwood, "Genealogy of Distant Reading," para. 30; and "Classics@Brown Participates in 'Linking Islands of Data' Network," Classics, Brown University, February 22, 2019, https://www.brown.edu/academics/classics/news/2019/02/classicsbrown-participates-linking-islands-data-network. Further, Brian Greenspan has used the archipelago to consider the prominent question of DH's utopianism. Greenspan, "Are Digital Humanists Utopian?," 393.
26 Chuck Jones, "Project Announcement: Linking Islands of Data," *AWOL: The Ancient World Online* (blog), February 18, 2019, http://ancientworldonline.blogspot.com/2019/02/project-announcement-linking-islands-of.html.
27 Other DH projects focused on routes and connectivity in the Mediterranean include Walter Scheidel and Elijah Meeks, ORBIS: The Stanford Geospatial Network Model of the Roman World, accessed August 22, 2020, http://orbis.stanford.edu; and Jenny Strauss Clay, Courtney Evans, and Ben Jasnow, Mapping the Catalogue of Ships, accessed August 22, 2020, http://ships.lib.virginia.edu/home. For important DH work on the Mediterranean that is engaged with broader currents in archipelagic thought, see DeMott, "Archipelago of the Maghreb."

28 Roberts and Stephens, "Archipelagic American Studies: Decontinentalizing," 3, 44n10.
29 On decolonial and postcolonial currents, see Risam, *New Digital Worlds*.
30 Noble, *Algorithms of Oppression*, 1.
31 These translations of Glissant are drawn from Wiedorn, *Think Like an Archipelago*, 113.
32 Underwood, *Distant Horizons*, ix–x.
33 Underwood, *Distant Horizons*, xi.
34 F. Frisbie, *Miss Ulysses* (1948), 233.
35 Hau'ofa, "Our Sea of Islands," 6, 15.
36 Kaiama L. Glover and Alex Gil (project wranglers), In the Same Boats, accessed August 31, 2020, https://sameboats.org/.
37 Glissant, *La cohée du Lamentin*, 37, 75; and Ted Underwood, *The Stone and the Shell: Using Large Digital Libraries to Advance Literary History* (blog), accessed August 31, 2020, https://tedunderwood.com/.
38 Corinne Segal, "Volunteers Are Helping Puerto Rico from Home, with a Map Anyone Can Edit," *PBS News Hour: Weekend*, October 1, 2017, https://www.pbs.org/newshour/nation/volunteers-helping-puerto-rico-home-map-anyone-can-edit.
39 Risam, *New Digital Worlds*, 4. As Marc Shell points out, the English term *island* contains two etymologies in disagreement with each other: via French it connotes a "'cutting' off," while the term's prior Norse origin involves the notion of "water-land." Shell, *Islandology*, 18.
40 Underwood, *Distant Horizons*, 143.
41 For the quotations and the epilogue respectively, see Crichton, *Jurassic Park*, 394–95 and 398–400.
42 In describing this corpus, we are using the word *article* to refer to any discrete piece of writing, ranging from traditional academic articles to book reviews to editors' introductions to a variety of other academic genres including brief mentions and indices. The 45,464 articles we visualize run from the journals' foundings to the end of 2019. The number of *Journal of American History* articles in the corpus (31,341) is over three times larger than that for *American Literature* (9,421) and over six times larger than that for *American Quarterly* (4,702). These disproportional tallies are explained by the large number of book reviews published in the *Journal of American History*. For instance, the table of contents for the *Journal of American History*'s December 2018 issue lists 150 items, only nine of which are traditional journal articles. We obtained these data for the three journals through three different steps. First, JSTOR's Data for Research service provided us with the bulk of the journals' print runs: *American Quarterly* from 1949 to 2012 (4,167 articles), *American Literature* from 1929 to 1999 (8,609 articles), and the *Journal of American History* from 1964 to 2012 (27,170 articles). Second, Duke University Press provided us with the data for *American Literature* from 2000 to 2017 (691 articles). Third, we collected the remaining data for the decade from their respective online platforms: the *Journal of American History* from 2013 to 2019 from the Oxford University Press website, *American Literature* from 2018 to 2019 from the Duke University Press website, and *American Quarterly* from 2013 to

2019 from Project Muse. We very much appreciate the cooperation of the different publishers and database providers in our research, and consistent with our agreement with JSTOR, we acknowledge the following: Data provided courtesy of JSTOR. We also appreciate the help of Jeremy Browne in Brigham Young University's Office of Digital Humanities for his help with obtaining the data in our third step.

43 We traced search terms within the corpus using regular expressions. Regular expressions allow for searching for very particular strings of text, similar to what one finds in a find-and-replace tool within a word processor. Insofar as regular expressions accommodate pattern matching on or around metacharacters (e.g., all digits or word boundaries), they allow for searching that is simultaneously more expansive and more precise. For example, our regular expression for *archipelago* finds many forms of the term, including singular (*archipelago*), plural (*archipelagos* or *archipelagoes*), adjectival (*archipelagic* or *archipelic*), possessive (*archipelago's*), and compound (*transarchipelagic* and *meta-archipelagic*). Each instance was saved to a spreadsheet, connected to the article in which it appeared, so we could monitor the performance of the code and iteratively eliminate false positives through refinements. We followed the same principles in designing the regular expressions for *island*, *ocean*, *mainland*, *continent*, and *transnational*. We created a much narrower regular expression for *sea*, one that only identifies the singular and the plural, *seas*. When preparing captions/legends for our graphs, we have reminded readers of the nature of our searching. Some captions/legends use an asterisk (*) to represent a wildcard character and indicate which side or sides of a word could be expanded upon. For the stricter search for *sea* and *seas*, the legends use *sea|seas*, where the pipe character functions as an *or*. Searching the corpus, as well as all other aspects of programming associated with our research, was done with Python, and the code is published at https://github.com/briancroxall/borderwaters.

44 *Continent* and *mainland* tallies for the three journals (2000s): *American Literature*, 109 and 5; *American Quarterly*, 132 and 19; and *Journal of American History*, 321 and 62.

45 See also Soto-Crespo, *Mainland Passage*, xi, on the vexedness of the term *mainland*.

46 It might also be used in transnational Americanist discussions, in phrases like *mainland China*.

47 Balaz, "Da Mainland to Me," 109.

48 For a description of the Literary History course, see Morretti, *Far Country*, 4–5.

49 This result is based on running the collocate tool to search *Far Country* within nine words of *American*. At distances of five and seven words, these three terms are also the top collocates for *American*. See Stéfan Sinclair and Geoffrey Rockwell, Voyant Tools, 2016, https://voyant-tools.org.

50 Moretti, *Far Country*, 91–93. For language on "a vast continent," Moretti quotes Perry Anderson, professor of history and sociology at the University of California, Los Angeles.

51 For Moretti on Slotkin, see Moretti, *Far Country*, 66.

52 Tallies for *sea* and *ocean* in *Journal of American History* during the 2010s are 198 and 247.

53 Tallies for *sea* and *ocean* in *American Literature* during the 2010s are 110 and 72.

54 For *island* in *American Quarterly*, tallies for the 1950s and 2010s are 83 and 207. For *sea* in *American Quarterly*, tallies for the 1950s and 2010s are 73 and 141.

55 In *American Quarterly*, the use of *ocean* moved from 36 articles in the 1990s to 110 articles in the 2010s. During the 2010s, *sea* was used in 141 articles in *American Quarterly*.

56 The relevant decade-by-decade tallies for articles containing *ocean* in *American Quarterly* are as follows: 39 in the 1950s, 40 in the 1960s, 39 in the 1970s, 36 in the 1980s, 36 in the 1990s.

57 Suarez, "Archipelagoes and Oceania."

58 Anonymous review included in Roopika Risam and Patrick Juola (ACH 2019 Program Committee cochairs), email message to Brian Croxall (Brian Russell Roberts cc'd), March 8, 2019.

59 These quotations are from Klein on distant reading as a means "of recovery or resistance." Klein, "Distant Reading after Moretti."

60 In the *Journal of American History*, the term *transnational* appeared in 435 of 6,123 articles published during the 2010s. For the same decade, in *American Quarterly*, it was 248 of 714, and in *American Literature*, it was 167 of 429.

61 For *American Quarterly*, the number of articles in the 2010s that used either *sea* or *ocean* or both was 189 (compared with 248 for *transnational*). For *American Literature*, the analogous *sea/ocean*/both figure was 153 (compared to 167 for *transnational*). For *Journal of American History*, the analogous figure was 392 (compared to 435 for *transnational*).

62 In the three journals, the tallies for *transnational* and *archipelago* during the 2010s are as follows: *American Literature*, 167 and 15; *Journal of American History*, 435 and 21; and *American Quarterly*, 248 and 46.

63 With regard to the individual uses of *archipelago* in the journals, it is not the case that each use seems significant to the article. For instance, an article might cite the British naturalist Alfred Russel Wallace's 1869 *The Malay Archipelago* without showing an apparent interest in archipelagoes or Indonesia. Further, in looking through individual uses of the term, we see a trend toward using it in the context of prison studies and related discussions, as scholars of prisons sometimes echo the structuring metaphor of Aleksandr I. Solzhenitsyn's 1973 *The Gulag Archipelago*. The consistent application of *archipelago* to multiple prisons reflects a tendency to think with the archipelago, even as prison studies, like DH, would do well to further look into archipelagic ontology.

64 Barnard, "Cod and the Whale"; Chang, "Borderlands in a World at Sea"; and J. Byrd, "Return to the South."

65 Moretti, *Graphs, Maps, Trees*, 8.

66 Glissant, *Poetics of Relation*, 208. Elsewhere Glissant admits that "distancings are necessary to Relation and depend on it." Glissant, *Poetics of Relation*, 157.

67 Roberts, "Archipelagic Diaspora."

68 For more on distinctions, see Roberts and Stephens, "Archipelagic American Studies: Decontinentalizing," 10–11. Distinctions aside, to this point it seems that the genus of transnationalism has made the archipelagic legible as one of a handful of transnational species. See, for instance, Gómez-Barris, *Beyond the Pink Tide*, 109. Indeed, archipe-

lagic thought in American studies has benefited from the legibility afforded by the metaframe of transnationalism: by invitation, Stephens and I published our initial articulation of archipelagic American studies in the *Journal of Transnational American Studies*: Roberts and Stephens, "Archipelagic American Studies and the Caribbean." See also Roberts, "Archipelagic American Studies."

69 Mandelbrot, *Fractal Geometry of Nature*, 97 and insert c16.
70 Pease offered this feedback in response to Anna Brickhouse's talk "Transatlantic vs. Hemispheric: Toni Morrison's Long Nineteenth Century," Futures of American Studies Institute, Dartmouth College, June 2009.
71 Somerville, "Great Pacific Garbage Patch," 322; and Somerville, "Where Oceans Come From."
72 See Martínez-San Miguel and Stephens, *Contemporary Archipelagic Thinking*. For archipelagic thinking as it has coalesced in island studies, see Stratford et al., "Envisioning the Archipelago"; and Pugh, "Relational Turn in Island Geographies." For archipelagic thinking and politics, see Carter, *Decolonising Governance*.
73 Suarez, "Archipelagoes and Oceania," 7–10; and Gillman, "Newer Newest Thing," 310. *Canoa* is a Taíno term which, via Spanish, has been incorporated into English as *canoe*. I am also referencing the term *waka* (also *vaka*, *aka*, or other variants) which occurs in over two dozen Polynesian languages; it is often translated into English as *canoe* or *boat*. Kirch and Green, *Hawaiki, Ancestral Polynesia*, 46–48. Keegan and Carlson, *Talking Taíno*, 13.
74 Blum, "Introduction," 4, 3.
75 Suarez, "Archipelagoes and Oceania"; and Perez, "Transterritorial Currents," 619. Stephens and I have also used the term "turn" in contemplating the place of the archipelagic in American studies: Roberts and Stephens, "Archipelagic American Studies: Decontinentalizing," 11. See also Roberts and Stephens, "Archipelagic American Studies and the Caribbean," 15–16.
76 For instance, this phrase is used twice in Goyal, *Cambridge Companion to Transnational American Literature*, 100, 157.
77 Brian Croxall, "The 'Next Big Thing' Ten Years Later: Digital Humanities at MLA 2019," Brian Croxall, April 16, 2019, https://www.briancroxall.net/2019/04/16/the-next-big-thing-ten-years-later-digital-humanities-at-mla-2019/.
78 Giles, "Archipelagic Accretion," 433.

BIBLIOGRAPHY

Adelman, Jeremy, and Stephen Aron. "From Borderlands to Borders: Empires, Nation-States, and the Peoples in between in North American History." *American Historical Review* 104, no. 3 (1999): 814–41.

Adelson, Leslie A. "Futurity Now: An Introduction." *Germanic Review: Literature, Culture, Theory* 88, no. 3 (2013): 213–18.

Aikau, Hōkūlani K., and Vernadette Vicuña Gonzalez, eds. *Detours: A Decolonial Guide to Hawai'i*. Durham, NC: Duke University Press, 2019.

Alaimo, Stacy. "The Anthropocene at Sea." In *The Routledge Companion to the Environmental Humanities*, edited by Ursula K. Heise, Jon Christensen, and Michelle Niemann, 153–62. New York: Routledge, 2017.

Alaimo, Stacy. *Exposed: Environmental Politics and Pleasures in Posthuman Times*. Minneapolis: University of Minnesota Press, 2016.

Alaimo, Stacy. "New Materialisms, Old Humanisms, or, Following the Submersible." *NORA: Nordic Journal of Feminist and Gender Research* 19, no 4 (December 2001): 280–84.

Alaimo, Stacy. "Trans-Corporeal Feminisms and the Ethical Space of Nature." In *Material Feminisms*, edited by Stacy Alaimo and Susan Hekman, 237–64. Bloomington: Indiana University Press, 2008.

Alaskan Boundary Tribunal. *Proceedings of the Alaskan Boundary Tribunal*. Vol. 6. Washington, DC: Government Printing Office, 1904.

Albrecht, Andreas. "Cosmic Inflation and the Arrow of Time." In *Science and Ultimate Reality: Quantum Theory, Cosmology, and Complexity*, edited by John D. Barrow, Paul C. W. Davies, and Charles L. Harper Jr., 363–401. Cambridge: Cambridge University Press, 2004.

Albrecht, Andreas, and Lorenzo Sorbo. "Can the Universe Afford Inflation?" *Physical Review D* 70 (2004): 1–10.

Allen, Chadwick. *Trans-Indigenous: Methodologies for Global Native Literary Studies*. Minneapolis: University of Minnesota Press, 2012.

Allison, James R., III. "Beyond It All: Surveying the Intersections of Modern American Indian, Environmental, and Western Histories." *History Compass* 16 (2018): 1–11.

Anderson, Benedict. *Imagined Communities: Reflections on the Origin and Spread of Nationalism*. Rev. ed. London: Verso, 1991.

Anderson, Sheila, and Tobias Blanke. "Taking the Long View: From e-Science Humanities to Humanities Digital Ecosystems." *Historical Social Research/Historische Sozialforschung* 37, no. 3 (2012): 147–64.

Anzaldúa, Gloria. *Borderlands/La Frontera: The New Mestiza*. San Francisco: Aunt Lute Books, 1987.

Arac, Jonathan. *Huckleberry Finn as Idol and Target: The Function of Criticism in Our Time*. Madison: University of Wisconsin Press, 1997.

Aravamudan, Srinivas. "Rogue States and Emergent Disciplines." In *States of Emergency: The Object of American Studies*, edited by Russ Castronovo and Susan Gillman, 17–35. Chapel Hill: University of North Carolina Press, 2009.

Arrington, Leonard J. *The Price of Prejudice: The Japanese-American Relocation Center in Utah during World War II*. Logan: Faculty Association, Utah State University, 1962.

Ascher, Marcia. *Mathematics Elsewhere: An Exploration of Ideas across Cultures*. Princeton, NJ: Princeton University Press, 2002.

Ascher, Marcia. "Models and Maps from the Marshall Islands: A Case in Ethnomathematics." *Historia Mathematica* 22, no. 4 (1995): 347–70.

Babcock, C. Merton. Introduction to *The American Frontier: A Social and Literary Record*, edited by C. Merton Babcock, 1–19. New York: Holt, Rinehart and Winston, 1965.

Bahrani, Ramin, dir. *FutureStates*. Season 1, episode 5, "Plastic Bag" (2009). Aired April 12, 2010 on PBS. https://www.pbs.org/video/futurestates-plastic-bag/.

Balaz, Joseph P. "Da Mainland to Me." *Chaminade Literary Review* 2, no. 2 (Spring 1989): 109.

Barnard, John Levi. "The Cod and the Whale: Melville in the Time of Extinction." *American Literature* 89, no. 4 (December 2017): 851–79.

Barr, Juliana, and Edward Countryman. "Introduction: Maps and Spaces, Paths to Connect, and Lines to Divide." In *Contested Spaces of Early America*, edited by Juliana Barr and Edward Countryman, 1–28. Philadelphia: University of Pennsylvania Press, 2014.

Barreiro, José, ed. "View from the Shore: American Indian Perspectives on the Quincentenary." *Northeast Indian Quarterly* 7, no. 3 (Fall 1990).

Barrish, Phillip J. *The Cambridge Introduction to American Literary Realism*. Cambridge: Cambridge University Press, 2011.

Barrow, John D., and Frank J. Tipler. *The Anthropic Cosmological Principle*. Oxford: Clarendon, 1986.

Barthes, Roland. *Critical Essays*. Translated by Richard Howard. Evanston, IL: Northwestern University Press, 1972.

Batongbacal, Jay L. "Defining Archipelagic Studies." In *Archipelagic Studies: Charting New Waters*, edited by Jay L. Batongbacal, 183–94. Quezon City: University of the Philippines Printery, 1998.

Baym, Nina. "Melodramas of Beset Manhood: How Theories of American Fiction Exclude Women Authors." *American Quarterly* 33, no. 2 (Summer 1981): 123–39.

Baym, Nina. *Women Writers of the American West, 1833–1927*. Urbana: University of Illinois Press, 2011.

Baym, Nina, Ronald Gottesman, Laurence B. Holland, David Kalstone, Francis Murphy, Hershel Parker, and William H. Pritchard. "Preface to the Second Edition." In *The*

Norton Anthology of American Literature, vol. 1, edited by Nina Baym, Ronald Gottesman, Laurence B. Holland, David Kalstone, Francis Murphy, Hershel Parker, and William H. Pritchard, xxvii–xxxi. 2nd ed. New York: Norton, 1985.

Baym, Nina, and Robert S. Levine. "Preface to the Eighth Edition." In *The Norton Anthology of American Literature*, vol. A, edited by Nina Baym and Robert S. Levine, xvii–xxvi. 8th ed. New York: Norton, 2012.

Beaglehole, Ernest, and Pearl Beaglehole. *Ethnology of Pukapuka*. Bernice P. Bishop Museum Bulletin 150. Honolulu: Bishop Museum, 1938.

Beckwith, Frank, Sr. "Escalante in Millard County." *Trek* (February 1943): 17–20.

Beckwith, Frank, Sr. "Landmarks of Pahvant Valley." *Trek* (December 1942): 17–20.

Beckwith, Frank, Sr. "Trilobite Fossils of Antelope Springs." *Trek* (June 1943): 14–16.

Bender, Bert. *Sea Brothers: The Tradition of American Sea Fiction from "Moby-Dick" to the Present*. Philadelphia: University of Pennsylvania Press, 1990.

Benítez-Rojo, Antonio. *The Repeating Island: The Caribbean and the Postmodern Perspective*. Translated by James Maraniss. 2nd ed. Durham, NC: Duke University Press, 1996.

Benjamin, Walter. *Illuminations*. Edited by Hannah Arendt. Translated by Harry Zohn. New York: Schocken Books, 1969.

Bennett, Jane. *Vibrant Matter: A Political Ecology of Things*. Durham, NC: Duke University Press, 2010.

Bernabé, Jean, Patrick Chamoiseau, and Raphaël Confiant. "In Praise of Creoleness." Translated by Mohamed B. Taleb Khyar. *Callaloo* 13, no. 4 (Autumn 1990): 886–909.

Bernstein, Robin. "Dances with Things: Material Culture and the Performance of Race." *Social Text* 27, no. 4 (Winter 2009): 67–94.

Bérubé, Michael. "American Studies without Exceptions." PMLA 118, no. 1 (January 2003): 103–13.

Billé, Franck. "Voluminous: An Introduction." In *Voluminous States: Sovereignty, Materiality, and the Territorial Imagination*, edited by Franck Billé, 1–35. Durham, NC: Duke University Press, 2020.

Bishop, Elizabeth. "The Map." In *The Complete Poems, 1927–1979*, 3. New York: Noonday, 1983.

Blacklock, Mark. *The Emergence of the Fourth Dimension: Higher Spatial Thinking in the Fin de Siècle*. Oxford: Oxford University Press, 2018.

Blum, Hester. "Introduction: Academic Positioning Systems." In *Turns of Event: Nineteenth-Century American Literary Studies in Motion*, edited by Hester Blum, 1–9. Philadelphia: University of Pennsylvania Press, 2016.

Blum, Hester. "The Prospect of Oceanic Studies." PMLA 125, no. 3 (May 2010): 670–77.

Blum, Hester. *The View from the Masthead: Maritime Imagination and Antebellum American Sea Narratives*. Chapel Hill: University of North Carolina Press, 2008.

Blum, Hester, Leslie Elizabeth Eckel, Maria Cristina Fumagalli, and Yuan Shu. Roundtable review of *Archipelagic American Studies*. *Journal of American Studies* 53, no. 2 (2019), e18, 1–11.

Boddy, Kimberly K., Sean M. Carroll, and Jason Pollack. "Why Boltzmann Brains Do Not Fluctuate into Existence from the de Sitter Vacuum." In *The Philosophy of Cosmology*, edited by Khalil Chamcham, Joseph Silk, John D. Barrow, and Simon Saunders, 228–40. Cambridge: Cambridge University Press, 2017.

Bogan, Eugene F. "Government of the Trust Territory of the Pacific Islands." *Annals of the American Academy of Political and Social Science* 267 (January 1950): 164–74.

Bogost, Ian. *Alien Phenomenology, or What It's Like to Be a Thing*. Minneapolis: University of Minnesota Press, 2012.

Bolton, Herbert E. "The Epic of Greater America." *American Historical Review* 38, no. 3 (April 1933): 448–74.

Bolton, Herbert E. *The Spanish Borderlands: A Chronicle of Old Florida and the Southwest*. New Haven, CT: Yale University Press, 1921.

Boltzmann, Ludwig. "On Certain Questions of the Theory of Gases." *Nature*, February 28, 1895, 413–15.

Bondi, H. *Cosmology*. 2nd ed. Cambridge: Cambridge University Press, 1961.

Bone, Martyn. "The (Extended) South of Black Folk: Intraregional and Transnational Migrant Labor in *Jonah's Gourd Vine* and *Their Eyes Were Watching God*." *American Literature* 79, no. 4 (December 2007): 753–79.

Bonilla, Yarimar. *Non-sovereign Futures: French Caribbean Politics in the Wake of Disenchantment*. Chicago: University of Chicago Press, 2015.

Bordelon, Pamela. "Zora Neale Hurston: A Biographical Essay." In *Go Gator and Muddy the Water: Writings by Zora Neale Hurston from the Federal Writers' Project*, edited by Pamela Bordelon, 2–49. New York: Norton, 1999.

Borges, Jorge Luis. "The Aleph." 1945. In *Collected Fictions*, translated by Andrew Hurley, 274–86. New York: Penguin, 1998.

Borges, Jorge Luis. "The Library of Babel." 1941. In *Collected Fictions*, translated by Andrew Hurley, 112–18. New York: Penguin, 1998.

Bottignolo, Bruno. *Celebrations with the Sun: An Overview of Religious Phenomena among the Badjaos*. Manila, Philippines: Ateneo de Manila University Press, 1995.

Bowles, Samuel. *Across the Continent: A Summer's Journey to the Rocky Mountains, the Mormons, and the Pacific States, with Speaker Colfax*. Springfield, MA: Samuel Bowles, 1865.

Boyd, Valerie. *Wrapped in Rainbows: The Life of Zora Neale Hurston*. New York: Scribner, 2003.

Brady, Mary Pat. "Border." In *Keywords for American Cultural Studies*, edited by Bruce Burgett and Glenn Hendler, 34–36. 2nd ed. New York: New York University Press, 2014.

Brathwaite, [Edward] Kamau. "Caribbean Culture: Two Paradigms." In *Missile and Capsule*, edited by Jürgen Martini, 9–54. Bremen: Universität Bremen, 1983.

Brathwaite, [Edward Kamau]. "Caribbean Theme: A Calypso." *Caribbean Quarterly* 4, no. 3/4 (March–June 1956): 246–49.

Brathwaite, Edward [Kamau]. *Contradictory Omens: Cultural Diversity and Integration in the Caribbean*. 1974. Reprint, Mona, Jamaica: Savacou, 1977.

Brathwaite, [Edward] Kamau. *ConVERSations with Nathaniel Mackey*. Staten Island, NY: We Press, 1999.

Brathwaite, Edward Kamau. *History of the Voice: The Development of Nation Language in Anglophone Caribbean Poetry*. London: New Beacon Books, 1984.

Braudel, Fernand. *The Mediterranean and the Mediterranean World in the Age of Philip II*. Vol. 1. Translated by Siân Reynolds. Berkeley: University of California Press, 1995.

Brickhouse, Anna. "Hemispheric Jamestown." In *Hemispheric American Studies*, edited by Caroline F. Levander and Robert S. Levine, 18–35. New Brunswick, NJ: Rutgers University Press, 2008.

Brown, Bill. "Thing Theory." *Critical Inquiry* 28, no. 1 (Winter 2001): 1–22.

Brubaker, Rogers. "The 'Diaspora' Diaspora." *Ethnic and Racial Studies* 28, no. 1 (2005): 1–19.

Bryant, Levi, Nick Srnicek, and Graham Harman. "Towards a Speculative Philosophy." In *The Speculative Turn: Continental Materialism and Realism*, edited by Levi Bryant, Nick Srnicek, and Graham Harman, 1–18. Melbourne: re.press, 2011.

Buck, Peter H. [also known as Te Rangihiroa]. *Vikings of the Pacific*. 1938. Reprint, Chicago: University of Chicago Press, 1959.

Bulosan, Carlos. *America Is in the Heart: A Personal History*. 1946. Reprint, Seattle: University of Washington Press, 1973.

Burnham, Michelle. *Transoceanic America: Risk, Writing, and Revolution in the Global Pacific*. Oxford: Oxford University Press, 2019.

Burns, Lorna. *Contemporary Caribbean Writing and Deleuze: Literature between Postcolonialism and Post-Continental Philosophy*. London: Continuum, 2012.

Bush, George W. "Establishment of the Marianas Trench Marine National Monument" (Proclamation 8335, January 6, 2009). *Federal Register: The Daily Journal of the United States Government* 74, no. 7 (January 12, 2009): 1557–63. https://www.govinfo.gov/content/pkg/FR-2009-01-12/pdf/E9-496.pdf.

Bush, George W. "Establishment of the Northwestern Hawaiian Islands Marine National Monument" (Proclamation 8031, June 15, 2006). *Federal Register: The Daily Journal of the United States Government* 71, no. 122 (June 26, 2006): 36443–75. https://www.govinfo.gov/content/pkg/FR-2006-06-26/pdf/06-5725.pdf.

Bush, George W. "Establishment of the Pacific Remote Islands Marine National Monument" (Proclamation 8336, January 6, 2009). *Federal Register: The Daily Journal of the United States Government* 74, no. 7 (January 12, 2009): 1565–75. https://www.govinfo.gov/content/pkg/FR-2009-01-12/pdf/E9-500.pdf.

Bush, George W. "Establishment of the Rose Atoll Marine National Monument" (Proclamation 8337, January 6, 2009). *Federal Register: The Daily Journal of the United States Government* 74, no. 7 (January 12, 2009): 1577–81. https://www.govinfo.gov/content/pkg/FR-2009-01-12/pdf/E9-505.pdf.

Butcher, John G., and R. E. Elson. *Sovereignty and the Sea: How Indonesia Became an Archipelagic State*. Singapore: National University of Singapore Press, 2017.

Byrd, Brandon R. *The Black Republic: African Americans and the Fate of Haiti*. Philadelphia: University of Pennsylvania Press, 2019.

Byrd, Jodi A. "A Return to the South." *American Quarterly* 66, no. 3 (September 2014): 609–20.

Byrnes, Corey. "The Infrastructure of Coral." *Verge: Studies in Global Asias* 6, no. 2 (Fall 2020): 29–34.

Cao, Zuoya. "Poetry and Zen: A Comparison of Wang Wei and Basho." *Tamkang Review* 24, no. 2 (Autumn 1993): 23–41.

Carby, Hazel V. "The Politics of Fiction, Anthropology, and the Folk: Zora Neale Hurston." In *New Essays on "Their Eyes Were Watching God,"* edited by Michael Awkward, 71–93. Cambridge: Cambridge University Press, 1990.

Card, Orson Scott. *The Folk of the Fringe*. New York: Doherty, 1989.

Carroll, Sean M. "Why Boltzmann Brains Are Bad." Preprint, submitted February 2, 2017. https://arxiv.org/pdf/1702.00850.pdf.

Carson, Rachel L. *The Sea around Us*. New York: Oxford University Press, 1951.

Carter, Paul. *Decolonising Governance: Archipelagic Thinking*. London: Routledge, 2019.

Cartwright, Keith. "'To Walk with the Storm': Oya as the Transformative 'I' of Zora Neale Hurston's Afro-Atlantic Callings." *American Literature* 78, no. 4 (December 2006): 741–67.

Castronovo, Russ. "Out of Order: Criticism and Anachronism." Paper presented on November 11, 2017, at the "Futures Past/Future Perfect: American Studies and Its Modes of Historicism" session of the 2017 American Studies Association Convention, Chicago.

Chakrabarty, Dipesh. "The Climate of History: Four Theses." *Critical Inquiry* 35, no. 2 (Winter 2009): 197–222.

Chang, David A. "Borderlands in a World at Sea: Concow Indians, Native Hawaiians, and South Chinese in Indigenous, Global, and National Spaces." *Journal of American History* 98, no. 2 (September 2011): 384–403.

Chang, David A. *The World and All the Things upon It: Native Hawaiian Geographies of Exploration*. Minneapolis: University of Minnesota Press, 2016.

Chen, Cecilia, Janine MacLeod, and Astrida Neimanis. "Introduction: Toward a Hydrological Turn?" In *Thinking with Water*, edited by Cecilia Chen, Janine MacLeod, and Astrida Neimanis, 3–22. Montreal: McGill-Queen's University Press, 2013.

Chōmei, Kamo no. *The Ten Foot Square Hut and Tales of the Heike*. Translated by A. L. Sadler. Westport, CT: Greenwood, 1970.

Christian, Barbara. "The Race for Theory." *Cultural Critique* 6 (Spring 1987): 51–63.

Cline, Howard F. "Imperial Perspectives on the Borderlands." In *Probing the American West*, edited by K. Ross Toole, A. R. Mortensen, John Alexander Carroll, and Robert M. Utley, 168–74. Santa Fe: Museum of New Mexico Press, 1962.

Cohen, Jeffrey Jerome. *Stone: An Ecology of the Inhuman*. Minneapolis: University of Minnesota Press, 2015.

Cohen, Margaret. "Literary Studies on the Terraqueous Globe." *PMLA* 125, no. 3 (May 2010): 657–62.

Collings, Michael. "Afterword: The Folk of the Fringe." In Card, *Folk of the Fringe*, 228–32.

Committee on Interior and Insular Affairs. *Investigation and Study of the Seaward Boundaries of the United States: Report of the Committee on Interior and Insular Affairs Pursuant to H. Res. 676, 82d Cong., Authorizing an Investigation and Study of the Seaward Boundaries of the United States*. Washington, DC: Government Printing Office, 1953.

Cooper, James Fenimore. *The Prairie: A Tale*. 1827. Reprint, New York: Signet Classic, 1980.

Corcoran, Patricia L., Charles J. Moore, and Kelly Jazvac. "An Anthropogenic Marker Horizon in the Future Rock Record." *GSA Today* 24, no. 6 (June 2014): 4–8.

Couture, Ruth, and Virginia McGowan, eds. *A Metaphoric Mind: Selected Writings of Joseph Couture*. Edmonton: Athabasca University Press, 2013.

Covarrubias, Miguel. *The Eagle, the Jaguar, and the Serpent: Indian Art of the Americas—North America: Alaska, Canada, the United States*. 1954. Reprint, New York: Alfred A. Knopf, 1967.

Covarrubias, Miguel. *Island of Bali*. 1937. Reprint, Singapore: Periplus, 2008.

Covarrubias, Miguel. *Negro Drawings*. New York: Knopf, 1927.

Covarrubias, Miguel. *Pageant of the Pacific*. [San Francisco]: Pacific House, 1940.

Cox, Paul Alan. *Nafanua: Saving the Samoan Rain Forest*. New York: W. H. Freeman, 1999.

Cox, Paul Alan, and Thomas Elmqvist. "Indigenous Control of Tropical Rainforest Reserves: An Alternative Strategy for Conservation." *Ambio* 20, no. 7 (November 1991): 317–21.

Craig, Robin Kundis. "Law Professor Amicus Brief in Massachusetts Lobstermen's Association v. Ross Regarding the Legality of the Northeast Canyons and Seamounts Marine National Monument." *Utah Law Faculty Scholarship* 105 (2018): 1–29.

Cribb, Robert, and Michele Ford. "Indonesia as an Archipelago: Managing Islands, Managing the Seas." In *Indonesia beyond the Water's Edge: Managing an Archipelagic State*, edited by Robert Cribb and Michele Ford, 1–27. Singapore: Institute of Southeast Asian Studies, 2009.

Crichton, Michael. *Jurassic Park*. 1990. Reprint, New York: Knofp, 2008.

Crutzen, Paul J. "Geology of Mankind." *Nature* 415, no. 6867 (2002): 23.

Crutzen, Paul J., and Eugene F. Stoermer. "The 'Anthropocene.'" *IGBP Newsletter* 41 (May 2000): 17–18.

Cruz, Denise. *Transpacific Femininities: The Making of the Modern Filipina*. Durham, NC: Duke University Press, 2012.

Culler, Jonathan. "Desert Island Texts." *Genre* 33, nos. 3–4 (Fall–Winter 2000): 247–56.

Cumings, Bruce. "Rimspeak; or, The Discourse of the 'Pacific Rim.'" In *What Is in a Rim? Critical Perspectives on the Pacific Region Idea*, edited by Arif Dirlik, 29–47. Boulder, CO: Westview, 1993.

Curiel, Barbara Brinson, David Kazanjian, Katherine Kinney, Steven Mailloux, Jay Mechling, John Carlos Rowe, George Sánchez, Shelley Streeby, and Henry Yu.

Introduction to *Post-Nationalist American Studies*, edited by John Carlos Rowe, 1–21. Berkeley: University of California Press, 2000.

Cusick, David. *David Cusick's Sketches of Ancient History of the Six Nations, Comprising, First, a Tale of the Foundation of the Great Island, (Now North America,) the Two Infants Born, and the Creation of the Universe*. 1828. Reprint, Lockport, NY: Turner, 1848.

Cutler, John Alba. "Borders and Borderland Literature." In *The Cambridge Companion to Transnational American Literature*, edited by Yogita Goyal, 157–73. Cambridge: Cambridge University Press, 2017.

Cutler, John Alba. *Ends of Assimilation: The Formation of Chicano Literature*. New York: Oxford University Press, 2015.

Cutler, John Alba. "The New Border." *College Literature* 44, no. 4 (Fall 2017): 498–504.

Cutter, Donald C. "The Western Spanish Borderlands." In *Historians and the American West*, edited by Michael P. Malone, 39–56. Lincoln: University of Nebraska Press, 1983.

Dana, Richard Henry, Jr. *Two Years before the Mast: A Personal Narrative*. 1840. Boston: Houghton Mifflin Company, 1911.

Danuredjo, Sumitro Lono Sedewo. *Hukum Internasional Laut Indonesia: Suatu Usaha untuk Mempertahankan Deklarasi 1957*. Vol. 2. Jakarta: Bhratara, 1971.

Danusaputro, St. Munadjat. "The International Sea System in Perspective." *Indonesian Quarterly* 3, no. 4 (July 1975): 3–43.

Danusaputro, St. Munadjat. *Tata Lautan Nusantara dalam Hukum dan Sejarahnya*. Bandung: Binacipta, 1980.

Danusaputro, St. Munadjat. "Wawasan Nusantara and the International Sea System." *Indonesian Quarterly* 2, no. 4 (1974): 52–87.

Darwin, Charles. *On the Origin of Species by Means of Natural Selection, or the Preservation of Favoured Races in the Struggle for Life*. London: John Murray, 1859.

Dash, J. Michael. "The Stranger by the Shore: The Archipelization of Caliban in Antillean Theatre." In Roberts and Stephens, *Archipelagic American Studies*, 356–70.

Dautel, Susan L. "Transoceanic Trash: International and United States Strategies for the Great Pacific Garbage Patch." *Golden Gate University Environmental Law Journal* 3, no. 1 (Fall 2009): 181–208.

Davenport, Matthew, and Ken D. Olum. "Are There Boltzmann Brains in the Vacuum?" Preprint, submitted August 4, 2010. https://arxiv.org/pdf/1008.0808.pdf.

de Certeau, Michel. *The Practice of Everyday Life*. Translated by Steven F. Rendall. Berkeley: University of California Press, 1984.

Defoe, Daniel. *Robinson Crusoe*. 1719. Edited by Evan R. Davis. Peterborough, Ontario: Broadview Editions, 2010.

de Hoyos, Angela. *Chicano Poems for the Barrio*. Bloomington, IN: Backstage Books, 1975.

de la Garza C., Luis Alberto. "A Covarrubias Chronology." In Williams and Chong, *Covarrubias in Bali*, 110–13.

Deleuze, Gilles. *Cinema 1: The Movement-Image*. Translated by Hugh Tomlinson and Barbara Habberjam. Minneapolis: University of Minnesota Press, 1986.

Deleuze, Gilles. "Desert Islands." In *Desert Islands and Other Texts, 1953–1974*, edited by David Lapoujade, translated by Michael Taormina, 9–14. Los Angeles: Semiotext(e) Foreign Agents Series, 2004.

Deleuze, Gilles, and Félix Guattari. *A Thousand Plateaus: Capitalism and Schizophrenia*. 1980. Translated by Brian Massumi. Minneapolis: University of Minnesota Press, 1987.

DeLoughrey, Elizabeth M. *Allegories of the Anthropocene*. Durham, NC: Duke University Press, 2019.

DeLoughrey, Elizabeth M. *Routes and Roots: Navigating Caribbean and Pacific Island Literatures*. Honolulu: University of Hawai'i Press, 2007.

de Maria y Campos Castelló, Alfonso, ed. *Covarrubias: Esplendor del Pacífico*. Mexico City: Conaculta, 2006.

Dembitz, Nanette. "Racial Discrimination and the Military Judgment: The Supreme Court's Korematsu and Endo Decisions." In *The Mass Internment of Japanese Americans and the Quest for Legal Redress*, edited by Charles McClain, 9–73. New York: Garland Publishing, 1994.

DeMott, Sarah. "Archipelago of the Maghreb: Mapping Mediterranean Movement from Transnational Migration to Transregional Mobility." In Martínez-San Miguel and Stephens, *Contemporary Archipelagic Thinking*, 161–75.

Deneen, Patrick J. "Was Huck Greek? The *Odyssey* of Mark Twain." *Modern Language Studies* 32, no. 2 (Autumn 2002): 35–44.

Department of the Navy, Office of the Chief of Naval Operations. *Report on the Administration of the Trust Territory of the Pacific Islands for the Period July 1, 1949, to June 30, 1950, Transmitted by the United States to the United Nations Pursuant to Article 88 of the Charter of the United Nations*. Washington, DC: Government Printing Office, 1950.

Diaz, Vicente M. "Voyaging for Anti-Colonial Recovery: Austronesian Seafaring, Archipelagic Rethinking, and the Re-mapping of Indigeneity." *Pacific Asia Inquiry* 2, no. 1 (Fall 2011): 21–32.

Dimacali, Timothy James M. "Sky Gypsies." In *Philippine Speculative Fiction III*, edited by Dean Francis Alfar and Nikki Alfar, 147–53. Pasig City, Philippines: Kestrel, 2007.

Dimock, Wai Chee. "Low Epic." *Critical Inquiry* 39, no. 3 (Spring 2013): 614–31.

Dimock, Wai Chee. "Planet and America, Set and Subset." In *Shades of the Planet: American Literature as World Literature*, edited by Wai Chee Dimock and Lawrence Buell, 1–16. Princeton, NJ: Princeton University Press, 2007.

Dimock, Wai Chee. *Through Other Continents: American Literature across Deep Time*. Princeton, NJ: Princeton University Press, 2006.

Dimock, Wai Chee. "Weak Theory: Henry James, Colm Tóibín, and W. B. Yeats." *Critical Inquiry* 39, no. 4 (Summer 2013): 732–53.

Djuanda, H. "Announcement of the Government on the Territorial Waters of the State of the Republic of Indonesia." 1957. Reproduced as appendix 1, in St. Munadjat Danusaputro, "Wawasan Nusantara and the International Sea System," *Indonesian Quarterly* 2, no. 4 (1974): 86–87.

Donahue, Micah. "Poe's Fluid, Terraqueous Landscapes: An Archipelagic Rereading of 'The Journal of Julius Rodman.'" *Poe Studies: History, Theory, Interpretation* 54 (2021).

Douglas, Edward M. *Boundaries, Areas, Geographic Centers and Altitudes of the United States and the Several States: With a Brief Record of Important Changes in Their Territory*. Bulletin of the United States Geological Survey 689. Washington, DC: Government Printing Office, 1923.

Douglas, Edward M. *Boundaries, Areas, Geographic Centers and Altitudes of the United States and the Several States: With a Brief Record of Important Changes in Their Territory and Government*. 2nd ed. Bulletin of the United States Geological Survey 817. Washington, DC: Government Printing Office, 1930.

Doyle, Laura. "Atlantic Modernism at the Crossing: The Migrant Labours of Hurston, McKay, and the Diasporic Text." In *Modernism and Race*, edited by Len Platt, 116–36. Cambridge: Cambridge University Press, 2011.

Drinnon, Richard. *Facing West: The Metaphysics of Indian-Hating and Empire-Building*. 1980. Reprint, Norman: University of Oklahoma Press, 1997.

Drucker, Johanna. "Why Distant Reading Isn't." *PMLA* 132, no. 3 (2017): 628–35.

Du Bois, W. E. B. "Criteria of Negro Art." 1926. In *African American Literary Theory: A Reader*, edited by Winston Napier, 17–23. New York: NYU Press, 2000.

Du Bois, W. E. B. *The Souls of Black Folk*. 1903. Edited by Brent Hayes Edwards. Reprint, New York: Oxford University Press, 2007.

Duck, Leigh Anne. "'*Go* There tuh *Know* There': Zora Neale Hurston and the Chronotope of the Folk." *American Literary History* 13, no. 2 (Summer 2001): 265–94.

Ducrocq, Albert. *The Origins of Life*. London: Elek Books, 1957.

Duffy, Simon B. *Deleuze and the History of Mathematics: In Defense of the "New."* New York: Bloomsbury, 2013.

Dusselier, Jane E. *Artifacts of Loss: Crafting Survival in Japanese American Concentration Camps*. New Brunswick, NJ: Rutgers University Press, 2008.

Dyson, Lisa, Matthew Kleban, and Leonard Susskind. "Disturbing Implications of a Cosmological Constant." *Journal of High Energy Physics* 10, no. 011 (2002): 1–20.

Eaton, Allen H. *Beauty behind Barbed Wire: The Arts of the Japanese in Our War Relocation Camps*. New York: Harper, 1952.

Eldredge, Niles. *Life Pulse: Episodes from the Story of the Fossil Record*. New York: Facts on File, 1987.

Eldredge, Niles, and Stephen Jay Gould. "Punctuated Equilibria: An Alternative to Phyletic Gradualism." In *Models in Paleobiology*, edited by Thomas J. M. Schopf, 82–115. San Francisco: Freeman, Cooper, 1972.

Ennis, Paul John. Introduction to *Post-Continental Voices: Selected Interviews*, edited by Paul John Ennis, 1–5. Winchester, UK: Zero Books, 2010.

Equiano, Olaudah. *The Interesting Narrative of the Life of Olaudah Equiano, or Gustavus Vassa, the African, Written by Himself*. 1789. In *The Classic Slave Narratives*, edited by Henry Louis Gates Jr., 15–247. New York: Signet, 2002.

Eshel, Amir. *Futurity: Contemporary Literature and the Quest for the Past*. Chicago: University of Chicago Press, 2013.

Euclid. *Euclid's Elements*. Translated by Thomas L. Heath. Ann Arbor, MI: Green Lion, 2007.

Evans, Sterling. Preface to *The Borderlands of the American and Canadian Wests: Essays on Regional History of the Forty-Ninth Parallel*, edited by Sterling Evans, xv–xxi. Lincoln: University of Nebraska Press, 2006.

Federal Writers' Project. *Florida: A Guide to the Southernmost State*. 1939. Reprint, New York: Oxford University Press, 1940.

Feinberg, Richard, Ute J. Dymon, Pu Paiaki, Pu Rangituteki, Pu Nukuriaki, and Matthew Rollins. "'Drawing the Coral Heads': Mental Mapping and Its Physical Representation in a Polynesian Community." *Cartographic Journal* 40, no. 3 (December 2003): 243–53.

Felski, Rita. *The Limits of Critique*. Chicago: University of Chicago Press, 2015.

Fiedler, Leslie. "Come Back to the Raft Ag'in, Huck Honey!" 1948. In *Adventures of Huckleberry Finn: A Case Study in Critical Controversy*, edited by Gerald Graff and James Phelan, 519–25. 2nd ed. Boston: Bedford/St. Martin's, 2004.

"Final Communique of the Asian-African Conference." In *Asia-Africa Speaks from Bandung*, edited by Ministry of Foreign Affairs, 161–69. [Jakarta]: Ministry of Foreign Affairs, Republic of Indonesia, 1955.

Fishkin, Shelley Fisher. "Crossroads of Cultures: The Transnational Turn in American Studies—Presidential Address to the American Studies Association, November 12, 2004." *American Quarterly* 57, no. 1 (2005): 17–57.

Fitzgerald, F. Scott. *The Great Gatsby*. 1925. Reprint, New York: Scribner, 1995.

Flores, Richard R. *Remembering the Alamo: Memory, Modernity, and the Master Symbol*. Austin: University of Texas Press, 2002.

Foucault, Michel. *The Order of Things: An Archaeology of the Human Sciences*. 1966. Reprint, New York: Vintage Books, 1973.

Foulcher, Keith. "*Sumpah Pemuda*: The Making and Meaning of a Symbol of Indonesian Nationhood." *Asian Studies Review* 24, no. 3 (2000): 377–410.

Franklin, Benjamin. *The Autobiography and Other Writings*. New York: Penguin Classics, 1986.

Freeman, Elizabeth. "Synchronic/Anachronic." In *Time: A Vocabulary of the Present*, edited by Joel Burges and Amy J. Elias, 129–43. New York: New York University Press, 2016.

Freud, Sigmund. *Civilization and Its Discontents*. 1930. Translated by James Strachey. New York: W. W. Norton, 1989.

Friedman, Nathan. "Political Props: Territorial Performance and the Chamizal Dispute." *MAS Context* 27 (Fall 2015): 168–85.

Frisbie, Florence (Johnny). *Miss Ulysses from Puka-Puka: The Autobiography of a South Sea Trader's Daughter*. Edited and translated by Robert Dean Frisbie. New York: Macmillan, 1948.

Frisbie, Florence (Johnny). *Miss Ulysses from Puka-Puka: The Autobiography of a South Sea Trader's Daughter*. Edited and translated by Robert Dean Frisbie. 2nd ed. Newport Beach, CA: Dockside Sailing, 2016.

Frisbie, Robert Dean. Introduction to F. Frisbie, *Miss Ulysses from Puka-Puka* (1948), vii–viii.

Gabrakova, Dennitza. *The Unnamable Archipelago: Wounds of the Postcolonial in Postwar Japanese Literature and Thought*. Leiden, Netherlands: Brill, 2018.

Gannett, Henry. *Boundaries of the United States and of the Several States and Territories: With a Historical Sketch of the Territorial Changes*. Bulletin of the United States Geological Survey 13. Washington, DC: Government Printing Office, 1885.

Gannett, Henry. *Boundaries of the United States and of the Several States and Territories: With an Outline of the History of All Important Changes of Territory*. 2nd ed. Bulletin of the United States Geological Survey 171. Washington, DC: Government Printing Office, 1900.

Gannett, Henry. *Boundaries of the United States and of the Several States and Territories: With an Outline of the History of All Important Changes of Territory*. 3rd ed. Bulletin of the United States Geological Survey 226. Washington, DC: Government Printing Office, 1904.

Garrison, Rebekah. "Settler Responsibility: Respatialising Dissent in 'America' beyond Continental Borders." *Shima* 13, no. 2 (2019): 56–75.

Gaynor, Jennifer L. *Intertidal History in Island Southeast Asia: Submerged Genealogy and the Legacy of Coastal Capture*. Ithaca, NY: Cornell University Press Southeast Asia Program Publications, 2016.

Gaynor, Jennifer L. "Liquid Territory: Subordination, Memory and Manuscripts among Sama People of Sulawesi's Southern Littoral." PhD diss., University of Michigan, 2005.

Geng, Jing. "The Legality of Foreign Military Activities in the Exclusive Economic Zone under UNCLOS." *Merkourios: Utrecht Journal of International and European Law* 28, no. 74 (2012): 22–30.

Getachew, Adom. *Worldmaking after Empire: The Rise and Fall of Self-Determination*. Princeton, NJ: Princeton University Press, 2019.

Ghosh, Ranjan, and J. Hillis Miller. *Thinking Literature across Continents*. Durham, NC: Duke University Press, 2016.

Giles, Paul. *Antipodean America: Australasia and the Constitution of U.S. Literature*. New York: Oxford University Press, 2013.

Giles, Paul. "Antipodean American Literature: Franklin, Twain, and the Sphere of Subalternity." *American Literary History* 20, nos. 1–2 (2008): 22–50.

Giles, Paul. "The Archipelagic Accretion." In Roberts and Stephens, *Archipelagic American Studies*, 427–35.

Giles, Paul. "The Deterritorialization of American Literature." In *Shades of the Planet: American Literature as World Literature*, edited by Wai Chee Dimock and Lawrence Buell, 39–61. Princeton, NJ: Princeton University Press, 2007.

Gillis, John R. *The Human Shore: Seacoasts in History*. Chicago: University of Chicago Press, 2012.

Gillis, John R. *Islands of the Mind: How the Human Imagination Created the Atlantic World*. New York: Palgrave Macmillan, 2004.

Gillis, John R. "Not Continents in Miniature: Islands as Ecotones." *Island Studies Journal* 9, no. 1 (2014): 155–66.

Gillman, Susan. "Black Jacobins and New World Mediterraneans." In *Surveying the American Tropics: A Literary Geography from New York to Rio*, edited by Maria Cristina Fumagalli, Peter Hulme, Owen Robinson, and Leslie Wylie, 159–82. Liverpool: Liverpool University Press, 2013.

Gillman, Susan. "Humboldt's American Mediterranean." *American Quarterly* 66, no. 3 (September 2014): 505–28.

Gillman, Susan. "It Takes an Archipelago to Compare Otherwise." In Roberts and Stephens, *Archipelagic American Studies*, 133–51.

Gillman, Susan. "The Newer Newest Thing: Reperiodizing, Redux." In *Timelines of American Literature*, edited by Cody Marrs and Christopher Hager, 307–16. Baltimore: Johns Hopkins University Press, 2019.

Gladwin, Harold Sterling. *Men out of Asia*. New York: McGraw-Hill, 1947.

Glissant, Édouard. *La cohée du Lamentin: Poétique V*. Paris: Gallimard, 2005.

Glissant, Édouard. "Europe and the Antilles: An Interview with Édouard Glissant," by Andrea Schwieger Hiepko. In *The Creolization of Theory*, edited by Françoise Lionnett and Shu-mei Shih, 255–61. Durham, NC: Duke University Press, 2011.

Glissant, Édouard. *Introduction à une Poétique du Divers*. Paris: Gallimard, 1996.

Glissant, Édouard. *Philosophie de la Relation: Poésie en étendue*. Paris: Gallimard, 2009.

Glissant, Édouard. *Poetics of Relation*. Translated by Betsy Wing. Ann Arbor: University of Michigan Press, 1997.

Glissant, Édouard. *Poétique de la Relation: Poétique III*. Paris: Gallimard, 1990.

Glissant, Édouard. "The Unforeseeable Diversity of the World." Translated by Haun Saussy. In *Beyond Dichotomies: Histories, Identities, Cultures, and the Challenge of Globalization*, edited by Elisabeth Mudimbe-Boyi, 287–96. Albany: State University of New York Press, 2002.

Glover, Kaiama L. *Haiti Unbound: A Spiralist Challenge to the Postcolonial Canon*. Liverpool: Liverpool University Press, 2010.

Goldstein, Alyosha. "Introduction: Toward a Genealogy of the U.S. Colonial Present." In *Formations of United States Colonialism*, edited by Alyosha Goldstein, 1–30. Durham, NC: Duke University Press, 2014.

Gómez, Myrriah. "Nuclear Alienation: A Literary Analysis of Race, Space, and Resistance Surrounding the Nuclear Coloniality of Los Alamos, 1942–2012." PhD diss., University of Texas at San Antonio, 2014.

Gómez-Barris, Macarena. *Beyond the Pink Tide: Art and Political Undercurrents in the Americas*. Oakland: University of California Press, 2018.

Gómez-Barris, Macarena, and Licia Fiol-Matta. "Introduction: Las Américas Quarterly." *American Quarterly* 66, no. 3 (September 2014): 493–504.

Gómez-Barris, Macarena, and May Joseph. "Coloniality and Islands." *Shima* 13, no. 2 (2019): 1–10.

Gott, J. Richard, III. "Boltzmann Brains—I'd Rather See Than Be One." Preprint, submitted February 2, 2008. https://arxiv.org/abs/0802.0233.

Goyal, Yogita, ed. *The Cambridge Companion to Transnational American Literature*. Cambridge: Cambridge University Press, 2017.

Grattan, Sean Austin. *Hope Isn't Stupid: Utopian Affects in Contemporary American Literature*. Iowa City: University of Iowa Press, 2017.

Greenspan, Brian. "Are Digital Humanists Utopian?" In *Debates in the Digital Humanities 2016*, edited by Matthew K. Gold and Lauren F. Klein. Minneapolis: University of Minnesota Press, 2016.

Grotius, Hugo. *The Freedom of the Seas; or, The Right Which Belongs to the Dutch to Take Part in the East Indian Trade*. 1609. Translated by Ralph van Deman Magoffin. New York: Oxford University Press, 1916.

Grove, Richard H. *Green Imperialism: Colonial Expansion, Tropical Island Edens and the Origins of Environmentalism, 1600–1860*. Cambridge: Cambridge University Press, 1995.

Gumbrecht, Hans Ulrich. *Production of Presence: What Meaning Cannot Convey*. Stanford, CA: Stanford University Press, 2004.

Gumbs, Alexis Pauline. *M Archive: After the End of the World*. Durham, NC: Duke University Press, 2018.

Guterl, Matthew Pratt. *American Mediterranean: Southern Slaveholders in the Age of Emancipation*. Cambridge, MA: Harvard University Press, 2008.

Habell-Pallán, Michelle. *Loca Motion: The Travels of Chicana and Latina Popular Culture*. New York: New York University Press, 2005.

Hakutani, Yoshinobu. *Haiku and Modernist Poetics*. New York: Palgrave Macmillan, 2009.

Hall, James Norman. *The Forgotten One and Other True Tales of the South Seas*. Introduction by Eugene Burdick. Boston: Little, Brown, 1963.

Hämäläinen, Pekka, and Samuel Truett. "On Borderlands." *Journal of American History* 98, no. 2 (September 2011): 338–61.

Handley, George B. *New World Poetics: Nature and the Adamic Imagination of Whitman, Neruda, and Walcott*. Athens: University of Georgia Press, 2007.

Handley, George B. "Toward an Environmental Phenomenology of Diaspora." *Modern Fiction Studies* 55, no. 3 (Fall 2009): 649–57.

Hansen, Jim. "Formalism and Its Malcontents: Benjamin and de Man on the Function of Allegory." *New Literary History* 35, no. 4 (Autumn 2005): 663–83.

Haraway, Donna J. "Situated Knowledges: The Science Question in Feminism and the Privilege of Partial Perspective." *Feminist Studies* 14, no. 3 (Autumn 1988): 575–99.

Haraway, Donna J. *Staying with the Trouble: Making Kin in the Chthulucene*. Durham, NC: Duke University Press, 2016.

Harman, Graham. "On the Undermining of Objects: Grant, Bruno, and Radical Philosophy." In *The Speculative Turn: Continental Materialism and Realism*, edited by Levi Bryant, Nick Srnicek, and Graham Harman, 21–40. Melbourne: re.press, 2011.

Harman, Graham. *Towards Speculative Realism: Essays and Lectures*. Winchester, UK: Zero Books, 2010.

Harman, Graham. *Weird Realism: Lovecraft and Philosophy*. Croydon, UK: Zero Books, 2012.

Harper, T. N. "Empire, Diaspora, and the Languages of Globalism, 1850–1914." In *Globalization in World History*, edited by A. G. Hopkins, 141–66. New York: Norton, 2002.

Hartle, James B., and Mark Srednicki. "Are We Typical?" *Physical Review D* 75, no. 123523 (2007): 1–6.

Hauʻofa, Epeli. "Our Sea of Islands." In Waddell, Naidu, and Hauʻofa, *New Oceania*, 2–16.

Hayles, N. Katherine. "Cognition on a Desert Island." *Genre* 33, nos. 3–4 (2000): 331–38.

Hegel, Georg Wilhelm Friedrich. *Lectures on the Philosophy of World History*. 1837. Translated by H. B. Nisbet. Introduction by Duncan Forbes. Reprint, New York: Cambridge University Press, 1975.

Heise, Ursula K. *Imagining Extinction: The Cultural Meanings of Endangered Species*. Chicago: University of Chicago Press, 2016.

Helmreich, Stefan. *Sounding the Limits of Life: Essays in the Anthropology of Biology and Beyond*. Princeton, NJ: Princeton University Press, 2016.

Hickel, Walter J. *Who Owns America?* Englewood Cliffs, NJ: Prentice-Hall, 1971.

Hickman, Jared. "Cosmic American Studies." *PMLA* 128, no. 4 (October 2013): 968–75.

Hill, Kimi Kodani, ed. *Chiura Obata's Topaz Moon*. Berkeley, CA: Heyday Books, 2000.

Hirabayashi, Lane Ryo. "Incarceration." In *Keywords for Asian American Studies*, edited by Cathy J. Schlund-Vials, Linda Trinh Võ, and K. Scott Wong, 133–38. New York: New York University Press, 2015.

Hirasuna, Delphine. *The Art of Gaman: Arts and Crafts from the Japanese American Internment Camps, 1942–1946*. Berkeley, CA: Ten Speed, 2005.

Hofmeister, Timothy, ed. "From Homer to *Omeros*: Derek Walcott's *Omeros* and *Odyssey*." Special issue, *Classical World* 93, no. 1 (September/October 1999).

Hofmeyr, Isabel. "Universalizing the Indian Ocean." *PMLA* 125, no. 3 (May 2010): 721–29.

Hohn, Donovan. "Moby-Duck, or, The Synthetic Wilderness of Childhood." *Creative Nonfiction* 35, no. 2 (2008): 74–130.

Holmes, Oliver Wendell. "The Chambered Nautilus." In *Illustrated Poems of Oliver Wendell Holmes*, 31–32. Boston: Houghton, Mifflin, 1885.

Homer. *The Odyssey*. Translated by E. V. Rieu and D. C. H. Rieu. Revised by D. C. H. Rieu. London: Penguin, 2003.

Howard, Jeffrey L. "Proposal to Add Anthrostratigraphic and Technostratigraphic Units to the Stratigraphic Code for Classification of Anthropogenic Holocene Deposits." *Holocene* 24, no. 12 (2014): 1856–61.

Hsu, Madeline Y. "Hierarchies of Migration Rights: Ideology and Law in the 1917 Barred Zone Act." Keynote address for Migration with(out) Boundaries: An Interdisciplinary Graduate Conference on Migration, Michigan State University, East Lansing, Michigan, October 6–7, 2017.

Hughes, Langston. *The Weary Blues*. New York: Knopf, 1926.

Huie, Shirley Fenton. *The Forgotten Ones: Women and Children under Nippon*. Pymble, Australia: HarperCollins, 1992.

Hurston, Zora Neale. "Crazy for This Democracy." In *Folklore, Memoirs, and Other Writings*, edited by Cheryl A. Wall, 945–49. New York: Library of America, 1995.

Hurston, Zora Neale. *Dust Tracks on a Road*. 1942. Reprint, New York: Harper Perennial, 1996.

Hurston, Zora Neale. *Tell My Horse*. 1938. Reprint, New York: Perennial Library, 1990.

Hurston, Zora Neale. *Their Eyes Were Watching God*. 1937. Reprint, New York: Perennial Classics, 1998.

Hurston, Zora Neale. *Zora Neale Hurston: A Life in Letters*. Edited by Carla Kaplan. New York: Doubleday, 2002.

Igler, David. *The Great Ocean: Pacific Worlds from Captain Cook to the Gold Rush*. New York: Oxford University Press, 2013.

Immerwahr, Daniel. *How to Hide an Empire: A History of the Greater United States*. New York: Farrar, Straus and Giroux, 2019.

Ingersoll, Karin Amimoto. *Waves of Knowing: A Seascape Epistemology*. Durham, NC: Duke University Press, 2016.

Ingraham, W. James, Jr., and Curtis C. Ebbesmeyer. "Surface Current Concentration of Floating Marine Debris in the North Pacific Ocean: 12-Year OSCURS Model Experiments." In *Proceedings of the International Marine Debris Conference on Derelict Fishing Gear and the Ocean Environment, 6–11 August 2000*, edited by N. McIntosh, K. Simonds, M. Donohue, C. Brammer, S. Manson, and S. Carbajal, 90–115. Honolulu: Hawaiian Islands Humpback Whale National Marine Sanctuary, U.S. Department of Commerce, 2001.

Ingstad, Anne Stine. *The Discovery of a Norse Settlement in America: Excavations at L'Anse aux Meadows, Newfoundland, 1961–1968*. Oslo: Universitetsforlaget, 1977.

Jackson, Mike, Mario Antonioletti, Alastair Hume, Tobias Blanke, Gabriel Bodard, Mark Hedges, and Shrija Rajbhandari. "Building Bridges between Islands of Data—An Investigation into Distributed Data Management in the Humanities." *Fifth IEEE International Conference on e-Science* (2009): 33–39.

Jagota, S. P. *Maritime Boundary*. Dordrecht: Martinus Nijhoff, 1985.

James, Jack, and Earle Weller. *Treasure Island, "The Magic City," 1939–1940: The Story of the Golden Gate International Exposition*. San Francisco: Pisani, 1941.

Johnson, Elizabeth R., and Irus Braverman. "Blue Legalities: Governing More-Than-Human Oceans." In *Blue Legalities: The Life and Laws of the Sea*, edited by Irus Braverman and Elizabeth R. Johnson, 1–24. Durham, NC: Duke University Press, 2020.

Johnson, James Weldon. "Life." In *Fifty Years and Other Poems*, 49. Boston: Cornhill, 1917.

Jones, Mark. "Perspectives: Albatrosses and Man through the Ages." In *Albatross: Their World, Their Ways*, edited by Tui De Roy, Mark Jones, and Julian Fitter, 138–47. Buffalo, NY: Firefly Books, 2008.

Jones, Terry L., Alice A. Storey, Elizabeth A. Matisoo-Smith, and José Miguel Ramírez-Aliaga, eds. *Polynesians in America: Pre-Columbian Contacts with the New World*. Lanham, MD: AltaMira, 2011.

Joseph, May. *Fluid New York: Cosmopolitan Urbanism and the Green Imagination*. Durham, NC: Duke University Press, 2013.

Kabutaulaka, Tarcisius Tara. "The Bigness of Our Smallness." In Waddell, Naidu, and Hauʻofa, *New Oceania*, 91–93.

Kaplan, Amy. *The Anarchy of Empire in the Making of U.S. Culture*. Cambridge, MA: Harvard University Press, 2002.

Kaplan, Amy. "A Call for a Truce." *American Literary History* 17, no. 1 (Spring 2005): 141–47.

Kaplan, Amy. "Manifest Domesticity." *American Literature* 70, no. 3 (September 1998): 581–606.

Kaplan, Amy, and Donald E. Pease, eds. *Cultures of United States Imperialism*. Durham, NC: Duke University Press, 1993.

Karem, Jeff. *The Purloined Islands: Caribbean-U.S. Crosscurrents in Literature and Culture, 1880–1959*. Charlottesville: University of Virginia Press, 2011.

Karuka, Manu. *Empire's Tracks: Indigenous Nations, Chinese Workers, and the Transcontinental Railroad*. Oakland: University of California Press, 2019.

Katayama, Taro. "Digressions." *Trek* (December 1942): 28–29.

Katayama, Taro. "Digressions." *Trek* (February 1943): 40–41.

Katayama, Taro. "Digressions." *Trek* (June 1943): 40–41.

Katayama, Taro. "Nightmare." *Trek* (December 1942): 25.

Katayama, Taro. "State of the City." *Trek* (December 1942): 2–11.

Kay, Marshall. *North American Geosynclines*. Geological Society of America Memoir 48. 1951. Reprint, New York: Geological Society of America, 1963.

Keegan, William F., and Lisabeth A. Carlson. *Talking Taíno: Caribbean Natural History from a Native Perspective*. Tuscaloosa: University of Alabama Press, 2008.

Keene, Donald. *World within Walls: Japanese Literature of the Pre-Modern Era, 1600–1867*. 1978. Reprint, New York: Columbia University Press, 1999.

Kent, Alicia A. *African, Native, and Jewish American Literature and the Reshaping of Modernism*. New York: Palgrave, 2007.

Kent, H. S. K. "The Historical Origins of the Three-Mile Limit." *American Journal of International Law* 48, no. 4 (1954): 537–53.

Keown, Michelle. *Postcolonial Pacific Writing: Representations of the Body*. London: Routledge, 2005.

Kerrigan, John. *Archipelagic English: Literature, History, and Politics, 1603–1707*. Oxford: Oxford University Press, 2008.

Kheng, Cheah Boon. *Red Star over Malaya: Resistance and Social Conflict during and after the Japanese Occupation of Malaya, 1941–46*. 4th ed. Singapore: National University of Singapore Press, 2012.

King, Tiffany Lethabo. *The Black Shoals: Offshore Formations of Black and Native Studies*. Durham, NC: Duke University Press, 2019.

Kirch, Patrick Vinton, and Roger C. Green. *Hawaiki, Ancestral Polynesia: An Essay in Historical Anthropology*. Cambridge: Cambridge University Press, 2001.

Kirschenbaum, Matthew G. "What Is Digital Humanities and What's It Doing in English Departments?" *ADE Bulletin* 150 (2010): 55–61.

Kirimura, Evelyn. "Toppats and Co." *All Aboard!* Spring 1944: 8–14.

Kirksey, Eben. *Emergent Ecologies*. Durham, NC: Duke University Press, 2015.

Ko, Dorothy. *The Social Life of Inkstones: Artisans and Scholars in Early Qing China*. Seattle: University of Washington Press, 2017.

Kolodny, Annette. *In Search of First Contact: The Vikings of Vinland, the Peoples of the Dawnland, and the Anglo-American Anxiety of Discovery*. Durham, NC: Duke University Press, 2012.

Koperski, Jeffrey. *The Physics of Theism: God, Physics, and the Philosophy of Science*. Malden, MA: John Wiley and Sons, 2015.

Kusumaatmadja, Mochtar. "The Legal Regime of Archipelagoes: Problems and Issues." In *The Law of the Sea: Needs and Interests of Developing Countries—Proceedings of the Seventh Annual Conference of the Law of the Sea Institute, June 26–29, 1972, at the University of Rhode Island, Kingston, Rhode Island*, edited by Lewis M. Alexander, 166–72. Kingston: University of Rhode Island, 1973.

Kusumaatmadja, Mochtar. "Supplementary Remarks." In *The Law of the Sea: Needs and Interests of Developing Countries—Proceedings of the Seventh Annual Conference of the Law of the Sea Institute, June 26–29, 1972, at the University of Rhode Island, Kingston, Rhode Island*, edited by Lewis M. Alexander, 172–77. Kingston: University of Rhode Island, 1973.

Lai, Paul. "Discontiguous States of America: The Paradox of Unincorporation in Craig Santos Perez's Poetics of Chamorro Guam." *Journal of Transnational American Studies* 3, no. 2 (2011): 1–29.

Lamming, George. *The Pleasures of Exile*. 1960. Reprint, London: Pluto Press, 2005.

Lamothe, Daphne. *Inventing the New Negro: Narrative, Culture, and Ethnography*. Philadelphia: University of Pennsylvania Press, 2008.

Lang, Julian. "Reflections on the Iridescent One." In *Abalone Tales: Collaborative Explorations of Sovereignty and Identity in Native California*, by Les W. Field, with Cheryl Seidner, Julian Lang, Rosemary Cambra, Florence Silva, Vivien Hailstone, Darlene Marshall, Bradley Marshall, Callie Lara, Merv George Sr., and the Cultural Committee of the Yurok Tribe, 84–106. Durham, NC: Duke University Press, 2008.

Larsen, Olga Popovic. *Reciprocal Frame Architecture*. Oxford: Architectural Press, 2008.

Latour, Bruno. *Facing Gaia: Eight Lectures on the New Climatic Regime*. 2015. Translated by Catherine Porter. Cambridge, UK: Polity, 2017.

Latour, Bruno. *We Have Never Been Modern*. Translated by Catherine Porter. Cambridge, MA: Harvard University Press, 1993.

Lebreton, Laurent C. M., B. Slat, F. Ferrari, B. Sainte-Rose, J. Aitken, R. Marthouse, S. Hajbane, et al. "Evidence That the Great Pacific Garbage Patch Is Rapidly Accumulating Plastic." *Scientific Reports* 8 (2018): n.p.

Lebreton, Laurent C. M., Joost van der Zwet, Jan-Willem Damsteeg, Boyan Slat, Anthony Andrady, and Julia Reisser. "River Plastic Emissions to the World's Oceans." *Nature Communications* 8, no. 15611 (June 7, 2017). https://www.nature.com/articles/ncomms15611.

Lee, Anthony W. *Painting on the Left: Diego Rivera, Radical Politics, and San Francisco's Public Murals*. Berkeley: University of California Press, 1999.

Levine, Caroline. *Forms: Whole, Rhythm, Hierarchy, Network*. Princeton, NJ: Princeton University Press, 2015.

Levine, Robert S., gen. ed. *The Norton Anthology of American Literature*. 9th ed. New York: W. W. Norton, 2016.

Levinson, Marjorie. "What Is New Formalism?" PMLA 122, no. 2 (March 2007): 558–69.

Lewis, Martin W., and Kären E. Wigen. *The Myth of Continents: A Critique of Metageography*. Berkeley: University of California Press, 1997.

Lewis, R. W. B. *The American Adam: Innocence, Tragedy, and Tradition in the Nineteenth Century*. 1955. Reprint, Chicago: University of Chicago Press, 1959.

Liebling, A. J. *The Earl of Louisiana*. 1961. Updated ed. Baton Rouge: Louisiana State University Press, 2008.

Liittschwager, David, and Susan Middleton. *Archipelago: Portraits of Life in the World's Most Remote Island Sanctuary*. Washington, DC: National Geographic, 2005.

Limón, José E. *American Encounters: Greater Mexico, the United States, and the Erotics of Culture*. Boston: Beacon, 1998.

Limón, José E. "Greater Mexico, Modernism, and New York: Miguel Covarrubias and José Limón." In *The Covarrubias Circle: Nickolas Muray's Collection of Twentieth-Century Mexican Art*, general editor Kurt Heinzelman, art curator Peter Mears, 83–102. Austin: University of Texas Press, 2004.

Linde, Andrei. "Sinks in the Landscape, Boltzmann Brains and the Cosmological Constant Problem." *Journal of Cosmology and Astroparticle Physics* 1, no. 022 (2007): 1–39.

Lionnet, Françoise. "Continents and Archipelagoes: From *E Pluribus Unum* to Creolized Solidarities." PMLA 123, no. 5 (October 2008): 1503–15.

Lipman, Andrew. *The Saltwater Frontier: Indians and the Contest for the American Coast*. New Haven, CT: Yale University Press, 2015.

Lippmann, Walter. *The Cold War: A Study in U.S. Foreign Policy*. 1947. Reprint, New York: Harper Torchbooks, 1972.

Lipsitz, George. "Our America." *American Literary History* 17, no. 1 (Spring 2005): 135–40.

Loe, Hikmet Sidney, ed. *The Spiral Jetty Encyclo: Exploring Robert Smithson's Earthwork through Time and Place*. Salt Lake City: University of Utah Press, 2017.

Loe, Hikmet Sidney. "*Spiral Jetty*, The Film." In Loe, *Spiral Jetty Encyclo*, 256–57.

Lohman, S. W. *Geology of Canyonlands*. Illustrated by John R. Stacy. Geological Survey Bulletin 1327. Washington, DC: Government Printing Office, 1974.

Lovecraft, H. P. "The Call of Cthulhu." In *Tales of the Cthulhu Mythos: Golden Anniversary Anthology*, 3–32. Sauk City, WI: Arkham House, 1990.

Lovelock, James. *The Revenge of Gaia: Earth's Climate Crisis and the Fate of Humanity*. New York: Basic Books, 2006.

Lowe, John. "Materials." In *Approaches to Teaching Hurston's* Their Eyes Were Watching God *and Other Works*, edited by John Lowe, 5–12. New York: Modern Language Association, 2009.

Lowe, Lisa. *Immigrant Acts: On Asian American Cultural Politics*. Durham, NC: Duke University Press, 1996.

Lowe, Lisa. *The Intimacies of Four Continents*. Durham, NC: Duke University Press, 2015.

Lubis, Mochtar. *Perlawatan ke Amerika Serikat*. Jakarta: Usaha Penerbitan Gapura, 1952.

Lutkehaus, Nancy C. "Miguel Covarrubias and the Pageant of the Pacific: The Golden Gate International Exposition and the Idea of the Transpacific, 1939–1940." In *Transpacific Studies: Framing an Emerging Field*, edited by Janet Hoskins and Viet Thanh Nguyen, 109–33. Honolulu: University of Hawai'i Press, 2014.

Lyons, Paul. *American Pacificism: Oceania in the U.S. Imagination*. New York: Routledge, 2006.

Lyons, Paul, and Ty P. Kāwika Tengan. "Introduction: Pacific Currents." *American Quarterly* 67, no. 3 (September 2015): 545–74.

Lyotard, Jean-François. "The Sublime and the Avant-Garde." In *The Continental Aesthetics Reader*, edited by Clive Cazeaux, 453–64. London: Routledge, 2000.

Mack, Doug. *The Not-Quite States of America: Dispatches from the Territories and Other Far-Flung Outposts of the USA*. New York: Norton, 2017.

Mahmud, Zaharah binti Haji. "The Malay Concept of *Tanah Air*: The Geographer's Perspective." In *Memory and Knowledge of the Sea in Southeast Asia*, edited by Danny Wong Tze Ken, 5–14. Institute of Ocean and Earth Sciences Monograph 3. Kuala Lumpur: University of Malaya, 2008.

Maldonado-Torres, Nelson. "Post-Continental Philosophy: Its Definition, Contours, and Fundamental Sources." *Worlds and Knowledges Otherwise* 1, no. 3 (Fall 2006): 1–29.

Malkin, Irad. *A Small Greek World: Networks in the Ancient Mediterranean*. New York: Oxford University Press, 2011.

Mallos, Nicholas. "Turning the Tide on Marine Debris." In *Gyre: The Plastic Ocean*, edited by Julie Decker, 74–96. London: Booth-Clibborn, 2014.

Mandelbrot, Benoit. *The Fractal Geometry of Nature*. 1982. Updated and augmented ed. New York: W. H. Freeman, 2006.

Mandelbrot, Benoit B. "How Long Is the Coast of Britain? Statistical Self-Similarity and Fractal Dimension." *Science*, n.s., 156, no. 3775 (1967): 636–38.

Mandelbrot, Benoit B., and Richard L. Hudson. *The (Mis)Behavior of Markets: A Fractal View of Financial Turbulence*. 2004. Reprint, New York: Basic Books, 2006.

Manovich, Lev. "The Science of Culture? Social Computing, Digital Humanities and Cultural Analytics." Preprint, May 23, 2016, 7. https://osf.io/preprints/socarxiv/b2y79/.

Marsh, Selina Tusitala. "Theory 'versus' Pacific Islands Writing: Toward a *Tama'ita'i* Criticism in the Works of Three Pacific Islands Woman Poets." In *Inside Out: Literature, Cultural Politics, and Identity in the New Pacific*, edited by Vilsoni Hereniko and Rob Wilson, 337–56. Lanham, MD: Rowman and Littlefield, 1999.

Martin, Craig. *Los Alamos Place Names*. 2nd ed. Los Alamos, NM: Bathtub Row, 2012.

Martínez, Oscar J. *Troublesome Border*. Tucson: University of Arizona Press, 1988.

Martínez-San Miguel, Yolanda. "Colonial and Mexican Archipelagoes: Reimagining Colonial Caribbean Studies." In Roberts and Stephens, *Archipelagic American Studies*, 155–73.

Martínez-San Miguel, Yolanda, and Michelle Stephens, eds. *Contemporary Archipelagic Thinking: Towards New Comparative Methodologies and Disciplinary Formations*. Lanham, MD: Rowman and Littlefield, 2020.

Marx, Leo. *The Machine in the Garden: Technology and the Pastoral Ideal in America*. 1964. Reprint, New York: Oxford University Press, 1967.

McCall, Grant. "Nissology: A Proposal for Consideration." *Journal of the Pacific Society* 17, nos. 2–3 (1994): 1–14.

McCallus, Joseph P. *Forgotten under a Tropical Sun: War Stories by American Veterans in the Philippines, 1898–1913*. Kent, OH: Kent State University Press, 2017.

McCarty, Willard. "Tree, Turf, Centre, Archipelago—or Wild Acre? Metaphors and Stories for Humanities Computing." *Literary and Linguistic Computing* 21, no. 1 (2006): 1–13.

McDougall, Brandy Nālani. "'We Are Not American': Competing Rhetorical Archipelagoes in Hawai'i." In Roberts and Stephens, *Archipelagic American Studies*, 259–78.

McGann, Mary, Doris Sloan, and Elmira Wan. "Biostratigraphy beneath Central San Francisco Bay along the San Francisco–Oakland Bay Bridge Transect." In *Crustal Structure of the Coastal and Marine San Francisco Bay Region, California*, edited by Tom Parsons, 11–28. Professional Paper 1658, US Department of the Interior, US Geological Survey. Washington, DC: Government Printing Office, 2002.

McGurl, Mark. "The New Cultural Geology." *Twentieth-Century Literature* 57, nos. 3–4 (2011): 380–90.

McGurl, Mark. "The Posthuman Comedy." *Critical Inquiry* 38, no. 3 (Spring 2012): 533–53.

McHenry, Donald F. *Micronesia: Trust Betrayed, Altruism vs Self Interest in American Foreign Policy*. New York: Carnegie Endowment for International Peace, 1975.

McIntyre, Angus. "The 'Greater Indonesia' Idea of Nationalism in Malaya and Indonesia." *Modern Asian Studies* 7, no. 1 (1973): 75–83.

McIntyre, James P. "Three Practical Jokes: A Key to Huck's Changing Attitude toward Jim." *Modern Fiction Studies* 14, no. 1 (Spring 1968): 33–37.

McKittrick, Katherine. *Demonic Grounds: Black Women and the Cartographies of Struggle*. Minneapolis: University of Minnesota Press, 2006.

McKittrick, Katherine. "Mathematics Black Life." *Black Scholar* 44, no. 2 (Summer 2014): 16–28.

McPhee, John. *Basin and Range*. 1981. Reprint, New York: Farrar, Straus and Giroux, 1982.

Meehan, Kevin. *People Get Ready: African American and Caribbean Cultural Exchange*. Jackson: University Press of Mississippi, 2009.

Meillassoux, Quentin. *After Finitude: An Essay on the Necessity of Contingency*. Translated by Ray Brassier. London: Continuum, 2008.

Meller, Norman. *The Congress of Micronesia: Development of the Legislative Process in the Trust Territory of the Pacific Islands*. With the assistance of Terza Meller. Honolulu: University of Hawai'i Press, 1969.

Melville, Herman. *Moby-Dick: An Authoritative Text (Norton Critical Edition)*. 1851. Edited by Harrison Hayford and Hershel Parker. New York: W. W. Norton, 1967.

Mentz, Steve, and Martha Elena Rojas. "Introduction: 'The Hungry Ocean.'" In *The Sea and Nineteenth-Century Anglophone Literary Culture*, edited by Steve Mentz and Martha Elena Rojas, 1–14. New York: Routledge, 2017.

Merivale, Patricia. "Audible Palimpsests: Coetzee's Kafka." In *Critical Perspectives on J. M. Coetzee*, edited by Graham Huggan and Stephen Watson, 152–67. New York: St. Martin's, 1996.

Merkl, Ulrich. *Dinomania: The Lost Art of Winsor McCay, the Secret Origins of King Kong, and the Urge to Destroy New York*. Seattle: Fantagraphics, 2015.

Mewburn, Charity. "Oil, Art, and Politics: The Feminization of Mexico." *Anales del Instituto de Investigaciones Estéticas* 72 (1998): 73–133.

Meyer, Kenneth A., dir. *The Golden Spike*. 1969. Remastered and revised, Tucson, AZ: Western National Parks Association, 2006.

Michener, James A. *Hawaii*. 1959. Reprint, New York: Random House, 2002.

Mignolo, Walter D. *Local Histories/Global Designs: Coloniality, Subaltern Knowledges, and Border Thinking*. Princeton, NJ: Princeton University Press, 2000.

Mignolo, Walter D., and Madina V. Tlostanova. "Theorizing from the Borders: Shifting to Geo- and Body-Politics of Knowledge." *European Journal of Social Theory* 9, no 2 (2006): 205–21.

Mignolo, Walter D., and Catherine E. Walsh. *On Decoloniality: Concepts, Analytics, Praxis*. Durham, NC: Duke University Press, 2018.

Milligan, Ian. *History in the Age of Abundance? How the Web Is Transforming Historical Research*. Montreal: McGill-Queen's University Press, 2019.

Minow, Martha. "The Enduring Burdens of the Universal and the Different in the Insular Cases." In *Reconsidering the Insular Cases: The Past and Future of the American Empire*, edited by Gerald L. Neuman and Tomiko Brown-Nagin, vii–xvi. Cambridge, MA: Harvard University Press, 2015.

Mitchell, W. J. T. "The Commitment to Form; or, Still Crazy after All These Years." *PMLA* 118, no. 2 (2003): 321–25.

Moore, Charles. *Plastic Ocean: How a Sea Captain's Chance Discovery Launched a Determined Quest to Save the Oceans*. With Cassandra Phillips. New York: Avery, 2011.

Moore, Charles James. "Synthetic Polymers in the Marine Environment: A Rapidly Increasing, Long-Term Threat." *Environmental Research* 108, no. 2 (October 2008): 131–39.

Moore, Raymond C., Cecil G. Lalicker, and Alfred G. Fischer. *Invertebrate Fossils*. New York: McGraw-Hill, 1952.

Moretti, Franco. *Distant Reading*. London: Verso, 2013.

Moretti, Franco. *Far Country: Scenes from American Culture*. New York: Farrar, Straus and Giroux, 2019.

Moretti, Franco. *Graphs, Maps, Trees*. 2005. Reprint, London: Verso, 2007.

Mori, Toshio. "Topaz Station." *Trek* (December 1942): 24–25.

Mori, Toshio. *Yokohama, California*. Caldwell, ID: Caxton Printers, 1949.

Morrison, Toni. *Playing in the Dark: Whiteness and the Literary Imagination*. New York: Vintage, 1993.

Morton, Timothy. *Hyperobjects: Philosophy and Ecology after the End of the World*. Minneapolis: University of Minnesota Press, 2013.

Morton, Timothy. "Molten Entities." In *New Geographies 08: Island*, edited by Daniel Daou and Pablo Pérez-Ramos, 72–75. Cambridge, MA: Harvard University Graduate School of Design, 2016.

Mullarkey, John. *Post-Continental Philosophy: An Outline*. London: Continuum, 2006.

Munavvar, Mohamed. *Ocean States: Archipelagic Regimes in the Law of the Sea*. Dordrecht: Martinus Nijhoff, 1995.

Muñoz, José Esteban. *Cruising Utopia: The Then and There of Queer Futurity*. New York: New York University Press, 2009.

Murdock, Luke S. *Palm Beach and West Palm Beach: The Palm Beaches, "Where Summer Spends the Winter."* West Palm Beach, FL: Long and Murdock, 1926.

NAACP. *Fourteenth Annual Report of the National Association for the Advancement of Colored People for the Year 1923: A Summary of Work and an Accounting*. New York: NAACP, 1924.

Nadarajah, Yaso, and Adam Grydehøj. "Island Studies as a Decolonial Project." *Island Studies Journal* 11, no. 2 (2016): 437–46.

Nagel, Alexander, and Christopher S. Wood. *Anachronic Renaissance*. Brooklyn, NY: Zone Books, 2020.

Nail, Thomas. *Theory of the Border*. New York: Oxford University Press, 2016.

Na'puti, Tiara R., and Michael Lujan Bevacqua. "Militarization and Resistance from Guåhan: Protecting and Defending Pågat." *American Quarterly* 67, no. 3 (September 2015): 837–58.

National Park Service and the American Samoa Government. *National Park Feasibility Study, American Samoa: Draft*. National Park Service and the American Samoa Government, July 1988. Accessed August 31, 2020. http://npshistory.com/publications/npsa/feasibility-study.pdf.

National Science and Technology Council. *The United States as an Ocean Nation: Scientific Research Priorities and Progress*. Edited by Mikkel Jorgensen. New York: Nova, 2013.

Navakas, Michele Currie. *Liquid Landscape: Geography and Settlement at the Edge of Early America*. Philadelphia: University of Pennsylvania Press, 2018.

Navy Department. *Information on the Trust Territory of the Pacific Islands, Transmitted by the United States to the Secretary-General of the United Nations Pursuant to Article 88 of the Charter*. Washington, DC: Navy Department, 1948.

Newman, William L. *Geologic Time: The Age of the Earth*. Washington, DC: United States Department of the Interior Geological Survey, Government Printing Office, 1977.

Niedenthal, Jack. *For the Good of Mankind: A History of the People of Bikini and Their Islands*. 2001. 2nd ed. Majuro, Republic of the Marshall Islands: Bravo Publishers, 2013.

Noble, Safiya Umoja. *Algorithms of Oppression: How Search Engines Reinforce Racism*. New York: New York University Press, 2018.

Noodin, Margaret. "Megwa Baabaamiiaayaayaang Dibaajomoyaang: Anishinaabe Literature as Memory in Motion." In *The Oxford Handbook of Indigenous American Literature*, edited by James H. Cox and Daniel Heath Justice, 175–84. New York: Oxford University Press, 2014.

Norris, Benjamin. "Re-asking the Question of the Gendered Subject after Non-philosophy." *Speculations: A Journal of Speculative Realism* III (2012): 7–42.

Noudelmann, François. "Literature: The Archipelago Perspective." *Interdisciplinary Literary Studies* 20, no. 2 (2018): 203–16.

Obama, Barack. "Northeast Canyons and Seamounts Marine National Monument" (Proclamation 9496, September 15, 2016). *Federal Register: The Daily Journal of the United States Government* 81, no. 183 (September 21, 2016): 65161–67. https://www.govinfo.gov/content/pkg/FR-2016-09-21/pdf/2016-22921.pdf.

Obama, Barack. "Pacific Remote Islands Marine National Monument Expansion" (Proclamation 9173, September 25, 2014). *Federal Register: The Daily Journal of the United States Government* 79, no. 188 (September 29, 2014): 58645–53. https://www.govinfo.gov/content/pkg/FR-2014-09-29/pdf/2014-23319.pdf.

Obama, Barack. "Papahānaumokuākea Marine National Monument Expansion" (Proclamation 9478, August 26, 2016). *Federal Register: The Daily Journal of the United States Government* 81, no. 169 (August 31, 2016): 60227–34. https://www.govinfo.gov/content/pkg/FR-2016-08-31/pdf/2016-21138.pdf.

Obama, Barack. "Stewardship of the Ocean, Our Coasts, and the Great Lakes" (Executive Order 13547, July 19, 2010). *Federal Register: The Daily Journal of the United States Government* 75, no. 140 (July 22, 2010): 43023–27. https://www.govinfo.gov/content/pkg/FR-2010-07-22/pdf/2010-18169.pdf.

O'Connell, D. P. "Mid-Ocean Archipelagos in International Law." *British Yearbook of International Law* 45 (1971): 1–77.

Oegroseno, Arif Havas. "Indonesia's Maritime Boundaries." In *Indonesia beyond the Water's Edge: Managing an Archipelagic State*, edited by Robert Cribb and Michele Ford, 49–58. Singapore: Institute of Southeast Asian Studies, 2009.

Okihiro, Gary Y. "Island Race." *International Journal of Okinawan Studies* 3, no. 1 (June 2012): 39–42.

Okihiro, Gary Y. *Island World: A History of Hawai'i and the United States.* Berkeley: University of California Press, 2008.

Okubo, Miné. *Citizen 13660.* 1946. Reprint, Seattle: University of Washington Press, 1983.

Orfield, Lester B. "The Citizenship Act of 1934." *University of Chicago Law Review* 2, no. 1 (December 1934): 99–118.

Osiander, Andreas. "Sovereignty, International Relations, and the Westphalian Myth." *International Organization* 55, no. 2 (Spring 2001): 251–87.

Otsuka, Julie. *When the Emperor Was Divine.* New York: Anchor Books, 2002.

Pacific House. "A Pageant of the Pacific." In *Pageant of the Pacific,* by Miguel Covarrubias, 5. 1940. Rev. ed. [San Francisco]: Pacific House, 1943.

Pacific Island Treaties: Hearing before the Committee on Foreign Relations . . . December 1, 1981. Washington, DC: Government Printing Office, 1982.

Pack, Frederick J. *Lake Bonneville: A Popular Treatise Dealing with the History and Physical Aspects of Lake Bonneville.* Bulletin of the University of Utah 30, no. 4. Salt Lake City: University of Utah, 1939.

Pack, Sasha D. *The Deepest Border: The Strait of Gibraltar and the Making of the Modern Hispano-African Borderland.* Stanford, CA: Stanford University Press, 2019.

Page, Don N. "Cosmological Ontology and Epistemology." In *The Philosophy of Cosmology,* edited by Khalil Chamcham, Joseph Silk, John D. Barrow, and Simon Saunders, 317–29. Cambridge: Cambridge University Press, 2017.

Page, Don N. "Is Our Universe Likely to Decay within 20 Billion Years?" *Physical Review D* 78, no. 063535 (2008): 1–6.

Page, Don N. "Susskind's Challenge to the Hartle–Hawking No-Boundary Proposal and Possible Resolutions." *Journal of Cosmology and Astroparticle Physics* 1, no. 4 (2007): 1–20.

Paine, Thomas. *Common Sense and Related Writings.* Edited by Thomas P. Slaughter. Boston: Bedford, 2001.

Paredes, Américo. "The Rio Grande." 1934. In *Between Two Worlds,* 15–16. Houston: Arte Público, 1991.

Paredes, Américo. *A Texas-Mexican Cancionero: Folksongs of the Lower Border.* Urbana: University of Illinois Press, 1976.

Parrington, Vernon Louis. *Main Currents in American Thought: An Interpretation of American Literature from the Beginnings to 1920.* 1927. Reprint, New York: Harcourt, Brace, 1930.

Pavlić, Edward M. *Crossroads Modernism: Descent and Emergence in African-American Literary Culture.* Minneapolis: University of Minnesota Press, 2002.

Pease, Donald. "Re-thinking 'American Studies after US Exceptionalism.'" *American Literary History* 21, no. 1 (Spring 2009): 19–27.

Perez, Craig Santos. *From Unincorporated Territory [hacha].* Kāneʻohe, HI: Tinfish, 2008.

Perez, Craig Santos. "Guam and Archipelagic American Studies." In Roberts and Stephens, *Archipelagic American Studies,* 97–112.

Perez, Craig Santos. "Transterritorial Currents and the Imperial Terripelago." *American Quarterly* 67, no 3 (September 2015): 619–24.

Perloff, Marjorie. "Removing the Eggshells: Rereading Wittgenstein on a Desert Island." *Genre* 33, nos. 3–4 (Fall–Winter 2000): 269–77.

Planck Collaboration. "*Planck* 2015 Results." *Astronomy and Astrophysics* 594, no. A13 (2016): 1–63.

Poirier, Richard. *A World Elsewhere: The Place of Style in American Literature*. New York: Oxford University Press, 1966.

Pollmann, Tessel. "Margaret Mead's Balinese: The Fitting Symbols of the American Dream." *Indonesia*, no. 49 (April 1990): 1–35.

Posmentier, Sonya. *Cultivation and Catastrophe: The Lyric Ecology of Modern Black Literature*. Baltimore, MD: Johns Hopkins University Press, 2017.

Posner, Miriam. "Data Trouble." Keynote address for DHU 4: Fourth Utah Symposium on the Digital Humanities, Weber State University, Ogden, Utah, February 2, 2019.

Pound, Ezra. "Hugh Selwyn Mauberley (Life and Contacts)." 1920. In *Modernism: An Anthology*, edited by Lawrence Rainey, 48–61. Padstow, UK: Blackwell, 2005.

Povinelli, Elizabeth A. *Geontologies: A Requiem to Late Liberalism*. Durham, NC: Duke University Press, 2016.

Pratt, Mary Louise. *Imperial Eyes: Travel Writing and Transculturation*. London: Routledge, 1992.

Price, Patricia L. *Dry Place: Landscapes of Belonging and Exclusion*. Minneapolis: University of Minnesota Press, 2004.

Pugh, Jonathan. "Island Movements: Thinking with the Archipelago." *Island Studies Journal* 8, no. 1 (2013): 9–24.

Pugh, Jonathan. "The Relational Turn in Island Geographies: Bringing Together Island, Sea and Ship Relations and the Case of Landship." *Social and Cultural Geography* 17, no. 8 (2016): 1040–59.

Quijano, Aníbal. "Coloniality of Power and Eurocentrism in Latin America." *International Sociology* 15, no. 2 (June 2000): 215–32.

Quintero Herencia, Juan Carlos. *La hoja de mar: Efecto archipiélago I*. Leiden: Almenara, 2016.

Radway, Janice. "What's in a Name? Presidential Address to the American Studies Association, 20 November, 1998." *American Quarterly* 51, no. 1 (March 1999): 1–32.

Raffety, Matthew. "Recent Currents in the Nineteenth-Century American Maritime History." *History Compass* 6, no. 2 (2008): 607–26.

Ramsay, David. "Dr. Ramsay's Oration." 1778. In *Principles and Acts of the Revolution in America*, edited by H. Niles, 374–83. 1822. Reprint, New York: Barnes, 1876.

Ransom, John Crowe. "Criticism, Inc." *Virginia Quarterly Review* 13, no. 4 (Autumn 1937): 586–602.

Ratuva, Sitiveni. "David vs Goliath." In Waddell, Naidu, and Hauʻofa, *New Oceania*, 94–97.

Rauzon, Mark J. *Isles of Amnesia: The History, Geography, and Restoration of America's Forgotten Pacific Islands*. Honolulu: University of Hawaiʻi Press, 2016.

Rebert, Paula. "Drawing the Line." In *Mapping Latin America: A Cartographic Reader*, edited by Jordana Dym and Karl Offen, 159–62. Chicago: University of Chicago Press, 2011.

Reeder, Tyson. "'Sovereign Lords' and 'Dependent Administrators': Artigan Privateers, Atlantic Borderwaters, and State Building in the Early Nineteenth Century." *Journal of American History* 103, no. 2 (September 2016): 323–46.

Rees, Martin. *Before the Beginning: Our Universe and Others*. Reading, MA: Helix Books, 1997.

Renan, Ernest. "What Is a Nation?" 1882. In *Nation and Narration*, edited by Homi K. Bhabha, 8–22. New York: Routledge, 1990.

Richard, Dorothy E. *United States Naval Administration of the Trust Territory of the Pacific Islands*. Vol. 3. [Washington, DC]: Office of the Chief of Naval Operations, 1957.

Riess, Adam G., et al. "Large Magellanic Cloud Cepheid Standards Provide a 1% Foundation for the Determination of the Hubble Constant and Stronger Evidence for Physics beyond ΛCDM." *Astrophysical Journal* 876, no. 85 (2019): 1–13.

Rifkin, Mark. *Beyond Settler Time: Temporal Sovereignty and Indigenous Self-Determination*. Durham, NC: Duke University Press, 2017.

Risam, Roopika. *New Digital Worlds: Postcolonial Digital Humanities in Theory, Praxis, and Pedagogy*. Evanston, IL: Northwestern University Press, 2018.

Rivet, Paul. *Los orígenes del hombre americano*. Translated by José Recasens. Mexico: Ediciones Cuadernos Americanos, 1943.

Riquet, Johannes. *The Aesthetics of Island Space: Perception, Ideology, Geopoetics*. Oxford: Oxford University Press, 2019.

Roberts, Brian Russell. "Archipelagic American Literary History and the Philippines." *American Literary History* 27, no. 1 (2015): 128–40.

Roberts, Brian Russell. "Archipelagic American Studies: An Open and Comparative Insularity." In *The Routledge Companion to Transnational American Studies*, edited by Nina Morgan, Alfred Hornung, and Takayuki Tatsumi, 51–60. London: Routledge, 2019.

Roberts, Brian Russell. "Archipelagic Diaspora, Geographical Form, and Hurston's *Their Eyes Were Watching God*." *American Literature* 85, no. 1 (March 2013): 121–49.

Roberts, Brian Russell. "Archipelagoes, Oceans, and Visual Theorizing." Lecture, Brigham Young University Art Department Lecture Series, Provo, UT, March 30, 2017.

Roberts, Brian Russell. "The Coloring of the Sea Almond and Other Archipelagic Legibilities." Presentation for the Critical Caribbean Studies Group, Rutgers–New Brunswick, April 17, 2013.

Roberts, Brian Russell. "On the Borderwaters and Watery Borders of a New World Order." *Verge: Studies in Global Asias* 7, no. 1 (2021): 31–39.

Roberts, Brian Russell. "What Is an Archipelago? On Bandung Praxis, Lingua Franca, and Archipelagic Interlapping." In Martínez-San Miguel and Stephens, *Contemporary Archipelagic Thinking*, 83–107.

Roberts, Brian Russell, and Michelle Ann Stephens, eds. *Archipelagic American Studies.* Durham, NC: Duke University Press, 2017.

Roberts, Brian Russell, and Michelle Ann Stephens. "Archipelagic American Studies and the Caribbean." *Journal of Transnational American Studies* 5, no. 1 (2013): 1–21.

Roberts, Brian Russell, and Michelle Ann Stephens. "Archipelagic American Studies: Decontinentalizing the Study of American Culture." In Roberts and Stephens, *Archipelagic American Studies,* 1–54.

Robinson, Greg. *The Great Unknown: Japanese-American Sketches.* Boulder: University of Colorado Press, 2016.

Robinson, Greg. "Writing the Internment." In *The Cambridge Companion to Asian American Literature,* edited by Crystal Parikh and Daniel Y. Kim, 45–58. New York: Cambridge University Press, 2015.

Rogers, Heather. *Gone Tomorrow: The Hidden Life of Garbage.* New York: New Press, 2005.

Roland, Alex, W. Jeffrey Bolster, and Alexander Keyssar. *The Way of the Ship: America's Maritime History Reenvisioned, 1600–2000.* Hoboken, NJ: Wiley, 2008.

Rooney, Ellen. "Form and Contentment." MLQ: *Modern Language Quarterly* 61, no. 1 (March 2000): 17–40.

Roosevelt, Theodore. *The Foes of Our Own Household.* New York: Doran, 1917.

Roosevelt, Theodore. *The Strenuous Life: Essays and Addresses.* 1900. Reprint, New York: Century, 1905.

Rosaldo, Renato. *Culture and Truth: The Remaking of Social Analysis.* Boston: Beacon, 1989.

Rosaldo, Renato. "Introduction: The Borders of Belonging." In *Cultural Citizenship in Island Southeast Asia: Nation and Belonging in the Hinterlands,* edited by Renato Rosaldo, 1–15. Berkeley: University of California Press, 2003.

Ross, Marlon B. *Manning the Race: Reforming Black Men in the Jim Crow Era.* New York: New York University Press, 2004.

Ryder, Robert T. "Oil and Gas Potential of the Chama–Southern San Juan Mountains Wilderness Study Area, Colorado." In *Mineral Resources of the Chama–Southern San Juan Mountains Wilderness Study Area, Mineral, Rio Grande, Archuleta, and Conejos Counties, Colorado,* 79–121. US Geological Survey Bulletin 1524. Washington, DC: Government Printing Office, 1985.

Sae-Saue, Jayson Gonzales. *Southwest Asia: The Transpacific Geographies of Chicana/o Literature.* New Brunswick, NJ: Rutgers University Press, 2016.

Saldívar, José David. *Trans-Americanity: Subaltern Modernities, Global Coloniality, and the Cultures of Greater Mexico.* Durham, NC: Duke University Press, 2012.

Sampson, Scott D., Mark A. Loewen, Andrew A. Farke, Eric M. Roberts, Catherine A. Forster, Joshua A. Smith, and Alan L. Titus. "New Horned Dinosaurs from Utah Provide Evidence for Intracontinental Dinosaur Endemism." PLOS *One* 5, no. 9 (September 2010): n.p.

Samuel, Nina. "On Seeing and Believing: Islands of Chaos and the Key Question of Scientific Visualization." In *New Geographies 08: Island*, edited by Daniel Daou and Pablo Pérez-Ramos, 90–97. Cambridge, MA: Harvard University Graduate School of Design, 2016.

Samuels, Willem. Introduction to *The Mute's Soliloquy: A Memoir*, by Pramoedya Ananta Toer, translated by Willem Samuels, xiii–xxii. New York: Hyperion, 1999.

Sanford, Dee S. *Marjum Pass*. Springville, UT: Art City, 1968.

Saranillio, Dean Itsuji. *Unsustainable Empire: Alternative Histories of Hawai'i Statehood*. Durham, NC: Duke University Press, 2018.

Sawczyn, Read. "The United States Immigration Policy toward Cuba Violates Established Maritime Policy, It Does Not Curtail Illegal Immigration, and Thus Should Be Changed So That Cuban Immigrants Are Treated Similarly to Other Immigrants." *Florida Journal of International Law* 13, no. 3 (Summer 2001): 343–60.

Schück, A. *Die Stabkarten der Marshall-Insulaner*. Hamburg: Kommissions-Verlag von H. O. Persiehl, 1902.

Schraubi, Globularius. "Yule Greetings, Friends!" *Trek* (December 1942): 12–16.

Schwyzer, Philip. Introduction to *Archipelagic Identities: Literature and Identity in the Atlantic Archipelago, 1550–1800*, edited by Philip Schwyzer and Simon Mealor, 1–7. Burlington, VT: Ashgate, 2004.

Scott, James Brown. "Introductory Note." In Grotius, *Freedom of the Seas*, v–x.

Scott, Julius S. *The Common Wind: Afro-American Currents in the Age of the Haitian Revolution*. London: Verso, 2018.

Semple, Ellen Churchill. *Influences of Geographic Environment, on the Basis of Ratzel's System of Anthropo-Geography*. New York: Holt, 1911.

Sharpe, Christina. *In the Wake: On Blackness and Being*. Durham, NC: Duke University Press, 2016.

Shaviro, Steven. "Non-phenomenological Thought." *Speculations: A Journal of Speculative Realism* 5 (2014): 40–56.

Sheldon, Rebekah. "Dark Correlationism: Mysticism, Magic, and the New Realisms." *symplokē* 24, nos. 1–2 (2016): 137–53.

Shell, Marc. *Islandology: Geography, Rhetoric, Politics*. Stanford, CA: Stanford University Press, 2014.

Sherrard-Johnson, Cherene. "'Perfection with a Hole in the Middle': Archipelagic Assemblage in Tiphanie Yanique's *Land of Love and Drowning*." *Journal of Transnational American Studies* 10, no. 1 (Summer 2019): 93–123.

Sigurðsson, Gísli. Introduction to *The Vinland Sagas: The Icelandic Sagas about the First Documented Voyages across the North Atlantic*, translated by Keneva Kunz, ix–xxxviii. London: Penguin, 2008.

Singer, P. W., and August Cole. *Ghost Fleet: A Novel of the Next World War*. Boston: Houghton Mifflin Harcourt, 2015.

Skaggs, Jimmy M. *The Great Guano Rush: Entrepreneurs and American Overseas Expansion*. New York: St. Martin's, 1994.

Skelton, R. A., Thomas E. Marston, and George D. Painter. *The Vinland Map and the Tartar Relation*. 1965. Reprint, New Haven, CT: Yale University Press, 1967.

Smith, Henry Nash. *Virgin Land: The American West as Symbol and Myth*. 1950. Reprint, Cambridge, MA: Harvard University Press, 1978.

Smith, Paul Chaat, and Robert Allen Warrior. *Like a Hurricane: The Indian Movement from Alcatraz to Wounded Knee*. New York: New Press, 1996.

Smithson, Robert. "Entropy and the New Monuments." 1966. In *Robert Smithson: The Collected Writings*, edited by Jack Flam, 10–23. Berkeley: University of California Press, 1996.

Smithson, Robert. "Fragments of an Interview with P. A. Norvell, April, 1969." In *Six Years: The Dematerialization of the Art Object from 1966 to 1972*, by Lucy R. Lippard, 87–90. 1973. Reprint, Berkeley: University of California Press, 1997.

Smithson, Robert, dir. *The Spiral Jetty*. 1970. New York: Electronic Arts Intermix, 2007.

Smithson, Robert. "The Spiral Jetty: The Essay." 1972. In Loe, *Spiral Jetty Encyclo*, 13–21.

Snyder, Gary. "The Rediscovery of Turtle Island." 1995. In *At Home on the Earth: Becoming Native to Our Place, a Multicultural Anthology*, edited by David Landis Barnhill, 297–306. Berkeley: University of California Press, 1999.

Solomon, Jack. "Huckleberry Finn and the Tradition of *The Odyssey*." *South Atlantic Bulletin* 33, no. 2 (March 1968): 11–13.

Solzhenitsyn, Aleksandr I. *The Gulag Archipelago, 1918–1956: An Experiment in Literary Investigation I–II*. Vol. 1. 1973. Translated by Thomas P. Whitney. New York: Harper and Row, 1974.

Somerville, Alice Te Punga. "The Great Pacific Garbage Patch as Metaphor: The (American) Pacific You Can't See." In Roberts and Stephens, *Archipelagic American Studies*, 320–38.

Somerville, Alice Te Punga. "Where Oceans Come From." *Comparative Literature* 69, no. 1 (2017): 25–31.

Sorensen, Leif. "Modernity on a Global Stage: Hurston's Alternative Modernism." *MELUS* 30, no. 4 (Winter 2005): 3–24.

Soto-Crespo, Ramón E. *Mainland Passage: The Cultural Anomaly of Puerto Rico*. Minneapolis: University of Minnesota Press, 2009.

Standiford, Les. *Last Train to Paradise: Henry Flagler and the Spectacular Rise and Fall of the Railroad That Crossed an Ocean*. New York: Crown, 2002.

Stark, Luke, and Anna Lauren Hoffmann. "Data Is the New What? Popular Metaphors and Professional Ethics in Emerging Data Culture." Preprint, May 2, 2019, 6. https://osf.io/preprints/socarxiv/2xguw/.

Steffen, Will, Paul J. Crutzen, and John R. McNeill. "The Anthropocene: Are Humans Now Overwhelming the Great Forces of Nature?" *AMBIO: A Journal of the Human Environment* 36, no. 8 (December 2007): 614–21.

Stephens, Michelle Ann. *Black Empire: The Masculine Global Imaginary of Caribbean Intellectuals in the United States, 1914–1962*. Durham, NC: Duke University Press, 2005.

Stern, Alexandra Minna. "Nationalism on the Line: Masculinity, Race, and the Creation of the U.S. Border Patrol, 1910–1940." In *Continental Crossroads: Remapping U.S.–Mexico Borderlands History*, edited by Samuel Truett and Elliott Young, 299–323. Durham, NC: Duke University Press, 2004.

Stevens, Wallace. *Letters of Wallace Stevens*. Edited by Holly Stevens. New York: Knopf, 1966.

Stratford, Elaine, Godfrey Baldacchino, Elizabeth McMahon, Carol Farbotko, and Andrew Harwood. "Envisioning the Archipelago." *Island Studies Journal* 6, no. 2 (2011): 113–30.

Strohl, Mitchell P. *The International Law of Bays*. The Hague: Martinus Nijhoff, 1963.

Suarez, Harrod J. "Archipelagoes and Oceania in Asian American and Pacific Islander Literary Studies." July 2018. In *Oxford Research Encyclopedia of Literature*, edited by Paula Rabinowitz, n.p. Oxford University Press USA, 2016. https://oxfordre.com/literature/view/10.1093/acrefore/9780190201098.001.0001/acrefore-9780190201098-e-874.

Sukarno. "Speech by President Sukarno of Indonesia at the Opening of the Conference." In *Asia-Africa Speaks from Bandung*, edited by the Ministry of Foreign Affairs, 19–29. [Jakarta]: Ministry of Foreign Affairs, Republic of Indonesia, 1955.

Sumida, Stephen H. "Reevaluating Mark Twain's Novel of Hawaii." *American Literature* 61, no. 4 (December 1989): 586–609.

Sun, Shirley. *Miné Okubo: An American Experience*. Oakland, CA: Oakland Museum, 1972.

Sutton, Peter, and Michael Snow. *Iridescence: The Play of Colours*. Port Melbourne, Australia: Thames and Hudson, 2015.

Suyemoto, Toyo. "Another Spring." With Susan B. Richardson. In *Last Witnesses: Reflections on the Wartime Internment of Japanese Americans*, edited by Erica Harth, 21–34. New York: St. Martin's, 2001.

Suyemoto, Toyo. "Gain." *Trek* (December 1942): 6.

Suyemoto, Toyo. *I Call to Remembrance: Toyo Suyemoto's Years of Internment*. Edited by Susan B. Richardson. New Brunswick, NJ: Rutgers University Press, 2007.

Suzuki, Daisetz T. "Buddhist Symbolism." In *Explorations in Communication: An Anthology*, edited by Edmund Carpenter and Marshall McLuhan, 36–42. Boston: Beacon, 1960.

Swanstrom, Lisa. "Digital Currents, Oceanic Drift, and the Evolving Ecology of the Temporary Autonomous Zone." In Martínez-San Miguel and Stephens, *Contemporary Archipelagic Thinking*, 191–212.

Szeman, Imre, and Dominic Boyer, eds. *Energy Humanities: An Anthology*. Baltimore: Johns Hopkins University Press, 2017.

Takaki, Ronald. *Strangers from a Different Shore: A History of Asian Americans*. Boston: Little, Brown, 1989.

Tally, Robert T., Jr., ed. *Geocritical Explorations: Space, Place, and Mapping in Literary and Cultural Studies*. New York: Palgrave Macmillan, 2011.

Teaiwa, Teresia K. "Bikinis and Other S/pacific N/oceans." *The Contemporary Pacific* 6, no. 1 (Spring 1994): 87–109.

Teaiwa, Teresia K. "What Remains to Be Seen: Reclaiming the Visual Roots of Pacific Literature." PMLA 125, no. 3 (May 2010): 730–36.

"Territorial Sea and Maritime Districts Ordinance 1939." Translated by the Secretariat of the United Nations. In *Laws and Regulations on the Regime of the Territorial Sea*, 194–201. United Nations Legislative Series, ST/LEG/SER.B/6. New York: United Nations, 1957.

Teves, Stephanie Nohelani. *Defiant Indigeneity: The Politics of Hawaiian Performance*. Chapel Hill: University of North Carolina Press, 2018.

Thompson, Lanny. *Imperial Archipelago: Representation and Rule in the Insular Territories under U.S. Dominion after 1898*. Honolulu: University of Hawai'i Press, 2010.

Tilley, Christopher. *A Phenomenology of Landscape: Places, Paths and Monuments*. Providence, RI: Berg, 1994.

Tinsley, Omise'eke Natasha. "Black Atlantic, Queer Atlantic: Queer Imaginings of the Middle Passage." GLQ: *A Journal of Gay and Lesbian Studies* 14, no. 2–3 (June 2008): 191–215.

Tocqueville, Alexis de. *Democracy in America and Two Essays on America*. Translated by Gerald E. Bevan. New York: Penguin, 2003.

Toer, Pramoedya Ananta. *Nyanyi Sunyi seorang Bisu: Catatan-catatan dari P. Buru*. Jakarta: Lentera, 1995.

Topaz Museum Board. "A Note on Terminology." In *The Price of Prejudice: The Japanese-American Relocation Center in Utah during World War II*, by Leonard J. Arrington, 1. 1962. Reprint, Delta, UT: Topaz Museum, 1997.

Trachtenberg, Alan. *Brooklyn Bridge: Fact and Symbol*. 1965. Reprint. Chicago: University of Chicago Press, 1979.

Traister, Bryce. "The Object of Study; or, Are We Being Transnational Yet?" *Journal of Transnational American Studies* 2, no. 1 (2010): 1–29.

Treaty with the Cook Islands on Friendship and Delimitation of the Maritime Boundary. Washington, DC: Government Printing Office, 1980.

Truett, Samuel. "Settler Colonialism and the Borderlands of Early America." *William and Mary Quarterly* 76, no. 3 (July 2019): 435–42.

Truman, Harry S. "Policy of the United States with Respect to the Natural Resources of the Subsoil and Sea Bed of the Continental Shelf" (Proclamation 2667, September 28, 1945). In *Submerged Lands: Hearings before the Committee on Interior and Insular Affairs, United States Senate, Eighty-Second Congress, First Session on S. J. Res. 20, 496*. Washington, DC: Government Printing Office, 1951.

Trust Territory of the Pacific Islands (U.S.): Administrative Divisions. Washington, DC: Central Intelligence Agency, 1974.

Tsao, Tiffany. *The More Known World*. Seattle: AmazonCrossing, 2017.

Tsao, Tiffany. *The Oddfits*. Seattle: AmazonCrossing, 2016.

Turner, Frederick Jackson. *The Frontier in American History*. New York: Holt, 1921.

Twain, Mark. *Adventures of Huckleberry Finn*. 1884. 125th anniversary ed. Edited by Victor Fischer and Lin Salamo with Harriet Elinor Smith and Walter Blair. Berkeley: University of California Press, 2010.

Twain, Mark. *Life on the Mississippi*. 1883. Reprint, New York: Harper and Brothers, 1901.

Twain, Mark. *Mark Twain's Letters*. Vol. 2. Edited by Albert Bigelow Paine. New York: Harper, 1917.

Ueda, Makoto. *Bashō and His Interpreters: Selected Hokku with Commentary*. Stanford, CA: Stanford University Press, 1992.

Underwood, Ted. *Distant Horizons: Digital Evidence and Literary Change*. Chicago: University of Chicago Press, 2019.

Underwood, Ted. "A Genealogy of Distant Reading." *Digital Humanities Quarterly* 11, no. 2 (2017).

United Nations. *The Law of the Sea: Official Text of the United Nations Convention on the Law of the Sea with Annexes and Index*. New York: St. Martin's, 1983.

US Bureau of the Census. *Census of the Philippine Islands Taken under the Direction of the Philippine Commission in the Year 1903*. Vol. 1. Washington, DC: Government Printing Office, 1905.

US Department of Energy and National Nuclear Security Administration. *Draft Site-Wide Environmental Impact Statement for Continued Operation of Los Alamos National Laboratory, Los Alamos, New Mexico (SWEIS)*. DOE/EIS-0380D. Vol. 2, bk. 2. Los Alamos, NM: National Nuclear Security Administration, June 2006. https://www.energy.gov/sites/prod/files/EIS-0380-DEIS-02-2006.pdf.

US Department of Labor, Bureau of Immigration. *Immigration Laws (Act of February 5, 1917): Rules of May 1, 1917*. Washington, DC: Government Printing Office, 1917.

US Department of the Interior/National Park Service. *General Management Plan/Environmental Impact Statement: National Park of American Samoa, Territory of American Samoa*. October 1997. Accessed August 13, 2020. https://www.nps.gov/npsa/learn/management/upload/npsagmpeis1997textop.pdf.

US Naval Civil Administration Unit, Marshall Islands. *Roster of Officers, Enlisted Men, Civilians and Dependents*. Majuro, Marshall Islands: US Naval Civil Administration Unit, August 1, 1950. Personal collection of Roger Knight.

van Dooren, Thom. *Flight Ways: Life and Loss at the Edge of Extinction*. New York: Columbia University Press, 2016.

van Dooren, Thom, Eben Kirksey, and Ursula Münster. "Multispecies Studies: Cultivating Arts of Attentiveness." *Environmental Humanities* 8, no. 1 (2016): 1–23.

van Zandt, Franklin K. *Boundaries of the United States and the Several States: With Miscellaneous Geographic Information Concerning Areas, Altitudes, and Geographic Centers*. Geological Survey Bulletin 1212. Washington, DC: Government Printing Office, 1966.

van Zandt, Franklin K. *Boundaries of the United States and the Several States: With Miscellaneous Geographic Information Concerning Areas, Altitudes, and Geographic*

Centers. Geological Survey Professional Paper 909. Washington, DC: Government Printing Office, 1976.

Vasconcelos, José. "La raza cósmica (Misión de la raza iberoamericana)." 1925. In *The Cosmic Race/La Raza Cósmica: A Bilingual Edition with an Introduction and Notes*, translated by Didier T. Jaén, 41–80. Los Angeles: Centro de Publicaciones, Department of Chicano Studies, California State University, Los Angeles, 1979.

Vazquez, Alexandra T. "Learning to Live in Miami." *American Quarterly* 66, no. 3 (September 2014): 853–73.

Venuti, Lawrence. *The Translator's Invisibility: A History of Translation*. 2nd ed. London: Routledge, 2008.

Verma, Ajit Ram, and P. Krishna. *Polymorphism and Polytypism in Crystals*. New York: John Wiley and Sons, 1966.

Vickers, Adrian. Foreword to *Island of Bali*, by Miguel Covarrubias, xix–xxiii. Singapore: Periplus, 2008.

Vickers, Adrian. *A History of Modern Indonesia*. Cambridge: Cambridge University Press, 2005.

Vickers, Adrian. "Word and Image in Miguel Covarrubias's *Island of Bali*." Keynote address presented at Miguel Covarrubias: Encuentros entre Antropología, Geografía y Arte, Universidad Nacional Autónoma de México, Mexico City, Mexico, August 23–24, 2017.

Waddell, Eric, Vijay Naidu, and Epeli Hau'ofa, eds. *A New Oceania: Rediscovering Our Sea of Islands*. Suva, Fiji: University of the South Pacific/Beake House, 1993.

Walcott, Derek. "Isla Incognita." 1973. In *Caribbean Literature and the Environment: Between Nature and Culture*, edited by Elizabeth M. DeLoughrey, Renée K. Gosson, and George B. Handley, 51–57. Charlottesville: University of Virginia Press, 2005.

Walcott, Derek. *Omeros*. New York: Farrar, Straus, Giroux, 1990.

Waligora-Davis, Nicole A. "'Myth of the Continents': American Vulnerabilities and 'Rum and Coca-Cola.'" In Roberts and Stephens, *Archipelagic American Studies*, 191–209.

Walker, Alice. *In Search of Our Mothers' Gardens*. New York: Harcourt, 1983.

Walker, Alice. "Zora Neale Hurston—A Cautionary Tale and a Partisan View." Foreword to *Zora Neale Hurston: A Literary Biography*, by Robert E. Hemenway, xi–xviii. 1977. Reprint, Urbana: University of Illinois Press, 1980.

Wallace, Alfred Russel. *The Malay Archipelago: The Land of the Orang-utan and the Bird of Paradise, a Narrative of Travel, with Studies of Man and Nature*. 1869. 4th edition. London: Macmillan, 1872.

Weheliye, Alexander G. *Habeas Viscus: Racializing Assemblages, Biopolitics, and Black Feminist Theories of the Human*. Durham, NC: Duke University Press, 2014.

Westermann, Andrea. "A Technofossil of the Anthropocene: Sliding Up and Down Temporal Scales with Plastic." In *Power and Time: Temporalities in Conflict and the Making of History*, edited by Dan Edelstein, Stefanos Geroulanos, and Natasha Wheatley, 122–44. Chicago: University of Chicago Press, 2020.

Wheatley, Phillis. *Complete Writings*. Edited by Vincent Carretta. New York: Penguin, 2001.

Whitehead, Alfred North. *Symbolism: Its Meaning and Effect, Barbour-Page Lectures, University of Virginia, 1927*. New York: Macmillan, 1958.

Whitman, Walt. *Leaves of Grass*. Introduction by John Hollander. New York: Library of America, 1992.

Widodo, Wahyu, Budi Anwari, and Maryanto. *Pendidikan Kewarganegaraan: Pengantar Teori*. Yogyakarta, Indonesia: Andi, 2015.

Wiedorn, Michael. *Think Like an Archipelago: Paradox in the Work of Édouard Glissant*. Albany: State University of New York Press, 2018.

Williams, Adriana. *Covarrubias*. Edited by Doris Ober. Austin: University of Texas Press, 1994.

Williams, Adriana, and Yu-Chee Chong. *Covarrubias in Bali*. Singapore: Didier Millet, 2005.

Williams, Terry Tempest. *Refuge: An Unnatural History of Family and Place*. New York: Pantheon, 1991.

Wilson, Rob. *Reimagining the American Pacific: From "South Pacific" to Bamboo Ridge and Beyond*. Durham, NC: Duke University Press, 2000.

Wineera, Vernice. "This Island." In *Into the Luminous Tide: Pacific Poems*, by Vernice Wineera, edited by Jay Fox, 4. Provo, UT: Brigham Young University, 2009.

Winkler, Captain. "On Sea Charts Formerly Used in the Marshall Islands, with Notices on the Navigation of These Islanders in General." 1898. In *Annual Report of the Board of Regents of the Smithsonian Institution, Showing the Operations, Expenditures, and Conditions of the Institution for the Year Ending June 30, 1899*, 487–508. Washington, DC: Government Printing Office, 1901.

Wright, Richard. *The Color Curtain: A Report on the Bandung Conference*. 1956. In *Black Power: Three Books from Exile*, by Richard Wright, introduction by Cornel West, 429–609. New York: HarperPerennial, 2008.

Wynter, Sylvia. "Beyond Miranda's Meanings: Un/Silencing the 'Demonic Ground' of Caliban's 'Woman.'" In *Out of the Kumbla: Caribbean Women and Literature*, edited by Carol Boyce Davies and Elaine Savory Fido, 355–70. Trenton, NJ: Africa World Press, 1990.

Wynter, Sylvia. "Beyond the Word of Man: Glissant and the New Discourse of the Antilles." *World Literature Today* 63, no. 4 (Autumn 1989): 637–48.

Wynter, Sylvia, and Katherine McKittrick. "Unparalleled Catastrophe for Our Species? Or, to Give Humanness a Different Future: Conversations." In *Sylvia Wynter: On Being Human as Praxis*, edited by Katherine McKittrick, 9–89. Durham, NC: Duke University Press, 2015.

Yaeger, Patricia. "Sea Trash, Dark Pools, and the Tragedy of the Commons." *PMLA* 125, no. 3 (May 2010): 523–45.

Yamada, Jim. "Falderol." *Trek* (June 1943): 42.

Yamada, Jim. "Lake Bonneville." *Trek* (February 1943): 35–37.

Yamada, Jim. "Portrait of an Artist." *Trek* (December 1942): 21–22.

Yanique, Tiphanie. "The Bridge Stories: A Short Collection." 2005. In *How to Escape from a Leper Colony: A Novella and Stories*, 15–30. Minneapolis: Graywolf, 2010.
Yoshihara, Mari. "Editor's Note." *American Quarterly* 67, no. 1 (March 2015): v–vii.
Yoshihara, Mari. "Editor's Note." *American Quarterly* 67, no. 3 (September 2015): vii–viii.
Zalasiewicz, Jan. *The Earth after Us: What Legacy Will Humans Leave in the Rocks?* With contributions from Kim Freedman. New York: Oxford University Press, 2008.
Žižek, Slavoj. *The Plague of Fantasies*. London: Verso, 1997.
Zulkarnain, Iskandar. "'Playable' Nationalism: *Nusantara Online* and the 'Gamic' Reconstructions of National History." *Sojourn: Journal of Social Issues in Southeast Asia* 29, no. 1 (March 2014): 31–62.

INDEX

Adventures of Huckleberry Finn (Twain), 38–39, 51–65, 75, 112, 157, 265–66
Aegean Sea, 13–17, 52, 95–97
Africa, 26–28, 62, 137
African Americans, 82–83, 88–89, 101. *See also* Blackness
Aikau, Hōkūlani K., 76
airspace, 22
Alaimo, Stacy, 179
"Albatross at Midway Atoll Refuge" (Jordan), 230
albatrosses, 223–39
Alcatraz Island, 245, 315n141
Alcoa, 233
All Aboard! (magazine), 163
America (as a term), 276n6
American Adam, The (Lewis), 46
American Encounters (Limón), 112
Americanist scholarship, 12, 25, 36–39, 46–70, 112, 222, 248–74, 276n6
American Literature (journal), 43, 258–70, 273
American Quarterly (journal), 38, 43, 46, 49–50, 255, 258–70
American Samoa, 4, 11, 21–22, 29, 65, 77–78, 240–42, 245–47
American studies, 23, 36, 45–54, 213, 249, 272, 276n6
American Studies Association, 24, 45, 112
American West, the, 52–62, 70–71
amphibians, 190–92, 196, 200–201
"Ancient Pond" (Bashō), 191–93
Anheuser-Busch, 233
Anthropocene, the, 211–12, 223–39
Antiquities Act, 226
Anzaldúa, Gloria, 25–28, 34–35, 111–12, 126, 129, 141, 145, 153, 237

Appalachia, 182
Arac, Jonathan, 64, 106
Archipelagic American Studies (Stephens & Roberts), 10–12, 254–55
archipelagic space, 17–25, 38, 48–54, 61–64, 83, 113, 121–23, 133, 176, 253
archipelagic thinking (archipelagic thought): Americanist scholarship and, 49–50, 61–62, 75, 80–81; borderlands and, 155–57; borderwaters and, 24–36, 113–15, 133–38, 147–48; definitions of, 13–23, 278n48; diaspora and, 86, 96; digital humanities and, 248–49, 253–58, 266, 269–73; ocean nations and, 1–13; temporality and, 162–65, 173, 198, 207–10, 213, 216–17, 220–22
archipelagos: a journal of Caribbean digital praxis, 253
archipiélados, 117–23, 130, 135, 153, 155, 158
Art Forms of the Pacific Area (Covarrubias), 119, 121
Asian-African Conference (1955), 131, 146, 151, 158, 237, 296n117
Asiatic Barred Zone Act, 29–31

Bahrani, Ramin, 234
Balaz, Joseph P., 260–61
Bali, 82–84, 117–19
Bamboo Roof (Ban), 80
Ban, Shigeru, 80
Bandung Conference. *See* Asian-African Conference (1955)
Barnard, John Levi, 268
Barton, Ralph, 152–53
Bashō, Matsuo, 191–93
Basin and Range (McPhee), 163
Batongbacal, Jay L., 60–61

Baym, Nina, 45–48, 51, 281n1
Beaglehole, Ernest, 68
Beaglehole, Pearl, 68
Beauty behind Barbed Wire . . . (Eaton), 185, 191
Beckwith, Frank, 166–67, 183–85, 188–90, 193, 196
Benítez-Rojo, Antonio, 23, 57, 84, 91, 222, 229
Benjamin, Walter, 14, 201
Between Two Worlds (Paredes), 113
Bevacqua, Michael Lujan, 81
Bikini Atoll, 146–47, 151–52, 157–58
birds, 228–39
birtherism, 8
Bishop, Elizabeth, 28
Blackness, 81, 101. *See also* African Americans
Blum, Hester, 273
Boas, Franz, 117
Bogost, Ian, 76, 171–73
Bolton, Herbert E., 25
Boltzmann brain paradox, 210–23, 243–44
Bonilla, Yarimar, 148
Border Field State Park, 113
borderlands, 24–35, 86, 111–12, 114, 129, 145–46, 149, 152–58, 278n62, 293n63
Borderlands/La Frontera (Anzaldúa), 25, 28, 111, 113, 153
borders: the Anthropocene and, 232–37; archipelagic thinking and, 18, 83, 121, 295n86; borderwaters and, 114, 117; coastal spaces, 126, 129; temporality and, 241, 244–47; United States, 21, 32–34; the United States and, 1–13. *See also* borderlands; borderwaters; US-Canada border; US-Mexico border
borderwaters: Americanist scholarship and, 53–54; the Anthropocene and, 232–33, 237; archipelagic thinking and, 24–36, 81, 117–23; coastal spaces and, 123–38; digital humanities and, 248–74; temporality and, 161–65, 247; the United States and, 1–13, 293n63. *See also* borders
Borges, Jorge Luis, 214, 217, 223
boundaries. *See* borders; borderwaters
Boundaries of the United States and of the Several States and Territories (USGS), 21

Boundaries of the United States and the Several States (USGS), 21–24
Brady, Mary Pat, 25
Brathwaite, Edward Kamau, 26–28, 59–60, 71, 108, 114, 162, 195, 257
Braudel, Fernand, 59–60
Braverman, Irus, 126
"Bridge Stories, The" (Yanique), 42, 210, 310n51
Buck, Peter H. *See* Te Rangihiroa
Buehler, Fidalis, 29
Bulosan, Carlos, 11
Buru Island, 136–39. *See also* Maluku Islands; Spice Islands
Bush, George W., 226–27, 235, 237
Butcher, John G., 30
Byatt, A. S., 42, 210, 229, 231–34, 238
Byrd, Jodi A., 268

"Call of Cthulhu, The" (Lovecraft), 187
cancer, 152, 158
Canyonlands National Park, 206
capitalism, 20. *See also* neoliberalism
Carby, Harby V., 83
Caribbean, the, 27–28, 60, 83–85, 91–98, 104, 210–23, 252–53
"Caribbean Theme" (Brathwaite), 27
Carpentier, Alejo, 51
Carroll, Sean, 215
Carson, Rachel L., 188
Carter, Paul, 136, 212
Cast Away (Zemeckis), 105
Central Utah Relocation Center. *See* Topaz internment camp
Chakrabarty, Dipesh, 189, 211
Chang, David A., 67, 268
Chicana/o studies, 25–26, 31–32, 34–35
Chōmei, Kamo no, 197–98
Christian, Barbara, 173
Citizen 13660 (Okubo), 165, 189
citizenship, 5, 11, 77, 79, 137, 187
Civilization and Its Discontents (Freud), 171
civil rights, 8, 82–83
Clark, John R. Kukeakalani, 108
class, 57

360 · INDEX

climate change, 20, 152, 170, 212, 224–25
Coca-Cola, 233, 238–39
Cohen, Jeffrey Jerome, 166, 171
Cohen, Yonatan, 1–2
colonialism: Americanist scholarship and, 56, 76; archipelagic thinking and, 14–15, 23, 67–68, 120–21, 134, 253, 287n132; borderwaters and, 10, 25–29, 36–37, 102, 115–16, 123–25, 136–38, 155; diaspora and, 91, 96; island spaces and, 85, 108; temporality and, 241–42, 245, 247. *See also* imperialism
colonial modernity, 10, 26, 91, 105, 118 207, 223–24. *See also* modernity
Color Curtain, The (Wright), 131
Columbian Exposition, 50
Columbus, Christopher, 37, 55–56, 67–70, 91–92
"Come Back to the Raft Ag'in, Huck Honey!" (Fiedler), 63
comics, 182–83, 244
Common Sense (Paine), 9–10
concentration camps, 176
consciousness, 217
contact zones, 88, 98, 114
Contemporary Pacific (journal), 273
continental exceptionalism, 8–12, 36, 48, 198, 219–22, 240, 257
continentalism: Americanist scholarship and, 46, 50, 58–62, 69–75; archipelagic thinking and, 18, 66–67, 81, 219, 255; borderwaters and, 35–38, 130, 133; digital humanities and, 258–62; frontier, 52–57; futurity and, 207–10; ocean nations and, 5–13; ontology and, 99–100, 102
continental philosophy, 164, 173, 300n22
continents. *See* continentalism
Contradictory Omens (Brathwaite), 28
Cook, James, 67
Cook Islands, the, 77–79
Cooper, James Fenimore, 52, 55
Copernicus, 221–23
cosmology, 212–23, 254, 308n32. *See also* theoretical physics
Covarrubias, Miguel, 41, 115–25, 136–37, 140, 148, 152–53

Cox, Paul Alan, 239–40
creolization, 14, 155
Croxall, Brian, 258, 266, 273
Crutzen, Paul J., 224–25
cubism, 127, 129, 141
Culler, Jonathan, 106
cultural geology, 161–63, 173
culture: archipelagic thinking and, 18, 23, 96, 119–21, 248; borderlands and, 47, 153, 158; borderwaters and, 24, 34–35, 38, 111, 114–15, 126, 129, 145; island spaces and, 83–86; temporality and, 163–64, 173
currents, 63–76
Cusick, David, 69
Cutler, John Alba, 26, 111, 149

Dana, Richard Henry, 63–64
Darwin, Charles, 194, 251–52
Dash, J. Michael, 135, 300n27
data, 253–55
Däwes, Birgit, 24
deep time, 58–60, 163–66, 168–69, 188, 192, 197, 209, 211–12. *See also* temporality
Defoe, Daniel, 105
Deleuze, Gilles, 28, 70, 74, 95, 108, 144–45, 161, 174, 217
Deloria, Philip, 24
DeLoughrey, Elizabeth M., 105, 107–8, 151, 154
democracy, 9, 99–100
demonic ground, 103
desert-islands, 62, 104–10, 217. *See also* island spaces
Detours (Aikau & Gonzalez), 76
diaspora, 82–104, 106–7, 109, 253
Diaz, Vicente M., 107, 252
digital humanities, 248–74
Dimacali, Timothy James M., 42, 210, 242–47
Dimock, Wai Chee, 21, 50, 58, 60–61, 164, 203–4, 207, 211
dinosaurs, 180–83, 258
Distant Horizons (Underwood), 255
Distant Reading (Moretti), 249–51
Dixie Cup Company, 233
Djuanda Declaration, 130–31, 133
Dow Chemical, 233

INDEX · 361

Du Bois, W. E. B., 26, 40, 49, 62, 85, 92, 95, 279n74
Duck, Leigh Anne, 88
Dust Tracks on a Road (Hurston), 82, 87–88, 93
Dutch East India Company, 125

Eagle, the Jaguar, and the Serpent . . . , The (Covarrubias), 153–56
Earth. *See* planet, the
Eaton, Allen H., 185, 191–93
Eckel, Leslie Elizabeth, 36
ecology, 116, 175–76, 183, 212, 224, 234–35, 307n12
Economy of the Pacific (Covarrubias), 119
education, 60
EEZ. *See* Exclusive Economic Zones (EEZs)
Eiriksson, Leif, 68, 73
Eirik the Red's Saga, 68
Eldredge, Niles, 183, 303n90
Elson, R. E., 30
Encyclopaedia Britannica, 251, 316n12
energy, 5, 213, 224, 308n33. *See also* natural gas
England, 10, 222, 230, 246, 249, 310n63
epistemology, 13, 15, 38, 70, 96, 112, 151, 164, 249
Equiano, Olaudah, 138
ethnicity, 9, 57, 121
Ethnology of Pukapuka (Beaglehole), 68
etymology, 13–15, 17, 96
Euclid, 114–17, 126–27, 134–36, 144, 149–51, 185. *See also* geometry
evolution, 193, 195–96, 206, 250–51
Exclusive Economic Zones (EEZs), 1, 3–5, 10, 22–24, 29, 32–35, 225, 227
Executive Order 9066, 162
Executive Order 13547, 225–26
exploration, 5, 16, 67, 72–75, 95–96, 137, 250–54

Falealupo Rainforest Preserve, 239–40
Far Country (Moretti), 261–62
Fauna and Flora of the Pacific, The (Covarrubias), 119, 141
Federal Writers' Project, 101
Felski, Rita, 160, 201
femininity, 46–47. *See also* women

Fiedler, Leslie, 63
Fiol-Matta, Licia, 49
Fishkin, Shelley Fisher, 112
Fitzgerald, F. Scott, 73
Fitzwilliam Museum, 254
Flagler, Henry, 100
Florida: A Guide to the Southernmost State (Federal Writers' Project), 101
Florida East Coast Railway, 93
foreshores, 165–80, 189–90, 196, 200, 202–3
Formations of United States Colonialism (Goldstein), 23
Fortune (magazine), 117, 189
fossils, 183–84, 186, 188–93, 196, 201, 238–39, 305n116
Foucault, Michel, 161–62
fractal geometry: archipelagic thought and, 216, 252–53, 256; borderwaters and, 116, 126–29, 142–43, 151, 155, 157–58; temporality and, 159–65, 199–200, 205, 220–21
Fractal Geometry of Nature, The (Mandelbrot), 128, 220
Franklin, Benjamin, 198
Freedom of the Seas . . . , The, (Grotius), 125
Freud, Sigmund, 171
Frisbie, Florence "Johnny," 39, 51, 63–76, 97, 109, 153, 161
Frisbie, Robert Dean, 64
frontiers, 18, 52–62, 65, 70, 74–75, 97, 233–34, 262
Fuiono Senio, 239–40, 242
Fukagai, Kozo, 175
futurity, 166, 203, 207–11, 229, 240–43, 307n21

Gadsden Purchase, the, 21
"Gain" (Suyemoto), 178
gender, 9, 26, 57, 88–89, 102, 115–16. *See also* women
genocide, 14
geography: Americanist scholarship and, 50, 58–60, 62; archipelagic thinking and, 19, 57, 60, 249–50; borderwaters and, 114, 138–39; island spaces and, 82–87, 109–10; ontology and, 98–104; parallax zones and, 87–90; temporality and, 160–62

362 · INDEX

geologic time, 166–71, 180–98, 202–11, 223–39
"Geologic Time Spiral, The" (USGS), 204–6, 307n8
geology, 163–64, 173. *See also* cultural geology; geologic time
geometry, 114–15, 149–51. *See also* Euclid; fractal geometry; mathematics
Getachew, Adom, 148
Ghosh, Amitav, 145
Ghost Fleet (Cole & Singer), 31
Giles, Paul, 86–88, 173, 273
Gillis, John R., 69, 161–62
Gillman, Susan, 50–51, 273
Gladwin, Harold Sterling, 154, 156
Glissant, Édouard: archipelagic thought and, 15–18, 24, 43, 51, 61–62, 81, 96, 109, 207–23; borderwaters and, 28, 122, 135, 145, 148, 155; continents and, 69–71; digital humanities and, 255–56, 268–69, 271
global warming. *See* climate change
Golden Gate International Exposition, 119–20, 159
Golden Spike National Historic Site, 202, 207
Goldman Environmental Prize, 240
Goldstein, Alyosha, 23
Gómez, Myrriah, 157–58
Gómez-Barris, Macarena, 49
Gonzalez, Vernadette Vicuña, 76
Gott, J. Richard, 212
Gould, Stephen Jay, 183
governance, 126, 136–38, 148, 165, 241–42
governmentality, 21–22, 129, 137, 145
Grass, Luis, 32
Great Gatsby, The (Fitzgerald), 73
Great Island, the, 69, 71. *See also* Turtle Island
Great Pacific Garbage Patch, 210, 228, 234, 237
Great Salt Lake, 167–70, 202, 207
Great Wave off Kanagawa, The (Hokusai), 269–72
Greeley, Horace, 5
Grotius, Hugo, 125, 141–42
Guam, 7–8, 10, 60

"Guam, Where America's Voting Rights End" (Perez), 7–8
Guano Islands Act of 1856, 11, 21, 65, 77
Guattari, Félix, 70, 74
Gulliver's Travels (Swift), 90
Gumb, Alexis Pauline, 238
Guntō: SekaiRon (Imafuku), 195
Guterl, Matthew Pratt, 50–51

Hague Tribunal, 126
Hakutani, Yoshinobu, 192
Hämäläinen, Pekka, 111–12
Handley, George B., 15, 69, 86
Hansen, Jim, 108
Haraway, Donna J., 213
Hau'ofa, Epeli, 97, 103, 120–22, 208, 227, 229
Hawai'i, 8–11, 63–64, 79, 138, 245
Hayles, N. Katherine, 107
Hegel, Georg Wilhelm Friedrich, 42, 62, 85, 162, 208–9, 222
Hellas, 91–92, 95, 98
Herzog, Werner, 234
Hickman, Jared, 213
Hiroshima, 152
Hōjōki (Chōmei), 197
Hokusai, 269, 272
Holmes, Oliver Wendell Sr., 220
"How Long Is the Coast of Britain?" (Mandelbrot), 126–28, 220
How to Escape from a Leper Colony (Yanique), 217
Huang, Hsinya, 24
Hughes, Langston, 117
humanities, 248–74
Humboldt, Alexander von, 51
Hurricane Maria, 8–9, 257
Hurston, Zora Neale, 40, 82–83, 87–89, 94–98, 104, 109, 117, 161, 268–69

I Call to Remembrance (Suyemoto), 178
identity, 97–98
Imafuku, Ryuta, 96, 195
immigration, 29–32, 187. *See also* refugees
Immigration Act of 1917. *See* Asiatic Barred Zone Act

imperialism: Americanist scholarship and, 48–49, 56; archipelagic thinking and, 7–12, 14, 65, 76, 79, 83, 90–91; borderwaters and, 25–26, 36–37, 123–24, 139, 143–44, 148; continentalism and, 209; island spaces and, 85–86; ontology and, 100, 102; temporality and, 241, 245. *See also* colonialism

imprisonment. *See* internment

Independent State of Samoa, 2–4, 66, 239–42, 245–47

Indigenous peoples: archipelagic thinking and, 14–17, 23, 121–22, 138; borderlands and, 153–55, 158; borderwaters and, 115–16, 136, 145, 151; continentalism and, 70, 74; navigation and, 107; ocean nations and, 12; ontology and, 172; temporality and, 241–42, 244–45, 247. *See also* Native Americans

Indonesia, 8, 60, 116–25, 129–33, 145, 295n86

infinity, 128–29, 161, 193–94, 199–200, 214–23, 241

Information Office of the Republic of Indonesia in New York City, 123–25, 129–31, 137, 292n42

inkstones, 185–86, 188–92, 194–96, 201, 305n116

Inouye, Komaye, 176–77

Insular Cases, 7–8, 24, 259–60

interlapping, 28, 31–32, 35, 37, 71–72, 74, 80, 97, 116, 158

internationalism, 85

international law, 1, 129, 133, 145

international waters, 31, 34

internment, 162–96

iridescence, 172–76, 183, 190, 195–202

Iroquois, 69, 71

Iseyama, Homei, 191, 195, 305n109

Ishizaki, Shigematsu, 185–86, 188–89, 191–92, 195, 304n97, 305n116

Island of Bali (Covarrubias), 117–19, 123

island spaces: Americanist scholarship and, 48–50, 55, 59–60; archipelagic diaspora and, 82–87; archipelagic thinking and, 15–19, 81, 216–23; borderwaters and, 28, 43, 45; diaspora and, 90–98; digital humanities and, 260–68; ontology and, 99–100,

102–4; parallax zones, 87–89; temporality and, 193–95, 200, 207. *See also* archipelagic space; archipelagic thinking (archipelagic thought); desert-islands

Island World (Okihiro), 48

"I Want to Be Recycled" (Keep America Beautiful), 233, 312n101

Japanese American National Museum, 190

Japanese Americans, 164, 178–79, 187

Jetñil-Kijiner, Kathy, 151–52, 157–58, 224

Jewish people, 96

Johnson, Elizabeth R., 126

Johnson, James Weldon, 193

Johnson, Lyndon B., 5

Jordan, Chris, 229–30

Journal of American History, 43, 258–70, 273

Joyce, James, 107

Juda (King), 147

Jurassic Park, 258

Kant, Immanuel, 162

Kaplan, Amy, 57

Karuka, Manu, 209

Katayama, Taro, 166, 173, 176, 180, 187–89, 198

Kay, Marshall, 19

Keep America Beautiful, 233–35

King, Tiffany Lethabo, 86–87, 287n132

Kissinger, Henry, 151

Kitashima, Tsuyako "Sox," 175

"Koch Island" (Mandelbrot), 128

Kusumaatmadja, Mochtar, 133–35, 294n71–72

Kwentillion (magazine), 244

labor, 101, 104

La cohée du Lamentin (Glissant), 96

Lai, Paul, 23

Lake Bonneville, 167–69, 173–74, 176–78, 180–82, 188

"Lake Bonneville" (Yamada), 167–69

Lamming, George, 107

"Landmarks of Pahvant Valley" (Beckwith), 167

language, 14–15, 26, 119, 185–87. *See also* translation

Laramidia, 181–82
"Las Américas Quarterly" (Gómez-Barris & Fiol-Matta), 49
Latour, Bruno, 34, 61
law. *See* international law; maritime law
Lectures on the Philosophy of World History (Hegel), 62, 208–9
Lewis, Martin W., 60
Lewis, R. W. B., 46
Liang, Iping, 24–25
liberalism, 9, 14
"Library of Babel, The" (Borges), 214, 217, 223
Liebling, A. J., 52
life, 193–96
Life (magazine), 117, 139–42, 148, 150
"Life" (Johnson), 193
Life magazine, 116
Life on the Mississippi (Twain), 112–13
Limón, José E., 112, 117, 129, 155, 157
Linking Islands of Data project, 254
Lionnet, Françoise, 70
Lipman, Andrew, 114
Lipsitz, George, 57–58
literature, 45–48, 58, 85, 249–50
Loe, Hikmet Sidney, 203
Lomax, Alan, 82
Los Alamos National Laboratory, 152–58
Louisiana Purchase, the, 21
Lovecraft, H. P., 187
Lovelock, James, 224–25
Lowe, Lisa, 9
Lubis, Mochtar, 131
Lutkehaus, Nancy C., 119
Lyons, Paul, 49–50, 70, 81

Machine in the Garden, The (Marx), 56–57
Mack, Doug, 241
Madagascar, 60
Magellan, Ferdinand, 67
Mahmud, Zaharah binti Haji, 135
Main Currents in American Thought . . . (Parrington), 61–62
mainlands, 89, 100, 249, 258–62, 294n72
"Malay Archipelago, The" (Covarrubias), 118
Malay Archipelago, the, 84, 91–92, 98, 118, 121

Maldonado-Torres, Nelson, 70, 164, 199
Malkin, Irad, 97
Maluku Islands, 37, 132. *See also* Buru Island; Spice Islands
Mandelbrot, Benoit, 126–29, 143, 161, 170, 176, 179, 199–200, 216, 220, 269
manifest destiny, 1, 5–7, 11, 240
"Map of American Culture Areas" (Covarrubias), 156
M Archive (Gumb), 238
Mariana Trench, the, 31, 35, 226
Marianas Trench Marine National Monument, 34–35, 226
maritime boundaries, 1–6, 77–78, 125–29, 143–45
maritime law, 125
Marshall Islands, the, 142–52, 157
Martínez-San Miguel, Yolanda, 155
Marx, Leo, 52, 56–58, 75
masculinity, 47. *See also* gender
Mataa, Ngatokorua à, 64
mathematics, 126–27, 144–45, 186. *See also* geometry
Mayr, Ernst, 250, 252
McCall, Grant, 218
McCarty, Willard, 251–52
McDonald's, 233
McDougall, Brandy Nālani, 16
McGurl, Mark, 21, 161, 164, 192, 203–4, 207, 211, 219
McKittrick, Katherine, 86–87, 89
McPhee, John, 163, 181–82, 192, 211
Mediterranean, the, 50–60, 65, 75, 96–97, 252, 254. *See also* Hellas
Mediterranean and the Mediterranean World in the Age of Philip II, The (Braudel), 59
Meillassoux, Quentin, 171–72, 186, 303n84
"Melodramas of Beset Manhood . . ." (Baym), 45–47, 51
Melville, Herman, 223–24, 229–32
Men out of Asia (Gladwin), 156
meta-archipelagoes, 84, 91–92, 98, 222–23
metaphysics, 166, 173, 179
Mexico, 117–23, 153–58
Miami Herald, 9

Michener, James, 138
Midway (Jordan), 229–30
Mifune, Toranosuke, 190–92, 195, 305n116
Mignolo, Walter D., 10, 26–27, 114
migration, 116, 137–38, 154
Millard County Chronicle, 166
(Mis)Behavior of Markets, The (Mandelbrot), 220–21
Mississippi River, 51–53, 112–13, 127, 136, 152–58
Miss Ulysses from Puka-Puka . . . (Frisbie), 39, 51, 63–81, 97, 102
Moby-Dick (Melville), 223–24, 229–32
Mochtar Kusumaatmadja. *See* Kusumaatmadja, Mochtar
Mochtar Lubis. *See* Lubis, Mochtar
"Modern European Literature" (Moretti), 249
modernity, 10, 26, 83, 91, 96, 105–6, 117–18, 223–24. *See also* colonial modernity
More Known World, The (Tsao), 37
Moretti, Franco, 20, 43, 249–52, 261–62, 268
Mori, Toshio, 166
Morrison, Toni, 101
Morton, Timothy, 199–200, 216
Mules and Men (Hurston), 105–6, 117
multiculturalism, 58
Museum für Völkerkunde, 149
Muslim ban, 8
Myth of Continents, The (Lewis & Wigen), 60
mythology, 35, 51–55, 74–75, 105–6, 116, 157–58

NAACP, 101
Naidu, Vijay, 208
Nail, Thomas, 114–15, 126
Na'puti, Tiara R., 81
nationalism, 5, 16, 82–83, 85, 133, 137, 148, 224–25
national monuments, 34–35, 76, 223–39
National Oceanic and Atmospheric Administration (NOAA), 2, 5, 10–11
National Park of American Samoa, 241–42
nation-states: archipelagic thinking and, 17–18, 83; borderwaters and, 1, 37, 100, 141, 146–47; national monuments and, 225–27; temporality and, 160, 245

Native Americans, 50, 70, 74–75, 155, 241, 245. *See also* Indigenous peoples
Native Dwellings of the Pacific Area (Covarrubias), 119
Native Means of Transportation in the Pacific Area (Covarrubias), 119–21, 131, 136
natural gas, 31
Navakas, Michele Currie, 102
navigation, 65–68, 107, 121, 141, 148–50, 157, 223, 246
Nazi Germany, 176
NED. *See A New English Dictionary on Historical Principles*
Negro Drawings (Covarrubias), 117
neoimperialism, 123–24. *See also* imperialism
neoliberalism, 14, 36, 280n97
New English Dictionary on Historical Principles, A, 14, 16
"New Horned Dinosaurs . . ." (map), 182
New Oceania, A, 97, 155, 208–9
New Yorker (magazine), 117
Ngā Upoko Tukutuku Reo Māori Working Group, 253
"Nightmare" (Katayama), 173–74, 180
nissology, 218, 284n73
Noda, Yuriko, 176–77
nonhuman species, 34, 113, 141, 146, 148, 151, 173, 179, 193–95
Noodin, Margaret, 77
Norris, Benjamin, 199
North America. *See* continentalism; Turtle Island
North American Geosynclines (Kay), 20
Northeast Canyons and Seamounts Marine National Monument, 226
Norton Anthology of American Literature, 45–48, 281n1
Not-Quite States of America, The (Mack), 241
Noudelmann, François, 18
Nuclear Claims Tribunal, 152
nuclear power, 146, 148, 157–58
Nuclear Survivors' Day, 151–52
nuclear testing, 116, 137, 151–52, 237
Nusakambangan Prison, 137
Nusantara Online, 253

Obama, Barack, 8, 10, 225–27
object-events, 200
object-oriented ontology, 164, 171–72, 216, 220. *See also* ontology
oceanic spaces: Americanist scholarship and, 49–50; the Anthropocene and, 224–39; archipelagic thinking and, 16, 120, 213, 216–18; borderwaters and, 28–31, 43, 113–18, 125, 144–46, 154; digital humanities and, 260–68; temporality and, 161, 171, 183, 189–91, 196; the United States and, 24. *See also* international waters; ocean nations
ocean nations, 1–13, 24, 133–36
Oddfits, The (Tsao), 37
Odyssey, The (Homer), 52, 55–57, 65–66, 91–92, 97, 107
OED. *See* Oxford English Dictionary
Oegroseno, Arif Havas, 130
Office of the Chief of Naval Operations, 144
Oki, Jim. *See* Schraubi, Globularius
Okihiro, Gary Y., 48
Okubo, Miné, 159–60, 162–63, 180–82, 189, 201
"Old Pond" (Bashō), 191–92. *See also* "Ancient Pond" (Bashō)
Omeros (Walcott), 97
On the Origin of Species (Darwin), 251
ontological amphibians. *See* amphibians
ontology: American, 65, 76; archipelagic thinking and, 13, 81, 223, 249; borderwaters and, 38; continentalism and, 69–70; island spaces and, 84, 108; ocean nations and, 11–12; temporality and, 161, 164, 171, 178; US geography and, 98–104. *See also* object-oriented ontology
OOO. *See* object-oriented ontology
Otsuka, Julie, 173–74
"Our Sea of Islands" (Hau'ofa), 97
"Our Sea of Plastic" (Santos Perez), 227–28
Outer Continental Shelf Lands Act, 226
Oversea Railway, 92–94
Oxford English Dictionary, 13–17, 95, 251–52

Pacific House, 119–20, 159
Pacific Remote Islands Marine National Monument, 34, 226

Pageant of the Pacific (Covarrubias), 131, 148, 159, 297n144
Paine, Thomas, 9–11, 99, 222, 246
Palace of Fine and Decorative Arts, 159
Palaeologus, Michael, 13
Pan American Unity (Rivera), 159
Papahānaumokuākea Marine National Monument, 34, 226–28, 230, 232, 234–35, 237, 245
parallax zones, 87–90, 96–97
Paredes, Américo, 113, 121
Parrington, Vernon Louis, 61–62
passports, 5–7
Pearl Harbor, 162
Pease, Donald, 272
Peoples of the Pacific (Covarrubias), 119, 121–22, 153, 297n11
PepsiCo, 233
Perez, Craig Santos, 7–8, 23, 49, 60, 227–29
Perloff, Marjorie, 106
Perrier, 230–39
phenomenology, 86, 95, 104, 108, 111, 180, 210–11, 303n84
Philippines, the, 29–34, 242–45
philosophy, 164–65, 173, 186
Philosphie de la Relation (Glissant), 122
planet, the: the Anthropocene and, 224; archipelagic thought and, 213–14, 217, 219–21; borderwaters and, 36–38, 115–17; island spaces and, 85–90, 94–95, 109–10; ontology and, 98–99, 104; temporality and, 204–5, 207, 211, 245–46; the United States and, 146
plastic, 227–39
"Plastic Bag" (Bahrani), 234
plate tectonics, 166
poetics, 60, 91, 171
Poétique de la Relation (Glissant), 135
Poirier, Richard, 47
political prisoners, 136–38
"Politics of Fiction, Anthropology, and the Folk, The" (Carby), 83
Pollack, Jason, 215–16
pollution, 227–39. *See also* plastic
postcontinentalism, 49–50, 54, 65, 74, 163–64, 199, 286n113, 300n22

postnationalism, 85
Pound, Ezra, 170
Povinelli, Elizabeth A., 200
Prairie, The (Cooper), 55
Pramoedya Ananta Toer. *See* Toer, Pramoedya Ananta
Pratt, Mary Louise, 88
prisoners. *See* internment
"'Programming' the Archipelago . . ." (Zulkarnain), 253
public lands, 23
Puerto Rico, 8–10, 256–57
Pukapuka, 71–81, 284n85

Quijano, Aníbal, 138
Quintero Herencia, Juan Carlos, 17, 138

race: Americanist scholarship and, 57; the Anthropocene and, 238–39; archipelagic thinking and, 16, 63–64, 83, 138; borders and, 26, 115–16, 139, 153; continentalism and, 8–10, 62; diaspora and, 95–98; geography and, 88–89, 288n20; internment and, 163, 165, 175; island spaces and, 85–86, 106; ontology and, 100, 102
radiation, 147, 152, 158
railroads, 7. *See also* Oversea Railway; transcontinental railroad
Rauzon, Mark J., 227
Reciprocal Frame Architecture (Larsen), 72
reciprocal framing, 71–72
recycling, 231–39, 312n91, 312n101
Rees, Martin, 214
refugees, 34. *See also* immigration
religion, 8–9, 86, 93–95, 171–72, 192, 239
Republic of Indonesia (Covarrubias), 123–25, 129–32, 137
Rifkin, Mark, 199, 242
Rimspeak, 119
"Rio Grande, The" (Paredes), 113
Risam, Roopika, 257
Rivera, Diego, 159, 162
Roberts, W. Adolphe, 51
Robinson Crusoe (Defoe), 105–7, 187, 200
Rockwell, Geoffrey, 261

Roosevelt, Franklin Delano, 8, 162, 176–79
Roosevelt, Theodore, 7, 11
Rosaldo, Renato, 113
Rose Atoll Marine National Monument, 34, 226
Roster of Officers, Enlisted Men, Civilians and Dependents (US Navy), 142, 150

Saldivar, José David, 113–14
Salt Lake Tribune, 175
Samoa. *See* American Samoa; Independent State of Samoa
Saranillio, Dean Itsuji, 241
scattering, 97–98, 195
Schraubi, Globularius, 187
Schwyzer, Philip, 29
"Sea Is History, The" (Walcott), 97, 208
seas. *See* oceanic spaces; *and specific seas*
"Sea Story" (Byatt), 42, 210, 229, 231–34, 238
Segal, Rafi, 1–2
Senio, Fuiono. *See* Fuiono Senio
Sessions, Jeff, 8, 260
set theory, 144–45
settler colonialism. *See* colonialism
sex and sexuality, 9, 57, 105–6
Shakespeare, 56, 58, 105, 249
Sharpe, Christina, 139
shells, 148–50, 162–65, 171–82, 190, 195–97, 200, 220, 256, 302n67–302n68, 303n82
shoals, 81, 85, 159–60
shorelines: Americanist scholarship and, 50; archipelagic thinking and, 16, 216; borderwaters and, 113, 116, 127–28, 145; island spaces and, 108; ontology and, 102–4; temporality and, 161, 166–68, 176, 180–81, 199, 202–3, 207–8, 246–47
"Significance of the Frontier in American History, The" (Turner), 54
Simmons, Henry, 101
Sinclair, Stéfan, 261
Six Nations. *See* Iroquois
Sketches of Ancient History of the Six Nations (Cusick), 69
"Sky Gypsies" (Dimacali), 42, 210, 242–47
slate carving, 184–86, 189–93, 199
slavery, 14, 104, 138

Small Axe: A Caribbean Journal of Criticism, 273
Smith, Henry Nash, 46, 51–52, 56, 58, 61
Smithson, Robert, 42, 202–7, 211
Smithsonian Institute, The, 166
Somerville, Alice Te Punga, 272
South China Sea, the, 31–33
sovereignty: archipelagic thinking and, 22, 24, 79, 148, 222; borderwaters and, 34, 113–16, 129–30, 141, 146–47, 151; ocean nations and, 5, 10–11; ontology and, 100–103; temporality and, 241–44
Sovereignty and the Sea (Butcher & Elson), 30
Spanish Borderlands, The (Bolton), 25
speculative realism, 164, 171, 216, 220
Spice Islands, 37, 56, 91–92, 132, 137. *See also* Buru Island; Maluku Islands
spices, 56, 91–92
Spiral Jetty (Smithson), 42, 202–9
state, the, 16–17, 30, 76, 114–16, 122, 133–34, 138, 149
Stephens, Michelle Ann, 10–11, 49, 216, 269
Stevenson, Robert Louis, 90
"Stewardship of the Ocean, Our Coasts, and the Great Lakes" (Obama), 225–26
stick charts (Marshall Islands), 121, 142, 148–51, 296n124, 296n126, 297n144
Stoermer, Eugene F., 224
Stone and the Shell, The (Underwood), 256
Strenuous Life, The (Theodore Roosevelt), 7
Suarez, Harrod J., 265, 273
subjectivity, 16, 94–95, 171–72
sublime, the, 89–90, 171, 199, 205, 223–24
Submerged Lands Act, 226
Suharto (president), 136
Sukarno (president), 123, 146–48, 151, 158, 237
Sumpah Pemuda, 133
Suyemoto, Toyo, 177–80, 182, 197
Suzuki, Daisetz T., 193
suzuri. *See* inkstones
Swanstrom, Lisa, 253–55
Swiss Family Robinson, The (Wyss), 90
Systematics and the Origin of Species (Mayr), 250

Tally, Robert T., Jr., 86–87
tanah air, 17, 133–35, 137–38, 141, 145–46
Tanforan Racetrack, 162
Teaiwa, Teresia, 64, 157
Tell My Horse (Hurston), 83, 93, 95
Tempest, The (Shakespeare), 56, 58, 75, 105
temporality: Americanist scholarship and, 58–60; archipelagic thought and, 210–23; borderwaters and, 18–21; desert-islands and, 106; foreshores and, 165–80; fractal geometry and, 159–65; geology and, 180–96; history and, 202–10; iridescence and, 197–201; plastic and, 232–33. *See also* deep time
Ten Foot Square Hut, The (Chōmei), 197
Tengan, Ty P. Kāwika, 49–50, 70
Tennyson, Alfred Lord, 55
Te Rangihiroa, 68, 153–54
terraqueous spaces, 12–21, 36, 112, 135, 145, 223, 278n62. *See also* watery spaces
"Territorial Map of the World" (Segal & Cohen), 1–4, 275n1
Territorial Sea and Maritime Districts Ordinance (1939), 125–26
territorial waters, 21–22, 32, 34, 76, 125–26, 141, 144, 247
Te Tawa o te Langi, 68–69, 71–72, 74
Teves, Stephanie Nohelani, 81
Te Whakakaokao, 253
Their Eyes Were Watching God (Hurston), 40, 83–110, 268–69
theoretical physics, 212–23. *See also* cosmology
Think Like an Archipelago (Wiedorn), 210
"This Island" (Wineera), 108–9
Thompson, Lanny, 65
Thousand Plateaus, A (Deleuze & Guattari), 70, 74
Through Other Continents (Dimock), 50, 58–60, 203
tides, 19, 89, 126–28 161–162, 169–71, 175–76, 200. *See also* foreshores
Tilley, Christopher, 86–87
"Timeline of the Far Future" (Wikipedia), 211–13
Tinsley, Omise'eke Natasha, 115, 279n63
Tlostanova, Madina V., 26

Tocqueville, Alexis de, 99–100
Toer, Pramoedya Ananta, 136–39, 147, 294n84
Topaz internment camp, 41, 162–201
Topaz Museum, 163–64, 302n67
Topaz Slate Club, 185, 188–89
Topaz Times, 163, 183, 185
topography, 76, 85–86, 93, 98, 145
Tocqueville, Alexis de, 9
Trachtenberg, Alan, 52, 58
Trans-Americanity (Saldívar), 113–14
transcontinental railroad, 7, 202, 207, 209
translation, 14–18, 21, 26, 185–86
transnationalism: Americanist scholarship and, 48, 50, 58–60, 75, 112; borderwaters and, 23, 36–37, 43, 85–86; digital humanities and, 260–74; temporality and, 159–61, 247
Treasure Island, 119, 159–60, 162, 201
Treaty of Paris (1898), 7, 29–30, 244–55
Trek (magazine), 163–67, 173, 177–78, 181–84, 187–88, 193, 196–98
"Trilobite Fossils of Antelope Springs" (Beckwith), 167, 183
trilobites. *See* fossils
Trinity nuclear test site, 137
Truett, Samuel, 111–12
Truman, Harry S., 143
Trump, Donald, 8–10, 36–37, 256–57, 300n26
Trust Territory of the Pacific Islands, 11, 22, 115–16, 139–41, 143–46, 148, 151
Tsao, Tiffany, 37–38
tsunamis, 170, 268
Turner, Frederick Jackson, 50, 54, 56–59, 61, 70, 97
Turtle Island, 50, 70–71, 74, 77, 81, 97, 245, 287n132, 315n141
Twain, Mark, 38–39, 51–64, 112–13, 129
Two Years before the Mast (Dana), 63–64

Ulysses (Joyce), 107
UNCLOS. *See* United Nations Convention on the Law of the Sea
Underwood, Ted, 255, 257–58, 271
United Nations Convention on the Law of the Sea, 2–3, 10, 17, 19, 22, 133, 135, 225

United Nations Environmental Assembly, 237–38
United Nations Security Council, 139
United States, the: Americanist scholarship and, 45–49, 54–55, 65; the Anthropocene and, 223–39; archipelagic thinking and, 18, 21–23, 66–67, 75–81, 90–98, 138, 151, 261–62; borderlands and, 26, 144; borderwaters and, 36–38, 83, 123–24, 130–32, 139–43, 276n6; continentalism and, 56–63, 70–71, 74; as an ocean nation, 1–13; temporality and, 207–8, 239–47
"United States is an Ocean Nation, The" (NOAA), 5–7, 11
United States military, the: archipelagic diaspora, 90–92; borderwaters and the, 31–34, 139–42, 145, 147, 151; continentalism and, 9; governmentality and, 22
United States Navy, the, 9, 141–43, 146–48, 151
universe, the, 215–20, 223–24
Unsustainable Empire (Saranillio), 241
US Army Corps of Engineers, 159
US-Canada border, 1–2, 126
US Geological Survey, 21, 23–24
US-Mexico border, 1–2, 25–26, 112–13, 139, 157, 293n63
US National Park Service, 240, 247, 307n15, 314n123
US Naval Civil Administration Unit, Marshall Islands, 142, 149–50

Vanity Fair (magazine), 117
Vasconcelos, José, 153, 155
Vazquez, Alexandra T., 49
Vikings, 67–69, 71, 73
Vikings of the Sunrise (Buck/Te Rangihiroa), 68
Vinland sagas, 67–69, 71, 73–74, 285n91, 285n99
Virgin Land (Smith), 46, 56
Vodou, 83, 93–94
Vogue (magazine), 117
Voyant Tools, 261

Waddell, Eric, 208
Walcott, Derek, 16, 37, 59–60, 97, 107–8, 155, 208

Walker, Alice, 104–6
Walsh, Catherine E., 10, 26
Wartime Civil Control Administration, 187–88
water. *See* watery spaces
watery spaces, 25, 31–34, 40, 56, 65, 69, 111, 117–28, 161, 292n22. *See also* terraqueous spaces
Watson, Derrick, 8
waves, 38, 128–29, 148, 161, 168, 175–76, 200
Wawasan Nusantara, 120–22
weak theory, 164
Weary Blues, The (Hughes), 117
Weheliye, Alexander G., 96
West, Jessamyn, 7
Western Interior Seaway, 180–82
Western Samoa. *See* Independent State of Samoa
Westphalianism, 134–37, 146
westward expansion, 52–62, 246, 315n144. *See also* frontiers
wet feet, dry feet policy, 32
Wheatley, Phillis, 100
Whitehead, Alfred North, 194–95
Whitman, Walt, 18, 56

Wiedorn, Michael, 17, 210, 216
Wigen, Kären E., 60
wilderness, 46–47. *See also* frontiers
Wilson, Rob, 24, 81
Wineera, Vernice, 108
Wing, Betsy, 135
Winkler (captain), 149–50
women, 45–47, 106. *See also* gender
Women Writers of the American West, 1833–1927 (Baym), 48
World and All the Things upon It, The (Chang), 67
Wright, Richard, 91, 104, 131
Wynter, Sylvia, 103–4, 290n71

Yaeger, Patricia, 25, 171
Yamada, Jim, 167–68, 170, 180, 182–83
Yanique, Tiphanie, 42, 210, 217–18, 220–21
Yokohama, California (Mori), 166
Yoshihara, Mari, 46, 49–50

Zapata, Emiliano, 153
Zen, 192
"Zora Neal Hurston—A Cautionary Tale and a Partisan View" (Walker), 105
Zulkarnain, Iskandar, 253